A HISTORICAL & THEOLOGICAL STUDY

JESUS
The Miracle Worker

GRAHAM H. TWELFTREE

InterVarsity Press
Downers Grove, Illinois

InterVarsity Press
P.O. Box 1400, Downers Grove, IL 60515
World Wide Web: www.ivpress.com
E-mail: mail@ivpress.com

InterVarsity Press® is the book-publishing division of InterVarsity Christian Fellowship/USA®, a student movement active on campus at hundreds of universities, colleges and schools of nursing in the United States of America, and a member movement of the International Fellowship of Evangelical Students. For information about local and regional activities, write Public Relations Dept., InterVarsity Christian Fellowship/USA, 6400 Schroeder Ra., P.O. Box 7895, Madison, WI 53707-7895.

Scripture quotations, unless otherwise noted, are from the New Revised Standard Version of the Bible, copyright 1989 by the Division of Christian Education of the National Council of the ̄hurches of Christ in the U.S.A., and are used by permission.

Cover photograph: Scala/Art Resource, N.Y.

ISBN 0-8308-1596-1

Printed in the United States of America ⊗

Library of Congress Cataloging-in-Publication Data

Twelftree, Graham H.
  Jesus the miracle worker : a historical and theological study /
Graham H. Twelftree.
    p. cm.
  Includes bibliographical references and index.
  ISBN 0-8308-1596-1 (paper : alk. paper)
  1. Jesus Christ—Miracles. 2. Jesus Christ—Person and offices.
3. Bible. N.T. Gospels—Criticism, interpretation, etc.
I. Title.
BT366.T54   1999
232.9'55—dc21   *99-22336*
                                                                           CIP

22	21	20	19	18	17	16	15	14	13	12	11	10	9	8	7	6	5	4	3	2	1
17	16	15	14	13	12	11	10	09	08	07	06	05	04	03	02	01	00	99			

CONTENTS

To
George Caird
Tony Denholm
Jimmy Dunn

Abbreviations

1QH	*Hôdāyôt (Thanksgiving Hymns)* from Qumran Cave 1
1QM	*Milḥāmāh (War Scroll)*
1QS	*Serek hayyaḥad (Rule of the Community, Manual of Discipline)*
1QSa	Appendix A *(Rule of the Congregation)* to 1QS
4Q246	Text 246 from Qumran Cave 4
4Q381	Text 381 from Qumran Cave 4
4Q521	Text 521 from Qumran Cave 4
4QD^b	Text 267 from Qumran Cave 4
4QPrNab	*Prayer of Nabonidus* from Qumran Cave 4
11QPsAp	Text 11 from Qumran Cave 11
11QTemple	*Temple Scroll* from Qumran Cave 11
ABD	D. N. Freedman (ed.), *Anchor Bible Dictionary*
Adv. Gent.	Arnobius *Adversus Gentes*
Adv. Haer.	Irenaeus *Adversus Haereses*
Ag. Ap.	Josephus *Against Apion*
Alex.	Plutarch or Lucian *De Alexandro*
Ant.	Josephus *Jewish Antiquities*
ANQ	*Andover Newton Quarterly*
ANRW	*Aufstieg und Niedergang der römischen Welt*
Apoc. Bar.	*Syriac, Greek Apocalypse of Baruch*
ATR	*Anglican Theological Review*
BAGD	W. Bauer, W. F. Arndt, F. W. Gingrich and F. W. Danker, *Greek-English Lexicon of the NT* (1979)
b. ʿAbod. Zar.	Babylonian Talmud tractate *ʿAboda Zara*
b. Ḥag.	Babylonian Talmud tractate *Ḥagiga*
b. Ber.	Babylonian Talmud tractate *Berakot*
b. B. Meṣ.	Babylonian Talmud tractate *Baba Meṣiʿa*
b. Ketub.	Babylonian Talmud tractate *Ketubot*
b. Pesaḥ.	Babylonian Talmud tractate *Pesaḥim*
b. Šabb.	Babylonian Talmud tractate *Šabbat*
b. Sanh.	Babylonian Talmud tractate *Sanhedrin*
b. Taʿan.	Babylonian Talmud tractate *Taʿanit*
BETL	Bibliotheca ephemeridum theologicarum lovaniensium
Bib	*Biblica*
BibLeb	*Bibel und Leben*
BibRev	*Bible Review*
BLE	*Bulletin de littérature ecclésiastique*
BLit	*Bibel und Liturgie*
BSac	*Bibliotheca Sacra*
BTB	*Biblical Theology Bulletin*

BVC	*Bible et vie chrétienne*
BZ	*Biblische Zeitschrift*
CBQ	*Catholic Biblical Quarterly*
CC	Origen *Contra Celsum*
CD	Cairo (Genizah text of the) *Damascus (Document)*
CurTM	*Currents in Theology and Mission*
Det. Pot. Ins.	Philo *Quod Deterius Potiori insidiari solet*
Deus Imm.	Philo *Quod Deus immutabilis sit*
Dial.	Justin *Dialogue*
ETL	*Ephemerides theologicae lovanienses*
EvQ	*Evangelical Quarterly*
EvT	*Evangelische Theologie*
ExpTim	*Expository Times*
Gen. Rab.	*Genesis Rabbah*
Gos. Thom.	*Gospel of Thomas*
HeyJ	*Heythrop Journal*
HTR	*Harvard Theological Review*
IBS	*Irish Biblical Studies*
Int	*Interpretation*
ITQ	*Irish Theological Quarterly*
JAAR	*Journal of the American Academy of Religion*
JBL	*Journal of Biblical Literature*
JR	*Journal of Religion*
JSNT	*Journal for the Study of the New Testament*
JSOT	*Journal for the Study of the Old Testament*
JTS	*Journal of Theological Studies*
Jub.	*Jubilees*
J.W.	Josephus *Jewish War*
KD	*Kerygma und Dogma*
L	Hypothetical source document used by Luke
LQ	*Lutheran Quarterly*
LSJ	Liddell-Scott-Jones, *Greek-English Lexicon*
LXX	Septuagint
M	Hypothetical source document used by Matthew
m. B. Meṣ.	Mishnah Talmud tractate *Baba Meṣiʿa*
m. ʿErub.	Mishnah Talmud tractate *ʿErubin*
m. Ḥag.	Mishnah Talmud tractate *Ḥagiga.*
m. Ketub.	Mishnah Talmud tractate *Ketubot*
m. Ohol.	Mishnah Talmud tractate *Oholot*
m. Šabb.	Mishnah Talmud tractate *Šabbat*
m. Taʿan.	Mishnah Talmud tractate *Taʿanit*
m. Yebam.	Mishnah Talmud tractate *Yebamot*
Migr. Abr.	Philo *De Migratione Abrahami*

MScRel	*Mélanges de science religieuse*
Neot	*Neotestamentica*
NovT	*Novum Testamentum*
NRT	*La nouvelle revue théologique*
NTS	*New Testament Studies*
Odes Sol.	*Odes of Solomon*
PGM	K. Preisendanz (ed.), *Papyri graecae magicae*
Philops.	Lucian *Philopseudes*
P. Oslo.	Papyrus Osloenses
P. Oxy.	Papyrus Oxyrhynchus
Pss. Sol.	*Psalms of Solomon*
Q	Quelle, a hypothetical source document used by Matthew and Luke
RB	*Revue biblique*
RelS	*Religious Studies*
Rer. Div. Her.	Philo *Quis Rerum Divinorum Heres*
RevExp	Review and Expositor
RevScRel	*Revue des sciences religieuses*
RHPR	*Revue de l'histoire et de philosophie religieuses*
RivB	*Rivista biblica*
RSPT	*Revue des sciences philosophiques et théologiques*
RTL	*Revue théologique de Louvain*
SBL	Society of Biblical Literature
ScEs	*Science et esprit*
SE	*Studia Evangelica* I, II, III (= TU 73 [1959], 87 [1964], 88 [1964], etc.)
SEÅ	*Svensk exegetisk årsbok*
Sib. Or.	*Sibylline Oracles*
SJT	*Scottish Journal of Theology*
SR	*Studies in Religion/Sciences religieuses*
ST	*Studia Theologica*
Str-B	[H. Strack and] P. Billerbeck, *Kommentar zum Neuen Testament*
t. Ber.	*Tosefta* Talmud tractate *Berokot*
t. Ḥul.	*Tosefta* Talmud tractate *Hullin*
t. Menaḥ.	*Tosefta* Talmud tractate *Menaḥot*
T. Levi	*Testament of Levi*
T. Sim.	*Testament of Simeon*
T. Sol.	*Testament of Solomon*
TD	*Theology Digest*
TDNT	G. Kittel and G. Friedrich (eds.), *Theological Dictionary of the New Testament*
TEV	Today's English Version

Tg. Ezek.	*Targum of Ezekiel*
Tg. Isa	*Targum of Isaiah*
TGl	*Theologie und Glaube*
ThStud	Theologische Studiën
TQ	*Theologische Quartalschrift*
TRev	*Theologische Revue*
TS	*Theological Studies*
TToday	*Theology Today*
TTZ	*Trierer theologische Zeitschrift*
TynBul	*Tyndale Bulletin*
TZ	*Theologische Zeitschrift*
VD	*Verbum domini*
Vit. Cont.	Philo *De Vita Contemplativa*
Vit. Mos.	Philo *De Vita Mosis*
WW	*Word and World*
y. ʿAbod. Zar.	Jerusalem Talmud tractate *ʿAboda Zara*
y. Ber.	Jerusalem Talmud tractate *Berakot*
ZKT	*Zeitschrift für katholische Theologie*
ZNW	*Zeitschrift für die neutestamentliche Wissenschaft*
ZRGG	*Zeitschrift für Religions- und Geistesgeschichte*
ZTK	*Zeitschrift für Theologie und Kirche*

Preface

Many books have been written on the miracles of Jesus. But it has been a long time since anyone has attempted a straightforward study that has both a historical—"Did it happen?"—as well as a theological—"What did, or do, they mean?"—perspective that would be intelligible and interesting for the specialist student as well as for the general reader. This book not only makes the bold claim to attempt just that but also takes the discussion of the Gospel miracle traditions into the arena of the quest for the historical Jesus.

I have in mind several different kinds of readers. There are the students writing essay assignments on the miracles of Jesus in one of the Gospels or in the ministry of the historical Jesus. Theological teachers can also expect to find the following pages helpful in gaining access to the contemporary study of the miracles of Jesus. Ministers, in the preparation of Sunday sermons or in a planned series of talks, may need to read background material on the miracle stories set in the lectionary. Also, with the increased interest in the miraculous among present-day Christians, I have in mind the reader who wishes to have at hand a readable introduction to the theological and historical study of the miracles of Jesus in the Gospels. Finally, I have in mind those wishing to inquire about research on the historical Jesus as it relates to his reported wonders.

Although I have not wished to sacrifice accuracy or completeness, I have not tried to be exhaustive in noting secondary literature. Endnotes have been kept to a minimum, generally citing only what I see as the most essential literature. Sadly much must be left unsaid and unacknowledged, especially my dependence on many commentaries on the Gospels. Nevertheless the bibliography at the end of this book will help those interested to take the next step in a greater understanding of their chosen aspect of the miracles of Jesus. Translations from the Bible are my own or are from the New Revised Standard Version.

A book makes its journey from author to reader with the generous help of many people. Over the years of writing I have relied on the advice of many kind readers and correspondents, some of them laboring over great slabs of very rough drafts. I offer my sincere thanks to Colin Brown, Bill Craig, Peter Davids, Tony Denholm, Dick France, Joel Green, Peter Head, Charles Holman, Robert Miller, Tanja Lang, Andrew Lincoln, Bill Loader, Scot McKnight, Christopher Marshall, Robert Menzies, Jeff Mountford, Philip Muston, John Painter, Moisés Silva, Stephen Silvester, Mark Stibbe, Bill Telford, Greg Trainor, Stephen Travis, Max Turner, Catherine Wait and Ben Witherington. Many of their comments in private communications either have changed my mind on points or have been woven (often unacknowledged) into the text. I trust I have not misrepresented them.

This is not the first time I have thanked the librarian (now Mark Sutherland) and staff members of Löhe Memorial Library, Luther Seminary (Adelaide), for their support of my research. I do so again, but with some sadness. For it was during the writing of this book that Pastor Trevor Zweck, the previous librarian, died far too young. I pay tribute to him as a unique librarian of excellence and as a keen supporter of scholarly research. The resources of other libraries and the kindness of their staff members have also greatly facilitated my work: the Adelaide College of Divinity Library, the Barr Smith Library of the University of Adelaide, the Bodliean Library in the University of Oxford, the British Library in London, the Flinders University Library in Adelaide, the Joint Theological Library in Ormond College in Melbourne, the King's College Library in the University of London, Moore Theological College Library in Sydney, Murdoch University Library in Perth, the State Library of South Australia in Adelaide and the Tyndale House Library in Cambridge. Thank you.

I also pay tribute to the unsung heroes at InterVarsity Press, especially to my long-suffering and efficient editor, Daniel G. Reid, for his patience, hard work and help in making what follows as readable as possible.

Twenty-five years ago the thrill and value of the study of human history were opened up for me by my teacher A. (Tony) F. Denholm, then professor in the Department of History, University of Adelaide. That excitement and value remain with me. It was then the late professor George B. Caird at Mansfield College, Oxford University, who in a callow beginner fostered an interest in the context of biblical studies with his remarkably broad knowledge and razor-sharp mind. My lifetime interest in the study of the historical Jesus was initially guided at Nottingham University under the friendly and patient hand of professor J. (Jimmy) D. G. Dunn. In grateful recognition of what I owe these three men, I dedicate this book to them. Of course, in doing so I would not wish to burden them with any responsibility for what I have written.

Graham H. Twelftree
Adelaide
August 5, 1998

PART 1

Miracles & the Modern Mind

One

Objectives & Issues

....

§1.1 Introduction

Studying the miracles of Jesus is important for at least three initial reasons: (1) the contemporary popular interest in Jesus; (2) the high proportion of space given to the subject of miracles in the Gospels in contrast to general scholarly neglect; and (3) that in ancient biographical writing a person's activities were important for understanding an individual's character.

1. Jesus and his miracles are in the news. Indeed, from earliest times there has been keen interest in the wonders reportedly performed by Jesus—with the puzzling exception of Paul, who, it is generally argued, tells us nothing about the miracles of Jesus.

The cover of *Time* magazine on April 10, 1995, carried the headline "The Message of the Miracles." In the article Nancy Gibbs writes, "As the faithful hunger for them, scholars rush to debunk and to doubt." Gibbs relates a number of stories of reported miraculous healings, along with the fact that 96 percent of the members of the Jesus Seminar agreed that the virgin birth never happened.

Time magazine has also summarized some of the scholarly views about Jesus: "He never cured any diseases. As for the other miracles? No loaves and fishes, no water into wine, no raising of Lazarus. And certainly no resurrection. What happened to his body then? Most likely it was consumed by wild dogs" (January 10, 1994).

The *Los Angeles Times* has carried reports arising in response to the sensation surrounding the controversial procedures and publications of the Jesus Seminar and some of its members.[1] The Jesus Seminar is a highly publicized—some would say deliberately provocative—scholarly "think tank" of two hundred "Fellows" or participants. Typically thirty to forty Fellows have met twice a year in various places since the Seminar first met in March 1985 at Pacific School of Religion in Berkeley, California.

The meetings have been dominated by discussions of the authenticity of the sayings and deeds of Jesus until a point is reached when nobody has anything further to say. Then a secret ballot is held, with each Fellow casting a colored bead into a box. In colloquial language, a red bead means "That's Jesus," a pink bead signifies "Sure sounds like him," a gray bead means "Well, maybe" and a black bead indicates "There's been some mistake" (that is, the material originated in the early church). The fellows of the Jesus Seminar assume that a saying or deed has to be "proven" to be authentic.

Not only is this method the cause of some alarm, so are the results that have been published so far. One popular article summarized them: "82% of the words attributed to Jesus were not spoken by him. Only one statement in the Gospel of Mark . . . is judged to have come from Jesus: 'Give to Caesar what is Caesar's, and to God what is God's' (Mark 12:17)."[2]

In the Fourth Gospel the Fellows were unable to find a single saying that could with certainty be traced back to the historical Jesus. They concluded that in this Gospel Jesus does little more than make claims for himself. "For that reason alone," says Robert Funk, the founder of the Jesus Seminar, "scholars regard the Fourth Gospel as alien to the real Jesus, the carpenter of Nazareth."[3]

However, on the historicity of the miracles of Jesus, the Fellows of the Jesus Seminar are, on a whole, more positive. They believe that Jesus practiced exorcism and that during his lifetime Jesus was considered a healer, though from today's perspective, they say, the cures are related to psychosomatic maladies. Yet the Fellows were unable to endorse any of the nature wonders as historical events, concluding that they are all fictions suggested by extra-Gospel models.[4]

Over against this, Jacob Neusner (Distinguished Research Professor of Religious Studies, University of South Florida) responds to these kinds of results as "either the greatest scholarly hoax since the Piltdown Man or the utter bankruptcy of New Testament studies."[5] Also, from March 31 to April 1, 1995, about 1,500 people packed Biola University's gymnasium in La Mirada, California, to hear Michael Wilkins and J. P. Moreland defend more traditional views about Jesus and his miracles in a "Jesus Under Fire" seminar.[6]

This confusing battle over Jesus and the reports of his miracles is causing consternation among some Christians at a popular level.[7] There are those who see the miracle stories in the Gospels as having their origin in eyewitness reports of Jesus' ministry.[8] Later in this chapter we will take account of Rudolf Bultmann's skeptical perspective (see §1.7), but the so-called left-wing Bultmannian, Fritz

Buri, exemplifies an even more radically negative position.[9]

This battle will not be resolved with more fury or by the throwing of more abuse and theological mud at opponents. Another way forward is instead to return to the text of the Gospels with (as far as possible) an open mind, using all the critical skills of the historian available.[10] Therefore part of the purpose of this book is to help unravel issues in the debate over the miracles of Jesus.

2. The study of the miracles of Jesus is also important because the Gospels portray Jesus as spending a large proportion of his time not only as a teacher but also as a miracle worker. If we open the Gospels at almost any place, we cannot avoid encountering the miracles and the miraculous.[11]

In his *Life of Jesus* Friedrich Schleiermacher (1768-1834) said, "If we reflect on the numerous miracles that are not recounted, on the numerous miracles that are narrated, and on the miracles that are described in detail, we must conclude that the performance of miracles required a large part of Christ's time during his life."[12] In our own time E. P. Sanders asks if we can determine the relative importance of miracles and proclamation in the general view of Jesus. Sanders says that if we have to arrange them in order, the miracles will win out. He goes on to say that it was the miracles that attracted the crowds to whom Jesus then proclaimed the good news. It is not, Sanders says, that Jesus was not a compelling speaker. Rather, if it is true he attracted large crowds, it was probably more because of his ability to heal and cast out demons than anything else.[13]

It is not surprising then that many have studied the miracles of Jesus since the advent of critical scholarship.[14] But it is staggering how little place is given to discussions of miracles in these studies, not only in years past but by those currently involved in the Third Quest for the historical Jesus.[15] For instance, Ben Meyer devotes only a few pages directly to the miracles of Jesus. Even Sanders devotes only one out of eleven chapters to Jesus' miracles. Donald Guthrie, a conservative scholar, did not discuss the miracles at all in his one-thousand-page *New Testament Theology*.[16] One of the minor though important objectives of this study is to redress this imbalance.

The glorious exception to this neglect of the miracles of Jesus is the magisterial treatment by John P. Meier in his study of Jesus.[17] This study will on many occasions depend on and interact with Meier's work. However, as Meier's program does not directly intersect with mine until part four, when I deal with the historicity of the miracle stories associated with Jesus, I will leave detailed interaction with him until then.

3. A study of the miracles of Jesus is important because in ancient biographical writing there was a deeply-rooted convention that what a person did was an important part of summing up the character of that person. This was more important than any reflection by a commentator.[18] Given that Jesus is portrayed

as working many miracles, any understanding of him, or at least how he was remembered in the traditions, must include a substantial discussion of his miracles.

For these reasons alone the miracles of Jesus merit our close attention. But even though the miracles that Jesus is said to have performed are center stage in this study, they do not exhaust the miraculous in the Gospels. Other stories of miraculous events in which Jesus is said to be involved include the virginal conception, aspects of the story of his baptism, the transfiguration, the resurrection and the ascension. There are also stories of Jesus having preternatural knowledge and stories of his followers' reporting appearances of the risen Jesus.[19] To this list we can add the sayings attributed to Jesus that relate to his conducting miracles (see §§10.10-16). On any account, a discussion of the historical Jesus ought to involve a significant discussion of his reported miracles and what they meant to him and the early Christians. This we intend to do.

§1.2 Purpose and Plan

This is by no means the first study concentrating on the miracles of Jesus. For example, during World War II Alan Richardson, then study secretary of the Student Christian Movement and later professor of Christian theology at the University of Nottingham, published *The Miracle-Stories of the Gospels* (London: SCM Press, 1941). In this small book Richardson sought to address what he saw as the real problem of the miracle stories: why the Gospel writers included so many miracle stories and what these stories meant.

More than twenty years later, Reginald H. Fuller, then professor of New Testament literature and languages at Seabury-Western Theological Seminary, Evanston, produced *Interpreting the Miracles* (London: SCM Press, 1963). Clearly it was written under the spell of Bultmann and form criticism. Franz Mussner, then professor of New Testament exegesis at the University of Regensburg in Bavaria, Germany, published *The Miracles of Jesus: An Introduction* (Notre Dame, Ind.: University of Notre Dame Press, 1968). Perhaps because it was ahead of its time in facing the question of the *ipsissima facta* of the ministry of the historical Jesus and being willing to do so without ignoring the miracles, this book has largely been ignored. However, from time to time we will make reference to this small book.

Although I do not pretend to be equal in skill to these great scholars, this study is intended to replace these older and smaller books, for much water has flowed under the bridge of scholarly New Testament research. With this in mind F. H. Bradley's words are salutary, as he expresses the well-known principle of historical inquiry: "The past varies with the present . . . since it is always the present upon which it rests."[20] Therefore it is important for those wishing to learn some basic things about the miracles of Jesus in light of contemporary research to have access to a book written by someone who is audacious enough to tackle the subject in an intellectual climate where the miraculous is still seen to be of interest only to naive fundamentalists or to people who predate the Enlightenment.

I am of two minds as I think of those who are reading this book. On the one hand, I am most anxious that you are able to read and become as excited as I am about one of the most interesting and important aspects of the reports of the ministry of the historical Jesus, what it meant for the early Christians and what could be some of the implications of the miracles of Jesus for us. On the other hand, my heart is in my mouth! There was a time in the recent history of interpreting the Bible when an attempt was made to unhinge the Christian faith and belief in Jesus from the vicissitudes of historical research.

Rudolf Bultmann once said, "As a matter of fact, the Easter faith has no interest in the historical question."[21] However, it was Wolfhart Pannenberg who reminded us that if faith is trust—trust in God working in our lives and the lives of people in the past[22]—our Christian faith is dependent to a large extent on what historians can recover about Jesus of Nazareth. I take it then that it is imperative to investigate the miracle stories from a historical perspective (see §10.2).

Some, however, may retreat from the question of historicity. They may fear that, in the face of rigorous historical inquiry, the "facts" may recede and the basis of their faith will have been reduced or made insecure. (This fear will be shown to be largely unfounded.) Some other readers, on finding questions raised about the historicity of some of the miracle stories as they are reported, may point out that I have damaged the trustworthiness of the Gospels, which in turn calls into question the material as a whole.

Neither conclusion needs to be drawn. First, the Gospels need be viewed not as untrustworthy but simply as different from what we may have once considered them to be. Indeed, no amount of faith can change the nature of the past or its record. Second, it would be unwise to suppose that our questions about the historicity of a report of one miracle or kind of story should necessarily raise questions about another story. Each must be examined in its own right.

Other readers may retreat from the inescapable historical inquiry for an opposite fear. They may fear that the miracle stories of Jesus will turn out to have a reliable historical base and be unavoidably part of the life of the historical Jesus. Therefore their perception of Jesus and God's action in the world would need to be redefined to include the miraculous, along lines that are in tension with their contemporary worldviews and how God is perceived to be involved or not involved in his creation.

So the purpose of this book is to introduce people to the miracles of Jesus by tackling four objectives:

1. To discuss how the Gospel writers understood the miracles of Jesus—what they understood to be the miracles' implication for their portrait of him, the place

the miracles had in their message about Jesus and what they understood the miracles to mean for their readers.

2. To try to determine how Jesus understood his miracles.

3. To see to what extent the miracle stories of Jesus in the Gospels reflect "what actually happened."[23]

4. To see where the other three objectives have led in relation to their implications for the quest for the historical Jesus.

These four objectives determine that we will be dealing only with those miracles reported *to be conducted* by Jesus, not with any of the miracles or miraculous phenomena *associated* with Jesus. We will not discuss a fuller contribution to the study of the historical Jesus, or a study of the miraculous in the Gospels, or a discussion of the general philosophy of miracles or the miraculous in the New Testament or in the Gospels.

In light of these four objectives, this book follows a simple plan. This first chapter deals with some preliminaries, including the problem of defining a miracle, and sets out the major issues we will face along the way, as well as noting the shadows cast over my enterprise by two giants in the study of miracles in the Gospels—Strauss and Bultmann.

One of the preliminary issues looms so large that we need a complete chapter to do it sufficient justice. That is, to a considerable extent, achieving our third objective—inquiring to what extent the miracle stories of Jesus in the Gospels reflect actual historical events—depends on the prior question of the possibility of miracles in any age. Without this discussion all we could establish would be that Jesus had a justifiable reputation as a powerful miracle worker. All we would be able to do in the discussion of the historicity of the miracle stories would be to make judgments about how reliable the reports of miracles are in reflecting what the observers thought they were witnessing.

But we stand in a different—not superior, it must be clear—position. We understand our world and experiences differently from those who witnessed the ministry of Jesus. Therefore it could be that what were reported as miracles in the Gospels we would report differently. Hence in chapter two it is necessary to take a brief excursion into a more philosophical field. This will enable us to establish whether the reports as miracle *qua* miracle stories remain meaningful to us at the turn of the millennium. If they are, we will be able to affirm the historicity of the reports considered to be historically authentic in reflecting at least in part what the observers thought they were witnessing.

Part two attempts to answer the question "How did each Gospel writer understand the miracles of Jesus?" Answering this question is the major task of this book. Rather than begin with questions relating to the historical Jesus, I have chosen to start from this point—with the first objective—because it enables us to begin with the Gospels as they stand. It will also enable the reader to become familiar with the stories as they appear before moving to the more difficult and potentially unsettling issue of historicity.

Furthermore, taking this starting point is more immediately productive for those who see it as a small, albeit difficult, step from doing a New Testament theology of miracles to constructing a contemporary theology of miracles. The Gospel of Mark will be discussed first, for it is generally recognized as the earliest; Matthew, Luke and John are taken in their order in the New Testament canon.[24]

Each chapter of part two includes a brief discussion of each miracle story from the perspective of the particular Gospel. There will also be a discussion of the major issues involved in each Gospel or a collecting of conclusions that arise from this discussion of the individual stories. Keeping in mind those readers who are seeking information on a single Gospel writer, each of these chapters is intended to stand alone and can be read without reference to the rest of the book. (The discussions and issues relating to Luke and the Fourth Gospel are so extensive that they each cover two chapters.)

To take into account the second objective (recovering Jesus' understanding of his miracles), part three deals first with some methodological issues (chapter nine), then with the meaning of the miracles for Jesus (chapter ten), asking the question, "What did Jesus think was the purpose and place of his miraculous works in the context of his overall ministry?" Answers to this question become contributions to the quest for the historical Jesus.

We need to pause here to note that the order in which we deal with the questions of how Jesus understood his miracles and in what way the stories in the Gospels reflect "what actually happened" is problematic. On the one hand, how Jesus understood his miracles depends on the way we answer the prior questions as to whether Jesus performed miracles and which, if any, of those stories now in the Gospels can be traced back to the historical Jesus. On the other hand, we need to decide how Jesus understood his miracles in order to judge which stories now reported in the Gospels cohere with his understanding and so are most likely to reflect an event in his life.

I will take the latter approach, dealing first with Jesus' understanding of his miracles, for we will be able to proceed with the help of a number of sayings generally agreed to be authentic. Notwithstanding, recognizing the circularity of our argument we must anticipate some of the conclusions from later in our study in discussing how Jesus understood his miracles.

In part four, having also argued that Jesus was a remarkably powerful miracle worker (chapter nine), we face the historiographically and, for some, emotionally difficult task of trying to see which, if any, of the miracle stories can be shown to contain reliable reminiscences of eyewitness reports of Jesus' ministry. This takes up my third objective. But I do not wish this part of the study to be seen as a selling out to skepticism. On the contrary, I hope it can be seen as a recognition that, in light of our changing world and the sharpened tools of inquiry, we must often return to check the historical nature and base of our faith.

Pursuing this third objective about historicity has in mind those who are unhappy with the extreme approaches to which I have already alluded: on the one hand, uncritically and defiantly taking the Gospels—including the miracle stories—to be "true" as they stand or, on the other hand, avoiding the issue of the miraculous in the Gospels' portrayal of Jesus and seeing the miracle reports as simply stories, myths or fables with interesting messages. In other words, this study attempts to take the slippery middle ground, which I find to be the one of integrity.

Finally, part five will accomplish the fourth objective. Not only will we draw some conclusions about the miracles of Jesus in the Gospels; we also will be able to make a contribution to the quest for the historical Jesus. As with those who follow William Wrede,[25] I consider what is usually called "New Testament theology" to be a historical enterprise. But I am also convinced that this enterprise—including our particular conclusions—have direct ongoing implications for Christians in our time in their practical work of theologizing and preaching. Space and my chosen objectives prevent my pursuing that enterprise beyond making some brief comments at the end of this book.[26]

No historical work can be undertaken without involving personal prejudices and presuppositions.[27] Indeed, to quote Albert Schweitzer, "There is no historical task which so reveals a man's true self as the writing of a Life of Jesus."[28] One of the attractions of the study of miracles for me is that it forces us to face some of the most difficult issues in the search for the historical Jesus, and it confronts me with my own prejudices. The resurrection aside, we are also forced to confront the contemporary significance of Jesus and his ministry in a way that no other aspect of Jesus' reported ministry requires.

§1.3 What Is a Miracle?

Different people have different definitions of miracles.[29] Although clear common denominators exist (see §17.10), not even the Gospel writers have exactly the same answer to the question "What is a miracle?" And the way a person today understands a miracle could be different from the way they were understood by the Gospel writers. Even David Hume—the one who brought the modern debate about miracles into sharp focus—had conflicting definitions.[30]

In attempting to understand the miracles of Jesus from his perspective and those of the Gospel writers, it is essential to have in mind views found in the Gospels, not our views or the views of others. To help distinguish between these views we will set out some of the better-known understandings of miracles that might inadvertently be overlayed on the New Testament writers. Our discussion here will not be conclusive, for we must wait until after completing our study to set out confidently how Jesus and the Gospel writers understood miracles.

1. *An astounding event.* In everyday life people use the word *miracle* to describe something that astounds them or causes them to wonder. John Macquarrie says, "In a minimal sense, a miracle is an event that excites wonder."[31] In New Testament times Josephus held this view (*Ant.* 18:63). Thomas Aquinas (1225-1274) also held this view, as did Augustine (354-430) in one of his conceptions of the miraculous.[32] There is no doubt that this view is found in the Gospels. For example, Mark and Luke say the crowd was amazed when Jesus cast out a demon at Capernaum (Mk 1:27; cf. Lk 4:36).[33]

2. *Conversion.* Some, including Augustine, see conversion and a life of true devotion to God as the primary miracle (*City of God,* 10:22). This may be a view reflected by Luke in relation to the conversion of Paul (Acts 9:1-22). As we will see in chapter five, it may also be reflected particularly in Luke's stories of those who were healed and praised God.

3. *A coincidence.* It is said that a miracle can be a coincidence. For example, R. F. Holland tells what is now the oft-quoted story of a little boy riding a toy car onto a railway track, where it gets stuck. An express train is due to pass with the signals in its favor. A curve in the track makes it impossible for the driver to stop his train in time to avoid any obstruction. The mother, on coming out of the house to look for her child, sees him and hears the approaching train. She runs forward shouting and waving. The little boy remains oblivious to the danger, for he is engrossed in peddling his car free.

The oncoming train stops just a few feet before the child, avoiding an accident. The mother thanks God for the miracle and continues to do so even after learning that there was nothing supernatural in the event. The reason the train stopped was because the driver had been taken ill and so released the control lever, automatically applying the brakes.[34] Some would argue that such a coincidence is produced not by chance but by God.[35]

Whereas coincidences allow Jesus to perform miracles—the case of Jesus being in the synagogue at the same time as the man with an unclean spirit (Mk 1:21-28) and the case of Jesus' delay in reaching the home of Jairus, which led to raising a dead girl rather than healing a sick girl (Mk 5:21-43)—a coincidence theory of miracle can account for very few of the reports of Jesus' miracles.[36] The large catch of fish (Lk 5:1-11; cf. Jn 21:1-11) and perhaps the storm being suddenly calmed (Mk 4:35-41) might be two such miracle stories. In Acts the earthquake and the opening of the prison doors for Paul and Silas could also be seen as coincidental (Acts 16:25-34).

4. *An unexplained observable event.* A miracle is often understood as an observable event that cannot be explained by natural law[37] or as an extraordinary event,[38] overriding or—as for David Hume—violating the laws of nature[39] or the usual pattern of nature.[40] This kind of view is not peculiar to Christianity or to modern philosophers, for it is found in, for instance, the writings of the fifth-century B.C. historian Herodotus.[41]

Augustine and Aquinas stress that a miracle is a violation not of nature but of what is presently known of nature or the usual apparent course of natural events, for nature has no order except that provided by God.[42] As A. E. Taylor put it, "Properly speaking, there are no laws of nature to be violated, but there are habits of expectation which any one of us, as a fact, finds himself unable to break through."[43] The concept of a miracle as something contrary to expectation is one we will often meet, notably for example in Luke 5:26 (see §5.9).

5. *An event not the result of ordinary causes.* Some, including theists and theologians such as Thomas Aquinas, often want to add that only God or his agents can work miracles.[44] Put another way, a miracle is an event that cannot be explained as a result of human abilities or any other force known to us.[45] Other people include the idea that a miracle is imprinted with some purpose of God that causes him to interrupt the ordinary course of nature.[46] Hume added that the event would still be a miracle even if no one noticed it.[47] The story of the so-called strange exorcist (Mk 9:38-39/Lk 9:49-50) raises the question of whether the Gospel writers thought any agents other than God or his representatives could perform miracles.[48]

6. *An inexplicable event that fits God's character.* It has been argued that although inexplicability or mystery is an element of the miraculous, it must fit a pattern. That is, not because of the degree of inexplicability a believer deems an event a miracle but because it fits a behavior pattern appropriate to the character of God.[49] We see this view often, especially in Luke, where in response to a miracle, the crowd or the individual concerned is said to give praise to God (see chapters five and six).

7. *An astonishing but rational event.* Paul Tillich (1886-1965) defined miracles in a way that did not involve any special activity by a god. Central to his definition is that, whereas a genuine miracle is first of all an event that is astonishing, unusual and shaking, it does not contradict the "rational structure of reality."[50] However, this in effect dissolves miracles as generally understood—both in everyday life and by most philosophers and theologians—in that a miracle is generally understood to override the anticipated patterns of nature.

Nevertheless it may be possible to argue that the story of the healing of the paralyzed man by Jesus' telling him that his sins were forgiven may override—for us—no anticipated pattern of nature (Mk 2:1-12). For it is frequently suggested that beneath the physical paralysis was a disease of the conscience, a sense of guilt that led to the bodily paralysis.[51]

8. *An eclectic definition.* It is not uncommon for some elements of these definitions of miracles to be combined in various ways. Richard Swinburne, for example, combines them for his definition of a miracle: "An event of an extraordinary kind, brought about by a god, and of religious significance."[52] We will see that this definition resonates well with the understanding of the so-called miraculous events reported in the Gospels.

It is not my purpose to show that any of these definitions is wrong or right in themselves. Yet we need to note that these ways of understanding miracles are modern constructs, or accepted by modern minds. While we may hold them, they may not in every case be appropriate for understanding Jesus and the Gospel writers. Therefore how helpful these definitions of miracles are in understanding what the Gospel writers understood Jesus to be doing in the "miracles" we will see in the discussion of each Gospel writer and then in the conclusions drawn at the end of this book (§17.10).

§1.4 Are the Miracle Stories Reliable?

The paramount issue for many is whether Jesus conducted miracles. Of course, we could say that because the Bible (the Word of God) reports Jesus (the Son of God) conducting miracles, then we have no reason to doubt the fact. In the words of Alan Richardson, "Our acceptance or rejection of the biblical miracles will depend upon our prior acceptance or rejection of the prophetic and apostolic testimony of the Bible concerning God's revelation in Christ."[53]

Before being tempted to criticize Richardson for his historical inquiry being theologically driven or determined, we can note that he wished to distance his approach from what he called the frivolous claim that this involves lifting the discussion out of the sphere of scientific and historical inquiry and accepting the view that Joshua made the sun stand still and that Elisha made the ax-head float. For Richardson, such a frivolous claim is made without recognition of the point that some reports of miracles are fundamental and others are not fundamental to the Christian faith.

However, not all readers of the Gospels (or this book) will be satisfied with such an answer, no matter how special one might claim the Bible or Jesus to be. To help as many readers as possible think through the issues relating to the miracles associated with Jesus in the Gospels, we will start from a position other than an assumed particular nature of Jesus and the Bible.

With the question in mind of whether Jesus conducted miracles, it could be, as has frequently been argued, that some or all of the miracle stories in the Gospels were not originally part of the Jesus tradition. They were added from non-Christian sources, or they were invented by the Gospel writers themselves or by other Christians before them. Part four will address this issue directly when we deal with the miracles of Jesus and history.

Similarly it could be said that although Jesus certainly conducted some miracles—for example the exorcisms and some of the healings that could have a natural explanation—it is unlikely that he performed such feats as giving sight to the blind or raising the dead or walking on water. Again, this will be the focus of our attention in part four.

The question of the reliability of the miracle stories also arises when we look at the unique approach of each of the Gospel writers. However, this arranging and editing of the traditions about Jesus ought not surprise us nor in itself cast doubt on the historical integrity of a story. The Gospels were written in a culture where reports of events were understood to be recitations that were to be performed anew—either in writing or verbally—rather than copied or repeated verbatim. As we can see from the way Plutarch (c. A.D. 50-120) conveyed stories of the lives of political and military figures, it was the normal editorial convention of the day to transmit stories of heroes in a way that enabled the writer to emphasize those aspects of a story in line with the message of his work.[54]

Again, this does not in itself cast any doubt on the historicity of the miracle stories in the Gospels. It means that the writers were "performing" these stories in order to stress their inherent aspects, especially to highlight a message they sought to convey. Nevertheless we need to pursue this issue a little further.

§1.5 Did—and Do—Miracles Happen?

For most of us reality is a one-level experience. Only what is "real" and visible to us is accepted as reality. No amount of faith can alter history and what has and can happen to us. However, in premodern—or what has been called the primordial—ways of understanding human experience, there was also an equally real, highly charged, invisible world inhabited by the gods. Important in this worldview is the connectedness or relationship between the two planes: in the way the terrestrial world depends on the other world for its existence—vibrates with its energy—and in the way the other world can be experienced in this world.[55]

With this understanding of the world, even if the miracles are understood as parables or allegories, or "types" (or "patterns") for the way God will act in the future,[56] their having happened is not usually questioned—they are taken at face value. I say "usually" because there is plenty of evidence that there were those who questioned the validity of reports of miracles.[57]

Over against this multidimensional interactive view of the world, a modern way of seeing life is often to take as real only what can be seen and verified by rational scientific argument.[58] Therefore for many post-Enlightenment readers of the Gospels, one of the first questions that arises is, Are the miracle stories we read accurate reflections of what happened? Or, as some have argued, have the stories been embellished or even added to the Jesus tradition, especially in light of wanting to portray Jesus as a Savior worthy of the attention of the Greeks, who were familiar with and valued such miracle stories and workers?

Or perhaps, as David Friedrich Strauss argued, since miracles are incompatible with reason and natural law, they are not historical records but myths—the expression or embodiment of an idea in a way that can be understood.[59] A similar view has been put bluntly by Bishop E. W. Barnes in writing about the author of the Gospel of Mark: "He was credulous inasmuch as the miracles, as they are narrated, cannot, in light of our modern knowledge of the uniformity of nature, be accepted as historical facts."[60] Reminiscent of Bultmann, John Macquarrie said, "The way of understanding miracle that appeals to breaks in the natural order and to supernatural interventions belongs to the mythological outlook. The traditional conception of miracle is irreconcilable with our modern understanding of both science and history."[61]

To a large extent the question of whether the miracle stories associated with Jesus can be taken as reliable reports of "what actually happened" will depend on whether our "modern" understanding of reality can be abandoned, even in the face of rational scientific argument. It may be that, as Marcus Borg has put it, we will have to set aside our modern vision of reality if our vision is not to be impaired. Writing of the New Testament, he says, "There is an 'otherness' in the texts—not only the otherness of a distant culture, but the otherness of an image of reality radically different from our own. An approach to the texts which does not see this does not see them fully."[62]

Since the issue of the historicity of the miracles is so important to many readers, it will, as I said, take up part four. This will be the most difficult section for many readers, for to aniticipate some results I conclude that in using the tools at the disposal of the analytical historian we often have too little data to make pronouncements with certainty on the historicity or nonhistoricity of the miracle stories in the Gospels. Nevertheless I will be arguing that the vast majority of the Gospel miracle stories can be read as reliable reports of those who witnessed the ministry of the Jesus of Nazareth (see §16.14).

However, all that will be concluded from the discussion and conclusions of these chapters dealing with the historicity of the miracle stories is that those who witnessed and reported the ministry of Jesus thought (perhaps mistakenly, some would say) that they were seeing miracles. So another step is required in our inquiry: to question whether it is reasonable to consider that the audiences of Jesus were correct to report that they were witnessing miracles. Or were they, at least in some cases, describing what we might see as psychosomatic illnesses and healings by a superior human being?[63] For as Dennis Nineham puts it, "'Miracle' in the modern sense of a decisive breach in an otherwise totally regular pattern of events will be inconceivable in such a society as ours."[64]

So, to repeat, to answer the question of whether miracles in the Gospels can be said to have happened, we must discuss the general possibility of miracles occurring. In center stage of this debate remains David Hume's infamous statement that "no testimony is sufficient to establish a miracle, unless the testimony be of such a kind, that its falsity would be more miraculous, than the fact, which it endeavours to establish."[65] This discussion will be taken up in chapter two.

§1.6 What Do the Miracles Mean?

This question arises because of the different meanings that have been attributed to the miracles of Jesus, including—so far as we recover his views—by Jesus himself.

1. One set of answers comes from *the Gospel writers*. Even a cursory reading of the four Gospels shows that each has a quite different perspective on the meaning of the miracles of Jesus. The ongoing development of redaction criticism[66] and narrative criticism[67] enables us to answer the question of what the miracles mean with fruitful results.[68] Through making use of these two tools in part two we will be able to elucidate what the four Gospel writers wanted to say about and through the miracle stories of Jesus. We will wait, however, until the end of the book to summarize the notions of miracle found in the Gospels (see §§17.2-7).

2. Another possible answer to the question of the meaning of the miracles comes from inquiring into *their meaning for Jesus* and what place he saw them having in his overall ministry. Here we find students of the New Testament giving a multitude of answers.

First, the so-called biblical theologians of a previous generation—for example, E. C. Hoskyns, Vincent Taylor, T. W. Manson, W. Manson, Alan Richardson and H. E. W. Turner—interpreted the healings and exorcisms as signs rather than as proofs of Jesus' Messiahship.[69] Second, Rudolf Bultmann saw the miracles as signs of the dawning of the coming kingdom.[70] On the other hand it can be argued, third, that the miracles were in themselves expressions of the presence of the kingdom of God.[71] A fourth way to look at the meaning of the miracles for Jesus is to consider their relationship to his teaching. Giving pride of place to Jesus' message, Gerhard Friedrich had this to say about the place of the miracles in Jesus' ministry:

> Miracles take place because the efficacious Word of God has declared the divine rule, and in it everything is sound and well. Hence the miracle is not the important thing. The important thing is the message which effects it. Signs accompany the Word. Their office is simply to confirm what is proclaimed. . . . Miracles, as *sēmeia* ["signs"], are a *verbum visibile* like the sacraments.[72]

Similarly it could be that, fifth, Jesus considered his miracles to be illustrations of his message. Also subordinating the miracles to the message, Herman Ridderbos, sixth, says that Jesus' miracles serve only as proofs of his power.[73] (The advantage of this view for some is that, in an age of supposed sophistication when the miracles of Jesus are considered an embarrassment, they can be left aside without damaging the integrity of the ministry of Jesus. In light of evidence from the Gospels, even from Matthew, we will be bound to take issue with this view.) At various points, especially in chapter ten, this study will assess these views in light of evidence from the Gospels.

3. A third way to answer the question of the meaning of the miracles is to ask, *What do the miracles mean today?* Or to put the question another way, What is the place of the miracles of Jesus in the proclamation of the good news about Jesus? Through history, broadly and in turn, miracles have been regarded (a) as the basis for believing the Christian message, then (b) as an apologetic crutch and more recently (c) as an embarrassment to the Christian message.[74]

(a) Regarding the miracles as a basis for faith, Origen (c. 185–c. 245) said that if the apostles had not appealed to the miracles of Jesus, they "would not have persuaded those who heard new doctrines and new teachings to leave their traditional religion and to accept the apostles' teaching at the risk of their lives" (*CC* 1:46).[75] This view can also be seen reflected in the book of Acts.

Similarly Quadratus (second century), who was probably the earliest Christian apologist seeking to give a reasoned account for the faith, thought the existence of the miracles of Jesus meant that Christianity could be defended as true against the attacks of Jews and pagans.[76] This view is found throughout the history of the interpretation of the miracles and has remained popular in some quarters. One example is William Paley (*View of the Evidences of Christianity* [1794]), who cannot conceive of divine revelation without miracles.[77] We will be asking if this view can be found among the Gospel writers (cf. §17.7).

(b) As a crutch or as one of the helps in knowing the truth of Christianity, miracles were given a fundamental place by John Locke (1632-1704). He said that reason aided by faith enables us to deduce truths from what we sense around us. But those things that are above reason, such as the resurrection of the dead, can be known only by a revelation from God. We know that a revelation is from God when the messenger that delivers it has credentials—miracles—given by God.[78] How this reflects views found in the Gospels will be seen in part two (cf. §§17.3-7).

(c) Dietrich Bonhoeffer (1906-1945) is an example of someone for whom the miracles were an embarrassment. In a letter to his friend Ebehard Bethge, he said that "mythological" concepts such as miracles are problematic for modern belief. Christians, in their coming of age, were supposed to be living in a world where God does not intervene through miracles: "God would have us know that we must live as men who manage our lives without him."[79] The next chapter establishes that there are no grounds for drawing this view from the Gospel writers. That Paul held a similar view we will debate in due course (§9.7).

Notwithstanding the importance of this problem of the meaning of the miracles today, because of the lack of space and the particular objectives of this study we will not discuss it in any detail. While not taking the position that "if history is done right the theology will take care of itself,"[80] I do consider that history (of the theology of the early church in the New Testament) done well is the principle contributor to contemporary theology. Therefore the results of our study can provide the major contours and some of the essential components in a discussion of the modern meaning of the miracles. In any case, this brings us to the next point.

§1.7 Shadows from the Past

Even though the miracles of Jesus have been neglected, particularly in the context of the search for the historical Jesus, there have been some important studies that we must take into account.[81] Indeed, a study of the miracles of Jesus cannot be undertaken except in the shadow of two monumental figures: Strauss and Bult-mann.[82]

1. *David Friedrich Strauss (1808-1874)*. The scene was set for the modern critical or historical study of miracles by the ground-breaking work of David Friedrich Strauss. As Albert Schweitzer said, the study of the life of Jesus falls into two periods—before Strauss and after Strauss.[83] To a large extent his work has remained the most important part of the background to all subsequent study of the miracles of Jesus.

In his theological and philosophical education at Blaubeuren and at the Tübingen theological college (Stift), Strauss was taught by Ferdinand C. Baur and influenced by Friedrich D. E. Schleiermacher and Georg W. F. Hegel. After becoming an assistant pastor and then a teacher in Maulbronn, in the spring of 1832 he moved back to the Tübingen Stift as a tutorial assistant, teaching in philosophy and working on his *Life of Jesus*. Sitting at the window of the tutors' room, which looked out upon a gateway arch, he wrote the two volumes, which were published in 1834.

Before Strauss the dominant interest in the study of the life of Jesus was the question of miracle and how a scientific treatment of the life of Jesus could proceed alongside the acceptance of supernatural events.[84] One solution—adopted by the first historical study of the life of Jesus by Herman Reimarus (1694-1768), for example—was to set aside the miracles. He does this (reminiscent of Hume), first, because miracles are unnatural events, as improbable as they are incredible, requiring as much examination as that which they are supposed to prove. Second, Reimarus set aside miracles because he said they contain nothing in themselves from which an inference can be drawn about doctrine.[85]

Strauss takes his starting point in the study of the miracles from the tension in the Gospels and Acts. He notes on the one hand a tension between the great number of miracle stories in the Gospels and, on the other hand—in response to the Pharisees' asking for a sign—Jesus appearing to repudiate the working of miracles in general, which accords with the fact that in the epistles the miracles of Jesus are unknown. The radical solution Strauss offered to this dilemma was that the miracles have no rightful place in history but are simply mythical elements in the sources.

Some of the stories are, in his view, *pure* myths in the sense that they, like the healing of the blind, have no historical foundation whatsoever. Other stories are *historical* myths in that they have at their core a historical fact that has provided the seed out of which the story grew. An example of this kind of myth would be the story of Peter's miraculous catch of fish (Lk 5:1-11) growing out of the statement of Jesus about his followers being called to be fishers of men (Mk 1:17). Strauss supports his case by a careful examination of all the categories of miracle stories in the Gospels.

In response to his publication, Strauss was relieved of his teaching post in the Tübingen evangelical seminary. In the hope of obtaining a theological teaching post and in light of some of his doubts about the severity of his conclusions, Strauss modified some of his conclusions. In a third edition of *The Life of Jesus Critically Examined* (1838-1839) he admitted the possibility of healings based on the unusual powers of nature, similar to animal magnetism or hypnotism. But that brought him no nearer orthodoxy.

In January 1839 he was invited to Zürich as professor of theology. However, in response to opposition from orthodox and pietist Christians, he was placed on a pension before he was inaugurated as professor or could even enter his office. In any case, in the 1840 edition of his life of Jesus, Strauss swept away his "compliance," declaring himself resolved to whet "my good sword, to free it from the notches made in it rather by my own grinding than by the blows of my enemies."[86] Strauss never returned to teaching, spending the remainder of his days writing theology and historical biographies.[87]

2. *Rudolf Bultmann (1884-1976)*. The other figure in whose shadow we still work as students of the Gospel miracles is Rudolf Bultmann. His father was a Lutheran pastor and his grandfather a missionary. There is no evidence that he ever considered a vocation other than serving the church through being an academic theologian. After studying in Tübingen, Berlin and Marburg he was appointed a New Testament lecturer in Marburg (1912). In quick succession he moved from assistant professor at Breslau (1916) to professor at Geissen (1920) to professor at Marburg (1921), where he remained until he retired in 1951.[88]

An important influence on Bultmann's life was Johannes Weiss (1863-1914), his *Doktorvater* ("doctoral supervisor"), who was a member of the *Religions-geschichtliche Schule* ("history-of-religion school"). This was a German school of thought, which flourished around the turn of the century and focused on studying early Christianity in the context of the religions of the eastern Mediterranean in the Hellenistic period. One of the implications of this is that, unlike Strauss, who treated the Old Testament as the most significant backdrop to the miracle stories, Bultmann turned to non-Christian and rabbinic stories as the early church's sources for its miracle stories. However, instead of arguing whether this material was used by the Gospel writers, it is implied that such stories were actually attributed to Jesus.

Another important figure in attempting to understand Bultmann is Wilhelm Bousset (1865-1920). Bultmann was Bousset's heir not only in succeeding him in the New Testament professorship at Giessen but also in his treatment of the miracles.[89] In *Kyrios Christos* (1913) Bousset sought to give a history-of-religions account of the history of faith in Christ from the beginning of Christianity to Irenaeus.[90]

In the section on the miracles of Jesus (pp. 98-106) Bousset asserts that the early Christian community not only inserted a stronger stress upon Jesus' person and the messianic idea; "it also above all surrounded this picture with the nimbus of the miraculous." On the (unargued) grounds that "the older part of the evangelical tradition . . . was probably a collection of the words of Jesus" and that the earlier passion narrative "has remained almost completely free of the miracu-lous," Bousset concluded that "the earliest tradition of Jesus' life was still relatively free from the miraculous."[91]

"On the question about the emergence of the miracle reports of the life of Jesus" he does not take Strauss's line in attributing it to the myth-making propensity of the early church. Rather, he says, "the fabrication of miracles in the life of Jesus probably took place as such a procedure usually takes place. People transferred to Jesus all sorts of stories which were current about this or that wonderworker and decorated gospel narratives that were already at hand with current miraculous motifs."[92] In other words, the community of Jesus' disciples fictionalized and surrounded the "picture of Jesus with the glitter of the miracu-lous."[93]

Bousset's grounds for this assertion were a number of asserted parallels in pagan literature, which were, in the main, from sources later than the Gospel traditions.[94] On these "the personal image of Jesus begins to work with magnetic power and to draw to itself all possible materials and narratives which were at hand in his environment."[95] In this, as we are about to see, he is Bultmann's precursor. How reasonable Bousset's assertions were we will see as this study proceeds.

Returning to Bultmann, a number of publications from his long career bear directly on issues relating to the miracles of Jesus.[96] In 1921, the year he went to Marburg, he published *Die Geschichte der synoptischen Tradition (The History of the Synoptic Tradition)*. Much of the book is taken up with the tradition of the sayings of Jesus, leaving only about thirty-five pages for the treatment of the miracle stories. Bultmann seeks to give an account of the history of the individual units found in the Synoptic Gospels—how they passed from a fluid state to the fixed form we find in the Synoptics.[97]

He says that he is entirely in agreement with Martin Dibelius (1883-1947), who maintained that form criticism does not consist of identifying individual units of tradition according to their aesthetic or other characteristics. Rather, form criticism is used "to rediscover the origin and the history of the particular units and thereby to throw some light on the history of the tradition before it took literary form."[98]

This view assumes that different forms of literature have arisen out of quite definite and different conditions in the early church and that there are recoverable "laws" about how oral tradition is modified. However, at the end of a long investigation E. P. Sanders concluded: "There are no hard and fast laws of the development of the Synoptic tradition. On all counts the tradition developed in opposite directions. It became both longer and shorter, both more and less detailed, and both more and less Semitic."[99]

Form critics—Bultmann included—have also tended to assume that having located the *Sitz im Leben* ("life situation") of a piece of tradition, they have located its historical origin. But this is to confuse form with content. We may be able to discover the use that has shaped material, but that tells us nothing about the material itself or its historical reliability.[100]

In short, Bultmann's method of using form criticism to trace the origin of miracle stories is fundamentally flawed. Indeed, much of his discussion of the miracles moves forward with assumptions and unsupported statements. For instance, without argument he says that in the story of the epileptic boy (Mk 9:14-27) two miracle stories have been combined, presumably because of the similarity of the illness and the healing.[101]

Further, there is no discussion of whether the great number of parallel miracle stories cited bear any real similarities to those in the Gospels. Nor is there any discussion of the dating of the parallels he cites or whether those responsible for the transmission of the Gospel miracle stories were aware of, or writing in, the same milieu as these parallels. Nevertheless because of his ongoing influence, we will often have cause in the discussion of the miracle stories of Jesus in part two to enter into more detailed debate with Bultmann's work in his *History of the Synoptic Tradition*.

Twenty years later, in 1941, the commentary *Das Evangelium des Johannes (The Gospel of John)* appeared. In this very readable masterpiece, with its undercurrent of existentialism, Bultmann was able to develop in more detail the form critical and, in particular, the history-of-religions approach to the miracles in John. Thus for example, the story of the changing of water into wine is said to be drawn from the Dionysian cult and adapted to illustrate Jesus' being the Revealer.[102] Again, our study of the miracles in the Fourth Gospel will benefit from interaction with Bultmann's treatment.

Another publication of the same year had a profound effect on the modern study of miracles: Bultmann's "The New Testament and Mythology."[103] Indeed, this essay initiated the modern debate on demythologizing. Regardless of the serious challenge from Strauss and the "history-of-religions" school, the problem of myth had been sidestepped. Myth was seen to be of little consequence, as it did not interfere with the essence of the message of Jesus. Bultmann undermined this state of affairs, however, by asserting that the message of Jesus cannot be separated from myth because it was conveyed through myth.

For Bultmann myth was a primitive, prescientific conceptualization of reality.[104] It was "the use of imagery to express the other worldly in terms of this world and the divine in terms of human life, the other side in terms of this side."[105] As this definition was criticized for being too all-embracing and for confusing myth and analogy (making it impossible to talk about God other than through symbols), Bultmann modified his concept of myth in terms of saying it is analogical, "for it assumes an analogy between the activity of God and that of the man."[106]

The point at which this impinges directly on this study is where he clarifies the meaning of his language. He says that mythological thought regards God's activity as interfering with nature. That is what Bultmann rejects:

> A miracle—i.e. an act of God—is not visible or ascertainable like worldly events. The only way to preserve the unworldly, transcendental character of the divine activity is to regard it not as an interference in worldly happenings, but something accomplished *in* such a way that the closed weft of history as it presents itself to objective observation is left undisturbed.[107]

Not only does this raise the question of whether the Gospel writers were as unsophisticated as Bultmann assumes in being unable to distinguish between language that was mythical or analogical and language that was not, it also has the effect of dissolving the idea of miracle in the Gospels; a similar result is obtained by Tillich's definition (see §1.3).

Ten years later, in 1951, Bultmann delivered the Shaffer Lectures at Yale University Divinity School and the Cole Lectures at Vanderbilt University. In their published form he drew attention to the changed worldview we have compared to the writers of the Gospels. It is not that our worldview is definitive but that the way of thinking is different. That is, it is not a question of whether the earth rotates around the sun or the sun around the earth. But it does make a decisive difference that modern people understand the motion of the universe to be obeying a cosmic law, a law that human reason can discover. Therefore, says Bultmann,

> modern man acknowledges as reality only such phenomena or events as are comprehensible within the framework of the rational order of the universe. He does not acknowledge miracles because they do not fit into this lawful order. When a strange or marvellous accident occurs, he does not rest until he has found a rational cause.[108]

Bultmann developed this line of thought in 1958 in what for any study of the miracles of Jesus is an important essay: "The Question of Wonder" ("Zur Frage des Wunders").[109] His case for the abandonment of the notion of miracle is so important that we will devote some discussion to it in the next chapter when we deal with the theological objections to the possibility of miracles (§2.4).

The works of these two figures—Strauss and Bultmann—have meant that the two issues of the mythical character of the miracles and the extra-Christian origin of the stories remain sticking points for the study of the miracles of Jesus in the Gospels. Throughout various parts of this study we will return to these issues. However, before proceeding further we need to address the fundamental issue of the general possibility that miracles occur.

Two

The Possibility of Miracles

....

§2.1 Introduction

Later in this study we will reach the point where we can say with some degree of confidence that, so far as one can judge, particular reports of miracles can be taken as arising in the ministry of the historical Jesus (see §16.14). But, it might be argued, those reports could have been mistaken. What were once thought to be miracles cannot now be seen as such, for miracles do not happen.

Therefore before we can be satisfied that we have a historically reliable reconstruction of the miracles of Jesus (as well as of his perspective on the miracles), we need to answer the preliminary, more philosophical question of the possibility of miracles in any era. We have to move from the question "Did they think these miracles happened?" to "Did these miracles happen?"[1]

But what sort of miracles need to be shown as being possible in order to establish the historicity of the miracles of Jesus? It might be granted that some of the stories portrayed as miracles—for instance, the exorcisms and healing from paralysis—may have natural explanations. But there are stories—such as those about the raising of the dead and walking on water—that remain the kinds of miracles that for many are stumbling blocks in relation to the issue of the possibility of miracles. They run counter to what we could ever normally expect to experience from the processes of nature.

It is not possible to respond to all the objections to the possibility of miracles.[2] Nor is it within the scope of this book to give a full account of the theist's positive case for miracles. Nevertheless if we are going to allow for the possibility of the historicity of the Gospel miracles, we have to engage in a debate on at least three important fronts—philosophical, theological and scientific—even though these fronts are not always clearly separate from each other. The most space will be given to interacting with philosophical and theological issues, for they are the most critical.

It is not our experience but the view of reality that we accept that determines whether we accept the miraculous. C. S. Lewis begins his book on miracles by citing the example of the only person he had met who claimed to have seen a ghost. Yet, he said, this person, who disbelieved in the immortal soul before she saw the ghost, continued to disbelieve after seeing it. Lewis agrees that she may have seen an illusion or a trick of the nerves. But the conclusion he draws is that "seeing is not believing."[3]

Neither, says Lewis, can history prove or disprove the miraculous according to the ordinary rules of historical inquiry. The ordinary rules of inquiry cannot be worked until we have decided whether miracles are possible and how probable they are.

In a similar vein John Vincent has reminded us that if history is about evidence, it is only about evidence that meets our approval. Consequently that evidence of which we do not approve might as well not exist. "We decide, even before looking at it, what can be evidence and what not."[4] As an example he cites miracles, stating that the body of evidence in favor of miracles could not be of higher quality: it is based on eyewitness testimony, it is contemporaneous, massive in bulk, from educated people, it is often disinterested and varies little over a large number of centuries.

He concludes that "the historical evidence for miraculous intervention could not be weightier. Our decision to disregard it is not a historical decision, not an induction from the evidence as it is. It is based on our non-historical or *a priori* belief (for belief it is) that there is no such thing as the miraculous."[5] Therefore, since historical inquiry depends on the philosophical view brought to the evidence, the philosophical question must come first.

§2.2 Philosophical Objections to Miracles
On one side we can array the philosophers who defend miracles: R. F. Holland, Richard Swinburne and R. C. Wallace, for example.[6] On the other side we can array a long catalog of writers who have proposed philosophical objections to miracles: Benedict de Spinoza, David Hume, Alastair McKinnon, Malcolm L. Diamond, Patrick Nowell-Smith and George Chryssides, for example.[7]

Hume's celebrated case is so similar to modern objections and has been taken up in one way or another by so many modern critics of the miraculous that he is a proper starting point. Indeed, answering Hume's objections clears away the vast majority of philosophical objections to the miraculous. Alastair McKinnon offers an example of another kind of philosophical objection. Interacting with these two philosophers will show that their objections have been reasonably met, so that the possibility of miracles is not so easily set aside as some suppose.

1. *David Hume (1711-1776)*. The post-Enlightenment argument against miracles was led by this Scottish philosopher and historian.[8] Section X of his *Enquiries Concerning the Human Understanding and Concerning the Principles of Morals* (1748) is headed "Miracles." Hume flattered himself that he had discovered an argument that, if found to be correct, would be an everlasting check to all kinds of superstitious delusions and, consequently, be useful for as long as the world endures.[9] Two hundred and fifty years later this section is still discussed probably more than anything else he wrote, not least because of its subtle, controversial, even scandalous nature.

Hume's main argument—an *a priori* one—against reports of miracles can be summarized as follows.[10] If someone reports an event, it must be weighed along with the likelihood of its taking place. Reasoning on the basis of past experience, the less likely an event is to have taken place, the more reliable the testimony must be if it is to be accepted. What makes the report of a miracle difficult to accept is that "a miracle is a violation of the laws of nature; and as a firm and unalterable experience has established these laws, the proof against a miracle, from the very nature of the fact, is as entire as any argument from experience can possibly be imagined."[11] Thus "no testimony is sufficient to establish a miracle, unless the testimony be of such a kind, that its falsity would be more miraculous, than the fact, which it endeavours to establish."[12]

Some uncertainty exists as to exactly what Hume was arguing here.[13] One view is that Hume was arguing *a priori* that miracles are impossible.[14] Another view is that Hume was claiming only that the evidence against a miracle is always strong enough to counter the evidence for the miracle and therefore prevent belief.[15] An intermediate position takes better account of the evidence in Hume: he argues not that miracles are impossible but that the standard of proof required to make a miracle claim plausible must be so high that the evidence against that miracle must always be overwhelmingly strong. Therefore belief in any miracle is irrational.[16]

At first sight Hume's case seems unassailable, so much so that intellectual orthodoxy has generally succumbed to its charm. In a book such as this there is not the space—neither is it necessary—to respond to all the points Hume makes. Rather, all I want to do is draw attention to the points that demonstrate Hume's case to be untenable. We begin with his definition of *miracle*.

According to Hume's definition of miracle, previously quoted, nothing could be deemed miraculous unless it was unique. On Hume's reckoning, a miracle must contradict the whole course of experience. But surely two or three exceptions to our experience would neither disprove the so-called law nor rule out the exceptions as being miracles.[17] Put another way, as A. E. Taylor says, "Properly speaking, there are no laws of nature to be violated, but there are habits of expectation which any of us, as a fact, finds himself unable to break through."[18]

Taking this point from another perspective, Hume's definition assumes that experience is consistent, infinite and infallible. More reasonably he says earlier that experience is not altogether infallible nor are all effects seen to follow with like certainty from a supposed cause.[19] Therefore, against Hume, we are unable so easily to set aside a report of an event because it flies in the face of experience. And it would be as irrational to go on claiming that if only we had more experience, the so-called miracle would not be seen as such, as it would be to accept uncritically any report of an event that was contrary to general human experience.[20]

A further difficulty in Hume's definition is that it depends on our excluding the possibility that a god may bring about or order events that run counter to our general experience of nature. However, if a god did so act that an event took place outside our expectations, no amount of testimony to the contrary would be relevant to weighing the evidence.[21]

To these difficulties in the definition we must add another: Hume is assuming that reports of miracles are verbal and based on memory, ignoring the possibility that miracles may be reported or reflected in and through subsequent events. For example, in the case of the resurrection of Jesus, not only are there evidences of verbal and written reports—in Paul and the Gospels—there is the evidence of the existence of Easter faith and the ongoing life of the church as testimony to the miracle.[22] Therefore on this point, against Hume, we unable to set aside the possibility of the occurrence of a miracle, for apart from verbal reports there may be more objective events and artifacts to bear witness to the miracle.

In light of this definition Hume said that "no testimony is sufficient to establish a miracle, unless the testimony be of such a kind, that its falsity would be more miraculous, than the fact, which it endeavours to establish."[23] Against this Keith Ward has rightly made the point that "if we have observed carefully, in good conditions, testimony will rationally outweigh expectations." He goes on to say that it must do so, for our expectations are, themselves, founded on testimony and on acceptance of thousands of reports from others.[24]

In the second part of Hume's treatment of miracles he gives four secondary *a posteriori* arguments against miracles. Here Hume is trying to show that, whether or not there might be evidence strong enough to conclude that a miracle has taken place, the evidence is so poor that it cannot even begin to serve as grounds for belief in miracles. First,

there is not to be found, in all history, any miracle attested by a sufficient number of men, of such unquestioned good sense, education, and learning, as to secure us against all delusion in themselves; of such undoubted integrity, as to place them beyond all suspicion of any design to deceive others; of such credit and reputation in the eyes of mankind, as to have a great deal to lose in case of their being detected in any falsehood; and at the same time, attested facts performed in such a public manner and in so celebrated a part of the world, as to render the detection unavoidable.[25]

He goes on to say that all these conditions need to be met for the acceptance of a report of a miracle. Although this last point might be accepted, it can be shown that there are many reports of miracles by sane and sensible witnesses. For example, of the fifty thousand cures reported in the town of Lourdes in the southwest of France, careful scrutiny has led to the declaration that fifty-eight of them were miraculous.[26] Also, Dr. Rex Gardner has reported a number of inexplicable healings of patients for whom prayer had been offered.[27]

Hume himself cites the great number of miracles that took place in France upon the tomb of Abbé Paris, the famous Jansenist: "The curing of the sick, giving hearing to the deaf and sight to the blind, were everywhere talked of as the usual effects of that holy sepulcher." He goes on to say that what was more extraordinary was that "many of the miracles were immediately proved upon the spot, before judges of unquestioned integrity, attested by witnesses of credit and distinction, in a learned age, and on the most eminent theatre that is now in the world."

Hume then asks what can oppose such a cloud of witnesses to these miracles. His answer is simply and dogmatically "the absolute impossibility or miraculous nature of the events, which they relate."[28] This is not a defense but rather an abandonment of his argument, retreating into dogmatism.

Second, Hume states that our confidence in reports of miracles is diminished in light of a human tendency to believe those reports because of the agreeable emotion of surprise and wonder they engender.[29] However, as Colin Brown has retorted,

> Hume's point just will not stand. It is irresponsible to brand all religious people as naturally prone to disseminate untruth whether wittingly or unwittingly. . . . He writes as if all believers are either deceivers or the deceived. He fails to take into account the possibility that some people, including religious people, are by nature skeptics.[30]

On the other hand, one of Hume's contemporary critics, George Campbell, made the point that "the prejudice resulting from the religious affection, may just as readily obstruct as promote faith in a . . . miracle."[31]

Third, Hume says that a strong presumption against reports of miracles is formed in noting that they arise mainly among ignorant and barbarous people.

Further, where civilized people do believe the reports, they will be found to have been received from their ignorant and barbarous ancestors.[32]

However, it is false to suggest that people in prescientific times were so unaware of what could be expected of the natural world that they uncritically accepted reports of the dead rising to life or the blind being made to see. Attention can also be drawn to the point already adumbrated that Hume has failed to take into account that some reports of miracles arise, as they still do, from informed skeptics.[33] Notably Hume has not taken into account his own example of relating miracles at the tomb of Abbé Paris.

Hume's fourth point against miracles is that conflicting religions all claim miracles in establishing their particular system. Therefore there is no testimony for any miracle that is not opposed by an infinite number of witnesses, each canceling out the others.[34]

In reply, it is simply not true that all religions are miracle-based. Furthermore, Hume incorrectly assumes that the evidence for miracles supporting one religion can be no greater than that in another religion.[35] Nor does Hume take into account the possibility that miracles could have different supernatural beings as their cause. It is also a mistake to assume that, at least in Christianity, the main purpose of miracles is to support its truth, and few Christians would deny that God is active in some way in religions other than Christianity.

In any case, as Richard Swinburne puts it, "evidence for a miracle 'wrought in one religion' is only evidence against the occurrence of a miracle 'wrought in another religion' if the two miracles, if they occurred, would be evidence for propositions of the two religious systems [being] incompatible with each other."[36] Swinburne is right: it is hard to think of a pair of alleged miracles of this kind. In short, there is no compelling reason that miracles cannot occur in relation to more than one religion.

As noted earlier, it is often assumed that the arguments of Hume and those who have followed him have never been answered and that those who have tried to assail Hume have been ill-informed and failed.[37] However, we have seen that a careful reading of Hume and an awareness of the writings of others raise some serious doubts about his case and conclusions.[38] Hume and those who follow him can be challenged at an informed and sophisticated level; it is justifiable to conclude that Hume has not closed the door to the possibility of miracles occurring.

2. Alastair McKinnon (b. 1925). McKinnon presents another example of a philosophical challenge to the possibility of miracle.[39] Hume was arguing that the standard of proof required to make a miracle claim plausible must be so high that the evidence against a miracle must always be overwhelmingly strong and that therefore belief in any miracle is irrational. On the other hand, Alastair McKinnon has argued that it is the concept of miracle itself that is incoherent.[40] One way of defining a miracle, he says, is as "an event involving the suspension of natural law." He says that the problem with this idea is that if the laws of nature are simply shorthand descriptions of how things happen, then, oddly, a miracle is an exception to what actually happened.[41]

However, McKinnon's approach is unsound. The terms *natural law* and *the actual course of events* cannot be interchanged. This assumes the actual course of events will conform to natural laws.[42] For a natural law alone cannot tell us what will or will not happen without us knowing that there are no other relevant forces present.[43]

McKinnon also says that there is another definition of miracle that is incoherent: that which says a miracle involves either the suspension of natural law or conflicts with our understanding of natural law. He claims that a person cannot believe both that a miracle happens and that it conflicts with his or her concept of nature. Either the person ought to surrender the idea of the historicity of the miracle or surrender how he or she understands nature.[44]

However, the laws of nature need not be suspended for a miracle to take place. It could be that some god has changed the conditions to which the laws apply and so introduced an event that nature would not otherwise have produced.[45] As impressive as McKinnon's arguments may be, they involve such contradictions that they have to be set aside.

Of course by no means have all the philosophical objections to accepting the possibility of miracles been discussed. However, the two examples cited, especially that of Hume, will serve as illustrations of its being possible to meet the objections of philosophers.

§2.3 Theological Objections to Miracles

We will not attempt to enter into a debate with all the theological objectors. Instead, we will take some of the key issues that have dominated the discussion to show that it remains reasonable on theological grounds to accept the possibility of miracles.

1. For three reasons *Rudolf Bultmann* argued that the idea of miracle has become untenable and must be abandoned.[46] First, he said that the concept of *Mirakel* ("miracle") had to be abolished because it has become impossible in light of our understanding of the processes of nature as governed by law. An event such as a miracle is untenable not because it would contradict all experience but because "conformity to law" or the universal validity of natural law—which is part of our understanding of nature as ontological, prescientific or premodern—is *"given in our existence in the world"* and something from which we are unable to free ourselves.[47] This unarguably presupposes that God does not or could not intervene in the natural processes. Unless we wish to adopt a form of deism, we must assert

God's freedom of ongoing involvement in his creation (cf. Ps 115:3).

Second, Bultmann said that miracle has become untenable because it is not a notion of faith but a purely intellectual notion. By this he means that miracles can be done by either Satan or God, wizards or prophets, for the miracle does not carry a label of its origin. Therefore before the miracle takes place the observer must know its origin. "But," says Bultmann, "to say that is to admit that understanding a wonder as a miracle is to abandon the idea of God's action as an inherent element in miracle."[48]

That there are events the biblical writers call miracles does not solve this ambiguity. "The fact merely makes necessary the use of critical methods which show that the biblical writers, in accordance with the presuppositions of their thinking, had not fully appreciated the idea of miracle and its implications."[49] In any case, in that the so-called miracles are "deeds of a man in the past they do not directly concern us. Seen as such they are not works of the Christ, if we understand by the work of Christ the work of redemption."[50]

To this it can be replied that the ambiguity of the origin of a miracle does not tell against its possibility. Also, it may be possible to see in the miracle itself the character of its origin. If it is considered evil and destructive, it could be assigned to Satan; if it were thought constructive or salvific, it could be assigned to God. Further, we cannot dismiss the miracles as dissociated from redemption. They are, to stay with Bultmann's language, part of the work of redemption no less than forgiveness and the resurrection. In line with this we will see that it was Jesus' view that his miracles, notably the exorcisms, were part of the coming of the kingdom of God (cf. Mt 12:28/Lk 11:20). Also, to attach any miracles to the man Jesus and thereby suggest that they do not concern us is to separate the risen Christ from the earthly Jesus in a way that is no longer generally considered legitimate.[51]

Third, Bultmann says that the concept of miracle has to be rejected because it is sinful to look for a miracle in a world that has an orderly course of nature. We can understand this point through Bultmann's example, the sin of the Jews asking for a miracle (1 Cor 1:22). In this case, asking for a miracle is a sin in that it is requiring God to certify himself through his achievement.[52] However, Bultmann has failed to note the difference between a demand for God to declare and prove himself in a particular way and the possibility of God graciously offering to declare—not prove—himself in a miraculous way in order to heal or raise the dead, for example.

While Bultmann argues for the abolition of the concept of miracle, he wants to preserve that of wonder *(Wunder)*. For Bultmann there is only one wonder—"the wonder of *revelation,* the revelation of the grace of God for the godless, the revelation of forgiveness."[53] Forgiveness is a wonder in that it is God's action in contradiction to the world process. In this there may be found no fault save in his restriction of wonder to forgiveness.

However, Bultmann's whole vendetta against "miraculous" events contrary to the expected order of nature can be seen as driven by his worldview, which he uses to determine uncritically what is historically true or possible and what is not. He says, in an oft-quoted passage, "It is impossible to use electric light and the wireless and to avail ourselves of modern medical discoveries, and at the same time to believe in the New Testament world of daemons and spirits."[54] This view is further revealed in other statements, such as: "Hardly anyone will support the historicity of a telepathic healing," and "An historical event which involves a resurrection from the dead is utterly inconceivable."[55] Bultmann's theological program directed against the miraculous can be seen to have failed.

2. For *John Macquarrie (b. 1919)* miracle has the meaning of a supernatural intervention to cause an event. In making his case against miracles, Macquarrie appears to echo Bultmann by first saying that the idea of the miraculous "is objectionable theologically because it goes back to a mythological outlook and expects God to manifest himself and prove himself in some extraordinary sensible phenomena."[56] He says that in establishing the claims of their faith, the early Christian writers wisely avoided putting too much weight on any appeal to miracles reportedly done by Jesus. He goes on to say that they were following the teaching and example of Jesus, who eschewed miracles to establish his claims.

Macquarrie cites the following examples of Jesus eschewing miracles: the temptation that Jesus throw himself down from the pinnacle of the temple (Lk 4:9-12), his condemning the kind of mentality that sought a sign (Mt 12:39), and his saying "If they do not listen to Moses and the prophets, neither will they be convinced even if someone rises from the dead" (Lk 16:31).

On the one hand, however, Macquarrie has failed to note that in each of these cases Jesus is portrayed as facing unsympathetic opponents. Also, if this material was permitted to stand as faithfully reflecting Jesus' attitude (and many would not permit it), it could be argued that Jesus was not going to allow others in their contrary willfulness to dictate the giving of signs only to have them then dispose of them.[57] On the other hand, there is plenty of evidence that Jesus reportedly performed miracles (the exorcisms, for example) knowing that they were seen, at least by the demon(iac)s, as evidence of his divine status (e.g., Mk 1:24; 3:11).

Further, as already noted, the particular playing down of miracles does not rule out the propriety of other appeals to miracles as revealing Jesus' significance,[58] as the writer of John's Gospel does at the end of his work: "These [signs] are written so that you may come to believe that Jesus is the Messiah" (Jn 20:31). Over against Macquarrie on this point it can be concluded that both Jesus and the early Christians were not averse to using the miracles to reflect on Jesus' status. Macquarrie's case turns out to be no more secure than Bultmann's.

3. Another theological objection is that if miracles were allowed, people would be so overwhelmed or coerced by the event that they could exercise no freedom in their believing.[59] Joseph Houston has recently reminded us that underpinning this argument is Søren Kierkegaard's contention that, properly, Christian faith has no objective support. Religious belief must involve a commitment-no-matter-what.[60] Two points can be made against this.

First, to follow Houston, "in the Bible people are condemned for cleaving stubbornly to vain traditions, for failing to see what new thing God is doing; and being open to correction, or ready for discovery, is part of the faithful person's attitude."[61] That is, faith involves people changing in light of a changing understanding of God.

Second, it is uncertain whether anyone ever has the complete freedom to believe or not. C. S. Lewis somewhere describes the compulsion to believe as his most free act: "[God's] compulsion is our liberation," he concluded in his autobiographical *Surprised by Joy*.[62] In any case, as the Gospel writers report, even the most striking miracle disclosing the hand of God can be rejected (e.g., Mk 6:1-5). In short, it is not credible to reject the possibility of miracles on the grounds that they would reduce human freedom: freedom is already in question, and what freedom there is does not seem always to be curtailed by the miraculous.

4. *Paul Tillich's (1896-1965)* theological objection was that miracles "cannot be interpreted in terms of a supernatural interference in natural processes. If such an interpretation were true, the manifestation of the ground of being would destroy the structure of being; God would be split within himself."[63] Hugo Grotius made the same point in his famous statement: "Natural law is so immutable that it cannot be changed by God himself."[64]

To this view we must reply that we cannot say it is impossible for God to alter what he has freely created. It would be a return to deism to suggest that the created order could either run by itself or that God was not always involved or could not be specifically involved in performing a miracle.[65]

5. There is another interesting theological objection to miracles: If God acts to perform miracles, why does he not act to prevent more evil?[66] One reply is that although God may love all human beings, he is under no obligation to assure complete equality regarding the temporal conditions of all humans. Further, it is not plausible to think that any human being has a claim on God either to prevent evil or to perform a miracle. To this is to be added the point that we humans cannot claim other than ignorance of all the reasons why God may act in any particular way. Nor can we say that God acts arbitrarily. The message of the book of Job is that it is rash for any person to presume to understand the ways and means by which God acts in the world. We cannot, in our finitude, even suggest why God does not intervene more often to perform miracles or prevent evil.[67]

6. Jesus' exorcisms are in the class of miracle that may be both most difficult to accept and most easily dispensed with. The vast majority of students of the Bible understand our world in a way that is, if not completely, fundamentally different from the so-called mythical world of the biblical writers.[68] If that is correct, then what are reported as exorcisms need now to be understood as mental illnesses cured by the healing word of Jesus, perhaps in a way similar to that of modern psychologists, who heal through the explaining and naming of the mental disturbance.

Yet the first-century assessment of sickness cannot easily be dispensed with as being uncritical.[69] It is easy to show that in some quarters the existence of demons was a matter of debate. For example, in the context of a discussion about healing, Lucian of Samosata (c. A.D. 120-c. 180) writes with a strangely modern ring: " 'Do you really think that certain incantations put a stop to this sort of thing . . . ?' They laughed at my remark and held me convicted of great stupidity." A little further on there is a discussion about demons: "You act ridiculously . . . to doubt everything. For my part, I should like to ask you what you say to those who free possessed men from their terrors by exorcising spirits so manifestly" (*The Lover of Lies* §16).

Not only was the demonic a matter of debate, there was a distinction often made between sickness and healing on the one hand and demon-possession and exorcism on the other.[70] Whether or not a person accepts the reports of Jesus' miraculous exorcisms as faithfully reflecting historical events depends on more than seeing that in the first century there was a critical assessment of sickness—even reflected in the Gospels. It also depends on whether or not the prevailing worldview of the intellectual elite of our society is an adequate model for understanding the experiences of sickness and healing.

In *A Rumour of Angels,* a brief but important book, Peter Berger pointed out that under the pressure of contemporary secularization the church has surrendered the supernatural. Yet Berger is able to cite a number of statistics, including some from a study in England in which 50 percent of the respondents had consulted a fortuneteller, one in six believed in ghosts, and one in fifteen had claimed to have seen one:

> There continue to be massive manifestations of that sense of the uncanny that modern rationalism calls "superstition.". . . For whatever reasons, sizeable numbers of the specimen "modern man" have not lost a propensity for awe, for the uncanny, for all those possibilities that are legislated against by the canons of secularized rationality.[71]

Further, a National Opinion Poll Ltd survey asked two questions of people in Britain. One was "Have you ever been aware of or influenced by a presence of a power?"

To this 36 percent of the sample gave a positive response. The other question was "Have you ever felt as though you were very close to a powerful spiritual force that seemed to lift you out of yourself?" To this the positive response was 31 percent.

Follow-up interviews revealed that some of this experience was thought to be of evil powers. This means it could be predicted that more than one-third of the British population believe they have had some kind of religious experience that is outside the prevailing scientific and secular descriptions of our society and consciousness.[72]

To answer the question at hand, the contemporary secular, scientific worldview, devoid of the supernatural, which has mesmerized the traditional church, is not adequate to describe and interpret the breadth of human experience. The distance between the first century and modern times is not as great as some believe (or hope!)—the people of the New Testament era did not always unthinkingly accept the supernatural or believe that demons caused all trouble or sickness. Nor is the contemporary world so devoid of such experience that we can dispense with the supernatural, including the notion of evil spiritual beings.

However, to allow the miracles of exorcism to stand as historically credible, we have to show that evil spiritual beings and their possession of people can be a credible part of our view of the world. The place to begin is with John Macquarrie's suggestion that creation involves a series of beings that occur in a kind of hierarchy, some beings standing closer than others to humans. He says that there is no reason we should suppose that the series of beings must terminate with humanity: "The panorama of creation must be far more breathtaking than we can guess in our corner of the cosmos, for there must be many higher orders of being whose service is joined with ours under God."[73]

Macquarrie does not use this argument to discuss demons or evil spirits because, as he says, they "have been eliminated through the secularization of our understanding of nature."[74] Yet we have just seen how this is not the case for many people. Nevertheless Macquarrie has provided one fruitful way of exploring the possibility of the existence of some form of super- or, perhaps better, subnatural evil spiritual beings.

The case is advanced by turning to an argument from religious experience. Philosophers have sometimes claimed that religious experience points to nothing beyond itself. Yet when discussing experiences of other kinds they would not adopt this attitude.[75]

Several contemporary philosophers, including Richard Swinburne, argue in relation to the existence of God that unless there is demonstration that very probably God does not exist, those who have religious experiences purportedly of God ought to believe them to be genuine. Even those who have not had any such experiences are faced with so great a weight of testimony of personal experiences purportedly of God that they must agree to the considerable probability of his existence. In short, "Religious perceptual claims deserve to be taken as seriously as perceptual claims of any other kind."[76]

With this argument in mind, and turning to the existence of evil spiritual beings, I would suggest that the material evidence collected by, for example, Kock, Richards, Montgomery and Perry contains perceptions made by reliable persons in reliable circumstances of experiences that we must take into account as we consider the existence of some form of evil spiritual beings.[77] Further, these reports not only advance the case for the existence of demons but also suggest that such beings are able to take control of people.

Further to this case, the notion of correspondence can be explored. Graham Dow—I think correctly—suggests that there is a correspondence between descriptions of present-day alleged demonic phenomena and the descriptions of the demonic in the New Testament.[78] For example, there is a correspondence between the present and New Testament accounts of demonic possession in the reported superhuman abilities of the sufferer, which completely disappear after healing.

Dow gives a second level of correspondence in that the New Testament writers, like our contemporaries, "show the ability to ascribe similar disorders on some occasions to demonic realities and on others not."[79] Then, third, Dow suggests another level of correspondence between the phenomena and the explanation offered—between the diagnosis and the cure. Thus in many instances to suggest the activity of a demon is the most satisfactory model for understanding the reality present.[80]

The evidence offered for the existence of evil spiritual beings and possession does not mean that we can define "demons," "evil spirits" or "possession" more precisely than to say that they are some form of evil agency often manifesting personal characteristics in control of human lives. A number of reasonable conclusions can be drawn from this discussion:

□ We could expect modern people to have encounters with the demonic in a way that is congruent with that echoed in the Gospels.

□ A miracle of exorcism could be expected to be part of the experience of a modern person.

□ We cannot deny the possibility of the miracle of exorcism in the ministry of the historical Jesus.

In the context of this study, the theological objections to miracles are particularly significant. Nevertheless we have seen that the objections put forward by Bultmann, Macquarrie, Tillich and others can be met quite readily. With so many Gospel miracle stories involving the demonic, countering the view that such phenomena are to be relegated to a prescientific age has been important.

§2.4 Scientific Objections to Miracles

The relationship between miracles and scientific laws has taken up much of the discussion about the concept of miracle.[81] Guy Robinson, for example, has objected to the notion or possibility of miracles on the ground that it would destroy the scientific endeavor.

He says that if a scientist allowed himself to employ the concept of an irregularity in nature, he would be finished as a scientist. Scientific development would either be stopped or made completely capricious because it would be a matter of whim whether an event was designated a miracle or a scientific theory needed to be modified.[82] This objection to the idea of miracle is based on the view that we have no way of knowing whether anomalies in our experience are to be regarded as miracles or whether we have incomplete knowledge of the natural world.[83]

In response to this objection, Robert Larmer proposed a test that makes it possible to distinguish between events that could be properly called miracles and events that indicate an inadequate understanding of the natural processes. In essence his test is as follows: supposing there is good evidence that the event that is an exception to regularity took place, if the event took place in a context in which it can be seen, on the one hand, to have moral and religious significance yet, on the other hand, is not consistently repeatable, we have evidence of a miracle taking place rather than an indication that natural processes are not fully understood.

Larmer admits the difficulty of applying this test, for there may exist reports of a miracle where it is difficult to decide whether the conditions for a miracle or a lack of understanding of the natural world have taken place. But at least the decision would not be based on a mere whim but on the application of a test, even if further understanding of the natural world changes our view of the event being a miracle. Further, there would come a point when it was irrational to maintain that a miracle had not taken place.[84]

Modern scientific endeavor is continually compelling us to modify our understanding of the processes of the natural world. Hence the so-called laws of nature, by which we describe the limits of our experience, are under constant revision. Nevertheless, there are some laws about which we know so much that an event reported contrary to them would be considered a miracle.

If we had good evidence, for example, of an instance of levitation, of the coming back to life of a person whose heart had stopped beating and all bodily processes had ceased for in excess of twenty-four hours, of water being turned into wine without mechanical or chemical assistance or of a person recovering from polio in a minute, we would not wish to revise the particular law of nature.[85] We would not even wish to suggest that one day these events might be explained scientifically. As Margaret Boden says, "Such a suggestion would be at least as blatant an act of faith as the wildest claim ever made in the name of religion."[86] Rather, from our experience of the world, we would agree that a miracle had taken place.

§2.5 Conclusions

Insofar as this discussion of some objections to the possibility of miracles can be taken as representative, we have been able to clear the ground of objections to the possibility of miracles. In part the argument has been that a view of the world that admits only its deistic physicality is inadequate in understanding our experience of it.

We could do a number of things to make a positive case for the possibility of miracles. The idea of "agency" could be clarified and developed,[87] for the idea of a miracle implies an immaterial agent with the ability to produce or influence events in our experience.[88] An argument or a body of evidence could be provided to support the existence of immaterial agents capable of such activity.[89] Then a worldview could be developed, one that accepts and explains all that is true in our experience of the natural world yet also includes a framework to make sense of the action of the immaterial agents.[90]

However, all we would need to accomplish in order to make a positive case for miracles is to make a case for the existence of the kind of God portrayed in the Gospels.[91] Indeed, as Norman Geisler put it clearly, "Miracles cannot be identified without a logically prior commitment (on whatever grounds) to the existence of God."[92] That is, we would need to support the theist—the person who believes in an eternal, necessary, personal, spiritual, loving creator-God distinct from creation yet continually active in sustaining the universe and the proper object of obedient worship.[93]

If there is such a God, we would expect him to interact with his creation, at least occasionally, on a personal basis in response to the prayers of his creatures. Yet we would not expect him to intervene in the natural order frequently, for that would remove the predictability of the consequences of our actions and cause us confusion.[94]

I will refrain from entering into the debate on the existence of this God. Instead, I refer to the overwhelming amount of literature on the subject and the reasonable cases made for the existence of such a God.[95] Further, my case would be helped if it could be supported with a reasonable defense of the doctrine of the incarnation.[96]

The import of all this is that *it is quite reasonable to suppose that miracles are possible*. Indeed, with Ninian Smart we can say that there is "no reason in the nature of things why occasional random and inexplicable events should not occur."[97] Further, *in view of the nature of the God of the Gospels and a reasonable defense of the doctrine of the incarnation, such miracles as are reflected in the Gospel stories are likely to have happened*. Whether particular miracle stories in the Gospels accurately reflect "what actually happened" will be discussed in part four.

§2.6 The Next Step

The next major part of this study needs to be an examination of the primary data: the miracle stories associated with Jesus in the four Gospels. We will not be seeking to recover the historical elements of the stories or trying to discern what Jesus thought of his miracles. Rather we will be trying to understand what each of the Gospel writers understood by the miracles and what part they played in the message they had for their readers.[98] Each of the Gospel writers will be treated separately and in turn.

Since the prime question will be "What do the Gospel writers say about the miracles?" my guiding critical methods of approach will generally be redaction criticism and narrative criticism, for we are primarily concerned with how the Gospel writers have gone about plotting their narratives and have handled the details of their material by shaping it to convey their message and with how the text would have presented itself to the first readers. The state of contemporary research and the differences among the Gospels will give rise to the distinct way I treat each Gospel. We begin with Mark, as it is generally agreed to be the first Gospel published.

PART 2

The Miracles of
Jesus in the Gospels

Three

The Miracles of Jesus
in Mark

....

§3.1 Introduction

Of all the neglected aspects of Gospel research, Mark's perspective on the miracles is not one of them.[1] Scholarly interest is not surprising: twenty miracle stories and summaries of healings account for almost one-third of Mark's Gospel[2] and nearly one-half of the first ten chapters,[3] a proportion greater than in any other Gospel.[4]

This proportion appears to be even greater than it is because, up to the central section on discipleship (beginning with the story of the blind man of Bethsaida; Mk 8:22-26), seventeen of the twenty pericopes occur. Further, some of these stories are strung together or set in single days, giving the impression that performing miracles occupied a great deal of Jesus' time. Despite the great attention given to the study of the miracles of Jesus in Mark, there is little agreement as to why and in what ways miracles are important to Mark.

§3.2 Miracles and Mark's Purpose

That Mark's purpose revolves in some way around the identity and mission of Jesus is axiomatic. The relationship between this purpose and his perspective on the miracles is far from clear, however.

For example, in explaining why Jesus was not recognized as the Messiah, William Wrede proposed that Mark introduced into his material the imposition of a ban on publicity regarding the miracles and other aspects of Jesus' ministry.[5] Johannes Schreiber understood the miracles in Mark differently. He took the miracle stories to represent a "divine man" Christology that was in competition with the self-emptying gnostic savior that Mark wished to promote.[6] But as we will see in the last section of this chapter, such proposals have not been widely accepted (§3.29).

It has long been postulated that in the earliest days of the church the miracle stories of Jesus served as material for evangelists as they portrayed Jesus as the Messiah[7] or demonstrated the preeminence of the "Lord Jesus," driving all other gods from the field.[8] Concomitantly it is argued or assumed that, following this tradition, the second Gospel is an evangelistic document for those outside the Christian community.[9] Indeed, the portrayal of Jesus as a suffering teacher-king would have been admired among Greco-Roman readers at large.[10]

Yet this is not the full story and is to be questioned.[11] For example, the points of tension in the Gospel—the question of fasting, the use of the Sabbath, ceremonial defilement, the ambition of James and John to sit with Jesus in glory[12]—would all be of little interest to those outside the church. Further, the teaching Mark gives on divorce, forgiveness, humility, trust, prayer and the stories on exorcism[13] are directed to Christians. Therefore on balance we can conclude that although Mark's prime concern was to communicate to a Christian audience, we should not, as Mary Ann Beavis cautioned, make too sharp a distinction between Mark's Christian and non-Christian audiences.[14]

Thus Mark's purposes were probably not directly or entirely evangelistic in nature; they were more likely to be predominantly pastoral in that he was trying to encourage his readers in their evangelism and life together. This means his interest in the miracle stories is unlikely to be primarily to convince outsiders of the identity of Jesus or the truth of his message. Rather, his use of the miracle stories will be a piece with his purpose, primarily to encourage his readers in their faith, evangelism and life together. The precise nature of this encouragement and the role of miracle stories in evangelism will become clearer as we proceed.

§3.3 The Story of Mark

It is now generally acknowledged that Mark's Gospel is more than a haphazard collection of short stories. Instead Mark is thought to have woven individual stories into a carefully plotted continuous narrative. Therefore as we now attempt to understand his theology of the miracles of Jesus, we will not only need to examine the sayings and stories themselves but do so in light of his single coherent story.[15] Further, as Mark does not often reveal the inner thoughts of his characters, including Jesus, his views on the miracles may be more easily gleaned from paying particular attention to the plot of his larger story, as well as various details in each story.

Little consensus exists regarding the overall plot and structure of Mark.[16] Nevertheless it is generally agreed that the story of Peter's confession at Caesarea Philippi marks a watershed in the Gospel (Mk 8:27-30).[17] As just noted, it is within the first section of Mark, prior to this summative confession, that most of the miracle stories are to be found. This means that not only does Mark want to portray Jesus as a miracle worker, or a powerful healer and exorcist, but the miracles make a major contribution to understanding who Jesus is. This conclusion will be confirmed and filled out as we proceed.

After the brief introduction (including the ministry of John the Baptist), Jesus breaks through Satan's temptation for him to remain silent (Mk 1:12-13). Jesus then begins his ministry by announcing that the kingdom of God has come near (1:14-15) and calls Simon, Andrew, James and John to follow him (1:16-20) immediately prior to conducting his first miracle.

§3.4 The Demoniac in the Synagogue at Capernaum (Mk 1:21-28/Lk 4:31-37)

Mark's placing this as the first miracle story, as well as the first public appearance of Jesus, signals to the reader the importance of miracles, exorcisms in particular, in understanding the ministry of Jesus.[18] Since Mark is writing about the "good news" of Jesus (Mk 1:1, 14-15) and the first public activity of Jesus is a miracle, we have the first hint that the miracles are not subsidiary to the gospel but at least coincident with it.[19]

Jesus is said to be known by the demons as the one who has come to destroy them and as "the Holy One of God" (Mk 1:24). This phrase was used at the time to denote a person—such as a prophet or holy man—thought to be from or living in the sphere of God.[20] In the context of Mark's Gospel it is of the same order as the title "Son of God." Thus Mark is using this story to confirm the identity of Jesus, initially spelled out by the heavenly voice as "my Son" (1:11).

The close relationship between the miracles and teaching of Jesus is demonstrated by the synagogue setting and highlighted when the amazed crowd asks "What is this? A new teaching—with authority!" (Mk 1:27). This point is probably important to Mark, for, as the vocabulary and grammar suggest,[21] these words are most likely from Mark's hand. What is "new" is that Jesus' teaching is realized or incarnated in exorcisms. Jesus is identified through both his teaching and his exorcisms.[22]

In saying Jesus' fame spread everywhere throughout the surrounding region of Galilee (Mk 1:28), Mark depicts the miracle as unable to be hidden—it leads to the preaching about Jesus.[23] Though faith is not mentioned, the spreading of Jesus' fame would, most naturally, be carried out by those who had confidence or faith—no matter how elementary—in his ability to heal. Through the brevity of his description and the response of the audience, Mark also draws attention to the extraordinary power of Jesus' exorcism ministry. With the very minimum of connection ("As soon as they left the synagogue," 1:29), Mark moves immediately to the next miracle story.

§3.5 Healing Simon's Mother-in-Law (Mk 1:29-31/Mt 8:14-15/Lk 4:38-39)

As the story begins the four disciples are still with Jesus (Mk 1:29),[24] a point that becomes increasingly important as Mark's story unfolds. In healing Simon's mother-in-law there is no direct mention of anyone's faith in Jesus. However, when Mark says that "they" (1:30)—most naturally the four disciples—told Jesus of her condition, he implies their faith or confidence in Jesus' healing power. The reader is to understand that this was sparked by being with Jesus in the synagogue.

This story too is characterized by the immediate and complete success of Jesus as a healer. The response of the healed woman is said to be one of service (*diakoneō*, Mk 1:31). Mark does not frequently use this word.[25] Its primary meaning is to serve someone generally[26] or to wait at table.[27] But the special nuance Mark wants to highlight is clear from its use in the strategic saying, "The Son of Man came not to be served but to serve, and to give his life" (10:45). In view of its connection here with the idea of dying or giving one's life, "service" in the present story takes on the idea of total devotion to Jesus in response to being healed by Jesus.

§3.6 Healings at Sundown—A Summary (Mk 1:32-34/Mt 8:16-17/Lk 4:40-41)

Mark ends the first day of Jesus' public ministry—a Sabbath dominated by two healings—with the first of the so-called summaries of Jesus' healings. Although Mark has included only two miracle stories so far, one of which was conducted in private (Mk 1:29-31), this summary creates the impression that these stories reflect a kind of ministry already much more extensive than the two miracles would indicate.[28]

News of Jesus' healing in the synagogue had so spread (cf. Mk 1:28) and—by implication—so generated faith in him that "the whole city" (1:33) was gathered around Simon's door with their sick and demon-possessed. Jesus is again portrayed as extraordinarily successful as a healer. (The "many" of 1:34 who were healed need not be exclusive, for an inclusive use of *polloi* has Semitic origins.)[29] Jesus' ability to heal implies that the crowd has faith,[30] for in a later summary (6:5-6) Mark says unbelief prevented Jesus from healing more than a few.

The summary of healings ends with the first of a number of Jesus' commands to silence that are associated with the healing stories (Mk 1:34). But here it is not a command to be silent about the healings, which have been unavoidably public. It is a command to the demons to be silent about the identity of Jesus.[31] Already Mark is establishing the paradox that, whereas in his healings Jesus' identity cannot be hidden, it cannot be fully understood save supranaturally.

We next read that the disciples, who found Jesus praying in a lonely place, told him that everyone was searching for him (Mk 1:37). In the context of Mark's narrative this was because Jesus was such a successful healer (1:32-34). However,

Mark has Jesus say that they must go to the neighboring towns "so that I may proclaim *[kēruxō]*[32] the message there also; for that is what I came out to do" (1:38). In the unity between teaching and healing that is emerging (cf. 1:27), there appears, at least superficially, to be a shift of emphasis away from healing to speaking.·

It could be that Mark is subordinating the miracles to what he considered to be Jesus' primary mission: teaching and proclaiming God's sovereign rule.[33] Perhaps Mark is portraying a tension between the public demand for Jesus' miracles and his call from God also to teach. Thus Cranfield, noting Calvin's view that the miracles were "appendages" to the Word, says that Jesus was rejecting the disciples' demand for Jesus to make the most of the opportunity to become a popular miracle worker.[34]

But a closer reading of the text leads to a different conclusion: that the miracles remain the focus of attention. In the two preceding stories Jesus has been portrayed as healing—first Simon's mother-in-law (Mk 1:27-31), then many who were brought to him that evening (1:32-34). Even though Mark says that Jesus went throughout Galilee proclaiming and casting out demons (1:39), Jesus is immediately portrayed healing a leper (1:40-45). Mark may be saying that both the miracles and the teaching are the message of Jesus.[35]

This can probably be taken one step further to suggest that, with Mark 1:38 describing the mission of Jesus simply in terms of proclaiming *(kērussein)* yet going on to describe him as exorcising and healing, as well as proclaiming (1:39, 40-45), Mark may wish to give the impression that healing and exorcism are neither separate nor distinct from the teaching but are the basis of the proclaiming and therefore more important than Jesus' speaking. That Jesus is portrayed in public as first a healer lends support to this theory. We will come across this theme again in the story of the cleansing of the leper.

This fluidity between word and deed—and deed as proclamation—is familiar in the prophetic traditions in the Old Testament. There are, for example, the actions of Isaiah walking about naked (Is 20), of Jeremiah smashing a potter's earthenware jug (Jer 19), and of Ezekiel eating a scroll (Ezek 2:8—3:3) and laying siege to a drawing of Jerusalem (4:1-4).[36] Even though none of these examples are of a miraculous kind, they do show the continuity between word and deed and, important for the point here, the understanding that an action can be proclamation.

§3.7 A Leper Cleansed (Mk 1:40-45/Mt 8:2-4/Lk 5:12-16)

In the Old Testament, leprosy is sometimes seen as a punishment for sin,[37] so Mark is probably telling a story not only about Jesus' ability to heal but also about his authority to forgive.[38] The way in which the leper approaches Jesus—begging him and kneeling—as well as how he addresses Jesus—"If you choose, you can make me clean" (Mk 1:40)—portrays a faith in Jesus' ability. As Mark tells the story, this faith does not arise from the miracle. Rather, trust in Jesus' ability precedes the request for healing and, by implication, forgiveness.

Because of the state of the text, Jesus' response to this act of faith (Mk 1:41) is not immediately clear. The majority of the manuscripts state that Jesus was "moved with pity" *(splanchnistheis)*, whereas others say that Jesus was "angry" *(orgistheis)*.[39] On the principle that the most difficult reading ought to be accepted, it remains to be explained why Mark describes Jesus as being angry. It could be that Mark understood the anger to be a ritual agitation or "pneumatic excitement" that a miracle worker might experience in reacting to situations of distress.[40] But this view has to be set aside for the lack of uniformity in the way the expression is used and because none of the examples leaves the impression of Jesus being taken over or controlled by a spiritual power that vents itself in such a variety of ways.[41]

Instead, it could be that Mark intends the righteous anger to be directed at the forces of evil for having distorted one of God's creatures.[42] Or it could be that Jesus is angry at the injustice done to the lepers by Israel.[43] Or Jesus may be responding angrily to people for breaking a divine sanction.[44] In fact we probably do not have to choose between these interpretations, for they are all likely to play a part in what Mark has in mind, though the next part of the story favors the suggestion that Jesus may have been angry over a breach of the law.

It remains a puzzle why Jesus "sternly charged" *(embrimaomai)* the healed man (Mk 1:43). It has been suggested that by this rarely used word[45]—probably in his tradition—Mark is conveying Jesus' displeasure or anger at the leper's infringement of the law by approaching Jesus. Or perhaps Jesus was expressing his frustration with evil and empathy toward the leper. Or it could be that he was verbalizing his attitude toward the battle with the forces of evil. Apart from the suggestion that Jesus was reacting to the leper's challenge to the law, none of these interpretations is supported by the text or the context.

The stern charge is a Middle Eastern command to silence, which functions like *epitimaō* ("sternly charged").[46] The hands were placed to the lips while breathing rapidly between the teeth,[47] perhaps equivalent to our placing a single finger across the lips and producing an extended "sh" sound. If this suggestion is correct, the sign calling for silence is verbalized in the command to say nothing to anyone (Mk 1:44). It could have been understood as both a response to the man's infringement of the law and a charge to silence.

The command to silence is followed by Jesus telling the man to show himself to the priest as a testimony to them (Mk 1:44). Mark could have meant this to be a positive witness to Jesus' power and his agreement with the Jewish law. Or included in this could have been a warning to the authorities against rejecting Jesus. Further, it might have been a condemnation of the Mosaic traditions, bringing cultic practices to an end. Alternatively the witness is likely to be thoroughly negative—a witness against them (cf. 6:11; 13:9).[48] This places Jesus in conflict with the religious leaders of Israel, a theme central to Mark's story. We will see this again in the next story of the healing of the paralytic.

In blatant disobedience to Jesus' command, Mark says that the healed man "began to proclaim *[kērussein]* it freely" (Mk 1:45). The miracle that Jesus had performed privately—no crowd is mentioned in the story—could not be contained or hidden. Notably (and in line with my suggestion that for Mark the miracles are paramount and can be the message) what is proclaimed is not a message distinct from or independent of the miracle but the miracle itself.

In addition, by using the word *proclaim* for the whole message of Jesus,[49] Mark is probably saying to his readers that the miracles give rise to the spread of the message about Jesus and therefore to some extent encapsulate the whole of the ministry of Jesus. This is confirmed in Mark's saying that the leper "spread the word" *(logos)*, a term that he also uses for the whole of Jesus' message.[50] Indeed, as we will see, the reported response of the leper takes us still further in realizing that for Mark the proclamation of Jesus is not independent of the miracles but arises out of them (see below).

The leper is told to present himself to the priest and make an offering for his cleansing (Mk 1:44). Because Mark is about to relate conflict over the law between Jesus and the authorities (2:1—3:6), he could be trying to demonstrate Jesus' concern for the law—an important issue in view of the following story.[51] However, that does not seem to be the major concern for Mark. More likely the procedure was seen to be part of the healing, enabling the man to be reunited with his people. This interpretation finds support in that the leper was cut off from his society (Lev 13-14).[52] Indeed, all three healings so far—a demoniac, a woman and this leper—have been of "outsiders" on whom Jesus has shown compassion.

Another puzzle is why the healed man, showing himself to the priest, could be "a testimony to them" (Mk 1:44). Mark is unlikely to be saying that the healed man is giving evidence to unbelievers of Jesus' status,[53] for that would directly contradict Jesus' previous charge to silence (1:43). More probably—especially in light of the ensuing conflicts with religious authorities over Jesus' obedience to the Sabbath regulations—the witness is to the man's healing being evidence of Jesus' obedience to the law.[54]

The conclusion to be drawn from this story is that, for Mark, a miracle of Jesus cannot be hidden. In fact, the result of this miracle is an overwhelming, positive interest in Jesus, so great that he is unable to enter a town openly without being surrounded by people (Mk 1:45). This predicament is continued and highlighted in the next story, where friends of a paralytic have difficulty getting him to Jesus through the crowds. This sharpens the tension for the readers between the teaching and the healing, for as people flock to be healed, Jesus is portrayed generally, and here in particular, as intending to teach them as well.

§3.8 A Paralytic Forgiven and Healed (Mk 2:1-12/Mt 9:1-8/Lk 5:17-25)

There has been considerable discussion about the unity of this story, for it deals with both the healing of a paralytic as well as an exchange between Jesus and his critics.[55] However, our concern is with the story as Mark presents it to his readers, which is dominated by a variety of responses to Jesus and his miracles.

The reader has been prepared for this story of a dramatic Sabbath healing by knowing already that Jesus is obedient to the law (Mk 1:44, see §3.7) and is a healer whose work cannot be hidden (cf. 1:45 and 2:2). Mark describes Jesus as being surrounded by people. Four people in particular express their faith in Jesus by overcoming their difficulty to get a sick person to him (2:5).

Although we have seen the theme consistently present in varying degrees in the miracle stories,[56] this is the first time faith has been explicitly mentioned since it was introduced as a key response to Jesus' ministry (Mk 1:15). The faith that Jesus acknowledges is not only (or even) that of the paralytic but of his bearers, for "their faith" (2:5) reads most naturally as referring to the four bearers, perhaps exclusive of the sick man. The paralytic's faith is evident only toward the end of the story, when he responds to Jesus' call to stand up (2:12). This is probably the first example of the vicarious faith of those closely related to a sick person.[57]

Their faith is probably not, in Mark's view, a naive trust in the power of a miracle worker, for they are said to be seeking to bring the man specifically to Jesus (Mk 2:4), who is, as we are about to see, more than a miracle worker in Mark.[58] Jesus addresses the man as "son" (*teknon*, 2:5), a word Mark uses for the disciples (10:24), perhaps showing that this encounter with Jesus results in discipleship for the man (that is, he had faith in Jesus). The paralytic is portrayed as exercising faith by his response of getting up and taking his mat home (2:12). However, this faith is not shown to be preexistent; it was elicited through Jesus' speaking to him.

From the healing stories so far, we might expect Jesus to heal by touch. Instead, Jesus speaks to him: "Son, your sins are forgiven" (Mk 2:5). As he has related no conversation to establish the need for forgiveness, Mark may wish to show Jesus having special insight into the needs of those he met. In any case, Mark is also demonstrating the common belief in the relationship between sin and sickness[59] and that forgiveness and healing are inseparable in Jesus' eschatological ministry. Forgiveness was thought to be the last great act in establishing salvation on earth.[60]

It could be that Jesus is declaring that God has forgiven the sins of the paralytic.[61] This would find a parallel in Nathan's declaring to David "The Lord has put away your sin" (2 Sam 12:13). However, in light of the ensuing debate with the scribes, there is no doubt that Mark is portraying Jesus as acting in the place of God—the

God of the Old Testament—in forgiving sin.[62]

The linking of healing and forgiveness and the general import of Mark 2:10 ("the Son of Man has authority on earth to forgive sins") mean that the reader can always take Jesus' ministry of healing as dealing not only with sickness but also with sin through forgiveness,[63] a point adumbrated in the cleansing of the leper. In this a parabolic dimension of the miracles is revealed.

Up to this point, all Jesus' activities in Mark are commensurate with his being a charismatic healer: gathering followers, teaching, casting out demons and healing.[64] But in forgiving sins Jesus' action is without parallel and is outside the scope of the law. Besides, there is nothing known in any Jewish literature of any person, including the Messiah, who can or would be able to forgive sin, except God. Therefore, although Jesus is being portrayed as a healer, he is more than that: in his healing (and forgiving) he is acting for God or, perhaps, even as God.[65]

Mark uses the term *Son of Man* to justify Jesus acting for God (Mk 2:10). There has been a prolix scholarly debate about this term.[66] The phrase "Son of Man" occurs fourteen times in Mark.[67] This is one of the two occasions when the phrase occurs prior to Peter's confession (cf. 2:28). Notably these two occurrences relate to Jesus' earthly authority to act in a unique way. In 2:28 the phrase relates to Jesus' lordship over the Sabbath.

In Daniel 7:14 the phrase is used of one "like a Son of Man," who has been given everlasting authority from God. Thus by means of this phrase Mark is drawing attention to this miracle, so demonstrating the unequaled authority of Jesus to act for God or in his place in forgiving sin. He reinforces this view by depicting the crowd glorifying God as a result of the miracle (Mk 2:12).

The incorporation of Jesus' reaction to the scribes (Mk 2:6-11) increases the range of responses Mark portrays to the miracles of Jesus: (a) those in the crowd (2:2) have responded positively to Jesus' healing of the leper (2:45) and are glorifying God (2:12), presumably expressing their faith in God (cf. 1:32; 6:5-6); (b) the four bearers have exercised vicarious faith; (c) the man himself has responded in faith, a fulfillment of the call of 1:15; and (d) the scribes have intimated that Jesus is acting blasphemously (2:7), a charge that will be echoed when Jesus is before Caiaphas (14:62-64).

This story is important because it holds together the themes of Jesus' preaching and his miracles—in being declared forgiven the man is healed of paralysis. Further, in the debate with the scribes, who are offended by Jesus' taking on the role of God, Jesus equates healing and forgiveness (Mk 2:9). Thus Mark is saying that the twin themes of speaking the good news of forgiveness and the healing from sickness are indissolubly linked—both are God's role and each is being carried out by Jesus. As in the last miracle story, in his healings Jesus is portrayed as being on the offensive against the religious authorities.

Following this miracle a number of stories revolve largely around Jesus' status in relation to God: his unique and absolute call of Levi (Mk 2:13-14),[68] his association with sinners and tax collectors (2:15-17), his not fasting (2:18-22) and his disregard for the Sabbath (2:23—3:6)—including a story of healing on the Sabbath (3:1-6), a story that concludes a section of controversies (2:1—3:6).[69]

§3.9 A Withered Hand Cured (Mk 3:1-6/Mt 12:9-14/Lk 6:6-11)

The last healing was the first story in the section of controversies. In this story the series of conflict stories comes to a climax (Mk 2:1—3:6).[70] The faith, or otherwise, of the sick man is not mentioned, save obliquely in his willingness to respond to Jesus' call to come to him (3:3) and to stretch out his withered hand (3:5). Thus as already seen in the last story, Jesus' miracles not only elicit faith but also draw out antagonism.

The miracle is not said to cause people to glorify God or even to reflect positively on Jesus. Instead, the Pharisees go out immediately to conspire with the Herodians against Jesus, seeking how they can destroy him (Mk 3:6). Thus again (cf. on 2:7 above) the shadow of the cross is cast over the miracles. Here the focus of attention is on Jesus' authority, which overrides the legal conventions of his adversaries. Immediately following this story Mark gives another of his summaries of Jesus' ministry.

§3.10 Crowds Come to Be Healed—A Summary (Mk 3:7-12/Mt 4:24-25; 12:15-21/Lk 6:17-19; 4:41)

This summary draws attention to the great popular appeal of Jesus as a healer, as well as to the very public nature of the miracles, especially through the telling of many cures (Mk 3:10) and of Jesus' exorcisms (3:11). This paragraph conveys the perception that Jesus' miracles extended beyond the preceding individual stories. The stories Mark has given are to be seen as mere isolated examples of a broader and more extensive ministry of miraculous healings and exorcisms.[71]

Jesus' command to the demons at the end of the summary ("not to make him known," Mk 3:12) is not a foil to highlight the impossibility of hiding the miracles, as in other commands to silence, but is a call not to publicize Jesus as the Son of God when he is, as yet, incompletely portrayed and understood as such. What can be taken as the end of a section on healing (1:21—3:6) is summarized here in a way that will be similarly repeated in 6:53-56.

In that Mark does not relate another miracle story until 4:35, this summary is important in irrefutably establishing the place and importance of miracles in the ministry of Jesus before turning to some of his teaching. As we will see in the next chapter, Matthew has reversed the significance, as well as the two panels of the healing-teaching diptych we have here in Mark (§4.2).

§3.11 The Twelve Appointed (Mk 3:13-19a/Mt 10:1-4/Lk 6:12-16)

Twelve of those who have heard Jesus' teaching and watched his healing are given authority to replicate two aspects of his ministry: preaching and casting out demons. That they receive authority only to cast out demons rather than to heal the sick generally, possibly reflects the fact that the majority of the healing stories Mark has included so far are exorcisms. More important, it is probably to draw attention to Jesus' healing ministry as being a battle with the demonic, a perspective that becomes more explicit in the next story.

§3.12 Jesus' Source of Authority for the Exorcisms (Mk 3:19b-30/Mt 9:32-34; 12:22-37/Lk 11:14-15, 17-23)

The issue in Mark over the identity of Jesus now comes to a point of crisis in the argument between Jesus and the religious leaders over the source of his authority (Mk 3:19b-30) and in a discussion on who can count themselves as his allies (3:31-35). On the one hand, the scribes attribute Jesus' success as an exorcist to his having Beelzebul or Satan. Mark has Jesus deny this in the statement that Satan could not cast out himself (3:24). On the other hand, Mark implies that Jesus' exorcisms are authorized by the Holy Spirit, the denial of which is the most tragic of sins (3:28-30).

Later Mark has Jesus say to his opponents, "Is not this the reason you are wrong, that you know neither the scriptures nor the power of God?" (Mk 12:24). Through using "power" here (which he uses in the plural of miracles)[72] with the qualifier "of God," Mark is obliquely affirming the divine origin of the miracles of Jesus. In this pericope Mark also explains the significance of the exorcisms by means of the parable of the strong man (3:27): Satan is being defeated, and those he has hitherto controlled are being taken from him by Jesus.[73]

Mark has portrayed the tension—yet indissoluble unity—in Jesus' ministry between the teaching and the miracles that cannot be hidden, as well as the antagonism the miracles generate. Now the graphic examples of miracles are balanced by an extended section of teaching on the nature of God's reign (Mk 4:1-34). In turn, this long teaching section will be further counterbalanced by yet another section of miracle stories (4:35—5:43), beginning with the story of the calming of a storm (4:35-41). Coming to that story presents us with the question of whether Mark has used two traditional cycles of miracle stories or, indeed, if he wishes his readers to understand the series of miracle stories found in 4:35—8:26 as two parallel sets of stories. If the latter, what does he wish to convey in the apparent parallelism?

§3.13 Pre-Markan Miracle Cycles

It is suggested that between the story of the calming of the storm (Mk 4:35-41) and the story of the feeding of the four thousand (8:1-10) are two roughly parallel cycles of stories that, with modifications, Mark has taken into his Gospel.[74] The attractiveness of this theory is seen when the stories are set out as follows:

Stilling a storm (4:35-41)	Walking on the sea (6:45-52)
Gerasene demoniac (5:1-20)	Blind man at Bethsaida (8:22-26)
Woman with a hemorrhage (5:25-34)	Syrophoenician woman (7:24b-30)
Jairus's daughter (5:21-23, 35-43)	Deaf-mute (7:31-37)
Feeding the five thousand (6:34-44, 53)	Feeding the four thousand (8:1-10)[75]

However, these two sets of miracle stories display only some degree of agreement with regard to content and vocabulary in the sea and feeding stories.[76] Most significantly the story of the blind man at Bethsaida (Mk 8:22-26) is obviously out of place in the above list. But according to this theory, the geographical reference ("They came to Bethsaida," 8:22) is taken as evidence that this story originally followed that of Jesus' walking on the sea, which also has a Bethsaida setting (6:45). However, that is hardly a convincing reason to relocate the story in the pre-Markan material. Following Robert Fowler, it is unlikely that there was such a cycle of miracle stories in Mark's tradition.[77]

Recovering Mark's intentions in these two apparent series of stories is more likely to come from noting the sequence of material as it is actually found in Mark and in what he himself has to say about the miracles. To begin with, when divided by the first miraculous feeding (Mk 6:30-44), the material that extends from the story of the storm (4:35-41) to just before Peter's confession (8:22-26) can be set out as follows:

Stilling a storm (4:35-41)	Walking on the sea (6:45-52)
Gerasene demoniac (5:1-20)	Healings at Gennesaret (6:53-56)
Jairus's daughter and	Pharisees on defilement (7:1-23)
the hemorrhaging woman (5:21-43)	Syrophoenician's daughter (7:24-30)
	Deaf-mute (7:31-37)
Unbelief and Jesus' rejection (6:1-6)	
Mission of the Twelve (6:7-13)	
John the Baptist beheaded (6:14-29)	
Feeding the five thousand (6:30-44)	Feeding the four thousand (8:1-10)
	Pharisees seek a sign (8:11-13)
	Disciples misunderstand (8:14-21)
	Blind man healed in two stages (8:22-26)

Mark's intentions in having two sets of stories here may be uncovered in two ways, the first way less certain than the second.

First, while Mark's actual progression of stories certainly does not reveal a tidy parallelism, it may be possible to see a broad pattern: sea miracles (Mk 4:34-41 and 6:45-52), exorcism stories (5:1-20 and 7:24-30), healing stories (5:21-43 and 7:31-37) and the miraculous feedings (6:30-44 and 8:1-10). Notably both cycles involve a misunderstanding and rejection of Jesus that is directly related to the miracles (6:1-6 and 8:11-21).

As Mark draws attention only to a parallelism between the feeding stories—in the discussion between Jesus and the disciples (Mk 8:14-21)—the clue to Mark's purpose in the paired narratives is probably to be found in this discussion. The plain import of Jesus' questions to the disciples about their incomprehension is that despite the enormity of the needs faced by Jesus and the disciples, on both occasions he was able to provide more than enough resources to meet their requirements. Thus through the arrangement of the two roughly parallel cycles of miracle stories, Mark has been developing the themes of Jesus' identity as well as the faith or trust of those who see the miracles.[78]

Following up this point in more detail, we can see that the first cycle of stories is generally characterized by a greater magnitude of miracle[79] (e.g., stilling a storm and taming an uncontrollable mad man) and the relative ease with which they are performed (e.g., the immediate obedience of the sea and the woman's mere touch of Jesus' garment). In the second set of stories, Jesus walks on the sea (no storm being mentioned) and feeds only four thousand. Is this diminution of the miraculous in their roughly parallel stories intended to draw attention to the need for faith? If so, when his ministry was not met by faith the result was a diminution of the miraculous.[80]

At the end of the two cycles of miracle stories, following the discussion about a sign and misunderstanding the miracles (Mk 8:11-21), there is the story of the two-stage healing of the blind man near Bethsaida (8:22-26). In light of what we have seen of the cycles and the fact that the receiving of sight can serve as a metaphor for receiving understanding, the generally recognized meaning of this story of a two-stage healing is clear: the disciples only partially understand the miracles. This is confirmed when we note that the next healing of blindness, which is complete and dramatic (10:46-52), follows the central section of Mark—the section on discipleship.

Another more certain way to discover Mark's intention in having two sets of stories is to pay attention to the settings of the stories, especially the two closest parallels—the two feedings—and their interpretation (Mk 8:14-21).[81] As we will see later, the feeding of the five thousand has an unmistakably Jewish setting, and the feeding of the four thousand has an unmistakably Gentile setting.[82] Also an examination of the other stories reveals that in some Jesus is among Jews and in some he is among Gentiles.

Thus through these two sets of stories, Mark is portraying Jesus on two parallel missions—one to the Jews and one to the Gentiles.[83] If we draw together these two ways of discovering why Mark has two sets of stories, we may be able to conclude that he is affirming the Gentile mission and, with less confidence, that he is affirming that when Jesus' ministry is not met with faith, the result is a diminution in the miraculous. We can now return to our discussion of individual stories within the first cycle of Mark's stories.

§3.14 Stilling a Storm (Mk 4:35-41/Mt 8:23-27/Lk 8:22-25)

After an extended section of teaching (Mk 4:1-34), this story begins both the first of the two so-called cycles of miracle stories (4:35—8:26) and the smaller collection of two pairs of miracle stories (4:35—5:20 and 5:21-43). In this way Mark—as he began to do from the first miracle story set in the context of Jesus' teaching in a synagogue (cf. 1:21-28)—is able to use this story to continue depicting Jesus as a man of both unique teaching and spectacular miracles.

This is also Mark's first so-called nature miracle. However, as we will see in §17.12, such categorizing of miracles was probably not obvious to Mark or to others in the first century.[84] One of the most striking aspects of the story is the magnitude of the miracle: the great storm, the boat filling and Jesus' instant and complete control of the situation. This story has the effect of setting the tone of expectation of the kind of miracle worker being portrayed in the following stories.

As the boat in Mark is always reserved as a place for Jesus and his followers to be together on a journey, it is reasonable to agree with those who see the boat as an image representing the church.[85] Through the storm Mark is probably depicting the church's suffering of preternatural attack, for in common with others of his time Mark believed that the elements were controlled by supernatural beings.[86] This perspective on the story is further endorsed when we note the way Jesus is said to speak to or "rebuke" (*pephimōso*, Mk 4:39) the wind and the sea as if they are demons, reminiscent of the language of the exorcisms (cf. *phimōthēti*, 1:25).

What Mark intended to convey by saying that Jesus was asleep during the storm (Mk 4:38) is variously understood: the Savior's unknown presence or his faith in the Father's care or Jesus' sovereignty and security. In that Mark later says that Jesus was able to calm the storm and that the disciples are therefore forced to question his identity, his sleeping probably signifies his sense of security in God's care, as well as his own sovereignty over the elements.[87] The contrast in responses to the situation between the serene Jesus and the faithless disciples also suggests that Jesus is being depicted as a man of extraordinary faith in God.[88]

The remarkable parallel in this story to that of Jonah, which has long been noted, makes it hard to avoid the conclusion that Mark had this Old Testament story in mind.[89] As the sleeping Jonah is roused and asked to pray for help (Jon 1:6), Jesus is awakened and speaks to the wind and sea (Mk 4:39).[90] Then, just like God in the Old Testament, Jesus gains authority over the natural elements.[91] In light of the rhetorical question of the disciples ("Who then is this?" 4:41), the readers of Mark are most likely expected to conclude that someone greater than Jonah has been described (cf. Mt 12:41/Lk 11:32).

In view of the testimony of demons (e.g., Mk 3:11) and of God himself (1:11), the readers can conclude not only that Jesus is the Son of God (cf. 1:1). What they must conclude will become clear in the parallel to this story: Jesus walking on the sea (6:45-52).

When the storm had been calmed, Jesus chastised the disciples for their lack of faith (Mk 4:40), a possible contrast to Jesus' serene faith. Faith is an important theme not only because it comes at the climax of the story. In each of the three stories of Jesus on the lake with his disciples—the lake calmed (4:34-41), walking on the lake (6:45-52) and teaching in the boat (8:13-21)—incomprehension and lack of faith are highlighted by Mark.[92] Later, in the story of the healing of the epileptic boy (9:19), Jesus will again chastise the disciples for their lack of faith.

According to Dibelius, the nature of this faith is "belief in the power of the miracle-worker . . . the confidence that Jesus, the great miracle-worker, excelled all other thaumaturges."[93] However, in light of the final question in the story ("Who then is this?" Mk 4:41), it is more likely that this faith is that which recognizes Jesus as the Son of God able to save his struggling followers from a preternatural storm in the church. The importance of this story in showing that Jesus can rescue his followers (and the church) from preternatural storms is brought to the readers' attention because this is the only story in which Jesus saves his disciples from distress.[94] The cycle of miracle stories continues without a break with another spiritual battle.

§3.15 The Gerasene Demoniac (Mk 5:1-20/Mt 8:28-34/Lk 8:26-39)

This story is tied to the preceding one (the calming of the storm) by means of Mark 5:1-2a (perhaps composed by Mark),[95] setting this healing story in Gentile territory so that Jesus' healing ministry is not confined to the Jews. The connection between this and the previous story also continues to draw attention to the contrast between the incomprehension of the disciples and the unmistakable power of Jesus in his miracles, which should have made his identity obvious. However, in this dramatic and vigorous miracle story, Mark turns from Jesus' conflict with and divine authority over preternatural beings operating through the natural elements back to his authority over spiritual beings in people (cf. 1:21-28).

There is no attempt to distance Jesus from contemporary exorcists: the technique of asking for the demons' name and commanding the demons to leave would have been familiar to Mark's readers.[96] In the demons' attempt to ward off Jesus' threat, Mark has the demons declare Jesus to be "Son of the Most High God" (Mk 5:7). By means of this title—already in his tradition[97]—Mark is able to continue weaving this thread of Jesus' sonship through his stories.

Mark contrasts the two different responses to the miracles of Jesus. On the one hand, the people beg Jesus to leave their district (Mk 5:17). They are said to be in awe, or afraid *(ephobēthēsan)*. In light of this, their request is probably understood to be based on their awesome fear of Jesus' power rather than simply over losing the pigs. Indeed, Mark's readers probably would not be surprised at this request, for if Mark intended his story to be read in light of Isaiah 65:4 (where God invites to join him those "who sit inside tombs, and spend the night in secret places; who eat swine's flesh"), this would have been understood as a story of the defeat of Gentile gods in preparation for Jesus' subsequent ministry in Gentile territory.[98]

On the other hand, the healed man is said to make the exact opposite request: he does not beg Jesus to leave but "that he might be with him" (Mk 5:18). The phrase is important to Mark, for he uses an almost identical phrase of Jesus' calling of the Twelve "to be with him" (3:14). Mark is probably saying that the correct response to a miracle or being healed is to become a follower of, or be devoted to, Jesus, a point already seen in the response of Peter's mother-in-law by the use of the word *service* (see above on 1:31).

Surprisingly Mark has Jesus refuse the man's request. He is sent home to his people to tell them "how much the Lord has done for you, and what mercy *[eleeō]* he has shown you" (Mk 5:19). In this apparent contradiction, Mark may be providing a model for his readers: although they cannot "be with Jesus" as the first followers were, they have the same responsibility to be obedient to Jesus to go out on mission, even if that is in their own area. That is, for Mark's readers, being on mission telling their people what the Lord has done, is equivalent to being "with Jesus."

Jesus' command to go home and tell how much the Lord had done for the man is contradicted by his telling in Decapolis how much Jesus had done for him. It is clear that Mark approves of this "proclaiming," for he uses *kērussein,* both of Jesus proclaiming his message (Mk 1:14, 38) and of the task Jesus calls his followers to carry out.[99] Within the plot of Mark this proclamation also prepares the way for another mission of Jesus to the Gentiles in 7:24—8:9.

Once again Mark is showing that the miracles of Jesus cannot be hidden. Notably, it is not simply a wonder that cannot be hidden; the salvation that Jesus brings in the healing cannot be hidden (cf. Mk 10:47-48), for *eleeō* ("to have mercy") was an eschatological term for God's salvation.[100]

Mark immediately continues with another miracle story, though not before Jesus crosses the lake (Mk 5:21), a reminder to his readers that Jesus has been in Gentile territory.

§3.16 Jairus's Daughter and a Woman with a Hemorrhage (Mk 5:21-43/Mt 9:18-26/Lk 8:40-56)

It is generally assumed—though probably incorrectly—that Mark has joined or sandwiched these two stories together.[101] The three clearest examples of this sandwiching of stories are the debate with the Pharisees and the concern of Jesus' family (Mk 3:21-35), the cursing of the fig tree and the cleansing of the temple (11:12-25) and the two stories here (5:21-43).[102] However, none of these three sets of stories shows any more evidence of Mark's editorial hand than does the rest of his writing.

Furthermore in each case the stories read naturally, as if they had always been remembered and told in this way. This is clearly suggested by the common themes or settings of each of the stories in the pairs. It remains an unproven hypothesis that Mark is responsible for sandwiching or joining any of these stories.[103] Nevertheless we will see that the sandwiching of stories has implications for Mark's understanding of the miracles.[104]

The theme of faith, which has been thoroughly explored by Christopher Marshall, is a prominent feature of both stories in this pericope.[105] Though not mentioned explicitly, the theme may first emerge for the readers in Jairus's "seeing" (*idōn*, Mk 5:22) or perceiving who Jesus is (see also 5:6; 9:20).[106] In any case, the motif of faith is more clearly expressed through the actions of Jairus.

Jairus is portrayed as a powerful, wealthy and influential member of society, who, in front of a large crowd, disregards his social position to adopt the same attitude of faith as the leper (1:40), the demonized (5:6) and the Gentile woman (7:25): he falls at Jesus' feet to beg him to heal his daughter. That Jairus is exercising faith is confirmed later when Mark has Jesus say that Jairus is to "believe" (*pisteue*, present tense), that is, continue believing in the way that he has begun.[107]

The nature of the faith that Mark is describing through Jairus's request is not in Jesus simply as a wonder worker but as a healer and savior. Mark uses the term *sōzein* ("to save" or "to heal," Mk 5:23) as the essence of Jairus's request, showing also that Jesus is being recognized as having divine origins.[108] Further, from Mark's perspective, the request that his daughter live (*kai zēsē*, 5:23) also takes the nature of the faith being described away from that of simply a miracle worker, or even a healer, to a trust in Jesus to mediate divine life and power (cf. 12:27), able to grant entry into the future kingdom (cf. 9:43-45; 10:17-30).

The priority of faith over other considerations is reinforced when Jesus disregards the station of Jairus by interrupting their journey to attend to a mere, frightened woman, who also displays faith.[109] Mark then portrays the man's faith as being tested both by Jesus' delaying (Mk 5:24b-34) and by the news of the death of his daughter (5:35a). The man's faith is further tested when the messengers raise doubts that Jesus—who is ironically described only as a "teacher"—will be able to raise his daughter (5:35b).[110]

In the face of this discouragement Jesus says, "Do not fear, only believe" (Mk 5:36). Thus Jesus' willingness to accompany Jairus to his home is portrayed as arising out of the expression of trust in Jesus' ability. The leader's faith is then further tried through the presence of mourners in his home (5:38), as well as by the doubting laughter of the crowd at Jesus' suggestion that Jairus's daughter is only sleeping (5:39). The man's faith is vindicated by the raising of his daughter (5:42).

Mark's vocabulary,[111] the mocking laughter of the crowd (Mk 5:40; cf. 15:29-32) and the presence of Peter, James and John (5:37; cf. 14:32) foreshadow elements of the passion narrative. In retrospect, Mark's readers may be expected to see in these two stories a symbol of Jesus' resurrection and an explanation of their being able to heal others as an experience of the power of Jesus' resurrection.

Once again Mark concludes a story with both the amazement of those who saw the miracle (Mk 5:42) and a charge from Jesus that the incident should not be made known (5:43a). Previously Mark has used this charge to highlight the way in which the wonders of Jesus escape privacy (1:43-45). Here, however, Jesus' order is not said to be disobeyed. This exception can probably be explained by noting that the story which follows (about the discussion, doubts and rejection of Jesus by people who knew him well, 6:1-6) would be incomprehensible if Mark had told of Jesus' miraculous powers' being noised abroad.[112] Further, in light of the casting of the passion's shadow over this story, this command to silence probably shows that Mark wishes faith in the miracles of Jesus to be tied to the Jesus of the cross and resurrection.

The theme of faith is also prominent in the story sandwiched within the one about Jairus's daughter—the healing of the woman who had been suffering from hemorrhages for twelve years (Mk 5:24b-34). In contrast to Jairus, whose faith caused him to humble himself to come to Jesus, this woman, who would have been socially and ritually isolated (Lev 15:7; Num 5:2), exercises her faith by breaking through her isolation in order to approach Jesus. Notably her healing probably involves her social reinstatement, for Jesus gives his explicit declaration of her permanent healing and finally addresses her as "Daughter" (Mk 5:34), a term of familial intimacy.

The woman's faith, which Jesus affirms at the end of the story ("your faith has made you well [or saved you]," Mk 5:34), is portrayed as arising because she had heard about Jesus (5:27)[113] and decided that a mere touch of his clothes would make her well, or save her. But many people are said to be pressing in on Jesus

(5:31), leaving the reader in no doubt that the only difference between the healed woman and the others pressing in on Jesus is her faith.

Mark has already mentioned the touching of Jesus' clothes as a method of healing in one of his summaries (Mk 3:10), and he will do so again in another summary (6:56). This story can be seen as a case study in the faith that is involved in this method of healing.[114]

Mark describes the healing of the woman as taking place because "power" (*dunamis*) had gone forth from Jesus. Hence Mark sees Jesus' ability to heal as depending on a substance independent of him, flowing from him to the sick person who has faith in his healing power. While this view may indicate the type of healing in Mark's tradition,[115] it is also a view Mark holds. A little further on, Herod talks about "these powers" at work in Jesus (Mk 6:14), which Mark's readers would probably associate with stories such as this healing of the woman with a hemorrhage (cf. 5:30).

Furthermore in the summary of healings at the end of chapter 6 Mark says, "They . . . begged him that they might touch even the fringe of his cloak; and all who touched it were healed" (Mk 6:56). It is not surprising then that Mark should refer to Jesus' miracles as "powers" when the people of Jesus' hometown comment, "What deeds of power are being done by his hands!" (6:2). More blatantly, at the end of the summary Mark says that "he could do no deed of power there" (6:5), and in 9:3 Jesus speaks of others doing a "deed of power" in his name. Yet this case study of the operation of "power" shows that, for Mark, it is not a method that is critical in this power transfer, it is Jesus and faith in him.

In the past the significance of this "power" terminology for understanding Mark's perspective on the miracles of Jesus has been explained by noting that the term *dunameis* was common in Hellenistic culture when referring to healings by physicians, gods or heroes.[116] This, in turn, has supported the view that Mark had a conceptual framework for the miracles of Jesus similar to that within "divine man" stories in Hellenistic culture.[117] However, the world was perceived by everyone, across the spectrum of ancient people, as pervaded by dynamic forces.[118]

Further, as already noted (§3.12), informing the nuances of "power" for Mark—hence his concept of miracles—is his connection *dunamis* with God. In 12:24 Jesus speaks of "the power of God," and, echoing Psalm 110:1 and Daniel 7:13, God is referred to as "the Power" (Mk 14:62). Mark's readers could not avoid concluding that, whereas the universe may be infused by many "powers" (cf. 13:25) and whereas healing power flowed from Jesus, it was the power or powers from the God of the Old Testament that enabled Jesus to heal those who responded in faith to him and his message (cf. 1:15).

These two interlocking or "sandwiched" miracle stories have highlighted the place of faith in receiving healing from Jesus. The next story of Jesus' rejection at

Nazareth (Mk 6:1-6a) also draws attention to the importance of faith in healing. Having related Jesus' rejection and that "he could do no deed of power there, except that he laid his hands on a few sick people and cured them" (6:5), Mark has Jesus marvel at their unbelief (6:6a). Then Jesus goes among the villages teaching (6:6b). He calls and sends out the Twelve (6:7-13). As an interlude while they are on mission, Mark tells the story of the Baptist's death (6:14-29).

§3.17 Feeding the Five Thousand (Mk 6:32-44/Mt 14:13-21/Lk 9:10-17; cf. Jn 6:1-15)

This story follows the execution of John the Baptist, wherein the question of Jesus' identity is raised again, especially concerning his relationship to Elijah (Mk 6:14-15). The reader is probably expected to call to mind similar accounts of Elijah and Elisha, particularly Elisha's feeding one hundred men with twenty loaves (cf. 2 Kings 4:42-44). The reader is probably to conclude that Mark was drawing attention to the greater miracle of Jesus. In the details of the story no further comparison is made between Jesus and Elijah or Elisha, perhaps to avoid the impression that Jesus *was* Elijah or Elisha.[119]

With this story, which begins with the apostles gathering around Jesus and telling him what they had done and taught (Mk 6:30), the preceding story of the call and sending of the Twelve (6:6a-13) is resumed. This alerts the reader to the significance of the role of the disciples in this story. The role of the disciples is also highlighted through the use of *didaskein* ("to teach") and *hosa poiein* ("how much to do") in 6:30. Since these words are otherwise used only of Jesus and since throughout the story Jesus is working primarily through the disciples, we are given the impression that the disciples are being portrayed as continuing the ministry of Jesus.[120]

The miracle story proper begins at verse 34, with Jesus coming ashore (still on the western, or Jewish, side of the lake, Mk 6:32-34) and seeing a large crowd. Mark says that Jesus had compassion on the crowd and develops this theme by referring to the people as sheep without a shepherd (6:34). This metaphor recalls God's leaderless and hungry people in the Old Testament (Num 27:17; 1 Kings 22:17; Ezek 34:5). By feeding the people, Jesus is shown to be the compassionate servant David whom Ezekiel expected would be their shepherd and feed God's people (Ezek 34:23). Also, Jesus the Messiah is shown to be compassionate in providing for the needs of God's people (Mk 6:43), as was God in providing manna for the Israelites when they were in the desert (Ex 16; Num 11).[121] An examination of the story of the feeding of the four thousand will show that this Jewish milieu is exchanged for a Gentile one (§3.22).

The absence of wine, the use of fish and the fact that Mark has not conformed this story to that of the Last Supper (cf. Mk 6:41 and 14:22)[122] argue against a thorough eucharistic interpretation of this feeding. Notwithstanding, by Jesus' taking, blessing, breaking and giving the bread, Mark's readers could hardly miss anticipating the eucharist and its portrayal of Jesus' self-giving. Indeed, in the preceding story of the death of John the Baptist (6:14-29) readers have been prepared for the theme of self-sacrifice.[123]

The first direction by Jesus is for the disciples to provide something for the people to eat (Mk 6:37), but they are unable to meet what is clearly an impossible demand. Nevertheless what the disciples could not provide Jesus is able to provide through the multiplication of the meager resources available to the disciples. The disciples' role also involved organizing and seating the people for the miracle and then distributing what Jesus had prepared. Is Mark teaching his readers how they are to behave in impossible situations—to prepare people for Jesus to provide for their needs? The difficulty of understanding the message of this story is highlighted in 6:52 (discussed in §3.18), where Mark says that the disciples did not understand about the loaves.

In having Jesus give direction to seat the people in groups *(sumposia)*, Mark uses a word that conveys the sense of a special bond between people, as at a drinking party.[124] This, linked with the numbers in the groups—fifty and a hundred—which call to mind Moses grouping the Israelites in Exodus 18:25 and the Messianic banquet in the Qumran literature (1QSa 2:11-22), suggests that Mark wants his readers to see Jesus as the Messiah providing for his people.

This draws attention to the probable Moses theme in the story. No more need be noted than the deserted place (Mk 6:31) and the groupings of people to suspect that Mark wants to portray Jesus as a figure understood in light of Moses: leading his people and abundantly providing for their needs.[125] However, the theme of feeding is wider than this, for in feeding his people as God fed his people, Jesus is portrayed as equal to God.[126]

From this story Mark goes immediately to that of Jesus walking on the sea. The voluntary self-giving or "powerlessness" of Jesus is tied with his being powerful enough to walk on the sea. He is, as we will see, more than a mere messenger from God.

§3.18 Jesus Walks on the Sea (Mk 6:45-52/Mt 14:22-33)

The story is preceded by Mark saying that Jesus went up on the mountain to pray (Mk 6:46).[127] The next time the disciples see Jesus they are terrified (6:50). It is hard to avoid seeing the parallel to Moses' going up the mountain to speak with God (Ex 34:2) and people's being afraid of him when he returned (34:30).

Why Mark says that Jesus intended to pass the disciples by as he walked on the sea is difficult to understand.[128] Without any support in the text and in contrast to the way Jesus usually deals with those in need—he shows compassion—various answers have been offered: that is what Jesus only appeared to be doing; he wanted to remain alone; he was testing their faith. Mark probably had in mind an echo of a Moses story that apparently forms the backdrop here.

In Exodus 33:17-23 God identifies himself and shows Moses his glory as he passes by. This was in response to Moses' asking for guidance, help and encouragement as the Israelites made their journey through the desert to the Promised Land. Thus Mark is most probably portraying Jesus as revealing his glory to his followers, which is enough to encourage them to continue on their journey.[129] This interpretation is confirmed, in part, by the disciples' fearful response to seeing what they assume to be a ghost (Mk 6:49-50).

Jesus makes a second attempt at self-revelation when he says, "Take heart, it is I *[egō eimi]*; do not be afraid" (Mk 6:50). In view of the context of this story, this is a probable parallel to the "I am" of the revelation of the divine name in Exodus 3:14.

Mark is using this miracle story to teach the readers that, even without his physical presence, Jesus' glory can encourage and help his followers on their difficult journey.[130] But he is also showing that in this epiphany Jesus has been revealed not only as directly empowered by God[131] but also as God uniquely present. This conclusion is corroborated by the Old Testament assertion that God can control the wind (Ps 104:4; 107:25-30) and that only God is able to walk on the waves (Job 9:8).

Jesus' walking on the sea (no storm is mentioned) is not the only miracle Mark portrays here. He also says that when Jesus got into the boat the wind ceased (Mk 6:51). From what we have noted about the story, this strongly suggests that the mere presence of Jesus was thought to bring the action of God on creation. Mark 10:32 is probably another example of Mark's view that Jesus' presence alone had a great impact: "Jesus was walking ahead of them; they were amazed, and those who followed were afraid."[132]

Despite depicting the clear revelation of who has been walking on the sea, Mark ends the story by saying that the disciples were astonished, for they did not understand about the loaves (Mk 6:52). The disciples should have understood Jesus' statement "It is I" *(egō eimi)* as a clear disclosure of his divine nature, but they did not. This means the disciples have misunderstood not simply a miracle, or the miracles in general, but who has been disclosed as performing the miracles.

In the feeding of the five thousand the disciples were to discover Jesus' divine identity. This first story in the second cycle of miracle stories was supposed to have answered the question posed at the end of the first story of the first cycle: "Who then is this, that even the wind and the sea obey him?" (Mk 4:41). However, the disciples appear to be increasingly without comprehension, hardly different from outsiders and opponents (cf. 3:5 and 6:52). Further, the readers of Mark are probably not only to see a miracle in this story but to understand from this story that Jesus is able to supply their needs even in the most desperate of situations and that, in turn, they should trust him.[133]

§3.19 Crowds Eager to Be Healed—A Summary (Mk 6:53-56/Mt 14:34-36)

Although this summary follows immediately after the story of Jesus' walking on the sea, Mark has Jesus in Gentile territory. The last time he was "on the other side of the lake" he performed a spectacular exorcism (Mk 5:1-20). This time Jesus is portrayed as overwhelmed by crowds of people wanting to be healed. Everywhere he went in the Gentile region people sought to be—and were—healed by him.

Whereas the disciples had failed to recognize Jesus in the feeding and the walking on the sea (Mk 6:50-52), the crowd "at once recognized him" (6:54) and brought their sick to him. Presumably Jesus was recognized because of the proclamation of the healed demoniac (5:19-20). As in the summary in 3:7-12, Jesus is quiescent in the healing of people—he takes no initiative. The people are healed merely by touching the fringe of his cloak (6:56; also see §3.16 on 5:30).

Through the frequent use of the imperfect tense (which denotes continuous action), such as "they heard,"[134] Mark gives the impression that what he reports here took place over an extended period of time. Also, by means of this paragraph Mark not only brings to a close a section on miracles but is able to illustrate the remarkable power of Jesus to work miracles—without his taking initiative and by people merely touching his clothing. Before the next set of miracle stories, beginning in 7:24, Mark has a discourse on defilement (Mk 7:1-23) that would be of particular interest to his non-Jewish readers.

§3.20 The Syrophoenician and Her Daughter (Mk 7:24-30/Mt 15:21-28)

As we have just noted, Mark sets the scene for this exorcism of a Gentile, as well as the following story of the healing of a deaf-mute, with a prior discussion between Jesus and some religious authorities on the nature of defilement (Mk 7:1-23). The point of the discussion is that a person's cleanliness and standing with God is not determined by external qualities (cf. 7:6-7, 21-22). In that a significant proportion of Mark's readers are probably Gentiles,[135] this discussion and the subsequent two healings would have been interesting and relevant in the sense of their being able to identify with the message of Mark.

Despite exegetical gymnastics that attempt to reduce the force of the word *dog* (*kunarion*) to mean "household pets," the plain reading of Mark 7:27 ("Let the children be fed first, for it is not fair to take the children's food and throw it to the dogs") is that Mark intends his readers to understand that Jesus refuses a Gentile's request for healing.[136] However, Jesus accedes to the woman's request when, in contrast to the timidity of a healed Jewish woman (5:33), she expresses her bold and strong faith in him.[137] Indeed, in his reply to the woman Jesus draws attention to her faith without actually using the word (contrast Mt 15:28): "For saying that, you may go—the demon has left your daughter" (Mk 7:29).

Mark's audience could conclude from this that although Jesus had been sent to bring salvation to the Israelites on the basis of their faith, the Gentiles were now also included.[138] Keeping in mind the enigmatic ending of Mark (cf. §3.29.9), it was impossible to exclude the Gentiles in light of what had happened to Jesus and what he had done.

§3.21 A Deaf-Mute Healed (Mk 7:31-37/Mt 15:29-31)

For this story, which follows immediately that of the Syrophoenician and her daughter, the setting remains Gentile territory. Again it is the Decapolis where the Gerasene demoniac has already proclaimed "how much Jesus had done for him" (Mk 5:20). Perhaps again (cf. 6:53-54) it is in view of the success of the demoniac's preaching that people are expressing their faith in Jesus by bringing a sick man to him.

Mark portrays the man as having a speech impediment (*mogilalos,* Mk 7:32)[139] and then being able to speak plainly (*orthōs,* 7:35) after being healed. The use of *mogilalos* probably draws attention to the eschatological dimension of the healing, for the only time the word is used in the Septuagint it is of those expected to be healed in the messianic age (Is 35:6). Although there is some tension between this description of the sickness *(mogilalos)* and the healing Jesus performs ("he even makes the deaf to hear and the mute *[alalos]* to speak," 7:37), in this tension Mark is able to heighten the miracle, as well as draw attention to Jesus' identity through the echo of Isaiah 35:6.

Once again Mark has Jesus heal a person in private (cf. Mk 5:30; 7:33). This is consistent with the pattern seen in the Gospel that, although a healing may have a private setting, it cannot be hidden. The variation on this theme here is that Mark says that the more Jesus ordered silence, the more keenly the miracle was proclaimed (7:36). This verse interrupts the flow of the narrative by its portrayal of people preaching about the miracle before they have been astounded by it.[140]

Thus this theme is important to Mark, for on the generally accepted principle that such conflicts are probably the responsibility of the final redactor,[141] he has most probably inserted this statement here. Indeed, unsuccessful hiddenness pervades this section of the Gospel. Mark sets up Jesus' extensive tour of Gentile territory as one that was to be kept secret (Mk 7:24, 31). Yet he says Jesus could not escape notice (7:24). Readers can conclude from this that Jesus and his ministry of healing could not be hidden, even from the Gentiles.

It has been argued that Jesus' command, "Ephphatha" (Mk 7:34), would have been seen by Mark as a foreign secret word with miracle-working power.[142]

However, this is unlikely, for Mark understands and translates this Semitic word for his Gentile readers as the unmysterious "Be opened."

The statement "He has done everything well" (Mk 7:37) at the end of the story may be intended to recall Genesis 1:31 where it is said that everything God made was very good. That would mean Mark is ascribing this miracle to the work of God in fulfilling the prophetic hope of restoring fallen creation.[143]

§3.22 Four Thousand Fed (Mk 8:1-10/Mt 15:32-39)

As there is no change in setting from the last story (Mk 8:1), in this second feeding story Mark has Jesus still in Gentile territory. Also, the mention of some of the crowd coming "from a great distance" (8:3; cf. Josh 9:6) may be intended to refer to the Gentiles. Interestingly, at the end of the first feeding story, which has a Jewish setting, Jewish baskets are described (*kophinos,* Mk 6:43), whereas at the end of this story *spuris* (8:8), a word used in everyday Greek for a basket, is used.[144] Therefore Gentile readers of Mark could conclude again that the fruit of Jesus' ministry was available to them as well as to the Jews.[145]

It is generally agreed that this story is a variant of the first feeding story,[146] but it most probably predates Mark. There are too many important word differences, and a similarity to the feeding in the Fourth Gospel, for Mark to have created this story (see §16.6).

The motivation for Jesus to act is said to be compassion (Mk 8:2), as it was for the first feeding (6:34). However, here the compassion is emphasized by means of the extended statement on the lips of Jesus: "I have compassion for the crowd," 8:2-3). Therefore the Gentile readers of Mark could not miss the message that they, no less than the Jews, who were the object of compassion in the feeding of the five thousand, are now the object of God's compassion and feeding in Jesus.[147] This impression would be enhanced for the readers in that here Jesus, instead of the disciples, takes the initiative in the feeding (8:2-3; cf. 6:5).[148]

Unquestionably the taking, breaking, giving thanks and distribution of the seven loaves anticipates the Last Supper and would have reminded the first readers of their eucharistic meals—heightened by Jesus "giving thanks" rather than looking up to heaven and "blessing" the bread, as in the former feeding story (cf. Mk 6:41). Further, the separating and subordination in the text of the mention of the few fish ("They had also a few small fish," 8:7) has the effect of sharpening the eucharistic reflections in the story. This in turn has the effect of drawing attention to the identity of Jesus and once again heightening the apparently (so far) impenetrable lack of faith of the disciples. Yet the grace and sovereignty of God are evident in that the faithless disciples are still offered a place in the distribution of the food (8:6).

The number of the loaves and baskets (seven) has caused extensive speculation.

The simplest explanation is that each loaf produced not only enough to satisfy the needy crowd, but enough remained to fill a large basket, and, as noted, the actual number may reflect a Gentile motif. This maintains the theme of Mark 7:36-37 ("He has done every thing well"), where the abundance of God's supply in meeting the needs of Gentiles is in view.[149]

At first sight the usual final acclamation of a miracle is absent—all Mark says is that "he sent them away" (Mk 8:9). However, in that Jesus would not initially send the crowd away because they would faint (8:3), this statement assumes that the large crowd of Gentiles has been fully and miraculously satisfied by the Messiah.

The discourse about the bread that follows (Mk 8:14-21), as well as the "again" in 8:1, clearly suggests that we are to read this second feeding story in light of the first. Despite their having been a part of the first feeding, the ignorance of the disciples stands out,[150] as it does in contrast to the faith of the Syrophoenician woman and those who brought the deaf-mute to Jesus. This feeding miracle is the setting for the ensuing debate with the Pharisees.

§3.23 The Pharisees Seek a Sign (Mk 8:11-13; Mt 12:38-39; 16:1-4/Lk 11:16, 29; Jn 6:30)

In Gentile territory Jesus has been met with faith, driven out a demon from a distance, given hearing and clear speech in a way expected by the Messiah and satisfied the needs of hungry crowds of Gentiles. On the other hand, in this story Jesus is confronted by the Pharisees—Jews—who request a God-given sign to authenticate his ministry (cf., e.g., Deut 13:1-6; Is 7:10-14).

It is unlikely that Mark is intending his readers to assume that the Pharisees are asking for another miracle like the ones he has just narrated (Mk 7:24—8:10). A closer reading suggests otherwise. So far Mark has used *dunamis* ("power") for the miracles of Jesus (6:2, 14); here he uses *sēmeion* ("sign," 8:11-12), which was a public event produced to certify divine truth.[151]

Also, readers can assume that the Pharisees are aware of Jesus' fame as a miracle worker. So the Pharisees are looking for a phenomenon quite different from the miracles so far described by Mark,[152] something reminiscent of the authenticating miracles of the Old Testament prophets.[153] They seek from heaven (that is, God) a mighty triumphalist deed of apocalyptic deliverance from slavery[154] that will—without their having to exercise faith—establish Jesus as the eschatological prophet.[155] Indeed, in the so-called eschatological discourse (Mk 13:1-37) Mark makes it plain that it is false messiahs and prophets who offer such signs (13:4, 22).

When Mark says that the Pharisees wish to "test" *(peirazō)* Jesus, he is probably suggesting the profound misunderstanding and distance between Jesus and those seeking the sign, for the previous and first use of "test" is of Satan's tempting Jesus (Mk 1:13). This perspective is reinforced in the use of the phrase "this generation" as a description for those questioning Jesus—a phrase used in the Old Testament of stubborn unbelieving people of God.[156] Jesus' question as to why this generation seeks a sign (8:12) may be designed to suggest that in all Mark has portrayed, the Pharisees—and readers—have enough evidence to see who Jesus is and what he can do. Jesus' refusal to give a sign is probably not related to any form of the so-called Messianic Secret.[157]

This story, coming between the feeding of the four thousand and the explanation of the feedings, demonstrates that neither the disciples nor the Pharisees understood the significance of the miracles. Jesus himself is the sign. No sign other than Jesus and his miracles can be given that unbelief can comprehend. Hence Mark says "he left them" (Mk 8:13), an act that prefigures the next story of Jesus warning his followers against the "yeast" of the Pharisees and Herod.

§3.24 Understanding the Miracles of Feeding (Mk 8:14-21/Mt 16:5-12)

The theme of faith and disbelief continues. The disciples had forgotten to bring enough bread. All they had in the boat was one loaf. On two previous occasions the disciples had faced the prospect of feeding large crowds of people (Mk 6:35-44 and 8:1-10). Each time their resources were meager. Yet each time Jesus took what the disciples had and was able to use it to feed the hungry crowds.

Now in this story (Mk 8:14-21), again faced with limited resources, Jesus warns the disciples to beware of the yeast of the Pharisees and Herod. In that Herod failed to grasp the significance of Jesus' miracles (6:14)—as have the Pharisees—Jesus' warning is probably against unbelief in the face of his very public miracles.[158] Thus Mark sees the miracles not only as eliciting faith[159] but as a summons to faith[160] and, by the association established in 1:15, to repentance as well. Jesus goes on to remind the disciples of what he had been able to do on the two previous occasions similar to this one and so asks them rhetorically, "Do you have eyes and fail to see?" and "Do you not yet understand?" (8:18, 21). However, despite the disciples' failure to understand, Jesus' ministry, including the care and teaching of the disciples, was to continue. These points are highlighted in the following story of the healing of a blind man.

§3.25 A Blind Man at Bethsaida (Mk 8:22-26)

The setting of Bethsaida[161] may have signaled some of its significance to Mark's readers. A little earlier Bethsaida was associated with a difficult crossing of the lake (Mk 6:45).[162] Thus in saying that Jesus and his disciples came to Bethsaida, Mark may have been alerting his readers to a story about difficulties in belief in Jesus' miracles. That is, healing—spiritual and physical—is less successful in an environment of unbelief.

Blindness was one of the most serious sicknesses in the ancient world, an affliction considered to be a little less serious than being dead (*b. Ned.* 64b). Its remedy has no precedent in the Old Testament, and there was no known cure.[163] Although it is likely that operations for cataracts existed by the third century B.C., it was thought that the cure for blindness required a miracle.[164] Physical blindness could also serve as a metaphor for spiritual or moral blindness (further see §3.27 on Mk 10:46-52). Thus a miracle story of the healing of a blind person would highlight the blindness of the disciples, as well as the power of Jesus and the arrival of the messianic age (cf. Is 29:18; 35:5).

Once again, in the bringing of a sick person to Jesus Mark shows that Jesus instills confidence or faith—a vicarious faith—in Jesus' ability to heal even the most difficult cases (Mk 8:22; cf. 2:1-12). The theme of faith is highlighted by having the blind man's companions "beg" or "pray" (*parakaleō*, 8:22) for Jesus to touch the man. In the ancient world *parakaleō* included the meaning of calling on God in times of great need (cf. Josephus *Ant.* 6:25).[165]

Why, when Jesus generally performed his healings in public, should Mark depict him leading the man out of the village to perform the miracle (Mk 8:23)? The explanation may be in the story of the illness and death of Jairus's daughter, when Jesus put out the laughing and disbelieving crowd of mourners before healing the girl (5:35-43). Mark may be telling his readers that Jesus wanted to remove the blind man from the unbelieving crowd of Bethsaida.

Another reason might have been the method of healing, for in the healing of a deaf man with a speech impediment, Jesus removed the man from the crowd, put his fingers in the man's ears, spat and touched his tongue, saying, "Ephphatha" ("Be opened," Mk 7:33-34). Similarly in this story Jesus is said to put saliva on the man's eyes (8:23). Perhaps then Mark wanted to tell his readers not only that a lack of trust was an impediment to healing but that the methods of healing Jesus used should not detract from an understanding that it was Jesus who performed the healing.

Jesus' question "Can you see anything?" followed by his again laying hands on the blind man is unique in the healing stories of Jesus and introduces the most striking and puzzling aspect of the story (Mk 8:25). As in the healing of the Gerasene demoniac (5:7-9)—though more obviously here—the healing takes place in two stages. The significance of this two-stage healing story for Mark is generally agreed to be found in its relationship to the story of Peter's confession, which immediately follows (Mk 8:27-30). However, there is no agreement on the nature of that significance.[166]

The way forward may be to note that what the disciples understand in the confession of Caesarea is the identity of Jesus (Mk 8:29-30). But what is not understood is the need for the death of Jesus and following him to the cross (8:31-34). Therefore complete insight involves faith in Jesus' messianic mission that includes suffering and death. That is, he is the crucified healer and is to be followed to the cross. This will be illustrated in the story of Bartimaeus (10:45-52).

Mark has presented us with another puzzle in Jesus' command in 8:26: "Then he sent him away to his home, saying, 'Do not even go into the village.'" Among the commands to silence, this is unique. It is neither a command to the demons to be silent about the identity of Jesus nor a command functioning as a foil to emphasize the man's inability to keep silent about the miracle. The man is said neither to follow Jesus on the way nor to speak about Jesus healing him.

One solution to the puzzle could be found in suggesting that the story is only a symbolic presentation of the healing of humanity's blindness by Jesus. From this it would follow that Jesus' prohibition is an indication of the significance of his saving action, which draws the people to whom he grants sight out of their world.[167] However, we cannot take this option, for Mark presents the story as a miracle. Nor is it a condemnation of the village.[168] That would serve no particular purpose in the context of the miracle story.

Rather, more simply, it is likely that in the command to silence Mark is continuing to draw attention to the theme of belief and disbelief associated with Bethsaida in this passage. That is, the man is being asked to dissociate himself from the town, which symbolized unbelief. In turn, Mark is again telling his readers of the importance of faith in relation to healing. Besides, through this small literary device Mark is able to pave the way for Jesus to go away alone with his disciples to Caesarea Philippi.

In the story of Peter's confession (Mk 8:27-33) we are able to see that in light of Jesus' teaching and healing—not least the unprecedented healing of a blind man—Jesus can be recognized as the Messiah. However, the disciples are ordered not to tell anyone about him (8:30) in the same way the demons have been ordered to be quiet, for they knew him. The reader is led to conclude that Jesus' identity as Messiah cannot be completely understood in light of the teaching and miracles alone. Yet in view of all that has been said about miracles so far, it is inconceivable to conclude that Mark is thereby disdaining the miracles. He simply wishes to include more than healing and teaching in the identity of the Messiah.

After Peter's declaration that Jesus is the Messiah, Mark spells out the costly implications of this for his followers (Mk 8:34—9:1). Then, after the declaration by the heavenly voice in the transfiguration "This is my Son" (9:7), Mark elucidates the implication for Jesus—suffering soon and then glory. In the ensuing miracle story of the epileptic boy Mark unfolds further implications for the disciples that Jesus is God's Son.

§3.26 The Epileptic Boy (Mk 9:14-29/Mt 17:14-20/Lk 9:37-43)

After the transfiguration, when Jesus, with Peter, James and John, rejoined the other nine disciples, they saw a large crowd around them and some scribes arguing with them (Mk 9:14). When Jesus asked about the nature of their argument (9:16), the answer did not, at first, seem entirely appropriate. Someone in the crowd answered for the disciples, saying that his disciples were unable to cast out a demon (9:17-18). However, on closer examination, the answer is entirely appropriate.

The first time that Mark records that Jesus taught and then performed an exorcism, a discussion was sparked about his authority being different from that of the scribes (Mk 1:21-28). Moreover, in the Beelzebul controversy Mark establishes that it is the Holy Spirit who authorizes Jesus' exorcisms (3:28-30). Importantly, in 3:15 the apostles are appointed in order to be sent (*apostellē*, subjunctive) with this same unscribelike authority to cast out demons. Then in 6:7-13 they are sent out on a successful exorcism and healing ministry (cf. 6:30). It would not be surprising then that in this story of the disciples' failure Mark means his readers to understand that the discussion with the scribes was about this unique authority, which, unaccountably, the disciples are unsuccessful in using.

This is confirmed by what Mark goes on to say. When the people saw Jesus they were immediately overcome with "awe" *(ekthambeomai)* and ran to greet him (Mk 9:15). For Mark, *ekthambeomai* (14:33; 16:5) contains a strong element of distress and is probably better translated "perplexed." Could it not be that Mark is saying that the crowd was perplexed at the disciples' failure in light of the debate they heard with the scribes about the authority the disciples had received from someone who so obviously had authority to heal? Mark is showing again (cf. 3:15; 6:7, 13) that he assumes that the miracles he relates are not to be seen as limited to the power of Jesus but are expected to be repeated successfully by his followers.

Mark uses the verb *ischuō*[169] ("to be strong" or "to have ability") in relation to the disciples' inability to perform the exorcism. While it has a similar meaning to *dunamai* ("to be able")—which Mark uses in verses 22 and 23 of Jesus' ability to heal—*ischuō* carries with it the idea of self-generated or innate strength.[170] In other words, the father said that the disciples did not possess the inner strength to perform the exorcism. This, the readers know, is precisely what the disciples were not given. This helps us understand Jesus' response about faith. Of all the miracle stories in Mark this one treats the subject of faith most thoroughly and thus requires our close attention.[171]

It is not exactly clear to whom Jesus is addressing the rhetorical double rebuke "You faithless generation, how much longer must I be among you? How much longer must I put up with you?" (Mk 9:19). However, since he addresses "them" and since the disciples are key characters in this story—and they have just been portrayed as failures—Mark probably intends his readers to understand Jesus to be speaking to the disciples. Therefore the error of the disciples (their lack of success in an exorcism) is that they have remained without faith. But the address may also be intended to reflect, to some degree, on the defective faith of the father.[172] Indeed, this interpretation is confirmed in the exchange between Jesus and the father.

In verse 22 the father asks Jesus to help if *(ei)* Jesus is able *(dunamai)*. In this "if" we see a hint of hesitancy or deficiency in the father's faith. It is probably significant that in this request Mark does not use the same word ("to be strong," *ischuō*) that was used of the disciples (Mk 9:18). Instead *dunamai* is used, which can be translated to have "power," with the sense of choice or possibility included. That is, in contrast to the failure of the disciples' ineffective, self-generated strength, the father asked Jesus to choose to do what he recognized he had the ability or power to do. Jesus said that whether or not he was able to heal the boy depended not on his ability—which all Mark's readers know is not in question—but on trust or faith (9:23).

While it may be possible to take the logic of this sentence to refer to the faith of Jesus,[173] it would be unique in Mark, and Mark has the father accept the challenge of the statement.[174] Thus the father's faith is in question, and the deficiency in the father's faith is in his uncertainty that Jesus is willing to heal.

The father's immediate response to Jesus is "I believe; help my unbelief!" (Mk 9:24). In view of the exorcism taking place right after this statement, it cannot be a confession of (complete?) unbelief.[175] Rather, it is a confession of faith which exonerates him from the cause of the failed healing and reinforces the disciples' culpability. Such a cry from the father was also probably a reminder to Mark's readers that although people are, of themselves, capable of responding to Jesus in trust (e.g., 1:15; 11:24), their faith needs supplementing by a further gift of faith.

Mark says that Jesus acted to heal when he saw the crowd "running together" (*episuntrechō*, Mk 9:25). This word is not known in Greek literature, though in the Fayum papyri (107:7, A.D. 133) *epitrechonti* is used as the title of a village inspector. Could it be that the members of the crowd—which in Mark's story were observers of what had happened—are to be understood as coming closer to observe Jesus' techniques, an indication that they misunderstood the nature of his healing ministry?[176] There is no evidence for the suggestion that the crowd was about to attack Jesus or the boy.[177]

The words of Jesus to the demon—"I command you" (*egō epitassō soi*, Mk 9:25)—highlight the decisive difference between Jesus' method and that of other exorcists. So far as I can discover, in all the ancient literature there is no evidence of an exorcist being represented as deliberately and specifically drawing attention to his own ability to cast out demons as Mark says Jesus does here. This means that, whereas Mark believed that in his exorcisms Jesus was empowered by the Holy Spirit (3:22-30), he was also telling his readers, paradoxically, that Jesus himself was an extraordinarily powerful self-sufficient exorcist.[178]

Jesus' taking the boy's hand (Mk 9:27) would have been understood as more than an encouraging touch. It was a means of transferring strength to the sick person.[179] Not only did Jesus take the boy's hand, he also "lifted him up" *(ēgeiren auton),* the same word Mark used for Jesus' being raised from the dead (16:6). This probably conveyed to the first readers the idea that, although the boy had not died (9:26), what had happened to him was akin to his being raised from the dead. That is, the removal of the demon, a minion of Satan, is no less significant or miraculous than bringing someone from death to life.

Furthermore, from the beginning—at least in retrospect—readers have probably seen here an allusion to the death and resurrection of Jesus. In death Jesus would then have been seen as trapped by Satan, but in the resurrection he would be freed by another and able to stand again.[180]

The end of the story reflects many other occasions when Mark says that Jesus gave private instructions to his disciples in light of their failure to understand his ministry.[181] Mark has depicted the disciples as involved in an intimate relationship with Jesus,[182] as receiving special instruction,[183] yet failing to understand him.[184] The theories attempting to explain Mark's intentions in this material have been almost endless. At the least the material indicates that, whereas those "outside" may have misunderstood, the disciples had no excuse for not understanding. They had been privy to all Jesus wanted to say and had seen his miracles.

Mark is probably saying to his readers that they have no excuse for failing to understand or to heal, for he has made plain who Jesus is and what is required of his followers. This included how success in healing could be assured. By implication, it should have been known that this kind of demon could be exorcised. The kind of demon thought to be involved was a mute-and-deaf spirit (Mk 9:25). Mute spirits were considered particularly difficult to exorcise.[185] Therefore, in a departure from the usual recommended method of commanding a demon to leave, Jesus says, "This kind can come out only through prayer" (9:29).

In light of Jesus' earlier chastising the failed disciples for their lack of faith (Mk 9:19), we could expect Jesus to say that this kind of demon could be driven out by faith, for in 6:5-6 the lack of healing by Jesus is directly attributed to a lack of faith in his hometown. But a lack of faith is only part of the reason for the failure of the disciples—prayer is also required. This combination of faith and prayer is obviously important to Mark, for in 11:24 he brings the two together as essential for receiving from God. From what Mark has said in this story concerning the importance of faith, prayer here would mean an expression of total trust in and dependence on the power and authority of the Holy Spirit given to the disciples of Jesus.[186]

A closer reading may reveal more about the disciples' failure. Mark depicts discipleship as being "with Jesus" (Mk 3:14; 5:18) and exorcism as arising out of being with Jesus (3:14-15; 6:6-13). In view of this as well as the difficulties experienced by the disciples when they are in the boat without Jesus (6:46, 51), we may infer from this story that Mark saw the disciples' failure as also due, to some extent, to the absence of Jesus from the situation. To put the same point another way, Mark may be inferring that the disciples are not yet ready for Jesus' absence (cf. 9:19).[187] This is analogous to the situation of Mark's readers. In suggesting the combination of prayer and faith as efficacious in exorcism, Mark may be offering a method of exorcism to readers who no longer have the physical presence of Jesus.[188]

The importance of this paradigmatic aspect of the story is reinforced by the fact that, apart from the introductory and closing stories, this is the only healing story in Mark's central section on discipleship. The next miracle story, the closing one in this section of Mark, is equally important in contributing to this theme of discipleship.

§3.27 Blind Bartimaeus (Mk 10:46-52/Mt 20:29-34/Lk 18:35-43)

This story is of particular significance in understanding Mark's view of the miracles of Jesus. It is the last of his healing stories, and it closes the carefully composed section of his Gospel on discipleship,[189] which began with the story of a man at first only partially healed of blindness (Mk 8:22-26). The reader is invited to see that what Jesus had been attempting to do in the first and last story is what Jesus has been doing in the whole section on discipleship: opening the eyes of blind disciples.[190]

This story also marks a decisive point of transition in Jesus' journey to the cross in the passion narrative. Three times in a single sentence (Mk 10:46) Mark draws attention to Jesus (as well as to his disciples and a large crowd) on a journey: they came to Jericho, they left Jericho, and Bartimaeus was sitting by the roadside. (Because of the significance of "way" or "road" *[hodos]*, Mark probably wants his readers to notice that Bartimaeus, who is said to be sitting alongside the road, is not yet a follower of Jesus.)

Mark would not have included this story simply because it was a difficult or miraculous healing. Its metaphorical meaning would have been just as important. Those who were morally and intellectually defective were said to be blind,[191] and those who did not know God's salvation were also said to be wandering around blindly (Is 42:16). In light of Mark's story of the so-called rich young ruler a little earlier in this section (Mk 10:17-22), it is interesting to note that in the ancient world wealth was thought to be the primary cause of intellectual and moral blindness.[192] Important for Mark's theme of the lack of understanding of the disciples, blindness was a metaphor frequently used for a lack of knowledge and understanding, especially about the future.[193]

Bartimaeus, the helpless beggar, is depicted as having faith and recognizing that Jesus can help him (Mk 10:47-48). In having Bartimaeus cry out to Jesus as the "Son of David" Mark may be identifying Jesus as the healer who brings salvation. The name "Son of David" may have called to mind not only the expected royal Messiah but also, by association, a Messiah like Solomon, who had a great reputation as a healer (cf., e.g., *T. Sol.*).[194] While "Son of David" is not a dominant title for Jesus in Mark, in that Jesus does not correct Bartimaeus it is clearly an aspect of Jesus' ministry that Mark wants to affirm: Jesus is recognizably a great healer, greater than any in the history of God's people. Yet the title is inadequate—it is the confession of a blind man[195] and it is a title shown to be correct, though inadequate, in Mark 12:35-37.[196]

Mark's readers would have understood the cry of Bartimaeus ("Jesus, Son of David, have mercy on me!") not simply—or even only—as a cry for healing.[197] A cry for "mercy" was a cry for God's anointed messenger to show love by removing God's wrath from his life and bringing salvation.[198] Later, Christians commonly used receiving sight as a way of talking about receiving salvation.[199]

The dramatic action of Bartimaeus in throwing off his cloak was a powerful symbol of throwing off the past (cf. Col 3:8-9).[200] Readers could hardly miss this being a graphic portrayal of the proper response to the call of Jesus to repent and believe (Mk 1:15). Blind Bartimaeus's cloak would have been his most treasured possession (cf. Ex 22:26-27), and when spread out before him it was his only means of collecting a livelihood.[201] Thus Bartimaeus's act is one of faith, placing his whole life in the hands of Jesus. Mark's readers may also have had in their minds the image of a person then putting on the cloak of the new master he was about to follow.[202]

Jesus' response to Bartimaeus is to ask "What do you want me to do for you?" (Mk 10:51). This is the same question Jesus has just asked of the disciples (10:36). The two different responses to Jesus' question highlight the blindness of the disciples and the faith of Bartimaeus. Whereas the disciples are preoccupied with sitting in places of honor in the future glory (10:37), Bartimaeus is sitting by the road that he is about to travel (with Jesus) to suffering—Jerusalem (10:52—11:1). Whereas the disciples understand Jesus' kingdom in terms of worldly power, the blind man understands Jesus' concern to be merciful healing and salvation. Whereas the disciples are self-confident, Bartimaeus is portrayed as a helpless beggar eagerly following Jesus.[203]

Bartimaeus was healed or, as the story emphasizes, received salvation because of his faith (*pistis*, Mk 10:52). When we look through the text we see a number of points where Mark has drawn attention to trust in what Bartimaeus says or does. Although many people sternly ordered him to stop calling to Jesus, he kept calling for mercy or salvation (10:48). When Jesus stopped to have Bartimaeus called over, he told Bartimaeus to "Take heart" *(tharsei)*, that is, be confident or trusting (10:49). When called, the blind beggar leaps up in response (10:50), and when asked what he wants, his request is like a prayer, using the reverent word: "Rabbouni [or "My teacher"], let me see again" (10:51).

Jesus responds by telling the man he can go, for his faith has made him well (Mk 10:52). By having Bartimaeus then follow Jesus, Mark shows the connection between faith and following Jesus, a connection also made by Mark in the early stages of his Gospel (1:14-20). This story becomes a model of what it means to connect faith and following—following Jesus in the way of the cross.[204]

Apart from the implications to be drawn from the passion narrative (cf. Mk 8:34-35), this is the last graphic demonstration of what it means to be a follower of Jesus, and the response to being healed or saved sums up much of what Mark has been saying about discipleship. In particular the proper response to being called by Jesus and receiving the miracle of God's merciful salvation from him is, like Bartimaeus, to follow Jesus voluntarily and unconditionally on the journey of discipleship, which will, for some, involve ultimate suffering. Such discipleship will be possible after the resurrection, when the followers of Jesus experience the presence of the risen Lord and have received the Holy Spirit (see 13:11).

§3.28 A Fig Tree Withered (Mk 11:12-14, 20-26/Mt 21:18-22; cf. Lk 13:6-9)

At chapter 11, after the healing of Bartimaeus, Jesus arrives in Jerusalem, the focus of Mark's attention being on the temple rather than on the city (Mk 11:11, 15, 27). Indeed, the miracle of the withered fig tree comes in two parts, separated by the story of Jesus cleansing the temple. Mark's readers can be expected to understand the cursing of the fig tree in the context of the cleansing of the temple.

The origin of this miracle story is variously understood,[205] but our concern here is Mark's understanding of the story. The importance of the story for Mark is to be gleaned from three facts: that this is his only destructive miracle story,[206] that it is associated with the temple and that it is the last miracle story he reports.

The fig tree could serve as a symbol of the Jewish nation, and this story recalls the Old Testament passages where Israel is castigated for not producing the fruit sought by God.[207] Therefore, for Mark, it is a piece with the cleansing of the temple and is perhaps a symbol of its future destruction.[208] Thus for Mark Jesus' cursing of the fig tree is to be associated with the view that Israel had failed to produce what the Messiah was looking for.

The major puzzle of the story is Mark's saying that it was not the season for figs (Mk 11:13).[209] In light of Jeremiah 8:13 ("When I wanted to gather them . . . there are no . . . figs on the fig tree") it could be that Mark is saying that God's people must always be producing the fruit he is looking for. The fruit Mark may have in mind is the recognition of or faith in Jesus as the Messiah. The preceding story of the triumphal entry, as well as the Gospel as a whole, suggests this.[210] Indeed, Jesus' response to Peter when the next day he points out the withered fig tree is "Have faith in God" (11:22), that is, faith in God that produces the fruit of recognizing who Jesus is.

§3.29 The Miracles in Mark

Before drawing our own conclusions we need to discuss two major contemporary views on Mark's perspectives on the miracles. First, some have argued Mark set out to disdain the miraculous and warn his readers against belief in miracles.[211] It is held that Mark wanted to encourage his readers to base their faith not on the power of Jesus but on his powerlessness. Evidence for this is said to be in the miracles being confined almost exclusively to the pre-passion period of Jesus' ministry, as well as in the so-called motif of secrecy (which I will mention in a moment) and in Jesus' refusal to give a sign (Mk 8:11-13).

That the miracles are confined primarily to that part of the Gospel preceding the passion is not an argument in itself against the miracles or their importance. Indeed, Mark uses miracles to accompany and thereby interpret the passion (Mk 15:33, 38; 16:1-8). He also uses the miracles to foreshadow (2:7; 6:6), encapsulate (9:26-27) and adumbrate Jesus' self-giving death.[212] So it cannot be concluded that the miraculous is dissociated from the powerless Jesus.

Moreover the refusal to give a sign is, as we have seen, a criticism not of miracles but of unbelief.[213] Even in the miracle stories, Jesus is presented not as powerless but as spectacularly powerful and successful—hardly a presentation designed to denigrate the miracles. Further, if Mark wished to disdain miracles and the miraculous, he would not have portrayed the disciples as miracle workers.[214] Nor would he have composed his summaries of Jesus' ministry with such a positive emphasis on the miracles if he were disdaining them or had no interest in them, apart from relating them because they were in his tradition.[215]

Rather than disdain the miracles, our study has shown Mark resolves to magnify their significance.[216] There can be little doubt that one of the major intentions of Mark is to portray Jesus as an exceptionally powerful miracle worker: "He radiates supernatural power almost as the sun radiates light."[217] Touching his clothing was sufficient to be healed (Mk 5:28; 6:56). Speaking to the wind and waves was sufficient to calm a storm (4:39). He could walk on the sea (6:47-52) and cause the blind to see (8:22-26; 10:46-52).

Besides, the sheer number of miracles is astounding. To follow Theissen, "Nowhere else do we have traditions of so many miracles by a single miracle-worker (with the exception of cult sanctuaries)." Theissen goes on to point out that the *Life of Apollonius* has only nine miracle stories.[218] This indicates that Mark is not only applauding the miracles but also portraying Jesus as an exceptionally popular miracle worker—so popular that crowds flocked to him, making it difficult for him to move about (e.g., Mk 2:2). Therefore a more reasonable account of Mark's attitude is to say that he highly values the miracle traditions and sees Jesus' miracle-working power as inseparable from his self-giving weakness seen in the passion narrative.[219] We will return to this point in a moment.

A second view of Mark's perspective on the miracles that must be discussed, if only briefly, is that he has taken up a collection, or collections, of miracle stories or an aretalogy. Mark has done this, so it is argued, either to portray Jesus as a "divine man" *(theios anēr)* or to correct such a Christology.

It is true that there were many healers in Mark's world who were said to perform miracles. Ludwig Bieler was the first to set out the Greco-Roman concept of the divine man *(theios anēr)*.[220] It was Beiler's view that the notion of a divine man became established in the Hellenistic period. The divine man was supposed to be a legendary or historical genius, a religio-philosophical hero, a human-become-*superman (Übermensch)* through being indwelt by the divine. The *theios anēr*, by definition, enjoyed supernatural gifts and powers.

However, there are grave doubts about the existence of such a special type of miracle worker.[221] It has been shown that the term *divine man* was not a technical or fixed expression and is relatively rare in ancient Greek literature. Further, the term is not ascribed to persons who were thought to be sacred or who distinguished themselves by conducting miracles.[222]

In short, the concept of a divine man who performed miracles proves to be a figment of imaginative scholarly research, and the search for Mark's understanding of miracles in relation to a *theios anēr* Christology—either to portray Jesus as a *theios anēr* or to correct such a Christology—proves to be misguided.[223]

In light of our examination of the data, and having dealt with these two major contemporary views, we are now in a position to draw together some conclusions about Mark's view of the miracles of Jesus that he wants to convey to his readers, especially to his Christian audience, whom he is encouraging in their faith, evangelism and life together. The following points emerge as the most significant.

1. *Who is Jesus?* Why has Mark given over such a high proportion of his Gospel to the theme and stories of miracles? Tied to this is the question of why the miracle stories are concentrated in the period before the passion.

Since so many themes are linked to the miracle stories in Mark (e.g., the Sabbath, the failure of the Jews, the inclusion of the Gentiles, the power of Jesus over sin and Satan, and the ability of Jesus to protect his followers), it is unlikely that there is a single answer to the question regarding the number of miracles in Mark. Nevertheless, I would like to suggest that Mark's linking of miracle stories to the question of Jesus' identity was the prime reason for the great number of miracle stories in his Gospel and for their concentration in the pre-passion ministry.

From the very first miracle story—the exorcism in the Capernaum synagogue (Mk 1:21-28)—Mark raises the question of the identity of Jesus: the unclean spirit addresses Jesus as the "Holy One of God" (1:24) and the observers ask the question, "What is this? A new teaching—with authority! He commands even the unclean spirits, and they obey him" (1:27). In 1:34 Mark says that Jesus would not permit the demons to speak because they knew him. Similarly in the story of the Gerasene demoniac, Jesus is addressed by the demoniac as "Son of the Most High God" (5:7). In the story of the healing of the paralytic the question of Jesus' identity is raised by means of the question "Who can forgive sins but God alone?" (2:7), and at the end of the story the crowd glorifies God (2:12).

In the story of the man with a withered hand Jesus is portrayed as someone who has the right to override the Sabbath (Mk 3:2). In 3:11 the unclean spirits shout that Jesus is the "Son of God." And Bartimaeus calls out to Jesus as the "Son of David" (10:47-48). At the end of the story of the calming of the sea, Mark has the disciples ask one another, "Who then is this, that even the wind and the sea obey him?" (4:41). Again, in his hometown the discussion arises as to who Jesus is in light of the deeds of power being done by his hands (6:2-3). And the powers or miracles were the center of Herod's questioning of the identity of Jesus (6:14).

It should not surprise us when these questions relating to Jesus' identity are unanswered; for heightened impact they are rhetorical—the readers know the answer (see, e.g., Mk 1:1). Through these questions the miracle stories are seen to be in the service of Mark's addressing the question of Jesus' identity.[224] Where there is an answer, it is that he is "of God" or the "Son of God" or acting in God's place (e.g., 1:24, 27; 2:7).

The so-called Beelzebul controversy (Mk 3:19b-30) adds another dimension to the identity of Jesus revealed in the miracles: he is the one empowered by the Holy Spirit (cf. 3:29). But Mark goes a step further than this. Most dramatically and clearly, the issue of Jesus' identity is addressed and taken to the extreme in the story of Jesus' walking on the sea (6:47-52). We saw that, in Jesus' intention to pass by the disciples, Mark was portraying Jesus not simply as God's Son or divine,[225] nor only as acting for God (cf. 2:7); he is God himself uniquely present.

If, for Mark, the self-giving Jesus is the Messiah—indeed, God himself present at work in the miracles (e.g., Mk 2:1-12; 6:48)—it is not surprising that he uses a vocabulary of eschatological salvation as part of his explanation of the meaning of Jesus' miracles. The Gerasene demoniac receives salvific mercy (5:19; cf. 10:48), and the giving of sight to Bartimaeus is the bringing of eschatological salvation (cf. 10:47-48). It is no wonder then that Mark sees the miracles as encapsulating the whole of Jesus' ministry and that they are "proclaimed" (1:45) in the same way Jesus proclaims his message (1:38-39).

To this partial answer as to why Mark has so many miracle stories—they identify

Jesus—we must add a further consideration. While there are many miracles before the passion narrative, apart from that of the cursing of the fig tree, no further miracle stories are related after it commences. This has the effect of leaving the reader with the impression that Jesus, the powerful miracle worker, identified as the Messiah and God, is being portrayed as choosing to offer himself powerless into the hands of the authorities in order to die (cf. Mk 10:45).

Indeed, in the miracle stories these are hints of this self-giving: the eucharistic themes in the stories of the feeding of the five thousand and then the four thousand are the most obvious examples (Mk 6:41; 8:6-7). A piece with this is the compassion that is portrayed in Jesus' healings. For example, we saw that in the first three healing stories Jesus is depicted as being compassionate toward "outsiders."[226]

A further part of the reason Mark has included so many miracle stories could be that in them he saw not the gospel being illustrated but that they were coincident with it—equivalent to the gospel itself. We saw this hinted at in that Mark is said to be writing about the gospel (Mk 1:1, 14-15) and that the very first public activity was the report of the performance of a miracle. This identity of miracle and gospel is also seen in the Beelzebul controversy (3:19b-30; further see point 6).

We are bound to conclude then that the highest matter on Mark's agenda in relating the miracle tradition is to reflect on Jesus' identity: the powerful Messiah—indeed, *God himself at work*—who gives himself to die for others. Jesus is the Son of God in his powerful miracles (e.g., Mk 3:11) as well as in his powerless death (15:39). In this, Mark's Christology is a piece with Paul's in describing Jesus as being in the form of God yet emptying himself, becoming obedient to the point of death (Phil 2:5-8).

The question of Jesus' identity being directly tied both to the miracle stories and to his passion as well shows that although the miracles are important to Mark, Jesus is more than a miracle worker. This leads to the next conclusion we must draw from our study.

2. *Miracles and teaching.* Although miracles are important to Mark, Jesus the miracle worker cannot be separated from Jesus the teacher. Part of Mark's agenda seems to be to establish not only the importance but also the place of the miracles, perhaps in the face of those who saw Jesus as only or primarily a teacher.

The first story of healing is set in the context of Jesus' teaching in a synagogue, and the crowd's subsequent amazement is over the teaching as well as the miracle (Mk 2:27). Yet Mark goes on to portray the crowds as seeking Jesus primarily as a healer (cf. 1:34 and 37). Jesus' response is to say that he must proclaim the message (1:38), even though Mark then says that Jesus went throughout Galilee speaking and exorcising (1:39).

A tension seems to be arising between Jesus' wishing to teach and his being sought as a healer. This finds its expression in that the next story is of yet another healing (Mk 1:40-45) and the story after that is of Jesus teaching at home yet being sought as a healer (2:1-12). In the next story of the healing of the man who had a withered hand (3:1-6), Jesus is in the synagogue, presumably where he intended to teach. This tension is resolved and a balance restored by Mark giving an extended section of teaching in chapter 4. Then, expressing the unity of healer and teacher, the frightened disciples address Jesus as "Teacher" when they request him to do something about the storm at sea (4:38). Similarly blind Bartimaeus, who expects Jesus to heal him, addresses Jesus as "my teacher" (or "Master," 10:51). As a healer then Jesus is addressed and sought as teacher (cf. 9:28), and in his teaching he is sought as a healer.

As a result of this study we can conclude that, in the face of those who may have seen Jesus only or primarily as a teacher, Mark probably wishes to establish the miracles as the most important components in Jesus' pre-Easter ministry. Indeed, the most significant impression left on the reader of Mark's Gospel is not that the miracles are superfluous[227] but that they are indispensably important in what Mark wishes to say about Jesus. We gain this impression from the sheer number of stories, the summaries, the concentration of miracle stories in the period preceding the passion narrative and the great popularity Mark attributes to Jesus the miracle worker, as well as the way he weaves together the twin roles of Jesus' teaching and healing. In Matthew we will see quite a different perspective.

3. *Jesus cannot be hidden.* Part of the popularity of Jesus is tied to the theme of his miraculous activity being unable to be hidden, despite his sometimes demanding those healed not to speak about what had happened. In relation to the miracles, these commands to silence are of two kinds.

On three occasions Jesus commands the demons to be silent (Mk 1:25, 34; 3:12). In one instance the command is part of the well-known technique of binding a demon (1:25; cf. 5:8). However, in 1:34 and 3:12 the demons are commanded to be silent because they know his true identity—the Son of God (cf. 1:11). As is often agreed, Mark is telling his readers that Jesus' true identity is improperly comprehended apart from his passion and death: the healer and exorcist without the suffering Jesus is a misunderstood Messiah.

The other kind of injunction is seen in the silencing of the cleansed leper (Mk 1:43-44) and the healed Gerasene demoniac (5:20). In both cases it is a conditional command to silence. The healed leper is sternly charged and told not to speak to anyone but to show himself to the priest and offer the sacrifice for his cleansing (1:44). The healed demoniac is directed to speak about what "the Lord has done" for him (5:19). However, both characters begin to speak freely and widely about Jesus (1:45; 5:20). Similarly in response to the man whose hearing and speech were healed, the crowd is said to have more zealously proclaimed it the more Jesus "ordered" them to tell no one (7:36).

Thus these injunctions to silence function as foils for Mark to highlight the impossibility of hiding Jesus' miracles ministry.[228] Even when there is no injunction, Jesus' fame spreads as a result of an exorcism in Capernaum (Mk 1:28). Also, after the feeding of the five thousand and his walking on the sea, Jesus is said to be recognized and besieged by crowds bringing their sick to be healed (6:53-56).

Part of the inability of Jesus the miracle worker to remain hidden is Mark's portrayal of Jesus' healing ministry spilling out into Gentile territory and the Gentiles receiving Jesus with acclaim equal to that accorded by the Jews.[229] In line with this conclusion it is notable that in the miracle stories where there is no command to silence such a command would be senseless or unnecessary when the miracles are said to take place in the presence of a crowd.[230] When there is no crowd, as in the story of the Syrophoenician woman's daughter (Mk 7:24-30), the story already has the motif of the news of Jesus reaching more widely than Jesus' immediate surroundings. Mark did not need to introduce the foil of silence to show that the message of Jesus' healing had spread or was unstoppable.[231]

4. *Conflict.* The first miracle story—the expelling of the unclean spirit in the Capernaum synagogue (Mk 1:21-28)—is one of conflict with the demonic. The theme of conflict surfaces again when Jesus tells the cleansed leper to show himself to the authorities as a witness against the religious leaders and their practices (1:44). Conflict also arises over Jesus' forgiveness of the sins of the paralytic (2:1-12). Thus in the miracles, as much as in other aspects of Jesus' ministry,[232] Mark sustains the view that Jesus was in conflict with the religious leaders, a conflict that saw its climax in the passion. The significance of this conflict, which is an offensive attack in the miracles, is at least that it highlights what had not so far been possible— healing and forgiveness. Both were now possible in the ministry of Jesus and, thereafter, in that of his followers.

5. *Miracles as models.* Earlier in this chapter I agreed with the argument that Mark's purposes were probably not directly evangelistic but pastoral in that he was trying to encourage his readers in their evangelism and life together (§3.2). This alerted us to his interest in using the miracle stories to encourage his readers along these lines. The precise nature of this encouragement has been seen in that the miracles were clear pointers to the identity of Jesus, who was to be followed, that faith in him is more than reasonable and that the miracles were sources of didactic models for the healing ministry of the readers.

It is not only that the miracle stories are interwoven with didactic themes. As shown in the clearest example—the healing of the epileptic boy (Mk 9:14-29)—the stories teach how the followers of Jesus are to conduct their healing ministry (9:29). In that story, prayer—an exercise in faith—is enjoined as a method of exorcism (9:29). In so far as the disciples are called to emulate the ministry of Jesus (cf

3:14-15), other miracle stories provide models for ministry. Further, by implication in the story of the strange exorcist, healing in the name or authority of Jesus is assumed to be the method of healing (9:38).

More generally the miracle stories teach Mark's readers how to carry out their healing ministry by modeling what they see in the stories of Jesus. This becomes apparent when we see that only after the called disciples (Mk 3:15) have been with Jesus the teacher and miracle worker are they sent out on mission—a mission patterned on Jesus' ministry (6:7-13). In this we can assume that the disciples will model Jesus' compassion (cf. 1:44; 8:2) and be able to heal because they have his authority to cast out demons (cf. 1:15) and power to heal the sick (cf. 5:30).

6. *Miracles as parables.* The Beelzebul controversy (Mk 3:19b-30) brings into clear focus another aspect of the miracles in Mark. They are not unequivocal heavenly signs (cf. 8:11-13) but parabolic in nature and ambiguous in their message.

From one perspective—the most obvious one—the exorcisms are the freeing and healing of sick people. From another perspective they are the destruction and plundering of Satan's kingdom in order that the kingdom of God can be realized (Mk 3:27). From yet another perspective the Beelzebul controversy shows that the miracles also provoked hostility, as they did in the case of the paralytic let down through a roof (2:1-12) and the man healed of a withered hand (3:1-6). Also, the exorcisms led the scribes to the conclusion that Jesus was empowered by Satan (3:22-30). Even the disciples did not grasp the meaning of the miracles, as for example in the cases of the calming of the storm (4:35-41), the feeding of the five thousand (6:51-52) and the feeding of the four thousand (8:14-21).

This ambiguity puts the reader in the same position in relation to Jesus' teaching, especially the parables of Jesus. That is, faith-insight is required to understand their meaning and significance (cf. Mk 4:10-12). As the words of Jesus can be perceived in a way that can bring understanding or misunderstanding, so the actions of Jesus in the miracles can elicit understanding or misunderstanding as to who he is and what the miracles accomplish (cf. 3:22-30).[233]

However, the miracles are parables only to a limited extent in that, in themselves, they also actualize what they symbolize. They actualize the kingdom of God and, for the eye of faith, point beyond to the identity of Jesus. Thus Mark does not view the miracles as final proof of the identity of Jesus (cf. 8:11-31).[234] It is not that Mark is ambivalent about the value of miracles.[235] It is rather that the perception of who Jesus is and the message of the ambiguous miracles require the insight of faith in Jesus. (This will lead to the next point, which has already been noted in passing.)

The parabolic nature of the miracle stories for Mark is also disclosed in his linking of healing and forgiveness and, as we saw, the general import of the statement "the Son of Man has authority on earth to forgive sins" (Mk 2:10). We took the position that this means the reader can always take Jesus' ministry of healing as dealing not only with sickness but with sin through forgiveness.[236]

7. *Miracles and faith*. While faith may not be the reason Mark has so many miracle stories (see above), Mark's portrayal of the miracles clearly links faith and miracles. It is notable that all five occurrences of the noun *pistis* ("faith") are part of a miracle story or connected with Mark's discussion of miracles: Jesus noted the faith of those bearing the paralytic (Mk 2:5); after stilling a storm Jesus asked why the disciples had no faith (4:40); it was the woman's faith that cured her hemorrhaging (5:34); the faith of Bartimaeus made him see (10:52); and in the context of explaining the cursing of the fig tree, Jesus tells his followers that if they have faith, whatever they say will take place (11:23-24). And in the story of the stilling of the storm Jesus is probably, at least in part, being depicted as the epitome of serene faith (4:35).

Christopher Marshall has rightly drawn attention to the importance of Mark 1:15 ("the kingdom of God has come near; repent and believe in the good news") in adumbrating that repentance and faith are the responses Mark anticipates in relation to all Jesus' activities—the miracles as well as the teaching. "Mark would accept no fundamental distinction between the *structure* of kerygmatic faith and miracle faith."[237]

In the stories of a leprous man coming to Jesus and begging on his knees for healing (Mk 1:40), of the four companions having sufficient confidence in Jesus' ability to heal to go to the trouble of letting a sick man down through a roof (2:4) and of sick people begging to touch even the edge of his clothes (6:54), Mark illustrates expressions of faith in Jesus. He also has examples of vicarious faith. In the story of the deaf-mute, some people begged Jesus to place his hand on the sick man (7:32). The story of the paralytic (2:3-5) and that of the blind man brought to Jesus in Bethsaida (8:22) also show faith being expressed on behalf of a sick person.

There are examples of satisfied suppliants responding in faith.[238] And in the discussion of the two feeding narratives (Mk 8:14-21) Mark shows that the miracles demand or are a summons to faith and, by association 1:15, repentance. Hence Mark has crowds coming to Jesus on the basis of their knowing about Jesus' miracles,[239] as well as individuals coming to be healed apparently on the basis of faith generated by reports of Jesus' miracles or even elicited by the words of Jesus as he begins to heal (cf. 3:5).

Clearly from Mark's perspective, faith or prayer—of the sick person or others—is integral in Jesus healing the sick. In fact, apart from the exorcisms, there is no healing story that does not include some expression of trust in Jesus either before, during or after the healing.

While there may be no internal development of the theme of faith,[240] in the story of Bartimaeus, Mark draws together and characterizes many of the connections between Jesus the miracle worker and the response that is expected. The man calls out in faith, he "repents" or throws off his old life and, on being healed, he unconditionally follows Jesus on the road of suffering discipleship (Mk 10:46-52).

We saw a similar response of total devotion to Jesus in response to his miracles illustrated by Peter's mother-in-law "serving" Jesus (Mk 1:31). Therefore Mark is portraying faith not as simply an awesome response to a wonder worker but as a response of someone to follow or serve or die to self (cf. 1:31; 10:45) or to be with Jesus on the basis of the eschatological salvation offered in healing (cf. 5:23; 7:37).

In his use of the miracles as a major stay in establishing the identity of Jesus and in his linking faith and miracles, the precise nature of Mark's use of miracles in his overall purpose to encourage his readers in their faith becomes transparent. For those who have some faith, yet need help in their unbelief through a gift of faith (cf. Mk 9:24), Jesus' initiative in miracles provides the encouragement to see who Jesus is and that he can be trusted completely as they respond to his call to repent and believe his good news (1:15), as well as to follow him absolutely to the end (cf. 10:50, 52).

But as the story of the forgiven paralytic shows (Mk 2:1-12), faith is only one of a number of possible responses to the miracles. Apart from this, Mark shows a variety of responses to Jesus' miracles: amazement (1:27; 5:20, 42), questioning of Jesus' identity (1:27; 6:2-3), service (1:31), disbelieving questioning (2:6-7), conspiracy to destroy Jesus (3:6), a recognition of Jesus' identity (3:11), fear (5:15), a desire for Jesus to leave the area (5:17), a desire to be with Jesus (5:18), proclaiming (5:20), unbelief (6:6), the conclusion that John the Baptist had come back to life (6:16), incomprehension (6:52; 8:21), popularity (6:54-55), astonishment (7:37) and a desire to follow Jesus.

In short, Marshall is right to say that the Markan miracle stories stand in a twofold relationship to faith: they illustrate the benefits of faith and are a summons to faith.[241]

8. *Miracle and unbelief.* I suggested that in mentioning Bethsaida as the setting for the healing of the blind man (Mk 8:22), Mark may be hinting at the difficulties of having faith in Jesus' miracles, especially in an environment of unbelief. Further, it may be possible to look back over the two cycles of miracle stories (4:35—8:10) and note a diminution of the miraculous. We may speculate that this was intended to draw attention to the need for faith: when Jesus' ministry was not met by faith there was a diminution in the miraculous.

It is among the Jews—those of "his hometown" (Mk 6:2)—that Mark most starkly portrays unbelief in response to Jesus (6:6): "He could do no *[edunato]* deed of power there, except that he laid his hands on a few sick people and cured them" (6:5). This irrefutably shows that Mark sees as essential faith in Jesus' not only being willing but able to perform miracles. This report may owe something to the disappointment early Christians experienced in their mission to the Jews.[242] However, this unbelief is probably best understood in light of reports of Jesus' miracles spilling over into Gentile territory, the high level of faith Jesus encountered among the Gentiles and Gentiles probably being prominent among Mark's readers. So these contrasts are best explained not so much as arising out of a failure of the mission to the Jews—for Mark reports many Jews responding with faith—as giving an explanation of the success of the mission of the Jews to the Gentiles.

9. *Miracles, fear and the good news.* We have seen that to be fearful *(phobeomai)* was a frequent response to the miracles in Mark. On being chastised for having no faith, the disciples are said to be "afraid" (Mk 4:41). On coming to Jesus and seeing the Gerasene demoniac in his right mind, the people from the towns are "afraid" and ask Jesus to leave their area (5:15). The woman who secretly and successfully sought to be healed of hemorrhaging comes to Jesus in "fear" and trembling (5:33). Then Jairus is told not to "fear," only believe (5:36).

This last instance best illustrates Mark's use of the word, especially in relation to the miracles. For Mark, fear is the awesome realization of the power evident and available in Jesus' miracles. Yet it also manifests an inability to respond positively to Jesus. It is the opposite of faith in him, a response to Jesus found in 11:33, where the chief priest, the scribes and the elders are unable to respond positively to Jesus. The importance of the word *fear* and its meaning is clear from Mark's use of it at the very end of his Gospel: the women flee the empty tomb saying nothing to anyone "for they were afraid."[243] The women are overcome with the awesome realization of the power associated with Jesus in what they have heard.

However, is not Mark also saying that although the initial response to awesome power evident in Jesus is one of dumbfounding, fearful awe, eventually as that awe turns to faith for a person, it is impossible to hide what had become evident in the miracle? The readers of Mark are testimony that the women did not remain fearful and were unable to remain silent, just as those who were healed could not conceal what had happened to them. The awe became faith, and the faith became the grounds for unstoppable proclamation of the good news of Jesus.

Four

The Miracles of
Jesus in Matthew

....

§4.1 Introduction

Having read Mark, we have already been introduced to all the miracle stories of Jesus found in Matthew, except for the ones concerning the healing of the official's son (Mt 8:5-13) and the finding of a coin in the mouth of a fish (17:24-27).[1] Yet the way Matthew presents the stories shows that he has particular and distinctive things to say and emphasize about the miracles as well as about Jesus himself. Matthew also reinforces the message we have in Mark that the miracles show Jesus to be God himself acting mightily and that the miracles are models for the ministry of his followers. We will also see that Matthew offers a massive modification to our understanding of Jesus being primarily a miracle worker, which we have received from Mark's interpretation of the miracle stories.

The bench mark for all subsequent discussion and understanding of the miracles in Matthew has been set by Heinz J. Held.[2] Like others before him Held noted the most obvious feature of Matthew's miracle stories: the majority are abbreviated by abridging the narrative while simultaneously expanding the discourse.

Few would question Held's conclusions that these changes are theologically motivated and carried out for the instruction of his readers. Moreover Held has correctly drawn attention to Matthew's concern for Christology, faith and discipleship in retelling the miracle stories. However, Held has misunderstood the importance of these themes and some nuances in the way Matthew has dealt with these key motifs.

In his contribution to the subject, Birger Gerhardsson concluded that in his mighty acts Jesus appears in Israel as a man with sensational authority and power.[3] Also, Gerhardsson says that it appears Matthew consciously divided the powerful acts into therapeutic and nontherapeutic miracles, interpreting them for two different theological purposes.

The individual healings are directed to those not (yet) disciples. In these mighty healing acts, Matthew brings out the authority of Jesus and its relation to the faith of persons in need. Gerhardsson notes that even though the nontherapeutic miracles are worked throughout for the disciples, the relationship between faith and Jesus' authority remains. Nevertheless Gerhardsson curiously says that it does not seem that Matthew's presentation of the miracles is strongly affected by apologetic intentions, though he goes on to conclude that "Matthew's aim was to present Jesus clearly and simply as the one who fulfils innumerable prophecies of the coming time of salvation. . . . Above all, the Jesus of the miracles is 'the Messiah, the Son of the Living God.' "[4]

One of the most striking and sometimes puzzling features of Matthew's Gospel is its structure.[5] Therefore we will begin our inquiry into Matthew's view of Jesus' miracles with a discussion of his structure and how it relates to his message about the miracles. Part of our discussion needs to pay particular attention to chapters 8 and 9, where his structure is most clearly seen and has an immediate impact on how a person understands the miracles in Matthew. But we must also take into account Matthew's narrative or plot,[6] a writer's more subtle tool for expressing intention. Then we will be prepared to "walk through" Matthew's story, stopping at each miracle story and summary that mentions miracles to note how the plot, his nuances, interests and details in the stories contribute to understanding Matthew's message in and through the miracles. Then we will be able to draw some conclusions about the miracles of Jesus in Matthew.

§4.2 The Structure and Story of Matthew

The accepted view that Matthew relies on Mark for the outline of Jesus' ministry necessitates an important conclusion about his understanding of the miracles. Whereas Mark mentions healing through exorcism as Jesus' first public act, Matthew does not mention miracles until the summary in 4:23-25. And there is no miracle story until that of the leper being cleansed in 8:1-4. Instead, the Sermon on the Mount dominates the early part of Matthew. This massive change portrays Jesus, initially, not as a healer who preaches but as a Moses-like prophet or teacher who heals.[7]

In this change Matthew has even omitted Mark's programmatic and paradigmatic exorcism story (Mk 1:21-28). Indeed, it is not until 8:28-34 that Matthew gives his readers an exorcism story. Already we can see what will be confirmed when we look at the individual stories: Matthew not only emphasizes Jesus the teacher-preacher over above Jesus the miracle worker, he also plays down the role of exorcism among Jesus' miracles.[8]

The Sermon on the Mount and the two subsequent chapters on miracles are held together by two almost identical summaries about Jesus' ministry of preaching and healing (Mt 4:23-25 and 9:35-36). This gives the impression that the Sermon on the Mount and the miracles of Jesus in chapters 8 and 9 form what could be called a literary diptych, or double panel, of the ministry of Jesus (cf. Clement *Paedagogos* 1:2:6).

Not only are the miracle chapters of 8 and 9 linked back to the teaching in chapters 5-7, but along with the Great Sermon the miracle stories prepare for the call and sending out of the disciples in chapter 10. This is done through the linking catch phrase "every disease and every sickness," which comes at the end of the cycles of miracle stories (Mt 9:35) and at the beginning of the commissioning of the disciples (10:1).

Also, two of the statements "and when Jesus had finished," which occur just before the miracle stories (Mt 7:28) and again after the instructions to the commissioned disciples (11:1),[9] bind together the chapters on miracles and the mission of the disciples. In this Matthew surely intended the teaching, along with the miracles, to function as a model not only for the ministry of the disciples but also for his readers. Thus the miracles form the second half of an integrated ministry of the Messiah, who instructs not only but also acts mightily to model a dual ministry for his followers.

Nevertheless, as will be shown more than once, for Matthew the preaching and teaching are main interests and are more important than healing. Jesus is established as a teacher-preacher in the Great Sermon before being shown to be the healer. The first statement of Jesus' ministry ("From that time Jesus began to proclaim," Mt 4:17) does not mention healing. The summary in 11:1 mentions only instruction *(diatassō)*, and the summary instruction at the close of the Gospel mentions only the requirement to teach (28:16-20). Indeed, the open-ended finish toward which the whole of Matthew's story moves portrays Jesus as commissioning his followers only to teach. Nothing is mentioned of healing (28:18-20).

Critical in Matthew's perspective on the miracles are chapters 8 and 9. To these we turn, focusing on the issues of structure.

§4.3 Chapters 8 and 9

Although it is sometimes proposed that Matthew's structure is modeled on Mark or is "centered" around a passage such as chapter 13 on the parables, it is most frequently suggested that Matthew is to be divided into five "books,"[10] each ending with a statement about how Jesus has finished speaking.[11] Notwithstanding the many critics of the "Baconian" structure,[12] as we have noted, two of the five summary statements just mentioned (Mt 7:28 and 11:1) tie these two chapters on miracles to that of the mission of the Twelve to form the second "book" of the proposed five. The implication of this is that these miracle stories become the backdrop to and—along with the teaching of Jesus—a model for the mission of the Twelve.

It is generally agreed that the miracles in chapters 8 and 9 have been collected into three groups of three stories, each group being followed by sayings of Jesus.[13] One way to set out the structure of these chapters is as follows:

A. Matthew 8:1-17
   (a) A leper healed (vv. 1-4)
   (b) A centurion's servant healed (vv. 5-13)
   (c) Peter's mother-in-law healed (vv. 14-15)
      *Summary of Jesus' ministry (vv. 16-17)
      *Would-be followers of Jesus (vv. 18-22)
B. Matthew 8:23—9:17
   (a) A storm calmed (vv. 23-27)
   (b) Two demoniacs healed (vv. 28-34)
   (c) A paralytic forgiven and healed (9:1-8)
      *The call of Matthew the tax collector (vv. 9-13)
      *The issue of fasting (vv. 14-17)
C. Matthew 9:18-34
   (a) A ruler's daughter raised and a woman healed (vv. 18-26)
   (b) Two men receive their sight (vv. 27-31)
   (c) A mute demoniac healed (vv. 32-34)
      *Summary of Jesus' ministry (v. 35)
      *The call for laborers (vv. 36-38)

H. J. Held argued that the first set of miracles dealt with Christology, the second set with discipleship and the third with faith.[14] Jeremy Moiser has proposed that Matthew used the Sermon on the Mount as the basis for his arrangement of the stories, so that the first triad of miracle stories illustrates Jesus' offer of new teaching, the second Jesus' words on prayer and the third Jesus' words on trust in God.[15] However, on examination, at least in relation to the first two cycles, these themes are not found to dominate the respective collections of miracles. Instead, each story contributes to a number of themes, often to one in particular—discipleship.

But Matthew's Gospel has more than a meaningful geometric structure that might be supposed from the analysis of the miracle chapters just set out. Matthew is a plotted story that develops from the introduction of the main character, follows his turbulent life and climaxes with his dramatic death and resurrection. While the immediate plot of Matthew is confined to the brief period of the story or life of the earthly Jesus,[16] it is set against a wider backdrop that begins with the people of Israel (e.g., Mt 1:2)—or perhaps even creation[17]—and ends beyond history (19:28; 25:46).

The ongoing significance of the story of Jesus reaches to every reader of Matthew, for Jesus never leaves the stage, and he promises to be with his followers to the end of the age (Mt 28:17-20). In fact, from early in the story we know that Jesus will be "with us" (1:23). Over against this thrust Matthew depicts Satan's challenge to Jesus (4:1-11), so that Matthew's main plot is set up to be the conflict between Satan and God in Jesus, the main character of the story,[18] although clearly in Matthew (not least in chapters 8 and 9) this "ultimate" conflict is played out at times in human characters (cf. 16:23; 27:40). Notable among the miracles, the exorcism stories portray this conflict most clearly.

We turn now to "walk through" Matthew's narrative, stopping at the stories and summaries covering miracles. Studying these stories and summaries uncovers Matthew's interest and message in relation to (and in) the miracle stories.

§4.4 The Miracles in Matthew

Through the first sentence and the ensuing genealogy (Mt 1:1-17) Matthew introduces Jesus as the Messiah and as a descendant of Abraham (the father and source of all blessing for the Jews) and of David (the king through whom God brought unity and security). The four sexually scandalous women who are mentioned (Tamar, Rahab, Ruth and the wife of Uriah) prepare readers for Mary's scandal. Like the other four women, she had a part to play in God's saving activity.

The question raised in 1:16 about Jesus' father (saying only that Joseph was the husband of Mary) is answered in the rest of the section, which tells of the birth of Jesus (Mt 1:18-25).[19] The section focuses on Jesus' origin—he was conceived by the Holy Spirit. We also learn that his name is Jesus—in Hebrew "Joshua," which is related to the verb "to save" (1:21). Thus we know not only that in the healings and miracles God has taken the initiative in bringing Jesus but also that, not least in his miracles, Jesus will in fulfilling Scripture be saving his people from their sins. Added to these themes, in the following paragraphs about Jesus' birth (2:1-12) and flight to Egypt (2:13-23) there are probably parallels between Jesus and Moses.[20]

In preparation for the ministry of this Jesus, John the Baptist calls many people to repent (Mt 3:1-12), and in his baptism Jesus enrolls as one of the purified and prepared people for what God will do (3:13-17). Having been launched on his mission, encountering the same tests as Israel, Jesus succeeds where Israel had failed and is further revealed to be God's true Son (4:1-11).

Matthew then describes Jesus' ministry as bringing light to the Gentiles and introduces his message of repentance because the kingdom of heaven had come near (Mt 4:12-17). But before any detail of that ministry is given, especially about teaching being part of God's purpose for his ministry, Matthew has Jesus call his first followers, who will replicate his ministry (4:18-22; 10:1—11:1).

With his introduction of Jesus complete, Matthew now provides an introductory summary to establish the main features of Jesus.

§4.5 A Summary Introduction (Mt 4:23-25; cf. 9:35-38)

There are a number of so-called summaries in Matthew,[21] not only summarizing the story up to that point but also tying together the narrative and geographically extending the ministry of Jesus. These summaries also function to give the story a sense of movement and highlight themes of interest to Matthew.

As we have noted, it is not until now, after thoroughly establishing the identity of Jesus and the broadest nature of his life and ministry as one dominated by conflict, that Matthew mentions the miracles. This delay in mentioning them should not cause a false impression of the nature of Jesus' ministry.

The significance of this first summary—about Jesus going throughout Galilee speaking and healing so that his fame causes great crowds to follow him—is that Matthew is setting this as the agenda for Jesus' ministry. In the parallel summary in 9:35, at the end of the two chapters of miracle stories, we see the nature of Jesus' ministry is highlighted as Matthew ties together the Sermon on the Mount and the miracle stories. Thus he presents Jesus' program as working miracles as well as teaching *(didaskein)* and proclaiming *(kērussein)*—between which there is no clear distinction for Matthew.[22] The exact repetition of the words "teaching in their synagogues, and proclaiming the good news of the kingdom, and curing every disease and every sickness" in both summaries (Mt 4:23; 9:35) further reinforces this impression that the Sermon and the miracles together form a whole in Jesus' ministry.

Yet as important as the miracles may be, it is the Great Sermon—which he closes with one of his transitional phrases ("Now when Jesus had finished saying these things")[23]—that dominates the initial phase of Matthew's portrayal of Jesus. Then with a first miracle story, Matthew balances the initial impression he has given his readers of Jesus as a great teacher by providing a series of stories depicting him as a great miracle worker.[24]

§4.6 A Leper Cleansed (Mt 8:1-4/Mk 1:40-45/Lk 5:12-16)

The leading story of Jesus' activity is that of a leper being cleansed. As will be shown, with this as the lead miracle story Matthew is able to show that in his miracles Jesus fulfills the law, carrying on that theme from the Great Sermon. Matthew's most significant addition to the opening statement in chapter 8 is about Jesus coming down from the mountain on which he delivered the Great Sermon.[25] It is natural to conclude that Matthew wished his readers to see a parallel between Moses and Jesus the healer.

Through the remainder of the story Matthew has abbreviated the descriptive elements. As a result, focus is redirected from the healing to the main character—Jesus—and the conversation between him and the sufferer.

In depicting great crowds following Jesus (Mt 8:1) Matthew is not only showing how responsive people were to Jesus' message or providing an audience for Jesus' sayings about faith in Israel (8:10). He is also foreshadowing the throng of disciples eventually to come from every nation to follow Jesus the great teacher who heals (28:19).[26]

The startling thing here, introduced by the words "And behold"[27] (Mt 8:2, author's translation), is that the Moses-like figure of Jesus descending from the mount of revelation is approached by a leper, a social and religious outcast (see Lev 13—14).[28] Further, the leper approaches Jesus in a worshipful manner[29] and begins his request to Jesus as a prayer—"Lord" (kurie).

This request is central to the significance of the story for Matthew. In saying "If you choose, you can make me clean" the leper is exercising his unrestrained faith in the power of the Lord Jesus to heal; perhaps this faith was generated in seeing who Jesus was in coming, like Moses, down the mountain. All that is in question, and on what the healing depends, is Jesus' willingness to heal. In response, instead of praying, as might be expected from the example of Moses (Num 12:13), Jesus does two things.

First, in contrast to Moses and Elisha (Num 12:10-15; 2 Kings 5:1-14), Jesus touches the leper (Mt 8:3). In so doing Jesus is portrayed as breaking the law.[30] However, just as his teaching was not intended to contradict the law but to reveal the divine intention in the law, so the touch of Jesus expresses the divine intention of healing. The willingness of Jesus to touch the man also emphasizes his association with the social and ceremonial outcast. Further, Jesus' power is evident in that he is not thereby diseased but instead cures the leper.

Second, Jesus says, "I will; be clean" (Mt 8:3, author's translation). That is, Jesus, who is the source of healing power, only has to will the cleansing to effect an immediate cure. The power to heal is not in what is said but in Jesus.

That Matthew has Jesus tell the cleansed leper to say nothing about his healing remains a puzzle. Having the leper obey the law of Moses and show himself to the priest and offer appropriate sacrifice provides a testimony (maturion) about what has happened.[31] Also Matthew is showing that the healing power of Jesus no more overturns the law than the new teaching of Jesus overturns the Torah (cf. Mt 5:17-20). This maintains the Moses theme in the Gospel. Jesus' compassion is also evident in the resocialization of the leper (cf. Lev 13—14).

In view of the Moses theme, the address to Jesus as Lord (Mt 8:2) as well as the expectation that lepers will receive healing when the Messiah comes (cf. 11:5), this story is an expression of the fulfillment of eschatological hope,[32] affirming that Jesus the healer is Jesus the Messiah. Further, this story is important to Matthew because, as we will see, he expects the followers of Jesus also to heal lepers. Only Matthew includes the healing of lepers among the instructions to the disciples sent out on mission (10:8). It is reasonable then to suppose that this story serves as a model for Matthew's readers in their ministry.

§4.7 A Centurion's Servant/Son Healed (Mt 8:5-13/Lk 7:1-10; cf. Jn 4:46-54)

Perhaps in order to maintain and develop the theme of Jesus' great authority, Matthew places this Q story of the centurion's servant or son *(pais)* here rather than use that of the paralytic brought by four friends, which he will take up in 9:1-8 (cf. Mk 2:1-12). Also, in contrast to Luke 7:1-3,[33] Matthew has the centurion himself confront Jesus rather than having him send elders of the Jews. For Matthew and his readers, this Roman centurion would have been an outsider coming in contact with and being accepted by Jesus (cf. *m. Ohol.* 18:7).

Matthew's abbreviation of the story removes references to elders of the Jews, applauding the centurion for his being worthy of Jesus' attention because of his love for the Jewish nation and for building a synagogue (cf. Lk 7:4b-5). This portrays Jesus responding not to earned attention but to a person with faith or a sense of humble undeserved need. This is heightened because the centurion is a high, commanding official—normally giving orders—here pictured as seeking help.

The centurion reports that his servant is terribly *(deinōs)* sick (Mt 8:6). This heightens both the severity of the illness and the consequent magnitude of Jesus' healing.[34] The centurion expresses his vicarious faith in Jesus' ability to heal by saying that Jesus only need to say the word for the healing to take place. Matthew's insertion here of "only" (*monos,* 8:8) highlights the centurion's confidence in Jesus' power.[35]

Contrary to his practice, Matthew has used the term *pais* ("son" or "servant") rather than *huios* ("son") for the servant.[36] Perhaps the double meaning of the term serves to suggest that the person is as much or more a "son" of the kingdom as those sons *(huioi)* who eventually will be thrown into outer darkness. This is, after all, the point of the story (Mt 8:12).[37]

Matthew does not often mention Jesus' emotional responses. Therefore in saying that Jesus marveled (Mt 8:10/Lk 7:9) Matthew draws particular attention to the faith of the centurion. Similarly, the addition of the distinctively Matthean "truly" or "amen" (*amēn,*[38] cf. Lk 7:9) also highlights Jesus' positive response to the faith of the centurion. Jesus' addressing his comments to those "following" *(akolouthousin)* him probably means Matthew wanted the followers among his readers to take particular note of Jesus' affirming the man's faith, which is contrasted with the lesser faith of the Jews: "In no one in Israel have I found such faith" (Mt 8:10).[39] Then, through the ensuing words of Jesus herein contrasting the many (in the future)[40] who come from east and west into the kingdom of heaven with the "sons of the kingdom" being excluded (8:12, author's translation; cf. Lk 13:28-30), Matthew is able to contrast the faith of the Gentiles with that of the "sons of the kingdom."[41]

This theme of faith is maintained in the closing stages of the story through Matthew's entire rewriting of the ending, which is no longer recoverable (cf. Lk 7:10). In Matthew, Jesus states bluntly that it is because of the centurion's faith that his slave has been healed. The importance of this theme to Matthew is obvious in that only twice is Jesus portrayed as granting the request of a Gentile, both times in response to faith (cf. Mt 15:21-28). Thus Jesus' call to the Jews is overcome, and the barrier between Jew and Gentile is shattered by faith.

Finally the powerful authority of Jesus is seen in the immediate healing of the servant—"in that hour"—from what was a severe affliction (Mt 8:13, cf. v. 6). Without a break Matthew begins another miracle story.

§4.8 Peter's Mother-in-Law Healed (Mt 8:14-15/Mk 1:29-31/Lk 4:38-39)

Not surprisingly Matthew abbreviates this story. The introduction is rewritten so that the focus is on Jesus: he enters Peter's[42] house alone, Andrew, James and John having been written out (cf. Mk 1:29). In Mark those in the house inform Jesus of the sick woman (1:31). Not in Matthew. No one tells Jesus of the woman and her troubles. He takes the initiative, and without being told he knows and understands her feverish and severe condition, captured in the word *beblēmenos*, "to be thrown aside on a sick bed" (Mt 8:14; Mark 1:30 in contrast has *katakleiō*, "to lie").

Whereas Mark says Jesus "raised her, taking her by the hand" (Mk 1:31, author's translation), Matthew highlights the healing power of Jesus by saying only that "he touched her hand" (Mt 8:15). Then Jesus' power is further acclaimed through the statement that "she got up" without, it is implied, any help. There is no hint of a delay or even a brief convalescence.

Finally, although in Mark 1:31 the woman serves "them," here she serves "him." In this Jesus is maintained as the focus of the story. At one level, for her "to serve" *(diakonein)* Jesus would have been understood as her waiting on him or preparing a meal for him.[43] But every other time Matthew uses the word it has a significance beyond mere meal preparation, and Jesus is always the subject of the service.[44] Matthew therefore probably intends the woman's actions to be discipleship or a service of worship in gratitude for being healed.

In this story Matthew has caused six verbs to stand out: three actions of Jesus and three responses. Jesus *comes* into the house, he *sees* the woman, and he *touches* her hand. As a result the fever *left* her, she *got up*, and she *served* him.[45] This minimalist rewriting of the story directs attention both to the person and to the power of Jesus.

Through these three healings in this first cycle of stories in chapters 8 and 9 some key themes have been highlighted, along with some interesting developments of the theme of faith. In all three stories the sufferers have been outsiders: first, a leper, then a Gentile and then a woman. Notably therefore the very first miracle in the Gospel benefits an outsider; encouragement to Matthew's Gentile readers to receive healing from Jesus.

Through these stories there has also been a progression in the way Matthew has depicted the faith and approach of these outsiders. In the first story the leper himself comes boldly and confidently to Jesus, asking in faith for his healing. In the second story the sick servant is too sick to come to Jesus. Instead his master goes and believes for his healing. The sufferer is healed not for his faith but for the faith of another person. In the third story, a woman, having been laid aside by the fever, is also too sick to come to Jesus. But notably there is no mention of faith: hers or anyone else's. Not even those in the house are said to believe for her or to tell Jesus of her plight. Jesus is depicted as asking absolutely no conditions to be prepared to heal her. Seeing her is enough to move him. Matthew now provides a summary of Jesus' ministry.

§4.9 A Summary (Mt 8:16-17/Mk 1:32-34/Lk 4:40-41)

At the end of the first cycle of stories these sentences summarize the events that concluded the day Matthew may have considered to begin with the Sermon on the Mount (Mt 5:4).[46] Following Mark 1:32-34, Matthew does not mention Jesus' teaching or preaching, and once again he reduces the emphasis on Jesus' healing of demoniacs, preferring to give the impression that Jesus healed a wide variety of sick people (cf. Mt 4:23-25).

In Mark they bring "all" the sick to Jesus and he heals "many" of them. In Matthew the impression that Jesus does not heal everyone is avoided by saying that "many" were brought and he healed "all" (see also Mk 3:10/Mt 12:15).

To his source Matthew has added "and he cast out the spirits with a word" (*logos*, Mt 8:16/Mk 1:33-34). This demonstrates both the ease with which Jesus is able to exorcise and, in the use of the word *logos*, the holding together of Jesus' teaching and healing as one consistent activity. It is reminiscent of the way Philo viewed Moses as having his speech and activities in harmony (*Vit. Mos.* 1:29).

The addition in verse 17 of the quotation from Isaiah 53:4 ("He took our infirmities and bore our diseases," author's translation) shows that the activities of Jesus are not simply wonders. They fulfill God's will prophesied in Scripture. The quotation also functions to associate Jesus with the Suffering Servant of Isaiah.[47] However, Matthew has not followed the wording of the Septuagint. Instead, he has translated the Hebrew to suit his purposes.

In the Hebrew, the writer speaks of the servant vicariously carrying the griefs and sorrows in himself. However, Matthew has the people healed simply by means of their sickness being taken away. This avoidance of the impression that Jesus vicariously carried sin or sickness acknowledges that Jesus' suffering and death are still to take place. Nevertheless the use of Isaiah 53 shows that the healings anticipate, or are even already possible because of, the coming sacrifice and that they are a piece with the vicarious death of Jesus the Servant.

Further, by associating the Servant of Isaiah with these healings, Matthew portrays Jesus not as a self-seeking, triumphant miracle worker but as a humble servant of God, one who associates with the outsiders and outcasts. Yet as the next story shows, unlike the weak Isaian Servant, the Matthean Jesus is a powerful man of mighty miracles.

Sandwiched, perhaps awkwardly, between this summary and the succeeding cycle of stories is a report primarily about two potential disciples whose intentions Jesus probes. One is told of the hardships (Mt 8:20) and the other of the absolute priority (8:21-22) of following Jesus. This, as we are about to see, renders the theme of discipleship as the backdrop for what follows in the second cycle of stories (cf. 8:18, 23).

§4.10 A Storm Calmed (Mt 8:23-27/Mk 4:35-41/Lk 8:22-25)

This story begins the second set of three miracle stories in chapters 8 and 9. Once again Jesus is taking the initiative by giving orders—here to go by boat to the other side of the lake (Mt 8:18, 23). The disciples are not simply with Jesus (Mk 4:36/Lk 8:22), they "followed him" (*ēkolouthēsan*, Mt 8:23). In this way Matthew's theme of discipleship is threaded into the story, linking it with the preceding story of two would-be followers (8:18-22), as well as to the healing of Peter's mother-in-law (8:14-15). This also makes the stilling of the storm a story about discipleship.[48]

The image of a storm was used not only of life's experiences in general[49] but of the experiences of the people of God in the Old Testament.[50] Further, the use of the word *seismos* ("earthquake") for the storm (Mt 8:24) probably signals that ongoing discipleship is a theme in the story.[51] There may also be a deliberate link between this story and that of the two houses in 7:24-27, which is also about the storm associated with ongoing discipleship.[52]

Notably the Dead Sea Scrolls use the image of a boat in a storm to describe the oppression of God's people in the end times,[53] and the early fathers likened the church to a ship.[54] As we have noted, the echo here of the description of the storm in Jonah 1:4-5 has long been recognized. Thus Matthew is most likely expecting his readers to see this story resonating with relevance in relation to the storms they faced.

In the story of the two houses, safety from the storm was guaranteed to those who heard and did the words of Jesus (Mt 7:24-27). Here safety is obtained by asking Jesus to calm the storm (8:25). Also, Jesus' being asleep during the storm may have been an allusion to another aspect of trust: the one who can sleep in troubled times is the one in control of the situation[55] or the one who has complete confidence in the power of God to oversee the situation.[56] Thus on being awakened Jesus can question the reason for the disciples' fear and express surprise at their little faith (8:26).

The disciples' initial address to Jesus is significant on a number of counts (Mt 8:25). First, it resembles the sailors' cry in Jonah 1:4, there directed to God. In the cry for help, Matthew is, then, probably assuming the divinity of Jesus. Second, in line with this, what was a question to the "Teacher" in Mark 4:37 is here a prayer to the "Lord" to be saved. Matthew's readers would not have lost the significance of the word *saved (sōzō)*. The previous (and first time) it was used was where the naming of Jesus was linked with his role of saving his people (Mt 1:21). This means that Matthew is telling more than the story of a calmed storm or even alluding to the storms of discipleship. It is also a snapshot of the significance of salvation—in the context of the church, by God, through Jesus, from the troubled storms of life.

In Mark the disciples are accused of having "no faith" (Mk 4:40). For Matthew to have Jesus say the disciples have "little faith" is not to salvage their reputation, nor is it part of a program to rehabilitate the disciples. Indeed, five times in his Gospel Matthew inserts the idea of the disciples' defective faith, three times using the term "little faith" deprecatingly.[57] For Matthew, being a disciple involves the expectation of having faith without any doubt (cf. Mt 21:21). The error of the disciples in this story is in not having sufficient faith in Jesus' power and authority to save them—the church—in their storms.[58] They should have had sufficient faith, for they had just witnessed the miracles in the first cycle of stories. We will come across a similar theme in the story of Peter walking on the water (see §4.23 on Mt 14:31).

Interestingly, Matthew does not mention a command of Jesus to the storm, but Mark does (Mt 8:26; cf. "Peace! Be still!" Mk 4:39). Neither does Matthew record any of the words of command to the demons, save the bold "Go!" in 8:32. It is not that Matthew is attempting to dissociate Jesus from anything that could be construed as magical.[59] More likely Matthew did not want it thought that Jesus' ability to control demonic and stormy situations was in what was said rather than in who said them. Matthew says simply that Jesus "commanded" *(epetimēsen)* the wind and the sea, the same word used of Jesus' command to the demons (8:26; cf. 17:18).

In common with others of his time, including the New Testament writers, Matthew believed that the elements were controlled or influenced by supernatural beings.[60] Thus again we suspect Matthew is using this story to represent Jesus' calming the spiritual storms that harass the church. Once again the response to Jesus' command is assumed to be immediate and is described in Old Testament terms of God controlling the chaos and sea.[61]

Designating those who marveled at the miracle as "men" *(anthrōpoi)* rather than disciples (Mt 8:27/Mk 4:41) is perhaps to suggest a contrast between the disciples (mere men of "little faith") and Jesus, who is obviously more than a man.[62]

The miracles have so far been for the benefit of individual outsiders and for those who were not followers of Jesus. These individuals have either been depicted as coming in faith (Mt 8:2, 10) or as responding positively (8:15). In contrast this miracle has been for the benefit of disciples, who display "little faith" in Jesus' miracle-working power or control of the situation, showing their lack of understanding of Jesus' identity.

§4.11 Two Gadarene Demoniacs Healed (Mt 8:28-34/Mk 5:1-20/Lk 8:26-39)

Immediately following the story of Jesus' calming the storm is this middle story of the second cycle of stories, which Matthew has drastically pruned from twenty to seven verses (cf. Mk 5:1-20). He maintains the severity of the sickness but only through mentioning that the two men were so fierce no one could pass that way. This gives greater notice to Jesus and draws attention to his fearless power.

The battle depicted in Mark between Jesus and the demon(iac)s has been reduced to a civil conversation in which there is no hint that the demons have disobeyed Jesus' initial command to come out of the man (cf. Mk 5:8-9). Matthew has also reduced Jesus' words and exorcistic technique to the single word "Go" (Mt 8:32). This brief command produces dramatic and instantaneous results: the demons leave the men for the herd of pigs, which then rushes into the water to destruction.

From Matthew's perspective, the Son of God does not need to use involved techniques for what appears to be an easy triumph. The effect again is to stress the authority of Jesus (cf. §4.10 on Mt 8:26). Matthew has also reworked the healed men's request to be with Jesus (Mk 5:18-20) so that they are overshadowed by the significance of Jesus and the response of the whole city begging Jesus to leave the area (Mt 8:33-34).

Most bewildering is Matthew's introduction of the second demoniac.[63] It could be that the multiplication of sick people is a piece with Matthew's writing to highlight Jesus' healing ability or is Matthew's way of conflating stories.[64] But so far no satisfactory, generally accepted explanation has been forthcoming for this Matthean practice.[65] Notwithstanding, an attractive suggestion is based on the observation that, in each of these cases, those to be healed declare Jesus to be the Son of David. Since Jewish law required two witnesses for a testimony to be believed, Matthew has supplied the second witness to give credibility to the confessions.[66]

The prefix "and behold" to the words of the demons (Mt 8:29, author's translation) is probably intended to signal their startling content—that the demons recognize Jesus' identity. The words of the demon in Mark—"Jesus, Son of the Most High God" (Mk 5:8)—have been changed to "Son of God" (Mt 8:29). Matthew never uses "Most High" with "God," perhaps because in the Septuagint it is generally used by Gentiles.[67] The result here is an emphasis on Jesus' status as God's Son.

Having identified Jesus, the demoniacs call out, "You have come here to torment us before the time" (Mt 8:29, author's translation). As with all writers of his time Matthew used little, if any, punctuation. Thus he may have intended the demoniacs not to ask a question but to make a statement: "You have come here to torment us before the time." In any case, Matthew has made two further important alterations to Mark 5:7, in line with wanting to highlight Jesus' true identity.

First, he has introduced the idea of Jesus "coming" *(erchomai)*. This idea was important to early Christians in expressing the "coming" of God's reign and his special anointed messenger.[68] The other alteration is the introduction of the idea that the demons' torment is "before time" *(pro kairou)*, that is, before the final judgment (cf. Mt 25:41). In Jesus the eschatological torture of the demons has already begun.[69]

A subtle change in the words of the demons from "Send us into the swine" (Mk 5:12) to "If you cast us out" (Mt 8:31) has the effect of portraying the demons demurring respectfully to Jesus rather than giving Jesus an ultimatum. The miracle causes the frightened herdsmen to flee into the city to "proclaim everything" *(apēngeilan panta)*, that is, the good news about what Jesus had done (8:33).[70]

Once again Matthew draws attention to the startling response of those who heard the report about the demoniacs by using "and behold" (Mt 8:34, author's translation). But the people from the city do not see the healed demoniacs. We are not even told they are healed (cf. Mk 5:15). Instead, the townspeople meet *(hupantēsin)* Jesus: he is the center of attention (Mt 8:34).[71] Matthew is portraying the crowd meeting not a mere miracle worker but the Son of God (cf. 8:29). In this climax to the story, Matthew has written out Mark's strong discipleship motif (Mk 5:18-20), to replace it with these more obviously christological concerns. At the end of this story Jesus gets into a boat, crosses the sea and comes to his own town (9:1), where the next story is set.

§4.12 A Paralytic Forgiven and Healed (Mt 9:1-8/Mk 2:1-12/Lk 5:17-26)

In this final story in the second cycle of three stories Matthew makes some important changes. At the turn of the century Johannes Weiss said Matthew's omission of the four friends tearing up the roof to let the sick person down in front of Jesus belongs "to the greatest riddle of Gospel criticism how Matthew could deny himself these living details" (cf. Mk 2:1-2).[72] These details would have highlighted the faith expressed in coming to Jesus. Nevertheless, perhaps Matthew's concern to delete all unnecessary details that may deflect attention from Jesus overrode such considerations.

There is no request from the man or his friends. Jesus takes the initiative for the healing, acting on the basis of "their faith" (Mt 9:2). Presumably simply bringing the sick person is to be understood as the act of faith. As in the story of the centurion's servant being healed, the faith exercised by someone else is sufficient grounds for Jesus to heal (8:10). Though, as in Mark's story (Mk 2:3-4), the lame man's faith may also be thought to be involved—the reader can assume that he is consenting and cooperating with being brought to Jesus. This is confirmed by Matthew saying "When Jesus saw their faith, he said to the paralytic . . ." (Mt 9:2).

To Jesus' address to the paralytic, "Son, your sins are forgiven," Matthew has added, "Take heart" (*tharsei*, 9:2/Mk 2:5) to encourage or acknowledge the faith of the man and those who brought him.[73] Having Jesus forgive the man, Matthew maintains the view expressed in his source and readily accepted at the time: sin and sickness were related, and in order for a cure to take place sins must first be forgiven (see §3.8 on Mk 2:5). Though not mentioned frequently, this is an important theme for Matthew. We saw that in Matthew 1:21 Jesus' whole ministry is put under the rubric of forgiving sins. And at the Last Supper Jesus says that his blood "is poured out for many for the forgiveness of sins" (26:28). Here then we are seeing an example of the forgiveness offered by Jesus applied to a specific life.

Matthew introduces the response of the scribes with "and behold" (author's translation). The startling point this introduces is the scribes' accusation of blasphemy (Mt 9:3). Presumably, as is clearer in Mark 2:6-7, the accusation of blasphemy arises because Jesus has not simply announced God's forgiveness but has acted in God's place by himself forgiving the man's sins.[74]

Perhaps to contrast the different responses to Jesus, Matthew uses the same word to describe Jesus' "knowing" or "seeing" *(idōn)* the faith of the paralytic and his friends (Mt 9:2) as he does Jesus' "knowing" the thoughts of the scribes (9:4; Mk 2:8 has *epignous*). The contrast between the two sets of characters is further heightened because Matthew adds "evil" to the description of the scribes (Mt 9:4/Mk 2:8).

To the apparently rhetorical question of whether it is easier to forgive sins or tell a paralytic to get up and walk, the answer could be, as Chrysostom long ago suggested, that the *healing* is more difficult, for it requires immediate proof

(*Homily on Matthew*, par. 29:2). Or it could be that *forgiving* is the more difficult task, for whereas many of God's representatives could heal a man's body, only God himself (given the nature of sin) can forgive sins. Furthermore the forgiveness of sins is difficult because, in the case of healing, the evidence will stand up or not and submit to ocular proof, but the proof that forgiveness has happened is more difficult to detect.[75]

Alternatively Matthew might think both actions equally difficult. In any case, highlighting the figure and authority of Jesus, he is portrayed as accomplishing both. For Matthew, Jesus' authority has already been given to him by God (cf. Mt 1:21). Jesus can exercise his authority as effectively before as after Easter (11:27; 28:18).

In contrast to the religious authorities, the crowd glorifies God for giving the authority they have seen to "human beings" (*anthrōpois*, Mt 9:8).[76] This dative could be translated "among people." At the level of the original story Matthew may have intended this to mean Jesus. Nevertheless, Matthew's readers probably understood the "human beings" to be the disciples.[77] This story thus serves as a paradigm for Matthew's readers in their ministry of healing and forgiveness.

Before proceeding to the final set of stories, we can look back on the major issues and themes noted in this second cycle of three miracle stories. Whereas the theme of discipleship pervades the whole of chapters 8 and 9, the suggestion that the theme of discipleship unifies this second cycle of miracle stories (Mt 8:23—9:8)[78] cannot be upheld. Instead, each story in this cycle draws special attention to Jesus and the response to his miracles.

1. In light of Jesus' calming the storm, the men's discipleship is reflected on poorly in that they marveled, "What sort of man is this, that even the winds and the sea obey him?" (Mt 8:27). No answer is given. So far as the theme of discipleship is in focus here (cf. *akolouthein* in 8:23) it is that discipleship involves storms and trusting God and Jesus, the one who can calm the storms.

2. After Jesus cures the two demoniacs, the people from the city do not wish to follow him but beg him to leave their area (Mt 8:34). Here Christology overrides any theme of discipleship, which at least might be echoed in the frightened swineherds reporting what had happened to the demoniacs, with the result that the whole town came out to meet Jesus (8:33-34).

3. After the paralytic is cured, there is a positive response from the crowd: they glorify God, who has given this kind of authority to people (Mt 9:8). But there is no hint of the theme of discipleship.

After the second cycle there follows the very brief report of Matthew's positive response to Jesus' call to follow him (Mt 9:9) and the Pharisees' misunderstanding the call of Jesus to be for sinners (9:10-13). Once again the obvious conclusion to draw from this range of responses is that Matthew considers that miracles in themselves neither cause faith or discipleship, nor dispel doubt. Rather they are in this second cycle nuanced reflections on Matthew's Christology, which he considers can lead to discipleship (9:9).

§4.13 A Woman Healed and a Girl Raised (Mt 9:18-26/Mk 5:21-43/Lk 8:40-56)

This story begins the third and final cycle of miracle stories (Mt 9:18-34) in chapters 8 and 9. With the opening words, "While he was saying these things" (*tauta*, 9:18) Matthew clearly wants the previous sayings about new wine not able to be contained in old wineskins (9:14-17) to provide the initial understanding for the ensuing cycle of miracles. For Matthew, this means that the coming and ministry of Jesus is unable to be confined within Judaism.

Matthew has changed Mark's setting of the story from the end of a sea journey (Mk 5:21) to a house (perhaps intended to be Matthew's), where Jesus was eating with the tax collectors and sinners (Mt 9:10). This highlights Jesus' association not only with leaders but also with outsiders, which was a theme of the first cycle of stories (cf. §4.8).

Matthew has drastically reduced the length of the story by about two-thirds. All that remains is the bare outline of Mark's story.[79] This turns the story into little more than a conversation between Jesus and those seeking healing. In turn, this focuses attention on Jesus and highlights his healing power. In the last third of the story a crowd is introduced to act as a foil for Jesus to express his confidence in healing the girl (Mt 9:23-24). Thus, although the theme of faith is important in this story, it has not determined its abbreviation.[80]

Nevertheless the theme of faith directed to the majestic and powerful Jesus is apparent from the beginning of the story. Whereas Mark says that the man "fell" (*piptei*) at Jesus' feet (Mk 5:22), Matthew says "he knelt" (*prosekunei*, Mt 9:18), which denotes a prostrating before a worthy or royal.[81]

The theme of faith is most explicit in the words of the ruler seeking healing for his daughter. In Mark the father requests Jesus' help "so that she may be made well and live" (Mk 5:23). With Matthew's turning the aorist tense of the two verbs into the single verb with a future tense, the father's expression of faith becomes unmistakable: "and she will live" (Mt 9:18). This indicates that faith, or confidence in Jesus' healing ability, rather than any achievement, is to be seen as evincing Jesus' willingness to heal (see also §4.7 on 8:5-13). Once again the disciples are said to follow Jesus as he goes to perform the miracle, indicating that this story is also about discipleship and is to be modeled by later followers of Jesus in their ministries.

The woman who met Jesus en route to the ruler's home is said to touch the "fringe" of Jesus' garment (Mt 9:20). In Mark she simply touches the garment (Mk 5:27). In mentioning the fringe or tassel, Matthew shows Jesus to be wearing appropriate clothing for a faithful Jew (Num 15:38-39; Deut 22:12). Having the woman say she needed "only" to touch his garment draws attention to the faith in Jesus expressed by the woman's action (contrast Mk 5:28). Though in eventually having Jesus say that it was the woman's faith that made her well, Matthew is making clear that touching the garment was not so much the means of healing as the expression of the woman's faith. Jesus alone is the healer, not any person's action.

By removing the conversation between Jesus and the disciples about power going out from him, the woman's statement of faith is immediately affirmed by Jesus' saying "Take heart, daughter, your faith has made you well" (Mt 9:22). For Jesus to identify the woman unaided without having previously seen her underlines the facility of supernatural knowledge Jesus is thought to have (cf. Mk 5:30-33).

The immediate healing Matthew reports is yet another facet of this story that highlights Jesus' healing power. That is, in being touched by an unclean woman, he was not contaminated.[82] Rather, she was healed.

In the scene change to the ruler's house, Matthew has yet again written out characters—this time the disciples—so that Jesus, the center of attention, enters the scene alone when healing is needed (Mk 5:40/Mt 9:25). Matthew's insertion of the flute players (Mt 9:23), who were required at a funeral (*m. Ketub.* 4:4; *m. B. Meṣ* 6:1), leaves the readers in no doubt that the girl had died and was not simply profoundly ill and at the point of death. This clear signal that a funeral was taking place provides a contrast to the words of Jesus that the girl is not dead, which the readers are plainly to understand as Jesus foreseeing that in the exercise of his healing power death is no more significant than is sleeping. The laughter of the crowd (Mt 9:24) underscores these themes and contrasts the faith of the father (and the woman) with the other characters.

Consistent with what we have seen so far, Matthew removes Jesus' special words of healing in his source (*talitha koum*, Mk 5:41/Mt 9:25). It is not that this would have been understood as magical. Rather, Matthew wants nothing to be seen as effective in healing other than Jesus himself. Also, in light of his didactic intention, Matthew would want to convey to his readers that in their emulation of Jesus' healing ministry they are not to rely on anything other than the power of Jesus.

In view of Jesus' message to John the Baptist about the dead being raised (Mt 11:5), which incorporates an echo of Isaiah 35:5-6, it is without doubt that Matthew saw this astonishing miracle as affirming Jesus to be the Messiah (Mt 11:23).[83] This is confirmed as we come to the second story in these cycles of miracles.

§4.14 Two Blind Men Receive Their Sight (Mt 9:27-31/20:29-34/Mk 10:46-52/Lk 18:35-43)

This brief story of two blind men[84] is probably a reworking of a parallel "doublet" in 20:29-34.[85] In turn, that story is probably Matthew's rewriting of Mark's story of Bartimaeus (Mk 10:46-52).[86] Assuming no other stories were at hand, the need of Matthew here was probably to provide a third story for this cycle of stories, balancing it with the other cycles.

Yet again the blind men "followed" Jesus (Mt 9:27). *Followed* is a favorite word of Matthew's, indicating the story's importance for the theme of discipleship. As noted in the discussion of the miracles in Mark, the significance of the cry for "mercy" (9:27) is a cry for salvation.[87] The title "Son of David" (Mt 9:27) in the cry of the blind men is clearly of great significance to Matthew.[88] The title or phrase is mentioned in the very first verse of the Gospel and occurs many times in Matthew.[89] Further, this is the only Gospel to have the phrase "*the* Son of David" associated with the Messiah.[90] Notably in all but two passages (21:1-17; 22:41-46) the context is a healing miracle. It is reasonable to conclude therefore that, for Matthew, the healing miracles reveal Jesus' true status: he is the Messiah (cf. 8:29).

This story contains another example of Jesus not complying immediately with the request for healing (cf. Mt 15:23 and possibly 8:7). This provides a foil to highlight and test the faith of the blind men. This theme may also explain Matthew's mention of Jesus entering a house—a move that would make it more difficult for the men to express their faith in Jesus—better than Jesus' need for privacy. Indeed, in this rewriting of the story (cf. 20:32-33) the theme of faith is clearest in Jesus' questioning of the men (9:28). The form of the question, "Do you believe that . . . ?" *(pisteuete hoti . . .),* may have been significant for Matthew in affirming that importance of faith, for it is typical of what are thought to be early creedal statements (cf. Rom 10:9; 1 Thess 4:4). This is further confirmed through Matthew's exchanging Mark's term *Master* for *Lord* as the blind men's address to Jesus. This is the usual way sick people address Jesus in Matthew.[91] So the question provides the means for the blind men to express the required faith in Jesus' healing power.

As in 20:34, Matthew has added mention of Jesus touching the blind eyes (Mt 9:29; cf. Mk 10:52). Nevertheless, the emphasis remains on Jesus healing in response to trust in him, for Jesus says, "According to *[kata]* your faith let it be done for you." This is very similar to his statements to the centurion (Mt 8:13) and the Canaanite woman (15:28), though they use "as" *(hōs)* rather than "according to" *(kata).* However, it is unlikely that Matthew means in "proportion to." More likely he means "in response to" your faith, as in 8:13 (cf. 15:28).

Rather surprisingly at first, Matthew adds—or perhaps uses Mark 1:43-45 (cf. Mk 10:52)—that Jesus strongly admonished the healed men: "See that no one knows of this" (Mt 9:30). Nevertheless, such a charge highlights the magnitude of the healing, for the healed men could not help but spread the fame of Jesus (9:31). As in Mark, what he has done cannot be hidden. Notably they do not spread the word (as in Mk 1:45) but spread abroad news of Jesus *(auton)*. For Matthew, it is Jesus who is unmistakably the healer and focus of attention.

§4.15 A Mute Demoniac Healed (Mt 9:32-34/12:22-24/Mk 3:22/Lk 11:14-15)

Immediately following, and to complete the final cycle of miracle stories in chapters 8 and 9, is yet another doublet, this time of Matthew 12:22-24. The brief story here captures many of the themes of all three cycles of miracle stories. There is the startling thing ("behold," author's translation) that an outsider and Jesus are associated; there is the expression of faith, in the man being brought to Jesus; there is the power of Jesus as well as the immediacy of the healing (9:32-33).

Highlighting the magnitude of Jesus' miracle, the crowds respond positively by saying that nothing like it had been seen in Israel (Mt 9:33). This also recalls the introduction to this cycle, where Jesus is said to have been speaking about his ministry's not being able to be contained in the Jewish tradition (9:14-18).

Yet in contrast to and in response to the crowd's positive acclamation, the Pharisees conclude that Jesus is empowered by the prince of demons—Satan (Mt 9:34). But Matthew leaves open this question of the source of Jesus' power-authority until John the Baptist's disciples question Jesus on his identity (11:2-6). However, the Pharisees' assessment remains steadfastly negative (cf. 12:24).

In this third and final cycle of miracles in chapters 8 and 9 we have seen Matthew convey to his readers the idea that the coming ministry of Jesus is unable to be confined within Judaism. Echoing the first cycle, Jesus associates not only with leaders but also with outsiders. He is portrayed as having enormous healing power, being worthy of faith—which on occasion is expressed and tested—as well as being worthy of a devotion befitting royalty. However, as was just noted, the Pharisees are said to conclude that Jesus was casting out demons by the ruler of the demons, showing that it is not possible to comprehend the power of Jesus from the methods or words of Jesus in his miracles.

§4.16 Chapters 8 and 9: In Summary

Before we continue with Matthew's story we can look back over all three cycles of miracle stories and observe a number of themes and interests in Matthew's presentation.

1. While there are ten miracles reported in chapters 8 and 9, which may echo the theme of a new Moses (see 5 below), it is the fact that Matthew has arranged his stories in three cycles of three that needs particular explanation.[92] Gerd Theissen suggests that geography has determined the arrangement of the stories. That is, Matthew 4:15 refers first to "the sea," then to the region "across the sea" and then to "Galilee of the Gentiles."[93] This, says Theissen, is precisely the journey Jesus

takes in chapters 8 and 9 (cf. 8:5, 28-34). This thesis, however, cannot stand.

First,[94] whereas Capernaum is prominent in chapters 8 and 9, it is not mentioned in 4:15-16 (though see Mt 4:13). Second, although in chapter 8 Jesus is by the sea (8:5-22), crosses to the other side (8:23-27) and lands in what may be Gentile territory (8:28), Theissen's suggestion does not take into account chapter 9.

As has already been noted, some have taken the view that each of the three cycles illustrates a theme: Christology (Mt 8:2-17), discipleship (8:18—9:17) and faith (9:18-31).[95] However, while these themes are apparent in these stories, they can hardly be said to dominate, unify or explain their respective cycles. Christology cannot explain the collection or reworking of the first three stories (8:2-17)—two stories in the second cycle (8:28—9:8; 9:14-17) are not about discipleship in any obvious way, and faith, though present as a theme (cf. 9:22, 29), is a motif not restricted to nor even a particular focus of the third cycle (see 8:26; 9:2). Indeed, faith as a theme was more prominent in the first cycle. More likely, and quite simply, we need only suggest Matthew has arranged these ten miracle reports (to illustrate a variety of themes) in three cycles of three stories out of his predilection for triads.[96]

Further, the probable reason Matthew has adopted the triad as one of his major patterns for the collection of miracle material is its popularity for the transmission of oral material. It could even be that Jesus favored the triad,[97] as did Mark, the pre-Markan author of the passion narrative and Simon the Just (*m. 'Abot* 1:3), with his three pillars of the world (the law, the temple worship and deeds of kindness) on which Matthew may have ordered his Great Sermon.[98]

2. Although until these cycles of stories Matthew has used neither the noun nor the verbs of "faith," the words and theme have now been woven through all three cycles.[99] For Matthew, faith is a practical confidence in Jesus' ability and willingness to heal, expressed in the sufferers' willingness to give practical expression to their confidence.

For the leper it was coming boldly to Jesus to request his healing (Mt 8:2). For the centurion it was stating his understanding of Jesus' ability (8:8). For the paralytic it was the willingness of some to carry him to Jesus (9:2). For the leader of the synagogue it was his confidence in coming to ask Jesus to raise his daughter to life (9:18). For the hemorrhaging woman it was to touch just the edge of Jesus' clothes (9:21). For the two blind men it was to follow Jesus indoors and be interrogated by him (9:28). And for the demoniac it was in being brought to Jesus (9:32).

In every case the object of confidence or faith is not God in general but specifically Jesus. Even the disobedient healed blind men spreading news about Jesus reinforces this focus on Jesus (Mt 9:30-31) rather than on, say, his message or words or technique. Nevertheless, in the last cycle what had been implicit in most stories, though not in the story of Peter's mother-in-law (8:14-15), is made explicit through Jesus' words to the blind men: "Do you believe that I am able to do this?" (9:28).[100]

3. There are also traces of another theme in these stories, clearer elsewhere, that Jesus responds to the sick out of mercy.[101] He encourages the timid woman by saying "Take heart" (Mt 9:22), and he eventually responds to the call of the blind men for mercy (9:27).

4. In these miracle stories the theme of Jesus fulfilling Jewish hopes or Old Testament prophecies, which dominates the early chapters of Matthew, gives way to the theme of the dramatic, unexpected newness of what Jesus is doing in his ministry (cf. Mt 9:16-17), as in the acclaim of the crowds that nothing like the healing of the blind had been seen in Israel (9:33b). Hence the Pharisees give voice to the attendant and key issues: the source of power-authority and the significance of the miracles. In their view the miracles show that Jesus is empowered by Satan (cf. 10:25; 12:22-32).

5. The Moses theme also features in the portrait of Jesus as a miracle worker in these two chapters.[102] If we count as two miracles the stories of the healing of the hemorrhaging woman and the girl being raised (Mt 9:18-26), which are in the one story, there are ten miracles recounted in chapters 8 and 9. This is the same number Moses performed in Egypt (Ex 7—12). Though Matthew does not press and develop this theme here (for instance, Jesus' miracles are not plagues, as in Exodus), he most probably wishes his readers to consider Jesus to be a new Moses not only because of the new law Jesus promulgates (Mt 5—7; esp 5:1-2) but also because of these "new" miracles (cf. 9:33b).

6. In these stories it is outcasts or outsiders (one is a Gentile) who are healed or respond positively to Jesus.[103] However, Jews generally do not respond favorably to Jesus.[104] Consequently the miracles function as part of Matthew's challenge to the Jews. A challenge that, according to chapters 11 and 12, they failed to take up.

7. Taking into account the sayings material following each of the three cycles of miracles, we would have to conclude that Matthew probably has various aspects of discipleship in mind throughout these stories.[105] At the end of the first cycle are two small stories about people wanting to follow Jesus (Mt 8:18-22). This picks up the theme present in the healing of Peter's mother-in-law, whose response to being healed is said to be "to serve" *(diakonein)* Jesus (8:15).

While the theme of discipleship does not unify the *second* set of stories from within, the story at the end of the second set of miracle stories is about the call to discipleship of Matthew the tax collector (Mt 9:9). This theme is immediately developed in the next story of Jesus reclining at table with tax collectors and sinners, a story in which Jesus says he has come to call sinners (9:10-13). Luke specifies this call as to repentance (Lk 5:32). But the unspecified call in Matthew (and in Mark 2:17) probably means that it is an all-encompassing call to discipleship—

which includes repentance—to the kingdom of heaven and to the messianic banquet (cf. Mt 22:1-14).

At the end of the third series of miracle stories Matthew leaves open the question of Jesus' authority. Instead of immediately settling that issue (cf. Mt 11:2-6), he provides another summary of Jesus' ministry. Notwithstanding, the major section (soon to follow) on the commissioning of the Twelve to emulate Jesus' ministry does give the third set of miracle stories in particular at least overtones of an interest in discipleship.

§4.17 A Conclusion and Summary (Mt 9:35-38)

These sentences provide the link between Jesus as a worker of miracles—unmistakably portrayed in the previous two cycles of stories—and his disciples, who are also called to be miracle workers. As in the summary preceding the Sermon on the Mount (Mt 4:23-25), here Jesus is depicted as an itinerant preacher-healer.[106] As this is also how the disciples are about to be portrayed (10:23) and expected to go on acting (28:19), Jesus is probably being depicted as a model for his followers.

Then through the saying about the need for laborers for the harvest, Matthew communicates the idea that Jesus wants others to accompany him in the task (Mt 9:37-38). The theme is developed in the ensuing story of the calling and sending out of the Twelve on mission (10:1-15). Also through this closing summary statement Matthew conveys the idea that Jesus' miracles have been performed out of compassion (9:35-36; cf. §4.16.3).

As we have noted (§4.15), Matthew delays solving the issue of the source of Jesus' power-authority that arose when he cast out a demon (Mt 9:32-34). Instead, in chapter 10 Matthew takes up the theme of discipleship in detail, portraying Jesus' followers as modeling his miracle working and receiving instruction for mission (10:1—11:1). However, Matthew returns to the issue of Jesus' source of power-authority in 11:2 with the Baptist's disciples asking about Jesus' identity and with sayings of Jesus on the theme (11:2-30). This authority claimed by Jesus is illustrated in the story of the disciples picking or harvesting grain on the Sabbath and by means of another miracle story.

§4.18 Jesus' Answer to John the Baptist (Mt 11:2-6/Lk 7:18-23)

Having dealt in detail with the theme of discipleship (Mt 10:1-42), Matthew draws a formal conclusion to this teaching (11:1) and returns to the question of Jesus' identity. He does this by having John the Baptist ask, "Are you the one who is to come?" (11:3).[107]

Because of the way Matthew has tied together the Great Sermon, the miracle stories and the material on discipleship (cf. §4.2), this question is set against the background of the whole of Jesus' ministry so far (Mt 4:23—11:1), not just his miracles. That is, John's question is said to arise out of hearing what Jesus was "doing" (*ta erga* ["works"] *tou Christou*, 11:2). In 11:4—"Go and tell John what you hear and see"—we see that for Matthew these "works of Christ" are the miracles as well as the preaching. Thus Jesus' reply (11:4), that there have been miracles of healing and the proclamation of good news, is not only a summary of the whole of his ministry but also a statement that, along with the proclamation, the miracles reflect on the nature and mission of Jesus.

Just what that identity is thought to be for Matthew has been variously understood as God, Son of man, a disciple of John, Elijah, the Messiah and no figure in particular.[108] In that Matthew takes the rare step of having just referred to Jesus as Messiah in the narrative (Mt 11:2; cf. 1:17), it is probable that he understands the miracles to be reflecting the fact that Jesus is the Messiah. Thus he says in 11:20 that Jesus "began to reproach the cities in which most of his deeds of power had been done, because they did not repent." For the miracles, he goes on to say (11:21-24), should lead people to repent.

§4.19 A Withered Hand Restored (Mt 12:9-14/Mk 3:1-6/Lk 6:6-11)

Continuing the theme that was begun with Jesus' answer to John the Baptist, the issue of Jesus' power-authority now comes to a head. The Pharisees' conflict with Jesus and their negative assessment of his miracles—which were voiced at the end of the three cycles of miracle stories in relation to the healing of the mute demoniac (Mt 9:32-34)—Matthew now explores more fully through chapter 12.

Once again there is a cycle of three stories,[109] of which the healing of the withered hand is the second. Each story begins with the mention of Jesus moving from one location to another (Mt 12:1, 9, 15) before there is a direct confrontation between Jesus and the Pharisees over his source of authority in 12:22-32.

The climax of the first story—about reaping grain on the Sabbath (Mt 12:1-8)—includes the principle that mercy is to take precedence over religious observance. The same theme is clearly echoed in the story of the healing of the withered hand (cf. Mk 3:1-6 and Q; Lk 14:5). Matthew inserts a question by Jesus: "Is it lawful to cure on the sabbath?" (Mt 12:10, perhaps based on the Q story, Lk 14:5). And Jesus concludes the debate with the statement "So it is lawful to do good on the sabbath" (12:12). This portrays him as a legal debater, superior to the Pharisees.

Hence a situation intended to trap Jesus has instead trapped the Pharisees. In this way the miracle is seen to arise out of Jesus' mercy. Also, Matthew has rewritten the story so that it appears more as a conversation than a miracle.

Although the Jewish sect at Qumran had a law that forbade rescuing an animal on the sabbath (CD 11:13-14), the assumption behind Jesus' question in Matthew is that animal rescue on the sabbath was generally permitted (cf. *b. Šabb.* 128b), while healing was not (cf. *m. Šabb.* 22:6). Indeed, Jesus is not appealing to any law but to the way Jews of the day generally treated their animals. In this merciful interpretation of God's intention in the law, Matthew has laid bare and highlighted the gulf between Jesus and the Jews—a gulf sufficient for the leaders to set out to annihilate him. Matthew has omitted mention of the Herodians (political supporters of Herod's dynasty) being implicated in the discussion to destroy Jesus (Mt 12:14/Mk 3:6), perhaps not to blur the primarily religious issues at stake.

The theme of faith is seen not only in the man's stretching out his dead hand but also in the man's hand being healed as a result of his act rather than by Jesus saying or doing anything. The power of Jesus, seen in the thoroughness of the miracle, is highlighted when Matthew adds that the hand was "whole like the other" (Mt 12:13, author's translation).

Once again we see that, while faith is often a precondition for receiving a miracle of healing (though see Mt 8:14-15), miracles do not necessarily generate faith (cf. §4.12). For those already entrenched in their religious heritage, a miracle only confirms their distance from understanding the source and nature of the event that had just taken place before them.

The conflict between Jesus and the Pharisees results in the Pharisees leaving to conspire against him (Mt 12:14). In the next story—a summary—Matthew has Jesus withdraw while he reflects on the significance of Jesus' ministry.

§4.20 Jesus Heals Many and Fulfills Scripture (Mt 12:15-21/Mk 3:7-12/Lk 6:17-19)

This is the first of three summaries in the middle of Matthew (cf. Mt 14:34-36; 15:29-31). Jesus has already been established as God's Son (3:17; cf. 1:1). Here, in the quotation from Isaiah 42:1-4, Jesus is said to be beloved, pleasing to God, anointed by his Spirit, having a great following of people and able to heal "all of them" (Mt 12:15). Yet in withdrawing from conflict and violence[110] and in ordering the healed man not to make him known, as well as in being described as dealing gently with a bruised reed, Jesus is pictured as one who is primarily a servant—in his ministry as well as in his death. In light of the last story of the sabbath healing of the man with the withered hand, this summary also shows the Pharisees to be in opposition to God and prepares the readers for further sharp conflict over an exorcism in the next story.

§4.21 The Blind and Mute Demoniac and the Debate with the Pharisees (Mt 12:22-30/9:32-34/Mk 3:22-27/Lk 11:14-15, 17-23)

In this story and interchange,[111] the conflict between Jesus and the Pharisees reaches one of its important climaxes. Comparing this story with its doublet in 9:32 and Luke 11:14, it is obvious that Matthew has introduced the idea that the demoniac was blind. Why has Matthew done this?

As we have noted already (see §3.25), of all the healing miracles in the New Testament, the only category not having an Old Testament precursor is the giving of sight to the blind.[112] Indeed, the fond hope was that in the age of the Messiah the blind would receive their sight.[113] Further, the only time when the theme of receiving sight occurs in the Old Testament, it is connected with the reception of speech (Is 35:5-6). Perhaps then, as an introduction to the controversy of Jesus' authority, Matthew wanted to highlight the messianic significance of this healing and so introduced the aspect of blindness. This suggestion is supported by the crowd's response to Jesus' healing: "Can this be the Son of David?" (Mt 12:23).

In contrast to the doublet to this passage in Matthew 9:32-34, the man is "cured" rather than demons being cast out. This could be so that Matthew could broaden the application of the accusation from exorcism to the more general activity of healing. Thus the whole, not just a part, of Jesus' healing ministry is seen to give rise to the question of Jesus' power and authority.

Unlike the crowd's positive response to the healing,[114] the Pharisees accuse Jesus of casting out demons by Beelzebul, the prince or leader of the demons (Mt 12:24). Although it seems from the dialogue Jesus would have heard the accusation of the Pharisees, Matthew enhances the portrait of Jesus by saying that he knew their thoughts (12:25 from Q; Lk 11:17).

In effect, Jesus' reply is that the accusation is illogical (Mt 12:25-26). As exorcisms are directed against Satan, to be empowered by Satan would be to render exorcisms ineffectual. Accordingly in verse 27 Jesus asks rhetorically, "By whom do your sons cast them [demons] out?" (author's translation). Whereas Matthew portrays Jesus as an extraordinary miracle worker, this verse shows he acknowledges that Jesus was not alone in being a successful exorcist. In the context of Matthew's story these exorcists would be the disciples or pupils of the Pharisees, making the accusation of the Pharisees doubly difficult, if not hypocritical, to maintain.

Over against the accusation of the Pharisees, the positive side of Jesus' exorcism ministry is spelled out in one of the most significant sayings in the Gospels: "But if in the Spirit of God I cast out demons, then has come [ephthasen] upon you the kingdom of God" (Mt 12:28/Lk 11:20, author's translation).

Back in verse 18, which quotes Isaiah 42:1, Matthew has written of the awaited eschatological Spirit, which was upon Jesus. Here in verse 28 Matthew is saying that the anointing of Jesus with the eschatological Spirit to effect exorcisms means that the long-awaited arrival of God's reign has actually come upon Jesus' hearers.

However, we cannot conclude that Matthew thought that Jesus' exorcisms signaled or accomplished the final and complete victory over Satan. The Jews of the first century believed in a two-stage defeat of Satan.[115] Following this received tradition, Matthew links the first stage of the defeat with the exorcisms of Jesus. The second and final stage of the defeat will be in the end time (cf. Mt 8:29).

In verses 27 and 28 we see what Matthew—and the tradition before him—thought to be the difference between Jesus and other healer-exorcists. The passage assumes they could not be distinguished by technique or appearance. The difference cannot even be the exorcisms of Jesus authorized by God and those of the Pharisees are not. The question in verse 27 about who authorizes the exorcisms only makes sense if their exorcisms are *not* authorized by Satan. It seems best to conclude that Matthew considers the exorcisms of Jesus distinctive simply because the eschatological Spirit is empowering him. This is the best explanation of the force of the emphatic "I" *(egō)* in verse 28.

Following his sources Matthew then takes up the parable of the strong man (Mt 12:29). In our discussion of Mark's version of this parable that this is a parable we saw of exorcism where the strong man, who obviously represents Satan, is being cast out (cf. §3.12). On this Matthew is in complete agreement with his tradition.

In this passage Matthew has been dealing with two responses to the miracles of Jesus. In the saying in verse 30—those who are not with him are against him—Matthew is following Q in affirming that in this dichotomy it is impossible to be neutral (cf. Lk 11:23). Response to the miracles manifests whether a person is either on the side of Satan or on the side of Jesus.

The increasing rupture between Jesus and the Jewish authorities continues to be reflected in sayings in the remainder of chapter 12 and in the parables of chapter 13, where in "an act of judgment, Jesus draws the veil of the parables over his teaching."[116] The great miracle worker of chapters 8 and 9, whose deeds caused the Pharisees to conspire to kill him, is now shown again to be the great teacher (cf. the Great Sermon). But again, as with the miracles, the teaching causes offense (Mt 13:57), so even in his hometown he could not do many deeds of power because of their unbelief (13:58).

In chapter 14 Jesus' tragic end is ominously foreshadowed in the martyrdom of John the Baptist (Mt 14:1-12). On hearing the news, Jesus again humbly withdraws in the face of hostility (cf. 12:15). But the crowds still seek him, as the next story shows.

§4.22 Feeding the Five Thousand (Mt 14:13-21/Mk 6:32-44/Lk 9:10-17; cf. Jn 6:1-15)

As we have come to expect, Matthew has abbreviated this story, though not as drastically as in some other cases. The story begins with the incredible popularity of Jesus (Mt 14:13-14)[117] as well as the compassion, rather than faith (see below), motivating Jesus to provide for the needs of people, both in his healing and feeding of people (14:14).[118]

The phrase "when it was evening" (Mt 14:15) is the first of a number of generally recognized echoes of the Last Supper in this story (cf. 26:20). The words that concern taking, blessing, breaking and giving the bread to his disciples also seem clearly to foreshadow the Last Supper (26:20-29). These echoes cannot be easily dismissed by the assertion that they are found in any Jewish meal, for the order of the important vocabulary is the same both in this story and in that of the Last Supper. Also, the mention of the time and Jesus handing the bread to the disciples goes beyond a description of a normal meal. Interestingly, this distribution echoes the early church practice of handing the bread and the wine to the deacons for them to distribute (cf. Justin *Apology* 1:65, 67).[119]

Further, Matthew has altered the vocabulary in his source and omitted mention of the fish in this distribution (Mt 14:19) to produce these last two parallels with the Last Supper (cf. Mk 6:41). This decreases the distance between this story and that of the Last Supper.[120] With the setting drawing attention to the compassion of Jesus, Matthew's readers would probably see—through the lens of the echoes of the Last Supper—Jesus' giving of his body in death as arising out of his compassion.

The most significant aspect of this miracle story is that Matthew probably intends it to be seen as an image of the eschatological banquet presided over by the Messiah or eschatological prophet. First, in at least two Jewish texts fish as well as bread are associated with the eschatological banquet (*2 Apoc. Bar.* 29:1-8; 4 Ezra 6:52; cf. Mt 14:19). Second, in the Qumran community the shared meals were seen to correspond to the eschatological banquet (1QSa). Third, there are parallels with the miraculous feeding by Elisha.[121] Thus with Matthew's interest in portraying Jesus as a prophet, he may intend his readers to see in this story echoes of Jesus, the eschatological prophet, presiding over the eschatological banquet.

Once again the theme of faith—here its deficiency—is evident. In Mark, the disciples are portrayed as misunderstanding Jesus' direction as to how the people are to be fed (Mk 6:37). Matthew gives no hint of the disciples' incomprehension. Matthew has Jesus say explicitly to the disciples that the people do not need to be sent away to buy anything. Instead, the disciples are to provide for the people. Thus the disciples' lack of faith (not their incomprehension) is immediately obvious. In their reply the disciples say they have little food with them—only five loaves and two fish. The deficiency of the disciples' faith is further heightened by Jesus' response. Mark simply says, "And he commanded them all to sit down" (Mk 6:39, author's translation). In Matthew the disciples' expression of lack of faith is followed by Matthew's addition: "But he said *(ho de eipen)*, 'Bring them [the five loaves and two fish] here to me' " (Mt 14:18, author's translation). This maintains the contrast between Jesus' ability and the lack of faith of the disciples in being able to deal with the situation.

At the very end of the story, where the number of those fed is mentioned, Matthew adds, "besides women and children" (Mt 14:21). This deliberately swells the size of the crowd. Also, as there is a similar phrase in Exodus 12:37,[122] Matthew may be wanting to allude to the exodus theme of God's provision for his people on a journey of faith.[123] But this story, and the next one linked closely to it, is showing Jesus to be more than Moses. In feeding the hungry he is a special figure. He is at least the Son of God and perhaps even God, as is clear from his walking on the sea in the next story.

§4.23 Jesus and Peter Walking on the Sea (Mt 14:22-33/Mk 6:45-52; cf. Jn 6:16-21)

As in his source, Matthew puts this story after that of the miraculous feeding so that his conclusion added to the end of the story sums up both: "Truly you are the Son of God" (Mt 14:33). Unlike his retelling of other miracle stories, Matthew has only slightly abbreviated this story. He has maintained Mark's strong word that Jesus "compelled" (*anankazō*, author's translation) the disciples to get into the boat and to go to the other side of the lake (14:22/Mk 6:45). With Matthew's theme of faith to the fore in many of the miracle stories, this word may have been used to show Jesus compelling the disciples into another situation in which their faith will be tested and stretched.

The phrase "going up on the mountain by himself to pray" (author's transla-tion) recalls Moses on Mount Sinai (Mt 14:23/Mk 6:46).[124] That Matthew probably intends his readers to notice again the Moses typology explains the insertion of the comment that Jesus "was there alone," for Moses is also said to be alone on the mountain (Ex 24:2). Further, it is noticeable that this miracle of Jesus took place at the same time as God's rescue of his people at the Red Sea—the fourth morning watch.[125]

The mention of Jesus praying has been taken over from his source (Mt 14:23/Mk 6:46). This simple statement belies its special significance for Matthew. It is the first time in Matthew that Jesus is specifically said to pray.[126] In light of how strongly related the fatherhood of God is to Jesus' teaching about prayer (Mt 6:5-14) and how the conclusion to this story draws attention to Jesus' sonship (14:33), the mention of Jesus' praying is probably to draw attention to Jesus' relationship with God. Thus Jesus' uniquely divine actions of walking on the sea and of saving his followers from destruction are seen to arise out of his intimate relationship with God the Father.[127]

When compared with Mark 6:46, Matthew stresses the distance between Jesus, praying alone on the mountain, and the boat being tormented or beaten by the waves (Mt 14:23). If the boat represents the church,[128] Matthew is probably drawing attention to an analogy: no matter how distant the Son of God may seem, he is still able to save the church when it is being buffeted by the storms of persecution or affliction.

In contrast to Mark 6:48, Matthew uses "beaten" *(basanizein)* in connection with those who are paralyzed (Mt 8:6) and the tormented demons (8:29), as well as this boat (14:24). Thus Matthew may be showing that storms suffered by the church are also within Jesus' ability to calm or cure.

As in Mark 6:48, Jesus walking on the stormy sea could only be seen as God himself coming to the distressed disciples. In the Old Testament it is only God who can save people from the sea (see §3.18 on Mk 6:45-52). Matthew has deleted Mark's enigmatic phrase, "and he wished to pass them by" (Mk 6:48, author's translation), perhaps because it would show Jesus not doing as he intended.

The theme of faith surfaces in Jesus' words to the terrified disciples, for, as we have seen, "take heart" (Mt 14:27) has been used to encourage faith (see §4.12 on Mt 9:2, 22).

At verse 28 Matthew introduces a story about Peter walking on the sea[129] sandwiched in the main story. The origin of the story has caused considerable debate. It has been suggested that it is a "haggadic midrash" that Matthew has composed on discipleship.[130] Others have seen the story as based on oral tradition[131] or on a resurrection story written back into the pre-Easter setting.[132] However, because so little knowledge of Matthew's sources is available and because there is so much distinctive Matthean vocabulary,[133] we can say no more than that what we have before us has been thoroughly reworked by Matthew.[134]

As Peter is probably the archetypal disciple for Matthew (cf. below on Mt 14:32),[135] his introduction here, along with the "take heart" (14:27) and the "little faith" mentioned in verse 31, means that this scene is probably a practical lesson in faith. It is notable that Matthew says Peter walked (temporarily) on "water" instead of "sea" (cf. Mk 6:47-49). As water is often used figuratively in the Old Testament to denote oppression,[136] it is perhaps reasonable to suppose that Matthew's readers would have read this as a lesson in faith in the face of evil and persecution.[137]

Peter's address to Jesus as "Lord" reflects what faith Peter does have in the one who is Lord of the destructive storm, which presumably is still raging as Peter makes his request (Mt 14:24, 28, 32), for in John it is implied that only God could walk on the sea (Jn 6:19-20).[138] And, for Matthew, Jesus' saying "It is I" *(egō eimi)* draws out a reflection on the identity of Jesus (cf. §3.18).

The precise lesson in Peter walking on the sea is difficult to determine. It cannot be that he is to be seen like Moses or the Son of God or even God, for his walking on the water is clearly dependent on Jesus (Mt 14:28-29), and he fails to maintain this ability and has to be rescued by Jesus (14:30-31). It could be a lesson in wrong faith. That is, Peter's modeling a desire to imitate Jesus was presumptuous, and Jesus' call to Peter is then a lesson in misplaced ambition. However, Peter is never reprimanded for leaving the boat.

On the other hand, it could be that Peter is to be imitated: like Peter, followers of Jesus are called to share in the Lord's power over the storms that threaten the life of the church. The ability to share this authority depends on having more than just "little faith"—that is, not doubting (cf. §4.10). This understanding correlates with the theme of 28:18, where the authority of Jesus (cf. Mt 11:27) is seen to be handed on to the disciples.[139]

Matthew states clearly that Peter was, initially, successful in joining Jesus in this divine mastery over the storm (Mt 14:29). However, what reduced Peter's faith and caused him to begin sinking was his seeing the wind. He cried out, "Lord, save me!" (14:30). Noting this, the first hearers of Matthew were likely to have been able to recall the psalmist's cry, "Save me, O God, for the waters have come up to my neck" (Ps 69:1). Nevertheless despite having "little faith," or doubting, Jesus is still present in the storm and rescues his followers from its destructive power.

Again an Old Testament motif seems to be echoed in Matthew's description of Jesus reaching out his hand to catch Peter. After God had tamed the storm and sea, the psalmist says, "He reached down from on high, he took me; he drew me out of mighty waters" (Ps 18:16). In this echo Matthew may be signaling his understanding of the nature of the storm for his readers, for Psalm 18 immediately goes on to say that God delivered the psalmist from his enemies, those who hated him (Ps 18:17-18).

At verse 32 Matthew returns to the principal story of the storm. Mark only mentioned that Jesus got into the boat (Mk 6:51). Matthew says "they"—Jesus and Peter—got into the boat. This makes Peter's representative status more obvious as he acts with Jesus to calm the storm.

The stilling of the storm once again draws attention to the identity of Jesus. In the Old Testament only God stills storms.[140] It is then thoroughly appropriate for Matthew to say that the disciples in the boat "worshiped" *(proskunein)* Jesus, saying, "Truly you are the Son of God" (Mt 14:33).

Of all Matthew's miracle stories, it is this one that portrays the highest Christology. The story begins by drawing parallels between Moses and Jesus. In the body of the story, it is not that Jesus acts for God. Rather, in Jesus, God is seen acting to calm the storm and to rescue his people. Alongside this Christology has been the theme of being a disciple in the face of paralyzing difficulties. The main lesson is that even followers with little faith—faith mingled with doubt—can rely on the Lord to save them, for storms are calmed when Jesus is with his followers. Further, we can extrapolate that in those moments when followers of Jesus hear his call and exercise more than little faith and are not deflected by the storm, they are able to participate in his divine authority over the storm.[141]

§4.24 The Sick Healed by Touching His Garment (Mt 14:34-36/Mk 6:53-56)

In this summary, which follows immediately after the story of Jesus walking on the sea, Matthew shows that Jesus is easily recognized as a powerful, almost magnetic source of healing.[142] To heighten the force of the passage and the image of Jesus, Matthew says that all were brought and all were healed. Jesus had only to be asked and he would heal, and the mere touch of his clothing made people well (Mt 14:35-36). This belief in the special or representative power of clothing is well attested in the Old Testament (14:37).[143]

Also, in his retelling of the story of Elijah choosing Elisha as his successor, Josephus says that on receiving Elijah's mantle "Elisha immediately began to prophesy" (*Ant.* 8:353-54). Matthew shared this view that clothing was an extension of and carried with it a person's power and authority.

As is clear from this summary, the miracles had made Jesus popular, but the Pharisees and scribes continue to attack Jesus, this time over his attitude toward Jewish purity laws (Mt 15:1-20). So again[144] Matthew has Jesus withdraw from the hostility. Then in the next story Jesus responds to a Gentile's persistent trust in him.

§4.25 The Canaanite Woman's Daughter (Mt 15:21-28/Mk 7:24-30)

Uncharacteristically, Matthew's story of 140 words is slightly longer than his source (Mk 7:24-30). But he has rewritten most of it in his own vocabulary, using only 40 of Mark's 130 words.[145] The theme of faith is once again clear. The woman seeking healing has her trust tested when Jesus does not answer her and when the disciples beg Jesus to send her away (Mt 15:23). It is further tested when Jesus says that he was sent only to the lost sheep of the house of Israel (15:24). Interestingly the phrase that the disciples use—"for she is crying after us" (Mt 15:23, author's translation)—gives the impression that Jesus and his disciples are trying to ignore her as they walk along,[146] which, if Matthew's intention, is a great test of the woman's faith.

In a response that draws attention to her continued faith in Jesus—the source of her salvation and healing—the woman kneels reverently before him and says, "Lord, help me" (Mt 15:25). However, Jesus tests her faith still further by saying that it is not good to take the children's bread and throw it to the dogs—a much stronger statement than in Mark ("Let the children be fed first," Mk 7:27).

But the woman's faith remains firm. Maintaining the metaphor, she replies that "even the dogs eat the crumbs that fall from their master's table" (Mt 15:27). This gives voice to Matthew's belief that though the place of Israel is not to be diminished Gentiles can receive salvation. For the third time she addresses Jesus as "Lord" and also "Master" (15:29), reflecting her trust in Jesus.

Finally Matthew makes explicit the theme of faith when Jesus says, "Woman, great is your faith! Let it be done for you as you wish" (Mt 15:28). Matthew notes the power of Jesus' ability by adding that the daughter was healed instantly (cf. Mk 7:30).

This story is remarkably similar to that of the healing of the centurion's servant (Mt 8:5-13). Both stories are healings from a distance of a Gentile's dependent. In both stories Jesus is initially reluctant to accede to the request until after extraordinary declarations of faith in extended conversations in which Jesus comments on Israel. Nevertheless, in view of the differences between the stories, Bultmann's suggestion that they are variants of a single story is incredible.[147] In one story a woman is involved, in another a centurion. In the first story a distressed paralytic servant is involved, in the other story a demon-possessed daughter.

In these, his only stories about healing and salvation being offered to Gentiles, Matthew focuses on the importance of faith and the place of Israel in God's offer of salvation. Matthew makes clear that Gentiles receive from Jesus on the basis of their faith, not on the basis of their being Jews. Also in these stories Matthew is able to mention Israel's special place in God's dealing with humanity, as well as Israel's failure to have the expected faith (Mt 8:10-12; 15:24, 26). This Gentile who receives healing from the Son of David is not an exception[148] but, as the following summary shows,[149] an example of the crowds of Gentiles who come to Jesus.

§4.26 Jesus Heals Many People (Mt 15:29-31/Mk 7:31-37)

In this final of three summaries in the middle of the Gospel (cf. Mt 12:15-21; 14:34-36) Jesus goes up a mountain, and, upon sitting down,[150] great crowds of Gentiles come to him with the sick. The list of the sick people may be reminiscent of the messianic expectations in Isaiah 35:5-6 (cf. Mt 11:2-6).[151] Thus again Matthew portrays the Moses-like figure of Jesus on intimate terms with God and not only a teacher but also a great healer. Putting the sick "at his feet" (15:30) could be Matthew's way of implying a recognition by the Gentiles of the lordship of Jesus.[152]

In the story that Matthew is probably using,[153] Mark has Jesus take the man aside, put his fingers into the ears, spit, touch his tongue, look up, sigh and say, "Ephphatha" (Mk 7:34). Matthew has the simple statement, "and he healed them" (Mt 15:30, author's translation), leaving aside Jesus' ordering them to tell no one (Mk 7:36). Thus rather than the theme of rejection dominating this and the other two summaries in the middle of Matthew,[154] attention is drawn to the awesome power of Jesus, as in the crowd's response of wonder and glorifying the God of Israel (Mt 15:31). In turn, the Moses-like Messiah is depicted in the next story sharing a foretaste of the heavenly banquet with the Gentile crowd.

§4.27 The Feeding of Four Thousand (Mt 15:32-39/Mk 8:1-10)

The first question to ask here is why Matthew has two feeding stories (cf. Mt 14:13-21). It cannot simply be that he is faithfully following Mark, for we have just seen that he has omitted, or at least probably radically rewritten, the story of the healing of the deaf-mute (Mk 7:31-37). He also omits the story of the blind man being healed near Bethsaida (see §3.25 on Mk 8:22-26). Rather, it could be that common themes in the two stories—the compassion of Jesus, the exodus theme, the Eucharist, faith in Jesus to provide, and Jesus' spectacular ability—are so important to Matthew that they need restating here. Perhaps most important, this feeding is a foretaste of the sharing of the messianic banquet with the Gentiles.

A new theme in this second feeding is provided by the immediately preceding summary (Mt 15:29-31). Jesus is the Moses-like Messiah who not only teaches but fulfills the Old Testament promises of the miraculous.

Instead of Jesus considering the error of sending away the crowd hungry (as in Mk 8:3), his compassion in performing miracles and his mastery are portrayed when he says, "I do not want to send them away hungry" (Mt 15:32). Although Matthew has slightly rewritten the disciples' question as to how they are to find sufficient bread in a deserted place, they still appear to misunderstand how the crowd is to be fed (15:33).

Mark does not mention the availability of fish until the bread has been distributed. Not only is Matthew able to condense the story slightly by mentioning the fish and bread initially (Mt 15:34; cf. Mk 8:5, 7); the mentioning of the bread and fish together could also be to make the feeding more nearly parallel to the Eucharist (see §4.22 on Mt 14:13-21).[155]

§4.28 The Pharisees and Sadducees Seek a Sign (Mt 16:1-4; 12:38-39; Mk 8:11-13/Lk 11:16, 29; Jn 6:30)

In contrast to the Gentiles flocking to Jesus for healing and praising the God of Israel (Mt 15:31), Matthew now portrays Jesus returning to the fray with the Jews. The sign that Jesus' opponents are seeking from heaven is probably to be understood as an event in the sky that will be unambiguously from God and clearly authenticate Jesus' claims.[156] In any case, as Davies and Allison say, "To the sympathetic reader, who has just finished with the feeding of the four thousand, the request for a marvellous sign is ludicrous, a symptom of acute spiritual blindness."[157]

Matthew has told of the remarkable claims of Jesus: that he can forgive sins (Mt 9:1-8); that eschatological signs are taking place in his ministry (11:4-6); that he has an intimate relationship with or knowledge of God (11:27); that his exorcisms mean that the reign of God is arriving (12:28); and that he is greater than Jonah and Solomon (12:41-42). Thus Matthew's readers would understand that, although all that he has told of Jesus' miracles has been on earth, they have been sufficient to make clear Jesus' heavenly identity. Indeed, in his response Jesus criticizes the Pharisees and Sadducees for not being able to interpret the signs of the times: the miracles he is performing around them in his ministry, which indicate his identity.

Jesus refuses their request, saying that the only sign they will (in the future) be given is the sign of Jonah:[158] his resurrection (cf. Mt 12:38). It is the crowds—including Gentiles—who have rightly discerned and responded to Jesus' miracles by glorifying God (15:31).

Once again Matthew is saying that miracles, in and of themselves, do not create faith. Thus Matthew never uses miracles to convince unbelievers. Rather, it is trust or faith in Jesus that enables miracles to take place and their significance to be understood (cf. Mt 13:56).[159] This aspect of the theme of faith is carried on in the next miracle story of the so-called epileptic boy. Matthew relates this story after Jesus has warned the disciples against the penetrating power of the evil teaching of the Pharisees and Sadducees (16:5-12) and set out his own teaching on his death and suffering (16:13-23), which show who he is and how to follow him (16:24—17:13).

§4.29 Jesus Heals an Epileptic Boy (Mt 17:14-20/Mk 9:14-29/Lk 9:37-43a; 17:6)

In the transfiguration, Matthew has just highlighted Jesus' heavenly status (Mt 17:1-13). In this story,[160] following that of Jesus' mountaintop experience (17:1-13), Matthew's interest in Jesus as a new Moses remains in the minds of the readers. Thus they are probably intended to pick up a parallel between Moses coming down from the mountain and finding unbelief (Ex 32) and Jesus coming down this mountain and also finding unbelief (Mt 17:17).

Once again Matthew abbreviates this story—sixteen verses have been pruned to seven (cf. Mk 9:14-29). Notably, the father's cry, "I believe; help my unbelief!" which could suggest a lack of faith on his part, is also deleted (Mk 9:24). It also could be that Matthew, as in the story of the healing of Peter's mother-in-law, does not want his readers to conclude that the faith of the person needing healing is always required (cf. Mt 8:14-15).[161]

One particularly important result of the abbreviation is his leaving out Jesus' extended command to the demon: "You spirit . . . never enter him again!" (Mk 9:25). Probably in order not to detract from Jesus' healing power (by having him use incantations of the time), Jesus simply "rebuked" the demon and it "came out" (Mt 17:18). The boy is cured instantly. In contrast to the story in Mark, there is no mention of the boy being left like a corpse before Jesus raises him up (Mk 9:26). In contrast to Mark—who often has the disciples involved in the healing—this is the only healing story in which Matthew has the disciples play an indispensable part. As we are about to see, Matthew is probably intending to give specific teaching on exorcism to his readers.

Two other important aspects of the story stand out as conveying Matthew's principal message to his readers. First, the father's call to Jesus, "Lord, have mercy on my son" (Mt 17:15), expresses the view that in coming to the Messiah for healing, salvation is received (see §4.25 on 15:22). A second prominent aspect of the story is the inadequate faith of the disciples, who could not heal the boy. Jesus' lament over the faithless generation is clearly directed to the disciples (17:17). As we have just noted, the father's faith is no longer an issue in the story; the final verse focuses on the little faith of the disciples (17:20). That is, in response to the disciples asking why they could not cast out the demon, Jesus says it was because of their little faith. Then to the end of the story Matthew adds the saying faith as (small as) a grain of mustard seed is sufficient to make anything possible for the disciples (17:20). A conclusion to draw from this is that faith to save, as opposed to faith to heal, needs only to be exceptionally small.

§4.30 A Coin in a Fish's Mouth (Mt 17:24-27)

To contemporary readers of the Gospel, this story stands out as odd. It is neither a healing nor a miracle of nature. Rather, it seems like a trick to prove a point. In view of the tension Matthew has portrayed between Jesus and the religious authorities and because this story follows a prediction of suffering, the point of the story is probably to be found in issues of the relationship between Judaism and the followers of Jesus.

Some hold that the tax imposed by the Romans is in question here.[162] Most, however, agree that the story concerns the half-shekel temple tax (Ex 30:11-16).[163] Although Jesus gives direction to catch a fish that will have the appropriate coin in its mouth, the story ends without the miracle being recorded. It is assumed that the coin will appear and enable Jesus to pay the tax.

In addition to these interpretations, it is generally assumed that this story is probably to be understood as a symbolic action or sign (Mt 17:24-27). But there is little agreement concerning what it signifies. Brown suggests that, as it is one of the three Petrine sections of Matthew, the story is connected to the theme of Peter's primacy.[164] The point of what Theissen calls a "rule miracle"[165] is that God's children, while keen to live in a way that does not offend, are free with respect to their heavenly Father.[166] In turn, and in light of the context of the passion prediction we have noted, this may have meant for Matthew that, while giving to the church was to be a matter of freedom, this freedom was constrained by a responsibility to others and was supplied by God.[167] After an extended section of teaching on humility and forgiveness (18:1-35), Matthew provides another brief summary statement.

§4.31 A Summary (Mt 19:1-2/Mk 10:1)

The mention of large crowds following Jesus and being cured by him comes in one of the five summaries marking the end of each of the five generally recognized major discourses and starting with "And when Jesus had finished these sayings"[168] (Mt 19:1, author's translation). As with the others, this indicates a new phase in Matthew's story. Here there is also a change of location—from Galilee to the region of Judea beyond the Jordan.

Through the addition of the adjective *many* to describe the crowds there comes an increased sense of Jesus' success. Also, Matthew says that the crowd "followed" rather than gathered around him (Mt 19:2; cf. Mk 10:1), giving the impression that the crowd had, to some extent, become disciples. What is of particular interest is that Matthew has changed his source (Mk 10:1) from Jesus teaching the crowd to "and he cured them there." Presumably, even though Matthew now turns his attention to Jesus leading his followers on the journey to Jerusalem, he still wants to maintain a balance in portraying him as healing as well as teaching.

§4.32 Two Blind Men Receive Their Sight (Mt 20:29-34/9:27-31/Mk 10:46-52/Lk 18:35-43)

On the journey to Jerusalem Matthew has Jesus make the great statement that "the Son of Man came . . . to give his life a ransom for many" (Mt 20:28). The subsequent story of healing, made possible because Jesus is on his way to death, serves to illustrate the ransom saying. As it does for Mark, this story comes at a pivotal point in Matthew's Gospel: just before Jesus enters Jerusalem. In the doublet of this story, the faith of the blind men is important (see §4.14 on 9:27-31). Here also faith is important in that the two blind men[169] continue crying out after being rebuked by the crowd (20:31).

The lordship or majesty of Jesus is also in focus, through Jesus' being followed by a large crowd and twice being addressed as Lord, as well as through immediate healing. The focus is also on Jesus and his call. Mark has the crowd convey news of Jesus' call, but in Matthew Jesus himself calls the men: "What do you want me to do for you?" (Mt 20:32).

Equally important is the compassion of Jesus in performing miracles or giving salvation through touching: "Moved with compassion, Jesus touched their eyes" (Mt 20:34). Then, as in the Markan version (Mk 10:52), on being healed and saved the blind men follow Jesus. But there is no mention of their throwing off their cloaks. Only the call of Jesus and the stark response of trust in his call to follow him to Jerusalem remains.

§4.33 The Blind and Lame Healed in the Temple (Mt 21:14-17)

Matthew has just heralded Jesus' entry into Jerusalem (Mt 21:1-11), which is followed by his entering the temple and driving out the merchants and money changers (21:12-13). Then in their place come the blind and the lame, whom Jesus heals (21:14). There is little doubt that this verse, which is unique to Matthew, is entirely from Matthew's hand.[170]

The association of the blind and lame with the temple echoes 2 Samuel 5:8, where David does not permit them in the temple.[171] By depicting their entry into the temple here—and Jesus healing them—Matthew is overturning such exclusion. In Jesus, God invites all into this saving presence.

This is the third time a healing story has included both a positive and a negative reaction to Jesus' ministry (cf. Mt 9:33-34; 12:22-24). Through these stories Matthew shows a progressive understanding of the implications of Jesus' healings. The positive reactions to the healings progress from a general statement of amazement ("Never was anything like this seen in Israel," 9:33) to a question ("Can this be the Son of David?" expecting a negative answer, 12:33) to the bold statement here by mere children ("Hosanna to the Son of David!" Mt 21:15). The accuracy of this appellation is strongly affirmed through Matthew's citing of Psalm 8:2.

As this is the last time Matthew mentions healing in his Gospel, this can be taken to be the climactic positive response to Jesus' miracles. It also provides the background for another negative response to Jesus' miracles, which leads to his condemnation and death, for the next day in the temple, the chief priests and the elders challenge him regarding the sources of his authority to do "these things" (Mt 21:23). However, before that story comes the story of Jesus cursing the fig tree.

§4.34 The Cursing of a Fig Tree (Mt 21:18-22/Mk 11:12-14, 20-26)

This, the last miracle story, is important because it follows and interprets Jesus' popular acclaim as he enters Jerusalem and then drives out money changers from the temple. In Mark 11:12 Bethany is the setting for this story. Matthew changes it to Jerusalem (Mt 21:18).[172] In Jeremiah 8:13 and Micah 7:1 fruitless fig trees symbolize the failure of God's people. Thus, here in Matthew, Jerusalem becomes the focus of the meaning of the curse: God's rejection of the fruitless city and its leaders.

In Mark the story is split in two, with the temple episode taking place between Jesus' curse of the tree and Mark's reporting of the results. In Matthew the power of Jesus is heightened in that the tree immediately withers. Notwithstanding, the main purpose of the story is clearly to illustrate how to be fruitful. That is, the story ends with Jesus saying that "if you have faith and do not doubt . . . [w]hatever you ask for in prayer with faith, you will receive" (Mt 21:21-22). Jesus' act—causing the fig tree to wither instantly—is therefore an example to his followers in the exercise of faith.

§4.35 The Miracles in Matthew

Being placed first in the New Testament canon has meant that Matthew's interpretation of the life and ministry of Jesus has dominated the perspective of the church. In turn, Matthew's understanding of the place of the miracles in the ministry of Jesus has probably determined that the miracles take second place in significance behind the teaching of Jesus. In the introduction to this study we saw an example of this in Friedrich's statement that "the miracle is not the important thing. The important thing is the message which effects it."[173] This leads to our first conclusion about the miracles in Matthew.

1. *Miracles and message.* The precise value or significance of the miracles of Jesus for Matthew is seen especially in chapters 8 and 9. It is almost universally agreed that the nine stories (containing ten reports of miracles) form the second panel of a two-part panel, or diptych (the other being the Great Sermon), in which the ministry of Jesus is introduced and typified.[174]

Indeed, through this device Matthew is able to do at least two things. On one hand, he is able to show that Jesus' ministry is to be understood as one of word and deed. On the other hand, in contrast to Mark he is able to give preeminence to the teaching above the miracles. We cannot avoid the conclusion that while the miracles of Jesus are indispensable to Matthew's portrait of Jesus, they are to take second place behind the teaching. It is this view that has become part of the orthodoxy of mainstream Christianity, as well as established in Jesus scholarship (cf. §§17.13 and 17.14).

2. *Abridged stories.* We have seen that Matthew's often minimalistic approach to rewriting the miracle stories focuses attention on Jesus. Thus while Held's understanding of Matthew's objective was that Christology was only one of Matthew's interests, our examination shows that it was Matthew's principal concern in the miracle stories. Here we find Matthew at one with his Markan tradition: the miracles identify Jesus.

The title "Son of David" was clearly of great significance to Matthew. It is mentioned in the very first verse of the Gospel, and Matthew is the only Gospel in which we find the phrase "*the* Son of David" associated with the Messiah.[175] In that the context of the title is mostly that of healing miracles, we can conclude that the healing miracles are revealing Jesus' true status as the Messiah.

But the Jesus of the miracles in Matthew is not only the Son of David or the Son of God, beloved and pleasing to God, or anointed by his Spirit, having a great following and able to heal. He is also God himself acting mightily among his people. So Jesus is astoundingly effective not because of what he says or does but because his simple authority arises out of who he is. Yet he is not a self-seeking, triumphant miracle worker but a humble servant acting out of compassion and associating with outsiders and outcasts.

We have just seen that through his Gospel Matthew has given us a progressive understanding of the implications of the healings. The positive reactions to the healings progress from "Never was anything like this seen in Israel" (Mt 9:33) to "Can this be the Son of David?" (12:33, expecting a negative answer). Then comes the bold statement by mere children: "Hosanna to the Son of David!" (21:15).

3. *The new Moses.* Jesus is also portrayed as the new Moses who not only teaches but, in fulfilling the hopes expressed in Isaiah 53, is the Messiah of word and deed. Perhaps influenced by Q (Mt 11:4-6/Lk 7:22-23) and being keen to see Scripture fulfilled (Mt 8:16-17; 11:4-6), Matthew broadens Jesus' healing so that Jesus is seen healing not just demoniacs but every kind of sickness.[176] Nevertheless the Messiah remains primarily a prophet-teacher who also heals every disease, though exorcism is not as significant as it is for Mark, one of his predecessors.

4. *A wonder worker?* From noting the responses of the crowds to Jesus' miracles—for example, in the use of *thaumasia* ("wonders") in Matthew 21:15[177]—Birger Gerhardsson concluded that "Matthew considers the mighty acts of Jesus as *miracles in the sense of extraordinary, sensational event.*"[178] However, whereas Matthew certainly reports this response, it is for him an incomplete understanding of Jesus.

For example, while the amazed disciples question who Jesus is only after he has calmed the storm and do not draw any particular conclusions about him (Mt 8:27), the immediately following stories present a crescendo of understanding and acclamation in view of Jesus' wonders: first the demons call him "Son of God" (8:29; cf. 12:23); then God is glorified in light of the paralytic being healed (9:8; cf. 15:31). It is never Matthew's intention that his readers should conclude that Jesus' mighty acts were those of a man with sensational authority and power (cf. point two above).

5. *The ambiguity of miracle.* While the crowds offer wide acclaim, the religious authorities respond negatively. Thus the miracles in themselves neither create faith nor dispel doubt. Instead, miracles only confirm the distance between Jesus and those who do not understand the source and nature of Jesus' miracles.

6. *Faith.* The theme of faith is important to Matthew, but not so important as to make it the only factor determining his transmission of any story.[179] We noted that Matthew proposes that miracles per se do not generate faith: they do not convince unbelievers. On the other hand, we have seen that it is trust, or faith, in Jesus that enables miracles to take place and their significance to be understood (cf. Mt 13:54-58). The origin of the faith seems to be in seeing Jesus for who he is, as in the case of the leper, who on seeing Jesus coming down the mountain knelt before him (8:1-2).

It is faith, not any achievement, that evinces the compassionate Jesus' willingness to heal. This means that salvation is also available for Gentiles who have faith. Yet sometimes Jesus grants healing without any mention of faith. This is seen in the three healings in the first cycle of stories in chapters 8 and 9, where there is a progression in the way Matthew has depicted faith.

In the first story, the leper comes boldly and confidently to Jesus, asking in faith for his healing. In the second story, the servant is too sick to come to Jesus. Instead, his master goes for him and believes for his healing. The sufferer is healed not for his faith but for the faith of a third person. In the third story a woman, having been laid aside with fever, is also too sick to come to Jesus. But notably there is no mention of faith—hers or anyone else's. Not even those in the house are said to believe for her or to tell Jesus of her plight. Jesus is depicted as asking absolutely no conditions for him to be prepared to heal her. Seeing her is enough to move him to heal her.

When it is evident, faith for Matthew is a practically expressed confidence in Jesus' ability and willingness to heal. At one point Matthew even has Jesus ask a prospective recipient of a miracle "Do you believe?" (Mt 9:28). Nevertheless the smallest imaginable amount of faith is all that is required. Even Gentiles, on the basis of their faith, are able to receive healing and salvation. Yet of the disciples— who are depicted on occasion as having little faith (cf. 8:23-27)—more than "little faith" is required if they are to model the ministry of Jesus as they receive and use the power he gives them, especially in relation to overcoming the storms and troubles of life, for that is the context in which "little faith" is used.[180]

7. *Miracles as models and prisms.* In chapters 8 and 9, each of the three cycles of miracle stories is followed by the teaching of Jesus. Here we see most clearly that Matthew uses the miracle stories as prisms to develop a number of themes relating to discipleship. For example, the miracles are probably models for the disciples to follow in their ministry. And in the case of the healing of Peter's mother-in-law, the healed one responds by serving Jesus.

In the first cycle of stories there were some key themes and interesting developments of the theme of faith. All three sufferers were outsiders: a leper, a Gentile and a woman. As the very first miracle story in the Gospel involves an outsider, Gentile readers would be encouraged in receiving healing from Jesus. We also saw in the first cycle of stories that there was a progression in the depiction of faith: the leper himself comes boldly and confidently to Jesus, then a master goes and believes for the healing of his sick servant, and then a woman, also too sick to come to Jesus but of whom there is no mention of faith, is healed with absolutely no prerequisites.

8. *Miracles: Embodiment and manifestation of salvation.* This leads to another aspect discovered about the miracles in Matthew: they are snapshots of the significance of salvation, or even of salvation itself—in the context of the church, by

God, through Jesus, from the troubled storms of life. This was particularly evident in the story of the calming of the storm (Mt 8:23-27). But in looking back, it is also true for the present, or in the eschaton, of almost all the other stories as well.

9. *The exorcisms.* In our discussion of miracles in Mark we saw how highly significant the exorcisms were. By comparison Matthew has played down Jesus as an exorcist to the point of being reticent about the stories. (Concomitantly he has played down the role of exorcism in the ministry of the disciples and early church.) I have argued elsewhere that perhaps this is because of the difficulties Matthew saw exorcists cause in the church (cf. Mt 7:15-23).[181] Nevertheless Matthew still believed that Jesus' ministry of exorcism was important, as it revealed his true identity and was the first stage in the defeat of Satan, was performed in the power of the eschatological Spirit and was evidence that God's new reign had arrived.

10. *"Little faith" and miracles in nature.* To some extent we can concur with Gerhardsson that individual miracles of healing are portrayed for those not (yet) disciples, whereas the so-called nature, or nontherapeutic, miracles were for the benefit of the disciples. However, we have seen that the stories of the feeding, while being lessons for the disciples, were performed for the crowds, and the miracle of the coin in the fish's mouth was for Jesus' benefit. Further, all the stories have been used by Matthew as lesson aids for his readers. Many of the stories are to be modeled by the followers of Jesus in their ministries.

The function of the nontherapeutic miracles may be gleaned from their connection to the four places where the followers of Jesus are reprimanded for having "little faith." Those followers worrying about clothing and food in the face of God's ability to provide are reprimanded for having "little faith" (Mt 6:30).[182] 'Having just witnessed the three miracles of the first cycle, the disciples are reprimanded for having "little faith" (8:26) in the face of the boat being swamped by waves. Peter is, at least initially, successful in walking on the water. But on noticing the strong wind he becomes frightened and begins to sink. Jesus reprimands him for having "little faith" (14:31), probably because he had just seen Jesus feed the five thousand with severely limited resources (14:13-21). Again, later, the disciples are chastised for having "little faith" (16:8) in light of their witnessing the feeding of the four thousand (15:32-39). Therefore it could be that the function of these nontherapeutic miracles is to teach followers of Jesus to have faith, rather than "little faith," in Jesus' ability to care for his followers in difficult life situations.

11. *The shadow of the cross.* Jesus, the new Moses, performs miracles and does so in the shadow of the cross. Thus especially the exorcisms cause the Pharisees to begin to plot against Jesus. The two feeding stories also foreshadow the suffering and triumph of Jesus in that they contain echoes of the Last Supper and, in turn, the eschatological banquet.

Five

The Miracles
of Jesus in Luke

The Stories

....

§5.1 Introduction

Luke has included twenty miracle stories of Jesus in his Gospel.[1] In three summaries Luke also mentions healing. The stories of the healing of the centurion's servant (Lk 7:1-10/Mt 8:5-13) and the mute demoniac (Lk 11:14/Mt 12:22) come from Q. Luke also includes some stories unique to his Gospel: the stories of the large catch of fish (Lk 5:1-11), the widow's son raised to life (7:11-17), the crippled woman freed (13:10-17), the man with dropsy healed (14:1-6), the ten lepers cleansed (17:11-19) and the replacing of the high priest's servant's ear (22:51). The remainder of the stories are from Mark.[2]

In order to understand Luke's perspective on the miracles of Jesus, we will need occasionally to take into account what he says in Acts about miracles in general and Jesus' miracles in particular (see §6.12). Surprisingly few studies have focused on Luke's overall treatment of the miracles of Jesus,[3] yet there have been numerous studies on individual miracle stories in the Gospel of Luke.

The miracles of Jesus are so significant for Luke and so many issues are involved that we will discuss his perspective over two chapters. This one will deal with the miracle stories in the context of his plot and arrangement of material. In the next chapter we will deal with the major issues that arise from our discussion here.

§5.2 The Stories and Luke's Plot

As I have said before, the purpose of our treatment of the miracle stories in each of the Gospels is not to provide a commentary on each story. Rather we will focus attention on those aspects of the stories that tell us most about the Gospel writer's understanding of the miracles and of Jesus as a miracle worker. Therefore our treatment of each story will continue to be relatively brief.

Further, if as we examine the individual stories we keep in mind Luke's plot, we can expect to discover some implications for his views on the miracles of Jesus. The plot is important to Luke. Though in the first part of his two-part work he may have been writing a kind of ancient Greco-Roman biography,[4] he has in mind the narrative (*diēgēsis,* Lk 1:1) form of literature with an identifiable, orderly plot governed by time, topic and causality.[5]

After the prologue, Luke introduces John the Baptist and Jesus (Lk 1:5—2:52). Between 3:1 and 4:13 Luke gives the political background to his story (3:1) and the religious preparation of John's ministry (3:2-20), as well as the anointing (3:21-22), genealogy (3:23-38) and tempting (4:1-13) of Jesus, God's Son. Then he relates the commencement of Jesus' public ministry (4:14-15).

§5.3 The Opening in Nazareth (Lk 4:16-30/Mt 13:53-58/Mk 6:1-6a)

The story of Jesus' public ministry is told in Luke 4:16—21:38. His ministry is introduced with him returning in the power of the Spirit from the wilderness and temptation experiences.[6] And Luke opens Jesus' ministry by presenting him as a Spirit-anointed healer and teacher of good news (Lk 4:16-44).

The ensuing two sections of first teaching (Lk 4:16-30) and then stories of healing (4:31-44) are introduced similarly.[7] This suggests that the introductory statement of 4:14-15 (about Jesus' returning in the power of the Spirit) relates both to the teaching and to the miracles. The readers could be expected to conclude that each equally arises out of Jesus being motivated by the Spirit of the Lord.

Early in the teaching section (Lk 4:16-30) is a clear statement on Luke's view of the nature of Jesus and the significance of the miracles of Jesus within his ministry. Jesus is said to read from the book of the prophet Isaiah:

The Spirit of the Lord is upon me,
    for he has anointed me.
He has sent me to preach to the poor,
    to proclaim to the captives release
    and to the blind sight,
to send away the oppressed released,
    to proclaim the acceptable year of the Lord.
    (4:18-19, author's translation)

Even though it is not a miracle story, the importance of this passage in understanding the mission and miracles of Jesus must not be missed.[8] Primarily we must note that Luke sees the ministry of Jesus arising out of his being anointed by the Spirit. This episode is the public introduction of Jesus. It is echoed in various ways throughout Luke,[9] and *euangelizein* ("to herald good news")—which Luke often uses to encapsulate Jesus' ministry[10]—is used for the first time here.

Already in this passage (and in pairing it with the teaching to follow, cf. Lk 4:16, 31) we see Luke balancing the teaching and miracles of Jesus in such a way that they are of equal significance. (This is in contrast to teaching being dominant in Matthew and miracles being dominant in Mark.) On further exploration of this theme we will see that this balancing of importance also extends to exorcism in relation to other forms of healing. Further, we will see that Luke develops the latent idea that the miracles of Jesus are not simply the work of God but the work of God as eschatological salvation (cf. 11:20).

In what is generally taken as the middle section of Luke (Lk 4:16—21:38), Jesus first conducts a Galilean ministry (4:16—9:50).[11] This initial deed of power—Jesus' second public activity—takes place in the synagogue in Jesus' hometown (cf. 4:23).

§5.4 A Demoniac in the Capernaum Synagogue (Lk 4:31-37/Mk 1:21-28)

As was already noted, Jesus' being said to return in the power of the Spirit (Lk 4:14) applies to his teaching as well as to his miracles. Thus we are to take this exorcism as an example (cf. 4:15) of the fulfillment of the prophecy read from Isaiah, most appropriately—as we will see from the next story—the line about captives being released (4:18). Even though he is following Mark 1:21-28 closely, Luke has made a number of changes to his source, some of which can be seen to have significance for his understanding of the miracles of Jesus.

In the introduction to this story, Luke says that the crowd was astonished at Jesus' "word" (*logos*, Lk 4:32), rather than at his "teaching" (*didaskōn*, Mk 1:22). Luke also uses the term *logos* for the words Jesus uses to perform the exorcism (Lk 4:36). It is unlikely that in choosing this word Luke wants to subordinate the miracles to the teaching of Jesus.[12] Rather, in view of the way word and activity are held together in the quotation from Isaiah (Lk 4:18) and the way this section is structured to balance teaching and miracles, Luke is probably expressing a balance and an inextricable link between the two aspects of Jesus' ministry.

The unclean spirit is not said to be "in" *(en)* the man (Mk 1:23); rather, the man is said to "have" *(echein)* an evil spirit (Lk 4:33). Perhaps this is to contrast one of the ways in which Luke says the (Holy) Spirit is associated with people (cf. 2:27; 4:1, 14).

To the words of the demoniac Luke has added the Greek particle *ea* (Lk 4:34; cf. Mk 1:24)—most likely an exclamation of displeasure[13]—highlighting the nature of the demoniac's response to Jesus' presence. Luke has retained the remainder of the words of the demons exactly as he found them in Mark. As for Mark, Luke takes the exorcisms of Jesus to be the destruction of demons.

However, Luke's description of what follows Jesus' exorcistic words is quite different from Mark's (Mk 1:26/Lk 4:35). Moving Mark's statement that the demon "cried out with a loud voice" to an earlier point (to 4:33) removes from the story the idea of struggle in the defeat of the demon. Instead of the demon convulsing the man (Mk 1:26)—which may have harmed him—Luke says that the demon threw the man down in the middle—that is, before them, probably as a way of demonstrating the reality of the cure. Luke says that the demon did the man no harm, indicating the power and gentleness of Jesus' ministry (Lk 4:35).

A change Luke makes to the amazed crowd's response to the healing is to add that the people were questioning not only the authority of Jesus (Mk 1:27) but also his "power" to command the unclean spirits to come out (Lk 4:36). This recalls Luke saying that Jesus returned to Galilee from the scene of temptation "filled with the power of the Spirit" (Lk 4:14), showing that this miracle arises out of Jesus being empowered by the (Holy) Spirit. Jesus' miracle is reported not just in Galilee (Mk 1:28) but in "every place in the region" (Lk 4:37; cf. 14).

§5.5 Simon's Mother-in-Law (Lk 4:38-39/Mk 1:29-31)

In saying that Jesus entered Simon's house after leaving the synagogue (Lk 4:38), Luke ties this to the previous story. In turn this makes it another example of Jesus' fulfillment of the Isaian prophecy of his ministry, arising out of the Spirit being upon him (4:18).

Although Luke is using only Mark as his source for this little story, he has exercised some freedom in relating it. For us, most notable about Luke's treatment of the story are the following points.

1. As he has not yet told the story of the calling of the disciples, Luke omits mention of them here (cf. Mk 1:16-20/Lk 5:1-11). Having Jesus enter the home alone has the effect of focusing attention on Jesus the healer.

2. The woman, Simon's mother-in-law,[14] is described as seized, shut up or hard pressed *(sunechein)* by the fever.[15] Since Luke uses the word for being held prisoner (Lk 22:63) and has described Jesus' ministry as proclaiming release to the captives, this story becomes another example of Jesus' Spirit-empowered ministry.

3. Luke's heightening of the severity of the sickness from a fever to a high *(megas)* fever[16] has the effect of increasing the ability of Jesus in the healing (Lk 4:38/Mk 1:30).

4. Jesus' ability is further heightened by the omission of Mark's saying that Jesus touched the woman (Mk 1:31). Here in Luke, Jesus heals only by what he says (Lk 4:39).

5. Luke says that Jesus "stood over her" (*epistas epanō autēs*, Lk 4:39) when he healed the woman.[17] It is possible that Luke says this simply because the woman was on a pallet.[18] Derrett says that Jesus stood over the woman to threaten the demon because Jewish impurity moved vertically upward and downward.[19] However, it is arguable that by this phrase Luke indicates that he is telling a straightforward exorcism story.

The practice of an exorcist standing over a patient may have its roots in Babylonian healings.[20] In the New Testament era it is directly paralleled in the magical papyri (e.g., *PGM* 4:745, 1229, 2735). In these documents the focus of attention in healing is often directed toward the head. Further, evidence that Luke may intend this report to be understood as an exorcism is his use of "rebuke" (*epitimaō*, Lk 4:39). This word is used in the Gospels apart from reference to exorcism.[21] However, it is also used in reports describing the action of an exorcist[22] and carries the idea of a "command by which God's agent defeats his enemies, thus preparing for the coming of God's kingdom."[23]

Thus in this brief story Luke relates this healing as an exorcism, the first of a number of examples we will come across in which he, while recognizing different kinds of healing, blurs the distinction between them. It is also an example of Jesus' Spirit-empowered ministry. Now, following Mark 1:32-34, Luke gives a summary report of Jesus' healings.

§5.6 Healings at Sundown—A Summary (Lk 4:40-41/Mt 8:16-17/Mk 1:32-34)

By means of the link word *rebuke* (Lk 4:35, 39, 41), the report is firmly tied to the preceding stories, which we have just discussed, and provides yet another example of the fulfillment of the Isaian prophecy. Into Mark's summary Luke has injected the idea that Jesus laid his hands on the sick. Strictly speaking, he does not say he laid hands on those who had demons,[24] for Luke has separated mention of the sick being brought to him (4:40) from the mention of demons coming out of many (4:41). (This maintains a consistency with the previous story, where Luke has Jesus stand over Simon's mother-in-law and rebuke the demon rather than touch her, as in Mark 1:31.)

The extent of Jesus' healing is widened and particularized at the same time by Luke saying that Jesus laid his hands "on each of them" instead of using the ambiguous "many" (Lk 4:40/Mk 1:34). Luke also adds the titles of Jesus used by the demons: "Son of God" and "Christ" (*christos*). This has the effect of linking this summary to the Isaian prophecy, where Jesus is said to be "anointed" (*echrisen*, Lk 4:18). Again this shows that the exorcisms were at least part of the release Jesus was thought by Luke to be proclaiming.

This brief summary brings to a close Luke's report of the beginning of Jesus' performing of miracles in Galilee (Lk 4:14-44). He concludes the section by giving the impression that Jesus' ministry will now be wider—to include Judea (4:44).[25] After these initial scenes of the Galilean ministry (4:16-44) Jesus' ministry will be portrayed as eliciting a number of responses. For example, as we will see in the next story, there is a call to discipleship in the context of a miraculous catch of fish (5:1-11), after which Jesus is addressed as "Lord" (5:8). Then a leper recognizes Jesus to be "Lord" (5:12). In turn, the leper's cleansing causes a sensation (5:12-16).

§5.7 The Large Catch of Fish (Lk 5:1-11; cf. Jn 21:4-14)

A similar story about a large catch of fish can be found in the Fourth Gospel (Jn 21:4-14). However, because of the differences in detail and vocabulary between the stories, it is unlikely there is any literary relationship between them. Rather, Luke and the publishers of the Fourth Gospel have probably had access to different versions of the same story.[26] The question as to which story is earlier is no longer answerable with confidence.[27]

Nevertheless, because it is less likely that an early Christian writer would take a story from after the resurrection and place it in the ministry of the earthly Jesus than the opposite, and because Luke is more likely to use a Galilean story in the body of his Gospel than in the Easter story (where Jerusalem is the focus of attention), the Fourth Gospel probably preserves the locality of the story, though not the time frame.[28]

Although the miracle is important in the story, for Luke the focus of attention is primarily on Simon and his call.[29] The miracle story is not so much an allegory, as it is for the Fourth Gospel (see §7.10), but a parable of Simon's future. Instead of Jesus agreeing to depart from the sinful Simon, he is forgiven—implied in the phrase "Do not be afraid" (Lk 5:10)[30]—and told that from now on it will be people he will be "catching" (*zōgrōn*, 5:10).

The relation of this story to that of the call of the disciples in Mark 1:16-20 is problematic, but that Luke omits that call story shows he probably sees this story as its equivalent. That makes the use of the word *catching* all the more significant. *Zōgreō* is "to take alive." The word has a compassionate nuance and is used for snatching people from danger.[31] In light of what fishermen do to fish after they are caught, Luke's metaphor is far more appropriate for Simon's call and future ministry![32] The miracle allows Luke to show—in contrast to the rejection of Jesus by his own people (Lk 4:16-30)—the magnitude of the success of Simon's following Jesus.

Thus Luke emphasizes the magnitude of the miracle: the disciples had been working all night (Lk 5:5), many fish were caught, the nets were beginning to break (5:6), a second boat was needed, both boats were filled, both boats began to sink (5:7), and all who witnessed this were amazed (5:9). From this story Luke goes immediately to another pair of miracle stories, held loosely together by *egeneto* ("it happened," 5:12, 17).

§5.8 A Leper Cleansed (Lk 5:12-16/Mk 1:40-45/Mt 8:2-4)

Just as Simon had a dramatic and life-changing encounter with Jesus, so this leper is another individual who encounters and is healed by Jesus. Since Luke will soon have Jesus list lepers being cleansed as an indication that the messianic age has arrived (Lk 7:22), this miracle story becomes an example of Jesus bringing the blessings of that age—a blessing, according to the rabbis, no less significant than raising the dead.[33]

Two features of the story help us see Luke's particular interest in it. First, Luke heightens the figure of Jesus in the healing by dramatizing the leper's approach to Jesus. He bows his face to the ground, rather than simply kneeling, and addresses Jesus as Lord (Lk 5:12/Mk 1:40). Second, Luke omits Jesus' emotional response to the leper (cf. Mk 1:41). Not only is this understandable if Jesus' response was said to be anger,[34] but in this omission Luke also is able to portray Jesus as acting not from emotion but from his will and power. This may explain why Luke also omits Jesus' violent dismissal of the cleansed leper (cf. Mk 1:43).

The response to Jesus' words of healing is immediate recovery (Mk 1:42/Lk 5:13). The authority of Jesus is further heightened in Luke's leaving out Mark's saying that the leper disobeyed Jesus' command to tell no one (cf. Mk 1:45): the leper is obedient to Jesus. Nevertheless, Luke is able to draw attention to the magnitude of the miracle through saying that, in any case, the news spread concerning Jesus (Lk 5:15).

§5.9 A Paralytic Forgiven and Healed (Lk 5:17-26/Mk 2:1-12/Mt 9:1-8)

This is the second in a pair of healing stories and the first in a series of five stories that involve disputes with the Pharisees,[35] here mentioned for the first time. Even though he does not mention them in the last story, Luke probably intends the previous story to be seen as part of the disputes with the religious authorities.

They are introduced in this story as spectators. (They are not in his source; Mk 2:2.) Saying they were "seated," the posture of a teacher, may suggest that they were already over against Jesus. And their coming from every village of Galilee, Judea and Jerusalem (Lk 5:17) is probably to be seen as having its ground in the report of what Jesus had just done—touching a leper and sending him cleansed to the priest. The mention of Jerusalem, the place of Jesus' passion, is probably a signal from Luke that the miracles of Jesus are part of the reason Jesus was crucified.

The phrase "and the power of the Lord was with him to heal" (Lk 5:17) is part of the web of words in this section that tie the miracles of Jesus to his being filled with the power of the Spirit (4:14) and the Spirit of the Lord being upon him (4:18). This theme is so important in Luke's understanding of the miracles of Jesus that not only will I repeatedly have cause to draw attention to it but we will return to it later in a special treatment of the current debate on the issues involved (see §§6.1 and 6.3).

For the present, we can note that Luke is implying an intermittency in the presence of the power of the Lord with Jesus. That this power is said to be for healing while Luke has just introduced Jesus as teaching is a further example of Luke tying healing and teaching together (cf. Lk 5:15).

In the body of the story Luke adds to his source (Mk 2:3) that those carrying the paralyzed man "were trying to bring him in and lay him before Jesus" (Lk 5:18), which emphasizes the keenness of people to gain access to Jesus and his healing ministry. Luke also adds that God "alone" can forgive sins (5:21/Mk 2:7), which has the effect of enhancing the divine act of Jesus in forgiving the man.

Though he is following his source, we must note that Luke sees faith as important in healing (Lk 5:20), as he will show in other stories.[36] Again, this is such an important feature of Luke's treatment of the miracles of Jesus that we will deal with it in more detail in the next chapter when we discuss issues relating to Luke's treatment of the miracle stories (§6.11).

Luke intensifies the response to Jesus' healing. First, the man is said to stand up "immediately" (Lk 5:25; cf. Mk 2:12). Unique to Luke is his saying that the healed man also glorified God (Lk 5:25), a Lukan feature found in other miracle stories.[37] This is, as we will see, part of Luke's program to show that God is at work in the healings of Jesus. Second, Luke says "all" the people glorified God (5:26). This awe is verbalized as: "We have seen strange things *[paradoxa]* today" (5:26). A *paradoxos* was something wonderful or remarkable, contrary to opinion or expectation.[38] Josephus also probably uses it of Jesus' miracles (*Ant.* 18:63).[39] Although it is the only time the word is used in the New Testament, it shows a contact with one of the concepts of miracle noted in §1.3. That Luke has the people say they saw these things "today" may be his connecting of this miracle with 4:21, where Jesus' ministry is portrayed as arising out of the eschatological Spirit's being upon him. After three other stories of disputes with the religious authorities (Lk 5:27-32, 33-39; 6:1-5), Luke includes another—a miracle story—in the same category.

§5.10 A Withered Hand Cured (Lk 6:6-11/Mk 3:1-6/Mt 12:9-14)

Through adding to his Markan source that this dispute story took place on the Sabbath, it is paired with that of the disciples plucking ears of grain on the Sabbath (Lk 6:1-5). As in the conflict over being able to forgive sin (5:17-25), this story shows that Jesus' Spirit-empowered miracles are more important than religious traditions and that Jesus—the Lord of the Sabbath (6:5)—is greater than David. More specifically, assuming that the Mishnah comment that "danger to life overrides the prohibition of the Sabbath" (*m. Yoma* 8:6) reflects a view familiar to Luke's readers, this miracle is shown to be bringing life to the man and conveys that the realization of God's intentions through Jesus is of the utmost importance.

The introduction of "the scribes and Pharisees" (Lk 6:7) into the story reinforces Luke's previous point that the miracles were part of the conflict between Jesus and the religious authorities. Luke's adding that Jesus knew the thoughts of the scribes and Pharisees further reflects on the character of Jesus—he is in complete control of the situation and has God-given insight into human thoughts.

Mark has Jesus' question to the scribes and Pharisees as "Is it lawful . . . to save *[sōsai]* life or to kill?" Luke has "Is it lawful . . . to save *[sōsai]* life or to destroy it *[apolesai]*?" (Mk 3:4/Lk 6:9). The use of *apolesai* over against *sōsai* in the context of a healing miracle creates a three-way link between healing, salvation, and the miracles (cf. 9:24).[40] After saying that Jesus spent the night in prayer before choosing the Twelve (Lk 6:12-16), Luke now gives a summary statement of Jesus' activity.

§5.11 Crowds Come to Be Healed—A Summary (Lk 6:17-19/Mk 3:7-12/Mt 4:24-25; 12:15-21)

This summary, taken from Mark 3:7-12 and thoroughly rewritten, is Luke's introduction to his Sermon on the Plain (Lk 6:20-49). In rewriting this summary Luke has reduced the importance of healing and balanced the healing and teaching aspects of Jesus' ministry by saying that people came "to hear him and to be healed of their diseases" (6:18). He also says that Jesus cured or healed *(therapeuō)* those who were troubled or harassed *(enochleō,* 6:18) by unclean spirits. What is interesting to note here is that the spirits are not said to possess the people and that their cure was not through driving them out or by exorcism but by healing them. This is another example of Luke's habit of blurring the distinction between healing and exorcism.

One of the most interesting features of this summary is the phrase "for power came out from him" (Lk 6:19). Indeed, the first issue we will discuss in the next chapter (§§6.2 and 6.3) in relation to Luke's treatment of the miracles of Jesus will take this phrase into account.

In the Galilean ministry that Luke is relating, he also establishes that Jesus is greater than John (Lk 7:18-23) through, for example, the miracle stories of the healing of the centurion's slave (7:1-10) and the raising of the widow's son (7:11-17), each of which we will discuss, as well as the conversation with John's disciples (7:18-23).

§5.12 A Centurion's Slave Healed (Lk 7:1-10/Mt 8:5-13; cf. Jn 4:46-53)

Having completed the Sermon on the Plain (Lk 7:1), Luke gives a series of stories drawing attention to the way Jesus' ministry is received by various people (7:1-50). Of these, three are of interest to us: this and the next miracle story (7:11-17), as well as the story of Jesus' answer to John the Baptist (7:18-23). There is a degree of parallelism between the two miracle stories in that individuals are supplicating for a suffering member of their household and both provide the immediate background for Jesus' reply to John the Baptist.

That Bultmann,[41] for example, among the form critics wished to categorize this story as an apothegm[42] cannot detract from the fact that Luke understands it to be a report of a miracle. That is clear from the conclusion he gives: "They found the slave in good health" (Lk 7:10).

The relationship between the stories in Matthew and Luke has caused some discussion. The evidence suggests that Q is the origin of the story for both writers.[43] If the double delegation to Jesus—first of Jewish elders (Lk 7:3) and later of friends (7:6)—was part of Q, it would be more difficult to explain Matthew's omission of it than Luke's creation of it. Therefore we can assume that Matthew has preserved the most original form of the story, with Luke inserting the aspect of the double delegation.[44]

The delegations have the effect of heightening the centurion's statement about his authority and acknowledgement of Jesus' authority. This in turn reflects on the main point of the story for Luke—the faith of the centurion. That is, the Jewish delegation does not add good works to the faith of the centurion[45] but heightens his faith (and humility) in conveying the message that despite his reported good works he is not worthy to have Jesus in his home. This faith is further highlighted by Luke having Jesus say "not even in Israel" (rather than "from no one in Israel") has such faith been found (Lk 7:9/Mt 8:10).

These probable Lukan changes[46] make the centurion's faith all the more extraordinary since he is clearly portrayed as a Gentile. This faith is expressed in his conclusion that his servant will be healed if Jesus would "only speak the word" (Lk 7:7). Jesus can heal by a single word or by speaking just as God can (cf. Ps 107:20), as is also illustrated in the next story.

§5.13 The Widow of Nain's Son (Lk 7:11-17)

When we deal with the historicity of this story (§14.3), I will argue that it predates Luke. It probably came from Luke's special source, L. Luke ties together this story of raising a dead person and the last parallel story (of an almost dead person) with "Soon afterwards" or, more accurately, "And it happened next" (*Kai egeneto en tō hexēs*, Lk 7:11).[47] This gives the impression of an escalating demonstration of the power of Jesus in preparation for his answer to John's disciples.

Luke gives the story pathos by saying that the dead man was an "only" child (a saying he uses three times, Lk 7:12; 8:42; 9:38) and that the mother was a widow (7:12). In turn Jesus' miracle working is motivated by pity or compassion (7:13), further evidenced in Luke's saying Jesus "gave him to his mother," a phrase straight from the story of Elijah (Lk 7:15/1 Kings 17:23 LXX), the implications of which we are about to note.

The response to the miracle comes in the keynote of this pair of stories, as Fitzmyer put it, which is sounded in Luke 7:16: "Fear seized all of them; and they glorified God, saying, 'A great prophet has risen among us!' and 'God has looked favorably on his people!' "[48] On many occasions Luke casts Jesus in the role of a prophet.[49] Although, as here, Jesus rejects that role when it is related to social reformation, he tolerates the title in relation to his miracles.

This makes us sensitive to the echoes of the Elijah cycle of stories in 1 Kings, especially that of the raising of the son of the widow of Zarephath (1 Kings 17:8-24), which has probably influenced Luke's writing here.[50] Further ahead in Luke's Gospel, Jesus' death is referred to as being "taken up" (Lk 9:51) in the same way Elijah is portrayed as being taken up to heaven (2 Kings 2:11) and also is expected to return. Thus by aligning this story to that of Elijah in his miracles Jesus is already being portrayed as the one who will be taken up by God to return again. As we have just recognized, this last pair of miracle stories thus gives the impression of an escalating demonstration of Jesus' power in preparation for John the Baptist's questioning about Jesus' identity.

§5.14 Jesus' Answer to John the Baptist (Lk 7:18-23/Mt 11:2-6)

Here and in the next two stories the issue for Luke and his readers is the relationship between Jesus and John the Baptist in God's plan of salvation (Lk 7:24-30 and 31-35). The issue is whether Jesus is the "coming one" (7:19,[51] author's translation), an expectation already put directly on the lips of John the Baptist in Luke 3:16. The meaning of this term for Luke has been understood in different ways: as a reference to God himself (cf. Zech 14:5), to the eschatological prophet, to a regal figure (cf. Zech 9:9), to a prophet like Moses and the messiahs (as in 1QS 9:11), to pilgrims coming to Jerusalem for a feast (cf. Ps 118:26), to an eschatological Elijah figure, the Son of Man who comes in judgment, or to the coming of the messiah in a secret manner.[52] Surely the answer is that Luke understands John's specific question not to be in exclusive relation to any particular tradition of messianic expectation but to relate to a collection of all hopes to be fulfilled in Jesus. However, verse 21, which we must discuss, shows that Luke is using this passage to identify Jesus as the Messiah.

Through the addition of verse 21—"In that hour he healed many" (author's translation)—Luke draws unavoidable attention to the place of the miracles in identifying Jesus, for the activities listed in this verse were expected of the Messiah (cf. §6.10). Luke has already said that John's question arises out of "these things" (Lk 7:18)—most naturally the preceding two miracle stories—and he will here take from Q Jesus' answer, which is principally a list of miracles. This addition, which mentions the giving of sight to the blind, also takes into account the fact that Luke has yet to report a story of Jesus giving sight to the blind (see §5.25 on 18:35-43). The phrase "the poor have good news brought to them" (7:22) recalls Jesus' reading of the scroll in the synagogue at Nazareth (4:18), thus reiterating the Spirit as the source of Jesus' miracles.

In the final statement of Jesus' answer, which is a beatitude—"And blessed is anyone who takes no offense at me" (Lk 7:23)—Luke recognizes that his readers may find offense in Jesus' identity being dependent not so much on his being a fiery reformer announced by Isaiah[53] but to a large extent at least here on his performing miracles, even though in Jesus' answer there has been repeated reference to Old Testament expectations.[54] Through the stories about John the Baptist (Lk 7:24-28 and 7:29-35) and that of Jesus' feet being kissed and anointed by a woman who is a sinner (7:36-50), Luke gives us a series of six stories on various receptions of Jesus.

At Luke 8:1 a new section of the Galilean ministry begins (cf. Lk 4:43). Jesus sets out on a tour of cities and villages with not only the Twelve but also some women who have been healed by him (8:1-3). In his travels Jesus teaches primarily in parables (8:4-18); Luke concludes that those who belong to Jesus' family "are those who hear the word of God and do it" (8:21). But again the teaching is balanced with a number of dramatic miracles (8:22-56), including the calming of a storm (§5.15). Also, in this Galilean ministry a demoniac is healed, a hemorrhage is stopped and a girl is raised to life.

§5.15 Stilling the Storm (Lk 8:22-25/Mk 4:35-41/Mt 8:23-27)

Following a report of Jesus' teaching during his tour (Lk 8:4-18), this story marks the beginning of a group of miracles that precede Jesus' sending out the Twelve with "power and authority over all demons and to cure diseases" and "to proclaim the kingdom of God and to heal" (Lk 9:1-2). Jesus illustrates the mission of the Twelve in this group of miracles.

When we discussed this story in Mark (see §3.14) we noted remarkable parallels with the story of Jonah. It is hard to doubt that Luke would also have had that story in mind here. Nevertheless in transmitting this story Luke is dependent on Mark and has made only minor changes to his source. However, as in Mark, not only is Jesus like the great figures of the Old Testament—Moses, Joshua and Elijah[55]—he is also portrayed as Lord of the elements, as the God of the Old Testament was similarly pictured and prayed to for protection.[56] As Jesus' exorcisms raised questions about his identity (Lk 4:36), so now his power over the storm raises similar questions (8:25). The issue comes to climax in Peter's confession that Jesus is "the Messiah of God" (9:20).

Another theme Luke picks up—though he expresses it more gently than Mark—is the question about the faith of the disciples. Whereas Mark has Jesus attribute the disciples' fear to a complete lack of faith, Luke portrays the disciples as failing to exercise their faith (Lk 8:25/Mk 4:40).

§5.16 The Gerasene Demoniac (Lk 8:26-39/Mt 8:28-34/Mk 5:1-20)

In this second of three stories of Jesus' great power, Luke has taken—with only minor modifications—an episode from Mark about Jesus' power over the demonic. In so doing Luke has Jesus recognized as "Son of the Most High God" (Lk 8:28). Nevertheless some of Luke's minor alterations shed light on his perspective on the miracles of Jesus and this story in particular.

In recounting the result of Jesus' miracle Luke adds that the man had been "healed" (*sōzein*, "to save" or "to heal," Lk 8:36). In using *sōzein* instead of simply following Mark in saying that the people reported "what had happened" (Mk 5:16), Luke conveys the idea that the man was not only healed but received salvation by being freed from the demoniac.

In reporting Jesus' command to the demoniac Luke says, "Jesus had commanded *[parēngeilen]* the unclean spirit to come out of the man" (Lk 8:29). Luke is particularly fond of *parēngeilen* ("charge" or "command") and uses it of a directive from an authoritative source.[57] The word has strong military associations, and its basic meaning has to do with passing an announcement along the ranks of command. This then would leave readers with the impression that Jesus was exorcising the demons in light of his being under authority. At this point readers would recall the story of the healing of the centurion's slave, which drew attention to Jesus healing because he was under authority and could command authority (Lk 7:8).

Luke says that the demons begged Jesus not to order them into the "abyss" (*abussos*, Lk 8:31). By using *abussos* Luke brings a whole new dimension to Mark's story. Although Luke does not clarify what he understands the abyss to be, from the present context and the word's use in the period,[58] he most probably means that the demons felt that in Jesus there was the potential for their final defeat and imprisonment in the "unfathomable deep." Rather than be so defeated, the demons request to be sent into the pigs (8:32). In this way Luke puts succinctly what he says throughout his two volumes: Jesus' ministry was not the final defeat of Satan and his minions but the first stage of that defeat (see §6.7).[59]

The final part of the story draws out what is only implied in Mark. Mark has Jesus tell the healed man to return to his people to tell them how much "the Lord" had done for him (Mk 5:19). Luke says more clearly that he was to declare how much "God" had done for him. Thus in declaring "how much *Jesus* had done for him" (Lk 8:39), Luke is able to make plain that, in Jesus' miracles, God is at work.

§5.17 Jairus's Daughter and a Woman with a Hemorrhage (Lk 8:40-56/Mt 9:18-26/Mk 5:21-43)

The third miracle story—actually a pair of stories—in this section reaches a climax when Jesus' power to work miracles is seen by Luke to extend beyond mere healing to raising the dead and to be so potent that it can heal by a touch without even his cooperation or knowledge.

In chapter 7 Luke has already given us a story of the raising of a dead person: there a son or servant (Lk 7:11-17), here a daughter. Such parallelism is common in Luke. Another parallel is the verb used in these stories—"to raise" the dead (8:54; cf. 7:14)—and in the story of the resurrection (24:6). This was probably to lead the readers to conclude that the power of God used in raising Jesus from the dead was the same power that Jesus used to raise the dead and that is also apparent in the post-Easter situation (cf. Acts 9:36-42; 20:7-12).

By Jesus' saying he perceived that "power" had gone out from him (Lk 8:46) and Luke's noting that Jesus was "filled with the power of the Spirit" (4:14), we are again to understand that the Spirit, or the power of the eschatological Spirit, has brought about a healing.

The climax of the woman's healing comes with Jesus saying that her faith had made her well. In the context here it cannot be that faith is the psychosomatic cause of the healing. Rather, it is the condition that opens a person to God's power.[60] So faith exists when there is no break in the pattern of divine initiative and human response by means of which a restored relationship to God is established.[61]

Even though Luke has taken it from his source, because he has used it before (Lk 7:50), our attention is drawn to the phrase "Go in peace" (8:48/Mk 5:34). Here this common farewell in Judaism[62] takes on the meaning of having received healing as well as, we can note, salvation from Jesus.

In response to hearing that the girl had died, Jesus tells the delegation, "Do not fear. Only believe." To this Luke adds, "and she will be saved" (*sōthēsetai*, Lk 8:50/Mk 5:36). Once again (cf. Lk 8:36) in the use of *sōzō* Luke sees the raising of the girl to be more than a resuscitation; it is experiencing God's salvation—eschatological salvation.[63]

Characteristic of Luke is his bringing pathos and gentleness to these stories. Here he adds that the girl was an only child (Lk 8:42/Mk 5:23); he removes the criticism of the doctors (Lk 8:43/Mk 5:26); the disciples' retort to Jesus' question as to who touched him is less insulting (Lk 8:45/Mk 5:31); and he explains why the crowd laughs at Jesus (Lk 8:53/Mk 5:40). This may tell us more about Luke himself being a gentle person, rather than any particular message he wished to convey in the miracle stories.

From these stories of Jesus' travels Luke turns increasingly to focus on Jesus' relationship with and teaching of the Twelve. This begins with him sending out the Twelve on mission (Lk 9:1-6) in the shadow of these miracles. When they return (9:10) he feeds the five thousand.

§5.18 Feeding the Five Thousand (Lk 9:10-17/Mt 14:13-21/Mk 6:32-44)

On their return from a mission of healing and teaching the Twelve are taken by Jesus on an unsuccessful attempt to retreat from the crowds. Nevertheless Jesus welcomes the crowd, speaking to them about the kingdom of God (Lk 9:10-11). Once again, even though he suppresses the motif of compassion in not mentioning that the crowds were like sheep without a shepherd (Mk 6:34),[64] Luke's pathos and gentleness are again evident in his adding that Jesus healed "those who needed to be cured" (Lk 9:11/Mk 6:34).

In omitting Mark's long story about the death of John the Baptist (Mk 6:17-29; cf. Lk 3:19-20), Luke is able to make the miracle of the feeding of the five thousand the response to Herod's question, "Who is this . . . ?" (Lk 9:9). And following this story the so-called Great Omission of Markan material from Luke (Mk 6:45—8:26) enables Jesus' question of his identity and Peter's confession (Lk 9:18-20) to arise out of this feeding story. Thus for Luke this story tells us who Jesus is, and Luke wants his readers to conclude that this Jesus is the "Messiah of God" (9:20). The stern charge to silence, which follows a few sentences after this story, and then the teaching that the Son of Man must also suffer (9:21-22) are probably meant to convey to the reader that Jesus—even though identified in the miracles—cannot be correctly identified or understood apart from the passion.

So what this miracle story tells us about Jesus is probably, at least partly, to be found in the echo of the Last Supper in the way Jesus takes, prays (in looking up to heaven),[65] blesses and distributes the food to the disciples (Lk 9:16; cf. 22:17-19). We cannot conclude that this feeding story and the Last Supper are one and the same; there are too many differences. Rather, in the Last Supper's being reflected in the miracle of the feeding and in the subsequent teaching on the need for Jesus to suffer, Luke is probably saying that in his miracles Jesus is not merely performing wonders but, in the echo of the coming suffering, is giving himself to sustain the needy (cf. §3.17).

The theme of the failure of the disciples to comprehend the identity of Jesus and its implications (perhaps meant to be understandable in light of their ignorance about his passion) is maintained in the story of the transfiguration (Lk 9:28-36) and in the miracle story that shows the failure of the disciples to model Jesus' healing (9:37-43a).

At this point (Lk 9:17) Luke departs from following Mark. In so doing Luke has left aside six miracle stories from Mark. This is at first surprising in view of the apparent importance of miracles in the Galilean ministry. The omission of five of these stories[66] occurs in the so-called Great Omission of Mark 6:45—8:26. The omission of this material is most probably not connected with the nature of the miracle stories nor with any deficiency in the version of Mark that Luke knew. Rather, in that Luke carefully limits the ministry of Jesus to Galilee in this part of the Gospel, the most likely explanation for the Great Omission is because it relates to Jesus' ministry outside Israel, in Phoenicia.[67]

Immediately following this story of the miraculous feeding is the question of Jesus' identity (Lk 9:18-20) and other teaching on discipleship (9:21-27). After the revelation of the identity of Jesus through the transfiguration (9:28-37, esp. v. 35) we see the miracle of the healing of the boy with the unclean spirit (9:37-43a), causing the crowd to be astonished at the greatness of God (9:43). To that story I now turn.

§5.19 The Epileptic Boy (Lk 9:37-43a/Mt 17:14-20/Mk 9:14-29)

As we saw to be the case in Matthew's version of this story (see §4.29), Luke has reworked and abbreviated this story. What stands out in Luke's account is Jesus' compassionate response to the man who begged Jesus to look upon his only child (Lk 9:38). Also prominent is Jesus' statement about a "faithless and perverse generation" (9:41). I have argued that Mark has this rebuke directed toward the disciples (Mk 9:19; see §3.26). However, in that Luke is specific in addressing the father ("Bring *your* son here"), the immediately preceding rebuke is clearly intended for him. That is, faith is a prerequisite to miracle. Luke's conformity of the first part of this saying to Deuteronomy 32:5 through the addition of the words "and perverse" strengthens the force of the saying. The message is that God (in Jesus) is being confronted by faithless and perverse people despite all they had seen God (in Jesus) do.

Although this is an exorcism story, Luke not only says Jesus rebuked the unclean spirit; he adds that Jesus "healed the boy" (Lk 9:42). Here we have another example of what will be discussed later: the blurring of the distinction between healings and exorcisms.

In adding that Jesus gave the boy back to the father (Lk 9:42/Mk 9:27) Luke makes a link back to the story of raising the widow's dead son (Lk 7:15), thereby helping build a picture of Jesus' compassion. Also, in concluding that "all were astonished at the greatness of God" (9:43), Luke continues to remind his readers that God is being seen at work in the miracles of Jesus.

This is the last miracle story in Jesus' Galilean ministry in Luke (Lk 4:16—9:50), which comes to a close with the disciples failing to understand a number of things: Jesus' speaking of his betrayal (9:43b-45); their relationships with each other (9:46-48); and their relationship to others (9:49-50). Jesus now journeys to Jerusalem (9:51—19:46).[68]

In this journey Jesus will be portrayed as often being in conflict with the scribes and Pharisees over issues such as his source of power-authority in the Beelzebul controversy (Lk 11:14-28), the demand for a miraculous sign (11:29-32) and the issue of healing on the Sabbath (13:10-17; 14:1-6). Yet some, such as one of the ten lepers (17:11-19) and even the blind man near Jericho (18:35-43), do recognize Jesus. This recognition of who Jesus is and his bringing the salvation of God is the dominant theme of these stories—a topic we will explore later.

§5.20 Controversy over Jesus' Authority for Exorcism (Lk 11:14-23/Mt 9:32-34; 12:22-30/Mk 3:22-27)

In the journey to Jerusalem Jesus performs an exorcism (Lk 11:14), which is seen to prompt the gibe that Jesus casts out demons by Beelzebul, clearly meant to refer to Satan (cf. 11:18). Among other things, Luke has Jesus say that this is a logical impossibility: Satan would be casting out Satan (11:17-18).[69]

The centerpiece of the passage is the saying "But if in God's finger I cast out demons, then has come upon you the kingdom of God" (Lk 11:20, author's translation). As we will discuss in §6.2, it is probable Luke has changed his Q source here from "Spirit" to "finger" (cf. Mt 12:28). In view of God's saying, for example, "I will stretch out my hand and strike Egypt with all my wonders" (Ex 3:20),[70] Luke may have had in mind a parallel between the miracles by which God, in Jesus, also released people from the bondage of Satan (cf. Lk 13:16). In so doing Luke has maintained an important view he holds on the relationship between Jesus and God.

Further, Luke has been at pains to show that Jesus was full of the Holy Spirit (Lk 4:1), that his ministry was in the power of the Spirit (4:14), that he was endowed by the Spirit (4:18) and that he rejoiced in the Spirit (10:21). In other words, Jesus is portrayed as the servant or instrument of the Holy Spirit. Jesus does not "have" or "control" the Spirit. Concomitantly Luke never talks of anyone (including Jesus) as "having" (echein) the Holy Spirit. The Holy Spirit is the controller, not the controlled. Returning to Luke 11:20, it is clear that Luke's retaining "Spirit" here may have given the impression that Jesus "used" the Holy Spirit to perform exorcisms in the same way contemporaries used gods or powerful names.

Also important in understanding Luke's perspective on the miracles—in Luke 11:20 the exorcism of Jesus—is the word ephthasen ("has come"). Albert Schweitzer, among others, took the term to mean that the kingdom of God was near.[71] With this verse in mind Bultmann said categorically, *"All that does not mean that God's Reign is already here; but it does mean that it is dawning."*[72] However, the plain sense of the word *ephthasen* and its accompanying saying is that the longed-for reign of God had actually arrived in the exorcisms that were being conducted by Jesus.[73]

Important here is the emphatic *egō* ("I")[74] by which Luke tells his readers that it is not simply the exorcisms that are important but the one who is performing them. This in turn means for Luke—and for Jesus as well, as we will see in §10.11—that *where the Spirit was operating in Jesus in performing the miracles of exorcism, the reign of God was not merely being illustrated but was being realized.*

Immediately following is the parable of the strong man (Lk 11:21-22), which shows that in the exorcisms Luke understood Jesus to be rescuing those who had been enslaved by Satan.

§5.21 The Sign of Jonah (Lk 11:16, 29-32/Mt 12:38-39/16:1-4/Mk 8:1-13; cf. Jn 6:30)

Not only does the exorcism just noted (Lk 11:14) provoke the criticism that Jesus is casting out demons by the ruler of the demons (11:15) but Luke has already added (cf. Mt 12:24/Mk 3:22) that it has also provoked in others the demand for a sign from heaven (Lk 11:16). By such an early link to this collection of sayings about the sign of Jonah, Luke may intend his readers to conclude that the exorcisms make a sign from heaven unnecessary.[75] The only sign of Jesus' identity and mission to be given will be a ministry such as the one just characterized by an exorcism.

In Luke 11:29-32 Jesus' refusal to give a sign other than the sign of Jonah raises the question of what way Jonah was a sign (cf. §3.23 and §4.28). As in the case of Luke 11:16, in the context of the whole passage (Lk 11:30-32) Jesus and his preaching is the sign, just as the person and preaching of the prophet Jonah was a sign from God sufficient to call people to repent.[76]

§5.22 A Crippled Woman Healed (Lk 13:10-17)

Jesus is still on his journey toward Jerusalem, during which much of the time he is teaching his disciples. Some of that teaching takes place in one of the synagogues (Lk 13:10). As if to balance the teaching with some healing by Jesus,[77] Luke introduces a woman in need of healing while Jesus is in the synagogue teaching. In contrast to the harshness of the Jewish authorities—characterized by the synagogue setting, which in 12:11 and 21:12 is even said to be the place of persecution—Jesus shows the graciousness of God (cf. 13:16-17) in the miracle of healing.

That even in the healing Jesus is involved in conflict at a cosmic level is suggested not only by the synagogue setting but in the way the healing is described. The woman is depicted as having a spirit that had crippled her (Lk 13:11) and as having been bound by Satan for eighteen years (13:16). Since we encountered this same perspective on the healings in Luke's story of the healing of Simon's mother-in-law (4:38-39), we cannot avoid noting Luke's view that healings as well as exorcisms are a piece in being essential in the defeat of the demonic.[78]

Furthermore, by juxtaposing this healing with the preceding parable of the growth of the fig tree (Lk 13:1-9), this theme is highlighted: as to the fig tree, so to this neglected daughter of Abraham will special attention or grace be extended.[79] Luke's conclusion to the story, that all Jesus' opponents were put to shame (13:17), echoes Isaiah 45:16. This, along with the crowd's rejoicing at "all the wonderful things" (cf. Ex 34:10), suggests Luke sees the healing as a fulfillment of Old Testament hope.

§5.23 A Man with Dropsy Healed (Lk 14:1-6)

Though separated from it by teaching—primarily about the end of the age (Lk 13:18-30)—and by a brief note concerning some Pharisees warning Jesus about Herod (13:31-35), this miracle story is parallel to the previous one: both healings are expressions of mercy taking precedence over regulations relating to the sabbath, and both are conducted on sabbaths in the presence of Jesus' opponents, shaming them in the first and silencing them here. The sabbath setting also highlights the divine authority being exercised by Jesus in the miracle (cf. Lk 6:5).

The story also provides a meal scene for the next four sections of this chapter (Lk 14:1-24), reinforcing the importance of the setting for this miracle. Meals are frequent in Luke.[80] In light of the significance of hospitality and the sharing of food in Luke[81] and the widespread use of the banquet as a messianic symbol,[82] as well as the parable of the great banquet in 14:15-24, this healing miracle becomes an expression of the fulfillment of eschatological hopes.

In passing we can note that *dropsy* (*hudrōpikos,* Lk 14:2), a term that had been used since Hippocrates, does not describe a disease. It refers to the symptom of the body swelling through the accumulation of fluid in the body cavities and tissue spaces caused by a disease of the heart, liver or kidneys, for example.[83]

§5.24 Ten Lepers Cleansed (Lk 17:11-19)

This story comes toward the end of what for the readers is the confusing or circuitous journey of Jesus to Jerusalem.[84]

The lepers initially call out to Jesus for "mercy" (Lk 17:13). In light of the mercy of God being seen as his salvation in the Old Testament,[85] this is a story about a salvation that includes healing.[86] Accordingly, when one of the lepers notices that he is healed, he "returns"[87] to Jesus praising God (17:15). To this action Jesus responds later in the story,"Your faith has made you well" (or "saved you," 17:19).

This use of *sōzein* ("to save") is the unavoidable clue that Luke wants his readers to understand that this leper was not merely healed. In his initial willingness to call to Jesus and probably also in his returning to praise God, he had also opened himself to God's salvation, which includes healing. That this returning to give thanks was one of the factors in the man being pronounced "saved" is obvious in that the other nine were not so pronounced.[88]

This story then is one of contrasts: between ungrateful Jews and grateful Samaritans (Lk 17:16); between those who receive healing from Jesus and those grateful few who also receive salvation (17:19). That is, for salvation to be received—to follow Marshall—"to faith must be added thanksgiving."[89] We are obliged to agree with Betz that healing and salvation are not the same thing for Luke in this particular story.[90]

§5.25 A Blind Man Healed (Lk 18:35-43/Mk 10:46-52/Mt 20:29-34)

In this the last major miracle story in Luke, still Jesus journeys toward Jerusalem, meeting a blind man on the outskirts of Jericho (Lk 18:35). Its importance to Luke can be judged not only by its being the last full miracle story before Jesus arrives in Jerusalem but also by its being Luke's only story of the healing of a blind person (discounting the general reference to Jesus giving sight to many who were blind in the presence of the delegation from John the Baptist, 7:21; cf. §5.14).

The context of this story is particularly telling in that what Jesus has just said about his impending death he also says is hidden from the disciples, who are not able to grasp what he said (Lk 18:31-34). Therefore the story of this blind man being healed and immediately following Jesus toward Jerusalem highlights not just the blindness of the uncomprehending disciples but also how obvious to their sight ought to have been Jesus' identity and power.

Luke makes a number of minor stylistic changes to Mark, his source. Some smooth out the story,[91] but most are of little significance.[92] However, some changes and details are of particular interest in understanding Luke's perspective on this and other miracles of Jesus.

1. In the Greek Old Testament (LXX) the word *boaō* was used for the needy cry of the oppressed and downtrodden to God.[93] So by using *boaō* ("I cry" or "I call" out) instead of *krazō* (also "I cry" or "I call" out), Luke is probably signaling to his readers that this man is calling out to God for help (Lk 18:38/Mk 10:47).

2. Mark has the man throw off his cloak, a symbol of leaving his past behind. Luke omits this detail (Lk 18:40/Mk 10:50). Was this to symbolize that, when compared to following Jesus, the past is of no significance?

3. Instead of having Jesus respond to the blind man's request by saying, "Go; your faith has saved you" (Mark 10:52, author's translation), Luke has Jesus say, "Receive your sight; your faith has saved you" (Lk 18:42). This makes Jesus' power

to heal the focus of attention rather than the man's faith, which is more closely related to his seeking Jesus in the face of the crowd's discouragement. Thus even though the word *power* does not appear here, this miracle is another instance of Jesus using Spirit-power to perform a miracle (cf. Lk 4:14)—a connection perhaps made even more obvious through the fulfillment of the eschatological expectation of sight being given to the blind (cf. 4:18; 7:22; Is 61:1).

As in Mark the blind man calls out to Jesus the "Son of David" to "have mercy" on him. In this address Luke is holding together Jesus the great healer with Jesus the bringer of salvation (cf. *sōzein*, Lk 18:42). Further, not only is Jesus the bringer of both, but healing can be salvation when the cure results in recognizing healing to be the work of God and in following Jesus (cf. §5.24 on 17:11-19). The final addition to the story of the healed man glorifying God and the people praising God (Lk 18:43) is a common way for Luke to draw attention to the miracle being the work of God.

§5.26 Healing the High Priest's Servant's Ear (Lk 22:50-51)

After healing the blind man (Lk 18:35-43) and meeting Zacchaeus (19:1-10), Jesus arrives in Jerusalem (19:11), where he ministers in the city and its temple (19:47—21:38). At that point Luke begins the passion narrative (22:1—24:53). Tucked away in the story of Jesus' arrest is the tiny story of one of the followers of Jesus using a sword to strike the slave of the high priest, cutting off his right ear. Having issued a reprimand to his follower, Jesus touches the slave's ear and heals him (22:50-51/Mk 14:47). This cameo not only shows that Luke wishes to portray Jesus as motivated by compassion but also highlights the compassionate character of Luke: "the scribe of the gentleness of Christ," as Dante described him.[94]

§5.27 A Parable in Place of a Miracle

At this point we can note that in Mark's Gospel Jesus curses a fig tree just before he arrives in Jerusalem (Mk 11:12-14, 20-26).[95] Not so in Luke, even though he is following the general arrangement of Mark. The omission of the story of the cursing of the fig tree has been variously explained.[96]

Some, for example, have suggested that the story was not in the version of Mark that Luke had before him. However, modern scholarship has widely tested and generally accepted the view that Luke knew the Gospel of Mark as we have it. Others have advocated that the miracle in Mark has been omitted because it conveyed the same message as the parable that replaces it (Lk 13:6-9). Adolf Jülicher went so far as to say the miracle was omitted because Luke recognized that it had no obvious religious significance.[97]

Luke, however, has exchanged the fig-tree miracle for a parable of a fig tree (Lk 13:6-9), most probably because of the clear, yet different, message inherent in each. On the one hand, no grace is offered in the Markan miracle story. The tree is barren, it is cursed, and on inspection the next morning, Jesus and the disciples see the tree withered from its roots (Mk 11:20). The message or implication is that Jerusalem and its temple have come under the judgment of Jesus (Mk 11:15-17).

On the other hand, for Luke, Jesus is less an instrument of judgment (cf. Lk 9:52-56) and more one who pleads for and offers grace (13:1-9). Indeed, at the point where Mark has the miracle of the cursing of the fig tree (Mk 11:12-14), Luke has Jesus weep over the city.[98] Similarly Luke gives Jerusalem a positive function in his story of salvation[99] and the life of the early church.[100]

Luke in turn softens opposition to the temple and the cultus he finds in Mark through the abbreviation of the "cleansing,"[101] omitting the reference to Jesus' forbidding anyone to carry anything through the temple (Mk 11:16) and removing the charge that Jesus threatened to destroy the temple (Mk 14:58 and 15:29-30). Only when the good news of Jesus moves beyond Jerusalem does Luke allow the temple to be denounced (Acts 7:48-51).[102] Thus, where Mark has Jesus perform a miracle by cursing the tree (and the temple), Luke has a parable of a tree that is offered a period of reprieve before the assumed fate (cf. Lk 23:26-31).

That Jesus is to be portrayed as one who offers grace rather than punishment may explain why he does not perform any miracles that inflict divine punishment.[103] In Luke 1:20 Zechariah is struck dumb because he did not believe the words of the angel Gabriel, and Acts has a number of punitive miracles,[104] perhaps the most striking difference between the miracle stories in Luke and those in Acts.[105] But none of these punitive miracles is portrayed as being at the hands of the earthly Jesus.[106]

It is notable that during Jesus' ministry in Jerusalem (Lk 19:11—21:38) Luke has no major miracle stories. Apart from the resurrection, the only miracle story in the passion narrative is that of Jesus replacing the right ear of the high priest's servant (Lk 22:50-51). Though miracles may have receded from Jesus' ministry, it cannot be concluded that miracles no longer have a place in Luke's understanding of God's economy. The abundance of miracles in Acts tells against that view.

Partly through the miracles Jesus' identity has already been established—their function has been fulfilled. Apart from the triumphal entry into Jerusalem (Lk 19:28-44) and his cleansing of the temple (19:45-48), Jesus' ministry in Jerusalem is dominated by the discourse about the coming destruction of the temple and the end of the age (21:5-36). In this material the miraculous happenings mentioned are no longer understood to draw people to trust in Jesus. Instead, miracles are said either to be dreadful portents (21:11) signaling the shaking of the universe (21:26) or to be used by leaders to deceive people (21:8).

§5.28 The Next Step

Through this examination of each of Luke's miracle stories in the context of his plot and arrangement of material, we have identified some of the themes and issues at the heart of his treatment of the miracles of Jesus. In the next chapter we will be able to explore these in more detail. We will also take up other issues in the contemporary debate about Luke that impinge upon his view of the miracles.

Six

The Miracles
of Jesus in Luke

The Issues

••

§6.1 Introduction

Luke's interpretation of the miracles of Jesus presents us with a number of interesting issues. For example, views on the meaning of the miracles for Luke range from Reginald H. Fuller, who says they are "the most important part of Jesus' biography prior to his passion,"[1] to Paul J. Achtemeier, who says Luke "attempts to balance Jesus' miraculous activity and his teaching in such a way as to give them equal weight."[2] Eduard Schweizer has argued that the miracles are never ascribed to the Spirit.[3] Max Turner has argued the opposite.[4] We will be able to assess the accuracy of these conclusions in light of our investigations in the previous chapter. Also, John M. Hull's view that Luke's tradition is "permeated by magic"[5] needs to be taken into account, for it has caused some debate.[6]

§6.2 The Spirit and Miracles

The story of the opening of Jesus' public ministry in Nazareth (Lk 4:16-30) has given rise to considerable debate in contemporary scholarship: Does Luke portray the Spirit as a direct source of Jesus' miracles of healing, exorcism or marvelous deeds?

Schweizer has stated, "Though the miracles are important for Luke, they are never ascribed to the Spirit."[7] This is, he says, because Luke shares with Judaism the view that the Spirit is essentially the Spirit of prophecy, preventing him from directly attributing miracles to the Spirit.[8]

To begin with, it is not difficult to show that in the Judaism of Luke's world the Spirit was at least occasionally seen to be the source of the miraculous as well as of prophecy. In translating the Old Testament the Septuagint uses "the Spirit of the Lord" *(pneuma kuriou)* where there is no doubt the miraculous is involved. For example, in Judges 15:14 "the Spirit of the Lord rushed on [Samson], and the ropes that were on his arms became like flax that has caught fire, and his bonds melted off his hands" (cf. Judg 14:6, 19). Also, the Spirit of the Lord is said to pick up and transport Ezekiel from one place to another.[9]

In the Targums, the Aramaic translations of the Old Testament, the Spirit is used in contexts where the miraculous is in mind, as in the story of Samson.[10] Although at a number of places Josephus omits references to the Spirit in contexts where the miraculous is mentioned,[11] he does portray the Spirit of God as the source of Elijah's ability to disable or wither a hand (*Ant.* 8:408; cf. 8:346). Pseudo-Philo also says that Kenaz, "clothed with the Spirit of power," was "changed into another man."[12] Clearly the Judaism of Luke's era did—even if infrequently—directly associate the Spirit with the miraculous. More specifically, it can be shown that Schweizer's statement that Luke never attributed miracles to the Spirit is incorrect.

It is argued that at 4:18 Luke changes Isaiah 61:1-2 and introduces Isaiah 58:6 to draw attention to the Spirit as the power for Jesus' preaching and, simultaneously, eliminates reference to the miraculous.[13]

First, it is suggested that the removal of "to bind up" *[iasasthai]* the broken-hearted (Is 61:1d) is motivated by a desire to sever any connection between the Spirit and physical healing.[14] There is no doubt that, for Luke, "to bind up" *(iaomai)* was a technical word for physical healing.[15] But Luke also uses *iaomai* metaphorically of healing dull hearts and ears that will not listen, as he does in Acts 28:27.[16] More important, the context of "broken hearts" in Isaiah 61:1 is most likely to have associated with it a metaphorical rather than a physical sense of healing.[17] Thus his removal of the word and phrase cannot easily be seen as due to his wishing to distance the Spirit from physical healing.[18]

Second, it is suggested that Luke has changed the "call" *(kalesai)* in Isaiah 61:2 to "proclaim" *(kruxai)* to emphasize that the Spirit's anointing is for proclamation. However, as we saw in the previous chapter, it is typical of Luke for Jesus' word of command to effect miraculous healings.[19] Thus Luke's change in this word is unlikely to be motivated by a desire to distance the miraculous from the anointing of Jesus with the Spirit.

Third, it is suggested that Luke has introduced the phrase "to let the oppressed go free *[aphesei]*" from Isaiah 58:6 because of its reference to forgiveness. As is well known, every other use of *aphesis* in Luke-Acts, as well as in the rest of the New Testament, is collocated with "sin," or as in Hebrews 9:22 contextually implies sin being forgiven. But collocated with "captives" *(aichmalōtois)* and "oppressed" or "broken" *(tethrausmenoi),* as it is in Luke 4:18, *aphesis* would reasonably mean release, freedom or liberty. Moreover, Luke never depicts sin as an oppressive burden. Instead it is the miraculous healings and exorcisms that Luke depicts as release, freedom or liberty.[20]

Clearly the changes Luke makes to Isaiah 61:1-2 and 58:6 do not appear to be intended to eliminate reference to miraculous healing. Indeed, there are two other aspects of Luke's quotation from Isaiah 61:1-2 that show he is doing the very opposite of distancing the miraculous from Jesus' empowerment by the Spirit.

First, one line has the words "and to the blind recovery of sight" (*kai tuphlois anablepsin*, Lk 4:18, author's translation). There is no doubt a metaphorical aspect to such a phrase.[21] However, in the story of the disciples of John the Baptist asking if Jesus was "the one who is to come" (Lk 7:20), Luke takes the idea literally. In the presence of the inquirers, Jesus is said to heal many, including the giving of sight to the blind (Lk 7:21). More significantly this literal giving of sight to the blind is then applied to the prophecy in Isaiah 61:1 (Lk 7:22). Further, in retelling Mark's story of the healing of blind Bartimaeus Luke adds to Jesus' command "Receive your sight" (*anablepson*, 18:42), using the same word as in 4:18.

Second, we saw in the story of the healing of Simon's mother-in-law the woman is described as seized, shut up or hard pressed *(sunechein)* by the fever (Lk 4:38; cf. §5.5). Since Luke uses this word for being held prisoner (Lk 22:63) and describes Jesus' ministry as proclaiming release to the captives because the Spirit of the Lord is upon him (4:18), it is hard to avoid the conclusion that Luke wants to make a connection between the Spirit and healing.

It is reasonable to assume, then, that in 4:18 Luke had in mind Jesus' miraculous healing. In turn and of great import then, the miraculous healings that form part of the backdrop to this verse are directly and deliberately linked with the Spirit's being upon Jesus, for the quotation begins, "The Spirit of the Lord is upon me" (Lk 4:18a).

Another passage said to show that Luke wished to distance the Spirit from the source of Jesus' miracles is Luke 11:20: "But if in God's finger [Matthew has "Spirit"] I cast out demons, then has come upon you the kingdom of God" (author's translation).[22] It was once generally agreed that Luke's "finger of God" was the original.[23] More recently, however, Matthew's "Spirit" is thought more likely to reflect the original.[24] In turn it is argued that Luke's change to "finger" was motivated by a desire to distance the Spirit from empowering Jesus' miracles.[25]

However, on the one hand, we can explain Luke's dropping "Spirit" (as he does in Lk 20:42) and replacing it with "finger." First, Luke is the only New Testament writer to take up the equivalent anthropomorphisms, the "hand of God"[26] and the "arm of the Lord" (Lk 1:31; Acts 13:17). Second, Luke has strong new exodus and Mosaic Christology themes that could explain his desire to take up the phrase "finger of God" here.[27] Similarly, third, the replacement of Spirit with finger brings out a parallel between the miracles of Jesus and those that brought Israel out of bondage.[28]

In any case, it is quite likely that the first readers of Luke would have understood the "finger of God" as referring to the "Spirit of God," for that was how the related "hand of God" was understood.[29] And we know from Acts that Luke uses "hand" of the Lord where he could have used "Spirit."[30]

On the other hand, in light of Matthew's using the phrase kingdom of "God" instead of his usual "heaven" and his likelihood of preferring "finger" if it was in his source—it would have enabled him to maintain his Moses typology (cf. Ex 8:19)—we can take Matthew's version with "Spirit" in it to be original.[31] From this exploration of Luke 4:18 and 11:20, there is no doubt Luke saw the Spirit as equally the source of Jesus' miracles and of his teaching.

There is a further passage to account for in the argument that Luke wanted to distance the Spirit from Jesus' miracles. It is Luke's placing of the saying about blasphemy against the Holy Spirit (Lk 12:10).[32] In Mark and Q the saying relates to the accusation that Jesus' exorcisms were possible because he was possessed by a demon. Luke positions the saying in the context of Jesus speaking to his followers about how they are to behave when encountering opposition. This change of setting is perfectly understandable as an extension of the meaning of the saying in its Markan and Q setting. That is, failure to witness with the Spirit in times of trial is also blasphemy against the Spirit.[33]

This is not the only case of Luke making such a change. In Mark 13:11 the Spirit is expected to provide the followers of Jesus with what to say when they are taken to court. Luke, however, changes this to Jesus giving wisdom on such occasions (Lk 21:15). Jesus' miracles are not in view here. Thus it is unnecessary to posit the view that Luke wishes to distance the Spirit from Jesus' miracles in his reworking of the blasphemy saying.

§6.3 Power and Miracles

Instead of the Spirit empowering miracles, Schweizer says, "Healing power is associated with the name of Jesus, with faith in Jesus, with Jesus Himself, with prayer, with bodily contact through the disciples, his shadow or his handkerchief, or more simply with the *dunamis* of Jesus."[34] This last point, that Luke attributes miracles to *dunamis* ("power"), is correct and easily established. That is, of the four places Luke attributes Jesus' miracles to *dunamis,* three of them are redactional.[35]

However, the issue is complicated by Luke using *power* and *Spirit* together.[36] It cannot be, as is sometimes argued, that Luke ascribes miracles to *dunamis* ("power") and reserves *pneuma* ("spirit") as solely the source of Jesus' proclamation, for in Luke 1:35 "the Holy Spirit" and "the power of the Most High" coming on Mary to conceive seem to be parallel or synonymous phrases.

Dunamis and *pneuma* are also used together in Acts 10:38: "God anointed Jesus of Nazareth with the Holy Spirit and with power; . . . he went about doing good and healing." It is difficult here to see how Jesus being anointed with the Holy Spirit and with power can be seen as separate sources for proclamation and miracles. Also, it cannot be that *dunamis* when combined with *pneuma* refers to persuasive speech, for Max Turner has drawn attention to the point that in Luke 1:35—the announcement of the conception of Jesus—no speech is in mind. Further, Turner has made the point that apart from Micah 3:8 "virtually *all* occasions where *dunamis* and *pneuma* appear closely collocated [they] refer to powerful or miraculous actions, not to speech (or at least, not to speech alone)."[37]

Even where pre-Lukan Christianity combined "power" and "Spirit" in referring to preaching, miracles were probably thought to be associated with the proclamation.[38] Therefore it is highly unlikely that by using *dunamis* Luke is attempting to distance the Spirit from being the source of Jesus' miracles.

There is the further nuanced suggestion that the Spirit is the source of power *(dunamis)*, which in turn is the source of Jesus' miracles.[39] However, this is unnecessary and complicates the phrase *hē dunamis tou pneumatos* (Lk 4:14) to mean "the power generated by the Spirit" instead of the more natural "the potency or ability given by the Spirit,"[40] as in Romans 15:13. It is then sound to conclude that, for Luke, miracles are to be attributed directly to the Spirit or to the power of the Spirit.

§6.4 Magic as the Power for Miracles

In noting *dunamis* as a source of Jesus' miracles, John M. Hull has argued for seeing Luke and Acts as a "tradition penetrated by magic."[41] To support his case Hull successively traces Luke's view of angels, demons and magical power. However, in relation to the motifs about angels and demons, Luke adopts essentially the same position as his sources, Mark and Q.[42]

Concerning *dunamis* Hull says that Luke regards it as "a substance, a *mana*-like[43] charge of divine potency, spiritual in so far as it emanates from the world of spirits, but actual, as vital as the beings who possess it."[44] Hull draws attention to Luke 5:17 ("the power of the Lord was with him to heal") and 8:46 ("someone touched me"). He concludes that *dunamis* works immediately and impersonally, responding to the contact of any believing person without the knowledge or approval of Jesus. Therefore, as difficult as it may be for us to comprehend, in light of 5:17 (just quoted), as we shortly will see, we probably ought to conclude that Luke supposed that Jesus experienced fluctuations in the availability of his power.[45]

According to Hull, the background to this conception is not to be found in the Old Testament. Rather, relying on Friedrich Preisigke's study of the story of the woman with a hemorrhage, Hull says that Luke's view springs from the universal idea of the magical miracles.[46]

To take up this last point, in following Preisigke, Hull has artificially forged a unity of conception across material from ancient Egypt to the church of the Middle Ages.[47] And Hull has such a broad definition of magic that it may include any sort of belief in angels and demons, and any exorcism is automatically described as magical.[48]

Whatever Luke's conception of *dunamis*, contrary to Hull there is clearly considerable influence from the Old Testament, for Luke uses *dunamis* in the two senses found in the Septuagint: in the sense of a miracle itself[49] and in the sense of "the host of heaven."[50] Luke also associates *dunamis* with God,[51] the Holy Spirit[52] and the returning Son of Man,[53] which reflects Septuagintal usage. That is, fifteen of twenty-five instances of *dunamis* in Luke and Acts seem to reflect Old Testament (Septuagintal) use.[54]

Nevertheless in light of references such as Jesus noticing that power had gone out of him (Lk 8:46) and the crowd trying to touch Jesus because power came out from him to heal them (6:19), it seems judicious to conclude, with Hull, that *dunamis* is a *mana*-like charge working impersonally, responding to the contact of any believer. However, this conception of *dunamis* has its origins in the Septuagint rather than in a universal idea of magical miracles.

Further, with Hull, it must be conceded that in 6:19 (the crowds "were trying to touch him, for power came out from him") Luke does not correct the impression that *dunamis* works immediately and impersonally. And in Acts, Luke gives the clear impression that *dunamis* appears to observers to operate this way. Thus Simon Magus believed and was so amazed when he saw the signs and great powers *(dunameis)* that took place in the laying on of hands that he offered money for authority *(exousia)* to dispense the Spirit through his hands (Acts 8:19).

Nevertheless, though it may appear that the Spirit is an independent substance, Luke corrects this view by having Peter say, "May your silver perish with you!" (Acts 8:20). Also, in the story of the woman with a hemorrhage, to whom healing power was transferred when she touched Jesus, a possible wrong conclusion is corrected when Jesus says to the woman, "Your faith has made you well" (Lk 8:48). Thus Luke recognizes that *dunamis* appears to function and is experienced as a *mana*-like substance. But it is more than that: it is the powerful presence of God's Spirit received for healing *through faith*. To that important issue we now turn.

§6.5 Miracles as the Mighty and Merciful Work of God

From the beginning of his Gospel, Luke's message is that, in Jesus (including his miracles), God is fulfilling his promise to bring salvation to his people.[55] In the first chapter, the "Benedictus" begins "Blessed be the Lord God of Israel, for he has looked favorably on his people and redeemed them" (Lk 1:67-79). In 1:78 this visitation of God is applied to the Messiah.[56]

We have seen that the link between God's work of salvation and the miracles of Jesus is made explicit in Luke's use of *sōzein* in the healing stories,[57] for the nouns *sōtēria* and *sōtērion* ("salvation") have broad meanings that include both salvation and healing.[58] And in the opening stories of Jesus' ministry God's healing is being brought by Jesus, the promised eschatological prophet (Lk 4:16-44, esp. v. 18), a theme reiterated in responses to the raising of the boy from Nain: "A great prophet has risen among us!" and "God has looked favorably on his people!" (7:16). Yet we cannot say that healing and salvation are synonymous; that is made clear in the story of the healing of the ten lepers. Only the one who turned back and praised God (17:15) is said to receive salvation (*sōzein*, 17:19; see §5.24).

Luke has rewritten the three healing stories in the opening stages of Jesus' ministry (Lk 4:31-37, 38-39, 40-44) to highlight miracles, exorcisms in particular, as the work of God.

1. In the first story Mark has the demon cry out after Jesus has commanded submission (Mk 1:26/Lk 4:31-37), but Luke omits this apparent disobedience to Jesus (4:35). At the end of verse 35 Luke adds that despite the violence of the situation the man was done no harm; Jesus was in control.

2. In the second story, the healing of Peter's mother-in-law, Luke also makes changes to draw attention to Jesus' power and authority (Lk 4:38-39). Mark 1:30 says that the woman was ill, but Luke says she was gripped or seized with fever (Lk 4:38). He also says that the fever was great. Then in verse 39, as a result of Jesus' healing, Luke adds that she was well immediately *(parachrēma)* and that she got up *(anastasa)*.

3. In the third story—relating an evening of healing (Lk 4:40-41)—where Mark simply says that the demons know him (Mk 1:34), Luke has the demons cry out, "You are the Son of God" (Lk 4:41). In view of Gabriel's declaration to Mary about the conception (1:35), Luke probably intends his readers to see Jesus as more than an adopted son of God in 4:41. The filial relationship is so unique that Luke appears in some ways almost to identify Jesus and God.[59]

That God is at work in the healings of Jesus is illustrated through other stories. First, when Peter realized that the large catch of fish had come about through Jesus, "he fell down at Jesus' knees, saying, 'Go away from me Lord'" (Lk 5:8). Although Luke uses *Lord* in dialogue as a polite form of address (e.g., 9:6; 19:8, 18), it is unlikely his readers would have failed to see more in Peter's address. Luke's use of *Lord,* the most frequent title for Jesus in Luke-Acts, is one of the devices he uses to focus attention on God being at work in the miracles of Jesus, for pre-Christian Jews occasionally used *Lord* to refer to Yahweh.[60]

Luke ends the story of the paralytic not only with the crowd glorifying God,[61] as in Mark (Mk 2:12/Lk 5:26), but with the healed man going home glorifying God (Lk 5:25).

On seeing the widow's son raised to life, Luke says, "Fear seized all of them; and they glorified God, saying, 'A great prophet has risen among us!' and 'God has looked favorably on his people!' " (Lk 7:16-17).[62]

In the story of the Gadarene demoniac (Mk 5:1-20/Lk 8:26-39), Mark has the demon attempt to put a spell on Jesus, warding him off with the words "I bind you by God" (Mk 5:7, author's translation). But Luke changes this to have the demon simply ask Jesus not to torment him (Lk 8:28). The natural conclusion the reader draws is that no demon ought dare attempt such a thing. In Mark 5:10 the demons address Jesus as they might any other exorcist, asking not to be sent out of the region (cf. Tobit 8:3). However, Luke heightens his eschatological characterization of Jesus by having the demons plead not to be sent into the abyss, the traditional place for demons to be locked until the final judgment (see §5.16). At the end of the story Mark has Jesus tell the man to go and tell "how much the Lord has done for you" (Mk 5:19). Luke dispels any ambiguity as to the identity of "the Lord," for the man declares "how much God has done for you" (Lk 8:39).

For Luke, the work of God is evident in his unique story of Jesus raising the widow of Nain's son (Lk 7:11-17). At the least the telling of the story is related to the story of Elijah raising the son of the widow of Zarephath (1 Kings 17:8-24).[63] Jesus acts authoritatively in telling the young man to sit up (Lk 7:8). The response is immediate (7:10). The response of the witnesses is to say not only "A great prophet has arisen among us" but also "God has looked favorably on his people" (7:16). As this story is a parallel to the preceding one about the healing of the centurion's servant (7:1-10), this response of God being at work in the miracles applies to both stories.

In the story of the epileptic boy (Mk 9:14-29/Lk 9:37-43), Luke has heightened the severity of the boy's condition (and hence heightened Jesus' power) through adding that the demon would hardly leave the boy (9:39). Whereas in Mark, Jesus questions the father about the illness, in Luke, Jesus does not need to ask any questions to effect the healing (Mk 9:21-22/Lk 9:42-43). And in Luke, Jesus heals the boy immediately rather than in two stages (cf. Mk 9:25-27 and Lk 9:42), even though there is a trace of the two-stage healing in Jesus' rebuking the unclean spirit *and* healing the boy (9:42).

Particularly in the stories of the man covered with leprosy (Lk 5:12-15), the crippled woman (13:10-17) and the ten lepers (17:11-19), Jesus expresses the mercy of God to outsiders who have been excluded by their sickness.[64] Others are shown to have been excluded from the merciful work of God by the sabbath. We have already seen in the story of Jesus healing the crippled woman that in the healing ministry of Jesus the sabbath and the synagogue no longer exclude people from God's merciful salvation (13:10-17). The story of the healing of the man with dropsy (14:1-6), similar in structure and content to that of the crippled woman, also shows the sabbath as a day of mercy and healing (14:5) in Jesus' ministry.[65]

This same conclusion—that for Luke the miracles are the mighty and merciful works of God—is evident in his frequent saying that as the result of a miracle the person was healed[66] or the crowd[67] praised or glorified God. Luke's most frequently used word here is *doxazō* ("glorify"). Using this word, which is derived from *doxa* (denoting the "divine and heavenly radiance"),[68] means that in the miracles Luke is portraying those healed and those who witness the miracles as able to share in the radiance and majesty of God.

In short, Jesus' bringing the salvation of God, the use of "Lord" for Jesus, the editorial changes to the miracle stories (especially their conclusions), the healings of Jesus that emphasize the inclusion of outsiders and the ensuing glorifying of God by the healed as well as the spectators show that in the miracles of Jesus the work of God is to be apprehended. Further, the recipients of the healings are among those able to receive salvation or able to participate in the reign or presence of God in Jesus' ministry.[69] This conclusion is required to be nuanced in light of the story of the healing of the ten lepers, which we saw to be one of contrasts: between ungrateful Jews and grateful Samaritans (Lk 17:16), and between those who receive healing from Jesus and those grateful few who also receive salvation (17:19). That is, healing and salvation are not necessarily identical. For salvation to take place, thanksgiving is to be added to faith.[70]

§6.6 The Place of Exorcism
We must deal specifically with the exorcism stories because of the notable difference between the understanding that Mark and Luke have of these stories.

Mark begins his Gospel by giving the impression that exorcism was the most significant feature of Jesus' ministry. However, as his Gospel progresses, this impression changes—exorcism becomes only one of a number of aspects of Jesus' ministry, as it is in Mark 4:1—5:43. Then in Mark 6:1—9:29 there are only two exorcism stories (Mk 7:24-30; 9:14-29). After the reference to the so-called strange exorcist (9:38-41), Mark drops all reference to exorcism. Jesus no longer confronts demonic sickness but rather confronts religious opponents, principally the scribes (e.g., Mk 11:27—12:34).

In contrast to this approach, Luke balances Jesus' exorcisms with the other

aspects of his ministry. Indeed, as his story progresses Luke increases the significance of exorcism and dealing with the demonic as an integral part of Jesus'
ministry in order to produce a balance.

First, Jesus' being full of, or empowered and led by, the Spirit[71] is shown to lead
him not only to preaching the kingdom of God[72] and to healing (Lk 4:18, 40) but
also to a ministry of exorcism (4:31-41). These three important aspects of Jesus'
ministry having been illustrated are then brought together in the summary of the
first stage of Jesus' public ministry (4:40-44).

Second, Luke recasts some of the healing stories as exorcisms in order to increase
the significance of exorcism (see also Lk 13:10-17). In the healing of Peter's
mother-in-law, Mark simply says that the woman had a fever and that Jesus healed
her by taking her by the hand and lifting her up (Mk 1:29-34). But Luke (4:38-41)
says that Jesus "rebuked" (*epetimēsen*, 4:39) the fever—a word we have seen to be
characteristic of a report describing the action of an exorcist.[73] Also, in contrast to
Mark saying that Jesus took the woman by the hand, Luke says that Jesus "stood
over her" and "rebuked" the fever (Mk 1:31/Lk 4:39). In this way not only has
Luke recast the story as an exorcism but by means of the word *rebuke* he has linked
the first three healing stories with an exorcism motif (4:35, 39, 41; see §5.5).

On the other hand, Luke also portrays Jesus' dealing with the demonic as if he
is performing a healing. Thus, as we have seen, in the summary of healings at the
beginning of the Sermon on the Plain he does not say that Jesus rebuked the
unclean spirits but healed "those who were troubled with unclean spirits" (Lk
6:18). In this we see that among the Gospel writers Luke has the least clear
distinction between healing and exorcism. Also, Luke not only blurs the distinction
between healing in general and exorcism in particular, but (and this may explain
why he so easily includes exorcism in the summaries of Jesus' healing ministry) he
in effect gives all sickness a demonic and cosmic dimension; in all healing God's
adversary is being subdued and the person released as is a prisoner from jail. This
is not to say, however, that Luke thought that all illness was caused by demons.[74]
There is, for example, no specific demonic dimension to the healing of the lepers
(Lk 5:12-16; 17:11-19).

Third, to sustain the impression that exorcism remained an important aspect of
Jesus' ministry, Luke inserts brief mentions of Jesus dealing with the demonic.
Thus, when the disciples of John the Baptist asked if Jesus was "he who is to come
or shall we look for another?" (Lk 7:20, author's translation), Luke adds the words
"In that hour he cured many of diseases and plagues and evil spirits, and on many
who were blind he bestowed sight" (7:21, author's translation; cf. Mt 11:3-4).
Also, the little biographical statement in Luke 13:32 ("Go and tell that fox,
'Behold, I cast out demons and perform cures today and tomorrow, and the third
day I finish my course'") has the effect of maintaining the high status of exorcism

in Luke's portrait of Jesus. The same end is served by Luke's introduction to the Sermon on the Plain, which says that people came to be cured of being troubled by evil spirits, as well as to hear Jesus (6:17-19).

Fourth, as we have noted, whereas Mark does not mention exorcism after referring to the so-called strange exorcist (Mk 9:38-41), Luke sustains the importance of exorcism through the Beelzebul controversy,[75] the story of the return of the evil spirit (Mt 12:43-45/Lk 11:24-26) and the story of the crippled woman whom Satan had bound (Lk 13:10-17).

Even though, apart from the story of the crippled woman, Luke did not introduce any conventional exorcism stories into the latter part of his Gospel, in these ways he has heightened the place of exorcism in his story and brought it into balance with other aspects of Jesus' ministry.

§6.7 The Significance of Exorcisms

With Jesus' exorcisms being so important among the miracles for Luke, it is necessary to inquire about their significance. One of the most important verses here is Luke 11:20: "But if in God's finger I cast out demons, then has come upon you the kingdom of God" (author's translation). Once again we are seeing that in Jesus God is at work or his presence is manifest (e.g., 8:37-39 and §5.20).

From the parable of the strong man (Lk 11:21-22), which follows this saying, it is assumed this coming of the reign or kingdom of God involves the destruction of the reign of Satan. Most probably as a parable of exorcism, the story of the strong man means that the defeat of Satan was, for Luke as for Jesus, taking place in the exorcisms. The use of *ekballō* ("I cast out") helps confirm this.

The Septuagint uses *ekballō* mostly in the context of an enemy, having frustrated or stood in the way of God's fulfilling his purpose for his chosen people, being cast out so that God's purpose can be fulfilled (cf. Ex 23:30; Deut 33:27-28). The use of *epitimaō* ("I rebuke") also shows that Luke thought Satan, God's enemy, was being defeated in the exorcisms of Jesus.[76] Further, in view of such passages as Exodus 3:20, 7:4-5, 8:19 and 15:6-18, it may be that in changing *Spirit* to *finger* (see §5.20) Luke wanted to bring out a parallel between the miracles by which God released Israel from bondage and the miracles by which God, in Jesus, also released people from the bondage of Satan.[77] Then, also, in the story of the woman with a spirit of infirmity, the release from the spirit meant being released from Satan's binding (Lk 13:11-12, 16).[78]

However, Luke did not see Jesus' exorcisms as the final defeat of Satan. A glance across Luke and Acts makes this clear. At the end of Jesus' healing ministry, Satan is still active and is said to enter into Judas (Lk 22:3), as well as demand to have Simon (22:31). In the portrayal of the post-Easter situation, Luke says that Satan had filled Ananias's heart (Acts 5:3). Later, Luke says that Paul's ministry was the delivering of the Gentiles from the power of Satan (26:18). And the material related to exorcism in Acts confirms the general perspective of the Luke-Acts corpus that Satan was not finally defeated in Jesus' ministry.[79]

This broad view is highlighted in a small editorial change Luke makes to the story of the Gadarene demoniac. Mark has the demon(s) beg Jesus not to send them out of the region (*chōra*, Mk 5:10). But Luke has "and they begged him not to command them to depart into the abyss" (*abussos*, Lk 8:31, author's translation). When we dealt with this story in §5.16 we saw that Luke probably means that the demons felt that in Jesus there was the potential for their final defeat and imprisonment in the "unfathomable deep." On being given leave, they enter the pigs instead (8:32). The pigs are drowned, and the demons enter their watery home. In this way Luke has spelled out in detail what he has said throughout two volumes: Jesus' exorcisms were not the final defeat of Satan and his minions; rather, they were the first stage of that defeat.

§6.8 A Balanced Ministry

Robert Menzies has argued that Luke—keeping within the bounds of pre-Pauline understandings of the Spirit—is mainly concerned with the primacy of "word" or verbal proclamation.[80] However, I have already argued for the close association in Luke between the (Holy) Spirit and Jesus performing miracles. Indeed, Luke could be described as seeking to portray Jesus as having a balanced ministry of "word and deed."[81]

Even though he wished to increase the status of exorcism among Jesus' miracles and in Jesus' ministry, Luke's principal aim was to portray a balance among the various aspects of his ministry. Thus the perspective of Jesus as simply, or primarily, an exorcist or healer is less sharp in the early stages of Luke than in Mark. Luke carries this out largely by beginning Jesus' ministry with him teaching in the synagogues (Lk 4:14-30, 33) rather than conducting an exorcism, as in Mark 1:21-28.

Then at the conclusion of the story of the Beelzebul controversy (Lk 11:14-28), which focuses on Jesus as an exorcist, Jesus responds to a woman in the crowd with "Blessed . . . are those who *hear the word* of God and keep it!" (11:28, author's translation).[82] Thus it is obvious Luke wanted his readers to understand that exorcism was an integral and important part of a wider ministry.

Further, Luke broadened the way Jesus confronted the demonic. The crippled woman is introduced not as having an evil or unclean spirit (cf. Mk 1:23/Lk 4:33) but as having a spirit of infirmity (13:11). Then Jesus' command is not to an evil spirit but to the woman: "Woman, you are freed from your infirmity" (13:12, author's translation). In the ensuing discussion with the ruler of the synagogue, who was indignant about Jesus healing on the sabbath, Jesus speaks of the woman being loosed from Satan's bindings (13:16).[83] And we have just seen again that by means of the word *rebuke* Luke provides all three initial healings with overtones of exorcism (cf. §5.5).

This broadening of Jesus' dealing with the demonic is encapsulated in a summary of Jesus' ministry in Acts 10:38: "how God anointed Jesus of Nazareth with the Holy Spirit and with power; how he went about doing good and healing all who were oppressed by the devil, for God was with him." Importantly, not only does this draw attention to exorcism, but the generalized reference to those "oppressed by the devil" confirms that, for Luke, the demonic is broader than "possession." In other words, for Luke all sickness has a dimension of the demonic (cf. Lk 13:10-17) or is evil even though it may not be (to repeat) caused by demons.

The bringing of exorcism into balance with other aspects of Jesus' ministry turns out to be part of Luke's endeavor to balance Jesus' teaching and his miracles so that they appear of equal importance. We have already seen other evidence of the giving of equal weight to miracles and teaching in the introduction to Jesus' ministry where, before taking up the initial miracle stories from Mark, Luke inserts a section of teaching, which itself propounds a balanced ministry of proclamation and healing (Lk 4:18). And this material, which precedes the call of the disciples (5:1-11), is a balanced section of first teaching (4:16-30) and then miraculous activity (4:31-44).

Then, in summaries of Jesus' ministry,[84] Luke takes the opportunity to portray a balance by adding mention of healing (cf. Acts 10:36-38). In the summary of Jesus' ministry at Luke 7:22, both healing and teaching are already found in his source Q (Mt 11:5), as they are at Luke 6:17-18 (Mk 3:7-12).

In his use of the particular stories from early in Mark, Luke carries through this balancing act. In Mark's story of the healing of the demoniac in the synagogue, the theme of Jesus' teaching is woven into the miracle story by having the crowd respond with amazement to the teaching as well as the exorcism (Mk 1:27). Luke, however, has the crowd respond quite separately and first to Jesus' teaching (Lk 4:31-32). Then in the exorcism story the mention of teaching is removed (Mk 1:27/Lk 4:36). The result is that each aspect of Jesus' ministry is dealt with discretely without subordinating one to the other.[85]

In the conclusion to the story of the cleansing of a leper, Mark says that the response to the news of the healing was so great that Jesus could no longer openly enter a town (Mk 1:44). However, Luke has the more generalized response: "But now more than ever the word about Jesus spread abroad." This is followed by Luke saying crowds would gather to hear him as well as to be healed (Lk 5:15). Similarly, the story of the healing of the man with a withered hand is introduced when Luke says that Jesus entered the synagogue not only to teach (cf. Mk 3:1) but also to heal (Lk 6:6). In introducing the story of the healing of the paralytic let down through the roof (5:17-26), Luke follows his source by having Jesus' teaching as the setting (5:17/Mk 2:2). The same can be said of his introduction to the Sermon on the Plain (Lk 6:17-19/Mt 4:24—5:2). Then in the introduction to the story of the feeding of the five thousand Mark says that Jesus began to teach the crowds who came to him (Mk 6:34). Luke strengthens the balance of healing and teaching by saying that Jesus "spoke to them about the kingdom of God, and healed those who needed to be cured" (Lk 9:11).

As further evidence of Luke's balancing of teaching and healing we can note the arrangement of chapters 6 and 7.[86] Apart from the insertion of the call of the first disciples at 5:1-11, Luke follows Mark's order of material from the first healing story until just before the Sermon on the Plain. At that point Luke simply reverses the order of the stories of the choosing of the Twelve (Lk 6:12-16) and Jesus healing multitudes by the sea (6:17-19; cf. Mk 3:7-19a). In this way the Sermon on the Plain (Lk 6:20-49) is bracketed by the healing of the multitude (6:17-19) and the healing of the centurion's slave (7:1-10). And in the healing of the multitudes Luke introduces the idea that the crowds come to Jesus not only because of what they had heard about him (cf. Mk 3:9) but also to be healed by him (Lk 6:17). Luke makes the same kind of change in his introduction to the story of the feeding of the five thousand (Mk 6:34/Lk 9:11).

The story of the crippled woman (Lk 13:10-17) is an interesting example of this balancing. The healing story includes Jesus responding to the leader of the synagogue, who is said to be indignant about healing on the sabbath. The story has been called a "hybrid form" created by transforming a paradigm with a talelike tendency to reveal Jesus as the Lord of divine powers.[87] Bultmann thought that the story exhibited the least skill in Lukan composition.[88] However, the contrasts in the story between (a) the ox or donkey (13:15) and the woman (13:11, 12, 16), (b) the merciful untying from the manger (13:15) contrasted with merciless Satanic binding with illness (13:16) and (c) the two bindings and loosings (13:12, 15, 16), as well as the connecting vocabulary of "synagogue," "sabbath," "eighteen years" and binding and loosing strongly suggest a thoroughly integrated story.[89] These factors, as well as the fact that the crowd's rejoicing came not at the conclusion of the miracle story but at the end of the whole complex story, suggest that this is another instance of Luke balancing the teaching and healing ministry of Jesus.[90]

This balancing of word and deed is seen throughout the Gospel and even in Acts. Near the end of the Gospel, in the story of the walk to Emmaus, those with Jesus state that Jesus was "a prophet mighty in deed and word" (Lk 24:19). And in the first verse of Acts Luke describes his Gospel as having been about "all that Jesus did and taught." Thus not only can it be concluded that Luke saw miracles as part of the whole of Jesus' ministry (note the healing of the servant's ear even during the passion narrative, Lk 22:51) but that these kinds of miracles were to continue among his followers.[91]

§6.9 Jesus' Methods of Healing

In each of the miracle stories Luke faithfully reflects the tradition he takes from Mark, though he heavily edits the contexts of the stories. Also, with few exceptions, Luke does not question that Jesus used the same techniques and procedures as his contemporaries.[92] For example, in the story of the healing of the woman with the spirit of infirmity (Lk 13:10-17), Luke says, "He laid his hands upon her, and immediately she was made straight" (13:13, author's translation). In view of the laying on of hands being understood as part of exorcism by the Qumran people (4QPrNab), Luke most probably saw Jesus' healing technique to be the same as those of his contemporaries.

Yet although Jesus may have been thought to use the methods of his contemporaries, Luke will not, as we have seen, have the procedure go so far as to allow the demon an attempt at putting a spell on Jesus. So, as we have noted in Mark 5:7, where the demon attempts to control Jesus by saying, "I adjure [or bind] you by God," Luke has the demon, less threateningly, beg *(deomai)* not to be tormented (see §5.16 on Lk 8:28). Thus Luke is not at all embarrassed about portraying Jesus as a man of his time who uses contemporary healing techniques. However, because Jesus' power and authority were the most important aspect of him as an exorcist, his techniques have been portrayed in such a way as to focus attention on his power and authority and the respect due to him.

§6.10 The Miracles Identify Jesus

1. At one level, and preeminently, the miracle stories reveal and validate Jesus' precise identity. Thus the main point of the story of the calming of the storm (Lk 8:22-25) is clear from the resultant fear and the concluding question of the disciples: "Who then is this, that he commands even the winds and the water, and they obey him?" In waking Jesus the disciples had already called him "Master" (*epistatēs*, 8:24). Only Luke uses this word.[93] Except for 17:13, when the ten lepers call out, it is used only by the followers of Jesus. Those who are not disciples say "Teacher." Thus *master* is clearly important for Luke in describing the relationship between Jesus and his disciples.

In the secular contemporary Greek literature *master* was used in a wide variety of ways: for a herder, an Egyptian taskmaster, a leader of a temple, a music teacher, the president of the Athenian college, a magistrate or governor of a city.[94] This suggests that *master* described a skilled authoritative professional commander or supervisor. In the disciples' fear-engendered question, "Who then is this?" such a description of Jesus is clearly intended to be inadequate even if accurate. The readers are expected to answer the disciples' question by concluding that as the God of the Scriptures had control of the natural elements,[95] so in the miracle of Jesus, God himself had calmed the sea.

Another example of the miracles revealing and confirming the precise identity of Jesus is when the disciples of John the Baptist question Jesus: "Are you the one who is to come?" (Lk 7:18). In Matthew this question arises after Jesus had been teaching the Twelve in preparation for their mission and John hears about Jesus' deeds (Mt 11:1-2). However, Luke precedes John's questions with the stories of the centurion's slave being healed (Lk 7:1-10) and the widow from Nain having her son raised from the dead (7:11-17). Then he says that on hearing about these deeds, John sent his disciples to ask about the identity of Jesus (11:18-19).

In Q, one of Luke's sources, Jesus answers the delegation from John by telling them to go and tell John what they hear and see of Jesus' ministry. However, as we noted in §5.14, Luke adds that at that moment Jesus healed many from sickness and plagues and evil spirits and gave sight to many blind people (Lk 7:21). This was the activity expected of the Messiah.[96] Thus both in the context of this question and in its answer, Luke assumes that the miracles of Jesus validate the identity of Jesus. That is, the miracles show Jesus to be the Messiah.

This theme has most probably also caused Luke to bracket the story of the feeding of the five thousand (Lk 9:12-17) with Herod's question ("Who is this?" 9:9) and subsequently Jesus' asking his disciples, "Who do the crowds say that I am?" (9:18-20). The correct answer comes in the heavenly voice as Jesus is praying, which shows that Jesus' identity, though clear in the miracles, is understood only through divine revelation (9:28-35).

The story of the healing of the ten lepers (Lk 17:11-19)[97] is written to bring out parallels to 2 Kings 5:1-19, so that it may have been told to show that Jesus surpasses Elisha. Then in Acts 2:22 (on which see §6.12.1), Luke says explicitly through Peter on the day of Pentecost that Jesus of Nazareth was "a man attested to you by God with deeds of power, wonders, and signs that God did through him."

2. At another level, Luke makes many changes through the miracle stories to identify Jesus as a man of compassion. When the demon comes out of the man in the Capernaum synagogue, Luke adds a compassionate touch to the story by saying that the demon causes no harm (Mk 1:26/Lk 4:35). The pathos of the story of the Gadarene demoniac and the consequent compassion of Jesus are heightened by describing the man not only as living among the tombs but also as having no clothes or home (Mk 5:3/Lk 8:27). Similarly, the epileptic boy is described as an "only child" *(monogenēs)* and the father "cries out" *(boaō)* and "begs" *(deomai)* Jesus for help (Mk 9:14-29/Lk 9:37-43a). In Luke, Jesus refers to the boy as a "son" *(huios)*, not "he," and, on being healed, hands the boy back to his father (Lk

9:41-42). In response to the trepid cry of the drowning disciples Luke has Jesus ask not "Have you still no faith?" (Mk 4:40) but the more compassionate "Where is your faith?" (Lk 8:25).

Not only is Jesus identified as compassionate; he is to be obeyed. As Mark tells the story, the demoniac in the synagogue is convulsed and cries out after Jesus rebukes and commands him to be silent (Mk 1:25-26). In Luke 4:35 the mention of the crying out with a loud voice is deleted, so the demoniac is seen to be silently obedient.

In Mark 1:44-45, despite Jesus' sternly warning him not to do so, the cleansed leper went out and began to proclaim freely his healing. However, Luke simply says that the report about Jesus spread abroad, absolving the leper from an implicit charge of disobedience (Lk 5:15).

Also, although Mark does not say whether the healed paralytic who had been let down through a roof went home as Jesus directed, Luke specifies that he "went home," thereby showing him to be obeying Jesus (Mk 2:11/Lk 5:25). Similarly, when he heals the man with a withered hand, Jesus calls to the man (Mk 3:3). Luke spells out that the man rose and stood there (Lk 6:8).

§6.11 Faith as the Preparation and Product of Miracle

That Luke held the view that miracles could be the basis for faith is most explicit and unavoidably obvious in Acts. For example, when the residents of Lydda and Sharon saw Aeneas healed, they all "turned to the Lord" (Acts 9:35).[98] Indeed, it is right to conclude that "at every point where the Gospel was first established among a certain people, the foundation was made in a miraculous context, with manifest showing of signs and powers worked by the hands of the Apostles."[99]

The most significant example in the Gospel of Luke expressing his view that miracles can be a basis of faith is in his construction of chapters 4 and 5. In Mark, the calling of the first four disciples follows immediately after Jesus has been introduced preaching the kingdom of God (Mk 1:16-20). However, Luke delays the call of the first disciples (Lk 5:1-11) until after Jesus has not only preached (4:14-30) but also performed a number of miracles (4:31-41), including the healing of Simon's mother-in-law (4:33-41). This significant change in the order of material gives the impression that discipleship, not least for Simon, is based not only on Jesus' teaching but also on his miracles.

This perspective is confirmed in the call story itself. After obeying Jesus' call to "put out into the deep water" (Lk 5:4) and catching so many fish that the nets were beginning to break, Simon "fell down at Jesus' knees" (5:8), an action understood to be one of worship. Also, the miracle—the large catch of fish—is not only a metaphor of catching people, it is also illustrative of its possibility and magnitude. There is no doubt that the miracle is the ground of faith and discipleship.

Then, when the Twelve are eventually sent out on mission in chapter 9, Luke displaces the story of Jesus' rejection (Mk 6:1-6a/Lk 4:16-30) so that the mission follows immediately after a series of dramatic miracle stories (8:22-56). Thus the mission is seen to arise out of the miraculous activity of Jesus they have seen. The disciples' mission can also be seen in terms of Jesus needing to enlist the help of others in light of his very successful early mission in the same way Barnabas enlists the help of Paul when he is confronted with enormous success in Antioch (Acts 11:19-26).[100]

Looking back through the miracle stories immediately prior to the call of Simon, we see that Luke has maintained his tradition or made small changes that turn the miracle stories into a basis of belief in Jesus. On being healed, Simon's mother-in-law is said to begin serving them (Mk 1:31/Lk 4:39). Luke may have taken this to mean that, as a result of the miracle, the woman became a follower of Jesus, for "to serve" *(diakonein)* was a way of expressing discipleship (cf. 8:3; 12:37).

In a summary of healings, Mark 1:34 says that Jesus cast out demons and would not permit the demons to speak because they knew him. However, Luke strengthens the link between the exorcisms and the declaration as to who Jesus was by depicting the demons crying out "You are the Son of God!" as they were coming out of the possessed (Lk 4:41).

The call of Levi (Lk 5:27-28) follows immediately after the miraculous healing of the paralytic, who had been lowered through a roof (5:17-26). In Mark, between this healing and the story of the call of Levi, there is mention of a crowd gathering to be taught (Mk 2:13). Luke has omitted this so that the call to discipleship follows immediately after the miracle. Indeed, Luke begins the story of the call of Levi by saying "after these things" (Lk 5:27, author's translation)—that is, after the miracle that takes place in the light of faith (5:20) and which caused people to glorify God (5:26).

The brief story of the ministering women is further evidence of Luke's view that miracles are a basis for belief or discipleship (Lk 8:1-3). The women who followed Jesus are introduced as having been healed of evil spirits and infirmities.

Throughout his Gospel Luke has also drawn attention to "seeing" what Jesus was doing, especially as a ground for response to his ministry. In 10:23 Jesus says, "Blessed are the eyes that see what you see!" Following this Matthew refers to ears being healed (Mt 13:16). In either dropping it from Q or not adding it, as Matthew has, Luke has emphasized the miracles in the ministry of Jesus. Then in the story of the triumphal entry into Jerusalem, Luke not only says that the crowd cried out but adds that it was because of "all the deeds of power that they had seen" (Lk 19:37).

Following his source Q, Luke also considers faith to be not only the *possible* but the *required* response to miracles. Thus the people of Chorazin and Bethsaida are condemned because they had not repented on seeing the deeds of power (Mt 11:21/Lk 10:13). Luke gives other examples of the requirement of faith not being met. In one of his cameos of life among the believers in post-Easter Jerusalem, the wonders and signs of the apostles cause fear (Acts 2:43). Although Stephen did great wonders and signs, he was seized and brought to trial and eventually stoned (6:8; 7:60). At Iconium, although signs and wonders were done by Paul and Barnabas, the residents of the city were divided. Only some appear to have believed (14:3-4).

A positive example Luke gives of the required response of faith is that of the Samaritan leper, one of the ten lepers (Lk 17:11-19). When the Samaritan saw that he was healed, Luke says he turned back praising God. Only then did Jesus say to the man "your faith has made you well" (17:19).

Faith is not only the correct and required product of miracle; faith is also the *preparation* for miracles. Thus in response to the centurion of Capernaum's comment about being under authority, Jesus says he has not found such faith in Israel. It is then said that the centurion's servant was found to be in good health (Lk 7:1-10). There are a number of instances of Jesus' saying that a person's faith had healed or saved them, or that they would be saved had they had faith, as in the case of the fearful storm-tossed disciples, for example.[101]

In returning to the story of the cleansing of the ten lepers (Lk 17:11-19) we find this double relation of faith to miracles well illustrated and that the question of the nature of faith is the context of this story (17:5-10). The final verse in the story, "your faith has made you well," shows that Luke thought faith was the preparation for the healing (17:19). But the one leper who, upon discovering that he was healed, returned to Jesus "praising God with a loud voice" also shows that faith is the proper response to a miracle of Jesus (17:15).

This verse (Lk 17:15) is one of a number of places where Luke shows that the object of faith is not in the miraculous powers of Jesus but in God. Thus, as we have already seen, Luke repeatedly has either the crowd or the healed person—or both—praise God for the healing.[102]

The relationship between healing and discipleship (and also Jesus' identity) is treated most vividly in the story of the giving of sight to the blind man near Jericho (Lk 18:35-43).[103] Luke drops the name Bartimaeus from the story, perhaps to allow the story to become a paradigm of discipleship and perhaps to draw attention to the following story of Zacchaeus (unique to Luke), where the conversion adumbrated in the healing of the blind man is spelled out.[104]

The blind man is told that Jesus of Nazareth was passing by (Lk 18:37). However, the blind man recognizes who Jesus is, first calling on him for mercy (that is, salvation) as "Son of David," then addressing him as "Lord" in his request to see—receiving sight being a metaphor for receiving salvation.[105] Jesus com-

mends the man for his faith, which has healed or saved *(sōzein)* him. The man's
faith not only enables him to see or be saved but to follow Jesus. He glorifies God,
as do the people. The miracle story becomes an illustration of the final verse of the
Benedictus: "to give light, . . . to guide our feet" (1:79).[106]

§6.12 The Miracles of Jesus in Acts

It is not the way Luke treats miracles generally in Acts that interests us here[107] but
how his treatment helps us understand his view of the miracles of Jesus. There are
two key passages that help in this regard: Acts 2:22 and 10:38.

1. In the first major speech in Acts, Peter says that Jesus was "a man attested to
you by God with deeds of power, wonders, and signs *[terasi kai sē meiois]* that God
did through him" (Acts 2:22).[108] In looking at the Septuagint and the literature
of the time, we discover two understandings of signs and wonders that are also
important to Luke. First, in the Septuagint, Deuteronomy has the largest number
of occurrences of the phrase. These signs and wonders do not authenticate the
prophet Moses as they do in Exodus (e.g., Ex 4:1-17). Rather, because they are
from God himself, they point to his saving power, which can be known in the
present.[109] Second, on just two occasions Philo uses the phrase "signs and
wonders" of the miracles of the exodus.[110] For Philo these miracles validate the
divine origin of an accompanying statement or revelation. Returning to Acts we
see that Luke has used both these understandings of signs and wonders.

First, Luke gives his first specific example of a sign in Acts 3:1-10 by means of
an extended story of Peter and John healing a man who had been lame from birth.
Not only is this miracle story called a sign (Acts 4:16), it also has echoes of Luke
7:22—the miracles performed by Jesus demonstrating to the disciples of the Baptist
that he was the coming one. Both Luke 7:22 and Acts 3:8 have echoes of Isaiah
35:6, indicating that this miracle, along with those of Jesus, is a present fulfillment
of promised salvation.

Second, although these signs and wonders are not intended by Luke as
conjuring tricks to induce belief, they do—and are intended to—cause observers
to respond with amazement and have the effect of causing belief, as in the case of
Philip, whose success in ministry is described as relying heavily on his producing
signs (Acts 8:6-7).[111] Therefore as his followers are modeling the ministry of Jesus
in the signs and wonders, Luke is portraying the miracles of Jesus as points at which
the saving power of God can be known in the present, as validating his divine origin
and ministry and as intended to induce faith.

However, with only a single occurrence of the phrase "signs and wonders" for
the miracles of Jesus, we are alerted to the probability that Luke was exercising
some caution in the miracles of Jesus being understood entirely from this perspective.[112] In line with this is the fact that he does not use the term in his Gospel, and

he uses it in Acts only when reflecting on a quotation from Joel 2:28-32. Indeed, as we will see when examining the miracles in the Fourth Gospel, the phrase was used of marvels such as showers of stones, stars shining for seven days, an eclipse of the sun and monstrous births (see §8.5). Thus though wishing to use two understandings of the miracles from the Septuagint to reflect on the miracles of Jesus, Luke's caution, as also for the other Gospel writers, is probably born out of a desire that his readers not associate the miracles of Jesus simply with the marvels of false prophets.[113]

2. Acts 10:38 has Peter again speaking. He summarizes Jesus' ministry: "how God anointed Jesus of Nazareth with the Holy Spirit and with power; how he went about doing good and healing all who were oppressed by the devil, for God was with him." It is probable that the "doing good and healing" is a single idea expressed in two terms (a hendiadys). Luke has just mentioned the preaching, and "doing good" *(euergetein)* is the practical rendering of service of a benefactor,[114] so apart from teaching, the whole of Jesus' ministry is seen as performing miracles.

Luke in turn sees all healing as dealing with the devil's oppression.[115] We have already seen in this chapter (§6.2) that, for Luke, the Holy Spirit is the source of power for the miracles of Jesus. And in Acts 10:36 Luke has just mentioned Jesus' preaching. So together the preaching and the miracles are seen as the work of God through Jesus as his representative.[116] Thus it is no surprise that verse 38 ends by saying "God was with him," so that the miracles are seen to arise out of being accompanied and aided by God.[117]

§6.13 Concluding Summary

Coming to the end of two chapters on Luke, readers are left with the distinct impression that, perhaps with the exception of the Fourth Gospel, the miracles of Jesus are much more important to Luke than to the other Gospel writers. From the outset, through his miracles (no less and no more than in his teaching), Jesus is identified and proved to be the eschatological prophet, Messiah and Lord. And despite the hesitation of some scholars, it is demonstrably obvious that Jesus is empowered by the eschatological Spirit to perform miracles, often in conflict with the religious authorities (e.g., Lk 6:7).

Through his arrangement of the material, Luke has made a distinctive impact on the miracle traditions about Jesus. He has included stories unique to his Gospel, brought stories into balance with the teaching of Jesus and made changes to individual stories that enhance their significance when compared to his tradition. We have seen that he has replaced the harsh story of the cursing of the fig tree with the story of grace about Jesus weeping for Jerusalem. Indeed, Luke records no punitive miracles at the hand of the earthly Jesus. He clearly distinguishes between the offer of grace in Jesus and the coming judgment of God. Jesus offers grace in his miracles rather than divine punishment.

Despite the significance of the miracles, Jesus performs no miracles during his ministry in Jerusalem (though see Lk 22:50-51). The miraculous happenings mentioned are no longer understood to identify Jesus and draw people to trust him. The identity of Jesus has been established. Instead, the miracles that are mentioned are said either to be dreadful portents (21:11) signaling the shaking of the universe (21:26) or to be used by leaders to deceive people (21:8). They also act as premonitions of a great punitive act of God on Jerusalem.

From Luke's perspective it is not possible to say that the miracles illustrate or demonstrate the good news of Jesus: they are, with the teaching, themselves the good news of Jesus.[118] Nevertheless, as with the writer of the Fourth Gospel,[119] Luke recognizes the ambiguity of the miracles of Jesus, for which he offers no resolution. We see this in the *dunamis* ("power") of miracles being portrayed as a *mana*-like or impersonal substance that independently responds to the wish of those who seek healing. Further, the ambiguity is demonstrated in the Beelzebul controversy (Lk 11:14-23) and in assuming that anyone can perform miracles (Acts 8:9-11).

Nevertheless Luke uses the miracles of Jesus to point to his true identity and to show that in the miracles God himself is at work. Thus, for Luke, healing and salvation—the same word *(sōzein)*—are a piece. Indeed, in light of stories such as the healing of the ten lepers (Lk 17:11-19), we see that the miracles can be salvation for those who have faith and that the miracles can take precedence over the words of Jesus and in themselves can be the good news.

For Luke, the proper preparation for receiving health or salvation is faith or trust in Jesus. We have seen that Mark believes a confession of Jesus as Lord or Christ in response to Jesus' miraculous activity is a defective faith (cf. Mk 6:14-16 and 8:27-30). But for Luke the proper response to healing or salvation is shown to be praise of God, faith in Jesus and a life of discipleship. In this Luke is nearest to the Gospel of John in seeing miracles as giving rise to trust in Jesus (Jn 4:53; 14:11). Like his contemporary Christians, Luke was convinced that Jesus' ministry of miracles was to be carried on by his followers.

S e v e n

The Miracles of Jesus in the Fourth Gospel

The Stories

··

§7.1 Introduction

The wealth of literature on the miracles or "signs" in the Fourth Gospel[1] is dominated by a number of issues. There are questions regarding the picture of Jesus the Fourth Gospel intends to portray through the miracles and also the meaning, significance and implication of the term *sign*. The question of faith and miracles remains an issue. Also, similarities between some of the miracle stories in John and those of the Synoptic Gospels, and some stories appearing only in the Fourth Gospel or the Synoptics, highlight the problem of the relationship between this Gospel and the Synoptics.[2] It has been suggested that the Fourth Gospel was written at a time when sacraments had replaced the miracles. The perennial question of a signs source being available to the writer and whether it was oral or written is also debated in the literature. These are some of the questions or issues from the miracle stories of the Fourth Gospel that we will discuss in this chapter and address specifically in the following chapter.

The importance of understanding John's perspective on the signs is seen in his statement "Although he had performed so many signs in their presence, they did not believe in him" (Jn 12:37). In this John is saying at least that the miracles are potentially important in leading to faith in Jesus. Then in 20:31 he says, "These [signs] are written so that you may come to believe." Although such passages as

12:37-50 stress public response to both word and deed, these statements make the miracles the cornerstone of Jesus' self-presentation in John.[3]

Something of John's outlook on the miracles is already unmistakable in the material immediately before his first sign story, the turning of water into wine. The paragraphs preceding this story end with Jesus saying that his followers will see greater things than they have so far seen: they will see "heaven opened and angels of God ascending and descending upon the Son of Man" (Jn 1:50-51). This is an allusion to Jacob's vision at Bethel (Gen 28:12), though John mentions no ladder, which decreases the distance between Jesus and God. John is saying that in what Jesus is about to do the disciples can expect to see the close and continuous unbroken relationship between Jesus on the one hand, and God and the heavenly world on the other hand. Notwithstanding, the mention of the mediating angels means that Jesus has a completely distinct existence in his earthly ministry.[4]

In what way (or ways) the disciples will see this close yet distinct relationship between God and Jesus and his ministry is intimated in the future tense "you will see" (*opsesthe*, Jn 1:51). For on the one hand, the future tense of "to see" is used of the time of the resurrection and beyond to the parousia.[5] On the other hand, John also uses "to see" in relation to the miracles in the ministry of Jesus (4:45; 6:2; 11:40). Thus Jesus' statement to Nathanael about seeing greater things signals early to the readers that in the miracles, as well as in the resurrection and expected parousia, John will be showing and anticipating the intimate yet independent relation of Jesus to God.[6]

John's perspective on the miracles may also be apparent in the framework he gives to his introduction. The first miracle story begins, "And the third day" (*kai tē hēmera tē tritē*, Jn 2:1, author's translation). This is usually translated "on the third day." Although John does not use this phrase in his stories of the resurrection, it most naturally alludes to the day of the resurrection when, in earliest Christian tradition, Jesus most unmistakably revealed his glory.[7] Thus for John this first sign may also reflect the same glory revealed in the future "third day."

Furthermore this time reference in 2:1 is probably intended to tie the first sign to the preceding paragraphs, which tell of a week[8] of revelation of the identity of Jesus.[9] Through these days—without his doing anything—Jesus is discovered, disclosed and presented as the Lord (Jn 1:23), the Lamb of God (1:29, 36), the Son of God (1:34, 49), the Messiah or Christ (1:41; cf. 25), the King of Israel (1:49), and the Son of Man (1:51). It is this Jesus, who in himself reveals the Father (14:9; 15:24), who at the climax of the week is about to perform the miracle, revealing God's glory.

Thus from the opening words of the Gospel and the initial few words of the first sign story, John's readers know that in the miracles, as well as in the resurrection and the parousia, Jesus will be revealing the glory of the Father and the intimate relationship, yet distinct existence, between God and Jesus: in the miracles Jesus will be continuously transfigured. Therefore not only will the miracles anticipate the glory of the Father to be revealed in the resurrection[10] but will in themselves be signs revealing the glory of the Father: the miracles are evidence of "his glory, glory as of a father's only son, full of grace and truth" (Jn 1:14). This is repeated by John at the close of the Gospel: the signs were written to lead people to believe that Jesus is the Messiah, the Son of God, and that through believing readers may have life (20:30-31).

The introduction to the Fourth Gospel also provides a clue to its plot:[11] "He came to what was his own, and his own people did not accept him. But to all who received him, who believed in his name, he gave power to become children of God" (Jn 1:11-12). As the Gospel progresses, an escalating hostility gives rise to an awareness that Jesus' impending death provides dramatic tension to the story. In turn, this hostility arises out of a failure to recognize Jesus for who he is. As we proceed we will see the importance that John and the Fourth Gospel place on the miracle-signs in establishing Jesus' identity.

§7.2 The Stories
It bears repeating that our purpose in examining each miracle story is not to provide a commentary on them. Our purpose is to draw attention to key issues, themes and interests in the interpretation of the miracles from this Gospel's perspective in order to build a picture of the understanding of the signs and their contribution to the portrait of Jesus. Thus many of the details of the stories need not detain us. Also, we are not yet concerned about the question of historicity. Regardless of the issue of historicity, however, we must know something of the historical background of these stories in order to understand how the stories would have been received by the first readers.[12]

§7.3 Turning Water into Wine (Jn 2:1-12)
This first public act of Jesus takes on an unavoidably programmatic status, and it is clearly important to John, for he refers to it later (Jn 4:46).[13] Thus an understanding of this story will probably contribute significantly to comprehending the importance and meaning of the other miracles, as well as the Johannine Jesus in general.

One of John's interests in this story is seen in his placing it immediately before, and tying it to, the story of the cleansing of the temple. At the end of both stories John says, "Many believed in his name because they saw the signs that he was doing" (Jn 2:23). They form a diptych as a prelude to Jesus' ministry.[14] The common theme of both stories is the contrast between the old order and the newness Jesus brings. What is new may be gathered by noting that Isaiah says there will be an abundance of wine in the eschatological feast (Is 25:6). The other Gospels also use the image of a feast to depict the kingdom of God.[15] Thus the new thing John is representing through this story and the story of the cleansing of the temple is probably the kingdom of God. This is also the subject of his exchange with Nicodemus (Jn 3:3, 5).[16] Thus Jesus is replacing the old purificatory rites of the Jews with his new wine.[17]

"There can be no doubt," says Bultmann, "that the story has been taken over from heathen legend and ascribed to Jesus."[18] He goes on to say that the motif of the story of changing water into wine is a typical motif of the Dionysus legend, and this provides the genesis of the miracle of Cana.[19]

Indeed, in the ancient literature Plutarch says that there was a spring at Haliartus with clear, sparkling, wine-colored, very pleasant-tasting water in which the newly born Dionysus was bathed.[20] Also, Pliny says that at Andros, on the festival known as *Theodosia,* a spring in the temple of Bacchus flowed with wine.[21] Pausanias says that at Elis the priests of Dionysus placed three large empty cauldrons in a sealed room to find them filled with wine when they returned the next day.[22] And Ovid says that Liber, the Italian god identified with Bacchus, gave the daughters of the Delian king Anius the power to turn things into wine,[23] a story associated with Dionysus.

However, from these references it is obvious that there are significant differences between the Dionysus legend and the story in John 2: the spring at Haliartus flowed with water, and the one at Andros flowed with wine, not water that had once been wine; and the empty cauldrons in the Elis temple were filled with wine rather than water subsequently changed into wine, key elements in John's story. These differences have convinced most scholars that John or his tradition is not dependent on the Dionysus legend for this story.[24]

Yet these stories that associate a god with the liberal and surprising supply of wine when water had been expected—widely circulating stories with which the readers of John could be expected to be familiar—would mean that John's readers would probably conclude at least that the one changing water into wine was superior to Dionysus.

Further, on the one hand, the first readers of John, also being familiar with the Old Testament, would have associated the failure of the supply of wine in this story not only with disaster but with God's judgment,[25] presumably on the failure of the Jewish law and religion.[26] For jars, once holding water and now holding the new wine, were used for the Jewish rites of purification (Jn 2:6).[27] On the other hand, the first readers of John would have associated the liberal supply of wine with God's general blessing,[28] as well as with "that day," the eschatological day of blessing that in Jesus was being shown to have arrived.[29]

Assuming a familiarity with Proverbs 9:5 ("Come, . . . drink of the wine I

[Wisdom] have mixed") and other wisdom writers, John's readers would also have been able to see here an echo of the function of Wisdom in the liberal supply of all of life's needs.[30] Thus the first readers of John would have seen in this miracle the coming of the expected reign of God and that Jesus—presented as Wisdom—was God's anointed one in that reign. That there were six (not the perfect number of seven) jars means that this coming, though liberal and one of blessing, waits its completion in the resurrection and parousia.[31]

However, also to be kept in mind in ascertaining the meaning of this story for John is the possibility that the first readers had been informed by the same context of thought evident in Philo. For as C. H. Dodd argued, the Fourth Gospel presupposes a range of ideas—such as the Logos concept, the use of symbolism, the importance of knowing God and so being a son of God, the emphasis laid on love and eternal life—which, despite varying treatment, has a remarkable resemblance to those of Hellenistic Judaism as represented by Philo.[32]

With this overlap of interest, what Philo says of Melchizedek is noteworthy in helping us see how the readers of John probably understood the changing of water into wine. In contrast to the miserly Ammonites and Moabites, Melchizedek, Philo says, will offer wine instead of water and give souls a pure draft so that they may become seized by that divine intoxication which is more sober than sobriety itself, for he is a logos priest having a share in the self-existent one (*Allegorical Interpretation* 3:81-82).

While neither the Dionysian material nor that from the Old Testament or from Philo can alone account for the story in John, it would be hard to deny that the readers of John would have seen that the Jesus portrayed in the story of water turning into wine was superior to other gods, that in Jesus Judaism had not so much been completed but surpassed and that the eschatological day of the coming of God's anointed had arrived, bringing God's joy.

Opinion varies enormously on the question of the presence of references to the sacraments in John. For example, Bultmann and most German scholars advocate a nonsacramental view, and Cullmann, with many of the British and French scholars, takes the opposing stance.[33] There are certainly no overt references to the sacraments or any account of the Last Supper in John. Yet it is difficult to imagine an early Christian writer or his audience not being familiar with the story of the Last Supper.[34]

Further, in light of such verses as John 3:5 (about being born of water), 6:51-58 (about eating Jesus' flesh and drinking his blood) and 19:34b-35 (about blood and water coming from Jesus' side), it is asinine to maintain that there are no intended references to the sacraments. Nor can we, with Bultmann, assign the key material in chapter 6 to an "Ecclesiastical Redactor,"[35] for the sacramental elements that appear elsewhere in chapter 6 establish a fundamental harmony with the remainder of the discourse.[36]

Returning to John's miracle story, the wine could be a pointer to the wine of the Last Supper.[37] This suggestion is found among Christians from early times,[38] and the possible internal hint to the Eucharist could be that the changing of water into wine takes place before the Passover (Jn 2:13).[39] Thus, though the word *wine* is not used either in the Pauline or Synoptic accounts of the Last Supper, in light of Jewish tradition it is obvious that Jesus would have been thought to have been using wine and that John is expecting his readers to see in this miracle an anticipation of the cross (cf. 2:1, 4) and its adumbration in the Eucharist. To this we add the unmistakable clue to the prolepsis of the Eucharist and the cross in Jesus' speaking of his "hour" (2:4).[40]

This interpretation arises more naturally from the text than the suggestion that the water and wine are to be seen as metaphors of the antithesis between the law and the Spirit.[41] Also, it is difficult to support the view that this story is a symbolic reference to the marriage between Christ and the church,[42] for there is no union between Jesus and Mary; they are simply present.[43] A more fruitful interpretation arises from noting that in the background of the story is the water. To follow Larry Jones, the water in the jars has a merely ceremonial function. But as this miracle transforms Jesus' followers into believers (Jn 2:11), so the water symbolizes and foreshadows what happens to the believers.[44]

Four other features of this story stand out as important in John's view of this and the other miracles of Jesus: its similarity to a Synoptic nature miracle; the exchange between Jesus and his mother; that the stone jars were for the Jewish rites of purification; and that this was the first of Jesus' signs intended to reveal his glory.

First, this story is similar to a Synoptic nature miracle in that no one is healed. Instead, a natural situation is dramatically changed. Though not a life-threatening situation, the turning of water into wine is not a "luxury miracle," contrary to Walter Bauer's suggestion, who contrasts it with the Synoptic nature miracles that are seen to arise out of concrete necessity.[45] The failure of wine at a wedding would have been acutely felt in a culture where unsatisfied wedding guests could expect in later reciprocating invitations to their weddings to receive not only gifts but an additional compensatory payment. Further, there would have been a loss of prestige for the bridegroom.[46] Thus, as in the Synoptic stories, even though it is not mentioned explicitly here (or anywhere in the Johannine miracle stories),[47] Jesus is possibly portrayed as acting out of compassion in performing a miracle.

At another level the miracle can also be seen not to be gratuitous or a luxury. It has for the readers in Asia Minor, as Ben Witherington suggests, the larger emblematic quality of displaying the social and theological significance of Jesus, who "eclipses and makes obsolete previous sources of life and health such as Jewish purification water."[48]

A second critical feature of the story is the exchange between Jesus and his mother. On hearing about the lack of wine, Jesus says to his mother, "Woman, what concern is that to you and me? My hour has not yet come" (Jn 2:4). However, Jesus' subsequent involvement in supplying wine—perhaps fulfilling his obligations as a guest to provide a gift[49]—means that this part of Jesus' reply should probably be translated more literally as a remonstration: "What have I to do with you, woman?"[50] The meaning of this phrase depends on its context.

At the historical level it may have meant, "You have no reason to blame me. The problem is taken care of."[51] However, our concern is with the significance of the rebuff for the Fourth Gospel. Jesus' mother is mentioned as one of the guests before he is introduced. Thus she, like the guests and water jars, is part of the scene of the story. Therefore, when she says "They have no wine," which is an implicit request for a miracle, she is partially identified with the crowd. It is this request for a miracle that elicits the gentle rebuke from Jesus. It must be seen as a gentle rebuke, for Jesus respectfully addresses other women in this way, as well as his mother at the foot of the cross (cf. Jn 4:21; 19:25-27; 20:13).[52]

At one level Jesus is refusing "to be prompted to act by any human agent, even when that agent is his own mother; he is driven by the will of the Father alone."[53] At another level, what Jesus' mother does not understand is that his "hour has not yet come." For John, Jesus' "hour" is his glorification in death.[54] Yet in two places John has Jesus say "the hour comes and now is" (Jn 4:23; 5:25; cf. 12:30-31). Thus in the miracles there is both a "now" (2:10) and a "not yet" (2:4) in relation to the revelation of glory.[55]

We can in turn expect John to portray evidence of that glory not only in the story of Jesus' death but also in the stories preceding it. This we have been told in the introduction (Jn 1:14), and this he does in the signs.[56] Thus in the context of this story, though it may not be time for a more complete revelation of his glory, Jesus risks being misunderstood by performing a miracle. This fear turns out to be unfounded, as the final sentence of the story shows: "His disciples believed in him" (2:11).[57]

Further, this means that the miracles are not only the signs of a future reality of God's glory but are in themselves the reality of God's present reign seen in Jesus' ministry.[58] Not surprisingly later John has the crowd say they cannot imagine the Messiah doing more signs than Jesus (Jn 7:31).

In any case, the mother of Jesus is not deterred. She says to the servants, "Do whatever he tells you" (Jn 2:5). John Ashton helps us understand the function of the mother of Jesus here:

This mixture of incomprehension and compliance is surely part of the *meaning* of the story. . . . In the context of an appeal to Jewish readers and listeners to come forward and declare themselves for Christ, the significance of Jesus' mother (or part of it at least) is as a representative of those who do just that, those for whom misunderstanding is not a permanent obstacle to discipleship.[59]

Jesus' refusing his mother's request, which later is granted, has a parallel in the story of the official begging Jesus to come and heal his son (Jn 4:46-54) and perhaps most clearly in 7:1-10. There Jesus is requested to go to Jerusalem. He at first declines, saying, "My time has not yet come" (7:6; cf. v. 8). This "time" would be Jesus' last journey to Jerusalem, where his glory would be unavoidably made clear. So by denying the request of his mother at the wedding, he was refusing to perform a single, all-sufficient sign that revealed the glory of the Father in his activity.[60] That glory, seen and foreshadowed in the signs (cf. 7:8)—which point toward the cross and beyond—was revealed supremely in the suffering, death and resurrection of Jesus and was expected to be seen again in the parousia (cf. 1:51).

Third, it is said that the stone jars were "for the Jewish rites of purification" (Jn 2:6). In view of John the Baptist's followers' strict observance of purification laws,[61] this could be part of a counter to a claim that John was the Messiah.[62] This is a strong possibility, for although we know of no such claim in the first century, it seems that John's later followers claimed him rather than Jesus as Messiah.[63] However, we need to note that a polemic against John the Baptist is only part of the portrait of the Baptist. The main concern in this Gospel is to show John as the ideal witness to Jesus the Messiah.[64]

Fourth, the story ends by saying more than that this sign revealed Jesus' glory and that his disciples believed in him (Jn 2:11).[65] John says that this was the first of his signs to reveal his glory. That is, we are being informed that all the signs of Jesus will reveal his glory and are to be seen in light of his "hour."[66]

As we have just noted, for John the suffering, death and resurrection reveal Jesus' glory most clearly. However, this is one of a number of clear statements in John we will note that show he saw the miracles pointing to the glory of Jesus, no less than the suffering, death, resurrection and anticipated parousia.[67] The believing response of the disciples to the miracle is an echo of the response of the disciples to the sign of the resurrection (cf. Jn 20:8, 29, 31), reinforcing the importance of the miracles, alongside the resurrection, as a legitimate basis for faith (see §8.8). They are a legitimate basis for faith because the signs show that "all previous religious institutions, customs and feasts lose meaning in his presence."[68]

Having established the faith of the disciples on the basis of their seeing his glory in the sign (Jn 2:11), John's story then moves Jesus from Cana to Capernaum. His mother, his brothers and his disciples are with him (2:12), leading the reader to imagine that in his ministry Jesus was still involved with his family and perhaps

John the Baptist (cf. 3:22-24), at least before his first journey to Jerusalem, where there is a dramatic confrontation between Jesus and the Jews over the abuse of the temple (2:13-25).

John gives the impression that Jesus performed more miracles in Jerusalem, for he says, "Many believed in his name because they saw the signs that he was doing" (Jn 2:23). However, in view of the disciples believing in Jesus after the turning of water into wine, the reader is left with the problem as to why Jesus does not trust himself to these people (2:24). John will present the same issue at the beginning of the next sign (4:43-45).

§7.4 Healing the Official's Son (Jn 4:46-54; cf. Mt 8:5-13/Lk 7:1-10)

After two days in Samaria (Jn 4:40, 43)[69] Jesus is said to go from place to place in Galilee. He is welcomed because at the festival in Jerusalem "they had seen all that he had done," presumably the signs (2:23). Since John inserts that "Jesus himself had testified that a prophet has no honor in the prophet's own country" (4:44),[70] it is likely that John is returning to the problem of the relationship between miracles and faith.[71] We will face this problem in the next chapter when we attempt to understand the relationship between miracle and faith in John (§8.8). For the moment, John has Jesus back in Cana for the second miracle.

A number of aspects of John's version of the story of the healing of the official's son call our attention to his purpose.[72] The first three are interrelated.

First, at the beginning of the story the setting is given as Cana,[73] where Jesus changed water into wine (Jn 4:4-6). At the end of the story this miracle is said to be the second sign (4:54),[74] also linking it with the story of the turning of water into wine. The link between these two stories is further strengthened by noting that at 5:1, after the healing of the official's son, John introduces a turning point in Jesus' public activity.[75]

Whether or not these stories are from a signs source (see §8.7), this link in the text alerts the reader to this present story's being understood in light of the first miracle story and, in turn, the introduction to the Gospel. It also explains why there is no further numbering of the miracle stories.[76] The two stories have a powerful "primacy effect," being part of the programmatic beginning to the whole of the ministry of Jesus that establishes the reader's first impression of Jesus' identity and mission.[77] In the prologue and introduction (Jn 1:1-51), without any action on his part, Jesus has been introduced, and we anticipate he will show himself to be, among other things, at one with God (1:51). As part of that introduction this discovery, in these two stories, is not so much sought for[78] as disclosed or more clearly unveiled through Jesus' miraculous actions.

Second, the man seeking healing is not a Roman centurion (as in Q) but a royal official *(basilikos)*, probably a Jew from Herod Agrippa's court.[79] By having a Jew seek healing, the rebuff by Jesus ("Unless you see signs and wonders you will not believe," Jn 4:48)[80] cannot be understood as his requirement of going first to the household of Israel (as in Mk 7:24-30). Instead, the issue turns on the lack of faith when signs and wonders are not seen or on the demand for miracles.[81] However, the criticism is not aimed directly or personally at the official, for the verbs are in the plural. So through these words John has Jesus address not only the audience in this story but also the readers of his Gospel.

In any case, the official ignores Jesus' rebuff and persists in his request, perhaps confirming that he was not seeking Jesus because of the signs he had seen. Indeed, when told his son would live, it is said, "The man believed the *word* that Jesus spoke to him" (Jn 4:50). At the end of the story, on discovering that his son is well, John says the official and his whole household believed (4:53). This faith is not criticized as inadequate, for as the official's persistence after the rebuff shows, his faith is not dependent on the miracles but on the word and deed of Jesus (see §8.8). This leads to another feature of this story.

Third, John focuses on the faith of the official: through the rebuff of Jesus (Jn 4:48); through taking Jesus at his word and returning home (4:50b); and through the final statement that he and his household believed (4:53). However, whereas the first sign led the disciples to trust in Jesus, this story leads the petitioner, as well as his household, to faith (4:53). Later, in 5:24, attention is drawn to the importance of the faith that takes Jesus at his word. In other stories faith comes as a result of seeing the miracle; in this story there is at least incipient faith before any miracle takes place.[82]

It has been suggested that John is showing that mere miracle-based faith is not genuine faith[83] or that John is portraying a progression of faith that reaches its pinnacle in faith in Jesus' word. The evidence of this story is simply that faith based on either Jesus' words or his miracles is possible and adequate (see §8.8).

Fourth, the miracle is portrayed as more spectacular than in the Synoptic Gospels. In contrast to the Q story (Mt 8:8-12/Lk 7:6-9), the miracle occurs without the father directly expressing any initial faith apart from the request for a healing (Jn 4:47). Also, instead of the simple statement in Matthew and Luke about the boy being healed that hour (Mt 8:13b) or being found in good health (Lk 7:10), John highlights and draws attention to the wonder of the healing by means of the servants of the official coming out to meet him and having a conversation about the boy being alive and the time of his healing (Jn 4:51-53).

Fifth, three times in the story John uses a variation of the phrase "your son will live" (*ho huios sou zē*, Jn 4:50, 51, 53). This repetition should probably be taken as the author's drawing attention at least to part of his purpose in the story. Because this is a sign (4:54) we can expect this coming to life to have more significance than for the life of the boy alone (see §8.5.3).

Already, between the first sign story and this one, Jesus has told Nicodemus that everyone who believes in him will not perish but have eternal life (Jn 3:16, 36). Also, in conversing with the Samaritan woman, Jesus has said that he offers water that will gush up to eternal life (4:14). Then, in the transition paragraph (4:43-45) between the story of the Samaritan woman and this one (which begins, "When the two days were over"), there is the possibility that John wishes the following story of the official's son to be an echo of the resurrection.[84]

In any case, this miracle story is the first one to act as a sign of the power of Jesus to give eternal life—to the point of raising the dead (cf. Jn 5:21-29). In this the story is not only a conclusion to what precedes it but also a foretaste of the signs and sayings to follow. This is confirmed by the work of Feuillet,[85] who has argued for taking this story of the healing of the official's son as the introduction to the next and central section of John (5:1—12:50), where the theme of Jesus giving life will appear in the discourses about the bread of life (6:22-71), the life-giving water (7:37-39) and the light that gives life (8:12).

What we are beginning to see here is that the miracles in John are not simply tangible illustrations of the message of Jesus. Nor can they be played down, as Bultmann tried to do, by seeing them as merely complementary or of secondary importance to the narratives.[86] The signs are the center of the life-giving ministry of Jesus, which, as we will see even more clearly in the later miracle stories, are explained in the discourses.

These first two miracle stories are not subsequently explained in any detail, in contrast to most of the other miracle stories being followed by or being part of a lengthy explanatory and analytical discourse.[87] They are, presumably, self-explanatory signs that establish the miracle-working nature of Jesus' ministry,[88] even though, by the Jews, they have been understood only as good works (Jn 10:33).

Even though the stories have not been explained by an accompanying discourse, two observations contribute to the readers' perception of these first two signs. The first observation is that they have a similar structure involving a problem (Jn 2:3; 4:46), a request (2:3; 4:47), a sharp rebuke (2:4; 4:48), a reaction (2:5; 4:50) and a consequence (2:5; 4:51-53), leading to a conclusion that each is a sign (2:11; 4:54).[89] Further, the important and climactic parallel is that each sign gives rise to faith—for the disciples (2:11) and the official (4:53).[90] We can maintain then that (correct) faith can be based on either Jesus' words or his works of miracles.

The second observation is that some of the significance of the first two signs is seen through their narrative context, where the Fourth Gospel moves Jesus from Cana and back to Cana. Each sign is part of a distinct movement in the narrative toward faith.[91] The first story, of the changing of water into wine, heads the first movement toward faith (Jn 2:1—3:36). The narrative moves from the lack of faith by the Jews (2:12-22) to partial faith by Nicodemus (3:1-21) to complete faith being exemplified in John the Baptist (3:22-36). This movement toward faith is in a Jewish context.

The second story, of the healing of the official's son, comes at the end of the second movement toward faith (Jn 4:1-54). Lack of faith is seen in the Samaritan woman (4:1-15), who then exhibits partial faith (4:16-26) before the villagers are shown to declare complete faith (4: 39-42). This second movement in the narrative is set in a non-Jewish context. Thus again, as we will be drawn to conclude from time to time, the signs are seen to be integral to this Gospel's moving readers toward faith.

§7.5 Healing the Paralytic at Bethesda (Jn 5:1-18)

As we have just seen, the second sign, as well as the first, has caused belief in Jesus (Jn 2:11; 4:53). These two signs took place in Galilee and were, to some extent, private events. Now Jesus' ministry is painted on a broader canvas. The second phase of Jesus' ministry is said to begin with his going up to Jerusalem at the time of a festival (5:1).[92]

Just as Jesus' public ministry was launched with a miracle, so the second major section of the Gospel begins with a miracle story. Again the unavoidable significance of the miracles for understanding Jesus are impressed upon the reader's mind, but now his identity is established against the background of intense conflict (cf. Jn 5:18).

Bultmann suggested that this story has stylistic features ("Semitizing" Greek, placing verbs at the beginning of sentences, and the lack of connecting particles) that show strong similarities with the other sections of the Gospel, which also probably come from the signs source.[93] With considerable yet unconvincing creativity, Fortna argued that this story was the seventh and last in the signs source.[94] Taking up the suggestions of others, Bultmann also pursued the idea that large sections of John have been displaced from their original positions. This includes chapter 6, which he argued should be placed between chapters 4 and 5. However, there is no textual evidence to support any of the displacements Bultmann proposes.[95] We are left to interpret the miracles from the order of the text as it stands.

With this story there is a change in the way John explains the miracles.[96] As we have already noted, until now he has given them little separate explanation; attention to their meaning has been confined to the way John tells the story and places it in his narrative. However, from this story on, apart from that of Jesus walking on the sea (Jn 6:16-21), John either appends to, or weaves into, his stories an often intricate explanation of their significance and implication.

We have seen that John emphasized that the official's profoundly ill son was healed by Jesus' words (Jn 4:50, 51, 53). Similarly in this story a profoundly ill man is healed by Jesus speaking to him (5:8). In its immediately following the story of the official's son being healed, this story emphasizes the life-giving word of Jesus. Thus the opening words of the Gospel, containing the statement that in him—the Word—was life, are here illustrated and demonstrated to be true (cf. 1:4).

As with other sign stories in John, the miraculous aspect is heightened. To begin with, the paralytic is described as having been sick for thirty-eight years (Jn 5:5). Also, the severity of his illness and hence the eventual magnitude of the miracle are repeated in the next verse, where Jesus is said to know that the man had been ill for a long time (5:6). And, again to emphasize the magnitude of the healing, the story concludes with John saying, "At once the man was made well" (*hugiēs*, 5:9). The word *hugiēs* occurs five times in the story.[97] Elsewhere in John it is found only in 7:23, which is linked with this passage by means of the sabbath theme, as well as those of healing and debating about the law with the Jews. The high concentration of this word here enables John to highlight the stark difference between the thirty-eight hopeless years of illness with the complete wholeness Jesus has brought to the man. Jesus is portrayed as standing above and apart from all others.

Particular features of this story have suggested to some writers that John intended a baptismal motif. In antiquity Tertullian (*De Baptismo* 5) held this view, and in modern times so did Cullmann, for example.[98] The case rests on a number of points.

First, the story is set over against the dipping in the healing pool near the Sheep Gate. Second, Cullmann sees the pool's becoming the scene of many Christian baptisms as corroborating evidence to support the baptismal motif intended by John.[99] However, this begs the question as to whether John had this motif in mind. Third, Tertullian found baptismal significance in the mention of the angel stirring the water, giving them healing powers (*De Baptismo* 5:5-6). However, not only do the waters not heal the man in this story, verse 4—which carries the reference to the angel—is almost certainly not part of the text of John.[100] From these points—apart from the setting—it is difficult to sustain a case that John intended this story to carry a baptismal motif.[101]

It is more likely that the water of the Pool of Beth-zatha is symbolic of the ineffective ordinances of the Jewish religion.[102] For, as we have seen in the story of the changing of water into wine, the water is likely to have been understood to represent the ineffective religion of the Jews. Here the water that was supposed to offer healing has not been effective in healing for thirty-eight years. The thirty-eight years may be an allusion to Deuteronomy 2:14, where thirty-eight years is said to be the time of wandering in the wilderness from Kadesh-barnea to Wadi Zereb, during which the entire generation of warriors died. The story could then be interpreted "parabolically" as the sick man being the embodiment of law-bound

Judaism.[103] However, Howard is probably right to say that

> unfortunately we are not told that this man had been waiting at Bethesda
> for all those years, and it is not easy to see why the Evangelist should suppose
> his readers would think of Deut. ii. 14 rather than of the period of forty years
> by which the wanderings of the Israelites in the wilderness were usually
> recalled (cf. Ps. xcv. 10).[104]

Dodd has also probably pressed the story too far by suggesting that the man's
inability to get into the water represents the law's inability to create the will to
live.[105]

Jesus' question, "Do you want to be made well?" (Jn 5:6), has caused some
discussion. Theodor Zahn's view that the question is a means of strengthening the
faltering will of the sick man is rightly criticized by Bultmann: the command to
take up his bed is what "fills the soul of the sick man with courage to believe and
his limbs with strength."[106] Haenchen's view is that the narrator has inserted this
question to establish contact between Jesus and the sick man, who is then able to
depict his deplorable situation.[107] It is more likely that John inserts or uses this
question to highlight what he draws attention to in the following narrative. Jesus
gives life to those he chooses, regardless of the initial presence of faith in the person
(5:21).

Jesus' words to the paralytic, "Stand up, take your mat and walk" (Jn 5:8), raise
the question of the story's relationship to that of the paralytic in Mark 2:1-12. The
Johannine story certainly has similarities to Mark in that the healing is not
represented as being related to or dependent on or even generating faith in the
person healed and in that both stories connect sin and sickness (Mk 2:5; Jn 5:14).
Yet unlike the Markan story, the significance of the healing in John is not said to
impress itself on the crowd (cf. Mk 2:12).

So, as is generally agreed, aside from the person being too lame to walk and
being told to stand up, take up his mat and walk, the stories are quite distinct from
each other. That is, the Markan story is set in Capernaum, not Jerusalem, and the
man is brought to a home and lowered through the roof, not deposited beside a
pool of water. Further, and fundamentally, the words common to both stories are
used quite differently. In Mark, Jesus' command is for the benefit of the bystanders;
in John they are for the man.[108]

The words "Stand up" *(egeire)* are almost certainly intended to mean more than
"Stand on your feet!" John uses *egeirō* thirteen times:[109] all but five of them have
to do with Jesus being raised to life.[110] Then in the narrative that follows this story
Jesus says, "Just as the Father raises the dead and gives them life, so also the Son
gives life to whomever he wishes" (Jn 5:21). From this we can conclude that John
sees Jesus' miracles as the work of God in his dispensation of life-giving power.

Also, the life-giving miracles are to be seen as pointing to,[111] or as a reflection of, the life-giving resurrection performed by God, and the resurrection is to be seen as a reflection of the life-giving miracles of Jesus. We have no reason to suppose, from John's perspective, that either the preceding ministry of miracles or the succeeding resurrection are to be seen as superior to the other. Both are equally life-giving works of the Father (cf. Jn 5:17). In such activities, as illustrated in this story, Jesus is giving life on a scale similar to the life God gave Jesus in the resurrection.

Thus, linking this story with that of the raising of Lazarus, Jesus says, "The hour is coming, and is now here, when the dead will hear the voice of the Son of God, and those who hear will live" (Jn 5:25). So this story of the paralytic prepares for the resurrection in that it prepares for the raising of Lazarus, in Jesus' going on to say, "Do not be astonished at this; for the hour is coming when all who are in their graves will hear his voice and will come out" (5:28-29).

The sick man's initial response to Jesus raises the issue of John's view of faith and miracles. Indeed, when Jesus speaks to the man his only response is one of complaint that he has no one to help him into the water (Jn 5:7). Clearly John is portraying a man who cannot have faith in Jesus, for he has no idea who is speaking to him (cf. 5:13).[112] Without the mention of exercising any faith, the man is healed (5:9).

Again John shows no interest in portraying the impact of the miracle on the crowd. The benefit of the miracle is limited to the man's healing. What John does draw attention to is the incredibly obtuse response of the Jews. They have seen the miracle, yet he portrays them as not having been affected by it. Instead, they chastise the man for working on the sabbath by carrying his bed (Jn 5:10). The blindness of the Jews in apprehending the miracle and its significance is highlighted in their asking who the person was who told him to pick up his bed and walk (5:12).

We have already noted that this story marks a change in the way John explains the miracles: this is the first sign that is followed by a discourse elaborating the significance of the miracle for John and his readers. The discourse takes place over three scenes. In the first scene the man carrying his mat on a sabbath is criticized by the Jews (Jn 5:10-13). This theme is developed a little in that Jesus is also said to be persecuted for "doing such things on the Sabbath" (5:16). Since the story itself carries little interpretation, this theme heightens the significance of the story and becomes a foil for the themes developed in the ensuing two scenes.

The second scene takes place in the temple, where Jesus finds the man who had been healed (Jn 5:14). It could be that the temple is the most likely place to look for people,[113] or perhaps John is saying that the man had gone to the temple to give thanks to God for his healing.[114] In Jesus' telling the man to sin no more, John implies that the man's sins up to that point have been forgiven.[115] Then, in telling the man "Do not sin any more, so that nothing worse happens to you" (5:14), John implies a connection between sin and sickness or trouble that is not always made by John. In fact, in the case of the man born blind, the connection is denied (9:2).

Importantly, through these words of Jesus to the healed man (Jn 5:14), John implies that the man understood the identity of his healer: in healing and forgiveness Jesus is revealed. For on being healed, "the man went away and told the Jews that it was Jesus who had made him well" (5:15). However, there has been much discussion as to whether the healed man is being portrayed positively. Read one way, the man is denouncing Jesus, for the Jews are "therefore" (*kai dia touto,* 5:16) said to start "persecuting Jesus."[116] It is most likely, however, that John intends this verse to convey the irony of the man's understanding and communicating Jesus' identity as being both the correct response to a miracle as well as the grounds for Jesus' persecution.

The third scene (Jn 5:15-18), the climax to the healing story, returns to the theme of the Jews objecting to Jesus "doing such things" on the sabbath. Jesus' reply—"My Father is still working, and I also am working" (5:17)—provokes the Jews all the more to seek to kill him because he called God his Father, making himself equal to God (5:18). The Jews can understand Jesus' claim to act like his Father only as blasphemy. "But," as Haenchen says, "the contrary is true. He can do nothing of himself. He is not a 'second God' or even the one true God. He exists only for God."

Haenchen rightly goes on to say that the term *obedience* is not suitable: "That suits a servant, but not a son, as the Evangelist understands this sonship. The son looks only to the Father, and does here on earth what he sees the Father do."[117] This specifies most clearly the meaning that John wants his readers to see in the healing: it was God in Jesus who was performing the healing. Already we can see that, for John, Jesus' miracles are the work of God himself, and God's work and revelation know no respite or limit (Jn 5:17; cf. 9:4).[118]

This scene is simply linked with the following discourse about Jesus and his Father (Jn 5:19-47) by *oun* ("then"). Through this discourse John continues portraying Jesus as totally dependent on God. Thus the miracles draw attention to Jesus having no independence, even if he is a distinct person: he is completely dependent on the Father (5:19-20). Again this discourse also specifies that Jesus' healing is analogous to the Father raising Jesus from the dead.

§7.6 Feeding the Five Thousand (Jn 6:1-15/Mk 6:32-44/Mt 14:13-21/Lk 9:10-17)

Once more Jesus is popular because of his signs.[119] Once more there is a misunderstanding of the significance of the signs.[120] As the previous sign had led to a conflict (Jn 5:17-18), so this story leads to a dispute (6:41-58). But this time the setting is Galilee rather than Jerusalem. The dispute is over belief in Jesus—the only significant source of conflict in the Fourth Gospel.[121] The conflict is so severe that its repercussions include some of his disciples dissociating from him (6:66).

As we consider the use of the feeding story, we cannot escape the question of the relationship of this feeding story to the feeding of the five thousand in the other Gospels. In common with the Synoptic stories, John has the broad agreements of a lake crossing, a miraculous feeding, the disciples leaving Jesus to attempt a crossing of the lake, the appearance of Jesus as he walks on the sea, the demand for a sign, a dialogue on bread and a messianic confession. There are also many smaller details of agreement between the stories.[122] Whereas C. K. Barrett urges that John is, therefore, shown to be dependent on the Synoptic Gospels,[123] most scholars hold the view that John is dependent on traditions parallel to those used by the Synoptic evangelists,[124] contact between the two being during the oral stages of their traditions.[125]

In this story John has particular interests he wishes to emphasize. The first is a negative point, followed by two positive ones.

It is notable that, whereas Mark gives a desert setting to this story (Mk 6:31, 32, 36), John does not. He says that they were on the other side of the Sea of Galilee (Jn 6:1-2). Therefore whether or not the setting in 6:1 is the work of John, he clearly does not wish his readers to see this miracle of feeding as a repetition of the nourishment of the Israelites in the wilderness. With the mention of Jesus going up the mountain (6:3) the Moses theme emerges: Jesus and Moses are to be contrasted.[126] John does not mention teaching, but the Moses theme, along with Jesus being said to sit down with his disciples (6:3), portrays Jesus as the Jewish teacher par excellence. Thus this story is to be seen as teaching.[127]

Second, once again John depicts the crowd following Jesus because of the signs (Jn 6:2). As John has said that Jesus would not entrust himself to "many who believed in his name because they saw the signs" (2:23), the reader has questions about John's view of the relationship between faith and miracles (see §8.8). With this in mind the reader is also prepared in advance for the crowd's misunderstanding of the implications of the miraculous feeding (6:15, 26).[128]

Third, in contrast to the Synoptic stories, Jesus takes the initiative in asking where bread can be bought to feed so many people (Jn 6:5). Whereas in Mark 6:34 Jesus is said to perform the miracle out of compassion, the only reason for the miracle in John is the wish of Jesus. Therefore Jesus remains in focus and in control, and the story is designed to teach directly about Jesus.

Fourth, the Passover setting stands out as significant for the Fourth Gospel. If we keep in mind the reference to the Passover (Jn 6:4) and the sacrificial death of the Lamb of God woven through the explanatory discourse in 6:51-58, the miracle can be seen as a sign of the movement from Moses to Jesus, from bread to flesh and from the provision of bread to the provision of the body of Jesus in his death.[129] Further, the mention of Jesus as the prophet who was expected to come (6:14; cf. 1:21; Deut 18:15) also suggests that John understood this miracle as an expression of the fulfillment of the expectation of the new, or second, exodus (cf. Jn 6:31).[130] To this must be added the probable allusions to Elisha in the multiplication of bread (2 Kings 4:42-44; cf. 4:1-4).

Thus the expectation John has in mind here may be an amalgamation of the two figures (cf. 1 Kings 19).[131] Or, to put it another way, considering jointly the three references to the nearness of the Passover (Jn 2:13; 6:4; 11:55), it can be seen that John is conveying to his readers that Jesus is wrongly perceived here as both an army feeder like Elisha and the prophet king like Moses (6:14).[132]

The eschatological dimension to the story is reinforced in the abundance of the provision of bread (Jn 6:12-13), reflecting the eschatological feast of Isaiah 25:6-9.[133] In turn, the potential connection between this story of the feeding of the five thousand and the Lord's Supper cannot be avoided. It is reinforced by the phrase "after the Lord had given thanks" in 6:23c.[134] This leads to the next point.

Fifth, the phrase "so that nothing may be lost" (*hina mē ti apolētai*, Jn 6:12) in Jesus' direction to gather up the leftover fragments most certainly has more significance than being of interest to environmentalists. Judas is said to have been lost (17:12), and at the end of this chapter, after the discussion on the meaning of the bread, some of the disciples are said to be lost (6:66). Can it then be concluded that "those who 'assimilate' the 'Bread of Life' do not perish, but live eternally"?[135]

Sixth, as we have noted, the importance for John of potential eucharistic motifs in this story have been discussed almost endlessly.[136] In light of the parallels of words and gestures of Jesus between the feeding stories in the Synoptics and the Last Supper,[137] it is arbitrary to resist the conclusion that the wording of the accounts of the Last Supper have colored the wording of the miraculous feeding here.

That John has in mind the Last Supper as he writes is also supported by the parallels of wording between his story and phrases concerning the Eucharist in another early Christian document—the *Didache*. The *Didache* has the lines, "Concerning the fragmented bread, 'We give thanks to you.' . . . As this fragmented bread was scattered on the mountains, but was gathered up" (*Didache* 9:4) and "After you are satisfied" (10:1).[138] What this means is that John's readers are able to have explained for them in the signs some of the significance of the cross. Here that significance is that the cross is the gift of the means of being eternally secure and fed.

That there is no actual fracture of the bread in John's story (Jn 6:11)[139] probably also alerts us to the eucharistic undercurrents. In the story of the cross John draws attention to Jesus' bones not being broken (19:36), as the Paschal lamb was without broken bones.[140]

A widely held view is that the last section of the discourse (on the Jews disputing the phrase about Jesus' flesh, Jn 6:52-58) is a sacramental exposition added by a later editor[141] or added by the Evangelist.[142] But even without the discourse on eating the flesh and drinking the blood of Jesus (6:51b-58), John's story of the miraculous feeding is most probably told in light of the Last Supper tradition.[143]

Seventh, in line with John's focus on Jesus taking the initiative in this miracle (in contrast to the story in Mark), Jesus also distributes the food himself without the aid of the disciples (Jn 6:11; cf. Mk 6:41). The only role of the disciples is to portray the helplessness of the human situation.[144] In saying the crowd received "as much as they wanted" (Jn 6:11, in contrast to the Synoptic tradition), the distribution itself becomes a minor or preliminary miracle: "The supernatural wealth of the host is revealed already at this stage."[145]

Finally, in view of this last miracle story in the Galilean ministry, the people are said to declare Jesus to be "the prophet who is to come into the world" (Jn 6:14; cf. 9:17). As we have just noted, this suggests that in his miracles Jesus is to be seen as fulfilling Old Testament hopes of the coming of a prophet like Moses.[146] Then in 6:15 John identifies the eschatological prophet—the Messiah—with the messianic king,[147] for the crowd is also said to attempt to make him king (cf. 12:13).

This double acclamation is in line with the messianic expectations of the time in that the populace anticipated a messianic prophet who would liberate them from their oppressors.[148] Having Jesus refuse this acclamation, however, emphasizes the nonpolitical nature of his kingship (cf. Jn 18:36). This refusal, as well as John's concluding the discourse with the disciples saying that his teaching was difficult (6:60) and with many of his disciples turning back and no longer following him (6:66), marks this story of the feeding and its interpretation as a turning point in John's overall story.[149] From this point the crowds are no longer shown to be closely associated with Jesus.

John is making clear that this miracle was a sign of the nature of Jesus' messiahship and rule. It was not political but spiritual (cf. Jn 12:13-16), though of course it will have political implications.[150] The spiritual nature of Jesus' kingship is confirmed in that the acclamation of Jesus as a prophet is not denied (6:14); only the interpretation that he must therefore be a temporal king is denied (6:15).

One of the principal themes of the passion story in John is the kingship of Jesus (cf. Jn 18:33-38). Therefore John is probably reinforcing the notion that Jesus' kingship cannot be understood apart from the cross event, which shows him to be king of another world (18:36). The correction of the simplistic and vulgar understanding of the miracles takes place immediately in the next story (6:16-21), as well as in the ensuing discourse on the bread (6:22-58).

There has been some discussion on the relationship between the miracle story and the discourse later in the chapter (Jn 6:25-71). General assent has been given to the view that from 6:31 (which introduces the theme of the manna in the wilderness) John gives a typical midrashic exposition.[151] The crowd, which had seen the miracle, asks for a sign so they can believe Jesus (6:30). They cite Exodus 16:15 as evidence that Jesus should reproduce the miracle of the manna if he is to be accepted as the Messiah (Jn 6:31). Jesus corrects his audience (6:31-33). Then occurs an exegetical debate in which Jesus explains the meaning of Exodus 16:15 (Jn 6:34-48). The discourse turns to revolve around the notion of "eating" (6:49-58).

From this discourse we can garner a number of points that bear on John's understanding of this miracle story and the miracles of Jesus in general. The key points are probably these:

1. As important as the miracles are in revealing the identity of Jesus, the miracles are not to be sought for their own sake. Rather, Jesus himself is to be sought (Jn 6:27, 35, 51-55).

2. Concomitantly, the readers will be sustained not by the miracles but by Jesus himself and his death (6:51-58).

3. Beyond himself and the miracles Jesus offers no evidence of his origin (Jn 6:41) or relationship to God (6:46).

4. Two Old Testament associations involving the Torah and Wisdom are probably used to illustrate the superiority of Jesus over the former dispensation. First, if the publishers of the Fourth Gospel were familiar with bread being a symbol for the Torah in rabbinic traditions[152]—the mention of it having not Moses but God give bread (Jn 6:32)—then it may be that this story is intended to illustrate the superiority of that which Jesus gives through his miracles and in himself. Second, the same conclusion is reached more confidently in noting that Wisdom and the manna are equated by Philo in language that resembles John's here: "The heavenly food of the soul, wisdom, which Moses calls 'mana,' is distributed to all who will use it in equal portions by the divine Word" (*Rer. Div. Her.* 191).[153] The probability of a Wisdom theme here in John—proposing the idea that Jesus and his miracles are superior to the former dispensation—is further enhanced by noting that in Proverbs 9:5 Wisdom is said to offer bread and wine.[154]

§7.7 Walking on the Sea (Jn 6:16-21; cf. Mk 6:45-52/Mt 14:23-33; also Mk 4:35-41/Mt 8:23-27/Lk 8:22-25)

Instead of immediately following the last story of the feeding with its associated discourse (eventually found in Jn 6:22-71), John concludes the feeding story by saying Jesus "withdrew again to the mountain by himself" (6:15). John then (along with Matthew and Mark but not Luke) proceeds here to tell the story of Jesus walking on the sea as a kind of interlude.

The existence of this division between a miracle and its associated discourse probably means that John is dependent on a tradition, for he would have been following his habit to join them together, and it would probably have been easier for John's readers to have the story and the discourse on bread kept together. Not surprisingly, therefore, Barrett proposes that John has derived his story of walking on the sea from Mark.[155]

In support of this can be cited a list of similarities between John and Matthew and Mark: the phrase "when evening came," getting into a boat, sea, wind, rowing, stadia, walking on the sea, and the sentence "It is I; do not be afraid." Yet the differences between John's story and the one in the Synoptics are considerable. The Synoptic story is told from the perspective of Jesus on land, who sees his disciples toiling in rough weather, whereas in John the disciples appear to be waiting for Jesus to come to them. Uncharacteristically in the Synoptics the miracle is greater than in John in that Jesus walks many stadia across the rough sea to the disciples (Mt 14:24) and calms the sea (Mk 6:51).[156] Also, although John's brevity cannot be taken as indicating that it represents a relatively undeveloped form of the story,[157] the many and significant differences between the stories strongly favor John's independence from the Synoptics in this story.[158]

As we have noted, this story of Jesus walking on the sea divides the story of the miraculous feeding from its accompanying discourse. Why then has John included this story? Or if it was in this position in his tradition, why did he leave it here?

It is not sufficient to say that John includes the story of Jesus walking on the sea "because it was firmly fixed in the tradition along with the miracle of the five thousand,"[159] for from what we know about the creativity of the Gospel writers, John would feel at liberty to remove a story if it did not suit his needs. Nor is it sufficient to say that John uses the story "to bring Jesus and his disciples back to Capernaum, where the discourse on the Bread of Life was held,"[160] for again we know that the Gospel writers can move their characters around more easily than by using a whole story. Nor can it be that John has Jesus remove the disciples from "becoming embroiled in a threatening messianic uprising."[161] The text does not support that. Indeed, John has the disciples, not Jesus, take the initiative in going down to the sea, embarking and starting to cross the sea (Jn 6:16; contrast Mk 6:45).

We may have the key to John's purpose in using the story in verse 22, where the point is repeated "that his disciples had gone away alone." For in the next verse John says, "It was now dark" (*skotia*, Jn 6:17). The striking symbolic use of "darkness" in the Fourth Gospel is instructive here.[162] In 1:5 the coming of the Word into the world is likened to light coming to darkness. In 8:12 John has Jesus say, "Whoever follows me will never walk in darkness but will have the light of life." And in 12:35 Jesus says, "If you walk in the darkness, you do not know where you are going."

In this story of Jesus' walking on the sea, having said "It was now dark," John immediately goes on to say, "and Jesus had not yet come to them" (Jn 6:17).

Noting that at the end of the ensuing discourse on Jesus' being the bread of life he says, "Among you there are some who do not believe" (6:64) and that in 12:46 Jesus says, "everyone who believes in me should not remain in the darkness," we can see that the darkness of the sea voyage is due to the disciples' not believing in or taking Jesus with them. Thus when the disciples wished to take Jesus with them it is said that they reached their destination (6:21). (This is not dissimilar to the point made by the Synoptic stories that the presence of Jesus brings calm and safety to the disciples.)[163]

This story is thus probably included to show that the miracles and Jesus cannot be separated from each other and that it is Jesus' true presence or, to put it another way, his followers' believing in him that enables the miracle of his life-giving presence to take place (cf. Jn 12:26). However, it is most probably reading too much into the Fourth Gospel here to conclude that the abiding presence of Jesus is a feature of the church's eucharistic teaching that, in turn, explains why this story is attached to that of the feeding.[164]

The theory that the Evangelist(s) thought that Jesus was walking by *(epi)* the sea and only appeared to be walking on the sea cannot be accepted.[165] (Certainly the Fourth Gospel uses *epi* in Jn 21:1 for Jesus walking by the sea. But that is clarified in 21:4, where it is said that Jesus was standing on the beach.) If John wanted to make it plain that Jesus was not "on" but "by" the sea, he could be expected to use *para* ("by") the sea.[166] Also, without Jesus' being said to walk on the sea, the story seems almost pointless and the disciples' fear (6:19) groundless.

An outstanding feature of the story is Jesus' response to the fear of the disciples when they see him walking on the sea. He says, "It is I *(egō eimi); do* not be afraid" (Jn 6:20). In the world of the Fourth Gospel, the phrase "It is I" was used in a number of ways.

For example, it could answer the question "Who are you?" (e.g., *Jub.* 24:22; Rev 1:17) or "What are you?" (e.g., Epictetus *Discourses* IV:8:15-16). Also, the phrase could be used to identify a speaker (e.g., "I am the truth" *PGM* 5:148).[167] Most of the "I am" statements of Jesus in John fall into this identificatory category.[168] And in these statements John has Jesus speaking of a unique relationship with God.

Most striking are those cases, such as the one here (Jn 6:20), that are in the absolute: "I am!"[169] In the context of Jesus' walking on the sea and saying "Do not be afraid" (a familiar Old Testament phrase in the mouth of God),[170] it is most likely that John's readers would have recalled Exodus 3:14, where God says to Moses, "I am who I am."[171] Therefore if John is not identifying Jesus with God here, he is certainly indicating an extremely close and unique relationship with God through which it is possible for God to speak in a unique uninterrupted way.[172] It can thus be concluded that in the miracle of Jesus walking on the sea the followers of Jesus are confronted by a person in whom they are confronting God himself.[173]

Once again there is a transitional passage in which the crowd seeks Jesus (Jn 6:22-24) "not because you saw signs, but because you ate your fill of the loaves" (6:26). They had missed the deeper significance of the miracles. As Culpepper says,

> The optimism of the early chapters collapses, and there is cause for real doubt as to whether Jesus will be able to execute his mission successfully. If it were not for the prologue and the early chapters, the reader would be fearful that the forces of unbelief were on their way to complete victory.[174]

Throughout chapter 7 conflict between the Jews and Jesus is sustained, and it reaches its most bitter intensity in chapter 8, when Jesus says his opponents have the devil as their father (Jn 8:44). They retort that he is a Samaritan and has a demon (8:48). They pick up stones to throw at him, but Jesus hides himself (8:59).

§7.8 Healing a Man Born Blind (Jn 9:1-7)
The overt antagonism between Jesus and his opponents is left behind for the moment. Instead, John picks up the theme of Jesus being the light of the world (Jn 8:12) as Jesus gives sight to a blind man.

The sign or miracle is narrated in John 9:1-7; the implications of the story are related in the remainder of the chapter (Jn 9:8-41), though within the story is the great interpretive statement "I am the light of the world" (9:5). Although the narrative begins with a general phrase ("As he walked along," *kai paragōn*, occurring only here in John), the story is related to, and used to illustrate, the saying (in 8:12) that Jesus is "the light of the world" (cf. 9:5). Thus the story becomes, in part at least, a symbol of a believer's salvation.[175] Certain aspects of the story reveal John's special interest in its contribution to his view of miracles.

First, there is the dialogue between Jesus and the disciples (Jn 9:2-6), which begins with the disciples asking if the man was blind because he or his parents sinned (9:2). That illness was a punishment for sin is a view well attested in Judaism, notably in the book of Job.[176] Whether John or Jesus viewed sickness as the result of sin cannot be ascertained from this passage.[177] Jesus' reply in the negative is specific to this particular man (9:3). At best, John might expect his readers to conclude that the question of theodicy is to be asked in each individual case. At the least John is expecting his readers to see in sickness the opportunity for the works of God to be revealed. In turn, this would cause people to trust Jesus as being the One sent by God (cf. 9:33).

Second, verses 4 and 5—about working while it is day—are so Johannine that it has been argued that they have come from the hand of the Evangelist.[178] Even though it may no longer be possible to be confident which particular verses John introduced into his sources, these verses stand out as characteristic of the Gospel and therefore important in understanding this story.

In the context of this story, the works of Jesus are the miracles; equally they are also the work of God (cf. §8.5.2). The urgency of working or performing miracles before the night of death comes refers both to the ministry of Jesus and, by implication (see Jn 9:5, "As long as I am in the world, I am the light of the world"), to the work of his followers in their post-Easter setting. Because this miracle is an expression of Jesus being and bringing light into the world (8:12),[179] verse 5 is an assurance to the readers that among them they can also experience the light—the miracles—of Jesus. Therefore, for John, Jesus remains in the world not only through the unity between Jesus and his followers (cf. 17:22) but also through miracles.

This view is also expressed in verse 4, the most likely reading of which is "*We* [not *I*] must work the works of him who sent *me* [not *us*]."[180] Whether or not the "We . . . us" was original or introduced by the Christian community,[181] it is likely that John is only associating the disciples with the work of Jesus[182] and saying that the work of God is to continue in the work of the followers of Jesus after Easter (cf. Jn 14:12).

Third, the urgency and importance of the miraculous work of Jesus is highlighted in that the miracle takes place on the sabbath (Jn 9:14). The physical preparations for the miracle—spitting on the ground and making mud with saliva—follow immediately the saying about urgency. This could be intended to show clearly that Jesus' actions were a breach of the sabbath laws.[183] But his healing ministry is so important that it overrides such considerations.

Fourth, the divided response of the Pharisees (Jn 9:16) is used to reflect on the miracle-working Jesus: he must be a sinner, for he breaks the sabbath; but a sinner could not cure the blind man. The divided response of the Pharisees also highlights the divided response the miracles of Jesus elicit: some people will have their eyes opened, and some will remain blind (9:25, 41).

The same theme occurs in verse 22: "The Jews had already agreed that anyone who confessed Jesus to be the Messiah would be put out of the synagogue" (*aposunagōgos*).[184] There has been debate on the significance of this verse for John's readers.[185]

On the one hand, it is argued as unthinkable that the synagogue already possessed such a test for heresy.[186] The claim is that there is no indication that the confession of Jesus as Messiah was a test issue between Jews and Christians before A.D. 70.[187]

On the other hand, in view of the possibility that Jesus spoke of his faithful followers being excluded by fellow Jews,[188] it is thought not intrinsically out of the question that, even during his ministry, opponents of Jesus attempted to silence and exclude his followers from claiming him to be a messianic figure of popular expectation.[189] Also to be noted is that Acts 9:2, a setting not long after Easter, has Saul on a mission to extricate followers of Jesus from the synagogues at Damascus on the basis that they belonged to "the Way" (perhaps to be understood as a messianic sect within Judaism).[190] Further, in a discussion about the authenticity of a Christian's experience of the Spirit (1 Cor 12:3), Paul may have in mind Christians who attempted to maintain their membership in the synagogue.[191]

Notwithstanding this debate, John has the saying about exclusion in the context of a miracle story. That is, John sees the response to the miracles of Jesus as dividing people between those who will confess him as the Messiah and those who will reject him and his followers.

Fifth, once again (cf. Jn 6:5) Jesus takes the initiative in performing the healing miracle of his own volition (9:6). He requires no one to direct or guide him in his ministry, save his Father (cf. 9:4).

Sixth, in contrast to the Pharisees, who three times express their ignorance (Jn 9:16, 24, 29), the blind man is portrayed as gradually understanding who Jesus is as the Son of Man.[192] He comes to faith and is then said to worship Jesus (9:35-38).[193] As Brown says, "The blind man emerges from these pages in John as one of the most attractive figures of the Gospels."[194]

Finally, if we take an overview of the story of the man, we see that it bears considerable resemblance to that of Jesus.[195] As with Jesus, his washing is followed by an illumination. Both share in being the subject of disputes over their identity and of division within their families. When interrogated, the man uses the same formula of self-identification as does Jesus—"I am"—and both figures produce hostile responses. As if prefiguring the trial of Jesus, the man is not believed when he testifies before the authorities.

Even though John left the theme of hostility at the start of this story, the Jewish leaders are portrayed as soon seeking evidence against Jesus. Even after the clear parablelike sayings about Jesus being the gate (Jn 10:9) and the good shepherd (10:14), opinions about Jesus are divided. Some did not think a healer could have a demon (10:21). Others said he had a demon (10:20), and there was an attempt to stone him (10:31), as well as a failed attempt to arrest him (10:39). But now the readers know that, despite the impending doom, no one other than Jesus will determine his fate: he will voluntarily lay down his life.[196]

§7.9 Raising Lazarus to Life (Jn 11:1-57)

In this story we reach the climax of the ministry of Jesus and approach his arrest, death and resurrection: the raising of Lazarus both causes and leads to the death and, hence, the resurrection of Jesus.[197] Whereas in the other Gospels Jesus is condemned in reaction to his ministry in general, in John the miracle of the raising of Lazarus is the direct cause of the Sanhedrin meeting to decide to destroy Jesus

(Jn 11:47). Also, if we understand the Gospel of John as being two major sections, this story is the last in the book of signs leading into the book of glory.

One of the distinctive features of this story is that, apart from the passion narrative, it is the longest continuous narrative in this Gospel. Also distinctive of this story is that, although John often follows a miracle story with the explanatory dialogue of Jesus, this sign story has the explanation woven through it. Further, the importance of this story also is seen in that all the miracles so far have been paired. (Two stories of Cana are paired, and so are two Galilean sea stories and two Jerusalem miracle stories.)[198] However, this one is left to stand alone and above, yet still among, the miracles of Jesus.

Sensing tensions within the story as we now have it, many students of the Gospel have charted possible histories of it.[199] For example, assigning the story to the signs source, Bultmann says that John used sayings from the revelation discourses to insert verses 4, 7-10, 16, 20-32 and 40-42.[200] Earlier Paul Wendland had postulated that the story arose from John's free additions to Synoptic material.[201] However, Dodd rightly says that "the interweaving of narrative and dialogue is complete. Any attempt to isolate a piece of pure narrative which may have served as nucleus soon becomes arbitrary in its treatment of the text." He concludes that there is no recoverable separate story from the pregnant dialogues between Jesus and the other characters in the story.[202]

The issue of historicity is never very far from our minds in this story, not least since the Synoptic Gospels make no mention of it. Notwithstanding, we must leave the issue of historicity for the discussion in §14.4, save to ask the related question about the relationship of this story to material in the Synoptics. For if there is a literary or tradition relationship between the two, we may be served in better understanding John's message in his redaction of material with which we are familiar. This will also provide guidance on the question of historicity.

It has been suggested that the story of the raising of Lazarus is a piece of fiction that was inspired by the story of the raising of the son of the widow of Nain (Lk 7:11-16).[203] Further, the characters of John's story are suggested to have been derived from the stories of the woman anointing Jesus' feet in Bethany (Mk 14:3-9) and Mary and Martha in Luke 10:38-42, as well as the parable of Lazarus and the rich man in Luke 16:19-31.[204] The strength of this suggestion lies in the final line of the parable of Lazarus: "If they do not listen to Moses and the prophets, neither will they be convinced even if someone rises from the dead" (Lk 16:31). This suggests that the coming to life of Lazarus would not lead everyone to faith, as is the case in the reaction of some of the Jews (Jn 11:46).

However, the broad objection to this proposal is that it presupposes that John relies on reshuffling Synoptic material rather than having an independent tradition.[205] But as we have noted, it is now coming to be agreed that John is probably reliant on traditions parallel to those used by the Synoptic Gospels. Indeed, the Lukan parable said to be behind this Johannine miracle could just as easily have arisen out of a miracle as the other way round.[206] Therefore in our search for the message of John in this story—and eventually its historical origins—we are left with the story as it is in John.[207]

Some of the significance of the story for John can be seen in noting that this last miraculous sign in the ministry of the earthly Jesus has a number of important contacts with the first miracle story. In the story of the changing of water into wine, the incident is said to be sparked by a comment that is not actually calling for Jesus to do anything: Jesus' mother tells him that the wine has run out (Jn 2:3). Here the sisters send a message to Jesus that the one whom he loved was sick (11:3). But in neither case does John portray Jesus as moved to do anything. Jesus' ministry is not determined by the clamor of those around him (cf. 7:3-10).

In both stories these statements are followed by Jesus' comments about the potential implication of the ensuing story for his destiny—his "hour" (Jn 2:4) or his "glory" (11:4). It is not that the miracles glorify Jesus or are his "hour" because they lead to his death.[208] Rather, as we have already seen, the signs in themselves, like the resurrection, even if on a smaller scale, equally reflect the purpose and glory of God and the Son.

Also, like the first sign, the raising of Lazarus is intended to bring about belief. Jesus says that he is glad he was not present while Lazarus was still alive "so that you may believe" (Jn 11:15; cf. 2:11). Then, at the end of the actual story of the raising of Lazarus, John says that many of the Jews who had seen what Jesus had done believed (11:45). However, as has been represented before (cf. 5:9b-18), some of the Jews reacted negatively to the sign by telling the Pharisees, who in turn called a meeting of the Sanhedrin to condemn Jesus (11:47). These contacts with the first sign story enable John to reinforce his view that the raising of Lazarus reflects the glory of Jesus and leads both to trust in and rejection of Jesus.

It is, Dodd rightly discerns, verse 4 that governs the whole story: "The illness does not lead to death; rather it is for God's glory, so that the Son of God may be glorified through it."[209] On one level, the illness of Lazarus does not lead to death. His four days in the grave do not prove to be his immediate end. Jesus raises him to life. On another level, the raising of Lazarus is portrayed as leading directly to the death of Jesus by the Sanhedrin immediately deciding to put Jesus to death. However, this death is not the end of Jesus either. He is, like Lazarus, raised to life again. On a further level, the story leads the disciples to their death. Thomas says to his fellow disciples, "Let us also go, that we may die with him" (Jn 11:16). We may be able to take this as an ironic truth, expressed in other parts of the New Testament, that in dying with Jesus his followers find life.[210]

Verse 4 is also important because it produces echoes in other places in this story

(Jn 11:13, 40), as well as through the remainder of the Gospel. God's glory is seen in the sign of the raising of Lazarus, and the Son's glory is seen in this story, revealing his relationship to the Father (11:41-42). Importantly, it leads to his death and eventual resurrection. Thus from now on the mention of the glorification of Jesus takes on a new meaning.[211] It is no longer seen through the lens of the miracles but is seen plainly for itself.

The glory expected to be seen in the raising of Lazarus (Jn 11:4) is not to be perceived automatically. On the one hand, Jesus says to Martha that she will see the glory of God if she believes (11:40). John portrays the expression of that belief in Martha's having to be involved in taking away the stone from the tomb (11:39, 41). On the other hand, the Pharisees, who reject Jesus, do not see his glory in this sign (11:45-53).

By means of verse 5, which says that although Jesus loved Lazarus he stayed two more days where he was, John is able to establish the idea, from the beginning of the story, that the greater work for Lazarus as well as the greater glory of Jesus was in raising a dead man rather than a sick man. The reader is also informed that the greater glory of and for Jesus will be in his death rather than in his ongoing life. Thomas's naive call for the disciples to follow Jesus, "that we may die with him" (Jn 11:16) expresses the truth that, for John, the followers of Jesus who wish to share in the glory of Jesus—perhaps through their own miraculous deeds (cf. 14:12)—must also share in the journey to the cross (cf. Mk 8:34; 10:52).

In the dialogue with Martha (Jn 11:21-28) John has the statement of Jesus, "I am the resurrection and the life. Those who believe in me, even though they die, will live, and everyone who lives and believes in me will never die" (11:25-26). This turns the miracle of the raising of Lazarus into a parable of the eternal life Jesus offers those—dead or alive—who believe in him. Those who die will rise in Christ, and those who believe in Christ in this life are able to experience life before death. Thus the believer is said never to die (11:26) because of having responded positively to the miracles of Jesus.

English translators have rendered Jesus' emotion in his dialogue with Mary variously as "greatly disturbed," "deeply moved," "troubled" and weeping (Jn 11:33, 35; cf. NIV).[212] But it cannot be denied that "the word *[embrimasthai]* . . . indicates an outburst of anger, and any attempt to reinterpret it in terms of an internal emotional upset caused by grief, pain, or sympathy is illegitimate."[213] This anger of Jesus, according to verse 33, arises when Jesus sees Mary and the Jews weeping. Presumably Jesus is weeping over their apparent disbelief in his power to raise Lazarus from the dead. This is confirmed in verse 37, where the Jews appear to misunderstand Jesus' emotion and express their surprise that Jesus cannot do anything for Lazarus. Consequently Jesus comes angrily *(embrimasthai)* to the tomb.

To this could be added the possibility that Jesus is troubled in the face of death.

That is, in 13:21 the word *tarassein* ("to be troubled") is used of how Jesus felt about being betrayed into the hands of Satan to die. On three other occasions when *tarassein* is used (Jn 12:27; 14:1, 27) it relates to facing death. Could it be then that Chrysostom (*John* LXIII:2) was correct in saying that this emotion of Jesus is his distressed response to the struggle with Satan? If so, there is a hint that the miracle of Jesus involves a struggle with Satan,[214] a theme familiar in the Synoptic miracle stories.

It has been common in John for the miracles to be portrayed as producing trust in Jesus, as well as misunderstanding and disbelief. The response to the raising of Lazarus is no exception (Jn 11:44-46). It is also common for John to convey two meanings in the words of his characters. In the words of Caiaphas—that it was expedient for one man to die to save the whole people (11:50)—we have a reasonable political statement as well as the climax to this story. The raising of Lazarus, the last sign in the ministry of Jesus, was to lead to his death on behalf of all (cf. Mk 10:45).

§7.10 The Large Catch of Fish (Jn 21:4-14; cf. Lk 5:1-11)

Most students of this Gospel agree that the statement in John 20:30-31 (about many other signs being done by Jesus but those in the Gospel being written so that the reader may come to believe) once formed the conclusion to the Gospel. Concomitantly it is also generally agreed that chapter 21 has been appended by someone other than the person or persons who published the first twenty chapters.[215] This passage's being an appendix from a different author alerts us to the possibility of a view of miracles distinct from the rest of the Gospel. (*Sēmeion*, for example, is not used in this Synoptic-like story; cf. Lk 5:1-11.)[216]

This story involves a double revelation through the miracle. At one level it is a story of a great catch of fish revealing the glory of God in Jesus. More profoundly it is the story of the appearance of the risen Jesus being revealed to his followers.

Most scholars believe that the present story of the large catch of fish arose out of the combination of two strands of tradition: one about a meal and the other about a catch of fish. There is less confidence that the strands can now be distinguished from each other.[217]

We have already noted that a similar story about a large catch of fish is found in Luke 5:1-11 (see §5.7). Because of the differences in detail and vocabulary between the two stories, we said, it is unlikely that there is any literary relationship between them. Instead, Luke and the publishers of the Fourth Gospel have probably had access to different versions of the same story. Also, we noted, the question as to which story is earlier is no longer answerable with confidence. However, because it is less likely that an early Christian writer would take a story from after the resurrection and place it in the ministry of the earthly Jesus than the opposite and because Luke is more likely to use a Galilean story in the body of his Gospel than in the Easter story, where Jerusalem is the focus of attention, it is more likely that the Fourth Gospel preserves the locality of the story.

Twice in the first verse and once at the end of the story (Jn 21:1, 14) the risen Jesus shows or reveals *(phaneroō)* himself to the disciples. From the use of this word in relation to other miracles—at the end of the story of the changing of water into wine where Jesus revealed his glory (2:11) and in the explanation of the healing of the blind man as a means of revealing God's work in the man (9:3)—we can expect that the author is using a further revelation of the nature of Jesus (cf. 1 Jn 1:2). The nature of that revelation of the risen Jesus is seen in Peter's confession: "It is the Lord!" (Jn 21:7). This comes in the context of Jesus directing and bringing harvest in mission.

Considerable allegorical significance has been seen in various aspects of the story. For example, S. Agourides sees Peter's nakedness as symbolic of his spiritual state since having denied Jesus; Peter's putting on clothing is symbolic of his conversion. His plunging into the sea hints at the exchange between Jesus and Peter concerning washing and purity, and the two-hundred-cubit swim is symbolic of Peter's repentance (Jn 13:9-11). But Brown's skepticism of such detailed allegorization ought probably to be shared by serious students of this Gospel.[218]

Yet regardless of whether or not the number of fish in verse 11 is a genuine recollection of a vivid detail, possibly some allegorical meaning in the number is intended. For such a precise number comes as a surprise; it catches us off guard, not having been told any other precise details in the story.[219] Of all the theories regarding the significance of the number of fish, that suggested by Augustine is as likely as any to be right, not least because it comes from an ancient rather than a modern mind.[220]

Augustine noted that 153 is the triangular number of 17. (That is, the sum of the numbers from 1 to 17 is 153.) In turn, the number 17 is the addition of 5 (the number of baskets multiplied) and 12 (the number of baskets collected after the feeding of the five thousand).[221] Thus if the story of the feeding of the five thousand is a reflection of the death of Jesus, this story is probably intended to reflect on the resurrection, for in the ancient world fish represented fruitfulness, life and immortality.[222] At the same time, the catching of fish may also focus on the gathering nature and expected great success of the mission of the church (cf. Mk 1:17).

Jerome (*Commentary on Ezekiel* 49:7) came to the same conclusion, saying that Greek and Latin poets—for example, Oppian of Cilicia—held the view that there were a total of 153 species of fish in the world. However, Robert M. Grant has discredited this view by noting that in Oppian the figure is 157.[223] Therefore pending a more convincing suggestion, it is perhaps best to stay with the interpretation that the number 153 is intended to reflect on the fruitfulness, life and immortality represented in the resurrection.

Verse 11, in which Simon Peter hauls the net ashore, contains two features of particular interest in understanding the Fourth Gospel's perspective on this story. First, since *haul (helkuō)* occurs in this Gospel five out of its six appearances in the New Testament, it is to be expected that the word is of special significance.[224] In John 6:44 and 12:32 the word is used of people being drawn toward Jesus through his death. The readers of the Fourth Gospel may then have seen in the use of the word here the idea that through the death of Jesus many are now being drawn to Jesus. With this in mind, this appended miracle story picks up the saying in 20:21—"As the Father has sent me, so I send you"—and becomes the Fourth Gospel's illustration that the Great Commission is successful through, perhaps, seemingly irrational obedience to Jesus.

A second important feature of verse 11 is the mention of the net not tearing (*schizō*, also at Jn 19:24). The most natural interpretation of the net not breaking is that the church is able to contain all who can be brought into its compass. However, to this understanding should probably be added the idea that the church will not be destroyed by division despite the great number of people, for earlier in the Gospel the noun *schisma* ("division") is used for the division Jesus caused in the crowd (7:43; 9:16; 10:19).[225] Also, we must not miss the possibility of the idea of the simple blessing on the life of his followers that this story may be intended to portray, for in *Testament of Zebulon* 6:6 a large catch of fish is a sign of God's blessing.

Since verse 13 says that Jesus "took the bread and gave it to them, and did the same with the fish," it is hard to escape the eucharistic symbolism of the story.[226] This verse is reminiscent of the parallel saying in the story of the feeding of the five thousand (Jn 6:11), which is also set by the lake and is generally recognized to be written in a way that conforms to the Last Supper.[227]

Verse 13 is preceded by the saying that no one dared ask who it was on the lakeside, for "they knew it was the Lord" (Jn 21:12). This is the same theme as at the end of Luke's Gospel: Jesus is recognized in the context of the breaking of bread (Lk 24:30-31). The publishers of the Fourth Gospel as we have it, like John before, saw miracles as revealing the identity and nature of Jesus as the one feeding his followers by means of his death. In contrast to John, at least from this one example, the publishers of the Fourth Gospel probably went beyond symbolism to understand the miracles allegorically.

§7.11 The Next Step

At the beginning of this chapter we noted some of the questions that arise from examining the signs, or miracle stories, in the Fourth Gospel: the picture of Jesus intended in the signs; the meaning and significance, as well as implication, of the use of the term *sign;* the question of faith and miracles; and the relationship between the miracles in John and in the Synoptics, for example. Having examined each of the stories, we can go on to answer these and other questions in the next chapter.

Eight

The Miracles of Jesus in the Fourth Gospel

The Issues

....

§8.1 Introduction

Having examined each of the miracle, or sign, stories in the Fourth Gospel, we now can not only draw together some conclusions but also enter into the discussions concerning some of the major issues arising in relation to the miracles of Jesus in the Fourth Gospel. This in turn will help us work toward understanding this Gospel's perspective on the miracles of Jesus. The first issue to be discussed will contribute most directly to an understanding of the nature of the signs.

§8.2 Are There Other Signs?

It has been suggested that the "many other signs" said to be performed by Jesus (Jn 20:30; cf. 21:24-25) are not to be identified exclusively or even primarily with the miracles.[1] Dodd, for example, argued to extend the category of sign to include the cleansing of the temple (Jn 2:13-21),[2] for up to this point in the Gospel Jesus has performed only one miracle or sign—the turning of water into wine. Yet at the conclusion of the story of the cleansing of the temple, John says, "many believed in his name because they saw the signs [plural] that he was doing" (2:23). Dodd's suggestion, however, has no basis in the text. We know from 20:31 that the writer thought that Jesus performed many other signs apart from those related in the Gospel. Thus this comment in 2:23 is probably also intended to refer to signs left unrecorded. In any case, it is unlikely that John thought the cleansing of the temple was a sign in the same way as the miracles, for in 4:54 he calls the healing of the official's son the second sign. Even if this verse is from John's signs source, it suggests that he did not consider any other actions of Jesus so far to be signs.

Brown has suggested another candidate for a nonmiraculous sign: the lifting up of the Son of Man being compared to the serpent of the exodus story (Jn 3:14-15). In favor of this view is that the comparison is drawn from Numbers 21:9, where in the Septuagint it is said that Moses set the serpent on a *sēmeion*.[3] However, John gives no overt hint that the lifting up of the Son of Man was a sign.[4]

In regard to the resurrection our conclusion needs to be different. In the story of the cleansing of the temple, the Jews ask Jesus for a sign to authorize his behavior (Jn 2:16). The sign John has Jesus offer is his resurrection (2:19-22).

To conclude, John sees the miracles as signs in a class of their own, and the death and resurrection are probably to be seen as another unique class of sign.[5] Therefore in that the words and actions of the Johannine Jesus have more significance than their prima facie meaning (cf. Jn 12:37; 18:32 [21:19]), the nonmiraculous actions of Jesus can be understood as "symbolic actions" rather than as Johannine "signs."[6]

§8.3 Why No Exorcisms?

When examining the miracles of Jesus in the Synoptic Gospels we found that exorcisms were so important that they could take a programmatic place in the story of Jesus' ministry (Mk 1:21-28) and virtually sum up his ministry (e.g., Lk 13:32). Whereas a miracle still takes a programmatic position in the Fourth Gospel (Jn 2:1-12), this Gospel, as well as the Johannine epistles and the Apocalypse of John, says nothing about exorcism[7] or about Jesus being an exorcist.[8] In view of the evidence that Jesus was widely known as a powerful and popular exorcist,[9] it does not seem reasonable to suggest that the author of John's Gospel knew nothing of this tradition.

Even if it is argued that none of the exorcism stories has its origin in Judea, the home of the the Beloved Disciple upon which this Gospel may depend, it is also unlikely to explain the absence of exorcism stories in the Fourth Gospel in light of the wide reputation of Jesus as a popular exorcist. Further, if we accept the emerging view that the Gospels were written not for particular audiences but for Christian readers at large,[10] we cannot conclude that the exorcism stories were omitted because they were of little interest to a particular community. We can only conclude that John has suppressed or deliberately ignored this tradition. Can this be explained?

It has been suggested that John was embarrassed about portraying Jesus as a man of his time using the healing techniques of his contemporaries.[11] However, that cannot be the case, for John is happy to include other techniques familiar to other healers: healing from a distance (Jn 4:46-54) and the use of spittle (9:1-7). It has also been suggested that "avoiding demon exorcism stories may have been John's way of avoiding the charge that Jesus affected exorcisms by the power of Satan."[12] This, however, is also unlikely, for John does not avoid the similar charge of Jesus having a demon and being mad (7:20; 8:48; 10:20). Rather, a number of aspects of Johannine theology have probably contributed to his deliberate suppression of Jesus' association with exorcism.[13]

First is the Johannine notion of the function of Jesus' miracles. The miracles are considered so to reveal the identity of Jesus that the readers would conclude that he was the Christ (Jn 20:30-31). Therefore, not only did John choose spectacular miracles (cf. 9:32),[14] but he chose miracles that were thought to be the work of God, such as the turning of water into wine or walking on the sea. By contrast, to associate Jesus with the relatively common healing of the demonized performed by many other healers of the time would have appeared banal and unconvincing. John P. Meier makes a similar point: "John's high christology of the eternal Word made flesh would sit uneasily with Jesus engaging in sometimes lengthy battles and negotiations with demons (who, after all, are only minions of Satan, Jesus' true adversary)."[15]

A second factor that has probably contributed to John not mentioning Jesus being an exorcist is his playing down of the theme of the kingdom of God.[16] In the Synoptic Gospels (and hence, presumably, large sectors of the early church), exorcism and the kingdom of God are so closely associated that for John to exclude one probably meant that he felt obliged to exclude the other (cf. Mt 12:28/Lk 11:20). To put the point another way, for John to mention Jesus performing exorcisms may have carried with it a particular view of the kingdom of God that would have diminished the notion of Jesus' kingship that John wanted to highlight.

Third, in the Synoptic Gospels the defeat of Satan is linked with Jesus' exorcisms (e.g., Mk 3:20-27). In John the battle with and the defeat of Satan—the grand cosmic exorcism as Meier calls it—is linked almost exclusively to the cross.[17] This shift in Johannine theology probably carried with it the need to remove reference to exorcisms, which other Christians—perhaps including his readers—would have associated with the defeat of Satan.

Nevertheless when discussing the story of the raising of Lazarus we saw that the word association involving "to be angry" (*embrimasthai*, Jn 11:33) and "to be deeply moved" *(tarassein)*[18] provides some evidence that John saw the miracle of the raising of Lazarus as a battle with Satan. However, in the nature of the miracle, this association looks forward to the cross rather than back to the other miracles as battlegrounds with Satan.

§8.4 The Position of the Signs

Apart from the eighth story in the appendix of the Gospel (Jn 21:4-14), all the other seven miracle stories occur in the first eleven chapters. Though this means that seven miracle stories may symbolize a perfection of accomplishment in Jesus' ministry, it leaves open the question as to why there are no miracle stories through most of the last half of the Gospel.

It is quite possible that, by relying on a signs source, John found material on signs exhausted by the end of chapter 11. However, John was creative enough not to find a signs source such a limiting factor. His distribution of signs is likely to be more intentional.[19]

The miracles in John are, in themselves, signs that reveal the glory of God through the action of Jesus, who is his Son, and that perform the work of his Father—as is particularly clear through the raising of Lazarus. The miracles were not then as Bultmann thought, "granted as a concession to man's weakness."[20] Of course, human need is the occasion for all the miracles, but meeting these needs turns out to be a subsidiary purpose. In John, God does not show himself without the splendor of miracles.[21] Thus the miracles also anticipate the larger and clearer sign—the death and resurrection of Jesus.

Perhaps therefore John allowed the story of the passion to be told uncluttered by other signs, which had served their purpose in relation to the great sign of the death and especially the resurrection of Jesus.[22] Now, in the latter part of the Gospel, the glorification of Jesus is no longer the seeing of his relationship with the Father through mighty miracles but rather his return to his Father.[23] Thus the signs of the first half of the Gospel reveal the identity of Jesus, whereas the sign of the second half of the Gospel reveals his destiny as the risen Lord ascended to his Father. This means that the signs were more than a preparation for the full revelation of Jesus in the second half of the Gospel.[24] They have a distinct, even if also a limited, function in revealing Jesus. Hence the separation of the signs from the sign in John.

§8.5 The Vocabulary of Miracle

One of the most obvious differences between the miracle stories of John and those we have encountered in the Synoptic Gospels is the distinctive vocabulary used. The two distinctive words of the language of miracles in the Fourth Gospel are *ergon* ("work") and *sēmeion* ("sign"). His avoidance of *dunamis* is significant, as are his single use of the phrase "signs and wonders" *(sēmeia kai terata)* and the way he uses *doxa* ("glory").

1. *Dunamis.* In the Synoptic Gospels *dunamis* ("power")[25] is frequently associated with the miracles of Jesus.[26] John omits the word altogether. That is not to say that John's vocabulary denies Jesus' powerful ability as a miracle worker, for

John uses *dunamai* ("to be powerful or able") more often than the other Gospel writers do.[27] For instance, in the healing of the blind man, the Pharisees recognize Jesus' "ability" to heal (Jn 9:16, 33). Certainly Jesus is often shown to have unlimited power or ability from God, as in the raising of Lazarus (11:37). But in this aspect of John's vocabulary, the miracles are not drawing attention to the personal power of Jesus. They are part of the powerful work of God (cf. 5:17-20).

2. *Ergon.* There are twenty-seven occurrences of *ergon* ("work")[28] in John's Gospel, nineteen of which refer to the work of Jesus.[29] Of these, only once is *ergon* used by someone other than Jesus: in 7:3 the brothers of Jesus say he should go to Judea so his disciples may see the "works" he does. The other eighteen times, *ergon* is used by Jesus to refer to doing his Father's "work." Indeed, Jesus does not say they are *his* works. Rather, when he refers to his work he always does so in the context of his relationship with the Father,[30] who gives Jesus the work (cf. Jn 5:36).

Sometimes John appears to use *ergon* of the ministry of Jesus in general.[31] In 17:4 *ergon* is on the lips of Jesus and sums up his entire ministry: "I glorified you on earth by finishing the *work* that you gave me to do" (cf. Jn 4:34). Sometimes these works are specifically the miracles.[32] Sometimes Jesus' words are presented as "works."[33] However, it is not possible to follow Bultmann in his program to demote the miracles of Jesus by identifying the "works" *(erga)* with the "words" of Jesus.[34] First, the Fourth Gospel distinguishes between works and words (see Jn 10:32-38; 14:8-12). Second, as just noted, there are too many examples of the works being specifically and conclusively miracles.

Rather, although the miracles are a distinct "work" of Jesus, John does blur the distinction among the miracles, words and entire work of Jesus. John may distinguish between "signs" and "works," but there is an overlap in the usage of the terms.[35] Thus in the miracles, as much as in the overall ministry of Jesus, God is to be understood as the author of what is seen in Jesus (Jn 14:10).

This intention of using *ergon* for the miracles is confirmed by noting the Old Testament background to the word. In the Septuagint *ergon* was used to refer to the work God did on behalf of his people, especially in his creation (Gen 2:2) and then salvation through the exodus (Ex 34:1; Pss 66:5; 77:12).[36] Thus in having Jesus identify his activity as "works" John is identifying Jesus and God. In the work of Jesus, including particularly the miracles, God himself is creatively at work to save his people. Also, in using *ergon* for the miracles, there is a slight possibility that John may be preserving the authentic voice of Jesus, for the Synoptics also use *ergon* of his miracles (see §4.18 on Mt 11:2; cf. Lk 24:19).

3. *Sēmeion. Sēmeion* ("sign")[37] is one of the most important and characteristic words of the Fourth Gospel.[38] In the Synoptic Gospels it is never used for the miracles of Jesus. Instead it is most often used of an eschatological sign that Jesus'

opponents unsuccessfully seek from him.[39] The Synoptic Gospels use *dunamis* to refer to miracles in the way the Fourth Gospel uses "sign."[40]

When the first three evangelists use "sign" for a miracle, they generally use the word in relation to the demand for Jesus to produce a sign to convince doubters of his credentials (e.g., Mt 12:38-39; Lk 23:8), but they never use it of a miracle of Jesus. They also use the word of the eschatological "signs of the times" (e.g., Mk 13:4). Whereas in the Synoptic Gospels Jesus consistently refuses to give such proof, in John, when asked for a "sign" to prove his authority, Jesus gives no rebuke (Jn 2:18; 6:30)[41] but appears to grant the sign (4:48). This is probably because, as we will see, John considers the "signs" to be a legitimate means for people to come to belief in Jesus.[42]

"Sign" occurs seventeen times in the Fourth Gospel, primarily referring to Jesus' miracles (cf. Jn 10:41), even though only at 4:48 and 6:26 is the word used by Jesus himself of the miracles.[43] All but two of the occurrences of "sign" appear within the miracle stories (cf. 5:2-9; 6:16-21), and all references but one are confined to chapters 2 through 12, where the miracle stories occur (cf. 20:31). The close association of sign and miracle is also seen in that only the healing of the paralytic at Bethesda (5:1-4), Jesus walking on the sea (6:16-21) and the catch of fish in the appendix (21:4-14) are not specifically called signs.

There is just one example of the Fourth Gospel using *sēmeion* in place of the Synoptics' *dunamis* (cf. Jn 10:41 and Mk 6:5). Further, with the probability that all but two of the uses of *sēmeion* are redactional (Jn 2:18 and 6:30),[44] the concept of sign is to be seen as theologically highly significant in John's understanding of the miracles of Jesus. Concomitantly, John the Baptist is said to perform no sign (10:41).

In Greek writings a "sign" from a god, though not necessarily having a miraculous component,[45] could identify a criminal by, for example, causing a shipwreck because of a guilty person on board. Also, a sign was an omen, as in the case of Oedipus being warned by an oracle that an earthquake with thunder and lightning would be a sign that his death was near. And the "daemon" that restrained Socrates from action is described as a divine sign.[46]

A sign could also be a ship's ensign (Euripides *Iphigeneia at Aulis* 253), a symptom of sickness (Philo *Det. Pot. Ins.* 43) or something in which a god was understood to communicate to a person (Plutarch *Alex.* 25:1). Apart from possibly the last example, this material does not seem to be of the same milieu as the writer of the Fourth Gospel. Rather, John's use of "sign" seems closer to and more easily understood in light of the Septuagint.[47]

In the Septuagint the word *sign* is almost always used of God showing himself to be the Almighty and Israel to be his chosen people through the events associated with Moses leading the Israelites out of Egypt.[48] Also, a sign could be either a natural or a supernatural event demonstrating the authenticity of the word of a prophet of God as well as the prophet himself.[49] Further, since an Old Testament sign could represent (cf. Ezek 4:1-3[50]) or announce things to come (e.g., Is 7:10-16), it is not surprising that for John the miracles of Jesus are also a foretaste of a future time of even greater things by God (Jn 14:12; see §8.9). This fits well with what we have already seen of the miracles in John. They are signs of something more than what can at first be seen:[51] that God himself is the author of the miracle whose character is revealed in the miracle, which authenticates the identity of Jesus and justifies and encourages trust in him. The signs reveal the glory of Jesus and so point to the death and resurrection of Jesus, where the glory of Jesus is also seen clearly.

Although "sign" is not used of the death and resurrection, when the Jews ask for a sign (Jn 2:18) Jesus refers to the resurrection. Perhaps "sign" is not used of the resurrection of Jesus because the resurrection is not pointing to anything beyond itself—it is the event itself that reveals the glory of Jesus.[52] Thus, as we have already suggested, it is right to see the signs as complemented by the great sign of the death and resurrection.

John's Gospel is not entirely alone in seeing the miracles as pointing to something beyond the event. The Synoptic Gospel writers also understand some miracles to have primarily a symbolic function. We saw that Mark understood the cursing of the fig tree to be a prophetic action regarding the rejection of Israel (Mk 11:12-14, 20-25). Luke has the story of the miraculous catch of fish, a prophetic action symbolizing the catching of people (Lk 5:1-11). In Matthew the miraculous appearance of a coin in the mouth of a fish is also probably to be understood as a symbolic action (Mt 17:24-27; see §4.29).

However, in the Synoptic Gospels a miracle was, with few exceptions, carrying out what it signified—the coming of the kingdom of God. In John, a "sign" is more than the miracle.[53] Being a symbol it points beyond itself[54] to the true identity or glory of Jesus and his filial relationship, or even identity, with the Father.

This sign function of the miracles gives them a function similar to the parables in the Synoptic Gospels in that they are enigmatic and potentially ambiguous. Their true significance is not immediately apprehended—they are being miscomprehended by some observers (e.g., Jesus' brothers reacted positively to his works but did not believe in him, Jn 7:3, 5), and many of the signs require explanation.[55]

However, having meaning beyond themselves does not mean that John (in contrast to the publisher of the Fourth Gospel) intended an allegorical interpretation of the miracle stories or the details in them. Rather, vivid detail, sometimes accurately describing historical settings or customs, is intended to contribute to vivid description,[56] making the stories unavoidably real and adequate for faith.

4. *Signs and wonders*. Only once does John use the phrase "signs and wonders"

(*sēmeia kai terata*): Jesus says, "Unless you see signs and wonders you will not believe" (Jn 4:48). Among educated Greeks of the period the phrase was used of purported marvels, such as lightning strikes, showers of stones, stars shining for seven days, dreams, an eclipse of the sun, monstrous births and a statue moving.[57] In view of this, John's single and negative use of the phrase probably means that he does not wish his readers to associate the miracles of Jesus simply with marvels or portents or false prophets of the time. In this John is in line with the perspective of the other Gospel writers (cf. Mk 13:22/Mt 24:24).

5. *Doxa.* After the prologue, only three times is *doxa* ("glory")[58] used in connection with the life of Jesus, and each of them concerns the miracles (Jn 2:11; 11:4, 40). The first miracle or sign ends with John saying that Jesus revealed his "glory" in doing the sign (2:11). In that the previous use of "glory" was 1:14 ("glory as of a father's only son, full of grace and truth"), the glory revealed is grace and truth that replaces the law of Moses (1:17) and the invisible reality of God seen specifically in Jesus' miracles.[59]

This view is confirmed in 11:4, where the raising of Lazarus is forecast as being for God's glory and the Son being glorified in it. Then in 11:40 Jesus says that Martha would see the glory of God in the miracle of the raising of Lazarus. Against Bultmann, we cannot avoid the conclusion that the glory is the miraculous power and that faith (cf. Jn 11:40) comprehends that glory.[60] Therefore we see again that in the miracles, no less than in his passion and return to the Father,[61] Jesus and God are being revealed for who they are.

§8.6 The Signs and Eschatology

The problem of eschatology in the Fourth Gospel[62] is that two contrasting views are juxtaposed: for example, John has Jesus say, "The hour is . . . now here" (Jn 5:25), yet a few verses later he says, "The hour is coming" (5:28). Bultmann resolved this tension by attributing the few references regarding future eschatology to a later ecclesiastical redactor[63] and concluding that the Evangelist has eliminated the traditional eschatology of primitive Christianity. Bultmann goes on to say that the "turn of the ages is now. . . . No future in this world's history can bring anything new, and all apocalyptic pictures of the future are empty dreams."[64] This solution is inadequate.

The pivotal saying of 11:25 (cf. Jn 5:21, 24) about Jesus being the resurrection and the life intertwines both present and future eschatology, and the difference between John and Bultmann's supposed ecclesiastical redactor is an illusion.[65] John emphasizes the truth of futurist eschatology.[66] Nevertheless John remains the best example of realized eschatology.[67] Alongside the resurrection of Jesus, the miracles of Jesus stand as the supreme examples of all that was expected in the eschaton to be fulfilled—even if only proleptically—in the ministry of Jesus. Because the raising of Lazarus, the prefigurement of Jesus' coming resurrection, is the final miracle in Jesus' earthly ministry, it becomes the prism through which readers view the other six signs: evidential pointers that the ministry of *Jesus has brought and is bringing what God promised and what will one day be fully realized.*[68]

§8.7 Was John Using a Signs Source?

In the early years of the twentieth century E. Schwarz and Julius Wellhausen both proposed that the signs composed the main part of a *Grundevangelium*, or rudimentary, Gospel to which the sayings material was later added.[69] In his commentary on John, Bultmann argued that, apart from the passion story, the author of the Fourth Gospel had a source for the discourses as well as for the miracles.[70] Though there was little agreement as to the extent of the signs source,[71] Bultmann had already suggested that the way forward was an investigation of the stylistic characteristics of the various layers of tradition in the Fourth Gospel.[72] However, when Eduard Schweizer examined thirty-three literary characteristics occurring only in John, he found that apart from rare cases they were distributed throughout the whole of John.[73] Then Eugen Ruckstuhl scrutinized the stylistic data and concluded that they were distributed throughout both strata of the Gospel and did not point to an author different from the Evangelist.[74]

Willem Nicol answered this attack on the signs source hypothesis by reviewing, extending and correcting the work of Schwiezer and Ruckstuhl. His conclusion was that in the miracle stories there is evidence of the influence of a style different from that of John, which he must have taken from tradition—a signs source.[75]

Robert Fortna saw in the apparent "aporiai" (discrepancies or unevenness in the text, e.g., between Jn 3:26 and 4:1-2) the key to identifying different writers in the Fourth Gospel, for the "aporiai" were less frequent in the proposed signs source.[76] In reconstructing the signs source, Fortna included the ministry of John the Baptist (1:19-34) and the call of the first disciples (1:35-50) at its beginning. On the grounds that the miraculous catch of fish (21:1-14) is said to be the third post-resurrection appearance (21:14), Fortna made it the third sign in the hypothetical signs source. Fortna also added the passion story to his reconstruction,[77] making the signs source more a primitive Gospel than a collection of miracle stories.[78] This proposal has the advantage of explaining the tension in John between the emphasis on miracles as revelations of the messiahship of Jesus and what is seen as the apparent devaluation of miracle-based faith (see §8.8). In this understanding, the statement of purpose in 20:30-31 relates to the signs source.[79]

However, Fortna and others who posit a signs source have not been without their critics.[80] The main clue to the existence of a signs source is the numbering of the first (Jn 2:11) and second (4:54) miracle stories. With 4:54 saying that the healing of the official's son was the second sign, yet ignoring 2:23, which says many people saw the signs (plural) that Jesus did, it is not unreasonable to postulate the existence of a source containing the first two miracles in John.[81] As we have noted, however, both numbered references to the signs (2:11 and 4:45) are probably entirely redactional, fundamentally undermining signs source theory.[82] Further, the inclusion of the miraculous catch of fish in a pre-Johannine signs source is inexplicable. It is a story from the post-Johaninne appendix, unknown to the writer who would have made use of a hypothetical pre-Johannine signs source.[83]

Mark Stibbe has suggested that there was no signs Gospel because there are Galilean miracles and Judean miracles—the latter occurring around Jerusalem (the healing of the paralytic at Bethesda, the healing of the man born blind and the raising of Lazarus), all of which lead to controversy with the Jewish authorities. Rather, there was a collection of Galilean signs/miracles.[84] However, in light of Stibbe himself recognizing that there is difficulty in distinguishing between tradition and redaction in John, we will leave aside his interesting proposal. Therefore, acknowledging an agnosticism regarding the sources of John in general,[85] we must go further and admit an agnosticism—if not skepticism—in relation to the postulated existence of a signs source for John 2—11.[86]

§8.8 Miracles and Faith

That there is some relation between miracles and faith in John is obvious: faith is connected to all seventeen occurrences of the word *sign*, for example.[87] However, the nature of that relationship is not immediately clear. While examining the stories of the water being turned into wine (Jn 2:1-11) and of the official's son being healed (4:46-54), we noted that, although John says the first sign revealed Jesus' glory and his disciples believed in him (2:11), in a transitional paragraph (2:23-25) John says Jesus would not entrust himself to the "many" who believed in his name upon seeing the signs he was doing (cf. 4:4).

The most common solution to this problem is to suggest that John is portraying various levels or stages of faith.[88] In this view, while not denigrating the signs, John is said to portray the faith that arises out of seeing the signs as a first, provisional or inadequate stage. Notwithstanding, John presents a number of reactions to Jesus and his miracles that bear on understanding the relationship between miracles and faith.[89]

First are those observers who refuse to see the signs with any faith.[90] For example, after hearing a report of the raising of Lazarus, the Pharisees are convinced by Caiaphas to seek the death of Jesus (Jn 11:45-53). In 12:37 John says that "although he had performed many signs in their presence, they did not believe in him." It cannot be that John is saying that all preceding faith based on the miracles is unbelief,[91] for he goes on to contrast it with the weak or uncertain faith of "many" (12:42). Rather 12:37 is probably John's summation of the Jewish nation's response as a whole to Jesus.[92] In light of 3:19-20, which is about people loving darkness rather than light, John explains this lack of belief to be the result of people loving their evil deeds rather than the light (cf. 12:43). In view of the signs, unbelief becomes a denial of the undeniable reality of Jesus' relationship with God as his Messiah and Son, and the genesis of his passion.[93]

Second, and similar, are those who see signs without believing. The initial response of the lame man by the pool is not one of faith but of complaint that he has no one to help him into the water (Jn 5:7). For John, as for others (e.g., Mt 8:14-15), a person without at least initial faith in Jesus is still able to receive or experience a miracle.

Third are those who see the signs as wonders or portents and believe in Jesus as a miracle worker.[94] John 2:23-25 is particularly important, for it, containing a number of expressions with a Johannine ring, is probably from John's hand.[95] In 2:23 John says that while Jesus was in Jerusalem many saw the signs and "believed in his name." Yet John criticizes this faith by adding that "Jesus . . . would not trust himself to them" (2:24). Since Jerusalem is the setting, to some extent this little paragraph sums up the previous scene. However, it is more a preparation for the Nicodemus story to follow, which enables us to understand the nature of the criticism of the faith related to miracles.[96] That is, Nicodemus's belief in Jesus was limited to his being a miracle worker from God (3:2-3), so he is criticized as uncomprehending. Similarly in the story of the feeding of the five thousand, in response to this kind of faith, Jesus withdrew (6:2, 14-15).

Fourth are those who see the true significance of the miracles enabling them to believe in Jesus and who see correctly who he is in relation to the Father.[97] From the so-called first ending of John—"these [signs] are written so that you may come to believe" (Jn 20:31)—it is clear John thought that the signs could elicit true faith and that they did so for the disciples.[98] At the conclusion of the first miracle John says that his disciples believed in him (2:11). Similarly the official whose son was healed is said to believe (4:53). The man born blind, on discovering that it was Jesus the Son of Man who healed him, believed and "worshiped him" (9:38). Further, in 10:38 Jesus is said to encourage the Jews to believe the miracles so that they may know and understand that the Father is in him and he in the Father (cf. 12:37).

In light of this we cannot agree with Eduard Lohse, who says that the author of the Fourth Gospel "points to a critical assessment of a faith born out of miracle; indeed, he denies such faith both permanence and lasting value."[99] Rather, it is John's view that faith "is not orientated to a set of facts or a doctrine, but that it grasps the divine action in Jesus"[100] (cf. Jn 5:17, 19c, 24a).

Fifth, there is another response to the miracles that John saw as positive. In John 10:38 Jesus says, "Even if you do not believe me, believe the works I do" (author's translation). That is, whereas the miracles are expected to lead to belief, it is belief in the words of Jesus that is seen as the ultimate form of belief-response to Jesus. This can be substantiated from other miracle stories.

In the story of the healing of the officer's son, Jesus at first responds negatively to the request to go and perform the healing: "Unless you [people] see signs and wonders you will not believe" (Jn 4:48). But the official persists, perhaps showing that he was not seeking Jesus because of the signs he had seen, thus indicating, in turn, that the criticism does not refer to him. Indeed, it is said that, when told that his son would live, "the man believed the word that Jesus spoke" (4:50). At the end of the story, on discovering that his son is well, John says that he and his whole household believed (4:53).

In the story of the raising of Lazarus, Jesus says, "Did I not tell you that if you believed, you would see the glory of God?" (Jn 11:40). In these two stories, as is often the case in the Synoptic miracle stories,[101] the belief in Jesus precedes the miracle. In each story the initial belief is in the words of Jesus. This correlates with the story of the man born blind. Before the healing takes place, the man responds obediently to Jesus asking him to wash in the pool (9:7). At the end of the story the man says, "Lord, I believe," and then John says that he worshiped Jesus (9:38). Thus John is affirming that those who encounter Jesus ought to trust his word. They will then witness the miracles. It is as if John is saying that belief in Jesus ought to be able to be based as much on the words as on the works (miracles) of Jesus.

Sixth are those who believe in Jesus without seeing any signs.[102] Thus Thomas is said to believe because he has seen Jesus, that is, the miracle of the risen Jesus. Jesus then says, "Blessed are those who have not seen and yet have come to believe" (Jn 20:29). This does not convey the notion that faith based on the resurrection is a superior, or ultimate, faith compared to that based on the miracles.[103] John's only other use of *makarios* ("blessed") is in 13:17, where he gives no indication that to be blessed is to receive more than eschatological salvation.[104] Rather, faith that recognizes the true identity of Jesus, whatever the basis of that faith—seeing the miracle-signs, hearing the words, witnessing the risen Lord or none of these—is sufficient for the blessing of salvation. The story of the man born blind shows that John considered there to be those who can receive a miracle without initial faith and see signs without initially even knowing who Jesus was (cf. Jn 9:11, 17).

In surveying these various ways that miracle and faith are related, we cannot say that all faith in or based on the signs is insufficient because belief needs the "word" as its proper basis.[105] This opinion does not do justice to the frequent correlation between word and miraculous work or sign;[106] nor does this view take into account the fact that John does approve of belief in the miracles (Jn 20:30-31).[107] John is convinced that the miracles adequately testify to Jesus' true identity (cf. 2:11; 10:25).

Rather, when belief in the miracles is deficient, it is because such belief sees the signs as proof only of the (divine?) miracle-working power of Jesus.[108] Hence taking into account the context of the story of Nicodemus (cf. Jn 2:23-25), the Jews are said to believe only "in his name" (2:23), rather than in "the name of the only Son of God" (3:18; cf. 1 Jn 3:23).[109] However, it needs to be noted here that John can simply state that belief in Jesus is sufficient (1:12). Nevertheless when that faith is deficient, it is corrected, as it is here (2:23-25; cf. 3:2, 18).

It is not correct to say that John attacks miracles[110] or considers signs inadequate for faith or that miracle-kindled and miracle-based faith is inadequate for salvation.[111] We cannot even follow Kümmel in saying that, "according to John, a belief that is awakened by miracles is only a first step and therefore an uncertain belief, which indeed has recognized the miracle worker, but has not seen the Father in Jesus and can only lead on to real faith."[112] In light of what we have seen, we also cannot follow Kümmel in saying that the crucial step toward salvation is a faith that requires no seeing.[113]

The clear statement of John 20:31—"These [signs] are written so that you may come to believe that Jesus is the Messiah, the Son of God"—means that *the signs alone are adequate for salvation and a full understanding of Jesus. The words* (cf. 6:33; 8:30) *or works of Jesus are adequate for faith.* What is inadequate, in some instances, is not the miracles but the response to them[114] and the limited understanding of Jesus that may arise from believing in Jesus on the basis of the signs.[115] Where there is fault it is not in the signs' ability to reveal the identity of the incarnation of the Father or in their ability to give rise to adequate faith. The criticism of John is of the individual who does not see.[116]

§8.9 Miracles and the Sacraments
We need to question Brown's view that in exalting a faith that has no dependence on miraculous signs John is appealing to the life-situation of the church of his time, where sacrament has largely replaced miracle as the vehicle of symbolic revelation.[117] For, in order to say this, Brown attempts to dismiss the relevance of 14:12: "anyone who has faith in me will do even greater things than these" (author's translation). However, verses 12 to 14 are in the future tense, referring to a time following the lifting up of Jesus to the throne of God. That is, they refer to the period of the post-Easter church.

Also, from John's use of *erga* ("works," see §8.5.2), the "works" in verse 12 are clearly intended to include the miracles of Jesus, so the greater works would naturally include the miracles of the followers of Jesus.[118] At the very least this verse is affirming the place of miracles among John's readers. Thus it is not possible to say, with Brown, that John writes in a setting where miracles have been replaced by sacraments or that "a faith not based on signs became a necessity when the period in which Jesus worked signs came to an end."[119]

§8.10 Who Is the Jesus of the Miracles?

While from the very first paragraphs the identity of Jesus is one of the major concerns of this Gospel, the traditional christological titles appear rarely in the miracle stories. In fact, some titles never occur here.

The word *prophet* occurs in the context of the story of the feeding of the five thousand (Jn 6:14), as does *king* (6:15). The phrase "I am the resurrection" is found in the story of the raising of Lazarus (11:25). The title (or at least word) *Lord,* which sometimes can be taken to mean no more than "Sir," also appears in the Lazarus story[120] and in the stories of the healing of the official's son (4:49), the healing of the paralytic (5:7) and the large catch of fish,[121] where Peter confesses, "It is the Lord!" (21:7). *Lord* is also associated with the stories of the feeding of the five thousand (6:23) and the healing of a man born blind (9:38). The least that could be concluded from this is that a number of the stories have been used to convey the view that in the miracles Jesus is being revealed as, and declared to be, Lord.

Even when the titles do not appear, on a number of occasions in the miracle stories the question of Jesus' identity is directly raised. After the healing of the man at the pool, there is a discussion about who the healer was: a law breaker, one doing the Father's will or God's Son (Jn 5:10-24). Having fed the large crowd, Jesus is heralded as "the prophet who is to come into the world" (6:14). As a result of healing the man blind from birth, the question is raised whether Jesus is from God or is a sinner (9:16).

More subtly the question of Jesus' identity is raised by means of parallels that John seems to draw between Jesus' miracles and other stories most probably known by his readers. Notably, as we have seen, the changing of water into wine would have been read in light of stories associated with Dionysus, Philo and the Old Testament so that Jesus would have appeared to be superior to all other gods (see §7.3). The changing of water into wine, the multiplying of bread, the washing to be healed and the raising of the dead, though being much more spectacular, are certainly reminiscent of the stories of Elijah and Elisha.[122] To this we can add the Moses-wilderness themes in the feeding story and the common use of "sign" in John, as well as in the Mosaic miracles (see §8.5.3).

The Jesus of the Johannine miracles is at least as significant as or greater than the expected eschatological prophets. Yet alongside these positive associations with Moses and Elijah, Jesus refuses to accept such identification (6:14-15). Any typology here is no more than a barely visible foundation of the Christology of the signs.[123]

At John 20:31 we have one of the clearest statements in this Gospel about the

Chistology of the signs: they are demonstrating that Jesus is the Messiah, the Son of God, in the close relationship with the Father adumbrated in the prologue. In contrast to the Synoptic Gospels, where the miracles are the fulfillment of the expectation of the coming of the kingdom of God, in this Gospel the miracles are signs that Jesus is the King. Going a step further we have seen that the Johannine miracles are, as in the stories of Moses, acts of God himself, so the reader can only conclude that Jesus is acting as God, or for and in God's place, even though he is never mentioned: "Jesus is everything, and therefore, the meeting with him is all that is needed."[124]

It is not surprising then that the Jesus of the Fourth Gospel is depicted as taking the initiative in performing the miracles.[125] On three occasions this is heightened by Jesus rebuffing those seeking a miracle, then acting on his own initiative (cf. Jn 2:4; 4:48; 11:6). Yet the Jesus of the signs is not just a god or divine being,[126] he is also a human being.[127]

In the most spectacular miracle, the raising of a dead man, Jesus weeps (Jn 11:35). Most starkly of all, John stresses the reality of the humanity of Jesus in his introduction to the Gospel. In 1:14 John says, "And the Word became flesh" *(kai ho logos sarx egeneto)*. The juxtapositioning of "Word" and "flesh"—*logos* and *sarx*—draws attention to great change in the manner of existence of the Word: a change from being in glory with the Father (cf. 17:5, 24) to being in "flesh."

Flesh is not simply a synonym for humanity. It stands for that which is earth-bound, transient and perishable, in contrast to that which is divine and of the Spirit (cf. Jn 3:6; 6:36).[128] In this verse John then affirms the Incarnation or humanity of Jesus in saying that the Word "dwelt" or "pitched his tent" among us. In this verse all doubts about the reality of the humanity of Jesus are removed: "It is a new and profoundly original way of confessing the Savior who has come 'palpably' (1 Jn 1:1) in history as a unique, personal human being, who has manifested himself in the reality of the 'flesh'. "[129] That this humanness is to be seen in the signs that are to follow is clear from John's then adding that "we have seen his glory" (cf. 2:11).

§8.11 Conclusions

1. When compared to the other Gospels, the most obvious feature about the miracle stories in John is that there are fewer of them and they take up less direct space than in the other Gospels.[130] Yet this relatively small amount of material belies one of the most important messages John conveys in the miracle stories: whereas the cross is the climax of the plot of John, the miracle-signs are the heart of Jesus' pre-Easter ministry.[131] Even the long discourse with Nicodemus is cast in light of inadequate responses to the signs (Jn 2:23-25; 3:3).

The centrality of the miracles in John can also be shown by noting that before the passion narrative, climaxing in the long and spectacular raising of Lazarus, the seven miracle stories are perhaps intended to symbolize a perfection of accomplishment in Jesus' ministry. Then, in this Gospel's structure a miracle is Jesus' first public act (Jn 2:1-11) rather than public teaching, as in Matthew and Luke. Further, the reference in 20:30 to Jesus doing many other signs gives the impression that performing miracles was typical of Jesus' ministry and leaves the reader to assume that further miracles occurred in the narrative gaps.[132] The same end is served by the summaries that mention the miracle-signs (2:23-24; cf. 10:42-44; 11:45).

2. Taking this last point a step further, the miracles do not illuminate the teaching of Jesus. The teaching—often related directly to and immediately following the miracle narrative—is required to explain what are portrayed as eschatological events.[133] Indeed, as in the case of the story of the feeding of the five thousand, the miracle is the teaching (cf. Jn 6:3). In short, again the miracles are the centerpiece of Jesus' activities before the cross.

3. Also, the type of miracle is generally quite different from that of the Synoptics.[134] We have seen that, in presenting God's revelation in Jesus' signs, John provides stories that are larger than life: for example, hundreds of gallons of water are turned into wine, a man is healed who could not walk for thirty-eight years, Lazarus was raised to life after being dead for four days.[135] Concomitantly the material reality of the miracles is stressed through these details.[136]

4. Further, the response of the crowds is distinctive. In the Synoptic Gospels the crowds are portrayed as pressing in on Jesus with their sick for him to heal and then they are shown to be amazed and awed at the miracles. In turn, the healings cause enthusiastic reports of Jesus' miracles, which are spread abroad. This is in contrast to the generally quieter and isolated activity of Jesus the miracle worker in the Fourth Gospel. Jesus stands portrayed as unharried by those around him, responsive only to his Father in carrying out his works. Something akin to the Synoptic astonishment and awe of the crowds as a literary device is present in John only following the feeding of the five thousand (Jn 6:14). This is not surprising, for in contrast to the Synoptics,[137] the proper response to a miracle is one of faith or trust (2:11; 4:50; 9:37; 11:45), worship (5:14) or confession (6:14).[138]

5. The close identity between Father and Son may explain John's abandoning of the Synoptic idea that Jesus' miracles were inspired by the Spirit: in Jesus the Father himself is encountered and not any gift of the Father.[139] We have seen that this high view of Jesus portrayed in the miracles is to be connected with Jesus being portrayed as taking the initiative in conducting the miracles.

Indeed, in this Gospel Jesus never directly accedes to a request. In four of the seven miracles, he takes complete initiative. In the others, even when he is petitioned he maintains the initiative by responding differently from what is expected.[140] (This is in contrast to the Synoptic miracles, where Jesus usually acts in response to a request.)[141] Jesus is so significant that his actions are not determined by anyone but the Father.[142] Apart from the possible indirect reference to compassion in the story of the changing of water into wine (Jn 2:3), Jesus is not even portrayed as being motivated by compassion, even when the disciples are caught in the storm (6:18).

Whereas in Jesus God himself is encountered and seen at work in activities that can only portray him as God himself among people, John maintains that Jesus is also a man. In 1:14 John has prefaced his work in such a way as to make plain that what they are beholding in the miracles is flesh.

6. The Synoptic miracles are inextricably linked to the coming of the kingdom of God. In such sayings as "If I by the Spirit of God cast out demons, then has come upon you the kingdom of God" (Mt 12:28/Lk 11:20, author's translation), the Synoptic writers are expressing the view that in the miracles themselves the kingdom of God is being established. The Synoptic miracles are not pointing primarily to anything outside themselves. They are what they signify, no less significant than—even if proleptic of—the death and resurrection of Jesus and the parousia.

But for John, the miracles also point beyond themselves—to the true identity or glory of Jesus and his filial relationship, or even identity, with the Father, still to be seen in the miracles of his followers and, eventually, in the parousia. Not surprisingly then the miraculous signs are not simply tangible illustrations of the message of Jesus. For the Fourth Gospel they are the centerpiece of the ministry of Jesus.

§8.12 The Next Step

At this point we have completed the first and major objective for this study: to discuss how the four Gospel writers understood the miracles of Jesus, what they understood to be the implication of the miracles for their portrait of Jesus, the place the miracles had in their message about Jesus and what they understood the miracles to mean for their readers, for example. We now can draw some conclusions about the common denominators in these interpretations and portraits, as well as point out the distinctive aspects of each writer's view of the miracles of Jesus. However, in order to avoid repetition I will leave this exercise until the end of the entire study (see §§17.1-7).

We turn now, looking behind the Gospels, to the historical Jesus and his reported miracles. As I pointed out in chapter one, after tackling the difficult issues of method I will deal with the meaning of the miracles for the historical Jesus. Not only is recovering the meaning of the miracles for the historical Jesus important in itself, but it also will provide us with part of the necessary framework to assess the historicity of individual stories or categories of stories. So we seek the historical Jesus not to set this portrait up over against the canonical Gospels as a "Fifth Evangelist." Rather, an understanding of the historical Jesus helps us to be more sensitive to the various Gospel trajectories on Jesus and to clarify the historical nature of the basis of our faith.

PART 3

Jesus & the Miracles

....

N i n e

Miracles & the
Historical Jesus

···

§9.1 Introduction

We are about to walk through a minefield, for here in part three the question is
whether the historical Jesus actually performed miracles. More accurately, the
question is whether those who witnessed the ministry of Jesus—and others in the
ancient world (Josephus, for example)—thought he conducted miracles. In part
four ("The Miracles of Jesus and History") we will go on to ask which, if any, of
the particular miracle stories, or parts of them, in the Gospels can be traced back
to the memories of those who witnessed Jesus' ministry, if he did indeed perform
miracles.

I have already concluded that it is quite reasonable to suppose that miracles are
possible and that, in view of the nature of the God of the Gospels and a reasonable
defense of the doctrine of the incarnation, such miracles as are reflected in the
Gospel stories are likely to have happened (see §2.5). This means that the task here
is not so much to seek the historicity of mighty works or prodigies. Instead, we
are seeking the historicity of events associated with the historical Jesus that involve
the direct and visible activity of God (see §1.3).

My susceptibility to criticism in undertaking this exercise is heightened by the
constraint of dealing with such large issues within the scope of a book of this size.
John Meier has undertaken a similar enterprise, but he took up about five hundred
pages in the process.[1] Meier, however, was concerned only with the first stage of
the program we have set here, not venturing to tackle the question of whether the
miracles of Jesus actually took place.

Yet doing here in a few pages what Meier attempted in many pages will, I hope, enable the general reader, as well as the student, to comprehend more readily what can be known about the deeds of Jesus we call miracles. We will interact with Meier's magisterial and monumental work, drawing conclusions on the question of historicity that will often be different from his.

As difficult as it is, this exercise is essential in understanding Jesus, his message and the essence of Christianity. Despite contemporary protestations, the basic understanding of who Jesus was, the truth of his message and the integrity of early Christianity were, as we sometimes saw in part two, thought to depend on Jesus having performed miracles. From the perspective of the Gospel writers, without the miracles of Jesus there would have been no Christianity.

In turn, for many of those who today want to continue on a biblical trajectory in their understanding and expression of Christianity, the historicity of the miracles remains of central significance. Therefore it is crucial that we embark on this part of our study with an inquiry into the historical veracity of Jesus' being seen as a miracle worker and to ask which, if any, of the accounts we now have in the Gospels can be traced back to the original reports of eyewitnesses.

In this exercise we will anticipate facing a barrage of attacks from a wide spectrum of readers. On the one hand, there will be those for whom even asking these questions is anathema and assumes a lack of faith in the "Word of God" as a reliable or infallible witness to the miraculous activity of the incarnate Son of God. However, this exercise is not intended to call into question either the value of the Bible or the identity of Jesus or his *ability* to perform miracles.[2] Rather, we are asking questions that will help us comprehend better the book in which we have invested so much value and help us understand the Jesus about whom it speaks and what he can mean for us.

Even though, compared to other figures from the distant past, we have a great deal of documentary evidence about Jesus, there is still much we do not know. The evidence or data available to us both in the New Testament and outside it is still very small compared to what we have for someone such as Washington, Napoleon or Gladstone. Therefore to be historians of integrity there will be times—perhaps many times—when we will have to say "I do not know" when it comes to asking whether or not a story reflects an event in the life of Jesus. Nevertheless, it needs to be stressed that doubt or uncertainty about the historical reliability of any one story does not necessarily lead to doubt regarding any of the other miracle stories. Each must be dealt with on its own merit.

On the other hand, there will be readers at the other extreme. For them there is no possibility of ascribing miracles to the historical Jesus: miracles do not and therefore did not happen.[3] They can be taken only as stories—similar to parables—through which the writers were teaching their readers truths about Jesus. (This was the focus in part two when we dealt with the Gospel writers' treatment of the miracle stories.)

Between these two extremes will be others who, though remaining open to the possibility of Jesus performing miracles in general, assert that we can no longer know whether particular miracle stories can be attributed to Jesus. Either our recoverable evidence is not sufficiently full or our tools of historical criticism are not sufficiently refined for us to reconstruct a credible picture of the historical Jesus that could include particular miracle stories. This perspective characterizes the Jesus Seminar, for example.[4]

§9.2 What Can We Know About the Past?

When encountering a miracle story in the Gospels, the questions in the minds of ordinary readers, as well as many students of the historical Jesus, are "Did it happen?" and "Did it happen like that?" This is the point at which we must face the problem of how and what we can know about anything—including the past. Putting the complex issues in their most simplistic form,[5] one view (usually called "positivism" or "naive realism") is that through careful observation we can gain unquestionable objective knowledge of things as they actually are—or were, in the case of history. In relation to our historical inquiry this view might be expressed by assuming that we can sidestep our presuppositions in reading a historical document, gaining direct passage to assured facts. That two different inquiries can produce different "facts" reveals the inadequacy of this model.

Another view about how we know things (called "phenomenalism") is that in our observations, including those concerning the past, all we can be certain of is our own impression of the text that we are reading or the data we are observing. Taken seriously, this view would give us confidence only of our own existence ("solipsism"). Caricatured in this way, the call for a new understanding and starting point of how we may gain knowledge is most easily understood. In our search for authentic historical reports of the ministry of Jesus, what we need is a way of making the transition from reader to text to author to report to event.

A way forward is made possible in the proposals of "critical realism," the title of a 1916 book by Roy W. Sellars.[6] When applied to historical inquiry such as the historicity of the miracles of Jesus, accepting the critical realist approach means that we hold that there is a past reality outside the historian and the data or documents (hence the appropriateness of the term *realism*). At the same time we accept that the only access we have to this past is by a recapturing or recreative understanding that develops through and alongside the process of interaction between the historian's data and the historian and his understanding of his world (hence the term *critical* is appropriate).[7]

Such a dialogue between the data and the historian rightly recognizes the fundamental place of a historian as the real criterion of history in the present world. As F. H. Bradley long ago put it, "The historian, as he is, is the real criterion; the ideal criterion . . . is the historian as he ought to be. And the historian who is true to the present *is* the historian as he ought to be."[8]

What this approach does is affirm that in historical inquiry we are concerned with a reality independent of us, whereas knowledge of it is not. This is not a selling out to phenomenalism by saying that what we discover is only a subjective matter. Rather, this understanding of critical realism acknowledges that we need to reflect critically on our initial observations of the data in light of what we consider likely to take place in the world—our world. This will involve a leap of the imagination—that is in tune with subject matter—from the observations to a hypothesis about a likely event.[9]

Thus for Ben Meyer the first salient trait of critical realism is its focus on the concrete structures of human operations, the human subject being the living norm against which all theories on life and the past are measured.[10] Put simply, for us this means that when we are considering the historicity of a miracle story, or an element of it, an essential task is the gathering of data not only by means of the traditional canons of authenticity but also by asking how the story relates to our experience of the world. Part of what will determine historicity is how the story relates to reality as we know it.[11]

This means that, as we attempt to satisfy the objective to recover "what actually happened" in relation to particular reports of miracles associated with Jesus, we will be able to do so not only as we critically reflect on their relation to the larger story of Jesus' ministry but also in considering the larger picture and its elements in relation to our own experiences of the story and stories of life. What this means in practical terms for this study is that we gain historical knowledge of particular miracle events as we discover things that fit with our particular experience. Hence our final decision as to whether miracle stories in the Gospels are authentic reports of miraculous events can be made only when we finally bring together the results of these two chapters on the historicity of the miracle stories with the earlier discussion on the possibility of miracles.

§9.3 The Angst of the Historians

As historians we face yet another issue as we ask "Did it happen?" and "Did it happen like that?" For many historians these simple questions can no longer be simply asked or simply answered because of other fundamental issues arising out of the revolution in historical studies and a state of anxiety among historians in our postmodern world.[12] The angst of the historians is symptomatic of the angst of the age.

Sometime in the middle of the twentieth century it began to be apparent to commentators on Western civilization that the aspirations of the social experiment that had it roots in the eighteenth century would not be attained. The resulting age of disappointment in which we live is characterized by a lack of confidence in what were once seen to be the unshakable beliefs and truths supplied by rationalism, science and technology. The confidence of historiographers, as will be seen, has also been shaken.

When it comes to writing history there is, for many, no confidence that a person can write anything other than a fictive reconstruction of an imagined past. To write other than fictive reconstructions, it is said, would be naive realism—an unfashionable view that the past exists independently of the contemplation of it.[13] No one doubts that writing about the past involves creating a form of literature. But are the writings of historians no more than literature, where no distinction can be made between fact and fiction?

I do not intend to dishonor the work of philosophers of history continuing an important debate about the nature of history by dismissing it with a cursory discussion. Nevertheless it is clear from a common-sense perspective that it is possible to write down something about the past—say the recent and remembered past—that others can read and determine whether or not, broadly, it is either fact or fiction. Therefore it is certainly possible, in principle, for history—or more specifically the writings of those interested in relating the past to others—to be more than a fictive construction of the writer's imagination.

For us this has two important implications. First, it is possible for the work of the Gospel writers to contain more than metaphor and the reconstructions of their own imaginations.[14] At least in the case of Mark, who was probably writing in the late sixties or early seventies, his work would have been open to the possibility of criticism from those who could check his writing from their memory of what happened. Second, it is possible for us to write about the Gospels and the historical Jesus in a way that can convey reliable or objective information about him as he would have appeared in the past, however incomplete that picture may be.

§9.4 Story and Event
More important in our search for those elements in the Gospel miracle stories that can be traced back to the ministry of the historical Jesus is the question of the relationship between a story and an event.

For some, while the past still exists in the memory of the fragments of the past, even given sufficient fragments—of all kinds—the past cannot be repeated or reconstructed in the mind of the historian and represented in historical discourse—a story. The view is widely held—by Hayden White, for example—that the past is not available to us as a story. Rather, it is the historians who provide the "verbal fictions, the contents of which are as much invented as found and the forms of which have more in common with their counterparts in literature than they have with those in the sciences."[15] In other words, the past is not a series of lived-out stories waiting to be turned into prose by the historian.[16] The past is invented for the present.

The pressing question is then, is a story so utterly different in form from a supposed series of past events that it cannot be recovered and represented in a story? Are stories that allegedly represent the past condemned to misrepresent or transform events they propose to depict? Or can stories be regarded as a representative extension of the primary features of an event and series of events?

Our individual experience of the present—and our memory of the past—is that it is a succession of interrelated events and interactions with people, places, objects and even ideas. Of course, it is not that our past or our present necessarily has a single plot or story. Our past may have an unlimited number of plots or stories that are able to represent the past faithfully. In the present, different people remembering or experiencing the same events would report a different though equally valid story. We can even tell a shared story of an event that is recognized by another person as a faithful, even if not exhaustive, account of what transpired.

Here we are approaching another key question: Can we show that history, as well as our individual lived experience, is able to be represented by a story or stories? For historical reality does not consist solely of individuals, so we cannot conclude that the storylike structure of our lives must be true of society or the past.[17] However, that we can use stories to represent history or the social past (other than our own) is clear when we note two things: first, we can personify social groups as having a life story; second, this life story is recognized to be intimately connected with the lives of individuals by their use of the first-person plural—"we"—when talking about their society.[18]

It is palpably true that a highly selective process is required to write a story about the past. Otherwise so much—an infinitely large amount—would have to be written down in order to reflect faithfully a series of events for a reader. But our common-sense experience of life and of the remembering and retelling of the past informs us that the selection of material for a story does not constitute the imposition of an unnatural narrative on an event or series of events. In the words of David Carr, "Narrative is not merely a possibly successful way of describing events; its structure inheres in the events themselves. Far from being a formal distortion of the events it relates, a narrative account is an extension of their primary features."[19]

The upshot of all this is that when we turn to the question of the historicity of miracle stories in the Gospels in part four we need not reject the idea that these very short stories could be faithfully reflecting the memory of someone who witnessed an event in the life of Jesus. So it remains one of our objectives to see which stories or parts of them can be considered faithful reflections of events in the life of the historical Jesus.

§9.5 Jesus and Miracles?

Before we attend to the question of the historicity of individual miracle stories associated with Jesus in the Gospels, a prior and fundamental question must be asked: Can it be shown that the historical Jesus generally performed extraordinary feats or miracles? It is sometimes suggested that whether Jesus actually performed miracles is largely irrelevant to us. Rather, the point is that the Gospel writers considered him a miracle worker and that it was important to them to portray him as such.[20] However, the question cannot be so easily sidestepped, for the Gospel writers place so much emphasis on the miracles of Jesus that if they did not occur, a large question mark is placed against all the Gospel writers' fundamental understanding of Jesus and their message about him. We have no choice but to face the question.

To begin with, it can be noted that in portraying Jesus as the Messiah his followers were not obliged to portray him as a miracle worker. For example, in *Psalms of Solomon* 17 the Davidic messiah is not expected to perform miracles. Even in portraying Jesus as a prophet[21] they would not need to associate miracles with Jesus, as in Luke 24:19, for example. John the Baptist, who was involved in the early days of the Jesus movement, is portrayed as a prophet.[22] Yet neither the Gospels nor Josephus (*Ant.* 18:116-19) portrays John as a miracle worker.

Coupled with this is the point that in the period of two hundred years on each side of the life of the historical Jesus the number of miracle stories attached to any historical figure is astonishingly small.[23] Werner Kahl concluded from his investigation of approximately 150 miracle stories from antiquity that we know of only one other case in the entire miracle story tradition before Philostratus's *Life of Apollonius* (written after A.D. 217) of an immanent bearer of numinous or preternatural power (and then in only a singular version of his miracle)—Melampous, according to Diodorus of Sicily (writing c. 60-30 B.C.). Other Jewish and pagan miracle workers of the period he categorizes as petitioners or mediators of numinous power.[24]

Therefore the attachment of so many stories to the traditions about the historical Jesus already predisposes us to the importance of asking the question about the possibility of his performing feats that we would call miracles. Indeed, from what we have seen, we can go so far as to say that it is unlikely that the miracle tradition about Jesus would have arisen had it not been for his conducting miracles—and so many of them.[25]

§9.6 The *ipsissima facta*

In the less troubled waters of the search for the authentic sayings—the *ipsissima verba*—of the historical Jesus, a growing list of criteria has been produced and discussed that can be applied to the sayings material in the hope of recovering reliable data.[26] In the last decade there has been a growing interest in systematizing what has been a relatively primitive methodology for investigating the historicity of the activities—the *ipsissima facta*—of Jesus.[27]

A recent discussion of historical method in relation to the deeds of Jesus has been given by Robert J. Miller.[28] In his summary of the state of the art of historical methodology, he provides eighteen theses that I will set out, often in my own words, and use as a backdrop to or basis for my approach.[29] (As they are not in every case self-explanatory, I will explain and discuss some of them briefly. Then I also will propose some modifications and additions to the theses.)

Burden of Proof
1. The concept of a burden of proof is a necessary part of method to prevent questions being decided beforehand or on insufficient evidence.
2. The only way to construe the burden of proof without deciding questions beforehand is to formulate it neutrally: the burden of proof falls on the one who makes a claim.

Demonstration
3. A position is demonstrated, when the reasons for accepting it "significantly" outweigh the reasons for not accepting it.
4. This leaves a large gray area where positions are held to be "likely" or "probable."

Historicity
5. A finding of historicity is essentially a default position, meaning that we have no other reasonable way to account for the presence of a story in the text.
6. This entails a presumption of unhistoricity, for an initial way to account for any story is to claim that the author of the Gospel made it up.
7. But this presumption is weak, for it does not fulfill the burden-of-proof thesis. However, unless there are good arguments for historicity, the lack of multiple attestation prevents us from considering it historical.

Multiple Attestation
8. Multiple attestation in independent sources demonstrates that a scene did not originate with the texts that contain it.
9. Multiple attestation may not be very useful in assessing the deeds of Jesus because Q and, for some, the Gospel of Thomas, which are important witnesses in the debate about sayings of Jesus, have few or no stories in them.

Dissimilarity

10. If a scene is not essential to the narrative design and does not employ christological themes distinctive to the Gospel, then we have narrative and thematic dissimilarity, which is preliminary evidence for historicity.

11. This preliminary evidence must be supported by literary evidence that the scene in question preexisted the Gospel in which it is found.

12. However, demonstrating that a scene preexisted a Gospel does not clinch the argument for historicity.

Plausibility

13. Implausible scenes are unlikely to be historical.

14. If the implausible features of a scene are redactional, there may be a plausible scene that preexisted the implausible one.

15. If such a plausible scene can be reconstructed, to strengthen the argument the present state of the text must be accounted for.

Coherence

16. If a historical saying implies a certain deed or the deed in question presupposes an authentic saying, then the deed should be considered historical.

17. If the meaning of a deed for Jesus is independently established as the same as the meaning of a historical saying, the deed should be considered historical.

18. The latter is complicated by the possibility that the meaning a given deed would have had for Jesus may not be the meaning it has in the Gospel.[30]

On these propositions I need to make some comments, as well as suggest additions, before proceeding with the broad question of whether Jesus performed miracles.

1. One of the fundamental issues involved in historical method is the question of who should bear the burden of proof—the so-called skeptical historian or the proponent of historicity.[31] In colloquial terms, is a document from the past guilty or innocent until proven otherwise?

On the one hand, we could make a general case for the historical reliability of the Gospel material. This might enable us to shift the burden of proof to those who wish to show that an element of the Gospel tradition is not historical. If we adopted this approach we could proceed under the assumption that elements of the Gospels were "innocent until proven guilty." However, this would reduce the confidence of many readers in the strength of our conclusions. In any case, to a large extent the general reliability of the Gospels arises out of the overall force of the reliability of the many individual sayings and smaller stories, including the miracles—which are the very issues at stake. Clearly this option is not open to us.

On the other hand, we could make the assumption that the Gospel writers' way of writing about Jesus involved a kind of historiography that so mixes event-report and interpretation that we are required to do an unraveling and questioning to establish for our satisfaction "what actually happened." Conceding to this approach—as we will in this study—could be said to lead inevitably to being held hostage to what is felt to be believable in terms of modern scientific worldview(s). That would be true if we did not, in turn, raise questions about the sufficiency of contemporary worldview(s) to understand our experience of the world and the past. Therefore it is important to recall that we have raised this fundamental question, if only in a relatively brief discussion in chapter two, as we sought—successfully, I hope—to establish the possibility of miracle.

So, in order to carry as many readers with me as possible, I shall accept the burden of proof to show that a story, or element of it, is historically reliable. That does not mean that we need to be unduly skeptical about the historical reliability of the Gospel material. However, it does mean that we will need to provide a reasonable argument for the cases for historical veracity we wish to make. Also, it does not mean that I can proceed without subjectivity and presupposition. But it does mean that I will be able to be more objective, and readers will more easily be able to identify and take into account my presuppositions.

Further, this approach does not mean that if I cannot prove historicity in any particular case, the story—or elements of it—must be discarded as necessarily historically unreliable. It must be stressed: We cannot move from "*un*proven" to "*dis*proven." Since the stories with which we are dealing are tiny, containing meager information, we will often not have enough appropriate material on which to make an informed judgment about historical reliability. Nevertheless, such an approach as I am adopting, even though I will often have to say "I don't know," does enable me to command a wider acceptance among readers for the historical veracity of material that, in our society, is inherently difficult to accept as such.

In any case, authenticity or certainty is a complex notion that ought to be expressed in terms of a range of possibilities along a spectrum. On one end of the spectrum is a confidence that a story most probably reflects an event in the life of the historical Jesus; on the other end is a conclusion that there is probably little relationship between a particular story and the ministry of the earthly Jesus.[32]

Nevertheless, rather than attempt the impossible—a decision on the historicity of single words and ideas—we will generally examine only the core and main features of the stories. This is working under the assumption not only that much of the possible original reports have been reworked by storytellers and writers but also that the cores of the stories have been less altered through their transmission than the settings and links with other stories. This approach also assumes that in determining the reliability of integral features of stories we are able to assume that we have a good indication of the stories' reliably reflecting reminiscences of the first audience of Jesus.

Notwithstanding, another assumption that underlies my approach is that both ancient storytellers and writers were—if they wished—able to transmit stories and elements within them with remarkable faithfulness.[33] This means I take it as justifiable, when dealing with the issue of historicity, to deal not only with the general sense of a story but, at times, with smaller elements of the narrative.

2. One of the major difficulties we face in discussing the historicity of the so-called miraculous deeds of Jesus is that we are dealing with stories of extraordinary events. That is, ordinarily they are to be seen as implausible.

Unless in chapter two we had called into question the assumption that pervades Western intellectual endeavor—that scientific naturalism or materialism is the only and sufficient description of human experience—it would not be possible to do other than rule out of court as implausible any notion or expression of miracle reflected in the Gospels. Therefore to some extent we will need to suspend judgment on the plausibility of these reports of miraculous deeds. I say "to some extent" because, even given the possibility of miracles, there may be deeds discussed that will seem implausible from a perspective other than its being thought miraculous.

3. The criterion of multiple attestation—Miller's theses 8 and 9—needs to be broadened to include the use of extracanonical material.[34] The degree to which we are certain of their independence of the Gospel is the degree to which this material is useful.

4. The test of dissimilarity as used by Miller in his theses (10-12) means a testing to see whether, for example, the Jesus portrayed in a scene or implied by a deed grates against the christological tendencies of the particular Gospel. If it did, this would count as evidence that the scene or deed was not invented by the Gospel writer.[35] A wider use of the test was described by Reginald H. Fuller. He said that we should eliminate from the authentic Jesus material—he had the sayings in mind—that which is paralleled in the Jewish traditions and in the post-Easter church as we know it from outside the Gospels.[36]

This test is valuable in recovering the distinctive aspects of Jesus' ministry. But it can hardly be useful in identifying that which is characteristic of Jesus, for this test cannot take into account the high probability that Jesus acted and spoke in ways that overlapped with Judaism. Also, in that the early church claimed to arise out of the words and works of Jesus, that which is distinctive of him over against the post-Easter community could hardly be taken to be characteristic of the Jesus of history. Therefore this test of dissimilarity, like a number of these other tests, can be of only limited value.[37]

5. Underlying the criterion of plausibility (theses 13-15)[38] is the view that "a scene depicting an event which severely strains our collective ability to believe that it happened is unlikely to be accepted as historical."[39] However, as Miller is right to add, "(1) judgments about plausibility are unavoidably subjective, and (2) implausible events do sometimes occur,"[40] as—we will be arguing—in the case of miracles in the Gospels.

6. The test of historicity from coherence is, for Miller (theses 16-18), that historicity can be argued on the grounds of an element's coherence with other similar elements in the Gospels. Rudolf Pesch argued that an event would need to be given meaning by an authentic saying for it to be considered historically reliable.[41] Presenting a slightly different nuance, Franz Mussner gave an example of this test in noting that miracle stories that cohered with Jesus' meals with sinners must be considered *ipsissima facta* of Jesus.[42] Of course, as Miller pointed out, this could not be the only test for historicity, for two items—or indeed a family of elements—could be due to the creativity of the Christians transmitting the material.

Nevertheless as Max Turner pointed out to me, this principle is important in a wider sense. That is, we are not able to answer the question of the historical probability of any given miracle without asking how it relates to—coheres with— the aims of Jesus in his Jewish restorationist context and in his collision with Judaism. From these comments on Miller's theses we turn to propose some additional tests for historicity in the following points.

7. Just as the historicity of some sayings is greatly enhanced because they were embarrassing for the early church to transmit, so it is with the activities of Jesus.[43] Therefore one indicator of historicity is that the report would have been embarrassing to transmit. Of course this is not to say that for a saying or deed of Jesus to be authentic it is required to be an embarrassment; rather if a saying or deed is embarrassing it is more likely to be an authentic part of the Jesus tradition than to have been created by the church.

8. The incidental transmission of sayings has proved a valuable criterion in establishing historicity. That is, as Arthur Marwick put it, "On the whole it can be said that a primary source is most valuable when the purpose for which it was compiled is at the furthest remove from the purpose of the historian."[44] This criterion will also be useful in our enterprise as it relates to the stories of Jesus' activities.

9. An important tool of historical method—analogy—had its decisive explication in Ernst Troeltsch's famous essay "Historical and Dogmatic Method in Theology" (1898).

Analogous occurrences that we observe both without and within ourselves furnish us with the key to historical criticism. The illusions, distortions, deceptions, myths, and partisanships we see with our own eyes enable us to recognize similar features in the materials of tradition.[45]

This principle has been taken up and helpfully restated by other historians. For example, Marc Bloch put it this way:

> In the last analysis, whether consciously or no, it is always by borrowing from our daily experiences and by shading them, where necessary, with new tints that we derive the elements which help us to restore the past.[46]

Therefore the historian cannot proceed by being mentally detached from the historical inquiry, or it would not be possible to form any reconstruction of the past. Even our limited or very different experience from the past enables us at least to begin that reconstruction.[47]

Yet the problem with using the principle of analogy to determine "fact from fiction" is that the historian's worldview is allowed to dominate that of the past.[48] This might eliminate from a reconstruction a genuine reflection of the past that was outside the experience of the historian. However, it is probable that no event in history can be contained, without remainder, by any analogue from any time. Further, it cannot be assumed that a historian's knowledge and experience contain all the possibilities of human knowledge and experience.[49]

This means, on the one hand, that we can legitimately use the principle of analogy only when we can identify an analogue for the event. On the other hand, we can only conclude that in so far as a report of an event falls outside our analogues and experiences, to that extent it remains beyond our grasp to make judgments about its historicity. That is, we cannot—using the principle of analogy alone—judge the story to be fictive. In that we are dealing with reports of the miraculous, the use of the principle of analogy depends to a large extent on our having been able to argue that there is the possibility of miracles in our time (see chapter two).

The principle of analogy leads naturally to take into account a further point. What we will be looking for in our historical examination of the miracle stories is an overall plausible story that, in turn, coheres with what we can otherwise recover about the historical Jesus.[50] With these things in mind we can turn to the question, "Did Jesus perform miracles?" We will not woodenly or mechanically apply the criteria and principles we have been discussing. Rather, in the chapters ahead they will continually inform our thinking and form the background to our discussions of historicity.

§9.7 Did Jesus Perform Miracles?

1. *Non-Christians and Jesus as miracle worker.* In that non-Christians would have had no vested interest in portraying Jesus as a miracle worker if in fact he was not, the surest point at which to begin our search for evidence that Jesus performed

miracles is outside the New Testament.

(a) In his *Jewish Antiquities* 18:63-64, written around A.D. 90, Josephus has a section purportedly on Jesus. Whereas Josephus most probably mentioned Jesus, Christian redactors and copyists have added to, subtracted from and altered the passage.[51] One of the lines about Jesus that is probably authentic runs thus: "He [Jesus] was one who wrought surprising feats" *(paradoxōn ergōn poiētēs)*.

In Josephus *paradoxōn* sometimes means "miraculous,"[52] as it does, for example, in his description of water gushing from a rock that Moses had struck with this staff[53] and in relating a story of Elijah blinding and then healing the eyes of the enemy.[54] *Paradoxōn* also means "strange" for Josephus, which could include the miraculous,[55] as it does on the only occasion it is used in the New Testament (Lk 5:26). Josephus has no particular reason to attribute miracles to Jesus. Indeed, from what he says about Moses, Elijah and contemporary false prophets offering "signs" *(sēmeia)* of deliverance *(J.W.* 2:259; 6:285), he does not even consider Jesus unique in this respect. We have then from Josephus evidence that Jesus was at least reputed to perform surprising feats, probably miracles.

(b) The *Babylonian Talmud* preserves a tradition that is probably to be associated with Jesus of Nazareth: "It has been taught[56] on the eve of the Passover Jesus was hanged. For forty days before the execution took place, a herald went forth and cried, 'He is going forth to be stoned because he has practised sorcery' *(b. Sanh.* 43a). By sorcery is probably meant the use of particular paraphernalia to perform healings (cf. *b. Sanh.* 67b).

Although this material does not give us contemporary evidence of Jesus being a miracle worker, it does give us (importantly) independent and indirect evidence in that it shows that Jesus was (or at least had come to be) remembered as a sorcerer-healer. However, it is probable that in Jewish-Christian debates the traditions have been confused such that Jesus' name has been only later and incorrectly associated with stories of other, often unorthodox figures.[57] Therefore this material is of doubtful value to us in our search for the historical Jesus.[58]

(c) In a similar category must be placed some lines from Origen in which he quotes Celsus from the end of the second century: "He was brought up in secret and hired himself out as a workman in Egypt, and after having tried his hand at certain magical powers he returned from there, and on account of those powers gave himself the title of God" *(CC* 1:38; cf. 1:160). Again this is too late to be considered as direct evidence, and Celsus may be dependent on Christian traditions in building his case.[59] However, it is certainly not material that would have been created by Christians. In any case, Celsus indicates a continuing tradition that Jesus was thought to have powers that enabled him to perform miracles.

(d) Another piece of indirect evidence that the historical Jesus performed miracles is in the continuing use of his name by healers.[60] Names, often of those considered to have been powerful healers—Solomon, for example (Josephus *Ant.* 8:46-49)—were used by later healers in their incantations for miracles.[61] Once again, though very late, the evidence from the rabbinic material is that Jesus was remembered as a healer, for the rabbis prohibited healing by Jesus' name.[62] And Arnobius, a Christian apologist who died about A.D. 330, says that Jesus' name was used in exorcisms in his day (*Adv. Gent.* 1:43).[63]

The relevant material from outside the New Testament is small but significant in giving us evidence that Jesus was known as or had a reputation as a successful miracle worker. In the case of Josephus, although his material has been transmitted and altered by Christians,[64] a core of evidence exists independent of Christian traditions. Though the rabbinic material is late, it is valuable in that it does not appear to be dependent on Christian traditions. In the case of evidence from Celsus, which comes to us through Christian traditions, we have information transmitted that would not have been created by Christians because of its offensive nature. In the case of Arnobius and other Christian writers, though we do not have independent evidence, we do have information that is transmitted incidentally to their purposes. Turning to the New Testament, we see that Jesus' reputation is well founded.

2. Paul and the miracles of Jesus. It is, at first, a great surprise to us that the earliest known Christian writer tells us so little—some would say nothing—about the miracles of Jesus. Indeed, Nikolaus Walter goes so far as to say, "It can be stated that we can detect no hint that Paul knew of the narrative tradition about Jesus."[65] In particular, a little later, Walter says that as far as we can see from Paul's letters, Jesus' actions played no role in his picture of Jesus' life and ministry "and certainly not his actions as a performer of miracles."[66]

Bultmann expressed a similar (though not such a severe) view in saying, "All that was important for him [Paul] in the story of Jesus is the fact that Jesus was born a Jew and lived under the Law (Gal. 4:4) and that he had been crucified."[67] This is an important issue, for if our earliest known Christian writer knows nothing of the miracles of Jesus, fundamental questions are raised regarding the historicity—and certainly importance—of the miracle tradition. For example, the miracle stories could have their origin no earlier than in the work of the author of Q or the pre-Markan material.[68]

Against this pessimistic view, however, are hints that Paul, while not giving us stories of Jesus' miracles, probably considered Jesus to have performed them.[69] First, Paul performs miracles as an integral part of his ministry[70] and regards himself as the representative and revealer of Jesus. Could not this imply that Paul knows that Jesus' ministry was also characterized by miracles?

Second, and in particular, does not Paul's summary of his own ministry ("what Christ has accomplished through me . . . by word and deed, by the power of signs and wonders, by the power of the Spirit," Rom 15:18-19) assume that his ministry, which included miracles, was a reflection of Jesus' ministry?[71]

Third, in 1 Corinthians 4:20 Paul says that the kingdom of God depends not on talk but on power *(dunamei)*. With the close association between powers, or miracles, and the kingdom of God in the Synoptic Gospels, it is not unreasonable to assume that Paul here is reflecting a knowledge of this association in the life of Jesus.

Fourth, 1 Corinthians 13:2 ("faith enough to move mountains," author's translation) probably echoes Jesus' saying about miracle-working faith.[72]

Also, negatively, it could be suggested that in writing of the deceptive "powerful signs and wonders" of the lawless one (2 Thess 2:9, author's translation) we may assume Paul believed that Jesus had such powers.[73]

Finally, that Paul would need to say something about the life of Jesus, including his miraculous deeds, is most likely because he probably would have found it impossible to proclaim a recently crucified man as Son of God without making reference to his words and deeds.

As limited as our information is, we can probably establish from these hints that Paul most likely considered that Jesus conducted miracles and that the miracles were an important part of both his teaching about Jesus and his own ministry. We can also probably establish—over against the view expressed by Bonhoeffer (see §1.6)—that Paul thought that the miracles of Jesus were significant because they were, along with the teaching of Jesus, a key component in the expression of the kingdom of God.

3. A final piece of evidence that Jesus performed miracles (as we will see when discussing the miracles in the Gospels) is that inside the New Testament all the Gospel traditions support the case that Jesus performed miracles: Mark, Q, M, L,[74] John and—if it existed—the Johannine signs source, as well as the appendix to the Fourth Gospel. The witness of various literary forms in the Gospels also gives support to the view that Jesus performed miracles. There are biographical sayings,[75] parables,[76] a dispute story,[77] sayings of instruction[78] and commissionings,[79] as well as the stories of exorcism, healing, raising the dead and so-called nature miracles, all of which we have already discussed in some detail.

These multiple attestations, from within and outside the New Testament, point to the high probability that the historical Jesus performed feats that were considered miracles.[80] Whether these "miracles" have natural or psychosomatic explanations,[81] *historians* may never conclusively know. But with Bultmann we can say that "the Christian community was convinced that *Jesus had performed miracles,* and told a good many miracle stories about him. . . . There can be no doubt that Jesus did the kinds of deeds which were miracles to his mind and to the minds of his contemporaries."[82]

Indeed, in light of this study so far we can say that this aspect of the life of the historical Jesus is well and widely attested in those ancient documents that refer to Jesus.[83] In view of the conclusions to the discussion of the possibility of miracles (chapter two) we can go a step further than Bultmann and propose that these feats and wonders can be taken to be miracles—the direct and visible activity of God.

§9.8 So Far . . .

In this chapter we have set out a number of things: an approach to the question on what we can know about the past and some criteria (or propositions), as well as items of evidence with which we can engage the data in the Gospels, in order to inquire whether the historical Jesus performed miracles. As a first step we have established that Jesus' reputation as a miracle worker is well founded. Whether the particular stories or (more likely) earlier parts of them can be traced back to the life of the historical Jesus is still to be discussed in part four.

Before then, a necessary intermediary step is to inquire into the meaning of the miracles for Jesus. This will provide part of the interpretative background against which to test whether elements of the miracle tradition have their place at the very bedrock of the traditions. This is the task of the next chapter.

Ten

The Meaning of the Miracles for Jesus

....

§10.1 Introduction

If we can be certain of anything about the historical Jesus it is that his contemporaries considered him to have performed wonders or miracles. That the early church considered these miracles to be more than simple cures and the marvels of a holy man is clear. John's Gospel, for example, talks about them as "signs" and says that they were recorded "so that you may come to believe that Jesus is the Messiah" (Jn 20:31). For Luke also the miracles are more than marvels of a mundane miracle monger—they are said to be the result of the (eschatological) Spirit of the Lord being upon Jesus (Lk 4:18).

This raises the question as to how Jesus may have understood his miracles. If he saw his miracles as more than isolated marvels, how did he understand them or what meaning, if any, did he give them? So the purpose of this chapter is to answer the question, What did Jesus think was the purpose and place of his miraculous works in the context of his overall ministry?[1]

As I will argue in a moment (§10.2), if we are able to ascertain the meaning of the miracles for Jesus we will have discovered something intrinsically valuable, for many Christians will want to allow that answer to inform their view of Jesus and the miracles. Further, and important in fulfilling the objectives of this study, knowing how Jesus viewed his miracles in general will help us test whether particular miracle stories, or parts of them, belong to the authentic material to be associated with the historical Jesus.

Two broad options are available in the attempt to recover Jesus' perspective on his miracles. The generally accepted way forward is through analyzing the more easily accessible sayings.[2] This I shall do later in this chapter. However, even though it is more difficult—in that we are dealing with stories of miracles—we shall take the other option first and examine Jesus' choice of miracles and his techniques.[3] In this way we may gain a broad understanding of Jesus' perspective on his work through the kinds of miracles he conducted and the methods he used or the way he went about them.

There is an unavoidable circularity in this approach: We have yet to discuss the historicity of individual stories, yet we will to some extent depend on those discussions to recover how Jesus viewed his miracles. This in turn will help us later test whether individual miracle stories can be accepted as fitting Jesus' perspective on his miracles. Hence in confronting an aspect of the limits of historical inquiry we will need to be circumspect in any claims and conclusions.

As we seek to recover the meaning and place of the miracles for Jesus in his ministry we must not allow our inquiry to become unbalanced to the point of concluding that miracles were the only activities he undertook. Jesus' activities are reported to be far more wide ranging than simply performing miracles. He is said to have been baptized, to call and eventually send out disciples, to engage in public debate with the religious authorities, to spend time eating with "sinners" and to ride into Jerusalem on a donkey, probably just before "cleansing" the temple.[4]

Notwithstanding, from what we have seen from the examination of the four Gospels, Jesus' activity that involves producing miracles is portrayed as such a large part of his ministry that it warrants special attention. This leads to the next point: it must be established that this exercise has value.

§10.2 Is the Historical Jesus Important?

Up to the beginning of the nineteenth century, the question, "What did the historical Jesus consider to be the meaning and place of the miracles in his ministry?" would have been meaningless to most readers of the Gospels. What could be read from the text was unquestioningly taken by most to tell the reader about the Jesus of history. But during the nineteenth century a historical revolution took place that was bigger in the character of human thought than the "revival of learning" we associate with the Renaissance.[5]

As was noted in §1.7, during the nineteenth century David Friedrich Strauss, who was not without his precursors, published his *Life of Jesus*. This brought thorough scientific historical research to the Gospels in the hope of sifting fact from fiction, or history from legend or myth. His work highlighted the distinction between the Jesus of history and the Jesus (or Christ) of faith reflected in the Gospels. Accepting this distinction, a task before the historian was to recover and reconstruct the historical Jesus.

Yet some have grave doubts about the possibility of such an enterprise,[6] not least because the earliest traditions did not seem to provide anything like enough material to produce even an outline sketch of the life of Jesus. Others thought the exercise pointless for Christian theology. For example, Bultmann is well known for having said that "we can know almost nothing concerning the life and personality of Jesus"[7] and also that all that mattered about Jesus was that he existed and was crucified, not the "what" of his life.[8]

In light of two of the major objectives in this study—to see to what extent the miracle stories of Jesus in the Gospels reflect "what actually happened" and also to try to determine how Jesus understood his miracles—it is important to ask if the historical Jesus and the miracle traditions that may be part of his life are only of antiquarian value or whether it is important for Christians to know which miracles Jesus performed and what he thought about them.

In his widely read book *The Real Jesus: The Misguided Quest for the Historical Jesus and the Truth of the Traditional Gospel,* Luke Timothy Johnson says that the most destructive effect of the Jesus Seminar and recent historical Jesus books has been "the perpetuation of the notion that history somehow determines faith, and that for faith to be correct, the historical accounts that gave rise to it have to be verified."[9] In a perspective reminiscent of Bultmann's, Johnson argues that this is simply not true, at least because of the fragility of historical reconstructions. But it is also not true that history somehow determines faith because the Christian faith is not directed at historical facts about Jesus or a reconstruction of him.

Johnson goes on to say that the faith of Christians is confirmed not by the establishment of facts about the past but by the reality of Christ's power in the present.[10] This, as I am about to argue, is only partly true. The very focus of the Gospel writers on the Jesus of Nazareth shows that the historical man Jesus is of great importance to post-Easter Christians.[11] But it is one thing to establish his importance for the Gospel writers; it is quite another to establish the importance of the historical Jesus for our time.

During the nineteenth century it was generally agreed that the historical Jesus was of great importance to the Christian faith. In this century the opposite position has generally been dominant. However, with some significant exceptions[12] recent decades have seen increasing numbers of scholars convinced that it does matter what we know about the historical Jesus.[13]

1. Ernst Käsemann, who is credited with inaugurating the "second" or "new quest" of the historical Jesus,[14] was concerned that, without a connection with the historical Jesus, Christianity ran the risk of falling into doceticism or becoming an ahistorical pietism.

2. Norman Perrin argued that the study of the historical Jesus provides content to Christian faith, which of necessity is faith in something, "and in so far as that

'something' is 'Jesus', historical knowledge can help provide the content."[15]

3. Perrin also argued that knowledge of the historical Jesus was important in providing a basis for discriminating among the proclamations claiming to be Christian. Perrin put it bluntly: "The true kerygmatic Christ, the justifiable faith-image, is that consistent with the historical Jesus."[16]

4. In a position similar to that of Perrin's, John Dominic Crossan said that the historical Jesus is important because the Christian faith is "(1) an act of faith (2) in the historical Jesus (3) as the manifestation of God."[17] From this perspective, in that the Christian faith does not even presuppose Easter but was present before it, the Christian faith cannot be defined primarily as faith in the kerygmatic Christ. Put positively, because the historical Jesus is seen as the manifestation of God, it follows that what he was like and what he was doing is a disclosure of God. Therefore knowing about the historical Jesus is of value.[18]

5. John Meier makes the distinction between the value of knowledge about the historical Jesus for *faith,* on the one hand, and *theology* on the other. Because the object of *faith* is Jesus Christ—risen and presently reigning and accessible to all believers, including those who will never study history or theology—historical scholarship about Jesus is of no significance. However, we must part company with Meier. Insofar as there is a continuity between the Jesus of history and the Christ of faith, faith will want to be informed about the Jesus of history. Notwithstanding, Meier's reasons for contemporary theology—faith seeking understanding—taking into account the quest for the historical reason, are worth noting.[19]

(a) It rules out reducing Christ to a cipher without content or to a mythic symbol by affirming that Christian faith is "adherence to a particular person who said and did particular things in a particular time and place in human history."

(b) It rules out pious and docetic tendencies to ignore Jesus' humanity and to emphasize his divinity by reminding us that Jesus was a fully human, first-century Jew living in Palestine.

(c) It rules out comfortable Christian domestications of Jesus by disclosing his nonconformist aspects, especially on religious issues.

(d) It rules out seeing Jesus as "a this-worldly political revolutionary" and prevents Jesus from being claimed by any ideology.

6. Another person expressing the view that it does matter what we know about the historical Jesus is Marcus Borg. He affirms that "one can be a Christian without historical knowledge of Jesus."[20] Yet he also is able to put the point simply and summarily in seeing the historical Jesus as important because how we as Christians think of Jesus shapes our understanding of the Christian life itself.[21]

In various ways these writers have given good reasons to maintain the ongoing significance of the historical Jesus for both the faith as well as for the theology of post-Easter Christians. Although Christians direct their faith toward the risen and present living Jesus, they dare not cut themselves adrift from the moorings of historical reconstructions of Jesus, even though they are fragile. Despite the propensity to project onto the historical Jesus our own hopes for a Messiah and the possibility of producing only what Martin Kähler called a "Fifth Gospel"[22] out of a scissors-and-paste reconstruction, it is important to try to recover the historical Jesus. Further, and fundamentally, if there is a continuity between the Jesus of history and the present living Jesus, we will do well to allow the Jesus of history, as well as of the Gospels, to inform our understanding of the Jesus we go on encountering.

If, as these voices are calling us to believe, the historical Jesus is important, there are remarkable implications for the study of the miracles of Jesus. These we will draw out in the conclusions at the end of this book. For the present our task is to see if we can say what Jesus understood to be the purpose and place of miracles in his ministry.

§10.3 Choosing Miracles

Just as Jesus' followers were not obliged to portray their Messiah as a miracle worker (see §9.5), so Jesus, to some extent, was not compelled to perform miracles, even though he may have been conscious of being a (or the) Chosen One of God. I say "to some extent," because as A. E. Harvey has suggested, "A person who knows himself to possess supernatural powers is not quite so free to decide whether or not to use them as a man who has knowledge is free to decide whether or not to teach. Such powers tend to impel their owners into action."[23] Nevertheless despite the sometimes realized potential that his conducting miracles would be misunderstood, Jesus still chose to perform miracles. We will see in a moment that the kinds of miracles he performed give us clues as to why, in general, he chose to perform miracles.

Given that there were many sick people in Palestine and given that he was a successful and sought-after healer, we can assume that Jesus made some choices about whom he healed and the kinds of miracles he performed. Those choices stand out when we place the list of miracle stories from the life of the historical Jesus (see §16.14) next to stories of other healers of the time.[24]

We cannot give the impression that Jesus was entirely free to choose which healings he conducted because of stories such as the healing of the official's son and the exorcism of the Syrophoenician woman's daughter, where against his will his healing was sought and eventually obtained. This situation may have arisen from what William Loader has suggested is a feature of Mark's presentation of Jesus, which, in turn, may have its roots in the life of the historical Jesus.[25] That is, like Peter in Acts 10, where Peter was reluctant to cross cultural boundaries to speak about Jesus to the Gentile Cornelius, Jesus also was reluctant to extend his healing ministry to Gentiles. His healing mission was to the Jews. Thus to some extent against his will, Jesus on occasion chose to heal.

Notwithstanding, whereas we are largely at the mercy of the Gospel traditions for our knowledge of the kinds of miracles Jesus conducted, the most conspicuous feature is that the most numerous category is that of exorcism. As there is nothing in the literature of the time that would suggest Jesus was bound to choose exorcism as the most common miracle he performed or that the early church focused on exorcism in its ministry, we can be fairly confident that this balance in the kinds of miracles is historically reliable. In view of the interpretation he gave his exorcisms—as a battle with Satan (see §10.11)—we are obliged to conclude that *Jesus saw his miracles—and hence at least a large part of his mission—as primarily a battle with the demonic and, concomitantly, an expression of the realization of the kingdom of God in the face of the defeat of Satan.*

§10.4 Raising the Dead
In chapter fourteen I will be arguing that, despite the profound difficulty we may have in accepting the historicity of stories of raising the dead, the stories of raising Jairus's daughter, the widow of Nain's son and Lazarus are probably to be seen as rightfully part of the authentic reports of Jesus' ministry.

On reviewing the miracles attributed to Hellenistic healers of roughly the same period as Jesus, the frequently alleged parallels to raising the dead are highly questionable.[26] The Jewish traditions know of no actual instances of this kind of miracle,[27] reserving it as the prerogative of God (cf. Ezek 37:13; *b. Ta'an.* 2a). Nevertheless it is notable that a Jewish tradition suggests that a rabbi of exceptional holiness might, in theory, be able to raise the dead.[28]

In view of this, two things are to be concluded about Jesus raising the dead. First, at the very least Jesus would have been considered by others—and we have to take the next step and say that Jesus would have considered himself—to be exceptionally spiritually powerful or uniquely close to God to be able to carry out such feats. Second, in light of the Old Testament expectations that in the last days the dead would be raised (see Is 26:19; Dan 12:1-3), Jesus would have considered himself to be part of the last days. To these we add an obvious third implication: Jesus would have deemed that the last days had arrived.

§10.5 "Nature" Miracles
In that Jesus made the choice to calm an angry sea, walk on the sea and feed thousands, we come to the same conclusion: Jesus most probably thought he was acting for or even as God. These acts also carry echoes of the exodus. It is not that

it would have been understood that in these "nature" miracles a new covenant was being inaugurated or an old one renewed.[29] Rather, what was primarily being expressed was the graciousness of God, and the gift and rescue nature of the powerful coming of God in Jesus' life and activity.

Similarly, it is well known that the disciples were the only ones said to witness these miracles. Even the miraculous feedings of the crowds are assumed to be recognized only by Jesus' followers.[30] In these stories Jesus is most clearly seen as acting in God's place. As God's most complete disclosure of himself was to his servant Moses (e.g., Ex 3:1-6; 19:1-25), so Jesus' most complete disclosure of himself was to his disciples.

That the vast majority of the miracles attributed to Jesus relate to relieving human suffering and need gives rise to the view that compassion was implicit in the historical Jesus' motivation for performing miracles. Also we can probably conclude that Jesus understood God's salvation to be focused on answering human suffering and need rather than in drawing attention to the miraculous power at his disposal.[31]

§10.6 The Cripples and Paralytics

A. E. Harvey notes that Jewish miracle workers certainly succeeded in curing diseases.[32] But he goes on to say that there is a notable absence of reports of the curing of the kind of lameness or paralysis that is common among the authentic reports of Jesus' miracles.[33] This not only accounts for some of the wonder and amazement his miracles are said to evoke but again identifies Jesus' miracles—at least some of them—as reflecting the hopes of the Old Testament for the messianic age (e.g., Is 35:5-6). In turn, we cannot avoid the conclusion that this was an impression that Jesus intended his observers to note from the kinds of miracles he conducted.[34]

§10.7 Faith

In our discussion of the miracle stories in chapters eleven through sixteen, we will often come across the theme of faith, which appears to have a legitimate place among the historical reminiscences of the historical Jesus. However, the frequent, almost universal connection between faith and miracles in the Gospels has meant that the degree to which the miracles have been difficult to handle critically is the degree to which faith has not featured in the discussions of the historical Jesus.[35] Yet when we compare the theme of faith and its association with miracles with the way it appears in ancient literature (broadly of the same period as the New Testament writers), there is a distinctive approach in the stories of Jesus. The approach is so distinctive—an approach not developed or modeled in the early church as reflected in Acts[36]—that we can be reasonably confident that the faith motif in the miracle stories is based on traditional material.[37]

An examination of miracle stories in Lucian, Plutarch, Strabo and the rabbinic material shows that faith is not required of the suppliant and is not the condition for miracle; it is the result or consequence of miracle.[38] To quote Theissen, "'Faith' in the ancient world is primarily an attitude to the miraculous event, whereas in the New Testament it is an attitude on the part of the people involved which is internal to the miraculous event."[39] In contrast to the Gospels, in the ancient, (roughly) parallel material, not faith in the miracle worker but confidence, hope or courage in relation to the healing process is required.

This brief discussion helps us see another aspect of what the miracles would have meant for Jesus. In that he generally expected faith or confidence in him to be the prior condition for a miracle, he would have been aware of his own pivotal role in the powerful presence of God being realized in his miracles. Put a slightly different way, he would have been conscious of the personal relationship with him that was a precondition for experiencing a miracle—as it was also an expected response to his miracles.

§10.8 Techniques

Turning to the methods adopted by Jesus in his miracles, it is notable that many of his techniques can be paralleled in his exact or near contemporaries. For example, Jesus' method of healing from a distance is paralleled in a report of Ḥanina ben Dosa (*b. Ber.* 34b), as is his sense of healing efficacy.[40] Ḥanina could tell that he was being successful by means of the fluency of his prayers, and Jesus could sense healing power going out of him (Mk 5:30). In this sense of efficacy we cannot say that Jesus would have seen himself as any different from other healers of his time. The same conclusion is to be drawn from noting that Jesus is reported to have used saliva in healings of the blind (Mk 8:23; Jn 9:6), for other healers, Jewish and Hellenistic, used saliva in their healings (see §§13.2 and 13.4).

However, in that Jesus did not use prayer in his healing, our conclusion has to be different. Even though the early church has enhanced Jesus' prayer life,[41] it did not appear to do so in relation to his healing techniques. At no point does the tradition seek to attribute or report prayer as part of Jesus' technique as an exorcist. And only in the story of the healing of the deaf-mute is Jesus portrayed as praying as part of his healing technique, in that he looked up to heaven (Mk 7:34).[42] (As we will note in §14.4, the prayer associated with the raising of Lazarus is not really part of Jesus' technique but is appended for the benefit of the bystanders.) Yet prayer is said to be an important part of the miracle-working technique of the Jewish holy men of the time.[43]

From this it is reasonable to conclude that Jesus would not have seen himself as simply one of the holy men.[44] Also, whereas Jesus may have seen God to be involved in what he was doing in his miracles, he believed that he was operating out of his own resources as a miracle worker.[45] Thus I cannot avoid the conclusion to which A. E. Harvey came in his Bampton Lectures of 1980: Jesus opted for methods of miraculous healing that were bound to be dangerously ambiguous.[46]

On the one hand, he used techniques common to other Palestinian holy men and performed miracles of a type familiar in the stories of Old Testament prophets or men of God. It is not surprising then that those in his audience were ready to give praise to God for what they saw. On the other hand, Jesus used techniques in his miracles that gave him an air of self-sufficiency and mystery, especially in his exorcisms. That this in itself would have raised suspicions about Jesus' orthodoxy may be inferred from later rabbinic thinking that any rabbi who performed a miracle to strengthen his own authority was highly suspect (*b. B. Meṣ.* 59b).[47]

§10.9 Jesus' Perspective

In the remainder of this chapter we will take the more assured path in attempting to understand Jesus' view of his miracles by examining a number of his sayings that relate to the miracles. We first need to make sure we are dealing with sayings that are reasonably likely to be reflecting the voice of Jesus. Then we will see if we can say what light these sayings throw on Jesus' understanding of his miracles.

The sayings that are most likely to be of value in this enterprise are:

☐ Jesus' reply to the charge of being empowered by Satan (Mt 12:27/Lk 11:19)
☐ The Spirit-finger saying (Mt 12:28/Lk 11:20)
☐ The parable of the strong man (Mk 3:27/Mt 12:29/Lk 11:21-22)
☐ Jesus' answer to John the Baptist (Mt 11:2-6/Lk 7:18-23)
☐ The "woes" on Chorazin, Bethsaida and Capernaum (Mt 11:20-24/Lk 10:12-15)
☐ Jesus' saying, "Tell that fox . . . !" (Lk 13:32)
☐ A sign from heaven (Mt 12:38-39; 16:1-4; Mk 8:11-13/Lk 11:16, 29; Jn 6:30).

Since the exorcisms most probably formed the bulk of the miracles of Jesus, we will begin by noting the three sayings that form part of the so-called Beelzebul controversy.[48] These sayings may help us understand how Jesus viewed his exorcisms. Although I will argue that the first two sayings originally belonged together, it is highly likely that the remainder of this paragraph is a collection of sayings.[49]

§10.10 Jesus' Reply to the Charge of Being Empowered by Satan (Mt 12:27/Lk 11:19)

Someone—we can no longer determine who—accused Jesus of casting out demons by Beelzebul, or Satan, the prince of demons (Mt 12:24/Lk 11:15). Jesus' reply as we have it in Luke 11:19 (which is most likely nearest to Q) reads as follows:

Now if I cast out demons by Beelzebul, by whom do your sons cast them out? Therefore they will be your judges. (author's translation)

That this is part of the bedrock of material giving us the authentic voice of Jesus is beyond reasonable doubt: (1) it is inextricably tied to a charge of Jesus being Satan-possessed; (2) it relativizes the exorcisms of Jesus by reference to other Jewish exorcists—both points highly unlikely to be invented by the early church; and (3) the antithetical parallelism of the question and statement is typical of Jesus' speech.[50]

Already we can see here something about Jesus' understanding of his exorcisms—he saw himself as one of a number of Jewish exorcists in Palestine. We can also see why he thought his exorcisms were successful. The question Jesus asks is "By whom do your sons [or followers[51]] cast them out?" (author's translation). The expected response would be "God," for the context of the debate gives only Satan or God as the alternatives, and "Satan" could not be expected because the debate assumes that Jesus and his contemporaries are doing the same thing by the same power.

The problem with this conclusion is that in the next verse (Mt 12:28/Lk 11:20) Jesus goes on to say that *his* exorcisms are—as I will argue—the arrival of the kingdom of God. How can he say this if he is empowered by God just like his contemporaries? Critics have rightly balked at the idea that Jesus thought the other Jewish exorcists were also marking the arrival of the kingdom of God.[52]

One solution to this problem has been to isolate these two sayings from each other in the ministry of Jesus.[53] But the question of Matthew 12:27—"By whom do your sons cast them out? Therefore they will be your judges" (author's translation)—is complemented by the saying of verse 28, and, as just noted, the two verses have the same initial structure and are part of an antithetical parallelism—a generally recognized feature of Jesus' speech. Also, we know of no early-church situation where this question is likely to have arisen.

Another solution is to suggest that the difference between Jesus' exorcisms and others was that he was more successful.[54] But there is nothing in the text that would suggest this. Nor does the text allow us to suppose that Jesus used different methods from his contemporaries.[55] Nor can we say that Jesus was aware of an "otherly" power as if this were particularly significant.[56] Such experiences were common to holy men.[57]

If we keep in mind that all this text is about—so far—is the source of power-authority for exorcism, not about the coming of the kingdom of God, we can focus on Jesus' saying—or implying—that in his exorcisms he, like his contemporaries, is empowered by God. This idea of Jesus being willing to accept and place on a level with himself other healers is not foreign in the Synoptic tradition. Notably at the end of this paragraph there is a negative version of a saying (Mt 12:30/Lk 11:23), also attached to the tiny report of the strange exorcist: "Whoever is not against us is for us" (Mk 9:40/Lk 9:50).

In short, this saying shows that Jesus saw himself on a level with other exorcists in that, like them, he believed that he was empowered by God. It also shows that Jesus' miracles, specifically his exorcisms, could be seen by the religious authorities to be grounds to seek his destruction.

§10.11 The Spirit-Finger Saying (Mt 12:28/Lk 11:20)
Immediately following the previous saying is this statement, which can be literally translated

> But if in God's Spirit [Luke has "finger"] I cast out the demons, then has come upon you the kingdom of God. (author's translation)

There is hardly a saying better known to students of the sayings of Jesus than this one. Nevertheless, before going further our first task is to see what level of confidence we can have in its being something Jesus may have said.[58]

A good case can be made that this saying is among those with the highest probability of coming from Jesus. (1) As we have twice noted, the saying seems tied to the previous verse for its sense and therefore is part of an antithetical parallelism—a character of Jesus' speech. (2) Its theme is that of the "kingdom," a theme central to the public ministry of Jesus.[59] (3) The fact that the kingdom of God is said to have come *already*—easily understood in Aramaic[60]—suggests that the saying arose in the ministry of Jesus. (4) Applying the criterion of dissimilarity (see §9.6), this association of the coming of salvation with exorcism is not something the early church cultivated.[61] Rather, it was the advent of Jesus, his death, resurrection and the coming of the Spirit that were more readily associated with the dawn of salvation.[62]

If with the vast majority of scholars[63] we take this saying as authentically Jesus' and that Matthew probably preserves the original saying (see §6.2), we can turn to the question of the meaning of this saying for Jesus. A prima facie reading suggests that Jesus saw some relationship between his exorcisms and the coming of the kingdom of God. A more careful reading reveals the following points:

1. From the Aramaic that can be reconstructed behind the word *ephthasen* in this verse,[64] at the very least we can say that Jesus understood his exorcisms to have something to do with the present coming of the kingdom of God, either its being realized or its being in the process of arriving.

2. Why Jesus thought his exorcisms were linked to the inbreaking of God's reign is less easy to establish. The verse has three components: the exorcist (where Jesus says "I," *egō*),[65] his source of power-authority (the Spirit) and the kingdom

of God. So did Jesus link his exorcisms with the coming of God's reign because he was the exorcist or because God's Spirit was his source of power-authority? It is probably a combination of both.

On the one hand, Jesus saw himself on the same side as his contemporary Jewish exorcists—with God (see Mt 12:27/Lk 11:19). Yet in contrast to his contemporaries, Jesus claimed that it was the *Spirit* of God who provided him with his power-authority.[66] So far as I can discover, no Jewish exorcist is known to have appealed to the Spirit as a source of power-authority for exorcism.[67] In this Jesus is making a unique claim.[68] That this claim would have been made in full knowledge of the expectation that in the last time the Spirit of the Lord would rest on the Messiah (Is 11:2)[69] makes it difficult to avoid the conclusion that Jesus was claiming that it was evident in his exorcisms that he was endowed with the eschatological Spirit and was therefore an eschatological figure himself.

3. Further, that Jesus says "I *[egō]* cast out demons" is also significant. This emphatic "I" is relatively infrequent on the lips of Jesus, so we can see that he was drawing attention to his view that the coming of the reign of God was linked to his exorcisms, not only because he was empowered by the Spirit of God but because he was the exorcist. In other words, on the strength of this saying we can conclude that Jesus did not think the kingdom of God was arriving where the Spirit was but where the Spirit was empowering him to perform exorcisms.[70]

4. From what we have said so far about this saying, for Jesus his exorcisms were not preparatory to the coming of the kingdom of God, nor were they signs or evidence of the coming of God's reign; they were more than signs or evidence. *The exorcisms were, in themselves, the kingdom of God expressed in the lives of those healed.* We shall find this confirmed in the next saying.

§10.12 The Parable of the Strong Man (Mk 3:27/Mt 12:29/Lk 11:21-22)

In Mark this parable reads as follows:

> But no one can enter a strong man's house and plunder his property without first tying up the strong man; then indeed the house can be plundered.

That this saying is faithfully reflecting something Jesus said is quite probable.[71] The comparison of a possessed person to a house is still common in the East,[72] and both Q and Mark have the saying.[73]

In the parable Satan is obviously understood to be the strong man, and the ideas of binding and loosing are quite natural and common in the ancient world in the context of dealing with demons.[74] Thus we have here a parable of an exorcism. In it Jesus is expressing the view that in his exorcisms Satan is being bound and the possessed person taken from him.

Long years of scholarly study of the New Testament may have dulled our senses to the significance of Jesus' understanding of his exorcisms. It is true that literature reflecting the thinking of the New Testament period shows that the demise of Satan, or the powers of evil, was expected in the messianic age.[75] However, when this literature is examined closely it emerges that all connections between a messianic individual, exorcism and the defeat of Satan are found in material that has been either edited or written by Christians.[76] We are bound to conclude that *it was Jesus himself who was the first to make the connection between exorcism and eschatology.* It was Jesus who made the connection between exorcism and the defeat of Satan, or the powers of evil.

Yet there is material in the Gospel traditions that assumes the continued existence of Satan until the end time, or last judgment.[77] Of all this material it is only the parable of the wheat and the tares that stands up to historical scrutiny to show that the historical Jesus associated the defeat of Satan and evil with the last judgment.[78] As small as the amount of material is, it is enough to show that, on the one hand, Jesus associated his exorcisms with the defeat of Satan yet, on the other hand, he sees the defeat of Satan as taking place in the last judgment.

The resolution of this tension is found in the literature read or written at the time. For example,[79] Isaiah 24:22 reads,

> They [the host of heaven][80] will be gathered together
>   like prisoners in a pit;
> they will be shut up in a prison,
>   and after many days they will be punished.

What is a simple picture of a two-stage defeat of these powers is clarified and developed in *1 Enoch* 10:4-6:

> The Lord said to Raphael, "Bind Azaz'el[81] hand and foot (and) throw him into the darkness!" And he made a hole in the desert which was in Duda'el[82] and cast him there; he threw on top of him rugged and sharp rocks. And he covered his face in order that he may not see light; and in order that he may be sent into the great fire on the day of judgment.[83]

Here the first stage of the defeat of Azaz'el is described as "binding," a preparation for the final and complete destruction of the leader of the evil minions.[84] This two-stage idea of the defeat of Satan and his angels fits well with what we see reflected of the views of Jesus. The key contribution of Jesus was that he understood his exorcisms as the first stage of that defeat. From this we can conclude that exorcism was of great importance, even of central importance, to Jesus. It is the essence of his conception of his ministry.

It is common to view the miracles—and exorcisms in particular—as "signs" or "signals" of the coming of the kingdom of God.[85] However, in light of the last two sayings discussed here it can be reiterated that Jesus did not see his exorcisms as signs in the sense that they pointed to something other than what they were. *The exorcisms are in themselves an expression of God's reign or kingdom.* The exorcisms do not prove that the end time of salvation has arrived;[86] they are the end-time salvation. Nevertheless, as the next passage shows, we are cautioned against thinking Jesus saw his exorcisms as of exclusive importance.

§10.13 Jesus' Answer to John the Baptist (Mt 11:2-6/Lk 7:18-23)

In this story, Matthew and Luke's source (Q) says that as a result of hearing about Jesus' activity John the Baptist through his disciples asked if Jesus was "the one who is to come, or are we to wait for another?" (Mt 11:3/Lk 7:19). Jesus' reply is reported as follows:

> Go and tell John what you hear and see: the blind receive their sight, the lame walk, the lepers are cleansed, the deaf hear, the dead are raised, and the poor have good news brought to them. And blessed is anyone who takes no offense at me.[87]

That we are here dealing with material that can be taken as faithfully reflecting the voice of Jesus would seem to be assured.[88]

1. It is very unlikely that the early church would have created a saying in which one of their major witnesses was seen, even as a foil, to doubt Jesus and his mission.

2. In that Jesus' reply is self-effacing, drawing attention to the state of affairs around him rather than to himself, avoiding all christological titles, rings true to the character of his ministry. Even though there is the christological title in John's question—"Are you the one who is to come *[ho erchomenos]?*"—it was not a set title for the Messiah in Judaism or in Q.[89]

3. Rather tellingly against this being a creation of the early church, there is no response from John the Baptist to what appears (from the final beatitude) to be a veiled threat to him.[90]

4. Also, the list of features of the new circumstances, while alluding to Old Testament prophecy,[91] is not derived by direct quotation or from listing the features of Jesus' ministry, for there is no mention of exorcism and the raising of the dead, and cleansing lepers is included.[92]

5. Finally the situation described is historically credible in that as soon as Jesus had begun to proclaim the kingdom of God, especially without its anticipated judgment expected by the Baptist, it would have been inevitable that John and his followers should question who Jesus was.[93]

If this material reflects the voice of Jesus, what does it tell us about his view of his miracles? To begin with, it is obvious that the mighty work he saw himself as performing—the blind receiving their sight, the lame walking, lepers being cleansed, the deaf hearing and the dead being raised—in some way reflected the hopes expressed in Isaiah of the new state of affairs God would bring about in the end time of salvation.

Through the allusion to Isaiah 61:1 ("the poor have good news brought to them") Jesus, it is likely, would be expressing two ideas. First, the miracles do not stand alone. They, together with the good news being brought to the poor, characterize the new state of affairs. Thus any portrait of Jesus that depicts him as primarily a teacher is not reflecting Jesus' understanding of himself in the Gospels. The Gospels report that he saw himself as God's key person bringing God's end-time reign primarily, though not exclusively, in the miracles he performed. Second, the miracles in turn involve God's anointed individual being at the center of these activities.

To go further we need to understand what "the one who is to come" (*ho erchomenos*) may have meant to Jesus.[94] In view of the variety of ways an eschatological "coming" is mentioned in the Old Testament,[95] it is most likely that Jesus would not have identified the word with any particular eschatological figure. This is confirmed by the enigmatic tone of the beatitude at the end of his reply—"And blessed is anyone who takes no offense at me" (Mt 11:6/Lk 7:23)—which makes no reference to a particular type of messianic figure.

Therefore all we can say with any degree of confidence from this passage is that Jesus understood that the miracles of his ministry were the fulfillment of the eschatological expectations of the Old Testament prophets and that this, in turn, showed that he was the key figure in what was happening. And we can see in the beatitude that Jesus expected his miracles to elicit a response to him.

This saying is also a point at which the relationship between Jesus' individual healings and the eschatological age can be seen clearly. One way of seeing that relationship is suggested by N. T. Wright. He says that the cures restore the healed individuals as members of the people of God. That is, these healings would have been seen as part of a total ministry of welcome that went with the inauguration of the kingdom.[96] It is true that many of the people Jesus healed came under one of the banned categories: the blind, deaf and mute, and lepers, for example. But the import of this saying of Jesus is not that people are being prepared for the new age or made eligible for entry. Rather, it is that as the eschaton has come, these individuals are experiencing it in their lives. Those healed have been caught in the wake of the coming of God's new powerful presence in Jesus.

§10.14 The "Woes" on Chorazin, Bethsaida and Capernaum (Mt 11:20-24/Lk 10:12-15)
The heart of this passage in Q probably read as follows:[97]

Woe to you, Chorazin! Woe to you, Bethsaida! For if the deeds of power done in you had been done in Tyre and Sidon, they would have repented long ago in sackcloth and ashes. But at the judgment it will be more tolerable for Tyre and Sidon than for you. And you Capernaum, will you be exalted to heaven? No, you will be brought down to Hades. (Mt 11:21-23/Lk 10:13-15)

Bultmann thought this piece to be a community formulation because it looks back on Jesus' activity as something already completed. But how this can be the case is not possible to determine from the text. Moreover, following Wellhausen, Bultmann says, "It would have been difficult for Jesus to imagine that Capernaum could be exalted to heaven by his activity."[98] But this assumes a particular understanding Jesus may have had of his miracles. Over against Bultmann we can give good reason for taking this tradition to be faithfully reflecting something Jesus said during his ministry.[99]

☐ The tradition of Jesus' miraculous activity in the area around the Sea of Galilee represented by these towns is firmly established in the Gospel traditions.

☐ The failure that is noted in the saying is that of a response to Jesus in his native Galilee.[100]

☐ The saying about Capernaum is consistent with the apocalyptic tone of other utterances of Jesus.

☐ The absence of the name *Chorazin* in the remaining Gospel traditions shows a lack of interest in this city in the life of the early church.[101]

☐ We have no other evidence of the early church conducting missions, including "power"-based missions in the towns mentioned here.[102]

☐ Concomitantly, a miracle-based mission is without real parallel in the Palestinian mission of the early church.

☐ As we have no evidence of an early church mission in the area, the failure here is to be related to Jesus' mission in Galilee, a portrayal not likely to have originated in the early church.[103]

In short, we can agree with Mussner that "if there is one pre-Easter logion, then it is the lament of Jesus over these three cities of his native Galilee! It belongs to the most authentic voice *(ipsissima vox)* of Jesus."[104] Having established that this material most likely comes from the words of the historical Jesus, we can see that Jesus believed his miracles were to lead people to repent (cf. 2 Kings 19:1; Is 58:5).[105]

The miracles are described as "powers" *(dunameis)*. As this word *powers* is not often used in the Gospels for Jesus' miracles[106]—never in the Fourth Gospel, where we might expect it—and because it probably stands for God in the Aramaic,[107] we see again that Jesus probably understood his miracles as the activity of God. Further, these "deeds of power" *(dunameis)* may have been understood to be or include so-called nature miracles, for in 1 Corinthians 12:9-10 Paul distinguishes between gifts of "healings" *(iamatōn)* and gifts of "powers" *(dunameōn)*.[108]

§10.15 "Tell that fox . . . !" (Lk 13:32)

At that very hour some Pharisees came and said to him, "Get away from here, for Herod wants to kill you." He said to them, "Go and tell that fox, 'Listen, I am casting out demons and performing cures today and tomorrow, and on the third day I finish my work.' "

The historical value of this saying in telling us about Jesus' views of his miracles is difficult to determine, not least because it is found in only one source and one of the key words, *cures (iaseis),* is a Lukan favorite.[109] Also, on the one hand, if the Pharisees are being unusually cast as allies of Jesus, we may have an indication of historical veracity.[110] Yet, on the other hand, if they are being portrayed as enemies of Jesus who are trying to get rid of him, the point is lost. However, as Luke seems to wish to portray Herod as wishing not so much to destroy Jesus but to see him (Lk 9:9; 23:8), this small story is at variance with Luke's usual portrayal of Herod and so could be reflecting words of Jesus. On balance, simply because of the difficulty in weighing what little evidence we have, I have to agree with members of the Jesus Seminar to leave this saying in the gray area of uncertainty and not rely on it for the authentic voice of Jesus.[111]

§10.16 A Sign from Heaven (Mt 12:38-39; 16:1-4; Mk 8:11-13/Lk 11:16, 29; Jn 6:30; cf. 2:12-22)

Scattered through the Gospels is material in which Jesus is asked for a sign, sometimes a sign from heaven. As the request for a sign is probably found in Mark, Q, John and perhaps Matthew's special source,[112] we have a saying that has a high degree of probability of being authentic. Also, though the word *sign* is common in John in relation to the miraculous, other than in this context the word is never used in the Synoptic Gospels in relation to the miraculous activities of Jesus. Taken with the good evidence for a Semitic source behind the Markan account, for example,[113] we have every confidence that Jesus was asked for a sign.

Further, that in all four Gospels the demand for a sign follows after a miracle suggests that the request rose out of a misunderstanding of the miracles Jesus had already performed, though in the Fourth Gospel the crowd does not actually witness any sign or miracle. Whether or not there was originally a reference to Jonah in Jesus' reply, as in the Synoptic Gospels, does not materially alter Jesus' refusal to give the requested sign.

However, as we saw in §3.23, the nature of the sign being requested of Jesus is probably not a miracle in the sense of a cure or an exorcism. Rather, according to the expectations of the time, his detractors were probably asking Jesus for some significant event in nature or catastrophic event in the sky that would unmistakably be from God and authenticate his claims.[114] In any case, Jesus' rejection of providing some "proof" of his identity by using his powers shows that, in contrast to some other religious leaders of the time, he did not want to use his powers to draw a following.[115]

Nevertheless we need to keep in mind that in Mark 2:1-12 Jesus comes very close to offering an "authenticating miracle" or proof. However, the miracle is not described as a sign and neither is Jesus' action described as an authenticating miracle to prove that he is a true prophet. Instead his actions demonstrate what he has already done, so that it is much more than a proof of his power—it is a sign that the sins of the man have been forgiven.[116]

§10.17 A Review

In reviewing these observations from various sayings relating to Jesus' understanding of his miracles, it is hard to avoid a particular conclusion: Jesus considered himself to be performing miracles. Further, this material gives the impression that Jesus considered performing miracles the main focus of his ministry and that exorcism was the epitome of his ministry. It is also hard to avoid the conclusion that, in light of his miracles, Jesus understood he was the anointed figure or Messiah from God involved in the eschatological happenings around him. But in view of the unpopularity of this course of inquiry, I have considerable hesitation in pursuing this theme.

Not only does the term *Messiah* not occur in the Old Testament—and only rarely in other Jewish material[117]—but the vast majority of Jews in the time of Jesus were not looking for a single Messiah, nor was there a *normative* concept of Messiah by which candidates were tested. Instead, there was a variety of ideas and expectations involving kings, priests and prophets.[118] Some of these messianic functions (e.g., eschatological high priest, all-powerful king, destroyer of the wicked[119]) neither Paul nor the four Gospel writers attribute to Jesus. Indeed, even if Jesus was conscious of being a messiah, or even the Messiah, he would probably not have announced it, for according to some texts only God was thought to know the time and identity of the Messiah.[120]

Nevertheless, to be true to the evidence we have been examining we cannot ignore the fact that, at least *because* of his miracles, *Jesus appears to have been conscious that he was God's key figure or Messiah* in a situation where he thought God's expected end-time reign was taking place in and through his activities.[121] And we can see especially in the answer to John the Baptist (Mt 11:2-6/Lk 7:18-23) and the "woes" (Mt 11:20-24/Lk 10:12-15) that, as Ben Meyer put it, "The whole of this activity [the mission of Jesus] was designed to elicit an act of faith-recognition."[122]

To the question of Jesus' view of the precise relationship between his mighty deeds and the coming of the kingdom of God, there have been a number of answers. The miracles have been seen as "signs" having little or no intrinsic significance save to point beyond themselves to the more important message of the kingdom of God.[123] Even though the Fourth Gospel understands the miracles to be signs, they are not intended to point to the less significant message of Jesus but to Jesus himself.[124]

Further, the sayings of Jesus we have been examining in this section, notably "if in God's Spirit I cast out the demons, then has come upon you the kingdom of God" (Mt 12:28/Lk 11:20, author's translation), suggest a different relationship between miracle and message. It is not that Jesus understood his miracles to be evidence of the dawning or nearness of the kingdom of God.[125] Nor can we agree with Marcus Borg that the coming of the kingdom of God refers to the power of the other realm active through Jesus the holy man, instead of the eschatological coming of the reign of God.[126] Rather, from our study *the miracles are themselves the eschatological kingdom of God in operation or made manifest.*[127]

This poses an important question: How are we to account for Jesus' self-consciousness in light of the great variety of messianic expectations and that miracles were not generally expected of the messiahs?[128] The answer is probably to be found in the coincidence of two factors. One factor is that Jesus is, as we have seen, presented as conscious of being empowered by God's Spirit (cf., e.g., Mt 12:28/Lk 11:20). The sense of this empowerment probably began with his baptism by John when he experienced the Spirit of God descend on him (Mk 1:9-11),[129] for it appears that at least on one occasion Jesus may have appealed to this experience as the source of his authority (cf. Mk 11:27-33).[130]

The other factor contributing to Jesus' self-consciousness is that he is portrayed as being aware that his miraculous activities have echoes in some of the Isaianic expectations of the messianic age.[131] Jesus took the initiative to include exorcism both as one of the expressions of the presence of the empowerment of God's Spirit and as part of the fulfillment of the messianic age. He may have done this by bringing together the idea of David being anointed by God's Spirit (Ps 110:1/Mk 12:36) and the view then current that Solomon (David's son) was a powerful exorcist.[132]

So despite the general hesitation of contemporary scholarship, in light of the evidence discussed here, we are bound to conclude that *in conducting his miracles,* both exorcisms and cures, *Jesus was aware that he was God's anointed individual at the center of these eschatological events.* For example, in view of the connection Jesus made between his exorcisms and the coming of the reign of God and his echoing of Isaiah 61:1 in his statements about what was taking place around him, *he must have been aware that he was the expected Messiah.*

It is with this point that we probably have the major reason Jesus chose to perform miracles at all: they were an inescapable yet ambiguous signal of his messianic significance. To this it must be added that the exorcisms exemplified Jesus' notion that his ministry was a battle with, and the first stage of the defeat of, Satan. Further, some of the miracles were able to highlight God's involvement in Jesus' activity, and others showed Jesus expressing compassion in the miracles.

The first part of this chapter, which sets out that Jesus' performing miracles (§10.2) and what he thought about them (§§10.3-16) really does matter, prohibits us from ignoring the results of this part of the study. I have already said something about this and will say more in the final part of this book. Before coming to that, keeping in mind the contemporary significance of the study of the miracles of Jesus, the next part will examine which stories or parts of stories can be traced back to the reports of those who witnessed the ministry of the historical Jesus.

PART 4

The Miracles of Jesus & History

Eleven

Jesus & Exorcism

··

§11.1 Introduction

Of the four objectives we set for the purpose of this book (see §1.2) two have been met. We have been able to set out (1) how the Gospel writers understood the miracles, and (2) how Jesus probably understood his miracles. Two objectives remain to be fulfilled: (3) determining to what extent the miracle stories of Jesus in the Gospels reflect "what actually happened" and (4) identifying this study's implications for the quest for the historical Jesus.

In this and the following five chapters I want to take the next step toward fulfilling the third objective. That is, having established that those who witnessed the ministry of Jesus thought he conducted miracles and that we have as part of our interpretative background Jesus' understanding of his miracles, we can now examine the miracle stories in more detail to see which elements of the Gospel traditions have a rightful place in the authentic material about Jesus.

Although no Gospel writer puts the "nature miracles" in a separate category,[1] Jesus' exorcisms[2] are often listed separately.[3] Therefore it is appropriate to treat these miracle stories separately. Apart from this category we shall follow the broadest categorization in our treatment: first, according to the kinds of human need treated (the crippled and paralytics, the blind, the dead and lepers, in chapters twelve through fifteen) and then the largest number of miracle stories that do not fit any particular prima facie categories (chapter sixteen).[4]

§11.2 Did Jesus Perform Exorcisms?

The historicity of the exorcism stories concerns us first simply because they take up such a large part of the miracle stories in the Gospels. For example, of the thirteen healing stories of Jesus in Mark, four of them are stories of exorcism.[5] Also important in my decision to treat this aspect of the portrayal of Jesus first is that Mark, the earliest Gospel writer, draws particular attention to this kind of miracle (e.g., Mk 1:39; 3:7-12). Further, even though (apart from Mt 12:22/Lk 11:14) Matthew and Luke provide no extra detailed stories of exorcism, they agree that exorcism was an important aspect of Jesus' ministry and go so far as to suggest that Jesus' dealings with the demon possessed is of central significance in understanding Jesus and his ministry. At least that is the case in Matthew 12:28/Luke 11:20 (see §10.11).

We commence with the obvious question of the general historicity of the exorcism stories. For an answer we will begin with evidence that is outside the New Testament.

1. Much of the evidence relating to Jesus and exorcism that we have from outside the New Testament is not entirely independent of Christian influences, even if only at the level of Christian transmission, as in the case of Josephus. Nevertheless we noted in §9.7.1d that incidentally embedded in some of this material is the idea that the names of those who were considered powerful healers were used by later healers. Some of those healers—including Jesus—were exorcists,[6] implying that Jesus was considered to be a powerful exorcist. The mention in the Babylonian Talmud that Jesus was killed because he practiced sorcery and Celsus saying that Jesus had certain magical powers (see §9.7) may betray a tradition that Jesus was thought to be an exorcist. So whereas the evidence is not extensive, it is conclusive that Jesus was remembered as a powerful exorcist.

2. Turning to the New Testament we find conflicting evidence. Whereas the Synoptic Gospels give a high priority to exorcism stories, the Fourth Gospel has nothing at all to say about exorcism or Jesus being an exorcist. We will look first at the evidence in the Synoptic Gospels.

(a) Stories of exorcism are attested independently in two Gospel traditions. Four stories are found in Mark,[7] making exorcism the most common category of healing in the oldest Gospel. Q, probably written between about A.D. 50 and 70, provides another brief exorcism story of a mute demoniac.[8]

(b) The Synoptics contain a number of authentic sayings of Jesus or his opponents that presume his ministry of exorcism (see §§10.10-12): (i) the charge that Jesus cast out demons by Beelzebul, the Prince of demons;[9] (ii) the saying that Jesus exorcised by the Spirit (Luke has "finger") of God (Mt 12:28/Lk 11:20); (iii) the parable of the strong man;[10] and with less certainty (see §10.15) we can add (iv) Jesus' warning to Herod, which mentions exorcisms: "Go tell that fox for me, 'Listen, I am casting out demons and performing cures'" (Lk 13:32).

Further, (v) there is a saying not of Jesus but of the disciple John: "Teacher, we saw someone casting out demons in your name, and we tried to stop him, because he was not following us" (Mk 9:38-39/Lk 9:49-50). Some have seen this comment about the so-called strange exorcist as arising in the early church,[11] principally on the grounds that the phrase "in your name" would not have been used in the pre-Easter Palestinian situation.

However, independently of the New Testament we know that the name of someone, usually a god, was thought to be efficacious in healing,[12] and the phrase has long been discovered independent of its Christian use.[13] The other phrase here that could indicate a post-Easter origin of this saying is "he was not following us." But there is overwhelming evidence that "to follow" was used in relation to the historical Jesus in the sense of "being one of the disciples" rather than of being part of the post-Easter community.[14]

Also Jesus' response to John: "Do not stop him; for no one who does a deed of power in my name will be able soon afterward to speak evil of me" (Mk 9:39)—which is inseparable from the previous verse—we note most probably goes back to the historical Jesus because of the Semitic manner of the expression.[15] Further, Luke has altered the next verse from "us" to "you" (Mk 9:40/Lk 9:50) in his attempt to apply this pericope to his *post*-Easter situation. All this is evidence not only that there was an exorcist who was a contemporary of Jesus but, indirectly, that Jesus himself was an exorcist.

The significance of this sayings material on exorcism stands out when we note that exorcism features surprisingly little in the reports of the ministry of the early church,[16] and it is not mentioned in any of the post-Easter commissionings by Jesus.[17] This means that it is difficult to argue that the early Christians were projecting their ministry back onto the historical Jesus. Instead, it is more likely that exorcism was part of the ministry of the historical Jesus.

3. Yet this evidence conflicts with the silence of the Fourth Gospel. As we have already noted, along with the Johannine epistles and Apocalypse, the Fourth Gospel says nothing about exorcism or Jesus performing exorcisms. In light of the evidence that a number of theological considerations have coalesced to bring about the Fourth Gospel's exclusion of exorcism from Jesus' ministry, we can conclude unhesitatingly that the historical Jesus was an exorcist.[18] Further, as his name was quickly taken up into the repertoire of other exorcists, we can also conclude that he was considered to have been a particularly powerful or successful exorcist.

I now dig a little deeper into the Synoptic traditions to see what can be recovered about Jesus as an exorcist. For even having argued that Jesus was rightly remembered as an exorcist, the question remains open whether the stories of exorcism found in the Gospels faithfully reflect events in the life of Jesus.

In the case of the exorcism stories, a great deal of material exists outside the Gospels with which to gain a more historically objective perspective than with any other category of miracle story. Therefore we will generally be able to discuss these stories in more detail than other miracle stories.

§11.3 A Demoniac in the Synagogue at Capernaum (Mk 1:21-28/Lk 4:31-37)

The setting given as Capernaum (Mk 1:21) could well be taken as part of the original report, for even John's Jerusalem-centered Gospel agrees with Mark that Jesus was active in teaching and working miracles in Capernaum (Jn 6:59). Q also has Capernaum as the focus of Jesus' Galilean ministry (Mt 11:23/Lk 10:15).

The presence of a demoniac in a synagogue has been doubted as historically unlikely.[19] But the chaotic and unpredictable character of demon possession could mean that, at times, the man showed no adverse symptoms of his condition.[20] Indeed, perhaps it was not until confronted by Jesus that it was evident the man was a demoniac. In any case, if the man was known to be demon possessed and subsequently associated with Jesus, we could have expected that Jesus may have been charged with encouraging an unclean person to be in the synagogue. The fact that Jesus was not so charged with this or with the work of practicing medicine on the Sabbath could be because the demoniac's advance on Jesus may have been seen as an attack (cf. Acts 19:16), against which Jesus would have been allowed to defend himself.[21]

There are a number of reasons for thinking that the man's crying out (Mk 1:23) is a piece of historical reminiscence in the story. Matthew, who as we concluded at the end of §4.35 is decidedly reticent about the exorcism stories and prunes the Markan stories, does not obliterate the consternation of the demoniacs. He recognizes it as an essential element in an exorcism story. Also, Mark shows no consistent use of this element of his stories. The variety of expressions[22] shows he had no desire at least to draw attention to this aspect of the story or to portray the demons as worshiping Jesus. Therefore it is not likely that the early church introduced the consternation of the demoniacs into the stories. It was already there.

The distress of the demon is verbalized as "What have you to do with us, Jesus of Nazareth? Have you come to destroy us? I know who you are, the Holy One of God" (Mk 1:24). The first part of this corresponds to the Semitic "Why are you bothering us?"[23] That is, it is to be understood as the demon's defense mechanism against Jesus as an exorcist in the way the phrase is used in 1 Kings 17:18 of the widow warding off Elijah.[24] That Mark does not use this mechanism consistently (cf. Mk 5:7) or conform it to 1 Kings 17:18 (the passage that best explains its meaning) and its not having a Semitic background speak in favor of its early origin.

That Jesus' name is involved in the expression of consternation is natural and to be expected, for the "name" was part of the prescription used in preternatural control.[25] The inclusion of "Nazareth" is also natural, for all Gospel writers use it to define the town of Jesus' origin,[26] and it is not a term used by any later Christian writer. When the term is used, it is restricted to the Palestinian church.[27] And if Matthew can be taken as representative of a tradition that has passed through early Palestinian Christianity, we have little evidence that the church showed particular interest in the title.[28] If Mark or the early church wanted to introduce a title for Jesus here, we would expect the more pregnant theological phrase "Son of God" (cf. Mk 3:11). Thus it seems reasonable to conclude that we are dealing with data that go back to the earliest memories of Jesus.

In that the question "Have you come to destroy *[apolesai]* us?" (Mk 1:24) is a description of Jesus and his mission, it could be seen to serve well the dogmatic purposes of the early church and be its creation. However, *apollumi* is not used in the New Testament in relation to the ministry of Jesus, and—apart from what can be judged to be part of the authentic Jesus material—there is no strand of tradition in the New Testament that thought the exorcisms were the final defeat of evil. Further, in antiquity the mention of spiritual entities or enemies could involve a description of them as well.[29] We are then dealing with a statement that has a high possibility of being in the original report of the exorcism.

The phrase "I know who you are, the Holy One of God" is in the same category (Mk 1:24). The "I know . . ." formula—a Hebrew idiom[30]—is well attested in incantations designed to gain control over spiritual beings,[31] and the phrase "the Holy One of God" has no recognizable tradition at all as a messianic title.[32]

Jesus' words to the demon include "Be silent, and come out of him!" (*phimōthēti kai exelthe ex autou,* Mk 1:25). With 1:34 (about Jesus not permitting the demons to speak) we may conclude that Mark understood this to be an injunction to silence. However, if the tradition wished to include the more general conception of ceasing to speak, it is surprising that it did not use *siōpa* ("be quiet"; cf. Mk 10:48) rather than *phimōthēti,* which is so strongly related to incantational restriction as opposed to talking. In any case, the crying out in the next verse would be a glaring oversight if this was an injunction to silence. More important, *phimētheti* is well known in the magical papyri to have the connotation of binding or restricting.[33] Therefore these words of Jesus are most likely part of the primary tradition of this story.

Jesus also says, "Come out of him" (Mk 1:25b). In view of there being so many expressions in the ancient literature that are parallel to this[34] and there being no discernible reason why this command should have been added to the tradition of the early church, I conclude that it also belongs to the bedrock of historical data in this story.

The violence of the demon's departure (Mk 1:26) is found in all other exorcism stories in Mark, but he shows no particular consistency of interest in its function.

In light of Matthew and Luke's hesitancy about the motif we can take it that, in all probability, it goes back to the earliest report of an exorcism.

On witnessing the healing, the crowd is said to be "astounded" or "amazed" (Mk 1:27). Only Mark uses this word *thambeomai*,[35] but in neither of the other cases does Mark seem to be responsible for the idea.[36] If we add to this observation the probability that even the mere presence of Jesus had such an impact on his hearers that they were said to be amazed or afraid,[37] far from dispensing with this motif as a stereotypical closing motif in the miracle stories taken over from Greek story telling,[38] we must conclude that here is a faithful reflection of part of an event that took place in the life of Jesus.

The Fellows of the Jesus Seminar "doubt that this episode represents a particular historical occasion."[39] However, from this discussion it is reasonable to conclude that insofar as this story reports a demoniac aggressively confronting Jesus in the Capernaum synagogue on a sabbath, after which followed a verbal exchange and a dramatic and violent exorcism that amazed the observers, it is a faithful reflection of an event in the life of the historical Jesus.

§11.4 The Gerasene Demoniac (Mk 5:1-20/Mt 8:28-34/Lk 8:26-39)

Explaining the setting of this story has been a recurring source of difficulty that impinges on the question of historicity. The manuscripts have a number of place names for the region: Gadarenes, Gerasenes, Gergesenes, Gergesines and Gergystenes, of which Gerasenes is probably to be preferred as the most likely reading in Mark.[40] The difficulty with this solution is that, as Meier comments, not even possessed pigs are likely to be able to jump into the Sea of Galilee from Gerasa, a distance of 33 miles (about 53 kilometers).[41] The problem of the location is as old as Matthew, who changed Mark's location from that of the Gerasenes to Gadara.

There is no solution to be found in noting that Mark gives the setting as the region of Gerasa, for Mark says the herdsmen ran to the city and the inhabitants returned, apparently on the same day, to find the man healed (Mk 5:14-15). The solution to the difficulty is either that the pigs episode was not originally part of this story (a solution we will reject) or more likely Mark probably did not know the area. Therefore the name Gerasene could have come about through the exchange of a similar sounding, little-known location for the one we have in the text.[42]

The most interesting aspect of this story is the episode of the pigs rushing to their death, which is generally agreed to be a secondary pagan feature added to an earlier Jesus story.[43] This seems to be thought to save Jesus from the indignity of being involved in the incredible and cruel story of the destruction of the pigs and hence the livelihood of the pig farmers. However, considerable doubt is to be cast on the two-story hypothesis that excludes the episode of the pigs from authentic Jesus material.

The pigs episode is not so much a proof of cure, as is found in, for example, the Hellenistic milieu of Apollonius of Tyana (Philostratus *Life* 4:20). Instead, as part of the cure, it was sometimes thought appropriate to transfer demons from a sufferer to an object, such as a pebble or piece of wood or a pot or some water. The newly "possessed" objects were then thrown away or destroyed to actualize or signify the demons' departure from the situation.[44]

In this particular story, the pigs, on being possessed, behave uncharacteristically in that they rush to the sea as a herd and in that they drown, for pigs do not normally herd and are able to swim. This then would have been seen as part of the miracle, for as J. Duncan M. Derrett says, "If such a thing happened any onlooker would say they were bewitched. Any professional pigkeeper would seize an opportunity to attribute this highly untypical behaviour to the supernatural."[45] As Jeff Mountford suggested to me in conversation, it could have been understood that the destructive nature or character of the demonic being(s) involved was simply transferred to the pigs, causing their drowning.

The historicity of this report depends to a large extent on accepting the reality of preternatural beings and their ability to cause such behavior. In another place I have argued for just such a case, which, if allowed to stand, makes a strong case for accepting the historicity of the episode of the pigs in this story.[46]

Also, it is worth noting that none of the Synoptic writers thought the episode of the pigs was out of character with the Jesus they were relating or they would have excluded it. Indeed, its distinctiveness can be seen as pointing to its strong claims to historicity. It is a feature reflected in other ancient exorcisms, yet it is not an aspect of Jesus' healings in which the early church showed particular interest.

Further, the proposition that this story as it stands does not fit the form of an exorcism story must be rejected.[47] The use of form criticism to determine which stories do and do not belong to a particular tradition is a highly questionable methodology.[48] Few stories, if any, show a pure form.

It is true that the episode of the destruction of the pigs is out of character with the other exorcism stories in the Gospels, for no other story has such a dramatic ending, nor is Jesus elsewhere reported as destroying people's livelihood.[49] However, we may have only a few of the exorcism stories that were once related to Jesus. Indeed, the importance Jesus gave to exorcism and the impression conveyed by the Synoptic Gospels indicate this.

Also, from different perspectives each of the four major exorcism stories can be seen to have its unique uncharacteristic feature, as we may expect with so few stories. Turning to other parts of the story, a number of features need to be discussed as possible indicators of authenticity.

First, that the Latin loan word *legiōn* ("legion," Mk 5:9, 15) appears here has also been seen as support for the secondary origin of the story.[50] However, it appears in Greek writings from the first century B.C., and there are many examples of it in Greek papyri.[51] Thus the use of the word cannot be employed to establish the origin of part of the story.

Second is the use of the phrase "Son of the Most High God," which is put in the mouth of the demoniac in the interaction with Jesus (Mk 5:7). The Qumran scrolls show that this title was used in Palestine of figures other than the Messiah or anointed one (4Q246). Though I can find no exact parallel to the phrase in the context of a demon's defense, "Most High God" is found in the magical-incanta-tional literature, and the appellation is not out of place here.[52] In the New Testament "Most High God" is attested in two different traditions as part of a demon's defense against Christian exorcists (here and in Acts 16:17). This, along with the fact that "Most High" is on the margins of New Testament traditions, points to the improbability that Mark or the early church needed to introduce it here in the demon's defense.

A third element that suggests this story goes back to the historical Jesus is the use of the word *horkizō* ("I adjure" or "bind"). It is entirely appropriate here[53] in that the demon is attempting to put a spell on Jesus to prevent him from performing the exorcism. Matthew 8:29 omits and Luke 8:28 softens the idea, suggesting they objected to the idea of a demon attempting to put a spell on Jesus. This gives credence to the originality of this feature of the story.

Fourth, the feature of Jesus' requesting the name of the demon points to the historical reliability of this story (Mk 5:9). It is a feature well attested in ancient literature,[54] yet it also shows Jesus' knowledge to be limited, not something a Christian story teller or copyist is likely to volunteer to a story.

Fifth, the difficulty of understanding the position and function of verse 8 ("For he had said to him, 'Come out of the man, you unclean spirit!'") turns out to be a factor in favor of the historicity of this aspect of the story. Without evidence—other than the assumption that two stories have been combined—it has been suggested that this verse is either out of place or an unnecessary afterthought.[55]

If the text is allowed to remain as it stands, however, the demoniac is reported as defending himself in verse 7 ("What have you to do with me?") over against Jesus' order, reported in verse 8 ("Come out"). Having failed in the first attempt for supremacy, Jesus then asks for the demon's name in verse 9 to gain the necessary power[56] to carry out the exorcism. This is not the only reported example of Jesus not always being initially and immediately successful in healing. We will see this same feature in the story of the blind man of Bethesda (Mk 8:22-26; see §13.2). Again, this kind of reflection on Jesus is highly unlikely to have been added to the story by the early church. In view of all these factors we can have a high level of confidence in this story's reflection of an actual event in the life of the historical Jesus.[57]

§11.5 The Syrophoenician Woman's Daughter (Mk 7:24-30/Mt 15:21-28)

Although not a consensus, this is a story that is often held to have been transferred to the pre-Easter Jesus tradition from one that had its origin in the time when the early church was struggling with extending the mission beyond the Jews.

As evidence for this, for example, the saying in Mark 7:27—that the children (Jews) should be fed first and then the dogs (Gentiles)—is perceived to be dependent on the theology of Paul and on the practice of missionaries in Acts.[58] But this is problematic. There is no reason that the practice of the missionaries in Acts could not be dependent on the memory of some teaching of Jesus such as we have here in Mark.

Also, Paul's saying that the Gospel was "to the Jew first and also to the Greek" (Rom 1:16) cannot be taken as encapsulating all of Paul's missionary strategy. Paul saw himself first and foremost as the apostle to the Gentiles, even though the synagogue provided a platform for his message to those Gentiles (Rom 11:13; 15:16).[59] In any case, it is again just as reasonable to suppose that Paul's theology or missionary practice is dependent on a tradition that is now reflected in such sayings as found in Mark 7:27 as to suppose that Mark or his predecessors have justified later traditions by projecting them back into the Jesus material.

Also, that the springboard for this story is Elijah's visit to the widow of Zarephath in the region of Sidon (1 Kings 17:8-24) is difficult to accept, for the points of contact between the two stories are limited.[60] Instead, a number of features of Mark's story point to the strong probability of a historical event behind the report.

First, that Jesus is said to be in Gentile territory is uncharacteristic of his ministry and therefore likely to be historically reliable, especially since Jesus is said to be in the *region* of Tyre rather than in the city, where at the time of the shaping of the Gospel material there was already a Christian community (cf. Acts 21:3-6).[61] If this story was created after Easter, it would have been natural to situate it in the city rather than in the countryside. Also, if Mark or any of his predecessors wanted to create a story to relate to Gentile readers, it is unlikely they would have chosen one about a woman in a society where women were not highly regarded.

Second, it is unimaginable that Mark, writing for Gentile readers, would have created the Jewish expression that the Gentiles were like dogs (Mk 7:27).[62] Further, this saying would not have been introduced into the story, for it cannot be understood apart from being in a story like the one in which it is now found.

Third, the offensive saying is ambiguous. Either it could be used to justify the later admission of Gentiles or to express disapproval of the extension of Christian privileges to the Gentiles. I wonder then whether a story whose import is so ambiguous would have been created for the express purpose of granting instruction on the Gentile problem. "Surely," as Davies and Allison put it, "an author unconcerned to record a pre-Easter episode would have done a better job of making his intentions clearly known."[63]

Fourth is the issue of the historicity of a healing from a distance. On the one hand, there is nothing in the story that necessitates a healing from a distance. On the other hand, such types of healing were known in both Jewish and Greek milieus, yet none of them appear to have any literary relationship with the one in Mark.[64] Therefore, to conclude, despite the hesitations of some,[65] this story has sufficient hallmarks of historicity to conclude that it most probably goes back to the reminiscences of Jesus' audience.[66]

§11.6 The Epileptic Boy (Mk 9:14-29/Mt 17:14-20/Lk 9:37-43)

Though it is sometimes suggested that this story is an amalgam of two earlier ones,[67] the evidence neither demands nor needs a two-story hypothesis. Having said this does not mean we should come under Meier's criticism of being so naive as to think we have a videotape of some event.[68]

It has been argued that this story has its origin in the Hellenistic mission of the early church.[69] However, once again features in Mark's story, in some cases, are so critical to it and arguably authentic that we can be confident the story as a whole faithfully reflects an incident in the life of Jesus.

First, the three descriptions of the illness fit the common form of an exorcism story in that the first one ("He has a spirit," Mk 9:17-18) sets out the need for healing, the second (about the boy falling on the ground, 9:20) is part of the consternation of the demoniac and dramatic confrontation with Jesus, and the third (the father saying the boy had been like that since childhood, 9:21-22) forms part of the technique of the exorcist obtaining the history of the condition. This may be seen as a case for the early church creating the story. However, the vocabulary of the descriptions does not betray any particular early church interests, and they do not conform to the pattern of descriptions elsewhere in Mark.[70]

Second to consider is the historicity of the rebuke in Mark 9:19: "You faithless generation." In the plural here it naturally applies to the disciples, the crowd not being the focus of attention. In view of Mark's portrayal of the disciples as failing in their understanding of Jesus, his portraying the father as crying out, the father's desperate cry, "I believe; help my unbelief!" (9:24) and other references to faith by those seeking healing,[71] it is likely that the rebuke was originally directed to the father. Along with this, the father's cry does not show Jesus in a kindly light in that he causes the father some grief. This indicates that the rebuke is probably to be associated with the original story.

Third, the details of Jesus' exorcistic technique in Mark 9:25 of commanding the demon to come out and never enter the lad again are readily paralleled in ancient literature.[72] Yet Mark and his tradition show no desire to be consistent in their representation of Jesus' exorcistic words so that they would conform to a literary pattern. And in view of the hesitancy of Matthew and Luke over this genre of Jesus' words (cf. Mt 17:18/Lk 9:42), we may be fairly confident that verse 25 is a genuine reflection of the words of Jesus.

Fourth to consider is the violent departure of the demon in convulsing the boy, leaving him like a corpse (Mk 9:26-27). Such reports were common in the ancient world[73] and are also found in other stories of Jesus (1:26; 5:13). It could be then that this element of the tradition was provided to accommodate the story to a widespread exorcistic technique. However, the element of violence not being consistently present suggests that the early Christians represented in this story were probably not motivated by this impulse. This, along with Matthew 17:18 and Luke 4:35 being reticent about this element in the story, means that it probably goes back to the original story associated with the historical Jesus.

Fifth, the story finishes with the disciples asking why they could not cast out the demon and being told "This kind can come out only through prayer" (Mk 9:28-29). Considering only the vocabulary would probably lead to the conclusion that Mark gave this ending to the story.[74] Yet the reference to prayer as a form of exorcism may not be Markan, for he does not show prayer to be an element in Jesus' or anyone else's technique. Notably the reported technique of the disciples is anointing with oil (6:13). On balance, it is probably right to conclude that the inconsistency between the motif of faith embedded in the story (9:19, 23, 24) and that of prayer in the final sentence means that Mark provided this conclusion.[75]

The features discussed and discovered to be historically reliable are in fact central to the integrity of the story. Thus, in that the descriptions of the illness, the rebuke, Jesus' technique and the violent departure of the demon are reliable recollections, it is most likely that this story as a whole carries a historical reminiscence of a healing of an epileptic boy that goes back to the Jesus of history.[76]

To these features can be added a further consideration that lends weight to the probability that here is a report on an event that took place in the life of the historical Jesus. That is, the application of the story in the early church, which is given in verses 28 and 29 about this kind of demon being able to be cast out only by prayer, is distinct from the story itself and not reflected in it. If the story had its origin in the life of the early church, we could expect that it would have reflected this conclusion, with, for example, Jesus being shown to pray as part of his technique.[77] In turn and in light of the earlier discussion of the rest of the story, we could not take up the option of a postresurrection story given the current conclusion in verses 28 and 29.

We have completed our examination of the four major exorcism stories.

Contrary to the conclusions of many critics, we have found that there is a reasonable case to be made for each of them to be taken to reflect an event in the life of the historical Jesus similar to the stories we now have.

§11.7 The Next Step

If the exorcism stories predominate the Gospel tradition, the healing of the crippled and paralytics is the next most numerous category of healing. To these we now turn to see what stories or elements of them can be argued to have their origin in the eyewitness accounts of the ministry of the historical Jesus.

T w e l v e

The Crippled & Paralytics

•••

§12.1 Introduction

In this chapter we gather together two kinds of healings in five reports of Jesus' healing ministry: a paralytic, a man with a withered hand, a paralyzed boy, a woman bent over who could not straighten herself and a paralyzed man sitting beside the pool of Bethesda. From a prima facie consideration it is difficult to determine whether we should be predisposed toward the historicity of these stories. A messianic hope was that such people would one day be healed (Is 35:6). So we might conclude that these healings have been added to the traditions by the early church, especially in view of there being a notable absence of reports of Jewish miracle workers curing lameness or paralysis.[1]

Further, in that many pagan shrines testified to the occurrence of these kinds of healing,[2] we may suspect that the early Christians would have been keen to portray Jesus as successful in this area. Yet with so many lame and paralyzed people in the ancient world,[3] it would be surprising if a person who thought of himself as a miracle worker did not perform healings for these people. Also, with Mark, Luke and John each independently attesting these kinds of healings, our predisposition is tipped toward their historicity. On balance then the question of historicity will have to be decided in relation to each story in turn.

§12.2 A Paralytic Forgiven and Healed (Mk 2:1-12/Mt 9:1-8/Lk 5:17-26)

There has been much discussion about the unity of this miracle story, for to some it appears to have been infiltrated by a dialogue involving controversy, casting doubt on the historicity of the miracle.[4] However, once again the use of a supposedly typical form of story to determine the integrity of another story is to be questioned. This assumes either that events could happen or be reported only in a certain way or that in conveying their stories first-century Gospel writers were unable to stray outside the confines of an arbitrary form proposed by twentieth-century scholars.

In any case, the common suggestion is that from the point in Mark when Jesus is said to see their faith (Mk 2:5a) until he says "Stand up" (2:9b), a section has been added (2:5b-9a) wherein Jesus is in opposition to the scribes. This supposed addition involved appending to the miracle story verses 10-11 about the Son of Man's authority to forgive sin. The point at issue turns on whether the words "Son, your sins are forgiven" (2:5b), which give the ensuing controversy sense, were part of the original story. If they were, there may be difficulty in removing the discussion with the scribes on the grounds of continuity of content.[5] Therefore in turn we have to inquire about the probability of Jesus saying to a sick person, "Son, your sins are forgiven."

In whatever way the words are understood, there is initial difficulty in attributing the words to Jesus. On the one hand, if the words were meant to be ones of encouragement that God forgives the man's sins,[6] it is unique. Instead, we would expect something like "Take heart" (as in Mt 9:2), but that would not explain the ensuing controversy with the scribes over Jesus' blasphemy in doing what only God can do (Mk 2:6).[7] On the other hand, if the words are to be understood as Jesus forgiving sin, that is unique in Mark and found elsewhere only in Luke 7:48.[8]

However, as Jeremias pointed out, such statistics mean nothing. In the pictures Jesus used in his teaching the subject of forgiveness is often present, as it is in his actions of eating with sinners.[9] That Jesus should be described as offering forgiveness to a man who is presented as sick and needing healing is not surprising in a world where sin and sickness were closely associated.[10] Therefore it can be expected that Jesus may have said something like, "Son, your sins are forgiven." Further, in light of Mark in particular not seeking to labor the point in his Gospel, it seems probable these words were part of the original story.[11] In turn, it is likely that the discussion about Jesus' authority to forgive sins was also part of that miracle story.[12]

What can be said about the historicity of the story as a whole? The approach to Jesus via the roof is perfectly possible in light of the nature of Palestinian houses. A slightly sloped roof of beams covered with reeds, matted layers of thorns and several inches of mud[13] would, as Mark says (Mk 2:4), need to be dug out for the man to be lowered down through the roof.[14] With Meier we can say that because of its strange circumstances it is likely that some event in the public ministry of Jesus stuck in the corporate memory to give rise to the story we now have.[15]

§12.3 A Withered Hand Cured (Mk 3:1-6/Mt 12:9-14/Lk 6:6-11)

The setting of this conflict with Jesus' opponents when he heals a man's withered hand is in a synagogue on the sabbath. Since Jesus' conflicts with his contemporaries over sabbath regulations are generally put beyond historical doubt, I am predisposed to accept the historicity of this story.

However, Geza Vermes casts doubt on the veracity of the story because Jesus only speaks to effect the healing; he does no "work" to infringe the sabbath.[16] But, the import of the rabbinic regulations is not that physical work is done but that someone comes to the aid of a person or practices medicine on one who is not in imminent mortal danger.[17]

That the story ends with the Pharisees conspiring with the Herodians to kill Jesus[18] does not impinge on the historicity of the story itself. Even if the conclusion to the story about conspiring to destroy *(apolesōsin)* Jesus was part of the original, *apollumi* can mean not only "to kill" but more naturally "to ruin or destroy."[19] And if Mark or his predecessors had meant to convey "to kill" we would have expected him to use the word *apokteinō*, which he has used earlier in this story (Mk 3:4) and does so later in reference to Jesus being killed.[20] In short, we cannot exclude the episode regarding the Pharisees and the Herodians on the grounds that Jesus' actions do not constitute reason to kill him, for Mark and his predecessors probably understood the healing to cause his opponents to seek to bring him down. That is readily understandable.

The story contains a number of Semitisms,[21] and the core of the story—Jesus' question to his opponents, "Is it lawful to do good or to do harm on the sabbath, to save life or to kill?" (Mk 3:4)—probably has at least a Palestinian origin in that it is composed of two antithetical parallelisms.[22] In turn, the saying is unlikely to have been transmitted without the miracle story. On its own, without the explanation provided by the context of the story, the saying would be essentially the same governing principle found in Judaism and therefore not likely to have been thought worth maintaining. Within the context of the miracle story the saying that healing brought life has the eschatological ring characteristic of Jesus' ministry.[23] So, with no evidence that healing on the sabbath was an issue for the early church, there is good reason to see this story as having its origin in the memories of Jesus' audience.[24]

§12.4 The Official's Servant/Son Healed (Mt 8:5-13/Lk 7:1-10; cf. Jn 4:46-54)

From the time of Irenaeus *(Adv. Haer.* 2:22:3) an important issue has been the relationship between the story in John 4:46-54 and that in Q, represented with minor variations in Matthew 8:5-13 and Luke 7:1-10. Are there two different events or only one behind these stories?

The major difference between the stories is that Luke has the centurion send a delegation to Jesus, whereas Matthew and John have the centurion meet Jesus. Luke has probably added this feature, for it bears the hallmarks of his hand, and in Luke the earthly Jesus never meets a Gentile. The specification in Matthew of the illness being paralysis is not evidence of a separate source but an example of Matthew's tendency to specify illnesses.[25] However, in light of the similarities seeming to be greater than the differences between the stories and most of the differences being open to logical explanations, it is reasonable to conclude that the same event lies behind all the accounts.

In that John sometimes has similarities to Matthew and at other times similarities to Luke, it can further be concluded that the Fourth Gospel and the Synoptics have given us independent traditions of the same parent event.[26] The import of all this is that we have a witness independent of the Synoptic traditions for this story and that behind Q and John is a single story.

Bultmann noted a number of features of this story: a Gentile makes a claim on Jesus; miraculous power is sought for a child by a parent; and the healing takes place at a distance from Jesus. From this he concluded that the Q story is a variation of the story of the healing of the Syrophoenician woman's daughter and that the scenes depicted in both are imaginary products of the church. Further (as we have noted) he says, "Hardly anybody will support the historicity of a telepathic healing."[27]

But Bultmann's position is not to be taken seriously. We cannot dismiss a story because the method of healing is not to the liking of the twentieth or twenty-first century.[28] Also, the differences between the two stories Bultmann has in mind are so great that few take his suggestion seriously.

With two independent traditions attesting this story, the possibility of there being a historical event behind the stories is enhanced. Further, more stylistic features suggest that the story has a Palestinian origin,[29] as does the story's freedom from antipathy between church and synagogue and the expectation that Jews will have faith.[30] Whereas there is evidence that the Jesus tradition tended to take on sayings about faith,[31] this one is of the rare type in the Gospels where Jesus is the explicit subject of the trust, a contrast to the early church usage where Jesus is more often the object of trust.[32] There are then good reasons for considering that the core of this story—a centurion who asked Jesus to heal his sick boy, which takes place at a distance—arose in the life of the historical Jesus.[33]

§12.5 A Crippled Woman Healed (Lk 13:10-17)
The question of the origin of this story has generated considerable discussion. Bultmann, for example, said the present story was perhaps modeled on the story of the healing of the man with a withered hand (Mk 3:1-6) and was composed on

the basis of an originally isolated saying in Luke 13:15 about untying animals from the manger to give them water on the sabbath.[34] But the only point of contact between the two stories is Jesus' defense of his healing on the sabbath, and Bultmann's evidence is simply that, based on the form of the sabbath healing of the man with a withered hand in Mark 3:1-6, the discussion ought to precede the account of the miracle. Once again, however, it is illegitimate to use modern constructions to determine the integrity or authenticity of a story. Indeed, the riddle in Luke 13:15 about untying and leading an animal to water could hardly exist without the following explanation about the woman being freed from Satan's grip.[35] It is quite possible then that miracle and discussion belonged together from the beginning of the story.

There is considerable evidence of Luke's hand throughout the story,[36] leading the Fellows of the Jesus Seminar, for example, to conclude that it is a Lukan composition.[37] However, there are details without theological purpose, that may point to a pre-Lukan tradition: the adversary is "the synagogue ruler" not Luke's usual antagonist—a Pharisee—and the woman is said to have been ill for eighteen years, perhaps simply a conventional number.[38]

That the story came from the life of the earthly Jesus has been doubted because sabbath practice was more rigorous than 13:15 suggests.[39] However, the Mishnah and Qumran documents give ample evidence of prohibitions that would form the background to a story such as this one.[40] Also, to follow Hengel, "There is not the least doubt that the underlying situation of conflict is based on the attitude of Jesus himself. Indeed, the later Palestinian community had a tendency to play down the sabbath conflict initiated by Jesus."[41] Therefore again, though it is not possible to trace with confidence the origin of all the details of the story, it is likely that behind the story we now have in Luke is the echo of an event in the life of the historical Jesus.

§12.6 Healing the Paralytic at Bethesda (Jn 5:1-18)

That the sick person here, as well as in Mark 2:1-11, is a man who cannot walk, whom Jesus tells to stand up, pick up his mat and walk, is not, as argued in §7.5, sufficient to suggest that Mark 2:1-11 is another source for this story.[42] John 5:1-18 is the only source for this story.

A pool fitting John's description has been unearthed in Jerusalem near St. Anne's church,[43] showing that the factual details in John 5:1-3 are accurate, betraying a knowledge of Jerusalem that militates against concluding a late or non-Palestinian origin of this story.[44] The Qumran Copper Scroll further confirms that Bethesda, or Beth-zatha, is an area of Jerusalem that had pools people could enter.[45] Although the Johannine story does not precisely conform to the form of a Synoptic story, the general similarity is unmistakable, so it is not likely to be a creation of the evangelist.[46] Sometimes John's characters are portrayed as clever (cf. Jn 3:1-2; 9:1-7), sometimes—as here—they are caricatured as dull, naive and obtuse (cf. 4:7-15; 6:5-9). Yet the personality traits in this story show no theological significance and are so realistic that we are predisposed to think the story had its origin in the life of the historical Jesus.[47]

§12.7 The Next Step

With these five stories of crippled and paralyzed characters being healed and the four major exorcism stories—all of which we have judged to contain in their cores reliable echoes of events in the life of the historical Jesus—we have covered the two categories of miracle that together have the most stories in them. We turn now to other healings and miracles, beginning with stories portraying the blind receiving sight.

Thirteen

The Blind

....

§13.1 Introduction

In the world of Jesus and his audience the blind were among the most tragic and needy of people. Besides being inherited, blindness was caused by insects, snake bites, wounds and punishment from war, exposure to lightning, illness, alcohol and even from self-infliction in trying to atone for sin. A few blind were wealthy. Some were able to make a living by singing or making music or poetry. Others kept alive by being slaves in copper and silver mines. The majority, because of their inability to move about well and make a living, generally lived in extreme poverty, begging for their existence. Though there may have been some operations for cataracts, curing blindness was thought possible only through the miraculous intervention of the supernatural.[1]

When it comes to the question of whether Jesus can generally be credited with healing the blind, we are again faced with the point, as with the healing of the cripples and paralytics, that it was expected that the blind would receive their sight in the messianic age.[2] Yet with so many blind people in the community, from what we already know about Jesus' compassion, it would have been surprising if Jesus had not attempted to heal them.

We have three stories in the Jesus tradition of the blind being healed, but restoring sight was not a type of healing the early church focused on. Indeed, Paul is the only one we know who was reported to be cured of blindness.[3] Whereas Luke includes recovery of sight in summaries of Jesus' ministry,[4] his summaries of life and healings in the early church do not include the blind seeing (e.g., Acts

5:12-16; 28:9). Therefore insofar as Luke can be representative, it seems unlikely that the early church has recreated its own interests and practices in its representation of the ministry of Jesus to the blind. Further, the idea that Jesus cured the blind is found in a number of forms of tradition and sources: a citation of the Old Testament (Lk 4:18); a Lukan summary statement of Jesus' ministry (Lk 7:21); a saying of Jesus from Q (Lk 7:22); and stories from Mark and John of the blind being healed, which we are about to discuss. We are therefore predisposed to consider positively the possibility that Jesus healed the blind.[5]

§13.2 A Blind Man at Bethsaida (Mk 8:22-26)
With so many parallels between this story and that of the man with a speech impediment (Mk 7:31-37),[6] it has been suggested this one is a variant of it.[7] But the differences between the two stories are so great it is virtually certain that we are dealing with two distinct stories.[8]

The major case to be made against the historicity of the healing story is that its two-stage character and the use of spittle mean that it was constructed to function not unlike some of the "recipes" of the Greek magical papyri.[9] However, the magical papyri are of an entirely different type of material. They do not contain stories like the Gospels and are truly like recipes in their approach to healing. There is no doubt that the stories of Jesus took on a didactic function (cf. Mk 9:28-29). However, it is highly questionable to assume, therefore, that the stories had their origin in such a purpose. Instead, we can give positive reasons why this story probably arose in the life of the historical Jesus.

The most positive historically telling aspect of the story is, it turns out, its two-stage form. It is unlikely a Christian storyteller or copyist would create a story in which Jesus is portrayed as initially or partially unsuccessful and needing a second attempt to secure the healing. Nor is it likely that a story would have been created where Jesus is portrayed as asking for information from the person being healed: "Can you see anything?" (Mk 8:23). It is more likely that the early church would have created a story in which Jesus was portrayed as all-knowing, as is suggested, for example, by the way Matthew removes the questioning of Jesus from the story of the epileptic boy (cf. Mk 9:21/Mt 17:17-18).

The setting, Bethsaida, is not as easily dismissed as Bultmann thought.[10] He saw a conflict in that he considered that Bethsaida's status as a city *(polis)* clashed with the story referring to it as a town *(kōmē;* Mk 8:23, 26).[11] However, in the New Testament there was no sharp distinction between a city and a town.[12] Also, recent archeological findings reveal that even after the creation of the city of Bethsaida-Julias by Herod Philip, the old fishing village of Bethsaida continued to function as a seaport for the city.[13] Along with this, both Mark and Q witness to the importance of Bethsaida in the ministry of Jesus, so it is quite probable that the setting Mark has for the story is to be traced back to the very earliest stage of this story.

That Jesus is said, on the one hand, to use saliva does not help in assessing the historicity of the story. To say it is an embarrassing form of healing[14] and therefore unlikely to be created by the early church is to use modern understandings of healing and saliva. Yet with Matthew appearing deliberately to omit the mention of spittle when he relates the story of the deaf-mute[15] and with spittle generally being accompanied by what would have been considered magical practices,[16] it is unlikely that Christians—as they are represented in the Gospel traditions—would create such a story. On the other hand, however, the use of saliva was common in the ancient world, so Mark or his predecessors may have been accommodating Jesus to the image of contemporary healers.[17]

On balance, the reference to healing through the use of saliva is probably an indication of historicity, for, as Meier put it, "Having Jesus spit in a person's face does not seem to fit any stream of christology in the early church,"[18] and it is discontinuous in relation to other miracle stories in that it is only here and in Mark 7:33 that spittle is a direct instrument of healing (cf. Jn 9:6).

To these points can be added that the description of people walking about like trees may go back to an Aramaic report.[19] Such a description in turn assumes that the man has experienced sight before. Thus there has been no attempt to heighten the miracle by saying that the man had been born blind.[20] In light of the two-stage nature of the healing, the setting, the use of spittle, and the description of the partial seeing of people looking like trees, we can conclude that this story is most likely reflecting an event in the ministry of Jesus.[21]

§13.3 Blind Bartimaeus (Mk 10:46-52/Mt 9:27-31/20:29-34/Lk 18:35-43)

There has not been much confidence in seeing this story as arising in the ministry of Jesus.[22] However, a number of signals in the story indicate that it not only predates Mark but probably goes back to the memories of Jesus' audience.

First, even indirectly identifying the sick person is not common in Mark's healing stories (cf. Mk 1:30; 5:22). Bartimaeus and Jairus are the only named individuals who seek a miracle from Jesus and, apart from the disciples, the only specifically named persons in the whole of the Synoptic traditions. (Lazarus is the only named person healed in the Fourth Gospel.) Compared to the apocryphal Gospels, the Synoptic tradition does not have a tendency to add names. For example, in this story both Matthew and Luke omit the name of the blind beggar (Mt 20:30/Lk 18:35). Further, the name Bartimaeus is Aramaic,[23] so it is more likely to have been in Mark's tradition than borrowed from among his readers.

Second, Bartimaeus addresses Jesus as "Rabbouni" (Mk 10:51). This is Aramaic for "my teacher" and not a title for Jesus of particular interest to the early church in that it occurs elsewhere only at John 20:16.

Third, only here in Mark is Jesus addressed as "Son of David" (Mk 10:47). Although used only once, the title "Son of David" can be readily understood. In the first century, Solomon the son of David had a reputation as a great healer. But the phrase had no pre-Christian messianic connections,[24] so when "Son of David" was taken up as a messianic title, it was associated not with healing but with the enthronement of Jesus.[25]

Fourth, contrary to what we would expect in Mark, the crowd (not Jesus) rebukes the blind man (Mk 10:48; cf., e.g., 3:12; 8:30).

The details of place (near Jericho) and especially of timing (shortly before the Passover) do not necessarily give us hints of historicity, for it may be Mark who has given this story its setting. Nevertheless in view of the signals we have identified, we can agree with Meier's judgment that the story is most probably basically historical and is "one of the strongest candidates for the report of a specific miracle going back to the historical Jesus."[26]

§13.4 Healing a Man Born Blind (Jn 9:1-7)

Although this story extends through most of John 9, the miracle itself is contained within three verses: John 9:1, 6 and 7. It is also transmitted almost incidentally. The similarities with Synoptic stories of the healing of the blind are few,[27] so that dependence on the Synoptics is quite unlikely.

In verses 2 and 3 a discussion is reported that arises out of the disciples asking Jesus a question about the cause of illness. It was not unusual for dialogue to be part of a healing story,[28] though these verses are unique in dealing with a question of speculative theology: theodicy about which John otherwise shows no interest. In Luke 13:1-5 there is a discussion with Jesus on a similar question. In both John and Luke, Jesus repudiates suffering as a basis for a moral judgment.

So although the language of these verses is Johannine, the dialogue is not unique to John, nor is he relating ideas that are of special interest to him. The dialogue is therefore likely always to have been part of the story. Verses 4 and 5 (about working while it is day and Jesus' being the light of the world) are far less certainly attributed, for they are heavily impregnated by Johannine ideas as well as language.

We do not need to comment further on the feature of Jesus being said to use saliva as part of the healing technique. When discussing the healing of the blind man at Bethsaida, we saw that, on balance, it was probably a faithful echo of Jesus' healing methods (see §13.2 on Mk 8:22-26).

The involvement of the patient in the healing process (here going to the pool of Siloam to wash, Jn 9:7) is not unique in the Gospels. In Mark 3:5 the man is asked to stretch out his withered hand. In Luke 17:14 the ten lepers are told to show themselves to the priests. However, the kind of involvement here in John is distinctive, and it is unlikely that early Christians would have created a feature of the story in which Jesus is portrayed as needing the help of the pool of Siloam to effect the healing. For this reason, even though washing in the pool carries the symbolism of baptism[29] and the name Siloam may mean "sent,"[30] it is unlikely that the story arose through lucky symbolic associations.[31]

Further, in favor of the historicity of the core of the story, C. H. Dodd noticed that in the course of the ensuing long dialogue, John has enriched the story with details: a man young enough for his parents to be alive; that he customarily sat and begged near the temple; and that the incident took place on the sabbath. Yet John did not take the liberty of introducing these details back into the core of the narrative.

We have few details in this story about which we can be historically certain. At a bare minimum it is probable that this story reflects an event in which Jesus was confronted by a man born blind, which raised a brief discussion. Jesus then made a saliva-based mud for the man's eyes, which the man washed off at the pool of Siloam, returning later, healed, to the scene.

Fourteen

Raising the Dead

....

§14.1 Introduction

The stories of the raising of the dead stretch the credulity of Western post-Enlightenment readers to the limit, if not beyond (see §2.4). Thus, not surprisingly, Heinrich Paulus (1761-1851) offered the natural explanation that all three stories of Jesus raising the dead were cases of suspended animation, even that of Lazarus, who was reported to have been in the tomb four days.[1]

But pointing out the confounding difficulty in this view—the texts of the stories do not support it—David Strauss concluded that the stories "are nothing more than mythi, which had their origin in the tendency of the early Christian church, to make her Messiah agree with the type of the prophets, and with the messianic ideal."[2] Or, as Rochais concluded, they are to be seen as theological inferences drawn from the resurrection of Jesus.[3] The following discussion will show the highly questionable nature of these views.

The early Christian tradition is not alone in transmitting stories of the raising of the dead. They are occasionally to be found in Jewish, Greek and, not surprisingly, the later Christian apocryphal literature.[4] Therefore it is considered that stories of the raising of the dead have made their way into the Jesus tradition from other traditions at a time when it was still in oral form.[5] Or they are considered myths, or they have their origin in the Old Testament stories. What this means is that there is no point in inquiring about the historicity of these stories. Though recognizing that this position is perfectly understandable, John Meier is right to question whether it takes into consideration three important points.[6]

1. As already noted in this study, what we take to be historically possible or probable is affected—perhaps even determined—by the culture in which our minds have been shaped. That is, most of us tend to accept certain things as possible or impossible, not because we have thoroughly investigated them but because authority figures around us seem to take them for granted. Thus though we may find it almost or completely impossible to entertain the idea of a dead person being brought back to life, pagans, Jews and Christians of the first century A.D. through the patristic and medieval period thought that it was plausible for special individuals to raise the dead.

Nevertheless such stories do not abound. The literature was most likely constrained by the view that this was rare or, as some thought, impossible. Much earlier, Aeschylus has the god Apollo say, "Once a man is dead . . . , there is no more rising" (*Eumenides* 647-48). So Christian and non-Christian traditions alike relate relatively few such stories—only a handful in the New Testament and a few in each of the other traditions.

2. Before too easily dismissing the stories of the raising of the dead as unhistorical, Meier also suggests we take into consideration the point that although the stories of raising the dead are relatively rare in the Gospels, they are neatly spread over a number of different literary sources. That is, Mark has the story of the raising of the daughter of Jairus (Mk 5:21-43), the L tradition has the story of the raising of the son of the widow of Nain (Lk 7:11-17), and Johannine tradition preserves the raising of Lazarus (Jn 11:1-46). To this multiple attestation we need to add the saying of Jesus to the disciples of John the Baptist in the Q tradition: "The blind receive their sight, the lame walk, the lepers are cleansed, the deaf hear, the dead are raised" (Mt 11:5/Lk 7:22). As Meier remarks concerning the raising of the dead, "Many a word and deed of Jesus in the Four Gospels lack attestation this widely based."[7]

3. Historians of the miracles of Jesus seek to establish, with varying degrees of certainty, whether certain stories in the Gospels rest on actual events in the life of Jesus reported by those who were in Jesus' audience. Meier is right to say that how those events were contrived or whether the audience was deceived is beyond our power to investigate.[8] However, I want to offer a caution that in the case of the Lazarus story those who transmitted the story were probably aware of the possibility of deception, for it is explicitly stated that Lazarus had been in the tomb for four days. To conclude: in light of these three points we are obliged at least to ask if there are reliable signs in the three stories that suggest they have their origin in the life of the historical Jesus.[9]

§14.2 Jairus's Daughter (Mk 5:21-43/Mt 9:18-26/Lk 8:40-56)

This story[10] presents us with a number of signs that it may go back to an event in the life of Jesus. One of the striking aspects of the story is the occurrence of the name Jairus. As was already noted, besides Bartimaeus, Jairus is the only individual named in the Gospels who seeks a miracle from Jesus. Since Codex Bezae (D) and some Old Latin manuscripts omit the name and it is lacking in Matthew, it has been regarded as secondary.[11] But the external support for the name of Jairus in Mark is impressive.[12]

When discussing the presence of the name Bartimaeus in Mark 10:46 I noted that the Synoptic traditions do not tend to introduce names (see §3.27). This suggests that the name Jairus was probably a part of the early traditions of this story. Also, even though the early church often struggled in its relationship with the synagogue, Jairus, the man of faith seeking healing from Jesus, is portrayed as "one of the leaders of the synagogue" (Mk 5:22). This suggests that this character was not created by the church.

Another sign of the antiquity of this story is the presence of the Aramaic command of Jesus to the dead girl, "Talitha cum" (Mk 5:41).[13] Even though Jesus' language was Aramaic, the Gospel traditions do not appear to seek to recreate the memory of his voice by introducing Aramaic words and phrases. The only other Aramaic word Jesus speaks in the Gospels is *ephphatha* ("Be opened," Mk 7:34). There are also other Semitisms in the story[14] that probably take the origin of the story at least back to a Palestinian setting.

Meier has pointed out the strange lack of any christological confession. The only possible christological confession is the people from Jairus's house telling of the death of the girl and saying, "Why trouble the teacher any further?" (Mk 5:35). A possible implication of this is that they believe Jesus is only a teacher and that raising the dead is beyond his capability.[15] The early church is unlikely to have created this aspect of the story.

The early church is also unlikely to have created a situation where the all-powerful Jesus is laughed at to the point of scorn *(katagelaō)*,[16] like an enemy, by those in the house whom he later throws out (Mk 5:40). Nowhere else is Jesus made the direct object of this scornful laughter, even when met by disbelief. Also, Matthew avoids the idea of Jesus being seen in the role of a controller of a crowd of mourners. He uses the passive voice ("when the crowd had been put outside," Mt 9:25), and Luke omits this feature altogether.

It is true that in an age when the science of medicine was inexact there was the danger of an erroneous diagnosis of death. However, presumably parents and others had watched the girl carefully before and after death, especially since theological significance was given to the time, manner and posture of death.[17] Further, professional mourners who were present would have been accustomed to recognizing signs of death.

Were it not for the fact that we are dealing with the raising of a dead person, we would more easily accept the clear signs that this story is one of the best candidates for being seen to have its origins in the stories the observers of Jesus' ministry told about him.[18] Further, the story coheres entirely with the Jewish "new exodus" expectations that form the coherent center of Jesus' understanding of the purpose of his ministry (cf. 4Q521).[19]

§14.3 The Widow of Nain's Son (Lk 7:11-17)

In weighing the historical veracity of the next two stories, one of the difficulties is that they have only one witness, in this case Luke. There is no doubt that this story is shot through with signs of Luke's theological interests. That is, as prophesied in Isaiah 40:5, God has come to bring salvation and healing to his people, especially to the poor, exemplified in the widow's plight (cf. Lk 3:6). Also, the story fits well with Luke's agenda at this point in his Gospel. Along with the story of the healing of the centurion's slave, it provides the basis on which, in the next story, Jesus can answer John the Baptist's disciples' question about his identity (Lk 7:18-23). Therefore it is sometimes suggested that Luke has created this story, perhaps by Christianizing Elijah's raising of the son of the widow of Zarephath (1 Kings 17:8-24).[20]

Indeed, the parallels between the stories are considerable: both Jesus and Elijah come to a town, a widow is met at the gate of the town, her son is brought back to life, and the healer is acclaimed.[21] At the very least it might be agreed that Luke's language has been influenced by the Old Testament story, as in the repetition of the phrase "and he gave him to his mother" (Lk 7:15b, author's translation).[22]

However, the differences between the two stories are considerable:[23] Luke's story does not contain the emotive background detail paralleling Elijah's knowledge and involvement in the life of the widow and her son; in Luke there is no history of the illness of the lad; the widow in Luke takes no initiative; and Jesus acts out of compassion rather than in response to faith or petition. Also, in contrast to Luke's story, Elijah acts in private, prays three times, then prostrates himself across the dead body, again praying.[24] These differences mean that it is unlikely Luke created his story out of this one. Nevertheless he was probably dependent on it for some of his phraseology.

There are also significant parallels between Luke's story and one by Philostratus about Apollonius (*Life* 4:45): the healer halted a funeral bier carrying a young person who had just died, large crowds were in attendance and, on being revived, the person speaks. On the strength of this, Bultmann proposed that Luke's story had its origin in a Hellenistic Jewish-Christian setting.[25] But the differences between the stories—for example, Apollonius revives a young newlywed, or about to be married lady, of a consular family, the crowd consoles the husband, and Apollonius touches and whispers a secret formula over the person—make it highly improbable that Bultmann's proposal has value.[26]

For the same reasons we must set aside the view that the raising of Jairus's daughter (Mk 5:21-43) or Peter's raising of Tabitha (Acts 9:36-43) provided Luke with the origin of the raising of the widow's son.[27] On the other hand, we can see some signs in Luke's story that at least it predates him.[28]

How Luke—not generally well informed about Palestinian geography[29]— should have known about this obscure town and its wall is difficult to explain apart from his learning about it in his tradition.[30] Another possible sign of the story predating Luke is the number of Semitisms in it.[31] Further, the story ends with the acclamation that Jesus is "a [not *the*] great prophet," a surprisingly insignificant title for Luke to use if it was not in his tradition (Lk 7:16). Indeed, with his earlier phrase "When the Lord saw her" (7:13), Luke overshadows the Christology of this story with this more profound title so that the readers will know that the appellation "prophet" is an insufficient designation for Jesus.

Also, Luke tends to avoid reproducing two similar stories. This is evident in his using only one of the feeding stories and in using the story of Jesus' feet being anointed but leaving out the one in which his head was anointed. In light of this it is unlikely that Luke would have created this raising when he has the story of Jairus's daughter in the next chapter. Indeed, Luke is the only Gospel writer to transmit two stories of the dead being raised. Together, all these factors are signs that this story predates Luke.

Whether any of these signals in the story allow us to progress to the next step and assign the story to the very earliest historical traditions about Jesus is difficult to determine. However, the location of the story in the completely obscure town of Nain, the realistic circumstantial detail of the mother's walking in front of the bier as they did in Galilee[32] and the Gospel writers' showing no evidence of creating resuscitation stories tip the balance in favor of concluding that this story goes back to the ministry of Jesus.[33]

§14.4 The Raising of Lazarus (Jn 11:1-57)

If ever a miracle story was to stretch the credulity of a modern reader, it would be this one. It is very tempting to rule out the possibility of genuine historical reminiscences in this case. Though some of the Fellows of the Jesus Seminar thought it remotely possible that the story was based on a historical event, "they were certain such an event did not involve the resuscitation of a corpse."[34] On the other hand, Westcott asserted boldly, "No explanation of the origin of the narrative on the supposition that it is unhistorical, has even a show of plausibility."[35] Van der Loos was right to say that, "Around the resurrection of Lazarus the critics are ranked in battle array, like an army round a beleaguered fortress."[36]

John has the story as his final, most profound sign and the direct cause of the intention to kill Jesus (Jn 11:57). Mark, on the other hand, uses the cleansing of the temple as the direct catalyst for the authorities to seek to kill Jesus (Mk 11:18). Yet this difference cannot be pressed too far as a sign of the unhistorical base of John, for Mark has already given notice of the intention of the authorities in 3:6.

That the Synoptic tradition does not mention the story is more difficult to explain. It is hard to believe that the Synoptic tradition did not know the story, especially if it was thought to have a critical effect on the arrest of Jesus, and was not necessarily interested in every aspect of what led to Jesus' arrest.[37]

It could be that this story is missing from the Synoptics because the authors did not want to record more than one event of the same kind, for their tradition already had a story of revivification in Jairus's daughter,[38] and Luke had a second in the widow of Nain's son (Lk 7:11-17). Or it could be missing because those responsible for the Synoptic tradition were seeking to protect Lazarus from reprisals from the Sanhedrin (cf. Jn 12:10-11).[39] Or a miracle of resurrection in Judea so soon before the Passion might have seemed theologically inappropriate.[40] In short, we do not know why the Synoptics have not carried this story any more than we do not know why other Gospel traditions do not carry some stories.

As we saw in §7.9, one explanation of the origin of this story is that it has been inspired by the parable of Lazarus and the rich man in Luke 16:19-31. However, we noted that the broad objection to this proposal is that it relies on a reshuffling of Synoptic material—a view that is generally not thought viable. Indeed, it is equally plausible that the parable has its origins in a borrowing from the miracle.[41]

Also to be noted, Lazarus was a common name,[42] and the only viable connections or parallels between the parable and the miracle story are the name Lazarus and the final saying of the parable about people not listening to Moses even if someone rises from the dead (Lk 16:31).[43] There is then nothing about this story that is any less likely to come from the early tradition about Jesus than from a Synoptic miracle story.[44]

The majority of Johannine scholars agree John took up a story that included mention of Lazarus's illness (Jn 11:1), the message sent to Jesus (11:3), his delay in responding (11:6), his intention to go and wake Lazarus (11:11-15), Jesus' arrival at Bethany (11:17-19), the scene at the tomb (11:33-39a), and the calling to and coming out of Lazarus (11:43-44).[45] Can we press the issue to see if this story would have come from the earliest memories of the ministry of Jesus?[46]

Once again it must be noted that the naming of the recipient of a healing is extremely rare in the Gospels. (That names are attached to two of what would have been thought to be the most difficult healings may indicate their rarity and a keenness for them to be remembered.) Similarly the statement "Now Bethany was near Jerusalem, some two miles away" (Jn 11:18) is a topographically accurate detail that is probably another indicator of reliable historicity in this story. The portrayal of Mary and Martha is remarkably similar to that found in Luke (Lk 10:38-42), suggesting at the least that Luke and John are drawing on a shared preexisting tradition.

Circumstantial details, such as Jesus' initial delay in coming to the aid of his friends (Jn 11:4), his joining in the mourning and weeping (11:35) and the hesitancy to take away the stone from the door of the tomb (11:39), point to a historically reliable story. Also, the deliberate delay of Jesus, which caused increased suffering, is unlikely to have been invented by early Christians, even though it could be put to theological use (11:4).

However, the presence of family members—the two sisters—may not be a pointer to historicity, for the presence of family members was so much a part of a death scene that it would be natural to narrate a story in this way.[47] Other indicators to historicity could be, for example, that the tomb was described as a cavern and that the grave clothes were precisely described as "strips of linen" and a "head-cloth." However, we need to entertain the possibility that they could equally be indicators of narrative skill.[48]

In the final analysis, despite any natural hesitation about the possibility of a dead person being raised to life after so long in the grave, the signs noted in this story point to the strong likelihood that in John 11 we are reading a story that—though perhaps greatly changed in its half-century or more history—had its origins in the life of the historical Jesus.

Fifteen

Lepers Cleansed

....

§15.1 Introduction

I have left this category of the healings until last, on the grounds that the smallest number of stories relate to Jesus' healing of leprosy: two stories, which, we will argue, are independent of each other.

One interesting difficulty in these stories is that we cannot be certain that the illness described in the Gospels as leprosy *(lepra)* is what we know as leprosy, or Hanson's disease. For "all references *lepra* seem to derive from the earlier Hippocratic concepts of a scaly, desquamating skin condition, with no indication that any such disease included the signs of true leprosy."[1]

Another difficulty is the major objection to their historicity that Rudolf Pesch has on the grounds that in portraying Jesus as the eschatological prophet, who echoes the miracle-working Elijah and Elisha, we most probably have constructs of the early church.[2] However, it seems historically well attested that Jesus acted as a prophet. His prophetic message was strongly eschatological, and he distinguished himself from other prophetic figures. So the picture of Jesus as an eschatological prophet is firmly rooted in traditions that go back to the life of Jesus, even though the idea was soon well developed. However, on the dissimilarity or discontinuity test—that we are on historically safe ground "when there are no grounds for deriving a tradition from Judaism or for ascribing it to primitive Christianity"[3]—Jesus' cure of lepers may be a legitimate part of the original Jesus tradition.

At the same time, apart from their representation of Jesus as a healer of lepers, the early church showed no interest in their healing. Also, this reported category of healing passes the test of coherence at two levels. On one level, I have already argued in §10.13 that within Jesus' answer to John the Baptist (Mt 11:2-6/Lk 7:18-23) we have an authentic saying of Jesus about healing lepers, to which his activity of healing lepers coheres. On another level, the reintegration of lepers into Israel-under-restoration dramatically coheres with the core new-exodus restoration hopes, while yet providing a distinctive form if measured by the criterion of dissimilarity.[4] Therefore there are good grounds on which to discuss favorably the possible historicity of the individual healing stories.

§15.2 A Leper Cleansed (Mk 1:40-45/Mt 8:1-4/Lk 5:12-16)

Peeling away possible later additions, we are left with a simple story that is consistent with the basic form-critical outline of a miracle story: the leper meeting and asking Jesus for his healing (Mk 1:40), the words and action of Jesus in healing the man (1:41), and the report of the immediate healing (1:42).[5]

There is little here on which to base a judgment about historicity. Although there is a version of the story in Papyrus Egerton 2, from about A.D. 150, this is most likely dependent on Luke's story,[6] leaving us with no witnesses apart from Mark. We may be able to place some weight on the mention of Jesus being angry or moved with pity at the approach and request of the leper. Taking the more difficult reading, as we argued in §3.7, it is more likely that Mark wrote that Jesus was "angry" (*orgistheis*; see §3.7)—probably for a variety of reasons—rather than "moved with pity" (*splagchnistheis*). If this is the case, it is unlikely that it has been added to the tradition.

Indeed, in support of this conclusion it can be noted that Matthew 8:2 and Luke 5:13 omit the idea from their versions of the story. Furthermore, Jesus is pictured as breaking the laws of uncleanness in touching the unclean.[7] Even though this touch brought cleansing, it is more likely that if this story was being created by the early church, they would have had Jesus speak the healing (cf. Lk 17:14) rather than touch a leper.

This is very little evidence on which to conclude a case for or against this story being from the earliest memories of the ministry of Jesus. However, on balance, I am inclined to favor concluding that this story has its origin in the ministry of the historical Jesus.[8]

§15.3 Ten Lepers Cleansed (Lk 17:11-19)

In assessing the origins of this story, the historian is again without the help of an independent witness. Only Luke preserves it. With so many words and phrases distinctive of Luke's hand,[9] it is not surprising that it has been seen as a totally Lukan creation, echoing the story of Naaman in 2 Kings 5.[10] But to suggest this does not account for the very odd statement at the beginning of the story that Jesus was going "through the middle of Samaria and Galilee" (Lk 17:11, author's translation).[11]

Samaria is south of Galilee, and Luke has already said that Jesus has left Galilee and entered Samaria (Lk 9:51-56). How this is to be explained remains a puzzle.[12] But it is implausible, if Luke was creating this story, for him to produce this muddle. It is more likely that he found it in his tradition.[13]

Equally puzzling is that over against so much of the story's exhibiting a Lukan style is the convergence of a number of curious features of language here that are unique in the New Testament.[14] Although some of the language may be influenced by the Greek Old Testament story of Naaman (2 Kings 5), Luke certainly had no monopoly on using the Septuagint. With the story having so many layers of theological meaning, Meier is probably right to conclude that Luke is reworking a story from L, one of his sources.[15]

That the story came from a reworking of the healing of the leper in Mark 1:40-45[16] can be disposed of easily. The two stories are too different, and Luke avoids doublets in his narrative.

When it comes to the question of whether this story has its origin in the life of the ministry of Jesus, again we have very little on which to make a judgment. René Latourelle's suggestion that Jesus' meeting of the lepers on the edge of the village is a hint of historicity does not take us far, for the marginalization of lepers was universally practiced.[17] In the end *historians* with limited tools have to leave open the question of the origin of this story and turn, in the next chapter, to a number of different kinds of stories.[18]

Sixteen

Other Healings & Miracles of Nature

....

§16.1 Introduction

A large number of miracle stories in the Gospels do not fit any particular category. It has been customary to call many of them nature miracles. But that is not a category familiar to Jesus or his first followers.[1] Other stories, such as the healing of Peter's mother-in-law, are healings of various kinds, not fitting any of the categories we have so far discussed. Some, such as finding a coin in the mouth of a fish, appear odd to modern minds.

Not least due to dealings with stories that often have only one witness, the task of the historian is greatly hampered in the quest for solid grounds on which to make decisions about historical veracity. More often than some may wish we will leave open the question of whether we are reading a story that had its origin in the life of Jesus. We will discuss the stories in the order that the earliest version appears in the Gospels, beginning with a story that appears only in Matthew.

§16.2 A Coin in a Fish's Mouth (Mt 17:24-27)

What is really a prediction of a miracle—when Jesus says that Peter will find a coin in the mouth of a fish—is also found in the *Epistula Apostolorum* 5 (mid-second century).[2] However, as this is probably not an independent story,[3] we are left with Matthew as our only witness to what Meier calls the miracle of the fiscally philanthropic fish![4]

The miracle prediction comes at the end of a discussion on paying taxes—probably the temple tax, for it was levied in the name of God and fits the requirement of the temple tax.[5] Though the discussion preceding the miracle (Mt 17:24-26) is thoroughly Matthean in its style and vocabulary,[6] it is unlikely, if writing after the destruction of the temple, that Matthew would have created a story about an obsolete tax.[7] If Matthew or his predecessors created this story, we would expect mention of the disciples' obedience and the ensuing amazement.[8]

Further, the situations implied in the story fit well with that of the ministry of Jesus.[9] (1) Jesus' comparing the burdensome temple tax (which was promoted as being paid to God) with secular taxes fits views of the time.[10] (2) The fatherly character of God portrayed in this story coheres more with a distinctive feature of Jesus' teaching than with the early church. (3) Jesus' attitude toward the temple is consistent with his reply to the question about the tribute money (Mk 12:13-17).

If this last point is valid, then the predicted miracle of the finding of a coin in the mouth of a fish in verse 27 need not be seen as Matthew's addition to the story to provide a corrective to head off a scandal.[11] Further, if the discussion on taxes in verses 24-26 is at least in part about provision by a fatherly God, the miracle prediction fits well with this theme, which is well attested in the Gospels.[12]

Also, we can see that the miracle prediction coheres well with what we know about the ministry of Jesus. Far from being a unique miracle (or prediction of a miracle) there are other miracles of provision attested across the Gospel traditions: the feeding stories, the large catch of fish and the turning of water into wine.[13] Therefore, though we may note with Davies and Allison that truth is stranger than fiction[14] and may be tempted to see this story as apocryphal[15]—belonging more to the realm of folk lore than authentic memories of the work of Jesus[16]—it is possible that this story does reflect an event in the life of the historical Jesus.

If the fish was one of the Tilapia—the so-called St. Peter's mouth-breeding fish, which has a tendency to take bright objects into its mouth—this might be considered a miracle of coincidence.[17] Having said all this, it may even be—seeing we are not told that Peter went to find the fish and the money—that Jesus' words were merely a playful comment on the disciples' lack of ready money and not intended to be taken literally.[18] Notwithstanding, on balance, as strange as it is to modern minds, we have here a story that probably has its origins in the life of the historical Jesus.

§16.3 Healing Peter's Mother-in-Law (Mk 1:29-31/Mt 8:14-15/Lk 4:38-39)

Even though this story—which does not fit any of the other categories of healing—is brief, it carries considerable theological significance: the immense and immediate power of Jesus' touch (a comment on the nature of Jesus), his raising the woman to new life (an image of his own resurrection) and her serving him (an image of discipleship). These factors would mitigate against the historicity of the story were it not for some inherent details that prompt a second look.

To begin with, its brevity, perhaps even transmitted incidentally by being attached to the story of the exorcism in the synagogue, speaks for its historicity. Second, incidental precise details that do not seem to have theological significance (entering the house of Simon and Andrew after the synagogue service and healing a clearly identified person, Peter's mother-in-law) point to the early origin of the story. Third, it can hardly be doubted that Peter had a mother-in-law. In 1 Corinthians 9:5 Paul writes of Peter taking his wife on missionary journeys. Fourth and more generally, following Latourelle, the story does not follow a prefabricated pattern—there is no dialogue or specific request for healing or report of an impression left on the observers.[19]

This story therefore has the hallmarks of faithfully reflecting an event that took place in the Galilean ministry of Jesus.[20] Indeed, for the Fellows of the Jesus Seminar, "This brief vignette comes as close as any to qualifying as a report of an actual happening."[21]

§16.4 Stilling a Storm (Mk 4:35-41/Mt 8:23-27/Lk 8:22-25)

Although both Matthew and Luke transmit this story, once again the historian is disadvantaged by having only Mark as the source upon which to rely. For some, this being a so-called nature miracle means that its historicity is in jeopardy.[22]

With post-Enlightenment arrogance Adolf von Harnack summarily dismissed the story as an illusion, saying that miracles no longer happen and "that a storm was quieted by a word, we do not believe, and we shall never again believe."[23] Since Jesus is thought to be presented as a god, many have concluded that this is a fictional tale produced by Christians. For example, Robert Funk reports that "the Fellows of the Jesus Seminar were unanimous in their judgement that the stilling of the storm was not based on an event in the life of Jesus."[24] Rationalist explanations, such as a natural calming that coincided with Jesus' command,[25] are equally inadmissible, for the text does not support them.

The Hellenistic world does not provide us with any account of a person calming a storm. The nearest parallel is the story of people anxious to share a voyage with Apollonius because he "was regarded as one who was master of the tempest and of fire and of perils of all sorts" (Philostratus *Life* 4:13). The fourth-century Jewish story of a storm calmed by a child praying led Bultmann to conclude that in the case of Jesus calming a storm we have an instance of an alien miracle story being transferred to Jesus. However, this suggestion is not realistic, for the Jewish story is late, as Bultmann recognized (c. A.D. 350), and it concerns a child.[26]

There are, on the one hand, two features in the story that argue for its originality: (1) the many Semitisms,[27] suggesting at least that an Aramaic community has been heavily involved in its creative transmission; (2) the vivid and picturesque details of the time of day, the disciples taking Jesus "just as he was," the allusion to other boats and the mention of the cushion,[28] none of which seem to have theological significance. On the other hand, there are two features of the story that could tell against it having its origin in the ministry of Jesus.

1. Many Old Testament themes are echoed—for example, a reversal of the Jonah story;[29] God's command of and calming of roaring seas[30]—which, at least, leads to the impression that the transmission of the story has been influenced by them.[31] But it will be difficult for many to imagine how the story could have arisen directly or indirectly from these texts.

2. Although it is the only story in the Gospels where Jesus saves his followers from trouble (allowing the story to pass the discontinuity test), it is similar to rescue stories in the early church (thus passing the coherence test), such as Peter being released from prison (Acts 12:6-19) and Paul being preserved in a shipwreck (Acts 27:13-44). However, apart from this theme there are not sufficient parallels between these stories to conclude that the stilling of the storm had its origin in the early church.

The evidence adduced in discussing historicity appears to be finely balanced, denying the possibility of confident results. Therefore *historians* once again have to leave open the question of the origin of this story.

§16.5 A Woman with a Hemorrhage (Mk 5:21-43/Mt 9:18-26/Lk 8:40-56)

Contrary to popular opinion, in the chapter on the miracles in Mark, I argued that before Mark received it, this story was woven together with that of the raising of Jairus's daughter (§3.16). Notwithstanding, this issue can be left to one side in trying to determine the likelihood of this story arising in the reports of those who witnessed Jesus' ministry, for this story is readily intelligible on its own.

The heart of the story is the woman touching Jesus' clothes to connect with his healing power. This is a method of healing commentators generally reject out of hand as impossible, or they attempt to rationalize it.[32] However, though the belief in the special powers or representative nature of clothing is well attested in the Old Testament,[33] mentioned by Josephus (*Ant.* 8:353-54) and also found in Acts 19:12, Mark, or any other Christian writer we know in the New Testament, does not seek to draw attention to the method. Indeed, it is unlikely that the early Christians would have invented a story about a woman breaking the Jewish purity regulations, stealing power without authority and possibly attempting to find a cure by handing on the disease,[34] without in any way drawing attention to these themes or speaking of the woman's positive motives in a way that would clear her of these possible indictments.[35]

Further, as unacceptable as it may be to modern minds, I have on numerous occasions seen people who are seeking Christian healing fall to the floor on being touched or almost touched, even by a person approaching unseen from behind the suppliant. Another hint of historicity comes in Jesus being portrayed as ignorant of who touched him. We could expect a story created by Christians to have Jesus know who touched him. Also, it is unlikely that the early church would have inserted into a story a scene where the disciples are rebuking Jesus, as they do in response to his question, "Who touched my clothes?" (Mk 5:30).

The originality of the story may also be endorsed by its structure: the miracle is attested in the woman's mind (Mk 5:29) and (simultaneously?) in Jesus' mind (5:30), followed by a dialogue between Jesus and his disciples (5:31) and with the woman (5:32-34), which includes her dismissal and the word of healing, even though the healing had already taken place (5:34). There is no characteristic applause from the crowd.

Although there is only one attestation, I would conclude that there are sufficient elements in this story to suggest it had its origin in the ministry of Jesus.[36]

§16.6 Feeding a Multitude (Mk 6:32-44/8:1-10/Mt 14:13-21/15:32-39/Lk 9:10-17/Jn 6:1-15)

As we already noted, C. K. Barrett urges that John is dependent on the Synoptic Gospels.[37] However, comparing this story in Mark with that in John,[38] the most reasonable conclusion is that John was not using the Gospel of Mark as we have it.[39] If he was, he would have to have been randomly selecting phrases from each story and unaccountably omitting key features, such as "breaking" the bread (Mk 6:41; 8:6) and particularly the idea of "wilderness," which would have been useful to his cause and is picked up later.[40] From this it can be concluded that John and Mark are independent witnesses to this story.

In Mark there are two feeding stories, which, though exhibiting differences, are so similar[41] that it is most likely that a single story lies behind them. Yet one story is not the reworking of the other. The Mark 6 version is closest to the John 6 version, so the Mark 8 story could be a reworking of the previous one.[42] But Mark 8:1-10 contains a surprising number of words and phrases that are unique in Mark, yet not of specific theological interest to him, and there are a few striking similarities to John's version of the story.[43] Further, if Mark were creating this story, we would expect the typical Markan rebuke of the disciples. But that does not come until the clearly redactional passage in 8:14-21.[44] It is best to come to the conclusion that Mark has given us two, and John a third, version of this story.[45]

What then of the historical reliability of what stands behind the reports? That this is the only miracle story that occurs in all four Gospels is not in itself helpful, for Mark and John are the only sources. One of the major objections to possible historicity is the suggested influence of the feeding attributed to Elisha (2 Kings 4:42-44),[46] and the parallels are significant:[47] (1) the miracle worker gives an impossible direction to feed a large group of people with a small amount of food; (2) there are two kinds of food mentioned; (3) an objection is raised; (4) the miracle worker persists in his request; (5) the miraculous feeding takes place; and (6) there is a surplus of food.

Yet there are important differences between the Jesus and Elisha stories: (1) the Elisha story has no details of setting and time; (2) there is no crowd following Elisha; (3) there is no background, preparation or motivation for the miracle in 2 Kings; (4) a man brings food to Elisha, but in the Gospels the disciples seek food after the story has begun; (5) the Old Testament story does not mention the crowd being seated or any preparation of the meal, two features often seen to be allusions to the Last Supper; (6) the disciples' objections precede Jesus' actual command to give food to the people; (7) the Gospel stories give details of the leftovers; and (8) the Elisha story is one of prophecy-fulfillment in structure, whereas in the Gospels it has a situation-miracle-demonstration structure.

So with Meier we can conclude that "while the Elisha story does share a number of basic elements with the primitive Gospel story, there is much in the Gospel miracle not found in and not derivable from 2 Kgs 4:42-44."[48] This means that, though we cannot preclude the influence of the Elisha story on the development of the one about Jesus, the later story probably does not have its origin in a reworking of the earlier one.

The same conclusion is reached evaluating the suggestion that the feeding stories have their origin explained by an appeal to the story of the Last Supper. On the one hand, with the mention of Jesus taking the bread, giving thanks and giving it to the disciples or crowd, it is inconceivable to me that, at any stage of their history, these stories could have been told without the hearers—even the Johannine readers—reflecting on the Last Supper.[49] But, on the other hand, the Passover meal cannot be seen as the source of any of the feeding stories: the fish motif is absent in the Last Supper stories, and the cup motif is absent in the feeding stories.[50] If the feeding is to be explained in light of the Last Supper, why weren't the anomalies corrected?

Returning then to the question of historicity, we have to take into account that the story is independently attested twice in Mark and once in John. In favor of taking these stories as reflecting an event in the life of Jesus is their cohering with the theme of Jesus speaking of the coming kingdom of God as a banquet and his table fellowship, which included being part of great meals.[51] Aside from this we have little upon which to base a decision. We cannot place much emphasis on the mention of the detail of the grass (Mk 6:39; Jn 6:9). At first sight this may seem to be an incidental detail reflecting an eyewitness account, but it could have been inserted as a reminder that in the messianic age the desert will be fertile (cf. Is 35:1), or it may reflect the shepherd's role of leading his sheep to lie down in green pastures.[52]

Nevertheless in light of our earlier discussion we cannot agree with the Fellows of the Jesus Seminar that "the multiplication of loaves and fish is magic: it is the equivalent of changing base metals into gold, if taken literally."[53] Rather, our discussion leads to the conclusion that it is quite possible that behind these three reports there lies a single reliable reflection of an event in which Jesus miraculously fed a large number of people. However, there is not sufficient evidence—*at least for a historian*—to be certain.

§16.7 Jesus Walks on the Sea (Mk 6:45-52/Mt 14:22-33; cf. Jn 6:16-21)

In his report of the discussions of the Jesus Seminar Robert Funk reports that "the Fellows of the Jesus Seminar agreed that walking on the water was not based on a historical event and that it originated as an epiphany and not as a miracle story." Funk goes on to say that, "almost to a person, the Fellows doubted that Jesus actually walked on water."[54] The difficulty of this miracle for modern minds to comprehend is seen by some of the incredible explanations offered. For instance, Karl Friedrich Bahrdt (1741-1792) said that walking on the sea is to be explained by supposing that Jesus walked toward the disciples over the surface of a great floating raft that they could not see.[55]

The story is attested independently by Mark and John,[56] and the story was early associated with the feeding of the crowd, so it certainly has a significant history prior to Mark and John using it. Vincent Taylor thought that the description—at least in the Markan account—of the hurried departure of the disciples under the constraint of Jesus, the reference to Bethsaida, the picture of the rowers buffeted by a contrary wind and their cry of fear on seeing Jesus suggested that the narrative had a factual base.[57] But such details could equally be the result of skilled storytelling, especially when they are theologically significant.[58] In any case, Taylor attempts to remove the miraculous element from the story by saying that in the original story "the action of Jesus in wading through the surf near the hidden shore was interpreted as a triumphant progress across the waters."[59] But the text does not allow us to draw this conclusion.

One of the outstanding features of the story is the great number of contacts with Old Testament themes concerning, for example, God walking on the sea,[60] such that Jesus is portrayed as acting as God. Such high Christology does not preclude the story from being early, for high Christology is evident in such early material as the pre-Pauline christological hymn in Philippians 2:6-11.[61] In any case, although the story may be infused with Old Testament themes, it is difficult to imagine how these contacts in themselves could give rise to this particular story.[62] Nevertheless the Old Testament contacts lead Meier to draw attention to two considerations that weigh heavily against the historicity of the story.[63]

1. Meier points out that the vast majority of the miracle stories of Jesus seek to

help an individual or group of people in great need rather than focus on Jesus' status or self-glorification, as this one does. Here the disciples are not seen to be in mortal danger but are simply straining at the oars in a heavy wind. Though all the miracles have implications for how Jesus is understood, this is usually implied rather than, as here, portraying Jesus as willing to reveal himself in the grand manner of the God of Job or Second-Isaiah. But in response to this point it must be asked: Is it not possible—indeed, highly likely—for Jesus to have conducted miracles that were not all of the same type? Could he not conduct a miracle for his exhausted followers?

2. Connected to Meier's point of the uniqueness of this miracle is that, though most of the other miracle stories are merely permeated with the "atmosphere" of the Old Testament or contain echoes to Old Testament stories, in this story allusions to Old Testament texts come to the fore and dominate.

Supposing Meier to be correct we would have to ask, What is the source of this story? It is generally thought that the most primitive version of the story is John's, which in turn shows many features of the postresurrection narratives.[64] However, the connection between the story of walking on the sea and that of the feeding is sufficiently strong and old that the latter is unlikely to have had its origin in a postresurrection story.[65] So Meier in turn suggests that, being early associated with the feeding story, it was created as a commentary on it. As the feeding was understood by the early church to prefigure the Last Supper and the celebration of the Eucharist, the story of the walking on the sea was created to draw out theological aspects of the Eucharist.[66]

In favor of this view Meier points out that many so-called high christological statements seem to have their origin in worship, as is evident in statements about Jesus' preexistence found in early hymnlike material. Thus the walking on the sea is "a symbolic representation of one way in which the church experienced the risen Christ in its celebration of the eucharist."[67]

I agree with Meier that the story of the walking on the sea stands out as distinct from the other miracle stories. However, we have little evidence that the early Christians created stories ex nihilo, and the examples of high Christology in hymnlike material cited by Meier bear no formal relation to the storylike material of the walking on the sea.

One answer to the dilemma about the historicity of the story would be to suggest that, although the author of the Fourth Gospel assumes it to be a miracle, it was not originally reported as a miracle story. Raymond Brown has noticed the lack of emphasis on the miraculous in the Johannine version.[68] Although the story as we have it in both Mark and John says—and probably means—that Jesus was walking "on the sea" (*epi tēs thalassēs*, Mk 6:49/Jn 6:19), not near it, this same phrase is used in John 21:1 to mean he was by the sea on the beach (cf. Jn 21:4).[69]

It then could be argued, keeping in mind the use of *epi tēs thalassēs* ("on the sea") and in light of the boat immediately reaching land as they wanted to take Jesus into the boat (Jn 6:21)[70]—and there being no acclaim of God or Jesus as the result of what happened—that Jesus was walking on the very edge of the sea (or in the shallows) as the disciples reached shore.[71] With this as the core of the tradition, it may be concluded that the story developed in light of Old Testament texts that were able to reflect a so-called high Christology.

However attractive, this is admittedly speculation. Approaching this story *with the tools and skills of a historian* we can go no further than to say that, as incredible as the story seems to modern minds, it cannot be ruled out of court as historically unreliable, for even the little information available (adduced, for example, by Vincent Taylor) points to the possibility of historicity. This possibility is increased and the uncertainty we faced when dealing with the feeding story is decreased when we take into account the corollaries between the stories of the feedings and walking on the water in Mark 6, 8 and John 6. There may have been a cluster of events—including a large feeding and Jesus walking on the sea—that occurred in the life of the historical Jesus.[72]

§16.8 A Deaf-Mute Healed (Mk 7:31-37/Mt 15:29-31)

If we remove from this story[73] the probable Markan introduction (about Jesus returning from the region of Tyre, Mk 7:31), we are left with a classic healing story without any indication of time or location. However, there are a number of aspects of this story that probably indicate we are reading a story that has good claim to go back to the reports of those who were in Jesus' audience.

First, there is vocabulary we find only here in Mark: "impediment,"[74] "took him aside," "put his fingers," *"ephphatha,"* "be opened," "opened," "released" and "plainly." This is a remarkable number of non-Markan words in such a short miracle story.[75] This indicates that we have a story dissimilar to the general interests of the early church. Yet as we noted in introducing the stories of Jesus cleansing lepers (§15.1), this story coheres with the Isaianic new-exodus theme of the ears of the deaf being unstopped and the tongue of the speechless singing for joy (cf. Is 35:5-6).

Second is Jesus' method of healing—using his fingers and spittle. Generally Jesus is portrayed as healing through a brief, powerful command (e.g., Mk 5:41). It is unlikely that early Christians would create a story to enhance the reputation of Jesus while showing him to be using the methods of other healers.

Third, it can be particularly noted that Jesus looked up to heaven (Mk 7:34). At the time, this was a gesture preceding prayer,[76] so readers would assume that prayer—silent or expressed in the sigh—was part of the healing technique of Jesus. The importance of prayer for the historical Jesus has been well demonstrated,[77] and the early church, particularly reflected by Luke, enhanced Jesus' prayer life.[78] But even though prayer was apparently used in early Christian healing (Jas 5:14-15; cf. Mk 9:29), at only one point do we find a prayer attributed to Jesus as part of his healing technique—the raising of Lazarus (Jn 11:41-42). Even then the prayer is not really part of the technique but is for the benefit of the bystanders. These considerations give us considerable confidence in the historicity of this aspect of the story of the healing of the deaf-mute.

Fourth, the Aramaic word *Ephphatha* ("Be opened!") is one of only two such words or phrases found in the miracle stories of Jesus (cf. *talitha koum* in Mk 5:41). There is no proof that these words were thought to be magical. Rather, as the stories of Jesus were translated into Greek, some Aramaic words (including also *abba*) remained, probably for emphasis and dramatic effect.[79] Over against the conclusions of the Jesus Seminar that this story may have originated as a story about a charismatic healer other than Jesus,[80] these considerations taken together augur well for this story's faithfully reflecting an actual event in the life of the earthly Jesus.

§16.9 A Fig Tree Withered (Mk 11:12-14, 20-26/Mt 21:18-19, 20-22; cf. Lk 13:6-9)

Considerable obstacles exist in taking this story as coming from the ministry of Jesus.

First, on the one hand, the closest parallel to this story is the parable of the fig tree (Lk 13:6-9), so it is often suggested that Mark has turned the parable into a miracle story.[81] Yet, on the other hand, the only point of contact between the parable and the miracle is the futile search for figs from a barren tree. Indeed, in the parable there is a period of grace for the threatened tree, whereas in the miracle the tree is condemned at once and withers. The moral to be drawn from the parable is a warning against spiritual unproductiveness. Yet the miracle is a warning against a deceptive show of productiveness and a lesson in faith, prayer and forgiveness (cf. Mk 11:20-24).

Further, for Mark—most probably the earliest Gospel—to be using a story in a later Gospel to present the earlier form of the story in such a chaotic way is a difficult assumption. On balance, it is unlikely Mark or his predecessors depended on the parable of the fig tree for the miracle story.

A second difficulty in accepting the historicity of this story is voiced by Robert Funk: "Causing an unproductive fig tree to wither seems uncharacteristic of the historical Jesus. A senseless miracle of retribution, triggered by a petty, even petulant, response, is scarcely a mode of behavior that comports with the Jesus who restored a withered limb."[82] That is, this story does not pass the test of coherence with those we have taken to be historical. Thus, though we find miracles in an early church setting that are destructive and punitive,[83] other than this story we find no other punitive miracles associated with Jesus in the Gospels.[84] This point is considerably weakened, though not I think destroyed, in light of the episode of the destruction of the pigs associated with the story of the healing of the Gerasene demoniac. In contrast to the cursing of the fig tree, the episode of the killing of the pigs was incidental to the miracle, only a part of the story, and not initiated by Jesus.[85] In the fig tree story we are faced with a narrative dominated by destruction initiated by Jesus.

Third, this miracle story does not pass the test of discontinuity, for not only are there many punitive miracles in the Old Testament and Apocrypha,[86] it also contains many echoes of Old Testament texts concerning blessing and judgment.[87] Thus the cursing of the fig tree fits the milieu of the Old Testament rather than with what many have come to see as characteristic of Jesus.

From what we have said so far, the most reasonable conclusion to draw from the evidence would be that if there is some activity of Jesus reflected in this story, it is most likely to be something along the lines of Jesus teaching his disciples some lessons in light of not finding figs on a tree, rather than a miraculous cursing of a tree. It was only later assumed that Jesus first cursed the tree.

Indeed, if we isolate this story from the wider context of Jesus' ministry and simply set it in a list alongside miracle stories that probably go back to the historical Jesus, it stands well apart from—does not "cohere" well with—what we have come to expect as saving, healing or helping events at the hands of Jesus.

However, to take up the suggestion of Max Turner,[88] the result is different when we set this story in the context of Jesus' critical appraisal of Judaism, his confrontation with Jerusalem (note the cleansing of the temple)[89] and his repeated warnings that the kingdom of God will burst in judgment upon a Judaism that embraces a separatist and nationalist "holiness" resistance movement. In this context the story of the cursing of the fig tree becomes the kind of prophetic symbolism or parable[90] that we might even anticipate, except that it is quite dissimilar to the remainder of Jesus' miracles.

A historian then, although unable to decide on the historicity of the story, certainly cannot dismiss the possibility of this story being an authentic reflection of an event in the life of the historical Jesus.

§16.10 The Large Catch of Fish (Lk 5:1-11; cf. Jn 21:4-14)

The following features are shared by Luke and John as they report this story:[91]

☐ The disciples have caught nothing after fishing all night.

☐ The disciples are told to put out their net(s) again.

☐ A large catch of fish results, though the nets are not damaged.

☐ Peter[92] expresses a response to what has happened, but the other disciples are silent.

☐ Jesus is called "Lord."

☐ The stories end with a mission call for Peter.

☐ The theme of missionary activity is common to both stories.

☐ The name Simon Peter appears in both, the only time the double name is used in Luke.

Yet the differences between Luke's and John's story are significant. For instance, Luke has it before, whereas John sets it after, the resurrection, and there are in Luke no crowds or other boats involved, nor is there a meal prepared on the beach by Jesus after which he asks Peter whether he loves him. Therefore good reasons exist for seeing John and Luke as preserving different versions of the same story. In turn, if we are dealing with two versions of the same story, the next obvious question to ask is who has preserved the most original.

It seems probable that some stories have made their way from their original post-Easter context to their present pre-Easter setting.[93] In the present story Peter says, "Go away from me, Lord, for I am a sinful man!" (Lk 5:8). This is a unique saying in the Gospels: a concrete confession of sin as the first and foremost reaction to meeting the earthly Jesus. In that Jesus is called "Lord," it is also an expression of high Christology. Though this is not impossible in the life of Jesus, it fits better in a post-Easter setting. Therefore it is more likely that the Fourth Gospel has preserved the oldest version of our story.[94] However, having come to this conclusion is not, in itself, to suggest that the story is historically unreliable.[95]

Contingent on the veracity of this story is the question of the historicity of a resurrection appearance that centers on Peter. That the risen Jesus appeared to his followers after Easter—not least to Peter—ought to be taken quite seriously. For not a generation after Easter, Paul gives independent witness to Jesus appearing not only to more than five hundred and the Twelve and James, but to Cephas/Peter as well (1 Cor 15:5-7). Notably Paul says he is handing on material he has received. He also says he is prepared to have his evidence scrutinized (1 Cor 15:6).

That the appearance to the disciples should take place in the context of a fishing expedition—and in Galilee—adds to the historical reliability of the story, for at least Matthew, Mark and the Fourth Gospel agree that Galilee was the focus of the resurrection appearances.[96] Therefore, though we cannot be certain about some of the details that may have been added for their allegorical or thematic value, such as the mention of the beloved disciple (Jn 21:7), bringing the story into parallel with the story of the empty tomb, on balance it is probable that the risen Jesus appeared to his followers and performed a miracle as broadly outlined in this story.[97]

§16.11 A Man with Dropsy Healed (Lk 14:1-6)

Although this story may be principally about a dispute between Jesus and some lawyers and Pharisees, the healing of the man with dropsy, which provides part of the setting for the controversy, is the focus of interest. Again, with Luke being the only witness to this story, we are at a disadvantage in seeking its historicity. Though this is the only time the word *dropsy*[98] occurs in the Old and New Testaments,[99] this is not in itself an impediment to a historical investigation.[100]

Notwithstanding, the preponderance of Lukan language has caused many critics to conclude that the story is the creation of Luke.[101] Without argument, Bultmann took it to be a variation of the story of the healing of the man with a withered hand (Mk 3:1-6).[102] Yet, though it could be argued that a miracle story may be created to provide the backdrop for a dispute between Jesus and his opponents, the stumbling block before such an easy dispensing of historicity is that it is inexplicable why Luke or any of his predecessors should choose such a healing as dropsy. It forms no part of Old Testament expectations, nor, so far as we know, was it a healing that was of any interest to the early church. The most natural conclusion to draw is that Luke has heavily rewritten a story that was found in his sources and that this cameo has its origins in the reports of the first witness of the ministry of the historical Jesus.

§16.12 Healing the High Priest's Slave's Ear (Lk 22:50-51)

All four Gospels record a story of one of those who was with Jesus when he was arrested drawing a sword to cut off an ear of the high priest's slave.[103] But only Luke says that Jesus "touched his ear and healed him" (Lk 22:51).[104] It is often said that Luke has only Mark as his source for this story.[105] Yet the miracle story is readily explicable as coming from Luke's hand: the first few words of the verse use a Septuagintal phrase ("answering, he said," cf. Gen 18:9), and the word *healed* is distinctively Lukan.[106] The word order of verse 50 ("the slave of the high priest"), however, is not only different from that in Mark, it is hard to attribute to Luke.[107]

Thus if Luke has access to another source here[108] the question is open as to the origin of this miracle story in miniature. Even though the story may cohere exactly with Jesus' "paradigm of mercy,"[109] it is just what we would expect of the gentle and compassionate Luke. Historians then are obliged to leave open the question of historicity, being unable with any certainty to trace the story back earlier than Luke's Gospel.

§16.13 Turning Water into Wine (Jn 2:1-12)

Meier has subjected this story to detailed scrutiny in order to determine whether it is probable that this remarkable feat at Cana in Galilee can be traced back to the ministry of Jesus.[110] He rightly notes how different this story is from other Gospel miracle stories: (a) instead of a clear request for a miracle, there is the laconic observation, "They have no wine!" (Jn 2:3); (b) Jesus plays no active part in performing the miracle, save giving directions (cf. the story of the large catch of fish); and (c) in the public response to the miracle, there is not the expected astonishment at the wonderful deed of Jesus. Instead, there is praise for the quality of the wine by an uninformed headwaiter. This leaves us puzzled as to how the disciples knew that Jesus had revealed his glory (2:10-11).[111] These aspects of the story, though not all unique, place it out of character with the other miracle stories and raise questions in our minds as to whether Jesus can be credited with changing the water into wine.

However, details such as this being the only miracle in which Jesus' mother features and in which a wedding is involved do not tell against its historicity.[112] Indeed, such unnecessary details could be said to point to the historical veracity of the report.[113] (Nevertheless we are about to question this in the next paragraph.) It cannot even be argued that this kind of miracle has no parallel in the Synoptic Gospels, for the feeding stories show that it was thought by the Synoptic writers that Jesus performed miracles of supply.[114]

The great difficulty in tracing this story back to the ministry of Jesus arises when we pare away those elements of the story that seem most likely to come from the hand of the Evangelist, for we are left with very little.[115] First, the mention of "the mother of Jesus" is probably redactional, for John consistently suppresses her name, referring to her in this way while sometimes mentioning others by name in the same verse.[116] Second, the pattern of request and apparent refusal by Jesus— also found in the stories of healing of the official's son (Jn 4:47-48) and the raising of Lazarus (11:3-6)—serves the Johannine theme of safeguarding Jesus' sovereign control over his life and the situation. Third, the headwaiter saying that he did not know "whence" (2:9, author's translation) the wine had come is most likely a Johannine idea, for *whence (pothen)* is generally used in John to refer to Jesus' heavenly origin.[117] (In paring away these three elements, we are dealing not only with issues of style but with content that is inextricably bound up with these elements of style.)

Nevertheless despite such a temptation I am not convinced that the stupendous nature of the report makes it suspiciously Johannine in origin. The "size" of a miracle in itself cannot be used to tell against its historicity. Also, the reference to the wine cannot be used to raise doubts about the reliability of the story because of its Old Testament echoes.[118] It is just as reasonable to see the echoes after the event as to construct a story to create the echoes. Indeed, in view of the social importance of weddings, it is highly likely that Jesus did attend a wedding.[119]

Another problem in trying to trace this story back to the historical Jesus is the fact that the figure of the headwaiter is unknown in the Jewish Palestine of Jesus' time.[120] On the one hand, we know of no custom or rule to which the headwaiter refers when he says, "Everyone serves the good wine first." On the other hand, we know that writers felt free to create fictitious customs.[121] Whereas this element of the story may have been introduced or enhanced, this cannot be used to tell against the historicity of the story as a whole. It is also strange that a small hill town in Galilee should be able to host such a large event (unless the story has been relocated from a Greco-Roman setting) and that Jesus and his mother are portrayed as giving orders to the hosts.

From a philosophical perspective it may be quite rational to consider this story to be based on a true story.[122] Nevertheless, keeping in mind the various factors mentioned here, *historians with limited critical tools* are left unable to pronounce with confidence for or against its historicity. We will therefore leave the door open on the question.[123]

§16.14 Some Results
Looking back over the last two chapters we can set out our results as follows:

A. Many stories can be judged with high confidence to reflect an event or events most likely in the life of the historical Jesus:
   1. A demoniac in the synagogue at Capernaum (§11.3; Mk 1:21-28/Lk 4:31-39)
   2. The Gerasene demoniac (§11.4; Mk 5:1-20/Mt 8:28-34/Lk 8:26-39)
   3. The Syrophoenician woman's daughter (§11.5; Mk 7:24-30/Mt 15:21-28)
   4. The epileptic boy (§11.6; Mk 9:14-29/Mt 17:14-21/Lk 9:37-43a)
   5. A paralytic forgiven and healed (§12.2; Mk 2:1-12/Mt 9:1-8/Lk 5:17-26)
   6. A withered hand cured (§12.3; Mk 3:1-6/Mt 12:9-14/Lk 6:6-11)
   7. The official's servant/son healed (§12.4; Mt 8:5-13/Lk 7:1-10; cf. Jn 4:46-54)
   8. A crippled woman healed (§12.5; Lk 13:10-17)
   9. Healing the paralytic at Bethesda (§12.6; Jn 5:1-9)
   10. A blind man at Bethsaida (§13.2; Mk 8:22-26)
   11. Blind Bartimaeus (§13.3; Mk 10:46-52/Mt 9:27-31/20:29-34/Lk 18:35-43)
   12. Healing a man born blind (§13.4; Jn 9:1-7)
   13. Jairus's daughter (§14.2; Mk 5:21-43/Mt 9:18-26/Lk 8:40-56)
   14. The widow of Nain's son (§14.3; Lk 7:11-17)
   15. The raising of Lazarus (§14.4; Jn 11:1-57)
   16. A leper cleansed (§15.2; Mk 1:40-45/Mt 8:1-4/Lk 5:12-16)
   17. Healing Peter's mother-in-law (§16.3; Mk 1:29-31/Mt 8:14-15/Lk 4:38-39)
   18. A woman with a hemorrhage (§16.5; Mk 5:21-43/Mt 9:18-26/Lk

8:40-56)

19. A deaf-mute healed (§16.8; Mk 7:31-37/Mt 15:29-31)

20. The large catch of fish (§16.10; Lk 5:1-11 and Jn 21:4-14)

21. A man with dropsy healed (§16.11; Lk 14:1-6)

22. A coin in a fish's mouth (§16.2; Mt 17:24-27)

B. Another group of stories has provided too little data to be pronounced with the same degree of confidence historically reliable. But it is important to repeat that it is not that there *cannot* be a reliable reflection of a miraculous event behind these reports. Rather, when historians ask the question "Did it happen?" the nature of historical research is such that these stories cannot, based on available data, be said with the same degree of certainty to reflect (or, indeed, not to reflect) an event in the life of the historical Jesus. Intellectual humility is required here.

23. Ten lepers cleansed (§15.3; Lk 17:11-19)

24. Stilling a storm (§16.3; Mk 4:35-41/Mt 8:23-27/Lk 8:22-25)

25. *Feeding a multitude (§16.6; Mk 6:32-44/8:1-10/Mt 14:13-21/Lk 9:10-17/Jn 6:1-15)

26. *Jesus walks on the sea (§16.7; Mk 6:45-52/Mt 14:22-33 and Jn 6:15-21)

27. A fig tree withered (§16.9; Mk 11:12-14, 20-26/Mt 21:18-19, 20-22/Lk 13:6-9)

28. Healing the high priest's slave's ear (§16.12; Lk 22:49-51)

29. Turning water into wine (§16.13; Jn 2:1-12)

Again, it is not that these stories do *not* reflect events in the life of the historical Jesus—they possibly do. The possibility may be greater with the two starred stories than with the others in this category (see §16.7). Notwithstanding, in these instances historians do not have the data or the tools and skills to say more.

§16.15 Taking Stock

We have come to the end of what for many, as I suggested at the outset of this part, will have been difficult chapters. We have been trying to pass judgment on the historicity of all the miracle stories attributed to Jesus and recorded in the Gospels. This exercise will have been difficult for some in that it assumes the possibility of miracles. Other readers will have found this discussion frustrating, for they will have concluded that I have "sold out" to those who do not take the Bible as "the Word of God."

Therefore I repeat something else already mentioned: this exercise has not been intended to call into question either the value of the Bible or the identity of Jesus or his *ability* to perform miracles. Indeed, in the words of Bishop A. E. J.

Rawlinson, "The broad truth of the Christian doctrine of the Incarnation once assumed, no wise person will proceed rashly to draw limits between what is and what is not possible."[124] Rather, I am asking questions that will help us comprehend better the book in which we have invested so much value and help us understand the Jesus about whom it speaks and what he can mean for us.

In part four we have been able to establish that, with varying degrees of confidence, the vast majority of the Gospel miracle stories can be traced back to those who witnessed and reported about the ministry of the historical Jesus. Also we have found no good evidence that any of the miracle stories are legendary or have their origins outside the Christian tradition. But as already stated, without taking into account the discussion of the possibility of miracles, these reports could be taken to be mistaken. In light of advanced knowledge of medicine, physical science and human behavior, what was once reported as miracles could now (it might be argued) be reported in other ways. This assertion prompted the brief philosophical discussion in chapter two.

Holding together what has been said in these chapters with the philosophical discussions of chapter two, it can be concluded not only that *reports have been recovered of miracles in the Gospels that can, with considerable confidence, be traced back to the ministry of the historical Jesus* but also that *there is good reason to accept these reports as being of genuine miracles—events that would not have occurred save through the intervention of God.* Further, it is almost universally held in the Gospel traditions that a great deal of Jesus' public ministry was taken up with performing miracles.

This conclusion, while of no surprise to some impatient readers, is of profound importance in any credible reconstruction of the historical Jesus. In simple terms, *it is not possible to do justice to the historically verifiable material in the Gospels without seeing the historical Jesus as being as much a miracle worker as a teacher and one who died and is risen from the dead.*

In the next and final chapter we will refine this statement, drawing together the threads from part four on the miracles of Jesus and history. We will also spell out the implications of this study for the quest for the historical Jesus.

PART 5

Conclusions

Seventeen

Jesus the Miracle Worker

....

§17.1 Introduction

What do the Gospel writers say about Jesus' miracles? How did Jesus understand his miracles? To what extent do the miracle stories in the Gospels reflect "what actually happened"? And what are the implications of the answers to these questions for the quest for the historical Jesus? These four questions have provided the stimuli for this historical and theological study of the miracles of Jesus. We will now set out in summary fashion the results of this study.

§17.2 The Miracles of Jesus in the Gospels

With chronology as our guide, we could have begun with an examination of the Jesus of history. Instead I chose to begin with the miracles in the Gospels. I took this as our point of departure because it enabled us to start with the Gospels as they stand (see §1.2). This approach has also enabled readers to become familiar with the miracle stories as they appear in the New Testament before moving on to more difficult and potentially unsettling issues relating to historicity. Beginning with the miracles also maintains an acknowledgment that it is the perspectives of the Gospel writers that provide the primary parameters of our understanding of Jesus and the miracles.

Therefore, as I said in chapter one, the first and major objective of this study has been to discuss how the Gospel writers understood the miracles: for example, what they understood to be the implication of the miracles for their portrait of Jesus; the place of the miracles in their message about Jesus; and what they understood the miracles to mean for their readers. It is answers to these questions that are most important in forming our views on the miracles of Jesus.

§17.3 The Miracles in Mark

Any study of the miracles in Mark has to take into account two views that are part of the modern debate about Mark: that Mark set out to pour scorn on the miraculous element in his tradition, and that Mark has attempted to portray Jesus as a "divine man."

1. One view is that Mark set out to pour scorn on the miraculous element in his tradition and to encourage his readers to put their faith in the powerlessness of Jesus instead of in his miracles. However, we saw that Mark uses miracles to accompany and thereby interpret the passion (Mk 15:33, 38; 16:1-8) and to encapsulate (9:26-27) as well as adumbrate Jesus' self-giving death (6:41; 8:6). That is not what we would expect if Mark was trying to dissociate the miraculous from the powerlessness of Jesus.

We also saw that the miracle stories and summaries presented Jesus as spectacularly powerful and successful, and the disciples are also portrayed as miracle workers. Clearly it is reasonable to conclude that Mark is not denigrating the miracles of Jesus, nor is he simply including them (even reluctantly) because they were in his tradition. He writes too positively of the miracles for that (e.g., Mk 1:27-28; 2:12; 4:41).

On the other hand, we have been able to show that Mark was attempting to stress the magnitude and significance of the miracles in Jesus' ministry. Jesus was so powerful in working miracles that a mere touch of his clothing brought healing and his words could raise the dead, so crowds flocked to him. Considering the amount of space given to the miracle stories, they are no less significant than—and, as has been shown, cannot be separated from—his self-giving weakness evident in his suffering, adumbrated in the miracle tradition.

2. Another view that must be considered in the study of Mark's miracles of Jesus is that Mark has attempted to portray Jesus as—or alternatively correct the view that Jesus was—a "divine man" *(theios anēr)*. But I repeat what I said earlier: the concept of a divine man who performed miracles proves to be a figment of scholarly imagination, and the search for Mark's understanding of miracles in relation to a *theios anēr* Christology proves to be thoroughly misguided.

In answer to the question, "What does Mark say about the miracles of Jesus?" we can set out the following points:

☐ *Who is Jesus?* The prime function of the miracles in Mark is to be the centerpiece in helping readers identify Jesus. In the stories, Jesus is "of God," "Son of God," one empowered by the Holy Spirit, the Messiah, one acting for God, and God himself uniquely present and active. Therefore the miracles, which encapsulate the whole of Jesus' ministry, bring eschatological salvation.

☐ *The powerful self-giving Messiah.* Because of the virtual absence of miracle stories after Jesus arrives in Jerusalem, the reader is left with the impression that Jesus' self-giving nature so far hinted at in the miracle stories is now given full rein. Jesus the powerful miracle worker—identified as the Messiah and God—chooses to offer himself, powerless, into the hands of the authorities in order to die "for many" (Mk 10:45). In other words, the miracles identify Jesus as the powerful Messiah—indeed, *God himself at work*—who gives himself to death for others.

☐ *Miracles as parables.* The miracles are not unequivocal heavenly signs but are parabolic in nature, ambiguous in their message. Ambiguity is seen in the miracles provoking a great variety of responses—from hostility and criticism to correct acclamations of Jesus' identity. We asserted that the ambiguity puts Mark's reader in the same position as in relation to the teaching: faith-insight is required to understand who the miracle worker is and what the miracles accomplish.

☐ *The kingdom in miracles.* As parables, the exorcisms represent, but are also in themselves, the freeing and healing of sick people, as well as the destruction and plundering of Satan's kingdom and the realization of God's kingdom.

☐ *The commands to silence* in Mark carry two themes. (1) Some of the commands to silence show that Jesus' true identity is improperly comprehended apart from his passion and death: the healer and exorcist without the suffering Jesus is an incomplete and misunderstood Messiah. Jesus is the Son of God in his powerful miracles as well as in his powerless death. (2) Other injunctions to silence function as foils for Mark to highlight the inability of Jesus' miracle ministry to remain hidden. They spill out into Gentile territory, and the Gentiles receive Jesus with acclaim equal to that accorded by the Jews.

☐ *Jesus the miracle worker.* Mark wishes to establish the importance of the miracles, perhaps in the face of those who saw Jesus as only or primarily a teacher. Thus as a healer Jesus is addressed and sought as teacher, and in his teaching he is sought as a healer. Nevertheless Mark is establishing that miracles are *primus inter pares* in relation to the teaching in his portrait of the ministry of Jesus.

☐ *Conflict.* In the miracles, as well as in other aspects of Jesus' ministry, Mark proposes the view that Jesus' ministry involved conflict[1]—conflict with Satan and with the religious leaders, a conflict that saw its climax in the passion. The theme of conflict is significant at least in that it provides a foil to show that healing and forgiveness, first seen in the ministry of Jesus, remain integral to the ministry of his followers.

☐ *Miracles and faith.* Though miracles may cause astonishment, disbelieving questions, conspiracy to destroy Jesus, fear, unbelief or a demand for Jesus to leave, it is repentance and faith that are the responses Mark applauds in relation to all Jesus' activities.

□ *Miracles and discipleship.* Faith or prayer—personal or vicarious—is so integral in Jesus' healing the sick that, apart from the exorcisms, there is no healing story that does not include some expression of trust in Jesus either before, during or after the healing. Faith is essential not only in Jesus being willing, but also in his ability, to perform miracles. In turn, the miracles are an encouragement—a summons or demand to repentance and faith—to be with Jesus, to follow him or to serve him on the basis of the eschatological salvation offered in the miracles.

□ *The Gentiles.* The high level of faith Jesus encountered among the Gentiles is probably a reflection of the prominence of Gentiles among Mark's readers rather than a failure of the mission to the Jews, for they also are shown to respond to Jesus in faith.

□ *Fear* is a frequent response to the miracles in Mark, for whom fear is the awesome realization of the power evident and available in Jesus' miracles. As is best illustrated in the final scene of the Gospel, the faith of Mark's readers shows that the response of awe to the miracle of the resurrection became faith, and faith became the grounds for unstoppable proclamation of the good news.

□ *Miracles as models.* Not only does Mark teach directly through the miracle stories but—in so far as the disciples are called to emulate the ministry of Jesus—the miracle stories also provide models for ministry.

§17.4 The Miracles in Matthew

Being placed first in the New Testament canon has meant that Matthew's interpretation of the life and ministry of Jesus has dominated the church. In turn, Matthew's understanding of the place of the miracles in the ministry of Jesus has probably determined the generally accepted view of the miracles. This leads to our first conclusion about the miracles in Matthew.

□ *Jesus the teacher.* Not least by arranging the nine miracle stories of chapters 8 and 9 to form the second panel of a diptych with the Great Sermon, Matthew not only proposes that Jesus' ministry is to be understood as one of word and deed but indicates that his readers are to give preeminence to the teaching above the miracles. This means that Matthew has left the unmistakable impression—which has established itself in mainstream Western orthodox Christianity—that in his portrait of Jesus the teachings are more important than the miracles.[2] Of all the Gospel writers, Matthew gives the miracles the least significance.

□ *Jesus is the new Moses.* Jesus also fulfills the hopes of Isaiah 53 as the Messiah of word and deed. Thus Birger Gerhardsson's conclusion—that "Matthew considers the mighty acts of Jesus as *miracles in the sense of extraordinary, sensational events*"[3]—is insufficient. The miracles in Matthew are of someone who is much more than this: he is the Messiah through whose miraculous deeds the reign of God is present.

❑ *Jesus as God.* Matthew's minimalistic rewriting of the miracle stories focuses attention on Jesus as God himself acting mightily among his people because of who he is. Yet Jesus is not a self-seeking, triumphant miracle worker. He is a humble servant acting out of compassion and associating with outsiders and outcasts.

❑ *Miracles, faith and Jesus.* Miracles in themselves neither create faith nor dispel doubt. Rather, they confirm a person's position in relation to Jesus. Yet faith is not any achievement that evinces the compassionate Jesus' willingness to heal. Nevertheless, probably to display his powerful independence, Jesus sometimes grants healing without any mention of faith. In the story of Peter's mother-in-law there is no mention of faith—hers or anyone else's. We noted that not even those in the house are said to believe vicariously or to tell Jesus of her plight. Jesus is depicted as asking absolutely no conditions to be prepared to heal her. Seeing her is enough to move him to heal her. And it is service rather than faith that is portrayed as her appropriate response to Jesus.

❑ *Faith, when it is evident, is a practically expressed confidence in Jesus' ability and willingness to heal.* The smallest imaginable amount of faith is all that is required. However, more than "little faith" is required of the disciples if they are to model the ministry of Jesus as they receive and use the power he gives them.

❑ *Salvation is available to the Gentiles.* Faith evinces the compassionate Jesus to act.

❑ *Exorcism.* Perhaps because of the difficulties Matthew saw exorcists causing in the church, he has downplayed the role of exorcism in the ministry of Jesus and the early church. However, as for Luke, Matthew still believed that exorcisms revealed Jesus' true identity and were the first stage in the defeat of Satan so that God could fulfill his purpose for his chosen people in bringing them the experience of the reign of God.

❑ *Miracles as models.* The miracle stories have been used by Matthew as lesson aids for his readers in their healing ministries.

❑ *Miracles and the cross.* More clearly than in the other Gospels, Jesus performs his miracles in the shadow of the cross, for the exorcisms cause the Pharisees to begin to plot against Jesus, and the two feeding stories foreshadow the suffering and triumph of Jesus in that they contain echoes of the Last Supper and, in turn, the eschatological banquet.

§17.5 The Miracles of Jesus in Luke

Examining the way Luke presents the miracles of Jesus has given rise to a number of interesting issues that have perplexed contemporary scholarship. The main features of our conclusions can be set out in the following statements:

❑ *The Spirit and miracles.* The agenda Luke sets for Jesus (Lk 4:18-19) and the saying about Jesus casting out demons by the finger of God (11:20, which he would have understood as God's hand, arm or Spirit), leave us in no doubt that Luke saw God's Spirit as the source of Jesus' ability to perform miracles. The significance of this conclusion is that the Spirit gives rise not only to prophecy but also to the miracles of Jesus. This is important in that we are not able to sideline the miracles of Jesus in Luke—they arise as much in response to the empowerment of the eschatological Spirit as does the teaching of Jesus. Though the Gospel of Matthew may permit post-Enlightenment Christians to ignore the miracles in any "essential" portrait of Jesus, Luke will not permit that intellectual luxury.

☐ *The miracles and "power."* Another way Luke attributed the miracles of Jesus to God was through the use of the word *power (dunamis)*. Luke's concept of power is not to be understood against a background of the universal idea of magical miracles. He understands "power" primarily in light of the Septuagint's associating power with God and the Spirit. Notwithstanding, this power is also understood as an impersonal force so powerful that it works independently of Jesus, as well as immediately and impersonally in response to the contact of a believer.

☐ *The ambiguity in miracle.* With the Fourth Gospel especially, and to a lesser extent with Mark, Luke recognizes the ambiguity of the miracles of Jesus—an ambiguity for which he offers no resolution. We saw this in his depicting the source of the miracles as being in the Spirit of God as well as in *dunamis* ("power"). In the Beelzebul controversy and in the notion of anyone being able to perform miracles (Acts 8:9-11), we also observe the ambiguity of miracles in Luke. Nevertheless Luke uses miracles to identify Jesus and to demonstrate that God himself is at work in them, for healing and salvation—the same word *(sōzein)*—are a piece in Luke.

☐ *The miracles and Jesus.* Not only do the miracles show Jesus to be the Messiah, to be a man of compassion, to be obeyed, to be Master (of his disciples), and to be in control of the natural elements, they also identify Jesus as God at work. This leads to the next point.

☐ *Salvation and the miracles.* That Jesus brings the salvation of God, the use of "Lord" for Jesus, the editorial changes to the miracle stories, that the healings include outsiders and that the response of the healed person or the crowd was to praise or glorify God show that the mighty and merciful work of God is to be discerned in the miracles of Jesus and that those healed are able to share in the radiance and majesty of God.

☐ *The importance of exorcism.* Though the importance of exorcism diminishes in Mark as the story of Jesus progresses, Luke on the other hand sustains its importance in a number of ways: by linking exorcism with Jesus' empowerment by the Spirit through the inclusion of exorcisms in his summary of the first stage of Jesus' public ministry; by recasting healings as exorcisms; by portraying exorcism as if Jesus is performing a healing; by inserting brief mention of exorcisms; and by including the story of the Beelzebul controversy.

☐ *The significance of the exorcisms* for Luke is that, as for Matthew, they show Jesus' ministry to be the first stage of the defeat of Satan so that God could fulfill his purpose for his chosen people in bringing them the experience of God's reign.

☐ *The miracles are the good news.* The miracles do not illustrate or demonstrate the good news of Jesus. They are themselves, with the teaching, the good news of Jesus.

☐ *Faith is the preparation and the product of miracle.* In spite of our hesitancy with regard to the faith-generating value of miracles, Luke unashamedly constructs his story of Jesus and edits the individual stories so that they become the ground of faith and discipleship. Equally firmly Luke considers faith to be not only the possible but the required preparation for and response to the miracles of Jesus. In a proper understanding of the miracles of Jesus and, in particular, for the miracle of healing to be salvation for the recipient, this faith is to be directed toward God.

☐ *A balance between word and deed.* For Luke there is no primacy of word over deed in the ministry of Jesus. Instead, there is a deliberate attempt to strike a balance between the significance of what Jesus said and what he did. Not only is exorcism brought into balance with the other healings of Jesus but Luke's editorial adjustments to the stories in his tradition and the arrangement of material reveal a balancing act of word and deed unique among the Gospel writers (which he also carries through into Acts).

☐ *Miracles in the church.* Like all his contemporary Christians (though more obvious to us through his account in Acts) Luke was convinced that Jesus' followers were to carry on his ministry of miracles.

§17.6 The Miracles in the Fourth Gospel

No other Gospel gives such a high profile to the miracles of Jesus. Yet no other Gospel has so few miracle stories. No other Gospel portrays the miracles as so profound and larger than life or other worldly. No other Gospel has such distinctive language in relation to the miracle tradition. And this is the only Gospel that gives no hint of Jesus being an exorcist. It is not surprising then that discussions about the miracles in this Gospel have been fraught with difficulty and that on some issues, such as historicity and the existence of a signs source, there are no clear answers.

Our summary of findings and conclusions on the miracles in the Fourth Gospel can be stated as follows:

☐ *The priority of miracle.* With the last Gospel in the canon we reach the other end of the spectrum from Matthew's perspective, who saw the miracles taking second place behind the teaching of Jesus. In the Fourth Gospel the miracles take center stage. The miracles are the centerpiece of the presentation of Jesus. They do not illuminate the teaching of Jesus; they are the message of Jesus, and the words of Jesus are required to explain what are portrayed as life-giving eschatological events.

□ *The miracles as signs.* By using the word *sēmeion* ("sign") for the miracles, the Fourth Gospel is saying that the miracles, like the parables of the Synoptic Gospels, are symbols pointing to something beyond the event to the true identity or glory of Jesus and his filial relationship, even identity, with the Father. Whereas non-miraculous actions of Jesus can be understood as "symbolic actions," the miracles stand in a class of their own as "signs" that God himself is the author of these extraordinary events that authenticate the identity of Jesus and elicit faith in him and the Father.

Also, because John has Jesus twice say "the hour comes and now is" (Jn 4:23; 5:25, author's translation; cf. 12:30-31), we are alerted to the glory of Jesus being seen not only in the story of Jesus' death but also in the signs.[4] The miracles are not only the signs of a future reality of God's glory but are, as in the Synoptic miracles, in themselves the reality of God's present reign seen in Jesus' ministry.

□ *The miracles as signs of the great sign.* In John's Gospel there is a progression of signs of roughly increasing magnitude reaching a crescendo in the raising of Lazarus. This final miracle-sign of the earthly Jesus, both prefigures the great sign of the death and resurrection and also is the prism through which to look back at the other signs and forward to the parousia. Thus the ministry of miracle-signs, though no less significant than the great sign, is nevertheless seen to anticipate the larger and clearer sign of the glory of God in Jesus: the great sign of the death and especially the resurrection of Jesus.[5] In turn, the great sign anticipates the final earthly sign of the return to the Father, which itself is an anticipation of the return of the Spirit and the parousia (Jn 13—14).

□ *Miracles and the identity and destiny of Jesus.* In the latter part of the Gospel the glorification of Jesus is no longer focused in his relationship with the Father—evident through the mighty miracles—but in his return to his Father. Thus the signs of the first half of the Gospel reveal the *identity* of Jesus, whereas the great sign of the second half of the Gospel—the death and resurrection of Jesus—reveals his *destiny* as the risen Lord ascended to his Father. This means that the miracle-signs were more than a preparation for the full revelation of the glory of God in Jesus in the second half of the Gospel. They have a distinct, even if also limited, function in revealing the Jesus who will die and rise. Hence the necessary separation of the signs from the sign in John, which is told uncluttered by miracles. Yet in both the miracle-signs and the great sign of the death and resurrection and the sign of the return to the Father, the glory of God in Jesus is being revealed.

□ *Miracles as the work of God.* The Septuagint uses *ergon* ("work") for the salvific work of God on behalf of his people. In using the same word for the whole ministry of Jesus, as well as for the miracles in particular, the Fourth Gospel conveys the idea that God is to be understood as the author of what is seen in Jesus' miracles.

Further, though the miracles are a distinct "work" of Jesus, John blurs the distinction between the miracles, the words and the entire work of Jesus such that in the miracles—as much as in the overall ministry of Jesus—God is to be understood as the agent of what is seen in Jesus.

□ *The Jesus of the signs.* The Jesus of the signs is never entirely or fully disclosed. Instead, at one level we are given hints of Jesus' identity by means of parallels echoed in the stories: parallels with Dionysus, Moses, Elijah and Elisha, for example. At another level we are to anticipate the identity of the Jesus of the signs as we look through the prism of these stories to the passion and ascension, where his glory will be fully revealed. He will have been revealed as "the Messiah, the Son of God," and the one who gives life (Jn 20:31).

However, at a further level what is being revealed is not a god or a divine being but a human being. Even in the most spectacular miracle—the raising of a dead man—Jesus is still a human being weeping, for he is "the Word [that] became flesh" (Jn 1:14)—an earth-bound, transient and perishable person. Yet—and we must say yet—there is such a close identity between Father and Son in the signs that, in Jesus, the Father himself is disclosed and encountered.

Such a high view of the Jesus of the miracles means that he takes the initiative in conducting the miracles. Also, Jesus is so significant that his actions are not determined by anyone but the Father. Jesus is not even portrayed as being motivated by compassion, even when the disciples are in a life-threatening storm.

In the Synoptic Gospels the kingdom of God is being established in the miracles—the miracles are not primarily pointing to anything outside themselves. For John, the Jesus he is portraying and the implication of the Word becoming flesh is far beyond what can be captured in even the most profound miracle. The miracles—even those of the passion and ascension and including those still to be performed by his followers—can only be signs pointing beyond themselves to the true identity or glory of Jesus, to his filial relationship, or even identity, with the Father and, eventually, to the parousia. The miraculous cannot simply be tangible illustrations or expressions of the message of Jesus. Even though they are the centerpiece of the ministry of Jesus, they are but signs.

□ *Miracles and faith.* John's Gospel illustrates a number of possible responses to Jesus in relation to the miracles: refusing to see the signs with any faith; similarly, seeing signs without responding in belief; seeing the signs, but only as wonders or portents and so believing in Jesus only as a miracle worker; seeing the true significance of the miracles, thus enabling belief in Jesus and an understanding of who Jesus is in relation to the Father.

Also, John expects those who encounter Jesus to trust his word. They will then witness the miracles. It is as if John is saying that belief ought to be able to be based not simply on *both* the words and the works (miracles) of Jesus but on the words alone, even though miracle-based faith can be sufficient.

There will be those (in the church) who believe in Jesus without seeing any signs, at first glance conveying the idea that faith in Jesus not based on the miracles is a superior level of faith. However, we have seen that this is not a criticism of miracle-based faith in itself. Rather, it is a caution that miracle-based faith may be a misunderstanding of who Jesus is. Also, this apparent criticism of miracle-based faith does not mean that the miracles (in the church) are dispensable or will cease and be replaced by the sacraments. Some will never believe without seeing miracles.

Also, there are those who see signs without even knowing who Jesus is, let alone believing in him in order to experience a miracle. A person without initial faith in Jesus is able to experience a miracle.

□ *No exorcisms.* It is not that this Gospel is embarrassed by the techniques of exorcism. Rather, (1) relatively commonplace exorcisms were not sufficiently spectacular to convey the work of God in Jesus. (2) In replacing the theme of the kingdom of God with the kingship of Jesus, the exorcisms associated with the kingdom were also laid aside. (3) The defeat of Satan is tied to the cross so that references to the exorcisms were probably necessarily removed.

□ *The Fourth Gospel.* At the start of our investigation of the miracles in this Gospel we said we would use the term *Fourth Gospel* for the Gospel as we have it and *John's Gospel* for the edition that ended at John 20:31. Insofar as chapter 21 is an appendix to the Gospel and does not read as a correction of it, we take it that the person, or persons, who published the Gospel as we now have it was in full agreement with what John had said about the miracles.

Nevertheless it is probable that the single miracle story of the Fourth Gospel (that of the large catch of fish) is to be understood not so much as functioning as a sign but as having its meaning revealed allegorically. If that is correct (see §7.10), the significant aspects of the story we noted that bear on the theology of miracles in the Fourth Gospel can be set out in this way:

1. The number of fish—whether or not it is a genuine recollection—is possibly intended to reflect the reality of the resurrection and the expected success of the mission of the church.

2. Connected to this, the story becomes the Fourth Gospel's illustration of the Great Commission in 20:21 ("As the Father has sent me, so I send you") being successful, even through seemingly irrational obedience to Jesus.

3. The church will be able to contain all who can be brought into its compass—without being destroyed by division.

4. The story may be intended to convey a blessing of fruitfulness on the life of the church.

5. In Jesus being recognized in the context of the taking and distributing of

bread, the publishers of the Fourth Gospel, as does John, see the miracles as revealing the nature of Jesus as the one whose death is the means of feeding his followers.

§17.7 The Miracles in the Gospels

Summarizing the results of this study of the miracles in the Gospels as we have, the variety of perspectives is apparent. Yet there are clear common threads in all the Gospels. The most obvious one is that the Gospel writers are all convinced that the miracles of Jesus carry in them the signature or fingerprints of the One who performed them. That is, *the miracles of Jesus reveal his identity as God himself at work: indeed, God is encountered in the miracles.* Thus the miraculous activity of Jesus is the eschatological work and message of salvation.

This revelation through and in the miracles themselves is not without ambiguity, for the responses to Jesus' miracles range from disbelieving antagonism to worshipful faith. That is, the miracles are a grounds not only for discipleship but also for the antagonism of Jesus' opponents. Notwithstanding, in all the Gospels the miracles can be the basis of faith, and all Gospel writers would probably agree with William Paley (cf. §1.6.1) that divine revelation is inconceivable apart from miracles.

All of the Gospel writers are agreed that the miracles of Jesus are more than the marvels of a prophet. We see this most markedly in their avoidance of the phrase "signs and wonders" to describe the miracles of Jesus. Neither Matthew nor Mark uses the term for Jesus' miracles (Mk 13:22/Mt 24:24), and John uses it only once in a slightly negative tone (Jn 4:48). Luke uses the phrase just once, most probably to allow the Septuagintal idea of the miracles being points at which the saving power of God can be known and to validate Jesus' origin and ministry, as well as to promote faith in Jesus.

At the risk of seeming simplistic, in Mark, the earliest Gospel, Jesus is the miracle worker who teaches and must also suffer. In Matthew, Jesus is the teacher who also performs miracles. Luke carefully balances Jesus' ministry of word and deed. Not so John (and the Fourth Gospel). Here Jesus is in such communion with, and is to be so identified with, God that he is first and foremost the author of the most stupendous wonders, which are signs of his unmistakable identity, origin and destiny seen preeminently in the sign of his death and resurrection.

Even if we should wish to set aside the historical Jesus as we construct our understanding of the nature of Christianity, we still have to contend with the four Gospels. These Gospels place the miraculous intervention of God into everyday life at such a high level—both for Jesus and for his followers—that most contemporary Christians will need to reassess the nature of the Christian life to include such a perspective.

§17.8 The Problems of History and Method

Achieving our remaining objectives takes us behind the message of the Gospels to the traditions of the Jesus about whom they write—to the meaning of the miracles for Jesus and to the question of the extent to which the miracle stories of Jesus in the Gospels reflect "what actually happened," as well as to how answers to these questions impact on the quest for the Jesus of history.

The order in which we deal with the questions of how Jesus understood his miracles and in what way the stories in the Gospels reflect "what actually happened" has been problematic. On the one hand, how Jesus understood his miracles depends on the way we answer the prior questions as to whether or not Jesus performed miracles and which, if any, of those stories now in the Gospels can be traced back to the historical Jesus. On the other hand, we need to decide how Jesus understood his miracles in order to judge which stories now reported in the Gospels cohere with this decision and so are most likely to reflect an event in his life.

I chose to take the latter approach, dealing first with Jesus' understanding of his miracles, for we were able to proceed with the help of general observations such as his choice of miracles and a number of sayings generally agreed to be authentic. Nevertheless, recognizing the circularity of my argument, we had to anticipate some of the conclusions from later in the study in discussing how Jesus understood his miracles.

In addressing the historical questions, I have been aware that some readers will have wanted to retreat in fear—the fear that the so-called facts of the faith will recede and their basis of faith will have shrunk, leaving them insecure. Such insecurities are unfounded.

In the first place, we have seen that at almost every turn there is good evidence that Jesus performed mighty works. We have to say "almost every turn," for there is, at first sight, the puzzling evidence from Paul. We saw it argued that Paul, our earliest known Christian writer, tells us nothing at all about the miracles of Jesus. However, we saw that at least in Romans 15:18-19 and 1 Corinthians 4:20 there are hints that Paul probably considered Jesus to have performed miracles and that these miracles were an important part of Paul's teaching about Jesus.

In the second place, insecurities in the face of the unsettling questions of historicity are unfounded. If we take our cue from the early Christians, their security came not only from their historical tradition but also from the conviction that the ongoing encounter with the risen Jesus was also intrinsic to the basis of faith.

The fears of readers in facing the historical questions turn out to be unfounded. Even with the very blunt tools of historical inquiry, we have shown that we can have considerable confidence in the great majority of the stories in the Gospels' being traced back to the historical Jesus.

However, there turned out to be some stories that provided too little data for us to be able to pronounce—with the same degree of confidence we had with the majority of stories—that they are most likely historically reliable. (There was just one story, the brief comment that involved the healing of the high priest's servant's ear, for which we have so little information that all that can be said at this stage of research is that it cannot be traced back earlier than Luke's Gospel.)

But I want to repeat that it is not that there *cannot* be a reliable reflection of a miraculous event behind even these stories. Rather, it is that when *historians,* with limited data and with obtund research tools, ask "Did it happen?" some stories cannot be said with equal certainty to reflect or not reflect an event in the life of the historical Jesus. As is often the case, we have had to acknowledge the limits of historical inquiry and exercise intellectual humility.

Also, I have been keeping in mind other readers who will want to retreat from the question of historicity for an opposite fear—the fear of discovering that the miracle stories can neither be dismissed as mythical nor as foreign accretions to the Jesus tradition. Nor can they be shifted to the periphery of the ministry of the historical Jesus. We have discovered this fear to be well founded, for in answer to the question "Did Jesus perform miracles?" we have to reply with an unequivocal and resounding "Yes!" We have seen that it is not a matter of so-called blind faith that enables us to say this.

From a historically critical examination of the Gospels, there is good evidence and grounds for saying that the historical Jesus not only performed miracles but that he was an extraordinarily powerful healer of unparalleled ability and reputation. We have good reason to agree with Ernest Renan that "it is probable that the hearers of Jesus were more struck by his miracles than by his eminently divine discourses."[6]

We have found no grounds whatsoever to agree with Norman Perrin's view that "we cannot, today, reconstruct a single authentic healing or exorcism narrative from the tradition we have."[7] Nor can we agree with Renan's statement that "the miracles of Jesus were a violence done to him by his age, a concession forced from him by a passing necessity."[8] To the contrary, essentially of his own choosing Jesus was a miracle worker, and the great mass of miracle stories can be shown to be recoverable reflections of the ministry of the historical Jesus.

The necessary conclusion, in light of our inquiry, is that *there is hardly any aspect of the life of the historical Jesus which is so well and widely attested as that he conducted unparalleled wonders.* Further, *the miracles dominated and were the most important aspect of Jesus' whole pre-Easter ministry.*

I have also been aware that some readers will have been impatient with my historical inquiry for different reasons. Some will consider the burden of proof in arguments about historicity—especially where the miraculous is said to be involved—to be on those who want to argue for authenticity. However, in order to carry as many readers with me as possible, I have accepted the burden of proof in all aspects of the inquiry.

I also took time to discuss how we can recover and represent the past, for in the last two centuries of critical biblical research and the development of the skills of modern historical research during the last century, it has come to be recognized that a prima facie reading of the text of Scripture does not always give us the information we would wish in order to reconstruct the past. Therefore in attempting to reconstruct "what actually happened" as well as views of the historical Jesus on his miracles, we need to undertake some preliminary inquiries and set out our method of approach.

Other readers will have been impatient because this approach will be thought to betray a lack of faith in the "Word of God" as a reliable or infallible record of the activity of the incarnate Son of God. But, as I said in §9.1, I have not intended to call into question either the value of the Bible or the identity of Jesus or his *ability* to perform wonders. Instead, what I have been trying to achieve is a better understanding of the book in which we Christians have placed so much value and to help us hear more clearly what it is saying about the Jesus of the miracles.

§17.9 The Meaning of the Miracles for Jesus

Another of my objectives—the second in this study of the miracles of Jesus—has been to determine how Jesus understood his miracles. There was a time not long ago when it was generally agreed that not only could we know almost nothing about the life of Jesus, we could know even less about his thought. But insofar as a person's words and actions reflect that person's thought, I have been asserting that it remains possible to be able to recover what Jesus thought about his miracles.

In light of some of Jesus' statements, such as

If in God's Spirit I cast out demons, then has come upon you the kingdom of God (Mt 12:28/Lk 11:20, author's translation)

or

Go and tell John what you hear and see: the blind receive their sight, the lame walk, the lepers are cleansed, the deaf hear, the dead are raised, and the poor have good news brought to them (Mt 11:4-5/Lk 7:22)

it is hard to avoid the conclusion that Jesus thought he was an (or the) anointed figure or Messiah from God, involved in the eschatological happenings around him. This may not be a popular course of inquiry at present. Yet to be true to the evidence from this study the fact cannot be ignored that, at least *because of his miracles,* Jesus appears to have been conscious that he was God's key figure or Messiah in a situation where he thought God's reign, expected at the end of time, was taking place in his activities.[9]

We also noted that, given the confines of his self-imposed Jewish mission, in making choices of the kinds of miracles he conducted and the methods he used, we can make some judgments about Jesus' understanding of his miracles. Thus the choice of exorcism as his principal category of miracle, along with its interpretation, shows that he saw his ministry as primarily a battle with Satan and his minions. (In the Fourth Gospel this is preserved, though the battle is centered in the cross, not in the exorcisms.)

Though performing exorcisms would not, initially, have been seen as obviously the work of a Messiah, Jesus' healing of cripples and paralytics would have been understood to reflect the messianic hopes of the Old Testament. Further, in the raising of the dead Jesus shows that he saw himself as doing the work of God. The same conclusion is to be drawn from his choice to calm a storm, walk on the sea and feed thousands with a small amount of food. This self-understanding is in line with Jesus' technique of not including prayer in his miracles but speaking to effect miracles, as if he was operating out of his own resources.

Asking the question about Jesus' view of the precise relationship between his miracles and the coming of the kingdom of God results in a number of answers (see §10.17). It is often said, for example, that the miracles are "signs" having little or no intrinsic significance save to point beyond themselves to the more important message of the kingdom of God or, as in the case of the Fourth Gospel, to Jesus himself. But our inquiries suggest that Jesus had a different understanding of the relationship between miracle and message. It is not that Jesus understood his miracles to be evidence of the dawning or nearness of the kingdom of God. Rather, *the miracles are themselves the eschatological kingdom of God in operation.*[10]

This issue has led to another problem. When we were discussing the meaning of the miracles for Jesus, there was a problem of accounting for Jesus' self-consciousness in view of the great variety of messianic expectations and for miracles' not generally being expected of messiahs. I suggested that the answer is probably to be found in the coincidence of two factors for Jesus: on the one hand, Jesus was conscious of being empowered by God's Spirit (cf., e.g., Mt 12:28/Lk 11:20); on the other hand, he appears to have been aware that his miraculous activities had echoes in some of the Isaianic expectations of the messianic age.

Therefore it seems to me that despite the general hesitation of contemporary scholarship, we are bound to conclude that *through the experience of the presence of the Spirit of God in him that enabled him to perform miracles, Jesus was uniquely aware that he was God's anointed individual or Messiah, who was at the same time at the center of these eschatological events that were expressions of God's reign or powerful presence.*

Strictly, all we had done in part two ("The Miracles of Jesus in the Gospels") was to establish that the Jesus of Nazareth was judged by observers to have conducted a great number of wonders or marvels. Therefore the third of our objectives, the most difficult, was to see to what extent the miracle stories of Jesus in the Gospels reflected "what actually happened." At the conclusion of chapter sixteen we listed the many stories (twenty-two of the twenty-nine) that I judged most likely to reflect an event or events in the life of the historical Jesus (see §16.14).

The remaining seven stories provided too little data to pronounce with the same degree of confidence that they are most likely historically reliable. But, to repeat, it is not that there *cannot* be a reliable reflection of a miraculous event behind these reports. Rather, it is that when examining this material it is not possible for historians to say with the same degree of certainty that these stories do (or do not) reflect an event in the life of the historical Jesus.

We stand in a different position from those of the first century in our understanding of the natural world. Thus we may conclude that what were then reported as miracles we would now report differently. Hence we took a brief excursion into a more philosophical field (see chapter two). This enabled us to establish the *possibility* of miracles. In conjunction with our examination of the Gospel stories associated with Jesus, it is more than reasonable to accept the vast majority of the reports in the Gospels to be historically authentic as miracle *qua* miracle stories.

Before drawing together the results on our fourth objective relating to the quest for the historical Jesus, three other issues need to be dealt with.

§17.10 What Is a Miracle?

In light of our study of the miracles in the Gospels, we can now give an answer to the question, "What is a miracle?" (§1.3). As we develop a definition of a miracle from the perspective of the Gospel writers, we can begin with what a miracle is not.

1. Hume's idea of a miracle being a "violation" of the laws of nature is foreign to the ethos of the Gospels. As noted by A. E. Taylor, who well expresses the assumptions of the Gospel writers, "Properly speaking, there are no laws of nature to be violated, but there are habits of expectation which any one of us, as a fact, finds himself unable to break through."[11]

Further, Hume's idea of a miracle being a violation of nature cannot be taken up, because a "violation" implies an ethically improper action.[12] There is no suggestion in the Gospels that Jesus' miracles were so considered, at least by his followers. Of course, his detractors are reported concluding differently, as, for example, when the sabbath was violated.

2. We also have to set aside the idea of coincidence as inherent in a definition of a miracle of Jesus in the Gospels. It is true that we have seen numerous cases where coincidence is part of the story, as in, for example, the story of the large

catch of fish (Lk 5:1-11; cf. Jn 21:1-11). However, in every story it is Jesus who is seen to be the cause of the miracle. Even Luke's story in Acts 16:25 of the earthquake setting Paul and Silas free would not have been seen as a coincidence, for earthquakes were evidence of God's presence (e.g., Ex 19:18; Is 29:6).

3. The idea that only God or his agents can perform miracles is also at least slightly at variance with what we have seen in the Gospels. In the story of the so-called strange exorcist (Mk 9:38-39/Lk 9:49-50) it is clear that those other than Jesus and his followers perform miracles. However, the essence of Jesus' reply is that the very performing of miracles makes the miracle worker his agent. Nevertheless in Luke's story in Acts of some exorcists—the sons of Sceva—attempting to perform miracles in the name of Jesus, the assumption is that they have been successful miracle workers outside the sphere of God or his agents (Acts 19:11-20).

4. In the first chapter we noted that Augustine (*City of God*, 10:22) saw conversion as the primary miracle (§1.3). However, though we have seen what may be termed *conversion* as part of a miracle story, that conversion is only the result of the miracle. This can be seen most clearly, for example, in the story of the healing of blind Bartimaeus.[13]

5. Turning to our positive conclusions about the notion of miracle in the Gospels,[14] at the very least we can say with John Macquarrie that a miracle is an event that *excites wonder* in the observers.[15] For underlying the concept of miracle in the Gospels is the idea of an event that is extraordinary or unusual, or even impossible, in light of the observed patterns of nature. Thus we find Matthew using the word *thaumasia* ("wonders") in 21:15 for the miracles of Jesus.[16] Luke 5:26 has the word *paradoxa* ("unexpected" or "remarkable things"), and in Luke 13:17 there is the word *endoxois* ("glorious things"). Behind these ideas is the Old Testament notion of *môpēt* ("portent," or "prodigious sign"), usually translated *teras* ("omen" or "wonder") in the Septuagint.[17]

6. But this is an incomplete understanding of the miracles of Jesus. Thus *teras* ("wonder") is never used alone of Jesus' miracles. Jesus is more than a man with sensational authority and power. He is seen as the "Son of God" (Mt 8:29; cf. 12:23) and is *reflecting the glory of God* in his healings (9:8; cf. 15:31).

7. Indeed, the Gospel writers are all convinced that the miracles of Jesus carry in them the signature or the fingerprints of the One who performed them. That is, the emphasis is on the One who is the source of the miracle.[18] On the one hand, they reflect the nature of Jesus as being from God or acting in his place. On the other hand, they reflect the nature of the powerful presence or reign of God evident in the activities of Jesus.

As part of this program Mark uses "power" *(dunamis)* or "powers" *(dunameis)*,[19] and John uses "sign" *(sēmeion;* see §8.5.3). Matthew and Luke use the

"Spirit (or finger) of God," giving clearest expression to this view in saying that the exorcisms of Jesus were the coming of the reign of God (Mt 12:28/Lk 11:20). So the miracles of Jesus are understood not only as a man of God performing wonders but as the power of God being uniquely appropriated in and by him.

□ *In short, for Jesus and the Gospel writers, a miracle performed by Jesus is an astonishing event, exciting wonder in the observers, which carries the signature of God, who, for those with the eye of faith, can be seen to be expressing his powerful eschatological presence.*

§17.11 The Origin of the Miracle Stories
One of the issues we have been facing from time to time is the theory that miracles have been invented and attached to the traditions about Jesus.[20] In his study of "The Form and History of Miracle Stories" Bultmann dealt with the ancient material that bears a resemblance to elements in the Synoptic miracle stories.[21] Bultmann was attempting to show that the early Christian tradition was dependent on Jewish and Hellenistic traditions for its miracle stories.

In *Jesus the Exorcist* I have already argued that Bultmann's case is unproven.[22] One of the solid conclusions of this study is that, although (as with any study of the past) the tools of critical history allow only varying degrees of certainty about the origin of the miracle stories of Jesus, *in no instance have we found there to be any reasonable grounds for seeing a Gospel miracle story as having its origin outside Christian traditions.*

§17.12 The Classification of Miracles
In discussions of the miracles of Jesus, it is customary to draw a distinction between the healings and so-called nature miracles.[23] The primary distinction between these two categories is seen to be that the nature miracles were witnessed or recognized only by the disciples, whereas other miracles were accessible to everyone. However, this distinction cannot strictly be held. For example, in the Johannine version of the feeding of the multitude, the crowd "saw the sign" (Jn 6:14).

Another suggested reason for the distinction between the healing and nature miracles is that the nature miracles are seen to be legendary and created by the early Christians.[24] Again, in view of the conclusions in §16.14, this distinction does not hold.

Even though we have no clear saying from Jesus (cf. §§10.9-16) that would suggest he performed what we call nature miracles,[25] the "deeds of power" *(dunameis)* said to be done in Chorazin and Bethsaida could have been intended to be or include "nature miracles" (§10.14). Also, Jesus' saying that a person of faith could command a mountain to be cast into the sea[26] "could indicate a conviction on Jesus' part that the spiritual powers at work in him and through him could affect and alter the course of nature."[27]

Further, the suggested close correspondence to Old Testament stories or the incorporation of significant Old Testament themes sets the so-called nature miracles apart. Yet in part two we found that Old Testament themes were apparent in many other stories.

Finally it is asserted that the miracles of revivification and the nature "miracles embody and promote beliefs and practices which unquestionably characterized the early church, making it possible to assign them a transparent, symbolic meaning."[28] But this could also be said to be true for the stories of, for example, exorcism, the opening of the eyes of the blind and the healing of lepers and the deaf. Consequently contrary to the convention adopted in many discussions of miracles, we have not seen any warrants in the Gospel traditions for delineating healing from the so-called nature miracles.

The miracle stories have been classified in other ways, for example,[29] according to function: those stories seeking to draw attention to Jesus (pure exorcisms and miracle stories) and those that give account of existing Christian communities. (For example, the story of Bartimaeus is thought to give account of the Jericho community.)[30] But this can only be deemed speculative.

Martin Dibelius distinguishes between paradigms and novellas, primarily on the basis of paradigms being characterized by the following: being rounded off by a deed or saying of Jesus; their brevity and simplicity; their emphasis on a saying of Jesus; and having approving words of the crowd. Novellas are distinguished by being longer and descriptive for their own sake, with proofs of success.[31] But on careful examination, such distinctions do not hold among the miracle stories.[32]

Rudolf Bultmann distinguished nature miracles from other miracle stories and also isolated those miracle stories (e.g., the healing on the sabbath) that are not told in the style of miracle stories but have been completely subordinated to the point of an apophthegm.[33] However, where there is teaching of Jesus in the miracle story, sometimes the teaching and sometimes the miracle is the "occasion" for the story.[34]

Further, miracle stories have been classified according to their objects (say, loaves of bread or a lake) or their characters (say, the lame or the blind).[35] There is also the suggestion that some miracles are those of assistance (such as walking on the sea) and some are those of power (as in the case of those in the Fourth Gospel).[36] Delling distinguishes cures, prodigies, epiphanies of gods, proof miracles demonstrating the supernatural, rescues and punishment miracles.[37] Theissen has categorized the miracle stories according to themes: exorcisms, healings, epiphanies, rescues, gifts and rule miracles.[38] However, apart from the exorcisms, the Gospel writers generally do not make distinctions among the kinds of miracle stories they relate (cf., e.g., Mk 1:32-34; Lk 7:22). Therefore any categorization other than this one would be an imposition on the Gospel writers.

§17.13 Miracles and the Historical Jesus

The fourth and final objective was to see what implications these inquiries might have for the quest for the historical Jesus. Though the canon of Scripture may be the measure for our faith—rather than our varying reconstructions of the historical Jesus—one of the reasons for our interest in the Jesus of history is to determine whether the Gospels' presentations of Jesus are broadly credible. If they are not, the basis of our faith is gone and we are of all people most to be pitied, for we cannot, with Rudolf Bultmann and Luke Timothy Johnson, sever faith from historicity any more than could the first Christians, who understood the credibility of the new faith to depend on the credibility of their historical tradition (e.g., 1 Cor 15:17-20). Their writings were historically intended. Thus our research enables us to set forth the following important preliminary conclusion: The Gospels have given a credible picture of Jesus as a miracle worker that coheres well with the historical Jesus we are able to reconstruct. In fact, contrary to the comfort of many modern readers, the Gospels of Mark and John, where the miracles are at the forefront of the portrait of Jesus' ministry, probably provide the most faithful reflections of the general character of the life and ministry of the historical Jesus.

1. *The First Quest.* We are regularly told that since the rise of "critical" scholarship the study of the historical Jesus has gone through a number of identifiable stages.[39] What is now known as the Old, or First, Quest for the historical Jesus is said to have begun in 1778, when Gotthold Ephraim Lessing published posthumously an anonymous article by Hermann Samuel Reimarus (1694-1768) called "On the Intention of Jesus and His Disciples."[40]

There followed significant contributions from, among many others, David Strauss (see §1.7) and Ernst Renan (1823-1892), who said, for example, that against his will Jesus was compelled to found his work upon miracle.[41] Another key figure was Johannes Weiss (1863-1914), who stated that it was through the impact of his powerful personality that Jesus aroused the sick.[42]

However, as is well known, confidence in this enterprise to recover the main features of the historical Jesus was dashed in the early twentieth century with the publication of Albert Schweitzer's magnum opus *The Quest of the Historical Jesus.* Schweitzer concluded that the Jesus who had been recovered was "a figure designed by rationalism, endowed with life by liberalism, and clothed by modern theology in an historical garb."[43] Partly in light of this devastating critique—that all historians had found (and, by implication, were likely to find) was a reflection of themselves—and partly because of the irrelevance of a Jewish apocalyptic prophet that had been reconstructed, as well as the argued irrelevance of the historical Jesus for faith, little place was given to the study of the historical Jesus for some time.

2. *The Second Quest.* However, on October 20, 1953, Ernst Käsemann (then a professor at Göttingen and later at Tübingen) delivered a lecture at a reunion of Marburg students in Jugenheim on "The Problem of the Historical Jesus."[44] Käsemann concluded "that there are still pieces of the Synoptic tradition which the historian has to acknowledge as authentic if he wishes to remain an historian at all."[45] He affirmed the importance of the historical Jesus: "The Gospel is tied to him, who, both before and after Easter, revealed himself to his own as the Lord."[46]

The first fruit of what James M. Robinson called the "New Quest"[47] was Günther Bornkamm's *Jesus von Nazareth* (1956). Bornkamm's reconstruction emphasizes the words of Jesus. Indeed, there is only a token mention of Jesus' activities in Bornkamm's eighth chapter. The result is that the works—including the miracles—play no significant role in Bornkamm's Jesus. Some of the highlights of this short-lived Second Quest have included Joachim Jeremias's *New Testament Theology* (London: SCM Press, 1971), Geza Vermes's *Jesus the Jew* (Glasgow, U.K.: Fontana, 1976; Vermes is also seen to be part of the Third Quest) and Edward Schillebeeckx's *Jesus: An Experiment in Christology* (New York: Crossroad, 1979).

In light of our study, what remains striking in the Second Quest—which still continues, for example, in its emphasis on Jesus the teacher—is the paucity of attention given to the miracles of Jesus that loom so large in the Gospel traditions. From studying the miracles of Jesus we can only conclude that Jesus research remained under the spell of Hume, Strauss and Bultmann in this neglect. "If," to follow Colin Brown, "Harnack's Jesus had the face of a liberal Protestant, and Schweitzer's the heroic demeanor of Nietzsche's superman, the Jesus of the New Quest was an existential philosopher whose presence in history was barely discernible behind the kerygma."[48]

3. *The Third Quest.* Sometime in the early 1980s, while some were still debating the presuppositions and methods of the Second Quest, what is now termed the Third Quest emerged.[49] It had its origins in convictions that, in light of a reexamination of the wealth of Jewish material and working as historians, it was possible to recover quite a lot about the historical Jesus, and what was recovered was of ongoing significance for believers. These were two things the orthodox Bultmann school denied.[50]

The Third Questers are also said to be distinguished from those involved in the Second Quest in their view that the Jewish background and its continuity with Jesus is vital to explaining why there were powerful interests seeking and able to kill Jesus. Further, the Third Quest is notable in that Jews, Christians and agnostics are all involved in a search for Jesus that is more historically, than theologically, driven.[51]

It is clear the Third Quest is not simply a characteristic of recent studies of the historical Jesus. Indeed, at the time of his writing N. T. Wright regarded twenty contributors as particularly important to the Third Quest: Hans-Dieter Betz, Marcus J. Borg, S. G. F. Brandon, George B. Caird, James H. Charlesworth, Bruce D. Chilton, Sean Freyne, Anthony E. Harvey, Martin Hengel, Richard Horsley, Marinus de Jonge, Gerhard Lohfink, John P. Meier, Ben F. Meyer, Douglas E. Oakman, John K. Riches, E. P. Sanders, Gerd Theissen, Geza Vermes and Ben Witherington III.[52] It is not necessary to discuss each of these contributions. Brief comments on three will be sufficient to reveal one of the major problems that has been carried from the Second Quest into this Third Quest for the historical Jesus.

(a) E. P. Sanders' book *Jesus and Judaism* reflects one of the significant tendencies in the Third Quest: it does not begin with or depend on the sayings of Jesus for its reconstruction of Jesus. Instead, Sanders sees the most sure starting point for his investigation to be in Jesus' activity in the temple in that it provides the thread between Jesus' intentions and his death.

Sanders goes on to give attention to other activities of Jesus. However—and here we encounter the major problem in the Third Quest that is of special interest to us—despite so much of the Gospel material relating miracle stories, Sanders has only a small chapter devoted to a discussion of miracles. Indeed, when in his more popular book *The Historical Figure of Jesus* (London: Penguin, 1993) he offers a list of statements about Jesus that are almost beyond dispute and that belong to the framework of Jesus' life, he makes no mention of the miracles (pp. 10-11).

Yet it is not that Sanders thinks that the miracles are unimportant. He agrees with Morton Smith that the miracles attracted the crowds to whom Jesus proclaimed the good news of salvation to "sinners."[53] One of the reasons the miracles end up not being important in Sanders's view of the historical Jesus is that they do not contribute very much to his understanding of why Jesus died. Notwithstanding our finding to the contrary,[54] the flaw in this approach is that it assumes that in discovering why Jesus was killed we have discovered what was most important to Jesus in his pre-Easter ministry and how he would have been viewed. It also seems to assume that in discovering why Jesus died we have a means to determine the shape of the pre-Easter portrait of Jesus, which, in Sanders's case, bears a striking resemblance to Albert Schweitzer's view of Jesus as the eschatological prophet or seer.[55]

(b) In *Jesus: A New Vision* (San Francisco: Harper & Row, 1987), Marcus J. Borg agrees that Jesus was a man of deeds like Ḥanina ben Dosa and Honi the Circle-Drawer. "Indeed, to his contemporaries, it was the most remarkable thing about him. During his lifetime he was known primarily as a healer and exorcist."[56] He goes on to say that despite the difficulty miracles pose for the modern mind, on historical grounds it is virtually indisputable that Jesus was a healer and exorcist. But when it comes to what he calls "spectacular" deeds, such as resuscitation of apparently dead people, stilling a storm, walking on the sea, feedings of thousands of people, a "miraculous" catch of fish and the withering of a tree, he says it is very difficult to accept them.

To follow Borg: first, the historical verdict about whether such events really happen will depend, in part, on whether we think even a charismatic can do these kinds of things. Second, the symbolic elements in the stories make it difficult to determine what Jesus actually did. Thus these stories must remain in a "historical suspense account."[57]

So in the end, and somewhat inconsistently, the miracles of Jesus hardly feature in Borg's image of the historical Jesus, who is "a vivid witness to the reality of the Spirit."[58] For Borg, Jesus was a Spirit-filled figure in the charismatic stream of Judaism, a teacher of wisdom, a social prophet, a model for human life, a disclosure of God as compassionate in his healing and critical of culture in his movement away from securities.[59] But he was not one whose ministry was dominated by performing wonders.

(c) John Dominic Crossan's *The Historical Jesus: The Life of a Mediterranean Jewish Peasant* (San Francisco: HarperCollins, 1991) has been immensely popular. His proposal is that Jesus was a Mediterranean, Jewish, Cynic peasant whose aims are seen not simply in his teaching but also in his offering of free miracles and in his eating freely with anyone.

Crossan says that Jesus proclaimed and sought to institute a brokerless and egalitarian kingdom. Jesus was neither the broker nor the mediator but only the announcer that neither of these should exist between humanity and divinity. "Miracle and parable, healing and eating were calculated to force individuals into unmediated physical and spiritual contact with God and unmediated physical and spiritual contact with one another. He announced, in other words, the brokerless kingdom of God."[60] So although his treatment of the miracles covers only one of the fifteen chapters of his book, Crossan agrees that Jesus healed and cast out demons and that this aspect of his ministry stood at the heart of his work and message about the kingdom.

The point of interest is that Crossan says that, in the wake of John's execution, Jesus began to speak of the kingdom as a power that could be felt in the exorcisms and healing and in the radically egalitarian ethos of the movement.[61] Thus Jesus' understanding of the kingdom of God is to be interpreted not against the background of an apocalyptic longing for a future new kingdom but against the wisdom tradition's recognition of a present kingdom in which the wise, good and virtuous share.[62] In turn, this has significant implications for Crossan's view of the miracles of Jesus. Instead of being in some way related to the breaking in of God's reign to contemporary life, they are Jesus' response to a colonial people under political and religious pressure.

Barry Blackburn has rightly raised serious questions about Crossan's thesis. For example, it outruns the evidence to suggest that Jesus pitted himself against an exploitative temple and priesthood, which claimed exclusive right to broker healing. Also, the egalitarian motive on Jesus' part is purely speculative. And that Jesus rejected the notion of an apocalyptic kingdom cannot stand in the face of the evidence.[63]

As I said a moment ago, our task is not to give a full critique of these contributions to the study of this historical Jesus. We have not accumulated sufficient evidence that would allow an interaction with these presentations other than from what would be a slender base. Instead we have used these three contributions as examples of the emphases of the Third Quest and, in particular, evidence that—in light of our study—there has been, in some cases, a triumph of the trivial or the peripheral in the reconstruction of the historical Jesus.[64]

Most significantly there remains a major problem in the portraits of Jesus offered by the Third Questers. I think it can be said of the Third Quest that we have looked down the well of history and seen a reflection of ourselves,[65] our values and the religious heroes of our own times, for the Jesus of the Third Quest also turns out to be a reflection of our contemporary religious heroes.

The Jesus of the Third Quest is an itinerant charismatic, a man of the Spirit in constant communion with his God, a model of modern spirituality. He is an individual standing over against the power elites of society and in conflict with the guardians of established religion. Jesus is a prophet producing social change by means of wise sayings, preaching an egalitarianism message, and favoring the minority groups in his social activities as he moves about the margins of Jewish society. His miracles of compassion, so far as they may be important, maintain his popularity on the periphery of society with the other cynical, eccentric Jewish holy men.

It is not that the Third Questers deny the historicity of at least some of Jesus' miracles. Indeed, however reluctantly, the vast majority of students of the historical Jesus affirm that Jesus performed mighty works.[66] Notwithstanding, the question of significance and balance must be redressed. For example, when answering the question of what we can say about Jesus that indicates he can still make a contribution to people living in a very different age and culture, James Dunn outlines what he sees as the three most important answers: Jesus the teacher; the Man who Shows us What God is Like; and Conqueror of Death. Incredibly he makes no mention of miracle.[67]

4. *The miracles and the Jesus of history.* I do not want to give the false impression that what we have achieved in this study will provide all the data for a balanced sketch of the historical Jesus, for the attention here has been too narrowly focused on the miracles of Jesus. No attention has been given to Jesus' other activities or

to his teaching or to why he died or to whether he rose from the dead. Nor have any miracles *associated* with Jesus been discussed: the virginal conception, aspects of the story of his baptism, and the transfiguration, for example. Nevertheless what we have discovered about the historical Jesus and the miracle tradition in the Gospels means that *the results, so far, of the Third Quest are wildly out of balance. A corrective is needed to reinstate the miracles of Jesus as a major component in a reconstruction of this historical figure.* Therefore in light of this study I offer the following statements as a contribution to that required corrective:

☐ The single most time-consuming aspect of Jesus' pre-Easter public mission was the performing of miracles. Concomitantly the performing of miracles was the major focus of his pre-Easter mission and was considered by his observers to be the most significant aspect of his ministry. (When he arrived in Jerusalem that changed—with the possibility of one or two exceptions—not least because Jesus' attention was now on his last days.)

☐ So great in number, so responsive to human need, so spectacular in scale and so profound in significance were his miracles recognized to be that Jesus attracted large crowds. He was pressed on every side to perform miracles, and people sought to touch him in the hope of making contact with his healing power.

☐ The milling crowds created such a fervor that they gave concern to both religious and political authorities. Hence within the miracle tradition we have the seeds of an explanation for the death of Jesus.

☐ Jesus was aware that he was God's uniquely anointed individual performing expressions of God's powerful presence. Further, Jesus considered that it was through his experience of the presence of the Spirit of God in him that he was able to perform miracles.

☐ Choosing exorcism as the vanguard of his miracle campaign unmistakably signaled that he understood his ministry as primarily one of a battle against Satan and his minions.

☐ These exorcisms gave graphic credence to his explanation that this activity was, itself, the first stage of the destruction of the kingdom of Satan and the arrival of the expected kingdom, reign or powerful eschatological presence of God. That is, Jesus understood the miracles to be not the adumbration of but themselves the expression and experience of the eschatological reign of God in operation.

☐ In choosing to perform miracles that were seen to reflect Old Testament hopes for the messianic age, Jesus deliberately drew attention not only to his own identity as a (or the) Messiah but also to the coming of the messianic age in his activity.

☐ Jesus chose to perform miracles that focused on answering human suffering and need, reflecting his compassion and the compassionate nature of the reign of God.

☐ Jesus' miracles contributed to his opponents seeking his destruction.

☐ The potential and actual misunderstanding of his miracles, and what they meant for who he was, compelled Jesus to explain their meaning and their implications for him and for those who had witnessed or experienced the impact of his powers. Much of the public teaching therefore, especially about the kingdom of God, arose out the need to explain the nature and significance of the wonders being witnessed.

☐ Insofar as we are able to include the so-called nature miracles in the authentic material that can be traced back to the life of the historical Jesus, they in particular can give clear indication that Jesus thought he was acting for God.

☐ Though Jesus' technique was simple, as were some of his statements, it showed that he did not see himself as entirely distinct from other healers.

☐ Jesus generally expected faith—that is, a confidence in or a positive personal attitude toward him—as the prior condition for his performing a healing.

☐ Jesus sometimes accepted into his group those who wanted to become his followers in response to being healed.

Despite the long-standing hesitancy to rely on the Fourth Gospel for historical reminiscences of the historical Jesus, this Gospel—even taking into account its intensified representation of Jesus—may be far nearer the historical reality than has hitherto generally been acknowledged. That is, the presentation of Jesus as primarily a performer of mighty works who is required to give an explanation in his teaching is probably a more accurate reflection of a historically reconstructed portrait of the earthly Jesus than we would gain through, for example, the Gospel of Matthew, where he is depicted as a teacher who performs miracles.

This is an unpalatable portrait for a culture, at least in the West, where members of the intellectual elite appear to be devoid of the expectation and experience of the miraculous. Nevertheless it appears that *any critical reconstruction of the historical Jesus must not only include but also, indeed, emphasize that he was a most powerful and prolific wonder worker, considering that in his miracles God was powerfully present ushering in the first stage of the longed-for eschaton of the experience of his powerful presence.*[68]

§17.14 And Finally . . .

If these results are correct—if miracles were the most important aspect of the pre-Easter life and ministry of Jesus and if he understood them to be more than mere marvels—there will need to be nothing less than a revolution in our understanding of the historical Jesus. He cannot be seen only, or even primarily, as a wise sage or as a wandering cynic or as a Jewish holy man. He was first and foremost a prolific miracle worker of great power and popularity, expressing in his activity the powerful eschatological presence of God.

Also, nothing less than a revolution will need to take place in our understanding of what constitutes a Christianity that proposes to be on a trajectory that is faithful to what is disclosed about Jesus in the Gospels and in the life of the historical Jesus.

What is now seen as Christianity, at least in Western traditional churches, as primarily words and propositions requiring assent and further propagation will have to be replaced by a Christianity that involves and is dominated by understanding God's numinous power to be borne uniquely in Jesus and also in his followers in the working of miracles.

Notes

Chapter 1: Objectives & Issues

[1] See, e.g., Josh Simon, "Who Was Jesus?" *Life*, December 1994, pp. 66-82; Mary Rourke, "Cross Examination: New Portraits of Jesus," *Los Angeles Times*, February 24, 1994, p. E1. For an "insider's" introduction to the Seminar, see Marcus J. Borg, *Jesus in Contemporary Scholarship* (Valley Forge, Penn.: TPI, 1994), pp. 160-81. See also Ben Witherington, *The Jesus Quest: The Third Search for the Jew of Nazareth* (Downers Grove, Ill.: InterVarsity Press, 1995), pp. 42-57; Luke T. Johnson, *The Real Jesus: The Misguided Quest for the Historical Jesus and the Truth of the Traditional Gospel* (New York: HarperCollins, 1996), pp. 4-5.

[2] James R. Edwards, " 'Who Do Scholars Say That I Am?' . . ." *Christianity Today*, March 4, 1996, p. 15.

[3] Robert W. Funk, Roy W. Hoover and the Jesus Seminar, eds., *The Five Gospels: The Search for the Authentic Words of Jesus: A New Translation and Commentary* (Sonoma, Calif.: Macmillan, 1993), p. 33.

[4] Robert W. Funk, *The Acts of Jesus: The Search for the Authentic Deeds of Jesus* (New York: HarperCollins, 1998), pp. 530-31. Also on the Jesus Seminar, see W. Barnes Tatum, *John the Baptist and Jesus: A Report of the Jesus Seminar* (Sonoma, Calif.: Polebridge, 1993).

[5] Jacob Neusner quoted in Richard N. Ostling, "Jesus Christ, Plain and Simple," *Time*, January 10, 1994, p. 38.

[6] John Dart, "Holy War Brewing over Image of Jesus," *Los Angeles Times*, October 28, 1995, pp. B4-5. Cf. Michael J. Wilkins and J. P. Moreland, eds., *Jesus Under Fire: Modern Scholarship Reinvents the Historical Jesus* (Grand Rapids, Mich.: Zondervan, 1995).

[7] See B. Schilling's review of twentieth-century approaches to the miracles in German New Testament scholarship: "Die Frage nach der Entstehung der synoptischen Wundergeschichten in der deutschen neutestamentlichen Forschung," *SEÅ* 35 (1970): 61-78.

[8] Cf. Gerhard Delling, "Das Verständnis des Wunder im Neuen Testament," *ZST* 24 (1955): 265-80 (reprinted in *Studien zur Neuen Testament und zum hellenistischen Judentum: Gesammelte Aufsätze 1950-1968*, ed. Ferdinand Hahn, Traugott Holz and Nicolaus Walter [Göttingen, Ger.: Vandenhoeck & Ruprecht, 1970], pp. 146-59); Gerhard Delling, "Botschaft und Wunder im Wirken Jesu," in *Der historische Jesus und der kerygmatische Christus*, ed. Helmut Ristow and Karl Matthiae, 3d ed. (Berlin, Ger.: Evangelische Verlagsanstalt, 1964), pp. 389-402; Franz Mussner, *The Miracles of Jesus: An Introduction* (Notre Dame, Ind.: University of Notre Dame Press, 1968).

[9] See the discussion in Schilling, "Die Frage nach der Entstehung der synoptischen Wundergeschichten." Also see William Edwin Winn and Nolan Pliny Jacobson, "Present Tendencies in Biblical Theology," *Religion in Life* 32 (1962-1963): 88-94; William O. Walker, "Demythologizing and Christology," *Religion in Life* 35 (1965-1966): 67-80; Charley D. Hardwick, "God and the Christian Self-Understanding," *JR* 50 (1970): 419-40.

[10] We cannot claim that more and better exegesis will bring peace in the battle over the miracles, for as in the field of ethics, careful exegesis is only part of the field of debate. Cf. Richard B.

Hays, *The Moral Vision of the New Testament* (Edinburgh, U.K.: T & T Clark, 1997), p. 3.

[11]Cf., e.g., C. H. Dodd, "Miracles in the Gospels," *ExpTim* 44 (1932-1933): 507.

[12]Friedrich Schleiermacher, *The Life of Jesus* (Philadelphia: Fortress, 1975), p. 192.

[13]E. P. Sanders, *Jesus and Judaism* (London: SCM Press, 1985), p. 164. Cf. Gerhard Lohfink, *Jesus and Community* (New York: Paulist, 1984), p. 13.

[14]See the survey by Barry L. Blackburn, "The Miracles of Jesus," in *Studying the Historical Jesus: Evaluations of the State of Current Research,* ed. Bruce Chilton and Craig A. Evans (Leiden, Neth.: Brill, 1994), pp. 353-94.

[15]On the wider discussion of the place of miracle in Christian theology, especially in the nineteenth and twentieth centuries, see Robert Bruce Mullin, *Miracles and the Modern Religious Imagination* (New Haven, Conn.: Yale University Press, 1996). On the neglect of the miracles in German scholarship, see Otto Betz and Werner Grimm, *Wesen und Wirklichkeit der Wunder Jesu: Heilungen—Ruttengen—Zeichen—Aufleuchtungen* (Frankfurt, am Main: Peter Lang, 1977), chap. 1. On the Third Quest, see Witherington, *The Jesus Quest,* and §17.13.

[16]Ben F. Meyer, *The Aims of Jesus* (London: SCM Press, 1979), pp. 154-58; Donald Guthrie, *New Testament Theology* (Downers Grove, Ill.: InterVarsity Press, 1981). There is also little space given to miracles in Leslie Houlden, *Jesus: A Question of Identity* (London: SPCK, 1992), John Dominic Crossan, *Jesus* (North Blackburn, Austl.: Collins Dove, 1993), and Markus Bockmuehl, *This Jesus: Martyr, Lord, Messiah* (Edinburgh, U.K.: T & T Clark, 1994). In *The Historical Figure of Jesus* (London: Penguin, 1993), pp. 132-68, E. P. Sanders devotes a chapter to miracles. But it is an uncertain chapter, mixing a treatment of how the New Testament writers viewed the miracles with a treatment of views that may originate in Jesus, contributing little to our understanding of the miracles of the historical Jesus. In *The Historical Jesus: A Comprehensive Guide* (London: SCM Press, 1998), Gerd Theissen and Annette Merz devote only 34 of 612 pages to the miracles of Jesus.

[17]John P. Meier, *A Marginal Jew: Rethinking the Historical Jesus,* 3 vols. (New York: Doubleday, 1991, 1994, forthcoming). Also focusing on the miracle stories of Jesus is Gerd Theissen, *Miracle Stories of the Early Christian Tradition* (Edinburgh, U.K.: T & T Clark, 1983). However, Theissen's aim, which is to develop the methods of classical form criticism by way of an analysis of the miracle stories (p. 1), is quite different from my historical and theological objectives.

[18]Graham N. Stanton, *A Gospel for a New People: Studies in Matthew* (Edinburgh, U.K.: T & T Clark, 1992), p. 70, noting his earlier works *Jesus of Nazareth in New Testament Preaching* (Cambridge, U.K.: Cambridge University Press, 1974), pp. 122-24, and *Characterization and Individuality in Greek Literature,* ed. Christopher B. R. Pelling (Oxford, U.K.: Clarendon, 1990).

[19]See the lists in Blackburn, "The Miracles of Jesus," pp. 353-54.

[20]F. H. Bradley, "The Presuppositions of Critical History" (1874), in *Collected Essays,* 2 vols. (Oxford, U.K.: Clarendon, 1935), 1:20.

[21]Carol Fellows, "An Interview with Rudolf Bultmann," *Christianity and Crisis* 26 (1966): 254, a view similar to that of Luke T. Johnson, *Real Jesus,* esp. pp. 142-43.

[22]Wolfhart Pannenberg, "Redemptive Event and History," in *Basic Questions in Theology,* 3 vols. (London: SCM Press, 1970-1973), 1:15-80.

[23]English translation of Leopold von Ranke's famous statement *"wie eigentlich gewesen,"* from the preface of *Geschichten der romanischen und germanischen Völker,* vols. 33-34 of *Werke* (Leipzig, Ger.: Duncker & Humbolt, 1874), taken from *The Varieties of History from Voltaire to the Present,* ed. Fritz Stern (New York: Meridian, 1956), p. 57.

[24]See the discussions by David Wenham, "Source Criticism," in *New Testament Interpretation: Essays on Principles and Methods,* ed. I. Howard Marshall (Exeter, U.K.: Paternoster, 1977), pp. 139-52, and Bruce Chilton, "Traditio-Historical Criticism and Study of Jesus," in *Hearing the New Testament: Strategies for Interpretation,* ed. Joel B. Green (Grand Rapids, Mich.: Eerdmans, 1995), pp. 37-60.

[25]See William Wrede, "The Task and Methods of 'New Testament Theology,' " in *The Nature of New Testament Theology,* ed. Robert Morgan (London: SCM Press, 1973), pp. 68-116.

[26]For the present, note can be made of R. Douglas Geivett and Gary R. Habermas, eds., *In Defense of Miracles: A Comprehensive Case for God's Action in History* (Downers Grove, Ill.: InterVarsity Press, 1997), and Gary S. Greig and Kevin N. Springer, eds., *The Kingdom and the Power: Are Healing and the Spiritual Gifts Used by Jesus and the Early Church Meant for the Church Today?* (Ventura, Calif.: Regal, 1993).

[27]Cf. Rudolf Bultmann, "Is Exegesis Without Presuppositions Possible?" in *Existence and Faith: Shorter Writings of Rudolf Bultmann* (London: Collins/Fontana, 1964), pp. 342-51.

[28]Albert Schweitzer, *The Quest of the Historical Jesus* (London: Black, 1911), p. 4.

[29]See also J. Kellenberger, "Miracles," *International Journal for Philosophy of Religion* 10 (1979): 146.

[30]Cf. A. E. Taylor, *Philosophical Studies* (London: Macmillan, 1934), p. 337; see also §2.2 and §17.10.

[31]Cf. John Macquarrie, *Principles of Christian Theology* (London: SCM Press, 1966), p. 225.

[32]Aquinas, *Summa Contra Gentiles,* 4:58-59; Augustine, *On the Profit of Believing,* p. 34. On Aquinas's view of miracles, see Joseph Houston, *Reported Miracles: A Critique of Hume* (Cambridge, U.K.: Cambridge University Press, 1994), pp. 21-32. On Augustine's view of miracles, see, e.g., Robert M. Grant, *Miracle and Natural Law in Graeco-Roman and Early Christian Thought* (Amsterdam, Neth.: North-Holland, 1952), pp. 215-20; Benedicta Ward, *Miracles and the Mediaeval Mind* (Aldershot, U.K.: Wildwood House, 1987), chap. 1; Houston, *Reported Miracles,* chap. 1.

[33]Cf. *existēmi* ("to be astonished"): Mt 12:23; Mk 2:12; 5:42/Lk 8:56; 6:51; *thaumazō* ("amazed"): Mt 8:27/Lk 8:25; Mt 9:33/Lk 11:14; Mt 15:31; 21:20; Mk 5:20; Lk 8:25; 9:43b; 11:14; Jn 7:21; *ekplēssomai* ("to be astounded"): Mk 6:2; 7:37; Lk 9:43; *phobeomai/phobos* ("to fear/fear"): Mt 9:8; 14:26, 27/Mk 6:50/Jn 6:19, 20; Mk 4:41/Lk 8:25; Mk 5:15/Lk 8:35. See also Theissen, *Miracle Stories,* pp. 60-72.

[34]R. F. Holland, "The Miraculous," *American Philosophical Quarterly* 2 (1965): 43.

[35]E.g., Robert A. H. Larmer, *Water into Wine? An Investigation of the Concept of Miracle* (Kingston, Can.: McGill-Queen's University Press, 1988), pp. 7-8.

[36]For a critique of the coincidence concept of miracle see Ian Walker, "Miracles and Coincidences," *Sophia* 22, no. 3 (1983): 29-36.

[37]See Margaret A. Boden, "Miracles and Scientific Explanation," *Ratio* 11 (1969): 138.

[38]E.g., Richard Swinburne, *The Concept of Miracle* (London: Macmillan, 1970), pp. 1-2.

[39]David Hume, *Enquiries Concerning the Human Understanding and Concerning the Principles of Morals,* ed. L. A. Selby-Bigge, 2d ed. (Oxford, U.K.: Clarendon, 1902), pp. 114-15.

[40]E.g., Aquinas, *Summa Theologiciae,* 1a2ae:105:7; cf. Pope Benedict XIV, "De Servorum Dei Beatificatione et Beatorum Canonizatione, iv: De Miraculis" (Bologna, 1738), cited by Swinburne, *Concept of Miracle,* p. 2. See also C. S. Lewis, *Miracles: A Preliminary Study* (London: Collins/Fontana, 1960).

[41]See Stephen Usher, *The Historians of Greece and Rome* (New York: Taplinger, 1970), p. 20, citing Herodotus *History* 2:120; 8:37; 9:110; 36:1.

[42]Augustine, *City of God,* 21:8; Aquinas, *Summa Contra Gentiles,* 3:100.

[43]Taylor, *Philosophical Studies,* p. 349; also cited in §1.3 and §17.10.

[44]Cf. Aquinas, *Summa Contra Gentiles,* 3:102; *Summa Theologiciae,* 1a:110:4; Hume, *Enquiries Concerning the Human Understanding,* p. 115 n. 1; Swinburne, *Concept of Miracle,* pp. 6-7; James C. Carter, "The Recognition of Miracles," *TS* 20 (1959): 175-97.

[45]Cf. Meier, *A Marginal Jew,* 2:512. Also Hume, *Enquiries Concerning the Human Understanding,* pp. 114-15.

[46]Noted by Antony Flew, "Miracles," *Encyclopedia of Philosophy* 5 (1967): 346; cf. Swinburne, *Concept of Miracle,* pp. 7-10. See Hume, *Enquiries Concerning the Human Understanding,* p. 115 n. 1.

[47]Hume, *Enquiries Concerning the Human Understanding,* p. 115 n. 1.

[48]Augustine thought magicians could work miracles; see Houston, *Reported Miracles,* pp. 13-14.

[49]Douglas K. Erlandson, "A New Look at Miracles," *RelS* 13 (1977): 423-24.

[50]Paul Tillich, *Systematic Theology*, 3 vols. (Welwyn, U.K.: Nisbet, 1953-1964), 1:130. A not dissimilar view of miracle that virtually dissolves the miraculous is that miracle involves a speeding up or enhancing of a natural process, say of healing, that already exists.

[51]See those cited by H. van der Loos, *The Miracles of Jesus* (Leiden, Neth.: Brill, 1965), p. 444.

[52]Swinburne, *Concept of Miracle*, p. 1. Cf. a similar definition by John Locke, "A Discourse on Miracles," in *The Reasonableness of Christianity*, ed. I. T. Ramsey (London: Black, 1958), p. 79.

[53]Alan Richardson, *Christian Apologetics* (London: SCM Press, 1947), pp. 174-75.

[54]On Plutarch's writing of his "lives" and its implication for our understanding of the way the Gospels were written, see Vernon K. Robbins, "Writing as a Rhetorical Act in Plutarch and the Gospels," in *Persuasive Artistry: Studies in New Testament Rhetoric in Honor of George A. Kennedy*, ed. Duane F. Watson (Sheffield, U.K.: JSOT, 1991), pp. 142-68, and Richard A. Burridge, *What Are the Gospels? A Comparison with Graeco-Roman Biography* (Cambridge, U.K.: Cambridge University Press, 1992). On Plutarch, see also C. P. Jones, *Plutarch and Rome* (Oxford, U.K.: Clarendon: 1971), and D. A. Russell, *Plutarch* (London: Duckworth, 1972).

[55]See the helpful summary by Borg (*Jesus in Contemporary Scholarship*, pp. 127-31) of Huston Smith, *Forgotten Truth: The Primordial Tradition* (New York: Harper & Row, 1976).

[56]See the summary in John Sweet, "Interpretation of the Miraculous," in *A Dictionary of Biblical Interpretation*, ed. R. J. Coggins and J. L. Houlden (London: SCM Press; Philadelphia: TPI, 1990), pp. 465-66.

[57]Further, see F. G. Downing, "Access to Other Cultures, Past and Present (on the Myth of the Cultural Gap)," *Modern Churchman* 21 (1977-1978): 28-42; John Barton, "Reflections on Cultural Relativism," *Theology* 82 (1979): 191-99; Graham H. Twelftree, *Christ Triumphant: Exorcism Then and Now* (London: Hodder & Stoughton, 1985), pp. 140-42.

[58]Logical positivism, most fashionable in the middle of the twentieth century, epitomizes this view. See A. J. Ayer, *Language Truth and Logic* (London: Gollancz, 1946); Jørgen Jørgensen, *The Development of Logical Empiricism* (Chicago: Chicago University Press, 1951); and Herbert Feigl and May Brodbeck, eds., *Readings in the Philosophy of Science* (New York: Appeleton-Century-Crofts, 1953).

[59]For a criticism of Strauss on myth and miracle, see James D. G. Dunn, "Demythologizing—The Problem of Myth in the New Testament," in *New Testament Interpretation: Essays on Principles and Methods*, ed. I. Howard Marshall (Exeter, U.K.: Paternoster, 1977), pp. 288-92. Cf. Ernest and Marie-Luise Keller, "David Friedrich Strauss and the Mythical Viewpoint," in *Miracles in Dispute: A Continuing Debate* (London: SCM Press, 1969), chap. 7; Werner Kahl, *New Testament Miracle Stories in Their Religious-Historical Setting* (Göttingen, Ger.: Vandenhoeck & Ruprecht, 1994), pp.14-15.

[60]Ernest William Barnes, *The Rise of Christianity* (London: Longmans, Green & Co., 1947), p. 108, cited by Antony Flew, "Miracles," p. 347.

[61]Macquarrie, *Principles of Christian Theology*, p. 226.

[62]Borg, *Jesus in Contemporary Scholarship*, p. 137.

[63]Cf. the discussion in Reginald H. Fuller, *Interpreting the Miracles* (London: SCM Press, 1963), pp. 12-13.

[64]Dennis E. Nineham, *The Use and Abuse of the Bible* (London: SPCK, 1978), p. 21.

[65]Hume, *Enquiries Concerning the Human Understanding*, pp. 115-16.

[66]John R. Donahue ("Redaction Criticism: Has the *Hauptstrasse* Become the *Sackgasse?*" in *The New Literary Criticism and the New Testament*, ed. Edgar V. McKnight and Elizabeth Struthers Malbon [Valley Forge, Penn.: TPI, 1994], p. 31) offers the following definition: "As redaction criticism has evolved, three elements have come to characterize it: (1) study of the editorial or composition activity of an 'author,' (2) as a key to theological intention (or in more neutral literary terms, ideology), (3) which is in response to questions or issues alive in a particular community within the last decades of the first century CE." Note the discussion and criticism of redaction by C. Clifton Black, "The Quest of Mark the Redactor: Why Has It Been Pursued, and What Has It Taught Us?" *JSNT* 33 (1988): 19-39, and *The Disciples According to Mark: Markan Redaction in Current Debates* (Sheffield, U.K.: Sheffield Academic, 1989), chap. 1.

[67]In narrative criticism we pay particular attention to the characters, setting, plot and subplots of a Gospel, acknowledging the writers as narrators of stories within their larger story, intending to convey a meaning or a number of meanings to readers. See, e.g., Mark Allan Powell, *What Is Narrative Criticism?* (Minneapolis: Fortress, 1990); Mark Allan Powell, "Narrative Criticism," in *Hearing the New Testament: Strategies for Interpretation,* ed. Joel B. Green (Grand Rapids, Mich.: Eerdmans; Carlisle, U.K.: Paternoster, 1995), pp. 239-55.

[68]See Christopher Tuckett, *Reading the New Testament: Methods of Interpretation* (Philadelphia: Fortress, 1987); the collection of essays from the journal *Interpretation* in Jack Dean Kingsbury, ed., *Gospel Interpretation: Narrative-Critical & Social-Scientific Approaches* (Harrisburg, Penn.: TPI, 1997); the collection of essays from the journal *JSNT* in Stanley E. Porter and Craig A. Evans, eds., *New Testament Interpretation and Methods: A Sheffield Reader* (Sheffield, U.K.: Sheffield Academic, 1997); Green, ed., *Hearing the New Testament.*

[69]See Fuller, *Interpreting the Miracles,* p. 14.

[70]Rudolf Bultmann, *Jesus Christ and Mythology* (New York: Charles Scribner's Sons, 1958), pp. 12-13. See also those listed in Graham H. Twelftree, *Jesus the Exorcist: A Contribution to the Study of the Historical Jesus* (Tübingen, Ger.: Mohr; Peabody, Mass.: Hendrickson, 1993), p. 169 n. 24.

[71]See Twelftree, *Jesus the Exorcist,* pp. 165-71. Cf. John M. Court, "The Philosophy of the Synoptic Miracles," *JTS* 23 (1972): 10.

[72]Gerhard Friedrich, "*kērussō . . . ,*" *TDNT* 3:714.

[73]Cited by Loos, *Miracles of Jesus,* p. 282.

[74]Cf. Colin Brown, *Miracles and the Critical Mind* (Grand Rapids, Mich.: Eerdmans; Exeter, U.K.: Paternoster, 1984), p. 281, citing Reinhold Seeberg, "Wunder," in *Realenzyklopädie für Protestantische Theologie und Kirche,* ed. A. Hauck (Leipzig, Ger.: Hinrich, 1908), 21:562.

[75]Augustine held a similar view. See Houston, *Reported Miracles,* pp. 9-11. Further, see also Brown, *Miracles and the Critical Mind,* p. 4 n. 6.

[76]Cited by Eusebius *The History of the Church* 4:3:1-2. On miracles in the early church, see G. W. H. Lampe, "Miracles and Early Christian Apologetic," in *Miracles: Cambridge Studies in Their Philosophy and History,* ed. C. F. D. Moule (London: Mowbray, 1965), pp. 203-18; Maurice F. Wiles, "Miracles in the Early Church," in *Miracles,* ed. C. F. D. Moule, pp. 219-34; Brown, *Miracles and the Critical Mind,* pp. 3-11; Rowan A. Greer, *The Fear of Freedom: A Study of Miracles in the Roman Imperial Church* (University Park, Penn.: Pennsylvania State University Press, 1989).

[77]William Paley, *A View of the Evidences of Christianity* (London: R. Faulder, 1807), pp. 2-5.

[78]Locke, "A Discourse on Miracles," p. 82. Further, see Houston, *Reported Miracles,* chap. 3. Cf. Aquinas, *Summa Theologiciae,* 2a2ae:6:1, who argued that as miracles did not always lead to belief, to be effective they required the assent of faith from God in a person.

[79]Deitrich Bonhoeffer, *Letters and Papers from Prison* (London: SCM Press, 1971), p. 360.

[80]N. T. Wright, *Jesus and the Victory of God* (London: SPCK, 1996), p. 118, caricaturing Sanders's position in *Jesus and Judaism* (London: SCM Press, 1985), p. 334.

[81]For a brief discussion of the "Six phases of the discussion of the miracles of Jesus," see Theissen and Merz, *Historical Jesus,* pp. 285-91.

[82]For a brief history of the study of miracles in general, primarily though not exclusively from a philosophical perspective, see Brown, *Miracles and the Critical Mind.* From a *religionsgeschichtliche* perspective, see Kahl, *New Testament Miracle Stories in Their Religious-Historical Setting,* chap. 2. For a history of the understanding of miracles in relation to faith, science and medicine, see Loos, *Miracles of Jesus,* part one.

[83]Schweitzer, *Quest of the Historical Jesus,* p. 10.

[84]Ibid.

[85]Charles H. Talbert, ed., *Reimarus: Fragments* (London: SCM Press, 1971), pp. 230-34. The most consistent rejection of all miracles and all that was supernatural—elements thought to intrude into the life of Jesus—was carried out by Heinrich E. G. Paulus (1761-1851); see Schweitzer, *Quest of the Historical Jesus,* pp. 28, 48-57.

[86]Preface to the 4th German edition, Stuttgart, Ger., October 17, 1840, David Friedrich Strauss, *The Life of Jesus Critically Examined* (London: SCM Press, 1973), p. lvii, cited by Colin Brown, *Jesus in European Thought 1778-1860* (Grand Rapids, Mich.: Baker, 1985), p. 186.

[87]Further, see Schweitzer, *Quest of the Historical Jesus*, pp. 68-120; Karl Barth, *Protestant Thought in the Nineteenth Century: Its Background and History* (London: SCM Press, 1972), pp. 541-68; Horton Harris, *David Friedrich Strauss and His Theology* (Cambridge, U.K.: Cambridge University Press, 1973); Brown, *Miracles and the Critical Mind*, pp. 121-22; Brown, *Jesus in European Thought 1778-1860*, chap. 10, esp. n. 1.

[88]Cf. Rudolf Bultmann, "Autobiographical Reflections," in *Existence and Faith* (London: Collins/Fontana, 1964), pp. 335-41.

[89]Cf. Brown, *Miracles and the Critical Mind*, p. 133.

[90]Wilhelm Bousset, *Kyrios Christos: A History of the Belief in Christ from the Beginnings of Christianity to Irenaeus* (Nashville, Tenn.: Abingdon, 1970).

[91]Ibid., p. 98.

[92]Ibid., p. 100.

[93]Ibid., p. 103.

[94]See the discussion in Brown, *Miracles and the Critical Mind*, pp. 130-33.

[95]Bousset, *Kyrios Christos*, p. 103.

[96]Cf. Eldon R. Hay, "Bultmann's View of Miracle," *LQ* 24 (1972): 286-300. Bernhard Bron, *Das Wunder: Das theologische Wunderverständnis im Horizont des neuzeitlichen Natur- und Geschichtsbegriffs* (Göttingen, Ger.: Vandenhoeck & Ruprecht, 1975), pp. 133-43.

[97]Rudolf Bultmann, *History of the Synoptic Tradition* (New York: Harper & Row, 1976), p. 3.

[98]Bultmann, *History of the Synoptic Tradition*, p. 4, citing Martin Dibelius, "Zur Formsgeschichte der Evangelien," *Theologische Rundschau* N.F. 1 (1929): 187.

[99]E. P. Sanders, *Tendencies of the Synoptic Tradition* (Cambridge, U.K.: Cambridge University Press, 1969), p. 272.

[100]Cf. Morna D. Hooker, "On Using the Wrong Tool," *Theology* 75 (1972): 573.

[101]Bultmann, *History of the Synoptic Tradition*, p. 211.

[102]Rudolf Bultmann, *The Gospel of John* (Oxford, U.K.: Blackwell, 1971), p. 120. Cf. Ernest and Marie-Luise Keller, "Rudolf Bultmann's Existentialist Interpretation: The Significance of Miracles in the Gospel of John," in *Miracles in Dispute*, chap. 11.

[103]Rudolf Bultmann, "New Testament and Mythology: The Mythological Element in the Message of the New Testament and the Problem of Its Re-interpretation" (1941), in *Kerygma and Myth: A Theological Debate*, ed. Hans Werner Bartsch (London: SPCK, 1957), pp. 1-44.

[104]A view taken from Christian Gottlob Heyne (1729-1812). See Werner G. Kümmel, *The New Testament: The History of the Investigation of Its Problems* (London: SCM Press, 1973), p. 101, and esp. Dunn, "Demythologizing—The Problem of Myth in the New Testament," pp. 285-307, esp. 294-95.

[105]Bultmann, *Kerygma and Myth*, p. 10 n. 2.

[106]Ibid., p. 197.

[107]Ibid.

[108]Bultmann, *Jesus Christ and Mythology*, pp. 37-38.

[109]Rudolf Bultmann, "The Question of Wonder," in *Faith and Understanding* (Philadelphia: Fortress, 1987), pp. 247-61.

Chapter 2: The Possibility of Miracles

[1]With such a question we move beyond Meier's program in which he did "not intend to delve into the vast philosophical questions surrounding the possibility and reality of miracles" (John P. Meier, *A Marginal Jew: Rethinking the Historical Jesus*, 3 vols. [New York: Doubleday, 1991, 1994, forthcoming], 2:521).

[2]For a wide-ranging and popular discussion of the possibility of miracles in light of many objections, see Norman L. Geisler, *Miracles and the Modern Mind: A Defence of Biblical Miracles* (Grand Rapids, Mich.: Baker, 1992). See also R. Douglas Geivett and Gary R. Habermas, eds.,

In Defense of Miracles: A Comprehensive Case for God's Action in History (Downers Grove, Ill.: InterVarsity Press, 1997).

[3]C. S. Lewis, *Miracles: A Preliminary Study* (London: Collins/Fontana, 1960), p. 7.

[4]John Vincent, *An Intelligent Person's Guide to History* (London: Duckworth, 1996), p. 13.

[5]Ibid., p. 13.

[6]R. F. Holland, "The Miraculous," *American Philosophical Quarterly* 2 (1965): 43-51; Richard Swinburne, *The Concept of Miracle* (London: Macmillan, 1970); R. C. Wallace, "Hume, Flew and the Miraculous," *Philosophical Quarterly* 20 (1970): 230-43.

[7]Benedict de Spinoza, *Tractatus Theologico-Politicus* (1670), in R. H. M. Elwes, *The Chief Works of Benedict de Spinoza*, 2 vols. (London: George Bell & Son, 1883, 1884), 1:81-97; David Hume, *Enquiries Concerning the Human Understanding and Concerning the Principles of Morals*, ed. L. A. Selby-Bigge, 2d ed. (Oxford, U.K.: Clarendon, 1902); Alastair McKinnon, " 'Miracle' and 'Paradox,' " *American Philosophical Quarterly* 4 (1967): 308-14; Malcolm L. Diamond, "Miracles," *RelS* 9 (1973): 307-24; Patrick Nowell-Smith, "Miracles—The Philosophical Approach," in *Philosophy of Religion: Selected Readings*, ed. William L. Rowe and William J. Wainwright (New York: Harcourt Brace Jovanovich, 1973), pp. 392-400; George D. Chryssides, "Miracles and Agents," *RelS* 11 (1975): 319-27. Further, on the contemporary philosophical debate about miracles, see Leon Pearl, "Miracles and Theism," *RelS* 24 (1988): 483-96.

[8]For a list of deists who attack the notion of miracle, see Colin Brown, *That You May Believe* (Grand Rapids, Mich.: Eerdmans; Exeter, U.K.: Paternoster, 1985), pp. 23-26.

[9]Hume, *Enquiries Concerning the Human Understanding*, p. 110. For a discussion on Hume's supposed originality, see David Wootton, "Hume's 'Of Miracles': Probability and Irreligion," in *Studies in the Philosophy of the Scottish Enlightenment*, ed. M. A. Steward (Oxford, U.K.: Clarendon, 1990), pp. 191-229.

[10]On Hume on miracles, see, e.g., Antony Flew, *Hume's Philosophy of Belief* (London: Routledge & Kegan Paul, 1961), chap. 8; John L. Mackie, *The Miracle of Theism: Arguments for and Against the Existence of God* (Oxford, U.K.: Clarendon, 1982), chap. 1; Antony Flew, *David Hume: Philosopher of Moral Science* (Oxford, U.K.: Blackwell, 1986), chap. 5; J. C. A. Gaskin, *Hume's Philosophy of Religion*, 2nd ed. (London: Macmillan, 1988), chap. 8; Joseph Houston, *Reported Miracles: A Critique of Hume* (Cambridge, U.K.: Cambridge University Press, 1994); Geivett and Habermas, eds., *In Defense of Miracles*.

[11]Hume, *Enquiries Concerning the Human Understanding*, p. 114. In a footnote he later offers another definition: "*a transgression of a law of nature by a particular volition of the Deity, or by the interposition of some invisible agent*" (p. 115, his emphasis).

[12]Ibid., pp. 115-16.

[13]See the discussions in Benjamin F. Armstrong, "Hume on Miracles: Begging Questions Against Believers," *History of Philosophy Quarterly* 9 (1992): 319-28; Chris Slupic, "A New Interpretation of Hume's 'Of Miracles,'" *RelS* 31 (1995): 517-36.

[14]Robert J. Fogelin, "What Hume Actually Said About Miracles," *Hume Studies* 16 (1990): 81-86.

[15]Antony Flew, "Fogelin on Hume on Miracles," *Hume Studies* 16 (1990): 141-44.

[16]So Joseph S. Ellin, "Again: Hume on Miracles," *Hume Studies* 19 (1993): 203-12.

[17]Cf. C. D. Broad, "Hume's Theory of the Credibility of Miracles," *Proceedings of the Aristotelian Society* 17 (1916-1917): 86; Robert A. H. Larmer, *Water into Wine? An Investigation of the Concept of Miracle* (Kingston, Can.: McGill-Queen's University Press, 1988), pp. 36-37.

[18]A. E. Taylor, *Philosophical Studies* (London: Macmillan, 1934), p. 349; also cited in §1.3 and in §17.10.

[19]Hume, *Enquiries Concerning the Human Understanding*, p.110.

[20]Cf. Grace M. Jantzen, "Hume on Miracles, History, and Apologetics," *Christian Scholars Review* 8 (1978): 324. See also J. Kellenberger, "Miracles," *International Journal for Philosophy of Religion* 10 (1979): 146-55.

[21]See Houston, *Reported Miracles*, pp. 133-34.

[22]Swinburne, *Concept of Miracle*, p. 35.

[23]Hume, *Enquiries Concerning the Human Understanding*, pp. 115-16.

[24]Keith Ward, "Miracles and Testimony," *RelS* 21 (1985): 133.

[25]Hume, *Enquiries Concerning the Human Understanding*, pp. 116-17.

[26]T. F. Casey, "Lourdes," *New Catholic Encyclopedia* 8 (1967): 1032-33.

[27]Rex Gardner, "Miracles of Healing in Anglo-Celtic Northumbria as Recorded by Venerable Bede and His Contemporaries: Reappraisals in Light of Twentieth Century Experience," *British Medical Journal* 287 (1983): 1927-33, cited by W. D. Davies and D. C. Allison, *The Gospel According to Saint Matthew*, 3 vols. (Edinburgh, U.K.: T & T Clark, 1988, 1991, 1997), 2:63, who also cite tales of the Brazilian priest Padre Pio (The Duchess of St. Albans, *Magic of a Mystic: Stories of Padre Pio* [New York: Clarkson N. Potter, 1983]) and the New Testament-like miracles of the Indian Guru Sai Baba (E. Haraldsson, *Modern Miracles: An Investigative Report on Psychic Phenomena Associated with Sathya Sai Baba* [New York: 1987]). See also John White, *When the Spirit Comes with Power* (London: Hodder & Stoughton, 1988); Richard Swinburne, *Is There a God?* (Oxford, U.K.: Oxford University Press, 1996), p. 120, citing D. Hickey and G. Smith, *Miracle* (1978), and Rex Gardner, *Healing Miracles* (London: DLT, 1986), on which see the editorial review in *ExpTim* 98 (1987): 194-95; Max Turner, *The Holy Spirit and Spiritual Gifts Then and Now* (Carlisle, U.K.: Paternoster, 1996), chap. 19.

[28]Hume, *Enquiries Concerning the Human Understanding*, p. 125.

[29]Ibid., pp. 112-14.

[30]Colin Brown, *Miracles and the Critical Mind* (Grand Rapids, Mich.: Eerdmans; Exeter, Penn.: Paternoster, 1984), p. 97.

[31]George Campbell, *Dissertation on Miracles* (Edinburgh, U.K.: A. Kincaid & J. Bell, 1762), p. 108.

[32]Hume, *Enquiries Concerning the Human Understanding*, pp. 119-21.

[33]For modern examples of reports of miracles, see, e.g., Francis MacNutt, *Healing* (Notre Dame, Ind.: Ave Maria, 1974); John Wimber, *Power Healing* (London: Hodder & Stoughton, 1986); Michael Perry, ed., *Deliverance: Psychic Disturbance and Occult Involvement* (London: SPCK, 1987).

[34]Hume, *Enquiries Concerning the Human Understanding*, pp. 121-22. See the discussion in Bruce Langtry, "Miracles and Rival Systems of Religion," *Sophia* 24, no. 1 (1985): 21-31.

[35]Cf. Larmer, *Water into Wine?* p. 108.

[36]Richard Swinburne, "Miracles," *Philosophical Quarterly* 18 (1968): 327.

[37]As does, e.g., Maurice Wiles, "The Reasonableness of Christianity," in *The Rationality of Religious Belief*, ed. W. J. Abraham and S. W. Holtzer (Oxford, U.K.: Oxford University Press, 1987), p. 48.

[38]See also, e.g., William P. Alston, "God's Action in the World," Essay 10 in *Divine Nature and Human Language: Essays in Philosophical Theology* (Ithaca, N.Y.: Cornell University Press, 1989), pp. 197-222; William L. Rowe, "Miracles and the Modern World View," in *Philosophy of Religion: An Introduction* (Belmont, Calif.: Wadsworth, 1978), chap. 9; Swinburne, "Miracles," pp. 320-28; Swinburne, *Concept of Miracle*.

[39]For other examples, see Larmer, *Water into Wine?* chap. 4; C. Stephen Evans, *The Historical Christ and the Jesus of Faith: The Incarnational Narrative as History* (Oxford, U.K.: Clarendon, 1996), chap. 7.

[40]McKinnon, " 'Miracle' and 'Paradox,' " pp. 308-14, on which see Larmer, *Water into Wine?* pp. 44-46.

[41]McKinnon, " 'Miracle' and 'Paradox,' " p. 309.

[42]Douglas K. Erlandson, "A New Look at Miracles," *RelS* 13 (1977): 417.

[43]David Basinger and Randall Basinger, *Philosophy and Miracle* (Queenstown, Ontario, Can.: Edwin Mellen, 1986), p. 11; Larmer, *Water into Wine?* pp. 45-46.

[44]McKinnon, " 'Miracle' and 'Paradox,' " p. 310.

[45]Larmer, *Water into Wine?* p. 46.

[46]Rudolf Bultmann, *Faith and Understanding* (Philadelphia: Fortress, 1987), p. 248. On

Bultmann on miracles, see Eldon R. Hay, "Bultmann's View of Miracle," *LQ* 24 (1972): 286-300. Cf. Hans Jonas, "Is Faith Still Possible? Memories of Rudolf Bultmann and Reflections on the Philosophical Aspects of His Work," *HTR* 75 (1982): 11-14.

[47]Bultmann, *Faith and Understanding*, p. 248 (his emphasis).

[48]Ibid., p. 249.

[49]Ibid.

[50]Ibid., p. 260.

[51]Cf. Marcus J. Borg, *Jesus in Contemporary Scholarship* (Valley Forge, Penn.: TPI, 1994), chap. 9.

[52]Bultmann, *Faith and Understanding*, p. 254.

[53]Ibid. (his emphasis).

[54]Rudolf Bultmann, "New Testament and Mythology," in *Kerygma and Myth: A Theological Debate*, ed. Hans Werner Bartsch (London: SPCK, 1957), p. 5.

[55]Rudolf Bultmann, *History of the Synoptic Tradition* (New York: Harper & Row, 1976), pp. 38-39; also cited by Hay, "Bultmann's View of Miracle," p. 298.

[56]John Macquarrie, *Principles of Christian Theology* (London: SCM Press, 1966), p. 228.

[57]So Houston, *Reported Miracles*, p. 87.

[58]Ibid., pp. 86-87.

[59]Cf. Reginald H. Fuller, *Interpreting the Miracles* (London: SCM Press, 1963), pp. 9, 44.

[60]Cf. Robert M. Adams, "Kierkegaard's Arguments Against Objective Reasoning in Religion," in *The Virtue of Faith* (New York: Oxford University Press, 1987), pp. 25-41, cited by Houston, *Reported Miracles*, p. 98; cf. p. 85 n. 8.

[61]Houston, *Reported Miracles*, p. 98.

[62]C. S. Lewis, *Surprised by Joy: The Shape of My Early Life* (London: Collins/Fontana, 1959), p. 183.

[63]Paul Tillich, *Systematic Theology*, 3 vols. (Welwyn, U.K.: Nisbet, 1953-1964), 1:129. See also Austin Farrer, *Saving Belief* (London: Hodder & Stoughton, 1964); Brian Hebblethwaite, *Evil, Suffering, and Religion* (London: Sheldon, 1976); Maurice Wiles, *God's Action in the World* (London: SCM Press, 1986).

[64]Hugo Grotius (1583-1645), *De Iure Belli ac Pacis* (1625), 1:10.

[65]Cf. Evans, *Historical Christ*, pp. 162-63.

[66]Christine Overall, "Miracles as Evidence Against the Existence of God," *The Southern Journal of Philosophy* 23 (1985): 347-53; Wiles, *God's Action in the World*, pp. 66-67.

[67]See Evans, *Historical Christ*, pp. 164-69.

[68]See, e.g., J. Keir Howard, "New Testament Exorcism and Its Significance Today," *ExpTim* 96 (1985): 105-9; Deinnis Nineham, *The Use and Abuse of the Bible* (London: SPCK, 1976); Rudolf Bultmann, "New Testament and Mythology," in *New Testament and Mythology and Other Basic Writings*, ed. Schubert M. Ogden (London: SCM Press, 1985), pp. 1-43.

[69]For what follows, see Graham H. Twelftree, "The Place of Exorcism in Contemporary Ministry," *Anvil* 5 (1988): 133-50, and also *Christ Triumphant: Exorcism Then and Now* (London: Hodder & Stoughton, 1985), chap. 5.

[70]See, e.g., Mk 1:34; 3:10-11; 6:13.

[71]Peter Berger, *A Rumour of Angels* (Harmondsworth, U.K.: Penguin, 1970), p. 39.

[72]See David Hay, *Exploring Inner Space* (Harmondsworth, U.K.: Penguin, 1982), pp. 118-19.

[73]Macquarrie, *Principles of Christian Theology*, p. 237.

[74]Ibid., p. 238.

[75]See Richard Swinburne, "The Evidential Value of Religious Experience," in *The Sciences and Theology in the Twentieth Century*, ed. A. R. Peacocke (Stockfield: Oriel, 1981), pp. 182-96.

[76]Ibid., p. 195.

[77]See K. E. Kock, *Christian Counseling and Occultism* (Berghausen: Ev. Verlag, 1972); John Richards, *But Deliver Us from Evil* (New York: Seabury, 1974); John W. Montgomery, ed., *Demon Possession* (Minneapolis: Bethel House, 1976); Michael Perry, ed., *Deliverance: Psychic Disturbances and Occult Involvement* (London: SPCK, 1987), esp. chaps. 9 and 10.

[78]Graham Dow, "The Case for the Existence of Demons," *Churchman* 94 (1980): 199-208.

[79]Ibid., p. 200.

[80]Ibid.

[81]See Herbert Burhenn, "Attributing Miracles to Agents—Reply to George D. Chryssides," *RelS* 13 (1977): 485. Also see Sir Nevill Mott, "Christianity Without Miracles?" in *Can Scientists Believe?* ed. Sir Nevill Mott (London: James & James, 1991), pp. 3-23.

[82]Guy Robinson, "Miracles," *Ratio* 9 (1967): 159.

[83]See Larmer, *Water into Wine?* p. 52.

[84]Ibid., pp. 52-56; Tan Tai Wei, "Recent Discussions on Miracles," *Sophia* 11, no. 3 (1972): 24; Jantzen, "Hume on Miracles, History, and Apologetics," p. 324.

[85]Cf. Swinburne, "Miracles," pp. 322-23.

[86]Margaret A. Boden, "Miracles and Scientific Explanation," *Ratio* 11 (1969): 140.

[87]Cf. J. P. Moreland, "Science, Miracles, Agency Theory and the God-of-the-Gaps," in *In Defense of Miracles*, chap. 8, and "Complementarity, Agency Theory, and the God-of-the-Gaps," *Perspectives on Science and Christian Faith* 42 (1997): 2-14. See also F. M. Bernard, "Accounting for Actions: Causality and Teleology," *History and Theory* 20 (1981): 291-312.

[88]Broadly, agents taken to be responsible for miracles could be divine or diabolic. See the discussion in Erlandson, "A New Look at Miracles," p. 422.

[89]So Swinburne, "Miracles," pp. 325-27.

[90]So Larmer, *Water into Wine?* pp. 88-92.

[91]Cf. Francis J. Beckwith, *David Hume's Argument Against Miracles: A Critical Analysis* (New York: University Press of America, 1989). I have in mind Archbishop Michael Ramsey's famous statement "God is Christlike and in him is no un-Christlikeness at all," A. M. Ramsey, *God, Christ and the World: A Study in Contemporary Theology* (London: SCM Press, 1969), p. 98, which inspired John V. Taylor's *The Christlike God* (London: SCM Press, 1992).

[92]Norman Geisler, *Miracles and Modern Thought* (Grand Rapids, Mich.: Zondervan, 1982), p. 75, cited by Brown, *Miracles and the Critical Mind*, p. 212.

[93]See, e.g., the first part of William J. Abraham, *An Introduction to the Philosophy of Religion* (Englewood Cliffs, N.J.: Prentice-Hall, 1985).

[94]Further, see Swinburne, *Is There a God?* pp. 114-15; Richard Swinburne, *The Existence of God*, 2d ed. (Oxford, U.K.: Clarendon, 1992), chap. 12.

[95]Cf., e.g., Swinburne, *The Existence of God*; Alvin Plantinga, *God and Other Minds: A Study of the Rational Justification of Belief in God* (Ithaca, N.Y.: Cornell University Press, 1990); J. P. Moreland and Kai Nielsen, eds., *Does God Exist? The Great Debate* (Nashville, Tenn.: Thomas Nelson, 1990); Hans Küng, *Does God Exist?* (London: SCM Press, 1991); Swinburne, *Is There a God?*

[96]Among the mass of material, see, e.g., Donald M. Baillie, *God Was in Christ: An Essay on Incarnation and Atonement* (London: Faber & Faber, 1956); Wolfhart Pannenberg, *Jesus—God and Man* (London: SCM Press, 1968); Thomas V. Morris, *The Logic of God Incarnate* (Ithaca, N.Y.: Cornell University Press, 1986); Hans Küng, *The Incarnation of God: An Introduction to Hegel's Theological Thought as Prolegomena to a Future Christology* (Edinburgh, U.K.: T & T Clark, 1987). See also the review article: Douglas Jacobsen and Frederick Schmidt, "Behind Orthodoxy and Beyond It: Recent Developments in Evangelical Christology," *SJT* 45 (1992): 515-41.

[97]Ninian Smart, *Philosophers and Religious Truth* (London: SCM Press, 1969), §2.57 (p. 48).

[98]As reading aloud was the principle means of "publication" in antiquity, our term *readers* (for the first-century audiences of the Gospels) needs to include the idea of "listeners." See Richard A. Burridge, "About People, by People, for People: Gospel Genre and Audiences," in *The Gospel for All Christians: Rethinking the Gospel Audiences*, ed. Richard Bauckham (Grand Rapids, Mich.: Eerdmans, 1998), pp. 141-42, citing, e.g., William V. Harris, *Ancient Literacy* (Cambridge, Mass.: Harvard University Press, 1989), p. 305.

Chapter 3: The Miracles of Jesus in Mark

[1]See the bibliography for the most important studies. For brief histories of the treatment of the

miracles in Mark, see Sharyn Echols Dowd, *Prayer, Power, and the Problem of Suffering* (Atlanta: Scholars, 1988), pp. 6-24; Edwin K. Broadhead, *Teaching with Authority: Miracles and Christology in the Gospel of Mark* (Sheffield, U.K.: Sheffield Academic, 1992), pp. 13-21.

[2]Mk 1:21-28, 29-31, 32-34, 40-45; 2:1-12; 3:1-6, 7-12; 4:35-41; 5:1-20, 21-43; 6:30-44, 45-52, 53-56; 7:24-30, 31-37; 8:1-10, 22-26; 9:14-29; 10:46-52; 11:12-14, 20-26.

[3]So Paul J. Achtemeier, "Person and Deed: Jesus and the Storm-Tossed Sea," *Int* 16 (1962): 169.

[4]Alan Richardson (*The Miracle-Stories of the Gospels* [London: SCM Press, 1941], p. 36) says that 209 of the 666 verses of Mark deal directly or indirectly with miracles.

[5]William Wrede, *The Messianic Secret* (Cambridge, U.K.: Clarke, 1971); cf. Christopher Tucket, ed., *The Messianic Secret* (London: SPCK, 1983), esp. James D. G. Dunn, "The Messianic Secret in Mark," pp. 116-31.

[6]Johannes Schreiber, "Die Christologie des Markusevangeliums," *ZTK* 58 (1961): 154-83. For brief surveys of Mark as correcting theology through his miracles, see Frank J. Matera, *What Are They Saying About Mark?* (New York: Paulist, 1988), pp. 23-29; Broadhead, *Teaching with Authority*, pp. 17-21.

[7]Reginald H. Fuller, *Interpreting the Miracles* (London: SCM Press, 1963), p. 46.

[8]Cf. Martin Dibelius, *From Tradition to Gospel* (Cambridge, U.K.: Clarke, 1971), p. 96.

[9]See, e.g., A. E. J. Rawlinson, *The Gospel According to St. Mark* (London: Methuen, 1925), pp. xi-xv; C. F. D. Moule, "The Intention of the Evangelists," in *New Testament Essays: Studies in Memory of T. W. Manson*, ed. A. J. B. Higgins (Manchester, U.K.: Manchester University Press, 1959), pp. 167. More recently see John Riches, "The Synoptic Evangelists and Their Communities," in *Christian Beginnings: Word and Community from Jesus to Post-Apostolic Times*, ed. J. Becker (Louisville, Ky.: Westminster John Knox, 1993), pp. 216-17.

[10]See Vernon K. Robbins, *Jesus the Teacher: A Socio-Rhetorical Interpretation of Mark* (Philadelphia: Fortress, 1984), pp. 187-91, cited by Mary Ann Beavis, *Mark's Audience: The Literary and Social Setting of Mark 4.11-12* (Sheffield, U.K.: Sheffield Academic, 1989), p. 171.

[11]Graham H. Twelftree, *The Way of Discipleship: Mark 8 to 10* (Sydney, Austl.: Albatross; Oxford, U.K.: BRF, 1993), pp. 12-13. For more detail, see Ernest Best, *Mark: The Gospel as Story* (Edinburgh, U.K.: T & T Clark, 1983), chap. 15. Cf. Ralph P. Martin, *Mark: Evangelist and Theologian* (Exeter, U.K.: Paternoster, 1972), pp. 156-62.

[12]Mk 2:18—3:6; 7:1-23; 10:35-45.

[13]Mk 9:14-29, 33-50; 10:10-12; 11:20-26.

[14]Beavis, *Mark's Audience*, p. 172.

[15]Thus in understanding Mark's message in relation to the miracles, we will be paying attention not only to the coherent, plotted narrative but also to those places where Mark seems to have been particularly creative in his authorship.

[16]Throughout this book I will take *plot* to be the connections of cause and effect and sequences of stories that generate the "narrative," or larger story, of the Gospel. For a discussion of the variety of definitions of *plot*, see R. Alan Culpepper, *Anatomy of the Fourth Gospel: A Study in Literary Design* (Philadelphia: Fortress, 1983), pp. 79-89. For recent discussions of issues relating to the plot of Mark, see, e.g., David Rhoads and Donald Michie, *Mark as Story: An Introduction to the Narrative of a Gospel* (Philadelphia: Fortress, 1982); David Rhoads, "The Story of Mark," *Bible Today* 34 (1996): 209-14; Donald Senior, "The Gospel of Mark in Context," *Bible Today* 34 (1996): 215-21.

[17]Cf., e.g., Frank J. Matera, *What Are They Saying About Mark?* (New York: Paulist, 1987), chaps. 4 and 5.

[18]Graham H. Twelftree, *Jesus the Exorcist: A Contribution to the Study of the Historical Jesus* (Peabody, Mass.: Hendrickson, 1993), p. 57 n. 2.

[19]Cf. Thierry Snoy, "Les miracles dans l'évangile de Marc: Examen de quelques études récentes," *RTL* 3 (1972): 449-66; *RTL* 4 (1973): 58-101.

[20]Cf. Num 16:3-5; 2 Kings 4:9; Ps 105:16 (LXX); Ben Sirach 45:6; CD 6:1; Rev 22:6. Further, see W. R. Domeris, "The Office of Holy One," *Journal of Theology for Southern Africa* 54

(1968): 35-38. Cf. K. Berger, "Jesus als Nasoräer/Nasiräer," *NovT* 38 (1996): 323-35, who argues that this phrase indicates that Jesus may have been known as a Nazarite.

[21]For detailed evidence, see Twelftree, *Jesus the Exorcist*, p. 59 n. 16.

[22]Cf. K. Kertelge, *Die Wunder Jesu im Markusevangelium: Eine redaktionsgeschichtliche Untersuchung* (Munich: Kösel, 1970), p. 56.

[23]Cf. Ulrich Luz, "The Secrecy Motif and the Marcan Christology," in *The Messianic Secret*, ed. Christopher Tuckett, p. 80.

[24]On the question of the singular (he) or plural (they) reading of Mk 1:29, see Robert A. Guelich, *Mark 1—8:26* (Dallas: Word, 1989), p. 61.

[25]Mk 1:13, 31; 10:45; 15:41.

[26]E.g., Mk 15:41; Rom 15:25; Heb 6:10.

[27]Cf. Josephus *Ant.* 11:163, 166.

[28]Cf. Charles W. Hedrick, "The Role of 'Summary Statements' in the Composition of the Gospel of Mark: A Dialog with Karl Schmidt and Norman Perrin," *NovT* 26 (1984): 298.

[29]C. E. B. Cranfield, *Saint Mark* (Cambridge, U.K.: Cambridge University Press, 1966), p. 87.

[30]Contrast Jack D. Kingsbury, *Conflict in Mark* (Philadelphia: Fortress, 1989), pp. 21-24. The absence of the word *faith* here and in the summaries (noted by Snoy, "Les miracles dans l'évangile de Marc") does not, as is implied by the reaction of the crowd (cf. 1:37; 3:7-8; 6:54-56), remove the motif of faith from the summaries.

[31]So Luz, "The Secrecy Motif and the Marcan Christology," pp. 77, 80-81.

[32]Used for the whole message of Jesus in Mk 1:14, 38, 39; 13:10; 14:9.

[33]So John T. Carroll, "Sickness and Healing in the New Testament Gospels," *Int* 49 (1995): 131.

[34]Cranfield, *Saint Mark*, p. 89.

[35]Cf. Guelich, *Mark 1—8:26*, p. 70: "Word and deed communicate Jesus' message summarized in 1:14-15."

[36]On prophetic actions in the Old Testament, see Morna D. Hooker, *The Signs of a Prophet: The Prophetic Actions of Jesus* (London: SCM Press, 1997), pp. 1-6, and W. David Stacey, *Prophetic Drama in the Old Testament* (London: Epworth, 1990).

[37]Num 12:10; 2 Kings 5:27; 15:5.

[38]Cf. Ernest Best, *Disciples and Discipleship: Studies in the Gospel According to Mark* (Edinburgh, U.K.: T & T Clark, 1986), p. 188.

[39]For more detail, see Bruce M. Metzger, *A Textual Commentary on the Greek New Testament* (Stuttgart, Ger.: United Bible Societies, 1994), p. 56; C. H. Cave, "The Leper: Mark 1.40-45," *NTS* 25 (1979): 246; Guelich, *Mark 1—8:26*, p. 72.

[40]So Gerd Theissen, *Miracle Stories of the Early Christian Tradition*, (Edinburgh, U.K.: T & T Clark, 1983), pp. 57-58.

[41]Mk 1:41; 3:5; 7:34; 6:34; 8:2; 9:19.

[42]So Guelich, *Mark 1—8:26*, p. 74, and those cited by him.

[43]Franz Mussner, *The Miracles of Jesus: An Introduction* (Notre Dame, Ind.: University of Notre Dame Press, 1968), p. 35.

[44]See further William Loader, "Challenged at the Boundaries: A Conservative Jesus in Mark's Tradition," *JSNT* 63 (1996): 55.

[45]Only at Mt 9:30; Mk 1:43; 14:5; Jn 11:33, 38.

[46]Mk 3:12; 8:30; 10:48

[47]E. E. Bishop, *Jesus of Palestine* (London: Lutterworth, 1955), p. 89.

[48]Further, see Edwin K. Broadhead, "Mk 1,44: The Witness of the Leper," *ZNW* 83 (1992): 257-65.

[49]Mk 1:14, 38, 39; 13:10; 14:9.

[50]Cf. Mk 2:2; 4:14-20, 33.

[51]Dennis E. Nineham, *St. Mark* (Harmondsworth, U.K.: Penguin, 1962), p. 87.

[52]Cf. Josephus *Ag. Ap.* 1:31; *J.W.* 5:227; *Ant.* 3:261, 265-68.

[53]Cf. H. van der Loos, *The Miracles of Jesus*, (Leiden: Brill, 1965), p. 89; H. Strathmann, *"martus,"* *TDNT* 4:503.

[54]So Nineham, *Mark*, p. 87.

[55]See the discussion in Guelich, *Mark 1—8:26*, pp. 81-84.

[56]See the earlier discussion of Mk 1:28, 30, 34, 40 (§§3.4, 3.6-7).

[57]Cf. Mk 5:36; 7:26, 29; 9:24. The call for repentance in Mk 1:15 need not conflict with this interpretation, for 1:15 does not exclude the possibility of vicarious believing.

[58]Contra H.-J. Klauck, "Die Frage der Sündenvergebung in der Perikope von der Heiling des Gelähmten (Mk 2,1-12 Par)," *BZ* 25 (1981): 235.

[59]See, e.g., Is 40:2; Jn 9:1-3; 1 Cor 11:30; *b. Ned.* 41a; and the discussion in Loos, *Miracles*, pp. 255-63.

[60]So Klauck, in "Die Frage der Sündenvergebung," 236-37, followed by Christopher D. Marshall, *Faith as a Theme in Mark's Narrative* (Cambridge, U.K.: Cambridge University Press, 1989), p. 89. Cf. Is 53:11-12.

[61]This is the view of, e.g., Joachim Jeremias, *New Testament Theology* (London: SCM Press, 1971), p. 114; Rudolf Pesch, *Das Markusevangelium*, 2 vols. (Freiburg, Ger.: Herder, 1980), 1:156.

[62]Cf. George Foot Moore, *Judaism in the First Centuries of the Christian Era: The Age of the Tannaim*, 3 vols. (Cambridge, Mass.: Harvard University Press, 1962), 1:535. See also §4.12 on Mt 9:3, where further data is given. For a discussion of this reading of Mark, see, e.g., Guelich, *Mark 1—8:26*, pp. 85-86, and Morna D. Hooker, *The Gospel According to St Mark* (London: Black, 1991), p. 86.

[63]Cf. Marshall, *Faith as a Theme*, p. 89.

[64]Cf. Martin Hengel, *The Charismatic Leader and His Followers* (Edinburgh, U.K.: T & T Clark, 1981).

[65]Cf. E. P. Sanders, *Jesus and Judaism* (London: SCM Press, 1985), pp. 240, 273, and *The Historical Figure of Jesus* (London: Penguin, 1993), p. 239.

[66]Cf., e.g., Hooker, *St Mark*, pp. 87-93; John J. Collins, "The Son of Man in First-Century Judaism," *NTS* 38 (1992): 448-66; Delbert Burkett, "The Nontitular Son of Man: A History and Critique," *NTS* 40 (1994): 504-21; Maurice Casey, "Idiom and Translation: Some Aspects of the Son of Man Problem," *NTS* 41 (1995): 164-82.

[67]Mk 2:10, 28; 8:31, 38; 9:9, 12, 31; 10:33, 45; 13:26; 14:21, 21, 41; 14:62.

[68]Only here does Mark use the stark *akolouthei moi*, "Follow me!"

[69]Cf. M. Albertz, *Die synoptischen Streitgespräche: Ein Beitrag zur Formsgeschichte des Urchristentums* (Berlin: Trowitzsch, 1921), pp. 5-6; J. Dewey, "The Literary Structure of the Controversy Stories in Mark 2:1—3:6," *JBL* 92 (1973): 394-401.

[70]Guelich, *Mark 1—8:26*, p. 133; Hooker, *St Mark*, p. 105.

[71]Cf. Hedrick, "Role of 'Summary Statements,' " p. 296.

[72]Mk 5:30; 6:2, 5, 14; cf. 9:39.

[73]Further, see Twelftree, *Jesus the Exorcist*, pp. 112-13.

[74]Further, see Paul J. Achtemeier, "Toward the Isolation of Pre-Markan Miracle Catenae," *JBL* 89 (1970): 265-91, and "The Origin and Function of the Pre-Marcan Miracle Catenae," *JBL* 91 (1972): 198-221. W. Schmithals (*Wunder und Glaube: Eine Auslegung von Markus 4,35—6,61* [Neukirchen-Vluyn: Neukirchener, 1970]) argued that Mk 4:35—6:31 was a self-contained unit that Mark incorporated into his Gospel with little alteration.

[75]See Achtemeier, "Toward the Isolation of Pre-Markan Miracle Catenae," p. 291.

[76]Cf. Robert M. Fowler, *Loaves and Fishes* (Chico, Calif.: Scholars, 1981), pp. 28-29.

[77]Ibid., p. 181.

[78]Cf. L. Wm. Countryman, "How Many Baskets Full? Mark 8:14-21 and the Value of Miracles in Mark," *CBQ* 47 (1985): 651.

[79]To the contrary, Eric K. Wefald, "The Separate Gentile Mission in Mark: A Narrative Explanation of Markan Geography, the Two Feeding Accounts and Exorcisms," *JSNT* 60 (1995): 3-26, esp. 16-17 n. 35.

[80]Cf. Countryman, "How Many Baskets Full?" pp. 643-55. Even though the sea may have been calm and, perhaps therefore, the report less miraculous, we will see that Jesus' identity is revealed to be even more significant than earlier.

[81]So Wefald, "Separate Gentile Mission in Mark," pp. 3-26.

[82]See the discussion in ibid., pp. 16-26.

[83]Jesus goes on a mission among the Gentiles on four occasions: (1) Mk 4:35—5:21; (2) 6:45-53; (3) 7:24—8:10; and (4) 8:13—9:30. See ibid., pp. 9-13.

[84]Cf. also Best, *Discipleship,* pp. 191-92.

[85]Cf. Gottfried Schille, "Die Seesturmerzählung Markus 4 35-41 als Beispiel neutestamentlicher Aktualisierung," *ZNW* 56 (1965): 36-37; Ernest Best, *Following Jesus: Discipleship in the Gospel of Mark* (Sheffield, U.K.: JSOT Press, 1981), 230-34. See also §4.10 on Mt 8:23-27.

[86]See, e.g., Ps 77:18; 104:7; Rev 14:18; *Jub.* 2:2; *2 Apoc. Bar.* 10:8; *1 Enoch* 72-82; *3 Enoch* 14:1-5; *PGM* 3:225-29.

[87]Cf. Guelich, *Mark 1—8:26,* p. 26.

[88]Contra Marshall, *Faith as a Theme,* pp. 238-39.

[89]See Leonhard Goppelt, *Typos: The Typological Interpretation of the Old Testament in the New* (Grand Rapids, Mich.: Eerdmans, 1982), pp. 72-73. Whether—as Robert M. Grant says in *Miracle and Natural Law in Graeco-Roman and Early Christian Thought* (Amsterdam, Neth.: North-Holland, 1952), p. 169—this story in Mark has its origins in the Jonah story is not our concern here (see §16.4).

[90]Cf. Pesch, *Das Markusevangelium,* 1:269.

[91]See, e.g., Gen 8:1; Ex 14:21; Job 38:8-11; Ps 33:7; 65:7; 74:13-14; 77:16; 89:9; 104:4-9; 107:25-30; Prov 8:22-31; Is 17:12-13; Jer 5:22; 31:35.

[92]Cf. B. M. F. van Iersel and A. J. M. Linmans, "The Storm on the Lake: Mk iv 35-41 and Mt viii 18-27 in the Light of Form Criticism, 'Redaktionsgeschichte' and Structural Analysis," in *Miscellanea Neotestamentica,* ed. T. Baarda, A. F. J. Klijn and W. C. van Unnik (Leiden, Neth.: Brill, 1978), 2:22.

[93]Dibelius, *From Tradition to Gospel,* p. 79.

[94]So van Iersel and Linmans, "Storm on the Lake," 2:18.

[95]So Joachim Gnilka, *Das Evangelium nach Markus,* 2 vols. (Neukirchen-Vluyn: Neukirchener, 1978-1979), 1:200; Ludger Schenke, *Die Wundererzählungen des Markusevangeliums* (Stuttgart, Ger.: Katholisches Bibelwerk, 1974), p. 173.

[96]See Twelftree, *Jesus the Exorcist,* §3.

[97]See ibid., p. 82.

[98]Cf. J. Duncan M. Derrett, "Contributions to the Study of the Gerasene Demoniac," *JSNT* 3 (1979): 9-10; Wefald, "Separate Gentile Mission in Mark," p. 14.

[99]Mk 3:14; 6:12; 13:10; 14:9.

[100]Cf. Is 54:8, 10; 55:3; 63:7; Ps 25:6; 85:7; 90:14; 130:7; Jer 31:3; Mic 7:20; 2 Macc 2:7; 7:29. Further, see Rudolf Bultmann, "*eleos*...," *TDNT* 2:480-81. See also §3.27 on Mk 10:47-48.

[101]E.g., Schenke, *Wundererzählungen,* p. 198; Dietrich-Alex Koch, *Die Bedeutung der Wundererzählungen für die Christologie des Markusevangeliums* (New York: de Gruyter, 1975), p. 139; James R. Edwards, "Markan Sandwiches: The Significance of Interpolations in Markan Narratives," *NovT* 31 (1989): 193-215; Tom Shepherd, "Intercalation in Mark and the Synoptic Problem," in *Seminar Papers: SBL* (Atlanta: Scholars, 1991), pp. 687-97; Tom Shepherd, "The Narrative Function of Markan Intercalation," *NTS* 41 (1995): 522-40 (who on p. 522 n. 1 cites some of the other contributors on intercalation). However, see, e.g., R. H. Stein, "The Proper Methodology for Ascertaining a Markan Redaction History," *NovT* 13 (1971): 193-94, who questions the assumption that Mark is responsible for these sandwiches.

[102]For other possible examples, see Howard C. Kee, *Community of the New Age* (London: SCM Press, 1977), pp. 54-56; Edwards, "Markan Sandwiches," p. 203; and Shepherd, "Narrative Function of Markan Intercalation," p. 522.

[103]Cf. K. Kertelge, *Die Wunder Jesu,* pp. 110-11.

[104]Cf. Marshall, *Faith as a Theme,* p. 93.

[105]Ibid., pp. 90-110.

[106]On the status of the word *Jairus* in the text and more on the theme of faith expressed in the name, see Rudolf Pesch, "Jairus (Mk 5,22/Lk 8,41)," *BZ* 14 (1970): 252-56.

[107]E.g., G. Rochais, *Les Récits de Résurrection des Morts dans le Nouveau Testament* (Cambridge, U.K.: Cambridge University Press, 1981), pp. 57-58, and William L. Lane, *The Gospel of Mark* (London: Marshall, Morgan & Scott, 1974), pp. 195-96, cited by Marshall, *Faith as a Theme,* pp. 95-96.

[108]Cf. Mk 8:35; 10:26; 13:13, 20; 15:30-31. On *sōzein* as a term for salvation, in antiquity and in the biblical literature in particular, see Werner Foerster and Georg Fohrer, "*sōzō...,*" *TDNT* 7:965-1024. On Mark's use of *sōzein* as a term for salvation, see Mk 8:35; 13:13, 20.

[109]So Marshall, *Faith as a Theme,* pp. 95-96.

[110]Cf. ibid., pp. 97-99.

[111]"To save" or "to heal" (*sōzein,* Mk 5:23, 28, 34), "to live" (*zaō,* 5:23), and "to rise" (*egeirein,* 5:41). Cf. 14:28 *(egeirein);* 15:30-31 *(sōzein);* 16:6 *(egeirein).*

[112]Cf. Luz, "Secrecy Motif and the Marcan Christology," p. 90 n. 18.

[113]Contrast Rudolf Bultmann (*History of the Synoptic Tradition* [New York: Harper & Row, 1976], p. 219), who says that the faith is directed to the miracle worker and not the person Jesus.

[114]Cf. Marshall, *Faith as a Theme,* p. 101.

[115]Cf. Vernon K. Robbins, "*Dynameis* and *Sēmeia* in Mark," *BibRev* 18 (1973): 10.

[116]Robbins, "*Dynameis* and *Sēmeia* in Mark," p. 11, following Walter Grundmann, "*dunamia ...*" *TDNT* 2:286-90.

[117]Robbins, "*Dynameis* and *Sēmeia* in Mark," p. 5. On the "divine man," see §3.29.

[118]Grundmann, "*dunamai ...*" *TDNT* 2:286.

[119]See the literature cited in Emil Schürer, *The History of the Jewish People in the Age of Jesus Christ* (Edinburgh, U.K.: T & T Clark, 1979), 2:515-16.

[120]Sanae Masuda, "The Good News of the Miracle of the Bread," *NTS* 28 (1982): 210.

[121]Cf. Stephen Barton, "The Miraculous Feedings in Mark," *ExpTim* 97 (1985-86): 113. See also Wefald, "Separate Gentile Mission in Mark," p. 19.

[122]Cf. Hermann Pasch, "Abendmahlsterminologie asserhalb der Einsetzungsberichte," *ZNW* 62 (1971): 225.

[123]Cf. Barton, "Miraculous Feedings in Mark," p. 113.

[124]Cf. Guelich, *Mark 1—8:26,* p. 341.

[125]For a more speculative approach, see Masuda, "Good News of the Miracle of the Bread," p. 208.

[126]Cf. Deut 8:1-5, 16; Prov 9:1-16; Ecclus 24; Wisdom of Solomon 16:20-21.

[127]The story begins with the statement that it was evening (Mk 6:47). A similar phrase being used in the previous story of the feeding of the five thousand (6:35) hardly allows sufficient time for the feeding, clean up and dismissal of the crowd, so Mark is likely to have placed the stories together (cf. Guelich, *Mark 1—8:26,* p. 349).

[128]For the range of suggestions, see Thierry Snoy, "Marc 6.48: '... et il voulait les dépasser,' " in *L'Évangile selon Marc: Tradition et rédaction,* ed. M. Sabbe (Gembloux: Duculot, 1974), pp. 347-63. Cf. Thierry Snoy, "La rédaction marcienne de la marche sur les eaux (Mk 6,45-52)," *ETL* 44 (1972): 205-41, 433-81.

[129]Cf. Guelich, *Mark 1—8:26,* p. 350, citing Ernest Lohmeyer, *Das Evangelium des Markus* (Göttingen, Ger.: Vandenhoeck & Ruprecht, 1963), pp. 133-34; J. Kremer, "Jesus Wandel auf dem See nach Mk 6, 45-52," *BibLeb* 10 (1969): 226-28; Pesch, *Das Markusevangelium,* 1:361. See also Theissen, *Miracle Stories,* p. 101.

[130]In this interpretation I am not suggesting that Mark did not think he was communicating something other than a historical event. On the dangers of allegorical readings of texts, see Francis Watson, "Toward a Literal Reading of the Gospels," in *The Gospel for All Christians: Rethinking the Gospel Audience,* ed. Richard Bauckham (Edinburgh, U.K.: T & T Clark, 1998), pp. 195-217.

[131]So John P. Heil, *Jesus Walking on the Sea* (Rome: Biblical Institute, 1981), p. 83.

[132]Cf. James D. G. Dunn, *Jesus and the Spirit* (London: SCM Press, 1975), pp. 76-77. See also Twelftree, *Jesus the Exorcist,* pp. 58-59 and notes.

[133]It is going too far to say that Jesus is depicted as able to preserve his followers from death (see

J. Kremer, "Jesus Wandel auf dem See," 221-32).

[134]*Ēkouon* ("heard," Mk 6:55); *eiseporeueto* ("entered," 6:56); *eisōzonto* ("were healed," 6:56).

[135]That Mk 7:3-4 explains Jewish customs—e.g., that the Pharisees and all the Jews do not eat unless they thoroughly wash their hands and that they do not eat anything from the market unless they wash it—assumes a significant number of Gentile readers who require such elucidation.

[136]See the discussion in Guelich, *Mark 1—8:26*, p. 386, and Hooker, *St Mark*, p. 183.

[137]Cf. Mary Ann Beavis, "Women as Models of Faith in Mark," *BTB* 18 (1988): 5-6; Elizabeth S. Malbon, "Fallible Followers: Women and Men in the Gospel of Mark," *Semeia* 28 (1983): 36-37.

[138]Cf. David Rhoades, "Jesus and the Syrophoenician Woman in Mark: A Narrative-Critical Study," *JAAR* 62 (1994): 343-75.

[139]Cf. BAGD, *"mogilalos,"* p. 525.

[140]So Koch, *Wundererzählungen*, pp. 72-73.

[141]Cf. Robert H. Stein, "The 'Redaktionsgeschichtlich' Investigation of a Markan Seam (Mc 1 21f.)," *ZNW* 61 (1970): 78-79, who gives Mk 2:13; 3:20 and 8:22 as examples of verses in conflict with other parts of a paragraph, indicating that Mark may be responsible for the verse in question.

[142]E.g., Theissen, *Miracle Stories*, pp. 63-65.

[143]So Guelich, *Mark 1—8:26*, p. 397, citing Gnilka, *Das Evangelium nach Markus*, and Joseph Ernst, *Das Evangelium nach Markus* (Regensburg: Pustet, 1981), p. 217.

[144]So Hooker, *St Mark*, p. 188.

[145]Masuda, "Good News of the Miracle of the Bread," pp. 211-12.

[146]Cf. Karl P. Donfried, "The Feeding Narratives and the Marcan Community," in *Kirche: Festschrift für Günther Bornkamm*, ed. Dieter Lührmann and Georg Strecker (Tübingen, Ger.: Mohr, 1980), pp. 95-103. See also the comparative chart in Raymond E. Brown, *The Gospel According to John*, 2 vols. (London: Chapman, 1971), 1:240-43. However, Fowler (*Loaves and Fishes*, p. 68) concludes: "The Feeding of the Five Thousand in its entirety was composed by the author himself." A more detailed examination of the vocabulary, style and themes of the story led Masuda ("Good News of the Miracle of the Bread," pp. 196) to conclude that the elements of the desert, five loaves and two fish, that they ate enough, that there were twelve basketfuls of leftovers and that the number of men who ate were five thousand are probably traditional elements.

[147]Cf. Wefald, "Separate Gentile Mission in Mark," p. 19. Wefald (pp. 22-23) draws attention to the numbers in the feedings being of special significance in highlighting the respective Jewish and Gentile milieu of each story: e.g., the twelve (Jewish) baskets of the feeding of the five thousand and the seven (Gentile; cf. Acts 6:1-6; 2 Kings 17; 25; Ezra 1; 6:3-5) baskets of the feeding of the four thousand.

[148]This contrasts with the resistance of the disciples (representing at least some of Mark's readers?) to the mission to the Gentiles. See Wefald, "Separate Gentile Mission in Mark," pp. 19-20, on Mk 4:35-41; 6:45-53; 8:14-21.

[149]Cf. Guelich, *Mark 1—8:26*, p. 408.

[150]Cf. Donfried, "Feeding Narratives and the Marcan Community," pp. 101-2.

[151]See Olof Linton, "The Demand for a Sign from Heaven (Mk 8, 11-12 and Parallels)," *ST* 19 (1965): 112-29, and §8.5.

[152]Cf. Richard A. Edwards, *The Sign of Jonah* (London: SCM Press, 1971), pp. 75-80; Kertelge, *Wunder*, pp. 23-27; James Swetman, "No Sign of Jonah," *Biblica* 66 (1985): 126-30; A. K. M. Adam, "The Sign of Jonah: A Fish-eye View," *Semeia* 51 (1990): 177-91 (including bibliography).

[153]Morna D. Hooker, *The Signs of a Prophet: The Prophetic Actions of Jesus* (London: SCM Press, 1997), pp. 5-6. See the references given in §4.28 n. 145

[154]Cf. Jeffrey Gibson, "Jesus' Refusal to Produce a 'Sign' (Mk 8.11-13)," *JSNT* 38 (1990): 53.

[155]Cf. the unfulfilled promises made by Theudas that the River Jordan would part at his command

(Josephus *Ant.* 20:97) and by an unnamed Egyptian that the walls of Jerusalem would fall down at his command (*Ant.* 20:169).

[156] Cf. Gen 7:1; Deut 32:5, 20; Ps 95:11-12.

[157] As suggested by, e.g., Cranfield, *Saint Mark,* p. 257, and Kertelge, *Wunder,* p. 26.

[158] Cf. Quentin Quesnell, *The Mind of Mark* (Rome: Pontifical Biblical Institute, 1969), pp. 254-57; Guelich, *Mark 1—8:26,* pp. 423-24.

[159] Contra Theodore J. Weeden, "The Heresy that Necessitated Mark's Gospel," *ZNW* 59 (1968): 45-58.

[160] Cf. Marshall, *Faith as a Theme,* pp. 59-61.

[161] Guelich (*Mark 1—8:26,* p. 431) says that a large scholarly consensus assigns this setting to Mark. If that is so, the significance of Bethsaida for Mark in this story is heightened.

[162] There is a slight possibility that Mark's readers may have been aware of a tradition that the people of Bethsaida had been castigated for their lack of belief, even though they had seen Jesus perform miracles (cf. Mt 11:21/Lk 10:13).

[163] However, see chapter 4, n. 105.

[164] Wolfgang Schrage, *"tuphlos . . . ," TDNT* 8:270-94.

[165] Further, see BAGD, *"parakaleō,"* p. 617.

[166] See Earl S. Johnson ("Mark VIII. 22-26: The Blind Man from Bethsaida," *NTS* 25 [1979]: 381) on the various ways the relationship has been understood.

[167] Luz, "Secrecy Motif and the Marcan Christology," p. 78.

[168] So J. Roloff, *Das Kerygma und der irdische Jesus* (Göttingen, Ger.: Vandenhoeck & Ruprecht, 1970), pp. 128-29.

[169] Used at Mk 2:17; 5:4; 9:18; 14:37. The noun *ischuros* is used at 1:7; 3:27.

[170] Here at least is Mark's understanding as to why Jesus' miracles reflect on his divine origin whereas those of the disciples do not reflect on any divinity of theirs. It is that the disciples' ability to perform miracles is derived from Jesus, but Jesus' ability derives directly from God (see, e.g., Mk 1:9-11). See also on Mk 9:25 in the text to follow.

[171] Cf. Eduard Schweizer, "The Portrayal of the Life of Faith in the Gospel of Mark," *Int* 32 (1978): 389, 396.

[172] Cf. Marshall, *Faith as a Theme,* pp. 117-18.

[173] Cf. Erich Klostermann, *Das Markusevangelium* (Tübingen, Ger.: Mohr, 1950), p. 91; Nineham, *Saint Mark,* p. 247. More widely on the debate about "the faith of/in Jesus," see the literature cited by Douglas A. Campbell, "Romans 1:17—A *Crux Interpretum* for the *Pistis Christou* Debate," *JBL* 113 (1994): 265-85; Brian Dodd, "Romans 1:17—A *Crux Interpretum* for the *Pistis Christou* Debate?" *JBL* 114 (1995): 470-73.

[174] Cf. Joachim Jeremias, *New Testament Theology* (London: SCM Press, 1971), p. 166.

[175] So, e.g., Paul J. Achtemeier, "Miracles and the Historical Jesus: A Study of Mark 9:14-29," *CBQ* 37 (1975): 480.

[176] The difficulty of understanding this reference to the crowd in light of the earlier mention of the crowd gathering around Jesus (Mk 9:14-15) has been part of the case for two stories being brought together here. Further, see Twelftree, *Jesus the Exorcist,* pp. 91-93.

[177] See the comments and literature cited in Vincent Taylor, *The Gospel According to St. Mark* (London: Macmillan, 1953), p. 400.

[178] Further, see Twelftree, *Jesus the Exorcist,* chap. 3.

[179] Cf. Mk 3:10; 5:21-34; 6:56.

[180] Cf. Susan R. Garrett, *The Temptations of Jesus in Mark's Gospel* (Grand Rapids, Mich.: Eerdmans, 1998), chap. 3.

[181] Mk 2:1; 3:20; 4:10-12, 34; 6:31-32; 7:17, 24; 8:10; 9:2, 28; 10:10; 13:3.

[182] Mk 1:16-20; 3:13; 4:35; 6:31-32; 9:2.

[183] Mk 4:34; 7:17; 8:31; 10:10.

[184] Mk 4:40-41; 6:52; 7:18; 8:14-21, 32-33; 9:5-6, 32; 10:24; 14:40.

[185] Cf. *PGM* IV:3037-44; XIII:242-44; Graham H. Twelftree, *Christ Triumphant: Exorcism Then and Now* (London: Hodder & Stoughton, 1985), p. 40.

[186]Cf. C. E. B. Cranfield, "St. Mark, 9.14-29," *SJT* 3 (1950): 62-63.

[187]Suggested to me in private correspondence by Christopher Marshall.

[188]Cf. Twelftree, *Christ Triumphant,* p. 122.

[189]Cf. W. Swartley, "The Structural Function of the Term 'Way' in Mark," in *The New Way of Jesus,* ed. W. Klassen (Newton: Faith & Life, 1980), pp. 74-77, and Best, *Discipleship,* pp. 1-16.

[190]So Marshall, *Faith as a Theme,* p. 139. See also John N. Suggitt, "Bartimaeus and Christian Discipleship (Mark 10:46-52)," *Journal of Theology for Southern Africa* 74 (1991): 57-63.

[191]Cf. Is 42:18-20; 56:9-10; 1QS 4:11; Philo *Rer. Div. Her.* 76; 250.

[192]Note esp. in Philo; cf. Schrage, "*tuphlos . . . ,*" *TDNT* 8:285-86.

[193]Further, see Schrage, "*tuphlos . . . ,*" *TDNT* 8:271-75.

[194]We need to exercise care here, for Vernon K. Robbins ("The Healing of Blind Bartimaeus [10:46-52] in the Marcan Theology," *JBL* 92 [1973]: 234 n. 65) reminds us "that we have no example in Judaism during or before the 1st century A.D. of the Son of David as a healer." Cf. Dennis C. Duling, "Solomon, Exorcisms and the Son of David," *HTR* 68 (1975): 235-52.

[195]Cf. Earl S. Johnson, "Mark 10:46-52: Blind Bartimaeus," *CBQ* 40 (1978): 197. See also Donald H. Juel, *A Master of Surprise: Mark Interpreted* (Minneapolis: Fortress, 1994), pp. 97-99.

[196]Cf. Robbins, "Healing of Blind Bartimaeus," pp. 224-43, esp. pp. 241-42.

[197]See also Michael G. Steinhauser, "The Bartimaeus Narrative (Mark 10.46-52)," *NTS* 32 (1986): 585.

[198]See, e.g., 2 Macc 2:7; 7:29; 8:27; *Pss. Sol.* 14:6; Ecclus 5:6; 16:11-12; Wisdom of Solomon 6:6; 11:9. Cf. Ferdinand Hahn, *The Titles of Jesus in Christology: Their History in Early Christianity* (London: Lutterworth, 1969), p. 255. See also earlier in the text on Mk 5:19.

[199]See, e.g., *Sophia of Jesus Christ,* 125-26.

[200]See further Eduard Lohse, *Colossians and Philemon* (Philadelphia: Fortress, 1971), pp. 141-42.

[201]Michael G. Steinhauser, "Part of a Call Story," *ExpTim* 94 (1983): 205.

[202]See an example in Eusebius *The History of the Church* 6:19.

[203]So Marshall, *Faith as a Theme,* p. 140.

[204]Cf. Paul J. Achtemeier, " 'And he followed him': Miracles and Discipleship in Mark 10:46-52," *Semeia* 11 (1978): 115-45. On "faith" in this story, see also Johnson, "Mark 10:46-52," 191-204.

[205]See William R. Telford, *The Barren Temple and the Withered Tree* (Sheffield, U.K.: JSOT, 1980), chap. 1, and William R. Telford, "More Fruit from the Withered Tree: Temple and Fig-Tree in Mark from a Graeco-Roman Perspective," in *Templum Amicitiae,* ed. William Horbury (Sheffield, U.K.: Sheffield Academic, 1991), pp. 264-304. Cf. also the discussion in §16.9.

[206]The healing of the Gerasene demoniac certainly involves the destruction of the pigs. However, that is only a peripheral element in a larger story.

[207]Is 34:4; Jer 5:17; 8:13; 24; 29:17; Hos 2:12; 9:10; Joel 1:7, 12; Mic 7:1-6.

[208]Cf. G. Wagner, "Le figuier stérile et la destruction de Temple: Mc 11/1-4 et 20-26," *ETL* 62 (1987): 335-42.

[209]Further, see Wendy J. Cotter, "For It Was Not the Season for Figs," *CBQ* 48 (1986): 62-66; Best, *Discipleship,* p. 180.

[210]Cf. Hooker, *St. Mark,* p. 262.

[211]E.g., Günther Klein, "Wunderglaube und Neues Testament", in *Ärgernisse: Konfrontationen mit dem Neuen Testament* (Munich, Ger.: Kösel, 1970), p. 56; Broadhead, *Teaching with Authority,* e.g., p. 183.

[212]See §§3.17 and 3.22 on Mk 6:41 and 8:6 respectively.

[213]Cf. Theissen, *Miracle Stories,* p. 296.

[214]Mk 3:15; 6:7, 13; 9:18; 11:23-24. Cf. Adela Yarbro Collins, *The Beginning of the Gospel: Probings of Mark in Context* (Minneapolis: Fortress, 1992), p. 61.

[215]Cf. Best, *Discipleship,* p. 181.

[216]Cf. Theissen, *Miracle Stories* (Ithaca, N.Y.: Cornell University Press, 1963), p. 293.

[217]T. A. Burkill, *Mysterious Revelation,* p. 58.

[218]Theissen, *Miracle Stories,* p. 293 n. 26.

[219]So also Paul Lamarche, "Les Miracles des Jésus selon Marc," in *Les Miracles de Jésus selon le Nouveau Testament,* ed. Xavier Léon-Dufour (Paris: Éditions du Seuil, 1977), p. 224.

[220]Ludwig Bieler, *Theios Anēr,* 2 vols. (Vienna: Oskar Höfels, 1935-1936). Further, see Barry L. Blackburn, "Divine Man/*Theios Anēr*," in *Dictionary of Jesus and the Gospels,* ed. Joel B. Green, Scot McKnight, I. Howard Marshall (Downers Grove, Ill.: InterVarsity Press, 1992), pp. 189-92, and Jack D. Kingsbury, *The Christology of Mark's Gospel* (Philadelphia: Fortress, 1983), chap. 2. See also H. D. Betz, "Jesus as a Divine Man," in *Jesus and the Historian: Essays Written in Honor of Ernest Cadman Colwell,* ed. F. T. Trotter (Philadelphia: Westminster, 1969), p. 124.

[221]For a survey of literature, see Morton Smith, "Prolegomena to a Discussion of Aretalogies, Divine Men, the Gospels and Jesus," *JBL* 90 (1971): 174-79. For a summary of the debate, see Jack D. Kingsbury, "The 'Divine Man' as the Key to Mark's Christology—The End of an Era?" *Int* 35 (1981): 243-57; Kingsbury, *The Christology of Mark's Gospel,* chap. 2; and Barry L. Blackburn, Theios Anēr *and the Markan Miracle Traditions* (Tübingen, Ger.: Mohr, 1991), esp. chap. 1.

[222]Peter Wülfing von Martitz, "huios . . . ," *TDNT* 8:338-39. See also David L. Tiede, *The Charismatic Figure as Miracle Worker* (Missoula, Mont.: Scholars, 1972); Carl H. Holladay, Theios Anēr *in Hellenistic Judaism: A Critique of the Use of This Category in New Testament Christology* (Missoula, Mont.: Scholars, 1977), e.g., p. 39, and the literature cited by Martin Hengel, *The Son of God* (London: SCM Press, 1976), pp. 31-32.

[223]For a survey of the history of this scholarship, see Dowd, *Prayer, Power, and the Problem of Suffering,* pp. 6-24.

[224]Cf. Burkill, *Mysterious Revelation,* p. 41.

[225]Cf. ibid., p. 96.

[226]Mk 1:21-28, 29-31, 40-45.

[227]So Kertelge, *Wunder,* p. 206.

[228]Cf. Luz, "Secrecy Motif and the Marcan Christology," p. 80. On the exceptions in 5:43 and 8:26, see above (§3.16 and §8.22, respectively).

[229]Cf. Mk 5:1-20; 6:53-56; 7:24—8:10.

[230]See Mk 1:29-31; 2:1-12; 3:1-6; 5:25-34; 9:14-29; 10:46-52.

[231]Cf. Heikke Räisänen, *The "Messianic Secret"* (Edinburgh, U.K.: T & T Clark, 1990), pp. 156-57.

[232]E.g., Mk 2:13-17; 11:15-18; 12:1-12.

[233]Cf. Marshall, *Faith as a Theme,* pp. 61-71.

[234]Contra Burkill, *Mysterious Revelation,* p. 41.

[235]Contra Koch, *Wundererzählungen,* pp. 180-93.

[236]Because Lk 13:1-5 (the story of the tower of Siloam) and Jn 9:1-3 (the introduction to the story of the man born blind) dissociate tragedy or sickness and sin, I could not draw this same conclusion for Luke and the Fourth Gospel.

[237]Marshall, *Faith as a Theme,* p. 54 (his emphasis).

[238]E.g., Mk 1:31, 45; 2:12; 10:52.

[239]E.g. Mk 2:2, 13; 3:7-12, 20; 5:31; 8:1.

[240]So Marshall, *Faith as a Theme,* pp. 226-28.

[241]Ibid., p. 59.

[242]Cf. Burkill, *Mysterious Revelation,* p. 59, citing Anton Fridrichsen, *Le problème du miracle dans le Christianisme primitif* (Strasbourg: Faculté de théologie protestante de l'Universitté de Strasbourg, 1925), pp. 51ff.

[243]I am assuming that Mark originally ended at 16:8. See Metzger, *A Textual Commentary,* pp. 102-6, and also Kurt Aland, "Der Schluss der Markusevangeliums," in *L' évangile selon Marc: Tradition et rédaction,* ed. M. Sabbe (Leuven, Bel.: Leuven University Press, 1974), pp. 435-70. For an attempt to argue the originality of Mk 16:9-20, see William R. Farmer, *The Last Twelve Verses of Mark* (Cambridge, U.K.: Cambridge University Press, 1974), on which

see the review by J. N. Birdsall, *JTS* 26 (1975): 151-60. For a discussion of major contributors to the debate about the ending of Mark, see Stephen Lynn Cox, *A History and Critique of Scholarship Concerning the Markan Endings* (Lewiston, N.Y.: Edwin Mellen, 1993).

Chapter 4: The Miracles of Jesus in Matthew

[1]See also the redactional statement "The blind and the lame came to him in the temple, and he cured them" (Mt 21:14), on which see §4.33.

[2]Heinz Joachim Held, "Matthew as Interpreter of the Miracle Stories," in *Tradition and Interpretation in Matthew*, ed. Günther Bornkamm, Gerhard Barth and H. J. Held (London: SCM Press, 1982), pp. 165-200, originally published in German in 1960.

[3]Birger Gerhardsson, *The Mighty Acts of Jesus According to Matthew* (Lund, Swe.: CWK Gleerup, 1979), p. 93.

[4]Ibid., p. 94.

[5]Cf. W. D. Davies (*The Setting of the Sermon on the Mount* [Cambridge, U.K.: Cambridge University Press, 1964], p. 14), who says that Matthew "reveals not only a meticulous concern, numerically and otherwise, in the arrangements of its details, but also an architectonic grandeur in its totality."

[6]For a discussion of "plot" in Matthew, see Frank J. Matera, "The Plot of Matthew's Gospel," *CBQ* 49 (1987): 244-53, esp. p. 233 n. 1; Mark A. Powell, "The Plot and Subplots of Matthew's Gospel," *NTS* 38 (1992): 187-204, esp. p. 187 n. 2.

[7]David M. Hay ("Moses Through New Testament Spectacles," *Int* 44 [1990]: 243) says that the popularity of the view that Matthew is depicting Jesus as the New Moses seems to be receding. See also those cited by Dale C. Allison (*The New Moses: A Matthean Typology* [Edinburgh, U.K.: T & T Clark, 1993], p. 18 n. 27), who nevertheless in light of his study concludes, "The Moses typology is no more the trunk of Matthew's Christology than it is only a distal twig. It is somewhere in between: I should liken it to a main branch" (p. 268).

[8]Cf. Graham H. Twelftree, *Christ Triumphant: Exorcism Then and Now* (London: Hodder & Stoughton, 1985), p. 123.

[9]On the debate surrounding the issue of Matthew's structure, see Ulrich Luz, *Matthew 1-7* (Minneapolis: Augsburg, 1989), pp. 33-46. See also David R. Bauer, *The Structure of Matthew's Gospel: A Study in Literary Design* (Sheffield, U.K.: Almond, 1988), chap. 2.

[10]The suggestion goes back to B. W. Bacon, *Studies in Matthew* (London: Constable, 1930), pp. 80-90. Bacon refers (pp. xiv-xvi) to precursors such as F. Godet, Alfred Plummer and Alan H. McNeile; especially noteworthy is John C. Hawkins, *Horae Synopticae* (Oxford: Clarendon, 1909), pp. 163-64, who suggests parallel fivefold sections in other Jewish literature; cf. B. W. Bacon, "The 'Five Books' of Matthew Against the Jews," *Expositor* 15 (1918): 56-66. See the discussion of the "five books" theory in Davies, *Setting of the Sermon on the Mount*, pp. 14-25. On the debate surrounding the issue of Matthew's structure, see Luz, *Matthew 1-7*, pp. 33-46. See also David R. Bauer, *The Structure of Matthew's Gospel: A Study in Literary Design* (Sheffield, U.K.: Almond, 1988), chap. 2.

[11]Mt 7:28; 11:1; 13:53; 19:1; 26:1.

[12]As well as Bauer himself. See Bauer, *Structure*, chap. 2.

[13]On the structure of chaps. 8 and 9, see Evert-Jan Vledder, *Conflict in the Miracle Stories: A Social-Exegetical Study of Matthew 8 and 9* (Sheffield, U.K.: Sheffield Academic, 1997), pp. 171-73. See the discussion of literature in W. D. Davies and Dale C. Allison, *The Gospel According to Saint Matthew*, 3 vols. (Edinburgh, U.K.: T & T Clark, 1988, 1991, 1997), 2:1-5.

[14]Held, "Matthew as Interpreter of the Miracle Stories," pp. 246-53. Also William G. Thompson, "Reflections on the Composition of Mt 8.1—9.34," *CBQ* 33 (1971): 365-88.

[15]Jeremy Moiser, "The Structure of Matthew 8—9: A Suggestion," *ZNW* 76 (1985): 117-18.

[16]Mt 1:1, 18; 28:1-20.

[17]Mt 19:4, 8; 24:21; 25:34.

[18]See Jack D. Kingsbury, *Matthew as Story*, 2d ed. (Philadelphia: Fortress, 1988), pp. 3-9; Powell, "Plot and Subplots of Matthew's Gospel," pp. 199-200.

[19]Cf. Margaret Davies, *Matthew* (Sheffield, U.K.: JSOT, 1993), pp. 30-31.

[20]See Hay, "Moses Through New Testament Spectacles," p. 243, and Allison, *New Moses*, p. 18 n. 27.

[21]See Mt 4:23-24; 8:16-17; 9:35-36; 12:15-21; 14:34-36; 19:1-2; 21:14-17, all discussed in the text to follow.

[22]Matthew makes no clear distinction between teaching *(didaskein)* and preaching *(kērussein)*. So Gerhardsson, *Mighty Acts*, pp. 23-24. Cf. John P. Meir, *Law and History in Matthew's Gospel* (Rome: Biblical Institute, 1976), pp. 95-96.

[23]Mt 7:28; cf. 11:1; 13:53; 19:1; 26:1.

[24]Christoph Burger ("Jesu Taten nach Matthäus 8 und 9," *ZTK* 70 [1973]: 272-87) incorrectly plays down this balance by confusing the dominant activity of Jesus (works of miracles) with themes. (Burger suggests kerygmatic and ecclesiological themes.)

[25]Mt 8:1; cf. Mk 1:40/Lk 5:12. The phrase "came down the mountain" (my trans.) occurs only here and in an almost exact parallel in Ex 34:29 (LXX, A) of Moses coming down from Mount Sinai (cf. Mt 17:9). Terence L. Donaldson (*Jesus on the Mountain: A Study in Matthean Theology* [Sheffield, U.K.: JSOT, 1985]) argues that the dominant typology in the mountain typology is Zion rather than Sinai, a view called into question by Dale C. Allison, "Jesus and Moses (Mt 5:1-2)," *ExpTim* 98 (1987): 203-5. A more reasonable conclusion is that Matthew has both mountains in mind.

[26]Cf. Robert H. Gundry, *Matthew* (Grand Rapids, Mich.: Eerdmans, 1982), p. 139.

[27]This favorite phrase of Matthew's (sixty-two times, seven in Mark and fifty-seven in Luke) is often used to introduce something surprising.

[28]See also Num 5:2; 2 Kings 7:3-10; 15:5; 2 Chron 26:16-21; 11QTemple 45:17-18; 46:16-18; 49:4; 1QSa 2:3-4; Josephus *Ant.* 3:261; *Ag. Ap.* 1:281.

[29]Matthew has rewritten the description of the leper approaching Jesus by using the word *proserchomai* ("to come"). The word's figurative use of approaching a deity (see Ex 34:32: Josh 14:6; Heb 7:25; 11:6; Philo *De Plantatione* 64; *Deus Imm.* 8) is probably intended, for Matthew has it here (8:2) with *proskuneō*, which for Jews was associated with the worship of God, kings and courts (e.g., Lev 9:5; Num 18:4; Deut 25:1; Jer 7:16; Heb 10:1; 1 Pet 2:4; Josephus *Ant.* 12:19. Note Mt 28:9; see also J. R. Edwards, "The Use of *Proserchesthai* in the Gospel of Matthew," *JBL* 106 [1987]: 65-74).

[30]See Lev 5:3; Josephus *Ag. Ap.* 1:281.

[31]J. Andrew Overman, *Church and Community in Crisis: The Gospel According to Matthew* (Valley Forge, Penn.: TPI, 1996), p. 113.

[32]This point stands even though we know of no pre-NT text anticipating the healing of lepers in the eschaton. There was a general expectation of healing (cf. Is 29:18; 35:5; 42:18; Str-B 1:593-95, and there is the specific mention of lepers being cleansed in Matthew 11:5.

[33]On the relation between the stories in Matthew, Luke and John, see Davies and Allison, *Saint Matthew*, 2:17-18, and §§5.12 and 12.4.

[34]Jesus' response could be either a statement ("I shall come and heal him") or a question ("Shall I come and heal him?"). A statement would show Jesus' compassion. However, Matthew probably intended Jesus' words to be a question expressing hesitation in responding. This accords with Jesus' negative response to the Gentile woman's request for her demon-possessed daughter to be healed (Mt 15:21-28). It is also in harmony with Matthew's view that Jesus' ministry was directed to the Jews (10:6; 15:24) and that, as a law-abiding Jew, Jesus would have eschewed Gentile hospitality (cf. Jn 18:28; Acts 10:28; 11:12; *m. Ohol.* 18:7).

[35]The statement of the centurion that he is under authority and can therefore command obedience (Mt 8:9) could imply that in not being under authority Jesus could more effectively command obedience. However, as the centurion begins with Matthew's rarely used *kai gar*, it should probably be given its full force of "for also" (cf. 26:73). That is, the centurion is implying that Jesus, also being under authority, can command the healing of this slave.

[36]Luke uses *doulos* ("slave," Lk 7:2) and John *huios* ("son," Jn 4:46).

[37]So Overman, *Church and Community*, p. 114.

[38]See Davies and Allison, *Saint Matthew*, 1:487-90.

[39]See also Ernst Haenchen, "Faith and Miracle," in *Studia Evangelica I*, ed. K. Aland et al. (Berlin, Ger.: Akademie, 1959), pp. 495-96.

[40]The verbs being cast in the future tense ("will come" and "will recline") point to the mission of the church when Gentiles will be able to take their place in the kingdom of heaven because of their faith.

[41]A Semitism referring to Jews. Cf. Lk 16:8; 1QM 17:8.

[42]The change of the common name of Simon to Peter is consistent with Matthew's habit of always identifying Simon as the one called Peter (Mt 4:18; 10:2; cf. 17:25) or combining it with the name Peter (16:6, 17); perhaps, though we cannot know, it was because a second Simon was known to Matthew's readers. Cf. Davies and Allison, *Saint Matthew*, 2:33.

[43]Cf. Lk 26:26-27; Philo *Vit. Cont.* 70: Josephus *Ant.* 11:163, 166.

[44]See Mt 4:11; 8:15; 20:28; 25:44; 27:55.

[45]Cf. Davies and Allison, *Saint Matthew*, 2:32. In correspondence Peter Head suggested to me a chiasm centered on Jesus' action:

Introduction: Jesus came into the house of Peter
A. he saw his mother-in-law
  B. lying down
    C. and full of fever
      D. and he took her hand
    C^1. and the fever left her
  B^1. and she got up
A^1. and she served him

[46]Matthew does not follow Mark in saying that it was a sabbath (Mk 1:21, 29). So Matthew has no need to include Mark's statement that the sick were brought to Jesus "when the sun had set" (Mt 8:16/Mk 1:32, auth. trans.).

[47]Is 53:4 is from the fourth Servant Song (Is 52:13—53:12).

[48]See Günther Bornkamm, "The Stilling of the Storm in Matthew," in *Tradition and Interpretation*, ed. Bornkamm, Barth and Held, pp. 52, 54-55; Overman, *Church and Community*, p. 120.

[49]E.g., Ps 65:5; 69:1-2; Is 43:2; 57:20; Dan 7:2-3; cf. Philo *Migr. Abr.* 148.

[50]E.g., Ps 29:3; 65:7; 89:9; 93:4; 107:25-32.

[51]That is, other New Testament writers used "earthquake" to describe the trials associated with the end times, e.g., Mk 13:1; Lk 21:11; Rev 6:12; cf. Mt 24:7.

[52]Matthew alters the singular "wind" in the story of the astilling of the storm to the plural, as it is in the story of the two houses (Mt 7:25).

[53]See 1QH 3:6, 12-18; 6:22-25; 7:4-5.

[54]See Davies and Allison, *Saint Matthew*, 2:69 n. 1. See also §3.14 on Mk 4:35-41.

[55]See B. Batto, "The Sleeping God: An Ancient Near Eastern Motif of Divine Sovereignty," *Bib* 68 (1987): 153-77.

[56]See Lev 26:6; Job 11:18-19: Ps 3:5; 4:8; Prov 3:23-24.

[57]*Oligopistos* ("little faith"), Mt 6:30; 8:26; 14:31; 16:8; *oligopistia* ("smallness of faith"), 17:20. See also 21:20 and 28:17.

[58]I am not here attempting to allegorize away the story; see the warning by Francis Watson, "Toward a Literal Reading of the Gospels," in *The Gospel for All Christians*, ed. Richard Bauckham (Edinburgh, U.K.: T & T Clark, 1998), pp. 195-217. That an allegorical or typological interpretation tends to negate history is a ghost of Strauss. I maintain, with Allison (*New Moses*, p. 267), that such interpretations do not settle, without further ado, the historical question. Here I am suggesting a message Matthew wished to convey through the story.

[59]Contrast John M. Hull, *Hellenistic Magic and the Synoptic Tradition* (London: SCM Press, 1974), chap. 7.

[60]See, e.g., Ps 77:18; 104:7; Rev 14:18; *2 Apoc. Bar.* 10:8; *Jub.* 2:2; *1 Enoch* 72-82; *3 Enoch* 14:1-5; *PGM* 3:225-29.

[61]Cf. Job 38:8-11; Ps 33:7; Prov 8:22-31; Jer 5:22; 31:35. See also Paul Frederick Feiler, "The

Stilling of the Storm in Matthew: A Response to Günther Bronkamm," *JETS* 26 (1983): 406.

[62] Cf. Gundry, *Matthew*, p. 157.

[63] Matthew also supplies a second blind person in Mt 20:29-34 (Mk 10:46-52), and in his editorial story at Mt 9:27-34 two blind men are involved (see also 21:1-22/Mk 11:1-10).

[64] So Stephen Travis to me in private correspondence.

[65] On the plethora of explanations, see Davies and Allison, *Saint Matthew*, 2:80, citing Georg Braumann, "Die Zweizahl und Verdoppelungen im Matthäusevangelium," *TZ* 24 (1968): 255-66.

[66] See James M. Gibbs, "Purpose and Pattern in Matthew's Use of the Title 'Son of David,' " *NTS* 10 (1963-1964): 456-57.

[67] So Davies and Allison, *Saint Matthew*, 2:81.

[68] E.g., Mt 6:10; 16:28; Lk 3:16; Jn 4:25; 7:28, 31. See the discussion in Davies and Allison, *Saint Matthew*, 1:604-5.

[69] Cf. *1 Enoch* 15-16; *Jub.* 10:8-9; *T. Levi* 18:12.

[70] See Mt 11:4; 12:18; 28:8, 10, and perhaps 2:8 and 28:11.

[71] *Hupantōsis* is used only three times in the New Testament: here, in Mt 25:1 (of the maiden "meeting" the bridegroom) and in John 12:13 (where the crowd "meets" Jesus as he enters Jerusalem with the refrain "Hosanna").

[72] Cited by Held, "Matthew as Interpreter of the Miracle Stories," p. 175 and n. 2.

[73] On the other two occasions Matthew uses "Take heart" *(tharsei)* to encourage or acknowledge faith. To the bleeding woman touching the edge of his clothing, Jesus says, "Take heart . . . your faith has made you well" (Mt 9:22). In the case of Peter attempting to walk on the sea, Jesus, encourages him by saying "Take heart, it is I, have no fear" (14:27, auth. trans.).

[74] See §3.8 on Mk 2:1-12 and Ex 34:6-7; Ps 103:4; 130:4; Is 43:25; Dan 9:9; Jn 10:31-33; 1QS 2:9; CD 3:18.

[75] Suggested to me in correspondence from Ben Witherington and Peter Head.

[76] Perhaps in order not to clutter the introduction to his story, Matthew only now introduces the crowds (Mt 9:8; cf. Mk 2:2). He says they were afraid *(ephobēthēsan;* cf. Mk 2:12, *existasthai,* "they were all amazed") and adds the editorial note on their glorifying God "who had given such authority to human beings" *(anthrōpoi,* 9:8; cf. Mk 2:12).

[77] In the story of the calmed storm those of "little faith" were clearly meant to be the disciples (Mt 8:26), representing subsequent followers of Jesus. Thus the "human beings" here most probably refer to the disciples and therefore to subsequent followers of Jesus being given authority to forgive sins.

[78] See Thompson ("Reflections" pp. 371-72, citing G. Bornkamm, X. Léon-Dufour and W. Grundmann), who notes that the theme is announced in Mt 8:18-22 and carried through in 8:23-27 but is somewhat submerged in 8:28-34 and 9:1-18, to reappear in 9:9 and sustained in 9:10-17.

[79] There is no crowd in either the setting or in the story itself among which the woman, in Mark, attempts unsuccessfully to hide (Mk 5:27, 30-31).

[80] As proposed by Held, "Matthew as Interpreter of the Miracle Stories," p. 178.

[81] Cf. BAGD. There is probably nothing to be made of Matthew's deleting the name Jairus and the change of "ruler of the synagogue" to "ruler" (Mk 5:22/Mt 9:18).

[82] See n. 30 above and Lev 15:25-31.

[83] Although Is 35:5-6 does not mention miracles or the Messiah (brought to my attention by Colin Brown)—and the Targums do not give Is 35:5 a miraculous dimension ("Then the eyes of the house of Israel, that were as blind to the law; shall be opened, and their ears, which were as deaf to listen to the sayings of the prophets, shall listen")—Mt 11:2-6 and Lk 7:21-22 take Isaiah to refer to the miracles of Jesus they are reporting.

[84] On Matthew having two blind people instead of one, see §4.11.

[85] On doublets—accounts or sayings appearing twice in a Gospel—see the list in John C. Hawkins, *Horae Synopticae* (Oxford, U.K.: Clarendon, 1909), pp. 80-107. For a discussion of doublets, see Hans-Herbert Stoldt, *History and Criticism of the Marcan Hypothesis* (Edinburgh, U.K.: T & T Clark; Macon, Ga.: Mercer University Press, 1980), pp. 173-84, and, briefly, Robert H. Stein, *The*

Synoptic Problem: An Introduction (Nottingham, U.K.: Inter-Varsity Press, 1988), pp. 107-8.

[86]For a more detailed discussion, see Davies and Allison (*Saint Matthew*, 2:133-34), who cite Augustine on the similarities between the Mt 20:29-34 story and that of Bartimaeus in Mk 10:46-52: "There is such similarity in occurrences that if Matthew himself had not recorded the latter incident (9.27-31) as well as the former (20.29-34), it might have been thought that the one which he relates at present has also been given by these other two evangelists." See also Gundry, *Matthew*, pp. 176-77.

[87]See §§3.5 and 3.29 on Mk 10:45. Cf. also Mt 8:25; 9:21-22; 14:30.

[88]On "Son of David" in Matthew, see Davies and Allison, *Saint Matthew*, 1:156 n. 32; Peter M. Head, *Christology and the Synoptic Problem: An Argument for Markan Priority* (Cambridge: Cambridge University Press, 1997), pp. 182-83.

[89]Mt 12:23; 21:9, 15.

[90]Mt 1:17, 20; 9:27-34; 12:22-24; 15:21-28; 20:29-34; 21:1-17; and 22:41-46.

[91]Cf. Mt 8:2, 6, 8; 9:28; 15:25, 27; 17:15; 20:30, 31.

[92]Hence in contrast to Erich Klostermann (*Das Matthäusevangelium* [Tübingen, Ger.: Mohr, 1927], p. 72) and Hans Joachim Schoeps (*Theologie und Geschichte des Judenchristentums* [Tübingen, Ger.: Mohr, 1949], p. 93), we are unable to see the major thrust of arrangement of the stories arising out of exodus motifs.

[93]Gerd Theissen, *Miracle Stories of the Early Christian Tradition* (Edinburgh, U.K.: T & T Clark, 1983), p. 210.

[94]For what follows, see Davies and Allison, *Saint Matthew*, 2:2.

[95]See Held, "Matthew as Interpreter of the Miracle Stories," pp. 246-53; Thompson, "Reflections," pp. 365-88.

[96]Triads are obvious in other places in Matthew. See the discussion in Davies and Allison, *Saint Matthew*, 1:62-72; cf. Dale C. Allison, "The Structure of the Sermon on the Mount," *JBL* 106 (1987): 423-45.

[97]See C. L. Mitton, "Threefoldness in the Teaching of Jesus," *ExpTim* 75 (1964): 228-30.

[98]For a more detailed discussion, see Davies and Allison, *Saint Matthew*, 1:70-71, 134.

[99]Mt 8:10, 13, 26; 9:2, 22, 28, 29.

[100]Contrast Davies and Allison (*Saint Matthew*, 2:140), who suggest that 9:28 introduces a new idea of faith being faith in Jesus rather than general faith in God.

[101]Cf. Mt 15:21-28; 17:15; 20:30, and in the summary at the end of the cycle of miracle stories, 9:36.

[102]See also Mt 2:20 (cf. Ex 4:19-20); 5:1-2 (cf. Davies and Allison, *Saint Matthew*, 1:423-24); 8:1 (cf. Ex 19:14; 32:15; 34:29); 11:27-30 (cf. Ex 33:12-13; Dale C. Allison, "Two Notes on a Key Text: Matt. 11:25-30," *JTS* 39 [1988]: 477-80); 17:1-8 (cf. Ex 24; 34). See also the discussion in Allison, *The New Moses*, pp. 207-13.

[103]Mt 8:1-4, 5-13, 14-17, 28-34; 9:1-8, 9, 10-13, 20-22, 27-31, 32-34. If the "ruler" (*archōn*) of 9:18-23 is a Jew, this is an exception showing that it was possible for Jews to respond well to Jesus. But those in the ruler's house certainly ridicule Jesus (9:24).

[104]Mt 8:18-22; 34; 9:3, 11, 24, 34. For a detailed discussion of the theme of conflict in these two chapters, see Vledder, *Conflict in the Miracle Stories*.

[105]Cf. A. Stewart-Sykes, "Matthew's 'Miracle Chapters': From Composition to Narrative, and Back Again," *Scripture Bulletin* 25 (1995): 55-65.

[106]Jesus is said to "go about" (9:35), the imperfect tense of *periagō*.

[107]In private correspondence Colin Brown suggested to me that John the Baptist was expecting that the Lord's anointed would bring deliverance to captives (Is 42:7; 61:1)—which would include himself—hence the message from prison.

[108]See the summary discussion in Davies and Allison, *Saint Matthew*, 1:312-14.

[109]Mt 12:1-8, 9-14, 15-21.

[110]Mt 12:14; cf. 4:12; 14:13.

[111]See Twelftree, *Christ Triumphant*, pp. 123-26; Graham H. Twelftree, *Jesus the Exorcist: A Contribution to the Study of the Historical Jesus* (Peabody, Mass.: Hendrickson, 1993), §10.

[112]Though in Tobit 11:7-15 Tobit is cured of blindness by his son with the gall of a fish.

[113]Is 29:18; (32:3); 35:5; 42:7, 16, 18-20; 43:8; 61:1 (LXX).

[114]The crowd's response is not to marvel (*thaumazein*, as in 9:33) but the stronger to be "amazed" (*existanto*), and it is put in the form of a question: "Can this be the Son of David?" Introducing the question with *mēti* suggests a skeptical question expecting a negative answer but open to the possibility of a positive one (cf. Mt 26:22, 25).

[115]See 2 Pet 2:4; Jude 6; Rev 20:1-3; and Twelftree, *Jesus the Exorcist*, pp. 218-24, 228.

[116]John P. Meier, *The Vision of Matthew* (New York: Crossroad, 1991), p. 90.

[117]In using *akolouthein* ("to follow") Matthew is portraying the masses following him with at least some positive, even if limited, understanding and discipleship.

[118]Cf. Mt 9:36; 15:62; 20:34; also 18:27.

[119]See the discussion in Gregory Dix, *The Shape of Liturgy* (London: Black, 1982), pp. 135-36.

[120]Cf. Held, "Matthew as Interpreter of the Miracle Stories," p. 187.

[121]2 Kings 4:42-44. First pointed out by Tertullian in *Adversus Marcionem* 4:21.

[122]On which see Davies and Allison, *Saint Matthew*, 2:493.

[123]This view is enhanced by noting that the setting of this feeding story is, like the exodus, a desert place (Mt 14:13-15). Further, the unpreparedness of the disciples (14:17) also recalls the exodus theme in that the Israelites left Egypt hurriedly, leaving little opportunity to prepare provisions properly (e.g., Ex 12:37-39).

[124]See Ex 24:2; 32:30-34; cf. Mt 5:1-2; 15:29; 17:1.

[125]Ex 14:24 (LXX); Mt 14:25.

[126]Cf. Mt 11:25-27, which, although a prayer, is portrayed as being for the sake of those observing.

[127]Cf. John P. Heil, *Jesus Walking on the Sea* (Rome: Biblical Institute, 1981), p. 33.

[128]See §3.14 and n. 85 above.

[129]For parallels in ancient literature, see Theissen, *Miracle Stories*, p. 101.

[130]E.g., Gundry, *Matthew*, p. 300; cf. F. W. Beare, *The Gospel According to Matthew* (Oxford, U.K.: Blackwell, 1981), p. 300; R. Kratz, "Der Seewandel des Petrus (Mt 14,28-31)," *BibLeb* 15 (1974): 86-101.

[131]E.g., George D. Kilpatrick, *Origins of the Gospel According to St. Matthew* (Oxford, U.K.: Clarendon, 1946), pp. 38-44; Eduard Schweizer, *The Good News According to Matthew* (London: SPCK, 1976), p. 321; Davies and Allison, *Saint Matthew*, 2:497.

[132]Raymond E. Brown, "John 21 and the First Appearance of the Risen Lord to Peter," in *Resurexit: Actes du symposium international sur la Résurrection de Jésus*, ed. E. Dharis (Rome: Libreria Editrice Vaticana, 1974), pp. 246-65.

[133]Davies and Allison (*Saint Matthew*, 2:497) list *kurie, keleuson me,* verb of perception + *phobeomai, krazō + legōn, katapontizomai, ekteinas tēn cheira, oligopiste, edistasas.*

[134]Though this is strictly a miracle not of Jesus but of Peter, we will discuss it here, for it has implications for Matthew's understanding of the main story.

[135]See also Karl P. Donfried, "Peter," *ABD* 5:256.

[136]E.g., 2 Sam 22:17; Ps 18:16; Is 8:6-7. Further, see Leonard Goppelt, *"hudōr," TDNT* 8:322.

[137]Cf. Goppelt, *"hudōr," TDNT* 8:323; similarly Gundry, *Matthew*, p. 299.

[138]Cf. Heil, *Jesus Walking*, p. 61.

[139]On the nature of this authority—the ability to do all things—see Davies and Allison, *Saint Matthew*, 3:682-83.

[140]See, e.g., Job 26:11-12; Ps 65:7; 89:6-10; 107:29; Jon 1:15; Wisdom of Solomon 43:23; also 4Q381.

[141]Cf. Held, "Matthew as Interpreter of the Miracle Stories," pp. 288-91.

[142]This summary, the second of three in the middle of Matthew (cf. 12:15-21; 15:29-31), which is based on Mark 6:53-56, omits many details: mooring the boat, disembarking, mention of the pallets, details of the sick coming from villages, cities and countryside, and their being placed in the marketplace.

[143]E.g., Gen 35:2; Num 20:25-26; 1 Sam 18:4; 1 Kings 19:19-21; 2 Kings 2:8; Ezek 44:19; Hag 2:12-13. Further, see Twelftree, *Christ Triumphant*, pp. 113-14.

[144]Cf. Mt 2:12, 14, 22; 12:15; 14:13; 15:21.

[145]Matthew has omitted reference to entering a house, perhaps in order for Jesus not to enter what would have appeared to be a Gentile home (Mk 7:24, cf. Acts 10:28). The explanation for changing the woman from a Syrophoenician to a Canaanite may be that in the previous verse Matthew has added "and Sidon" to Mark's "Tyre" (Mk 7:24). The phrase "Tyre and Sidon" was associated with pagans (cf. Jer 25:15-28; 47:1-7; Joel 3:1-8; 1 Macc 5:15; Judith 2:28). Thus a change to "Canaanite" would heighten the significance of Jesus dealing mercifully with a woman who was a complete outsider. Matthew's addition—"Have mercy on me, O Lord, Son of David" (15:22/Mk 7:25; see also Mt 12:27; 17:15; 20:30-31; cf. T. Sol. 20:1)—may be to remind the readers that the Gentiles, as well as the Jews, are able to recognize that Jesus the healer is the source of their salvation.

[146]Cf. T. W. Manson, The Sayings of Jesus (London: SCM Press, 1949), p. 201.

[147]Bultmann, History of the Synoptic Tradition, p. 35.

[148]Contra Meier, Vision of Matthew, p. 105. For Matthew, "Galilee" (Mt 15:29) is associated with the Gentiles; see 4:13-18 and Gundry, Matthew, pp. 317-18.

[149]After the healing of the Syrophoenician woman's daughter, Mark tells the story of a deaf man with a speech impediment being healed (Mk 7:31-37). Matthew's omission of this story is often explained as due to Matthew's dislike of magical procedure (cf. Julius Wellhausen, Das Evangelium Marci [Berlin, Ger.: Georg Reimer, 1903], p. 64, cited by Held, "Matthew as Interpreter of the Miracle Stories," p. 207; Hull, Hellenistic Magic, pp. 116-41; Davies and Allison, Saint Matthew, 2:561). However, the presence of the so-called messianic secret, Jesus' groaning and his being disobeyed, as well as the use of a summary here to increase the parallelism between the two feeding stories, may be sufficient to explain Matthew's decision to turn Mark's story into this summary (cf. Gundry, Matthew, p. 317; Davies and Allison, Saint Matthew, 2:561).

[150]See Mt 5:1; cf. 14:23; 17:1.

[151]The words "and many others" give the impression of increasing the range and number of those healed.

[152]See also Mt 5:35; 22:44; 28:9; and Gundry, Matthew, p. 318.

[153]See n. 140 above.

[154]T. J. Ryan, "Matthew 15:29-31: An Overlooked Summary," Horizons 5 (1978): 31-42.

[155]That the fish are "small fish" (the diminutive ichthudion, rather than "fish," ichthus) could be to enhance the magnitude of the miracle through the disciples' disappointment in what they can provide.

[156]Cf. 4 Ezra 5:4; 7:6; Mt 24:27; Mk 13:24; Lk 21:11, 25; Rev 12:1, 3. See also Str-B 1:640-41, 977-1015.

[157]Davies and Allison, Saint Matthew, 2:579.

[158]For a discussion of "the sign of Jonah," see Morna D. Hooker, The Signs of a Prophet: The Prophetic Actions of Jesus (London: SCM Press, 1997), chap. 2.

[159]Cf. Davies and Allison, Saint Matthew, 2:584.

[160]See also Twelftree, Christ Triumphant, pp. 129-31; Twelftree, Jesus the Exorcist, §9.

[161]Also, in the abbreviating, the scribes have been written out, the crowd's role is insignificant, and the conversation between Jesus and the father has gone, a conversation that could have reflected negatively on Jesus' lack of foreknowledge of the boy's illness.

[162]E.g., R. J. Cassidy, "Matthew 17.24-7—A Word on Civil Taxes," CBQ 41 (1979): 571-80.

[163]E.g., William Horbury, "The Temple Tax," in Jesus and the Politics of His Day, ed. Ernst Bammel and C. F. D. Moule (Cambridge, U.K.: Cambridge University Press, 1984), pp. 265-86; Richard Bauckham, "The Coin in the Fish's Mouth," in Gospel Perspectives 6: The Miracles of Jesus, ed. David Wenham and Craig Blomberg (Sheffield, U.K.: JSOT, 1986), pp. 219-52.

[164]Raymond E. Brown, "The Gospel Miracles," in New Testament Essays (Ramsey, N.J.: Paulist, 1965), p. 177, n. 30.

[165]Theissen, Miracle Stories, p. 316.

[166]Davies and Allison, Saint Matthew, 2:741.

[167]For other interpretations, see ibid., 2:739-40.

[168]Mt 7:28; 11:1; 13:53; 19:1; 26:1. That there are five discourses, see, e.g., Bauer, *Structure*, chap. 8; Davies and Allison, *Saint Matthew:* 71-72.

[169]On Matthew providing a second blind man for this story, see §4.11.

[170]Cf. Gundry, *Matthew*, p. 413.

[171]See also 1QSa 2:19-25; 1QM 7:4-5; 4QD[b]/CD15:15-17; *m. Ḥag.* 1:1.

[172]The significant differences between Matthew's and Mark's versions of this story can be accounted for in Matthew's redaction. See Davies and Allison, *Saint Matthew*, 3:147-50.

[173]Gerhard Friedrich, "kērussō ...," *TDNT* 3:714.

[174]Cf. Davies and Allison, *Saint Matthew*, 2:1.

[175]Mt 12:23; 21:9, 15. Further, see §4.14 on Mt 9:27-31.

[176]Dennis C. Duling, "The Therapeutic Son of David," *NTS* 24 (1978): 333-39.

[177]See also Mt 8:27; 9:1-8, 33; 12:23; 15:31.

[178]Gerhardsson, *Mighty Acts*, p. 15 (his emphasis).

[179]Implied by Held, "Matthew as Interpreter of the Miracle Stories," p. 178.

[180]Ulrich Luz ("The Disciples in the Gospel According to Matthew," in *The Interpretation of Matthew*, ed. Graham N. Stanton [Edinburgh, U.K.: T & T Clark, 1995], p. 125) takes "little faith" too broadly to refer to a lesson in miracles in general for the church, where miracles are sometimes absent.

[181]Twelftree, *Christ Triumphant*, pp. 123-31.

[182]If, as is most likely, the Sermon on the Mount is addressed to disciples (cf. Mt 5:1; Luz, "The Disciples in the Gospel According to Matthew," p. 122), those reprimanded in 6:30 are disciples.

Chapter 5: The Miracles of Jesus in Luke: The Stories

[1]Lk 4:31-37, 38-39; 5:1-11, 12-16, 17-26; 6:6-11; 7:1-10, 11-17; 8:22-25, 26-39, 40-56 (two stories); 9:10-17, 37-43a; 11:14-26; 13:10-17; 14:1-6; 17:11-19; 18:35-43; 22:51.

[2]Lk 4:40-41/Mk 1:32-34; Lk 6:17-19/Mk 3:7-10 and Lk 7:21, which Luke has inserted into the tradition. Further, in 8:2 he notes "some women who had been cured of evil spirits and infirmities" and "Mary, called Magdalene, from whom seven demons had gone out."

[3]See, e.g., Ulrich Busse, *Die Wunder des Propheten Jesu: Rezeption, Komposition und Interpretation der Wundertradition im Evangelium des Lukas* (Stuttgart, Ger.: Katholisches Bibelwerk, 1977); J. A. Grassi, *God Makes Me Laugh: A New Approach to Luke* (Wilmington, Del.: Michael Glazier, 1986), pp. 38-47; Howard C. Kee, *Miracle in the Early Christian World: A Study in Sociohistorical Method* (New Haven, Conn.: Yale University Press, 1983), pp. 190-220; Walter Kirchschläger, *Jesu exorzistisches Wirken aus der Sicht des Lukas: Ein Beitrag zur lukanischen Redaktion* (Klosterneuburg, Aus.: Österreichisches Katholisches Bibelwerk, 1981); Robert C. Tannehill, *The Narrative Unity of Luke-Acts: A Literary Interpretation*, 2 vols. (Philadelphia: Fortress, 1986), 1:75-99; Charles H. Talbert, *Reading Luke: A Literary and Theological Commentary on the Third Gospel* (New York: Crossroad, 1982), pp. 58-60.

[4]The debate on the biographical nature of the Gospels has been renewed by Richard A. Burridge (*What Are the Gospels? A Comparison with Greco-Roman Biography* [Cambridge, U.K.: Cambridge University Press, 1992]), who notes that "Loveday Alexander's detailed study suggests affinities with prefaces in Greek scientific monographs, although such affinities do not negate the 'biographical content of the Gospels and Acts' (p. 194, citing Loveday Alexander, "Luke's Preface in the Context of Greek Preface-Writing," *NovT* 28 [1986]: 70).

[5]So Jack D. Kingsbury, *Conflict in Luke: Jesus, Authorities, Disciples* (Minneapolis: Fortress, 1991), p. 34.

[6]Lk 4:1-15/Mt 4:1-11; cf. Mk 1:12-15.

[7]Lk 4:16: "And he came to Nazareth" (auth. trans.); 4:31: "And he went down to Capernaum" (auth. trans.).

[8]See C. J. Schreck, "The Nazareth Pericope: Luke 4:16-30 in Recent Study," in *L'Évangile de Luc—The Gospel of Luke*, ed. Frans Neirynck (Leuven, Bel.: Leuven University Press, 1989), pp. 399-471.

[9]Lk 4:43-44; 7:22; 14:21; 16:16.

[10]See Lk 4:43; 7:22; 8:1; 16:16; 20:1.

[11]At 4:44 Luke has "Judea" instead of Mark's "Galilee." See Bruce M. Metzger, *A Textual Commentary on the Greek New Testament* (Stuttgart, Ger.: United Bible Societies, 1994), pp. 114-15. To follow I. Howard Marshall, *The Gospel of Luke* (Exeter, U.K.: Paternoster, 1978), pp. 198-99 (his emphasis):

> This can hardly refer to the southern district of Judaea, as distinct from Galilee . . . ; it is improbable that a ministry in the south should be interpolated here. . . . Judaea here means Palestine as a whole *including* Galilee . . . , but it is questionable whether so sharp a distinction should be drawn between the two parts of Jesus' ministry. Rather v. 43 indicates that Jesus' ministry is directed to the Jews as a whole; the point is theological rather than geographical.

[12]Heinz Schürmann, *Das Lukasevangelium: Erster Teil: Kommentar zu Kap. 1,1-9, 50* (Freiburg, Ger.: Herder, 1969), pp. 244-46.

[13]See BAGD, "*ea*," p. 211.

[14]Luke alludes to the change of Simon's name to Peter in Lk 6:14. Prior to that Luke does not use the name Peter alone. Further, see Joseph A. Fitzmyer, *The Gospel According to Luke,* 2 vols. (Garden City, N.Y.: Doubleday, 1981, 1985), 1:549.

[15]In the New Testament the word is used at Mt 4:24; Lk 4:38; 8:37, 45; 12:50; 19:43; 22:63; Acts 7:57; 18:5; 28:8; 2 Cor 5:14; Phil 1:23. For parallels to this description of sickness, see J. H. Moulton and G. Milligan, *The Vocabulary of the Greek Testament* (London: Hodder & Stoughton, 1930), p. 606.

[16]Cf. Galen (*Differentiis febrium* 1:1), who distinguishes between high and low fever. See John M. Creed, *The Gospel According to St. Luke* (London: Macmillan, 1930), pp. xx, 71.

[17]For this paragraph, see Graham H. Twelftree, "*EI DE . . . EGŌ EKBALLŌ DAIMONIA . . .,*" in *Gospel Perspectives 6: The Miracles of Jesus,* ed. David Wenham and Craig Blomberg (Sheffield, U.K.: JSOT, 1986), p. 394 n. 17.

[18]So Marshall, *Luke,* p. 195.

[19]J. Duncan M. Derrett, "Getting on Top of a Demon (Luke 4:39)," *EvQ* 65 (1993): 99-109.

[20]Cf. R. C. Thompson, *The Devils and Evil Spirits of Babylonia,* 2 vols. (London: Luzac, 1903-1904), 1:103, 119-21.

[21]Mt 8:26/Mk 4:39/Lk 8:24; Mt 16:20/Mk 8:30/Lk 9:21; Mt 16:22/Mk 8:32; Mt 19:13/Mk 10:13/Lk 18:15; Mt 20:31/Mk 10:48/Lk 18:39; Mk 8:33; Lk 9:55; 17:3; 19:39; 23:40.

[22]Mt 17:18/Mk 9:25/Lk 9:42; Mk 1:25/Lk 4:35 (39); cf. Mt 12:16/Mk 3:12; Mk 1:34/Lk 4:41.

[23]Howard C. Kee, "The Terminology of Mark's Exorcism Stories," *NTS* 14 (1967-1968): 244; cf. p. 243.

[24]Contrary to the view of, e.g., Fitzmyer, *Luke I—IX,* p. 553, and John Nolland, *Luke 1—9:20* (Dallas: Word, 1989), p. 213.

[25]See n. 11 above.

[26]Although the scholarly consensus does not agree, Marshall (*Luke,* p. 200) says, "There is no real evidence that forbids" the possibility that Luke and the Fourth Gospel are relating stories that go back to two different traditions. See the summary of discussions in Frans Neirynck ("John 21," *NTS* 36 [1990]: 321-29), who says, "There is no doubt . . . that the similarities between Luke 5 and John 21 are important and that some kind of relationship can hardly be denied" (pp. 322-23). Of course, it is possible that in the span of Jesus' ministry there was more than one large catch of fish. But the issue here is that the similarity between the stories means that the stories in Luke 5 and John 21 are most probably dealing with the same tradition. See also the discussion in Nolland, *Luke 1—9:20,* p. 220.

[27]See the discussion in Raymond E. Brown, *The Gospel According to John,* 2 vols. (London: Chapman, 1971), 2:1091.

[28]See Günther Klein, "Die Berufung des Petrus," *ZNW* 58 (1967): 1-44, esp. pp. 24-34.

[29]On which see S. O. Abogunrin, "The Three Variant Accounts of Peter's Call: A Critical and Theological Examination of the Texts," *NTS* 31 (1985): 587-602.

[30]Cf. Marshall, *Luke,* p. 205.

[31]See, e.g., Josh 6:26 (LXX); Num 31:18; 2 Chron 25:12; 2 Tim 2:26; Polybius 3:84:10; Josephus *J.W.* 2:448; *Ant.* 9:194; 20:210.

[32]Cf. Charles W. F. Smith, "Fishers of Men: Footnotes on a Gospel Figure," *HTR* 52 (1959): 187.

[33]See Str-B 1:593-96.

[34]On the state of the text in relation to "pity" *(splanchnistheis)* or "anger" *(orgistheis)*, see §3.7 on Mk 1:41.

[35]Lk 5:17-26, 27-32, 33-39; 6:1-5, 6-11.

[36]*Pistis* is related to miracles at Lk 5:20; 7:9; 8:25, 48; 17:5, 6, 19; 18:42; cf. Acts 3:16; 14:9; *pisteuō* at Lk 8:50.

[37]Cf. Lk 5:26; 7:16; 13:13; 17:15; 18:43; Acts 4:21.

[38]See BAGD, *"paradoxos,"* p. 615.

[39]On the state of this text, see Graham H. Twelftree, "Jesus in Jewish Traditions," in *Gospel Perspectives 5: The Jesus Tradition Outside the Gospels,* ed. David Wenham (Sheffield, U.K.: JSOT, 1985), pp. 301-8.

[40]Cf. Nolland, *Luke 1—9:20,* p. 261.

[41]Rudolf Bultmann, *History of the Synoptic Tradition* (New York: Harper & Row, 1976), p. 38.

[42]This "category of story in the synoptic tradition was called 'paradigm' by Dibelius, 'apophthegm' by Bultmann, 'pronouncement story' by Taylor. This is a brief account, told with a minimum of extraneous detail and designed to lead up to a single saying of Jesus, the 'pronouncement,' which forms the climax of the story" (Christopher Tuckett, *Reading the New Testament: Methods of Interpretation* [London: SPCK, 1987], p. 97).

[43]See the summary in Marshall, *Luke,* p. 277, and Fitzmyer, *Luke I—IX,* pp. 648-49. See also §12.4.

[44]On the Lukan language in the double-delegation insertions, see Siegfried Schulz, *Q: Die Spruchquelle der Evangelisten* (Zürich, Switz.: Theologischer Verlag, 1972), p. 238 n. 410.

[45]So Ernst Haenchen, "Faith and Miracle," in *Studia Evangelica I,* ed. Kurt Aland et al. (Berlin, Ger.: Akademie, 1959), p. 496.

[46]Cf. Nolland, *Luke 1—9:20,* p. 318.

[47]On the textual uncertainties here, see Metzger, *A Textual Commentary,* p. 119.

[48]Fitzmyer, *Luke I—IX,* p. 648.

[49]E.g., Lk 3:16; 4:24; 7:16, 19, 39; 9:8, 19; 13:33; 22:64; 24:19; further see Raymond E. Brown, "Jesus and Elisha," *Perspective* 12 (1971): 84-104; Fitzmyer, *Luke I—IX,* pp. 213-15.

[50]Cf. A. George, "Le miracle dans l'oeuvre de Luc," in *Les miracles de Jésus,* ed. X. Léon-Dufour (Paris: Éditions du Seuil, 1977), pp. 252-53.

[51]Cf. Gen 49:10; Ps 118:26; Dan 7:13; Hab 2:3; Zech 9:9.

[52]See the brief discussion in Bultmann, *History of the Synoptic Tradition,* pp. 156-57 n. 3; Fitzmyer, *Luke I—IX,* pp. 666-67; Nolland, *Luke 1—9:20,* pp. 328-29.

[53]Cf. Fitzmyer, *Luke I—IX,* p. 665.

[54]Cf. Is 26:19; 35:5; 61:1; Mal 3:1. See also, e.g., §5.13.

[55]See Ex 14:15-16; Josh 3:10-13; 2 Kings 2:8.

[56]Cf. Ps 89:8-9; 93:3-4; 106:8-9; 107:23-30; Is 51:9-10.

[57]*Parēngeilen* occurs in Luke-Acts: Lk 5:14; 8:29, 56; 9:21; Acts 1:4; 4:18; 5:28, 40; 10:42; 15:5; 16:18, 23; 17:30; 23:22, 30. Further, see Graham H. Twelftree, *Christ Triumphant: Exorcism Then and Now* (London: Hodder & Stoughton, 1985), pp. 112-13.

[58]See esp. 2 Pet 2:4; Jude 6; Rev 9:1, 2, 11; 11:7; 17:8; 20:1, 3 and also *1 Enoch* 10; 18:11-16; *Jub.* 5:6-11.

[59]Also see Twelftree, *Christ Triumphant,* p. 105.

[60]See Schürmann, *Das Lukasevangelium: Erster Teil,* p. 492.

[61]So Nolland, *Luke 1—9:20,* p. 360.

[62]See Judg 18:6; 1 Sam 1:17; 2 Sam 15:9; 1 Kings 22:17; Acts 16:36; Jas 2:16. Luke uses the LXX form *poreuou* rather than the *hupage eis eirēnēn* that he finds in his source (Mk 5:34). In this way Luke is able to give the sense of living in peace rather than simply departing from the situation.

[63]See the discussion of *sōzō* by Ben Witherington, *The Acts of the Apostles: A Socio-Rhetorical*

Commentary (Grand Rapids, Mich.: Eerdmans; Carlisle, U.K.: Paternoster, 1998), pp. 842-43.

[64]This is assuming that Luke's source is Mark. See the brief discussion in Fitzmyer, *Luke I—IX*, pp. 761-63.

[65]See Joachim Jeremias, "*airō . . .*," *TDNT* 1:185 n. 1.

[66]Mk 6:45-52; 7:24-30, 31-37; 8:1-10, 22-26.

[67]See the brief discussion in Fitzmyer, *Luke I—IX*, pp. 770-71.

[68]On the issues surrounding the Lukan journey to Jerusalem, see David P. Moessner, *Lord of the Banquet: The Literary and Theological Significance of the Lukan Travel Narrative* (Minneapolis: Fortress, 1989).

[69]On Lk 11:16, see §5.21.

[70]Cf. Ex 7:4-5; 8:19; 9:3, 15; James D. G. Dunn, *Jesus and the Spirit* (London: SCM Press, 1975), p. 46. For what follows, see Twelftree, *Christ Triumphant*, pp. 100-101.

[71]Albert Schweitzer, *The Quest of the Historical Jesus* (London: Black, 1911), p. 345. Cf., e.g., R. H. Fuller, *The Mission and Achievement of Jesus* (London: SCM Press, 1954), pp. 37-38; E. Grässer, "Zum Verständnis der Gottesherrschaft," *ZNW* 65 (1957): 3-26. Rather puzzlingly Hans Conzelmann (*An Outline of the Theology of the New Testament* [London: SCM Press, 1969], p. 107 n. 2) "excludes any idea of the imminence of the Kingdom."

[72]Rudolf Bultmann, *Theology of the New Testament*, 2 vols. (London: SCM Press, 1952-1955), 1:7 (his emphasis).

[73]Further, see Graham H. Twelftree, *Jesus the Exorcist: A Contribution to the Study of the Historical Jesus* (Peabody, Mass.: Hendrickson, 1993), pp. 218-19. For the hope of the binding of the powers of evil or the demise of Satan in the Messianic Age, see, e.g., Is 24:21-22; *1 Enoch* 10:4-6; 1QS 4:18-19; and James D. G. Dunn and Graham H. Twelftree, "Demon-Possession and Exorcism in the New Testament," *Churchman* 94 (1980): 220 and n. 31.

[74]On the status of *egō* in the text, see the apparatus of Nestle-Aland, *Novum Testamentum Graece* (Stuttgart, Ger.: Deutsche Bibelstiftung, 1993), p. 196.

[75]So Marshall, *Luke*, p. 473.

[76]Cf. Fitzmyer, *Luke X—XXIV*, p. 933.

[77]Cf. Paul J. Achtemeier, "The Lukan Perspective on the Miracles of Jesus: A Preliminary Sketch," in *Perspectives on Luke-Acts*, ed. Charles H. Talbert (Danville, Va.: Association of Baptist Professors of Religion; Edinburgh, U.K.: T & T Clark, 1978), pp. 156-57.

[78]Cf. Howard C. Kee, *Miracle in the Early Christian World: A Study in Sociohistorical Method* (New Haven, Conn.: Yale University Press, 1983), p. 204.

[79]Cf. Joel B. Green, "Jesus and a Daughter of Abraham (Luke 13:10-17): Test Case for a Lucan Perspective on Jesus' Miracles," *CBQ* 51 (1989): 651-52, citing St. Gregory Hom. 31; M.-J. Lagrange, *Evangile selon Saint Luc* (Paris: Lecoffre, 1927), p. 381; and Marshall, *Luke*, pp. 556, 560.

[80]See the references for eating, meals and table fellowship in Luke-Acts in Jerome H. Neyrey, "Ceremonies in Luke-Acts: The Case of Meals and Table Fellowship," in *The Social World of Luke-Acts: Models for Interpretation*, ed. Jerome H. Neyrey (Peabody, Mass.: Hendrickson, 1991), pp. 361-62.

[81]See H. Moxnes, "Meals and the New Community in Luke," *SEÅ* 51 (1986): 158-67; Dennis E. Smith, "Table Fellowship as a Literary Motif in the Gospel of Luke," *JBL* 106 (1987): 613-38.

[82]See George Foot Moore, *Judaism in the First Centuries of the Christian Era*, 3 vols. (Cambridge, Mass.: Harvard University Press, 1927-30), 2:363-65; Joachim Jeremias, *Jesus' Promise to the Nations* (London: SCM Press, 1967), pp. 59-65.

[83]BAGD, "*hudrōpikos*," p. 832, and literature cited. The TEV catches the nuance of Lk 14:2 well: "A man whose legs and arms were swollen came to Jesus."

[84]On the puzzling location given to this story, see §15.3. See also n. 68 above on the journey to Jerusalem in Luke.

[85]See Rudolf Bultmann, "*eleos . . . ,*" *TDNT* 2:479-85.

[86]See the discussion in Ben Witherington, "Appendix 2: Salvation and Health in Christian Antiquity: The Soteriology of Luke-Acts in Its First-Century Setting," in *Acts of the Apostles,*

[87]pp. 821-43.

[87]*Hupostrephō* is never used by Luke to signify repentance. Contrast Fitzmyer (*Luke X—XXIV,* p. 1151), who suggests that Luke wishes us to understand that the leper repented.

[88]Cf. Hans Dieter Betz, "The Cleansing of the Ten Lepers (Luke 17:11-19)," *JBL* 90 (1971): 325.

[89]Marshall, *Luke,* p. 649.

[90]Betz, "The Cleansing of the Ten Lepers," pp. 314-28.

[91]Christoph Burger, *Jesus als Davidssohn: Eine traditionsgeschichtliche Untersuchung* (Göttingen, Ger.: Vandenhoeck & Ruprecht, 1970), pp. 107-12.

[92]See the list in Fitzmyer, *Luke X—XXIV,* p. 1213.

[93]See E. Stauffer, *"boaō,"* *TDNT* 1:625-26.

[94]Cited by Fitzmyer, *Luke I—IX,* p. 257. Cf. §5.17.

[95]Cf. §§3.28 and 4.43.

[96]On what follows, see particularly William R. Telford, *The Barren Temple and the Withered Tree* (Sheffield, U.K.: JSOT, 1980), pp. 229-33.

[97]Adolf Jülicher, *Die Gleichnisreden Jesu,* 2d ed., 2 vols. (Tübingen, Ger.: Mohr, 1910), 2:446.

[98]See Lk 19:41-44; cf. 13:31-35; 23:26-31.

[99]See Lk 1:9, 21, 22; 2:27, 37, 46; 18:10; 19:47; 21:37, 38; 22:52; 24:53.

[100]See Acts 2:46; 3:1-26; 5:42; 21:17-26; 22:17-21; 24:17-19; 25:8. Luke also portrays the temple as a place for Jesus' teaching: Lk 19:47; 20:1; 21:37, 38; 22:53.

[101]See Mk 11:15-17/Lk 19:45-46.

[102]Cf. R. E. Dowda, cited by Telford, *Barren Temple,* p. 232. By the latter part of Acts the temple becomes the background to hostility between the Jews and Paul. See Acts 21:27-30; 24:6, 12, 18; 25:8; 26:21. Cf. Joel B. Green ("The Demise of the Temple as 'Culture Center' in Luke-Acts: An Exploration of the Rending of the Temple Veil," *RB* 101 [1994]: 514), who notes that the only clear negative comments on the temple are in Lk 21:5 and 25:45. The former verse deals with the future destruction of the temple and the latter with the rending of the temple curtain, the symbolism looking forward to a time when the temple would no longer be dominant. Contrast Philip F. Esler, *Community and Gospel in Luke-Acts* (Cambridge, U.K.: Cambridge University Press, 1987), p. 156, who sees Luke's attitude to the temple as "fundamentally ambivalent."

[103]On these miracles, see R. M. Gen, "The Phenomenon of Miracles and Divine Infliction in Luke-Acts: Their Theological Significance," *Pneuma* 11 (1989): 3-19.

[104]Acts 5:1-14; 9:1-21; 12:20-23; 13:4-12.

[105]Cf. Hardon, "The Miracle Narratives in Acts of the Apostles," *CBQ* 16 (1954): 306.

[106]The punitive miracles of the deaths of Ananias and Sapphira (Acts 5:1-11) and Paul's temporary blindness (9:8-9) are portrayed as being carried out by Peter and the risen Jesus respectively.

Chapter 6: The Miracles of Jesus in Luke: The Issues

[1]Reginald H. Fuller, *Interpreting the Miracles* (London: SCM Press, 1963), p. 87.

[2]Paul J. Achtemeier, "The Lukan Perspective on the Miracles of Jesus: A Preliminary Sketch," in *Perspectives on Luke-Acts,* ed. Charles H. Talbert (Danville, Va.: Association of Baptist Professors of Religion; Edinburgh, U.K.: T & T Clark, 1978), p. 156.

[3]Eduard Schweizer, *"pneuma,"* *TDNT* 6:406. See also his "The Spirit of Power: The Uniformity and Diversity of the Concept of the Holy Spirit in the New Testament," *Int* 6 (1952): 259-78.

[4]Max Turner, "Jesus and the Spirit in Lucan Perspective," *TynBul* 32 (1981): 3-42, esp. pp. 14-25; Max Turner, "The Spirit and the Power of Jesus' Miracles in the Lucan Conception," *NovT* 33 (1991): 124-52; Max Turner, *Power from on High: The Spirit in Israel's Restoration and Witness in Luke-Acts* (Sheffield, U.K.: Sheffield Academic, 1996), esp. pp. 105-18.

[5]John M. Hull, *Hellenistic Magic and the Synoptic Tradition* (London: SCM Press, 1974), p. 87.

[6]See, e.g., Achtemeier, "Lukan Perspective on the Miracles of Jesus," pp. 162-64; David E. Aune, "Magic in Early Christianity," *ANRW* II.23.2 (1980): 1507-57, esp. p. 1543; E. P. Sanders and Margaret Davies, *Studying the Synoptic Gospels* (London: SCM Press; Philadelphia:

Trinity, 1989), p. 281; Susan R. Garrett, *The Demise of the Devil: Magic and the Demonic in Luke's Writings* (Minneapolis: Fortress, 1989), pp. 26-29.

[7]Schweizer, *"pneuma," TDNT* 6:406.

[8]Ibid., 6:409. See also his "Spirit of Power," pp. 259-78, and his *The Holy Spirit* (London: SCM Press, 1981), pp. 58-64. These views have also been championed by G. J. Haya-Prats, *L'Esprit Force de l'Eglise* (Paris: Éditions du Cerf, 1975); A. George, *Etudes sur l'oeuvre de Luc* (Paris: Gabala, 1978), and "L'Esprit Saint dans l'oeuvre de Luc," *RB* 85 (1978): 500-42; Robert P. Menzies, *The Development of Early Christian Pneumatology with Special Reference to Luke-Acts* (Sheffield, U.K.: JSOT, 1991), rev. and exp. as *Empowered for Witness: The Spirit in Luke-Acts* (Sheffield, U.K.: Sheffield Academic, 1994); see also his "Spirit and Power in Luke-Acts: A Response to Max Turner," *JSNT* 49 (1993): 11-20. For a critique of these views, see, e.g., Turner, "Jesus and the Spirit in Lucan Perspective," pp. 3-42, esp. pp. 14-25, and "The Spirit and the Power of Jesus' Miracles," pp. 124-52.

[9]E.g., Ezek 3:14; 8:3; 11:1; 43:5.

[10]*Targum Jonathan* Judges 14:6, 19; 15:14.

[11]Josephus *Ant.* 3:200; 5:287, 294, 301; 8:333.

[12]Pseudo-Philo *Liber Antiquitatum Biblicarum* 27:9-10; cf. 36:2. In so far as creation is considered a miracle, it can also be noted as being associated with the Spirit: *2 Apoc. Bar.* 21:4; 23:5; 4 Ezra 6:39-41.

[13]Martin Rese, *Alttestamentliche Motive in der Christologie des Lukas* (Gütersloh: Mohn, 1969), pp. 143-46; Haya-Prats, *L'Esprit Force de l'Eglise,* pp. 40, 172-73; Menzies, *Development of Early Christian Pneumatology,* pp. 154-77, and *Empowered for Witness,* pp. 139-56.

[14]Rese, *Alttestamentliche Motive,* p. 214; cf. pp. 144-45, 151-52.

[15]E.g., Lk 5:17; 6:17; 22:51; Acts 3:11. Also see Albrecht Oepke, *"iaomai," TDNT* 3:203.

[16]The figurative use of *iaomai* is also well attested in the ancient literature, e.g., Job 5:18; Heb 12:13; 1 Pet 2:24; Josephus *Ant.* 2:119; *1 Enoch* 10:7; *1 Clement* 16:5; 56:7. Also see Oepke, *"iaomai," TDNT* 3:203.

[17]Cf. Turner, "The Spirit and the Power of Jesus' Miracles," p. 147.

[18]Just why Luke omitted Is 61:1d ("to bind up the broken hearted") remains a mystery. See Turner, "The Spirit and the Power of Jesus' Miracles," p. 147, citing D. L. Bock, *Proclamation from Prophecy and Pattern: Lucan Old Testament Christology* (Sheffield, U.K.: Sheffield Academic, 1987), pp. 106-7.

[19]E.g., Lk 4:31, 39; 5:13, 20; (cf. 7:7); 7:14; 9:42; 13:13; 18:42. Note where the speech-act is introduced by Luke, e.g., 5:24; 6:10; 7:7; 18:42.

[20]In Luke 13:10-17 the woman described as having been bound *(deō)* by Satan is said to be freed *(apoluō)* by Jesus. In Acts 10:38 Jesus is said to heal all those oppressed *(katadunasteuomenoi)* by the devil.

[21]David P. Seccombe, *Possessions and the Poor in Luke-Acts* (Linz, Aus.: SNTU, 1982), pp. 59-61; M. Dennis Hamm, "Sight to the Blind: Vision as Metaphor in Luke," *Biblica* 67 (1986): 457-77.

[22]Cf. Menzies, *Development of Early Christian Pneumatology,* pp. 185-89, and *Empowered for Witness,* pp. 161-66.

[23]E.g., C. K. Barrett, *The Holy Spirit and the Gospel Tradition* (London: SPCK, 1966), pp. 62-63; T. W. Manson, *The Teaching of Jesus* (Cambridge, U.K.: Cambridge University Press, 1967), pp. 82-83; Joachim Jeremias, *Die Sprache des Lukasevangeliums* (Göttingen, Ger.: Vandenhoeck & Ruprecht, 1980), p. 201.

[24]Cf. the literature cited by Menzies, *Development of Early Christian Pneumatology,* pp. 186-87 and notes. See also §10.11.

[25]Menzies, *Development of Early Christian Pneumatology,* pp. 185-89, and *Empowered for Witness,* pp. 161-66.

[26]Lk 1:66; Acts 4:28, 30; 7:50; 11:21; 13:11.

[27]See Turner, "Jesus and the Spirit in Lucan Perspective," pp. 26-28; Jean Marie van Cangh, "Par l'Esprit de Die—Par le Doigt de Dieu Mt 12,28 par. Lc 11,20," in *Logia: Les paroles de Jesus—The Sayings of Jesus,* ed. Joel Delobel (Leuven, Bel.: Leuven University Press, 1982), pp. 339-41.

[28]See Ex 7:4-5; 8:19; 9:3, 15. On the Old Testament interchange of "finger" and "hand" of God, see C. C. Caragounis, "Kingdom of God, Son of Man and Jesus' Self-Understanding," *TynBul* 40 (1989): 9.

[29]See *Tg. Ezek.* 1:3; 3:22; 8:1; 40:1; Robert G. Hamerton-Kelly, "A Note on Matthew XII, 28 par. Luke XI, 20," *NTS* 11 (1964-1965): 168; and Turner, "The Spirit and the Power of Jesus' Miracles," p. 145.

[30]See Acts 4:28-30; 11:21; 13:11; and Dunn, *Jesus,* pp. 45-46.

[31]Contra John P. Meier, *A Marginal Jew: Rethinking the Historical Jesus,* 3 vols. (New York: Doubleday, 1991, 1994, forthcoming), 2:410-11.

[32]Mk 3:28/Mt 12:31-32/Lk 12:10. Cf. Menzies, *Development of Early Christian Pneumatology,* pp. 190-98, and *Empowered for Witness,* pp. 163-68.

[33]Cf. H. von Baer, *Der heilige Geist in den Lukasschriften* (Stuttgart, Ger.: Kohlhammer, 1926), p. 138, and those cited by Turner, "The Spirit and the Power of Jesus' Miracles," pp. 142-43 and notes. The temptation to fail in witnessing, which Luke could be addressing, may be evident in Acts 4:29.

[34]Schweizer, *"pneuma," TDNT* 6:407.

[35]Lk 4:36/Mk 1:26; Lk 5:17/Mk 2:2; Lk 6:19/Mk 3:10. Cf. Lk 8:46/Mk 5:30.

[36]Lk 1:17, 35; 4:14; cf. Acts 1:8; 4:7, 8; 10:38.

[37]Turner, "The Spirit and the Power of Jesus' Miracles," p. 139 (his emphasis).

[38]Cf. 1 Thess 1:5; 1 Cor 2:4; Turner, "The Spirit and the Power of Jesus' Miracles," p. 139.

[39]Menzies, *Development of Early Christian Pneumatology,* p. 126, and *Empowered for Witness,* p. 115.

[40]Turner, "The Spirit and the Power of Jesus' Miracles," p. 141.

[41]Hull, *Hellenistic Magic,* chap. 6.

[42]So also Sanders and Davies, *Studying the Synoptic Gospels,* p. 281.

[43]*Mana* or *mania* was used by the Greeks for what we would call something magically inspired. See LSJ.

[44]Hull, *Hellenistic Magic,* p. 105.

[45]Without evidence Hull (*Hellenistic Magic,* pp. 107, 115) attributes this view to the historical Jesus.

[46]Hull, *Hellenistic Magic,* pp. 108-9; cf. Friedrich Preisigke, *Die Gotteskraft der früchristlichen Zeit* (Berlin: Walter de Gruyter, 1922), republished in *Der Wunderbegriffe im Neuen Testament,* ed. A. Suhl (Darmstadt: Wissenschaftlich Buchgesellschaft, 1980), pp. 210-47.

[47]Turner, "The Spirit and the Power of Jesus' Miracles," pp. 136-37 and n. 33.

[48]So Howard C. Kee, *Miracle and Magic in New Testament Times* (Cambridge, U.K.: Cambridge University Press, 1986), p. 114. On defining magic, see Graham H. Twelftree, *Jesus the Exorcist: A Contribution to the Study of the Historical Jesus* (Tübingen, Ger.: Mohr; Peabody, Mass.: Hendrickson, 1993), §24.

[49]Lk 10:13; 19:37; Acts 2:22; 8:13; 19:11; cf. Ps 77:14; 145:4.

[50]Lk 21:26/Mk 13:25; cf. Is 34:4(B).

[51]Lk 5:17; 22:69; cf. Ps 21:13; 54:1; 140:7.

[52]Lk 1:17, 35; 4:14, 36; 24:49; Acts 1:8; 10:38; cf. Ps 33:6; Is 61:1-2.

[53]Lk 21:27; cf. the use of *exousia* in Dan 7:13-14, which Luke associates with *dunamis* in Lk 4:36.

[54]So Sanders and Davies, *Studying the Synoptic Gospels,* p. 282. Lk 4:36; 5:17; 6:19; 8:46; 9:1; 10:19; Acts 3:12; 4:7; 6:8; 8:10 remain to be considered.

[55]On *salvation* in Luke-Acts, see, e.g., Ralph P. Martin, "Salvation and Discipleship in Luke's Gospel," *Int* 30 (1976): 366-80; Neal Flanagan, "The What and How of Salvation in Luke-Acts," in *Sin, Salvation and the Spirit,* ed. Daniel Durken (Collegeville: Liturgical, 1979), pp. 203-13; Joel B. Green, " 'The Message of Salvation' in Luke-Acts," *Ex Auditu* 5 (1989): 21-34; Mark Allan Powell, "Salvation in Luke-Acts," *WW* 12 (1992): 5-10.

[56]Cf. Lk 10:23-24; 19:44; Acts 2:22; 10:38.

[57]Lk 6:9; 8:36, 48, 50; 17:19; 18:42; on which see §§5.10, 16, 17, 24, 25.

[58]See Lk 19:9; Acts 4:12; 13:25, 47. Cf. Robert C. Tannehill, *The Narrative Unity of Luke-Acts: A Literary Interpretation,* 2 vols. (Philadelphia: Fortress, 1986), 1:87.

[59] Cf. Lk 8:39; 9:43; also see Acts 20:28 and text to follow.

[60] See George Howard, "The Tetragram and the New Testament," *JBL* 96 (1977): 63-83; Joseph A. Fitzmyer, "The Semitic Background of the New Testament *Kyrios*-Title," in *The Semitic Background of the New Testament* (Grand Rapids, Mich.: Dove, 1997), chap. 5.

[61] Cf. Lk 2:13, 20; 4:15; 19:37.

[62] Cf. Lk 5:25, 26; 7:16; 13:13; 17:15; 18:43; cf. Acts 4:21.

[63] Cf. Nolland, *Luke 1—9:20,* p. 321. T. L. Brodie ("Towards Unravelling Luke's Use of the Old Testament: Luke 7.11-17 as an *Imitatio* of 1 Kings 17:17-24," *NTS* 32 [1986]: 247-67) argues that Luke's story is an imitation of the Old Testament story.

[64] Joel B. Green, "Jesus and a Daughter of Abraham (Luke 13:10-17): Test Case for a Lucan Perspective on Jesus' Miracles," *CBQ* 51 (1989): 634-54, esp. pp. 649-52.

[65] Cf. ibid., pp. 649-51.

[66] Lk 5:25; 7:16; 13:13; 17:15; 18:43.

[67] Lk 5:26; 7:16; (cf. 13:17); 18:43.

[68] Gerhard Kittel, "*dokeō* . . . ," *TDNT* 2:237.

[69] Cf. Powell, "Salvation in Luke-Acts," pp. 5-6.

[70] Marshall, *Luke,* p. 649. Cf. Hans Dieter Betz, "The Cleansing of the Ten Lepers (Luke 17:11-19)," *JBL* 90 (1971): 314-28.

[71] Lk 1:35; 3:16, 22; 4:1, 14, 18.

[72] Lk 4:43; cf. 1:33 and 4:18.

[73] Cf. Howard C. Kee, "The Terminology of Mark's Exorcism Stories," *NTS* 14 (1967-1968): 232-46.

[74] As does Busse, *Die Wunder der Propheten Jesus,* pp. 79-80, 111.

[75] Mt 12:22-20/Mk 3:22-27/Lk 11:14-23; Graham H. Twelftree, *Christ Triumphant* (London: Hodder & Stoughton, 1985), pp. 98-99.

[76] See Lk 4:35, 39, 41; 9:42.

[77] Cf. Luke 13:16; James D. G. Dunn, *Jesus and the Spirit* (London: SCM Press, 1975), p. 46.

[78] M. Dennis Hamm, "The Freeing of the Bent Woman and the Restoration of Israel: Luke 13.10-17 as Narrative Theology," *JSNT* 31 (1987): 23-44.

[79] Acts 5:16; 8:7; 16:16-18; 19:11-20.

[80] Menzies, *Development of Early Christian Pneumatology,* and *Empowered for Witness,* chap. 8.

[81] Cf. Leo O'Reilly, *Word and Sign in the Acts of the Apostles: A Study in Lucan Theology* (Rome: Editrice Pontifical Università Gregoriana, 1987), p. 217.

[82] Note also Lk 4:40-44; 6:17-26; 7:18-23; 8:1-3; 9:1-2; 10:8-9.

[83] Cf. John Wilkinson, "The Case of the Bent Woman in Luke 13:10-17," *EvQ* 49 (1977): 195-205.

[84] Lk 5:15/Mk 1:45; Lk 5:17/Mk 2:1-2; Lk 9:11/Mk 6:34.

[85] Cf. Achtemeier, "The Lukan Perspective on the Miracles of Jesus," pp. 156-57.

[86] Cf. ibid., p. 157.

[87] Martin Dibelius, *From Tradition to Gospel* (London: Clarke, 1971), pp. 97-98.

[88] Rudolf Bultmann, *The History of the Synoptic Tradition* (New York: Harper & Row, 1976), pp. 12-13.

[89] F. Godet, *A Commentary on the Gospel of St. Luke,* 2 vols. (Edinburgh, U.K.: T & T Clark, 1976), 2:120; Green, "Jesus and a Daughter of Abraham," pp. 647-49.

[90] Green, "Jesus and a Daughter of Abraham," pp. 644-49.

[91] E.g., Lk 9:1-2; 10:9; Acts 3:1-10, 11-26; 5:12-16; 8:4-8; 14:3, 8-10; 16:16-18; 19:11-20.

[92] Lk 4:33-37/Mk 1:23-28; Lk 8:26-39/Mk 5:1-20; Lk 9:37-43a/Mk 9:14-29.

[93] Lk 5:5; 8:24, 45; 9:33, 49; 17:13.

[94] See Albrecht Oepke, "*epistatēs,*" *TDNT* 2:622.

[95] See §3.14, n. 91 above.

[96] Cf. Is 35:5; 4Q521. Further, see A. E. Harvey, *Jesus and the Constraints of History* (London: Duckworth, 1982), p. 115.

[97] See Betz, "The Cleansing of the Ten Lepers," pp. 314-21; Wilhelm Bruners, *Die Reinigung*

der zehn Aussätzigen und die Heilung des Samariters, Lk 17.11-19 (Stuttgart, Ger.: Katholisches Bibelwerk, 1977).

[98]See also Acts 2:43-47; 5:12-16; 8:6-7, 13; 9:42; 13:12; 16:30, 33; 19:17, 20.

[99]John A. Hardon, "The Miracle Narratives in Acts of the Apostles," *CBQ* 16 (1954): 311.

[100]So Charles H. Talbert, *Reading Luke: A Literary and Theological Commentary on the Third Gospel* (New York: Crossroad, 1982), p. 60.

[101]See also Lk 7:50; 8:25, 48; 17:19; 18:42.

[102]Lk 5:25-26; 7:16; 9:43; 13:13; 17:15, 18: 18:43; 19:37.

[103]Roland Meynet, "Au coeur du texte: Analyse rhétorique de l'aveugle de Jéricho selon saint Luc," *NRT* 103 (1981): 696-710; Hamm, "Sight to the Blind," pp. 463-65.

[104]Cf. Hamm, "Sight to the Blind," pp. 463, 475.

[105]For details, see ibid., pp. 457-77. Cf. §6.2.

[106]See Meynet, "Au coeur du texte," pp. 697-706.

[107]A number of studies have appeared on the miracles in Acts and Luke-Acts. E.g., Hardon, "Miracle Narratives in Acts," pp. 303-18; G. W. H. Lampe, "Miracles in the Acts of the Apostles," in *Miracles: Cambridge Studies in Their Philosophy and History,* ed. C. F. D. Moule (London: Mowbray, 1965), pp. 163-78; John Fenton, "The Order of the Miracles Performed by Peter and Paul in Acts," *ExpTim* 77 (1966): 381-83; Achtemeier, "The Lukan Perspective on the Miracles of Jesus," pp. 153-67; Frans Neirynck, "The Miracle Stories in the Acts of the Apostles: An Introduction," *ETL* 48 (1979): 169-213; O'Reilly, *Word and Sign.*

[108]Also at Acts 2:(19), 2:43; 4:30; 5:12; 6:8; 7:36; 14:3; 15:12. See Graham H. Twelftree, "Signs, Wonders, Miracles," in *Dictionary of Paul and His Letters,* ed. Gerald F. Hawthorne, Ralph P. Martin and Daniel G. Reid (Downers Grove, Ill.: InterVarsity Press, 1993), pp. 875-77.

[109]Deut 4:34; 6:22; 7:19; 11:3; 26:8; 29:3; 34:11; see also 28:46.

[110]Philo *Vit. Mos.* 1:95; *Leg. All.* 2:218; *see also Vit. Mos.* 1:210.

[111]See also Acts 8:13; 9:42-43; 16:30; 19:20. Contra J. Roloff (*Das Kerygma und der irdische Jesus: Historische Motive in den Jesus-Erzählungen der Evangelien* [Göttingen, Ger.: Vandenhoeck & Ruprecht, 1970], pp. 198-200), who does not see the miracles having any missionary purpose.

[112]Why Luke should use not only the phrase "signs and wonders" (Acts 4:30; 5:12; 14:3; 15:12) but also "wonders and signs" (2:19, 22, 43; 5:8; 7:36) remains a puzzle. It could be that, as Karl H. Rengstorf suggested, we have different traditions (*"teras," TDNT* 8:125).

[113]The use of the phrase "signs and wonders" for the miracles performed by the followers of Jesus (Acts 2:43; 4:30; 5:12; 6:8; 14:3; 15:12) may be a way of distinguishing Jesus' miracles from those derivative miracles of his followers.

[114]Cf. BAGD, *"euergeteō,"* p. 320.

[115]Josephus (*Ant.* 6:211) describes the restoring of health by driving out evil spirits and demons as "doing good."

[116]So I. Howard Marshall, *Acts* (Leicester, U.K.: Inter-Varsity Press, 1980), p. 192.

[117]Cf. C. K. Barrett, *The Acts of the Apostles,* 2 vols. (Edinburgh, U.K.: T & T Clark, 1994, 1998), 1:525.

[118]Contra J. Łaach, "Funkcja cudów w ewangelii Łukazowej," *Collectanea Theologica* 55 (1985): 39-44.

[119]Jn 6:26; 9:16, 30, 34; 11:46-47; cf. §8.5.3.

Chapter 7: The Miracles of Jesus in the Fourth Gospel: The Stories

[1]I will use "Fourth Gospel" for the Gospel as we have it and "John's Gospel" for the edition that ends at John 20:31.

[2]Although this issue will not be addressed directly in this chapter, Adelbert Denaux, ed. (*John and the Synoptics* [Leuven, Bel.: Leuven University Press, 1992]), says in the preface that at the Colloquium that formed the basis of this book, there was "a growing consensus that the author of the Fourth Gospel was related to and/or in one way or another dependent upon one or more of the Synoptic Gospels" (p. viii). Recently on the problem of the relationship between

John and the Synoptics, see Robert Kysar, *The Fourth Evangelist and His Gospel: An Examination of Contemporary Scholarship* (Minneapolis: Augsburg, 1975); George R. Beasley-Murray, *John* (Waco, Tex.: Word, 1987), pp. 87-88; D. Moody Smith, *Johannine Christianity: Essays on Its Setting, Sources and Theology* (Edinburgh, U.K.: T & T Clark, 1987), pp. 39-61; D. Moody Smith, *John Among the Gospels: The Relationship in Twentieth-Century Research* (Minneapolis: Fortress, 1992); Ismo Dunderberg, *Johannes und die Synoptiker: Studien zu Joh 1—9* (Helsinki, Fin.: Suomalainen Tiedeakatemia, 1994). For the view that "the Fourth Gospel was written, not for a Johannine community isolated from the rest of the early Christian movement, but for general circulation among the churches in which Mark's Gospel was already being widely circulated," see Richard Bauckham, "John for Readers of Mark," in *The Gospel for All Christians: Rethinking the Gospel Audiences,* ed. Richard Bauckham (Grand Rapids, Mich.: Eerdmans, 1998), p. 171.

[3]Cf. Willem Nicol, *The Sēmeia in the Fourth Gospel: Tradition and Redaction* (Leiden, Neth.: Brill, 1972), p. 3; Rudolf Bultmann, *The Gospel of John* (Oxford, U.K.: Blackwell, 1971), pp. 113-14.

[4]Cf. Ernst Käsemann, *The Testament of Jesus* (London: SCM Press, 1968), p. 70; Ernst Haenchen, *John,* 2 vols. (Philadelphia: Fortress, 1984), 1:166; Beasley-Murray, *John,* p. 28.

[5]Jn 16:16, 17, 19; cf. 20:18, 25. Cf. William R. G. Loader, *The Christology of the Fourth Gospel* (Fankfurt am Main, Ger.: Peter Lang, 1989), pp. 121-23.

[6]Udo Schnelle (*Antidocetic Christology in the Gospel of John* [Minneapolis: Fortress, 1992], p. 75) restricts the "greater things" to the miracles and activities of Jesus.

[7]Cf. C. H. Dodd, *The Interpretation of the Fourth Gospel* (Cambridge, U.K.: Cambridge University Press, 1953), pp. 299-300. It is notable that the only other occurrence in the New Testament of the exact phrase *tē hēmera tē tritē* is in 1 Cor 15:4, where Paul is handing on a tradition about Jesus being raised on the third day.

[8]Jn 1:29, 35, (41?), 43. Further, see C. K. Barrett, *The Gospel According to St John* (London: SPCK, 1978), p. 190. Cf. V. Parkin, " 'On the Third Day There Was a Marriage in Cana of Galilee' (John 2.1)," *IBS* 3 (1981): 134-44.

[9]John Ashton, *Understanding the Fourth Gospel* (Oxford, U.K.: Clarendon, 1991), p. 266.

[10]So Raymond E. Brown, *The Gospel According to John,* 2 vols. (London: Chapman, 1971), 1:cxxxix.

[11]On the plot of John, see R. Alan Culpepper, "The Plot of John's Story of Jesus," in *Gospel Interpretation: Narrative-Critical and Social-Scientific Approaches,* ed. Jack Dean Kingsbury (Harrisburg, Penn.: TPI, 1997), pp. 188-99, and R. Alan Culpepper, *Anatomy of the Fourth Gospel: A Study in Literary Design* (Philadelphia: Fortress, 1983), pp. 77-98; also see Mark W. G. Stibbe, " 'Return to Sender': A Structuralist Approach to John's Gospel," *Biblical Interpretation* 1 (1993): 189-206.

[12]J. Duncan M. Derrett (*Law in the New Testament* [London: DLT, 1970], p. 228 n.1) notes the contrary view that many writers say it is vain to "speculate about the historical conditions of a fact which does not belong to strict history." He cites A. Loisy, G. H. C. MacGregor and R. H. Strachan.

[13]Cf. A. Geyser, "The Semeion at Cana of the Galilee," in *Studies in John Presented to Professor Dr. J. N. Sevenster* (Leiden, Neth.: Brill, 1970), p. 13.

[14]So Bultmann, *John,* p. 112.

[15]E.g., Mt 5:6; 8:11-12; Mk 2:19; Lk 22:15-18, 29-30a.

[16]Cf. Dodd (*Interpretation,* p. 297), who ties together 2:1—4:42 with the theme "The Old things have passed away, see, the new have come!" (2 Cor 5:17).

[17]Cf. Dodd, *Interpretation,* p. 297; Raymond E. Brown, *New Testament Essays* (New York: Paulist, 1965), p. 70 n. 52; Raymond F. Collins, "Cana (Jn. 2:1-12)—The First of His Signs or the Key to His Signs?" *ITQ* 47 (1980): 79-95.

[18]Bultmann, *John,* p. 118.

[19]Cf. Wilhelm Bousset, *Kyrios Christos* (Nashville: Abingdon, 1970), p. 103.

[20]Plutarch *Lysander* XXVIII:4.

[21]Pliny *Natural History* II:231; XXXI:16.

[22]Pausanius *Description of Greece* VI:xxvi:1-2.

[23]Ovid *Metamorphoses* XIII:650-54.

[24]Cf. Martin Hengel ("The Interpretation of the Wine Miracle at Cana: John 2:1-11," in *The Glory of Christ in the New Testament,* ed. L. D. Hurst and N. T. Wright [Oxford, U.K.: Clarendon, 1987], pp. 83-112), who rejects the choice between a Jewish background and a Dionysian background because the Dionysian and pagan wine god traditions had long penetrated Jewish culture (p. 112).

[25]E.g., Is 16:9-10; 24:11; Jer 48:33; Joel 1:5; Amos 5:11; Mic 6:15; Zeph 1:13.

[26]So Barnabas Lindars, *The Gospel of John* (London: Oliphants/Marshall, Morgan & Scott, 1972), p. 128. Note that it is not that the wine originally offered was in question but that it had failed; so had the Jewish law and religion.

[27]Cf. Rudolf Schnackenburg, *The Gospel According to St John,* 3 vols. (New York: Burns & Oates; Freiburg, Ger.: Herder, 1968), 1:332.

[28]E.g., Gen 27:28; 49:11; Deut 7:13; Ps 104:14-15; Eccles 9:7; Joel 2:23-24.

[29]Jer 31:12; Joel 3:18; Amos 9:13-14; Zech 10:7; cf. Mk 2:22; *2 Apoc. Bar.* 29:5; *Sib. Or.* 2:313-21; 3:619-23, 744-45; 8:209-12.

[30]Cf. Martin Scott, *Sophia and the Johannine Jesus* (Sheffield, U.K.: JSOT, 1992), p. 183.

[31]See the discussion in the text on John 1 and on 2:4.

[32]Dodd, *Interpretation,* pp. 54-73.

[33]Oscar Cullmann (*Early Christian Worship* [London: SCM Press, 1953], p. 69 n. 1) cites Maurice Goguel, Walter Bauer and C. T. Craig, as well as the church fathers Cyril of Jerusalem and Cyprian as taking his position. See the discussion in Brown, *New Testament Essays,* chap. 4.

[34]On the endlesss discussion of the issue of the eucharistic motifs in this Gospel, see, e.g., Günther Bornkamm, "Die eucharistische Rede im Johannes-Evangelium," *ZNW* 47 (1956): 161-69; Wilhelm Wilkens, "Das Abendmahlzeugnis im vierten Evangelium," *EvT* 18 (1958): 354-70; B. Gärtner, *John 6 and the Jewish Passover* (Lund, Swe.: CWK Gleerup, 1959); G. H. C. MacGregor, "The Eucharist in the Fourth Gospel," *NTS* 9 (1962-1963): 111-19; Oscar S. Brooks, "The Johannine Eucharist: Another Interpretation," *JBL* 82 (1963): 293-300; Eduard Schweizer, "Das johanneische Zeugnis vom Herrenmahl," in *Neotestamentica* (Zürich, Switz.: Zwingli, 1963), pp. 371-96; T. E. Worden, "The Holy Eucharist in St. John," *Scripture* 15 (1963): 97-103; 16 (1964): 5-16; J. K. Howard, "Passover and Eucharist in the Fourth Gospel," *SJT* 20 (1967): 329-37; James D. G. Dunn, "John 6: A Eucharistic Discourse?" *NTS* 17 (1971): 328-38; Rudolf Schnackenburg, "Das Brot des Lebens," in *Tradition und Glaube,* FS K. G. Kuhn (Göttingen, Ger.: Vandenhoeck & Ruprecht, 1971), pp. 328-42; Barnabas Lindars, "Word and Sacrament in the Fourth Gospel," *SJT* 29 (1976): 49-63.

[35]Bultmann, *John,* pp. 138 n. 3, 234, 677 n. 6.

[36]So Brown, *New Testament Essays,* p. 57.

[37]Cullmann, *Early Christian Worship,* p. 69.

[38]Further, see Maurice F. Wiles, *The Spiritual Gospel* (Cambridge, U.K.: Cambridge University Press, 1960), pp. 42-43.

[39]Noted by Brown, *New Testament Essays,* p. 70.

[40]Cf. Jean Zumstein, "Le signe de la croix," *Lumière & Vie* 41 (1992): 68-82.

[41]Heinrich Seesemann, *"oinos,"* *TDNT* 5:163 n.12, citing Karl L. Schmidt and E. Hirsch.

[42]So Bruce Vawter, "The Johannine Sacramentary," *TS* 17 (1956): 151-66; cf. David M. Stanley, "Cana as Epiphany," *Worship* 32 (1957-1958): 83-89.

[43]So Brown, *New Testament Essays,* p. 69.

[44]Larry Paul Jones, *The Symbol of Water in the Gospel of John* (Sheffield, U.K.: Sheffield Academic, 1997), p. 220.

[45]Walter Bauer, *Das Johannesevangelium,* 3d ed. (Tübingen, Ger.: Mohr, 1933), p. 46, followed by Eduard Lohse, "Miracles in the Fourth Gospel," in *What About the New Testament?* ed. Morna Hooker and Colin Hickling (London: SCM Press, 1975), p. 68.

[46]For details, see Derrett, *Law in the New Testament,* p. 237.

[47]Nicol, Sēmeia *in the Fourth Gospel,* p. 43.

[48]Ben Witherington, *John's Wisdom: A Commentary on the Fourth Gospel* (Louisville, Ky.: Westminster John Knox, 1995), p. 78.

[49]See Derrett, *Law in the New Testament,* p. 236.

[50]On this Semitism, see Brown, *John,* 1:99.

[51]Similarly Derrett, *Law in the New Testament,* p. 242.

[52]See Scott, *Sophia and the Johannine Jesus,* p. 179; Witherington, *John's Wisdom,* p. 79.

[53]Haenchen, *John,* 1:172, citing, e.g., Jn 5:19, 30; 7:6; 8:25.

[54]Jn 7:30; 8:20; 13:1; 17:1; cf. 7:6.

[55]So also Francis J. Moloney, *The Gospel of John* (Collegeville: Liturgical, 1998), p. 69.

[56]Jn 2:11; 11:4 (cf. 9:3), 11:40; 12:41, 43.

[57]So Ashton, *Understanding the Fourth Gospel,* p. 270.

[58]Cf. Schnelle, *Antidocetic Christology,* p. 80.

[59]Ashton, *Understanding the Fourth Gospel,* pp. 268-69 (his emphasis).

[60]Cf. Cullmann, *Early Christian Worship,* p. 67.

[61]Cf. Jn 3:25-26; Mk 2:18-22; Josephus *Ant.* 18:116-17.

[62]So Geyser, "The Semeion at Cana of the Galilee," p. 18.

[63]See Pseudo-Clementine *Recognitions* 1:54, 60, cited by Walter Wink, *John the Baptist in the Gospel Tradition* (Cambridge, U.K.: Cambridge University Press, 1968), pp. 100-101. Cf. Brown, *John I—XII,* pp. 46-47.

[64]See further in Wink, *John the Baptist,* pp. 105-6.

[65]Most probably entirely redactional. See the argumentation in Schnelle, *Antidocetic Christology,* pp. 78-79.

[66]Cf. Collins, "Cana (Jn. 2:1-12)," p. 91.

[67]Contrast Robert T. Fortna ("Source and Redaction in the Fourth Gospel's Portrayal of Jesus' Signs," *JBL* 89 [1970]: 166), who isolates Jesus' death as the chief sign.

[68]Brown, *John,* 1:104.

[69]Francis J. Moloney ("From Cana to Cana [John 2:1—4:54] and the Fourth Evangelist's Concept of Correct [and Incorrect] Faith," in *Studia Biblica 1978 II: Papers on the Gospels,* ed. E. A. Livingstone [Sheffield, U.K.: JSOT, 1980], p. 206 n. 22) insists that this reference to "days," as well as that in Jn 2:1, connects the Cana miracles with the resurrection. If correct, this strengthens the case for the cross being foreshadowed in the Johannine signs.

[70]Against Barrett (*St John,* p. 246); e.g., initial difficulties in this transitional passage cannot be solved by postulating that Jesus' "own country" is Jerusalem or Judea. See Jn 1:46; 7:41-42. Further, see Haenchen, *John,* 1:234.

[71]Cf. Haenchen, *John,* 1:234; Witherington, *John's Wisdom,* p. 126.

[72]Against the majority view (see the discussion in Schnackenburg, *St John,* 1:471-75) that this story is a variant of the healing of the centurion's son in Mt 8:5-13/Lk 7:1-10, see Witherington, *John's Wisdom,* pp. 127-28, citing his "Principles for Interpreting the Gospels and Acts," *Ashland Theological Seminary Journal* 19 (1982): 35-61.

[73]Generally agreed to be redactional. See Bultmann, *John,* p. 206; Wilhelm Wilkens, *Zeichen und Werke* (Zürich, Switz.: Zwingli, 1969), p. 33, and others cited by Schnelle, *Antidocetic Christology,* p. 83 n. 50.

[74]Most probably entirely redactional. See Schnelle, *Antidocetic Christology,* p. 87 and n. 77.

[75]André Feuillet, *Johannine Studies* (New York: Alba, 1964), pp. 39-43.

[76]Cf. Schnelle, *Antidocetic Christology,* p. 93 and n. 110.

[77]So Beasley-Murray (*John,* p. 67) and Culpepper (*Anatomy of the Fourth Gospel,* p. 91), who cites Meir Sterberg, *Expositional Modes and Temporal Ordering in Fiction* (Baltimore, Md.: Johns Hopkins University Press, 1978), pp. 102-4, for a discussion of "primacy effect."

[78]Contrast John Painter, *The Quest for the Messiah,* 2d ed. (Edinburgh, U.K.: T & T Clark, 1993), chap. 4; cf. Robert C. Tannehill, ed., "Pronouncement Stories," *Semeia* 20 (1981): 1-13.

[79]On *basilikos,* see Josephus *Life* 400-401; *J.W.* 1:45; and Schnackenburg, *St John,* 1:461 n. 15.

[80]Widely thought to be redactional. See Schnelle, *Antidocetic Christology,* p. 84 and n. 55.

[81]Cf. ibid., p. 85.

[82]Against Nicol, Sēmeia *in the Fourth Gospel,* p. 43.

[83]Lohse, "Miracles in the Fourth Gospel," p. 66.

[84]So Marie Emile Boismard, *Du baptême à Cana (Jean, 1,19-2,11)* (Paris: Éditions du Cerf, 1956), p. 107, cited by Schnackenburg, *St John,* 1:462 n. 2.

[85]See Feuillet, *Johannine Studies,* pp. 44-51.

[86]Rudolf Bultmann, *Theology of the New Testament,* 2 vols. (London: SCM Press, 1952-1955), 2:60.

[87]Cf. Peter Riga, "Signs of Glory: The Use of *'Sēmeion'* in St. John's Gospel," *Int* 17 (1963): 417. On this indicating a different source, see Mark W. G. Stibbe, *John's Gospel* (London: Routledge, 1994), pp. 79-82.

[88]Cf. Schnelle, *Antidocetic Christology,* p. 91.

[89]Noticed in passing by Walter Bauer, *Das Johannesevangelium* (Tübingen, Ger.: Mohr, 1933), p. 78, and explored in Moloney, "From Cana to Cana," pp. 190-91.

[90]Moloney ("From Cana to Cana," p. 191) attempts to see the mother of Jesus and the official as the believers on the basis not of the miracle but of the word of Jesus. This ignores the faith evident in the persistence of the official (Jn 4:48-49) and the climactic position of 2:11 and 4:53, where the miracle is the basis of (uncriticized) faith.

[91]Here I am following the general observation of Moloney ("From Cana to Cana," esp. p. 200) but not his conclusion that "true faith means a radical openness to the *word* of Jesus" (p. 202, emphasis added). See also Moloney, *John,* pp. 151-58.

[92]That Jn 5:1 begins a new section is clear from "after this" (cf. Jn 6:1; 7:1; 13:7; 19:38; 21:1). See Haenchen, *John,* 1:243.

[93]Bultmann, *John,* p. 238 n. 1.

[94]Robert T. Fortna, *The Gospel of Signs* (Cambridge, U.K.: Cambridge University Press, 1970), pp. 102-9.

[95]Barrett (*St. John,* p. 24) notes the exception of the Sinaitic Syriac in Jn 18:13-24.

[96]On the different form of story here and the related issues of source this raises, see Stibbe, *John's Gospel,* pp. 79-82.

[97]Jn 5:[4], 6, 9, 11, 14, 15.

[98]Cullmann, *Early Christian Worship,* pp. 84-85 and notes.

[99]Ibid., pp. 86-87, citing Joachim Jeremias, *The Rediscovery of Bethesda: John 5:2* (Louisville, Ky.: Southern Baptist Theological Seminary, 1966), p. 24.

[100]This is apparent for three reasons: the verse contains a number of non-Johannine words or expressions; it has been transmitted to us in a diversity of forms; and, most important, it is absent from the earliest and best witnesses. Cf. Bruce M. Metzger, *A Textual Commentary on the Greek New Testament* (London: United Bible Societies, 1971), p. 209.

[101]So, e.g., Brown, *John,* 1:211; Brown, *New Testament Essays,* pp. 64-66.

[102]Dodd, *Interpretation,* p. 319.

[103]So Emanuel Hirsch, *Das vierte Evangelium in seiner ursprünglichen Gestalt verdeutscht und eklärt* (Tübingen, Ger.: Mohr, 1936), pp. 156-58, cited by Haenchen, *John,* 1:255.

[104]W. F. Howard, *The Fourth Gospel in Recent Criticism and Interpretation* (London: Epworth, 1931), p. 184, followed by Bultmann, *John,* pp. 241-42 n. 7. So also J. H. Bernard, *Gospel According to St. John,* 2 vols. (Edinburgh, U.K.: T & T Clark, 1928), 1:229.

[105]So Barrett, *St. John,* p. 254.

[106]Bultmann, *John,* p. 242 n. 2.

[107]Haenchen, *John,* 1:245.

[108]Cf. Bernard, *St. John,* 1:231.

[109]Jn 2:19, 20, 22; 5:8, 21; 7:52; 11:29; 12:1, 9, 17; 13:4; 14:31; 21:14.

[110]Jn 5:8; (5:21?); 7:52; 11:29; 13:4; 14:31.

[111]Cf. Haenchen, *John,* 1:256.

[112]So C. H. Dodd, *Historical Tradition in the Fourth Gospel* (Cambridge, U.K.: Cambridge University Press, 1963), p. 177.

[113]So Bultmann, *John,* p. 243 n. 5.

[114]So B. F. Westcott, *The Gospel According to St John* (London: John Murray, 1896), p. 83.

[115]So Barrett, *St. John,* p. 255.

[116]Cf., e.g., Bultmann, *John,* p. 243 and n. 10; Haenchen, *John,* 1:247-48.

[117]Haenchen, *John,* 1:258.

[118]Cf. Lohse, "Miracles in the Fourth Gospel," p. 69.

[119]Jn 6:2; cf. 2:23-25; 4:43-45.

[120]Jn 6:15; cf. 2:23-25; 4:43-45, 48.

[121]Culpepper, *Anatomy of the Fourth Gospel,* pp. 91-92.

[122]See the detailed list in Brown, *John,* pp. 240-43. Cf. Dodd, *Historical Tradition,* pp. 199-211; Schnelle, *Antidocetic Christology,* pp. 105-6.

[123]Barrett, *St. John,* p. 271; cf. also Schnelle, *Antidocetic Christology,* p. 115.

[124]E.g., Bultmann, *John,* p. 210; Dodd, *Historical Tradition,* pp. 196-222; Schnackenburg, *St John,* 2:21-23, 28; Fortna, *Signs,* pp. 63, 66. See also n. 2 above.

[125]Cf. Paul N. Anderson, *The Christology of the Fourth Gospel: Its Unity and Disunity in the Light of John 6* (Tübingen, Ger.: Mohr, 1996), p. 192.

[126]Brown, *John,* 1:232.

[127]Cf. L. Th. Witkamp, "Some Specific Johannine Features in John 6.1-21," *JSNT* 40 (1990): 47.

[128]Schnackenburg, *St John,* 2:13-14.

[129]Cf. Edwyn Clement Hoskyns, *The Fourth Gospel,* ed. Francis Noel Davey, 2d ed. (London: Faber & Faber, 1947), p. 281.

[130]Cf. Beasley-Murray, *John,* p. 87. See also Barrett, *St. John,* p. 277.

[131]So Brown, *John,* 1:235; cf. Nicol, *Sēmeia in the Fourth Gospel,* pp. 89-90.

[132]See further Anderson, *The Christology of the Fourth Gospel,* pp. 172-73.

[133]Cf. Beasley-Murray, *John,* p. 88.

[134]On the status of this verse in the text, see Barrett, *John,* p. 285, and Bruce M. Metzger, *A Textual Commentary on the Greek New Testament* (Stuttgart, Ger.: United Bible Societies, 1994), p. 182.

[135]Anderson, *Christology of the Fourth Gospel,* p. 174.

[136]See, e.g., Bornkamm, "Die eucharistische Rede im Johannes-Evangelium," pp. 161-69; Wilkens, "Das Abendmahlzeugnis im vierten Evangelium," pp. 354-70; Gärtner, *John 6 and the Jewish Passover;* MacGregor, "The Eucharist in the Fourth Gospel," pp. 111-19; Brooks, "The Johannine Eucharist," pp. 293-300; Schweizer, "Das johanneische Zeugnis vom Herrenmahl," pp. 371-96; Worden, "The Holy Eucharist in St. John," *Scripture* 15 (1963): 97-103; 16 (1964): 5-16; Howard, "Passover and Eucharist," pp. 329-37; Dunn, "John 6: A Eucharistic Discourse?" pp. 328-38; Schnackenburg, "Das Brot des Lebens," pp. 328-42; Lindars, "Word and Sacrament," pp. 49-63.

[137]See the chart in Brown, *John,* 1:243.

[138]See further, C. F. D. Moule, "A Note on *Didache* IX 4," *JTS* 6 (1955): 240-43.

[139]This was pointed out to me by Mark Stibbe in private correspondence, who noted that there was no fracture in this Gospel—the bread is not broken (6:11), neither are his bones (19:36) or the net (21:11). The different vocabulary and that the third example comes from Jn 21 means we need to exercise caution before seeing a pattern here.

[140]See Ex 12:46; Num 9:12; Ps 34:20.

[141]E.g., Bultmann, *John,* pp. 218-21.

[142]Brown, *John,* 1:51-58.

[143]Against Bultmann, *John,* pp. 234-37.

[144]Cf. Nicol, *Sēmeia in the Fourth Gospel,* p. 43.

[145]David Daube, *The New Testament and Rabbinic Judaism* (Salem, N.H.: Ayer, 1984), p. 38.

[146]Further, see Anderson, *Christology of the Fourth Gospel,* pp. 174-79.

[147]Against Wayne A. Meeks, *The Prophet-King, Moses Traditions and the Johannine Christology* (Leiden, Neth.: Brill, 1967). See the discussion in Nicol, *Sēmeia in the Fourth Gospel,* p. 88 n. 2.

[148]Cf. Richard A. Horsley, "Popular Messianic Movements Around the Time of Jesus," *CBQ* 46 (1984): 471-95, and *Bandits, Prophets, and Messiahs: Popular Movements at the Time of Jesus* (San Francisco: Harper & Row, 1985), chaps. 3 and 4.

[149]So Dodd, *Historical Tradition*, pp. 213-15, 221-22. Later, in the story of the entry into Jerusalem, John will again show that in acclaiming Jesus as king (Jn 12:13) they misunderstood the nature of Jesus' messiahship and were not able to believe in him even though they saw the signs.

[150]On the implications of Jesus' kingship not being "of this world," see David Rensberger, "The Politics of John: The Trial of Jesus in the Fourth Gospel," *JBL* 103 (1984): 395-411.

[151]Peder Borgen, "Observations on the Midrashic Character of John 6," *ZNW* 54 (1963): 232-40.

[152]Str-B 2:483-84.

[153]Noted by Dodd, *Interpretation*, pp. 336-37.

[154]Cf. *Exodus Rabbah* 25:7, where Prov 9:5 is associated with Ex 16:4: "I am going to rain bread from heaven for you." See Peder Borgen, *Bread from Heaven: An Exegetical Study of the Concept of Manna in the Gospel of John and the Writings of Philo* (Leiden, Neth.: Brill, 1981), pp. 154-58.

[155]Barrett, *St. John*, p. 279.

[156]For more detail, see Brown, *John*, 1:253-54. For a discussion of the differences between the Markan and Johannine story, see Anderson, *Christology of the Fourth Gospel*, pp. 179-83.

[157]Brown, *John*, 1:254.

[158]For a discussion of the differences between the Markan and Johannine story, see Anderson, *Christology of the Fourth Gospel*, pp. 179-83.

[159]So Barrett, *St. John*, p. 279.

[160]So ibid.

[161]So Beasley-Murray, *John*, p. 89.

[162]Contra Lindars, *John*, p. 246.

[163]So ibid., p. 245.

[164]So ibid.

[165]Cf. Bernard, *St. John*, 1:185-86.

[166]So George Giffordt, "*Epitēs thalassēs*," *ExpTim* 40 (1928-1929): 236.

[167]Further, see Bultmann, *John*, p. 225 n. 3.

[168]E.g., Jn 6:35, 41, 48, 51; 8:12; 10:7, 9, 11, 14; 15:1, 5.

[169]Cf. Jn 8:24, 28, 58; 13:19.

[170]Gen 26:24; 46:3; Jer 1:8, 17; 42:11; 46:28. Further, see esp. David Mark Ball, "*I Am*" *in John's Gospel: Literary Function, Background and Theological Implications* (Sheffield, U.K.: Sheffield Academic, 1996), pp. 181-82.

[171]Cf. Ball, "*I Am*" *in John's Gospel*, p. 185. To the contrary, see Barrett, *St. John*, p. 281; Loader, *Christology*, p. 45; Kenneth L. McKay, " 'I Am' in John's Gospel," *ExpTim* 107 (1996): 302-3.

[172]Further, on the *egō eimi* phrase, see Eduard Schweizer, *Egō eimi* (Göttingen, Ger.: Vandenhoeck & Ruprecht, 1939); Daube, *The New Testament and Rabbinic Judaism*, pp. 325-29; Dodd, *Interpretation*, pp. 93-96, 349-50; H. Zimmermann, "Das absolute *egō eimi* als die neutestamentliche Offenbarungsformel," *BZ* n.s. 4 (1960): 54-69, 266-76; Brown, *John*, pp. 533-38; Schnackenburg, *St John*, 2:79-89; Ball, "*I Am*" *in John's Gospel*.

[173]Cf. Schnackenburg (*St John*, 2:88), where he suggests that John sees Jesus as "God's eschatological revealer in whom God utters himself."

[174]Culpepper, *Anatomy of the Fourth Gospel*, p. 92.

[175]Cf. Bruce H. Grigsby, "Washing in the Pool of Siloam—A Thematic Anticipation of the Johannine Cross," *NovT* 27 (1985): 227-35.

[176]See also Ex 20:15/Deut 5:9; cf. Lk 13:1-5; Jerusalem Targum on Deut 21:20. Considering Ps 58:3 and Jer 1:5, rabbis discussed cases in which a child had already sinned in its mother's womb (*Gen. Rab.* 63:[39c]). Further, see Str-B 2:527-29.

[177]Cf. Günther Bornkamm, "Die Heilung des Blindgeborenen (Johannes 9)," in *Geschichte und Glauben*, 2 vols. (Munich, Ger.: Kaiser, 1971), 2:68.

[178]E.g., John Bligh, "The Man Born Blind," *HeyJ* 7 (1966): 132-33; Haenchen, *John*, 2:41.

[179]Cf. Culpepper, *Anatomy of the Fourth Gospel*, p. 93.

[180]Cf. Metzger, *A Textual Commentary* (1994), p. 194.

[181]So Bultmann, *John*, p. 331 n. 7.

[182]So Brown, *John*, 1:372.

[183]So Bultmann, *John*, p. 332, citing Str-B 2:534 on Jn 9:16.

[184]Also at Jn 12:42; 16:2.

[185]E.g., J. Louis Martyn, *History and Theology in the Fourth Gospel* (New York: Harper & Row, 1968), chap. 2. More recently see Richard A. Burridge, "About People, by People, for People: Gospel Genre and Audiences," in *The Gospel for All Christians: Rethinking the Gospel Audiences*, ed. Richard Bauckham (Grand Rapids, Mich.: Eerdmans, 1998), pp. 136-37.

[186]So Barrett, *St. John*, p. 361. Cf. Martyn, *History and Theology*, pp. 40-41.

[187]So James D. G. Dunn, *The Parting of the Ways: Between Christianity and Judaism and Their Significance for the Character of Christianity* (London: SCM Press, 1991), p. 221; also Wolfgang Schrage, "*aposunagōgos*," *TDNT* 7:848-52.

[188]Cf. Mt 5:11; 10:32-3; Lk 6:22; 12:8-9. Cf. Beasley-Murray, *John*, p. 154.

[189]Cf. J. N. Sanders and B. A. Mastin, *The Gospel According to St John* (London: Black, 1968), p. 242.

[190]Cf. in Acts 18:25 "the Way of the Lord" (cf. 18:26) and its use in self-definition at Qumran (1QS 9:17-18; 10:21; CD 1:13; 2:6). See also Eero Repo, *Der "Weg" als Selbstbezeichnung des Urchristentums* (Helsinki, Fin.: Suomalainen Tiedeakatemia, 1964).

[191]See the discussion by J. Duncan M. Derrett, "Cursing Jesus (I Cor. XII.3): The Jews as Religious 'Persecutors,' " *NTS* 21 (1975): 544-54. On expulsion from synagogues in the time of Jesus, see Emil Schürer, *The History of the Jewish People in the Time of Jesus Christ* (Edinburgh, U.K.: T & T Clark, 1979), 2:431-33.

[192]On the Son of Man here as "the one who mediates the salvation of the kingdom of God, which in this Gospel is chiefly represented as eternal life; his function as executor of the judgment which accompanies the revelation of the divine sovereignty, now and in the future," see Beasley-Murray, *John*, p. 159; also, Martyn, *History and Theology*, pp. 131-35, Barrett, *St John*, p. 354, and Schnackenburg, *St John*, 2:253, who are cited by Beasley-Murray.

[193]On the status of Jn 9:38-39 in the text, see Metzger, *A Textual Commentary* (1994), p. 195.

[194]Brown, *John*, 1:377.

[195]So also Bligh, "The Man Born Blind," p. 141.

[196]Jn 10:18; cf. 10:11, 15, 17.

[197]On this story, see in particular Stibbe, *John's Gospel*, pp. 75-106, and "A Tomb with a View: John 11.1-44 in Narrative-Critical Perspective," *NTS* 40 (1994): 38-54.

[198]Cf. Stibbe, "A Tomb With a View," p. 41.

[199]See the summaries in Haenchen, *John*, 2:67-68.

[200]Bultmann, *John*, pp. 395-96 nn. 2, 4.

[201]Paul Wendland, *Die urchristlichen Literaturformen* (Tübingen, Ger.: Mohr, 1912), pp. 305-7.

[202]Dodd, *Interpretation*, p. 363.

[203]Alan Richardson, *The Gospel According to St. John* (London: SCM Press, 1959), p. 139.

[204]See Roderic Dunkerley, "Lazarus," *NTS* 5 (1958-1959): 321-27; Wilhelm Wilkens, "Die Erweckung des Lazarus," *TZ* 15 (1959): 22-39.

[205]So Brown, *John*, 1:429.

[206]So Dunkerley, "Lazarus," pp. 321-27.

[207]The story of the raising of a young man at Bethany in *The Secret Gospel of Mark*—see Morton Smith, *Clement of Alexandria and a Secret Gospel of Mark* (Cambridge, Mass.: Harvard University Press, 1973)—is not generally thought, as Smith argued, to be independent of the Fourth Gospel. See Raymond E. Brown, "The Relation of 'The Secret Gospel of Mark' to the Fourth Gospel," *CBQ* 36 (1974): 466-85; H. Merkel, "Appendix: The 'Secret Gospel' of Mark," in *New Testament Apocrypha*, 2 vols., ed. Wilhelm Schneemelcher (Cambridge, U.K.: Clarke; Louisville, Ky.: Westminster John Knox, 1991), 1:106-9; John K. Elliott, *The Apocry-*

phal New Testament (Oxford, U.K.: Clarendon, 1993), pp. 148-49 and literature cited.
[208]Contra, Brown, *John*, 1:431.
[209]Dodd, *Interpretation*, p. 363. For the opinion that the words of Jesus in v. 4 are to be consigned to Johannine redaction, see Schnelle, *Antidocetic Christology*, p. 127.
[210]Cf., e.g., Mk 8:34; Rom 6:8; 2 Cor 4:10; 5:14.
[211]So Bultmann, *John*, p. 398. Cf. Jn 12:16, 23, 28, 13:31-32; 17:1, 4-5.
[212]See the discussion in Beasley-Murray, *John*, p. 193.
[213]So Schnackenburg, *St. John*, 2:335.
[214]Cf. Brown, *New Testament Essays*, p. 182. Cf. §8.3.
[215]Notable exceptions are Walter Bauer and Adolf Schlatter and, more recently, Stephen S. Smalley, "The Sign of John XXI," *NTS* 20 (1973-1974): 275-77. See also the discussion in Haenchen, *John*, 2:229.
[216]This is not to deny that a careful reading of 21:1-14 indicates several conscious links with the Gospel of John as a whole (e.g., the use of the verb *phanerō* for the revelation of Jesus, the unnamed disciple in v. 2, the possible link between the bread and the fish of 21:9 and 6:1-15) and especially with events reported in 20:1-29 (e.g., links with the experience of Mary Magdalene and the time when it took place, and the return of Simon Peter and the Beloved Disciple, who behave as they did in 20:3-10). (Cf. Moloney, *John*, p. 551.)
[217]See the discussion in Brown, *John*, 2:1084-85.
[218]See ibid., 2:1096-97.
[219]Cf. Kenneth Cardwell, in Paul Trudinger and Kenneth Cardwell, "153 Fishes: A Response and a Further Suggestion," *ExpTim* 102 (1990): 11.
[220]On the various suggested interpretations of the number of fish (153), see Westcott, *St John*, pp. 306-7; Bultmann, *John*, p. 709 n. 2; Brown, *John*, 2:1074-76; Trudinger and Cardwell, "153 Fishes," pp. 11-14; and Beasley-Murray, *John*, pp. 402-4.
[221]See Mathias Rissi, " 'Voll grosser Fische, hundertdreiundfünfzig,' Joh 21:1-14," *TZ* 35 (1979): 73-89.
[222]So Beasley-Murray, *John*, p. 404.
[223]Robert M. Grant, "One Hundred Fifty-three Large Fishes," *HTR* 42 (1949): 273-75.
[224]Jn 6:44; 12:32; 18:10; 21:6, 11; Acts 16:19.
[225]The theme of schism is reminiscent of 1 John. See, e.g., Brown, *New Testament Essays*, pp. 103-9.
[226]Cullmann (*Early Christian Worship*, p. 15) notes "that later the symbol of the fish was associated with the Eucharist."
[227]So, e.g., Brown (*John*, 2:1099-1100), who also draws attention to the Eucharistic symbolism of the meal. Barrett (*St. John*, p. 582) is more cautious: "The eucharistic allusions are more remote than some modern expositors suppose."

Chapter 8: The Miracles of Jesus in the Fourth Gospel: The Issues
[1]E.g., Bruce Vawter, "Johannine Theology," in *The Jerome Bible Commentary* (London: Chapman, 1969), p. 833.
[2]Cf. C. H. Dodd, *The Interpretation of the Fourth Gospel* (Cambridge, U.K.: Cambridge University Press, 1953), pp. 300-303; Francis J. Moloney, "From Cana to Cana (John 2:1—4:54) and the Fourth Evangelist's Concept of Correct (and Incorrect) Faith," in *Studia Biblica 1978 II: Papers on the Gospels*, ed. E. A. Livingstone (Sheffield, U.K.: JSOT, 1980), p. 189, citing S. A. Panimolle, *Lettura Pastorale del Vangelo di Giovanni, Lettura pastorale della bibbia* (Bologna: Dehoniane, 1978), 1:201, and I. de la Potterie, "Structura primae partis Evangelii Johannis (capita III et IV)," *VD* 47 (1969): 137-40. See also Andreas J. Köstenberger, "The Seventh Johannine Sign: A Study of John's Christology," *Bulletin for Biblical Research* 5 (1995): 87-103.
[3]Raymond E. Brown, "The Gospel Miracles," in *New Testament Essays* (New York: Paulist, 1965), p. 184 n. 56.
[4]Robert T. Fortna ("Source and Redaction in the Fourth Gospel's Portrayal of Jesus' Signs,"

JBL 89 [1970]: 166) suggests that the death of Jesus is the chief sign by which he gives life (Jn 3:14-15; 13:32).

[5]See §§7.3, 4, 5, 6, 9.

[6]On "Symbolic Action" in John, see Craig R. Koester, *Symbolism in the Fourth Gospel* (Minneapolis: Fortress, 1995), pp. 74-122.

[7]On what follows, see Graham H. Twelftree, *Christ Triumphant: Exorcism Then and Now* (London: Hodder & Stoughton, 1985), pp. 88-90, and "Demon, Devil, Satan," in *Dictionary of Jesus and the Gospels,* ed. Joel B. Green, Scott McKnight and I. Howard Marshall (Downers Grove, Ill.: InterVarsity Press, 1992), p. 171.

[8]Edwin K. Broadhead ("Echoes of an Exorcism in the Fourth Gospel?" *ZNW* 86 [1995]: 111-19) makes the interesting, though not wholly convincing, case that Jn 6:66-71 may carry echoes of a Synoptic exorcism tradition.

[9]Graham H. Twelftree, *Jesus the Exorcist: A Contribution to the Study of the Historical Jesus* (Tübingen, Ger.: Mohr; Peabody, Mass.: Hendrickson, 1993), §16.

[10]Richard Bauckham, ed., *The Gospels for All Christians* (Edinburgh, U.K.: T & T Clark; Grand Rapids, Mich.: Eerdmans, 1997).

[11]Vincent Taylor, *The Gospel According to St. Mark* (London: Macmillan, 1959), p. 171.

[12]D. Moody Smith, *The Theology of the Gospel of John* (Cambridge, U.K.: Cambridge University Press, 1995), p. 108, citing Mk 3:22; cf. Jn 8:48-49.

[13]See also Twelftree, "Demon, Devil, Satan," in *Dictionary of Jesus and the Gospels,* p. 171.

[14]Cf. Ernst Käsemann, *The Testament of Jesus* (London: SCM Press, 1968), p. 22.

[15]John P. Meier, *A Marginal Jew: Rethinking the Historical Jesus,* 3 vols. (New York: Doubleday, 1991, 1994, forthcoming), 2:637 n. 18.

[16]John mentions the kingdom of God only at Jn 3:3, 5.

[17]Meier, *A Marginal Jew,* 2:637 n. 18. Jn 6:70; 12:31; 13:2, 27; 14:30; 16:11.

[18]Jn 12:27; 13:21; 14:1, 27; cf. §7.9.

[19]Cf. Käsemann, *Testament of Jesus,* p. 22.

[20]Rudolf Bultmann, *Theology of the New Testament,* 2 vols. (London: SCM Press, 1952, 1955), 2:56.

[21]So Käsemann, *Testament of Jesus,* p. 21.

[22]Douglas K. Clark ("Signs in Wisdom and John," *CBQ* 45 [1983]: 208) regards the seventh and greatest sign in Wisdom 19:1-9 (of death by drowning of the Egyptians and the passing of the Israelites through the Red Sea to new life) as corresponding to the greatest sign of Jesus' death and passing over to new life. However, this correspondence between Wisdom and John depends on counting the Johannine signs of the feeding and walking on the sea as one sign (p. 205).

[23]See Jn 13:31; 16:14; 17:1, 5, 24.

[24]So Peter Riga, "Signs of Glory: The Use of '*Sēmeion*' in St. John's Gospel," *Int* 17 (1963): 408-10, and Henri van den Bussche cited by Riga.

[25]On *dunamis,* see Walter Grundmann, "*dunamai . . . ,*" *TDNT* 2:284-317, and Gerhard Friedrich, "*dunamis,*" in *Exegetical Dictionary of the New Testament,* 3 vols., ed. Horst Balz and Gerhard Schneider (Grand Rapids, Mich.: Eerdmans, 1990), 1:356.

[26]See Mt 11:20, 21, 23; 13:54, 58; Mk 6:2, 5, 14; Lk 5:17; 10:13; 19:37; and §§3.16, 23; 6.3, 4.

[27]Matthew twenty-seven times, Mark thirty-three, Luke twenty-six and John thirty-six.

[28]On *ergon,* see Georg Bertram, "*ergon . . . ,*" *TDNT* 2:635-52; Willem Nicol, *The Sēmeia in the Fourth Gospel: Tradition and Redaction* (Leiden, Neth.: Brill, 1972), pp. 116-19, and those cited by Gilbert van Belle, *The Signs Source in the Fourth Gospel: Historical Survey and Critical Evaluation of the Semeia Hypothesis* (Leuven, Bel.: Leuven University Press, 1994), pp. 379-80.

[29]Jn 4:34; 5:20, 36 (twice); 7:3, 21; 9:3, 4; 10:25, 32 (twice), 33, 37, 38; 14:10, 11, 12; 15:14.

[30]See Jn 3:35; 5:20; 12:45; 14:19-21; 17:1-4; cf. Karl H. Rengstorf, "*sēmeion . . .*" *TDNT* 7:248.

[31]Jn 7:3; 10:37-38; 14:11; 15:24; cf. 9:3; 10:25.

[32]Cf. Jn 5:20; 6:21; 9:4; 10:32-33; 14:11-12.

[33]Jn 5:36-38; 8:28; 14:10; 15:22-24.

[34]Bultmann, *Theology of the New Testament*, 2:59-61.

[35]See van Belle, *Signs Source in the Fourth Gospel*, p. 386.

[36]Cf. Riga, "Signs of Glory," p. 419.

[37]On Sēmeia, see Rengstorf, *"sēmeion . . ." TDNT* 7:243-57; Wilhelm Wilkens, *Zeichen und Werke* (Zürich, Switz.: Zwingli, 1969), pp. 30-45; Nicol, *Sēmeia in the Fourth Gospel*, esp. pp. 113-16; Brown, *New Testament Essays*, pp. 180-86; Udo Schnelle, *Antidocetic Christology in the Gospel of John* (Minneapolis: Fortress, 1992), pp. 144-48; van Belle, *Signs Source in the Fourth Gospel*, pp. 379-83.

[38]C. K. Barrett, *The Gospel According to St John* (London: SPCK, 1978), p. 75.

[39]See Mt 12:38, 39; 16:1, 4; Mk 8:11, 12; Lk 11:16, 29; 23:8. The Synoptics also use *sign* for the work of false prophets (Mk 13:22/Mt 24:24) and the "signs" of the coming of the Son of Man (Mk 13:4/Mt 24:3/Lk 21:7, 11, 25). Further, see Rengstorf, *"sēmeion . . ." TDNT* 7:231-39.

[40]Cf. van Belle, *Signs Source in the Fourth Gospel*, p. 381.

[41]Cf. Nicol, *Sēmeia in the Fourth Gospel*, pp. 45-46.

[42]Jn 2:23; 3:2; 6:2, 24; 7:31; 9:16; 12:18. So Gary M. Burge, *The Anointed Community: The Holy Spirit in the Johannine Tradition* (Grand Rapids, Mich.: Eerdmans, 1987), pp. 78-79. See also n. 26 above.

[43]In contrast to *ergon*, *sēmeion* is not used of the entire ministry of Jesus. In a number of places (Jn 12:33; 18:32; 21:19) a statement of Jesus serves "to signify" *(sēmainein)* how he or Peter will die.

[44]Cf. Schnelle, *Antidocetic Christology*, p. 148.

[45]So R. Formesyn, "Le sèmeion johannique et le sèmeion hellénistique," *ETL* 38 (1962): 861-68.

[46]From Molly Whittaker, " 'Signs and Wonders': The Pagan Background," *SE* 5 (1968): 155.

[47]So also Formesyn, "Le sèmeion johannique," pp. 856-94.

[48]E.g., Deut 26:8; Jer 32:20-21; Cf. Philo *Vit. Mos.* 1:210; Josephus *Ant.* 274-80. Also Graham H. Twelftree, "Signs, Wonders, Miracles," in *Dictionary of Paul and His Letters*, ed. Gerald F. Hawthorne, Ralph P. Martin and Daniel G. Reid (Downers Grove, Ill.: InterVarsity Press, 1993), p. 875.

[49]E.g., Ex 3:12; 4:1-9; 1 Sam 10:1-9. Cf. George R. Beasley-Murray, *John* (Waco, Tex.: Word, 1987), p. 33.

[50]Cf. Dodd, *Interpretation*, p. 141.

[51]R. Alan Culpepper, *Anatomy of the Fourth Gospel: A Study in Literary Design* (Philadelphia: Fortress, 1983), p. 182:

> Unlike symbols, signs more or less arbitarily stand for or point to something other than themselves. There is no intrinsic connection between a sign and the thing or person to which it points. The meaning of the sign must be learned, and whereas a symbol may point to many things, to be effective, a sign can point to only one.

[52]Cf. Barrett, *St John*, p. 78.

[53]Contrast Dodd, *Interpretation*, p. 140.

[54]Against Nicol, *Sēmeia in the Fourth Gospel*, p. 62

[55]Cf. Bultmann, *Theology of the New Testament*, 2:44-45, 60; Riga, "Signs of Glory," pp. 402-10.

[56]Cf. Nicol, *Sēmeia in the Fourth Gospel*, pp. 44-45.

[57]Polybius *Hist.* 3:112B; Livy XXII:36; Suetonius 88, 94, 96; Dio Cassius 45:2; Tacitus *Annals* 14:2; 15:47; *Histories* 1:4; 1:86:1. Cf. Selly Vernon McCasland, "Signs and Wonders," *JBL* 76 (1957): 149-52.; Whittaker, "Signs and Wonders," pp. 155-58; Twelftree, "Signs, Wonders, Miracles," p. 875.

[58]On *doxa*, see Gerhard Kittel, *"doxa . . . ," TDNT* 2:237, 247-51; David Hill, "The Request of Zebedee's Sons and the Johannine *DOXA*-Theme," *NTS* 13 (1967-1968): 281-85; George B. Caird, "The Glory of God in the Fourth Gospel: An Exercise in Biblical Semantics," *NTS* 15 (1968-1969): 265-77.

[59]So Nicol, *Sēmeia in the Fourth Gospel*, p. 122.

[60]So ibid., p. 121. Contrast Rudolf Bultmann, *The Gospel of John* (Oxford, U.K.: Blackwell, 1971),

p. 119.

[61]Jn 2:4; 7:39; 12:16, 23, 28; 13:31-32; 17:1-2.

[62]On which see G. Stählin, "Zum Problem der johanneischen Eschatologie," *ZNW* 33 (1934): 225-59; Rudolf Schnackenburg, *The Gospel According to St John*, 3 vols. (New York: Burns & Oates; Freiburg, Ger.: Herder, 1968), 2:114-17, 426-37, and the bibliography in Ernst Haenchen, *John*, 2 vols. (Philadelphia: Fortress, 1984), 1:241-42.

[63]Bultmann, *John*, p. 261.

[64]Ibid., p. 431.

[65]Cf. Käsemann, *Testament of Jesus*, pp. 15-16.

[66]See Barrett, *St John*, pp. 68-69.

[67]So Raymond E. Brown, *The Gospel According to John*, 2 vols. (London: Chapman, 1971), 1:cxviii.

[68]Cf. Beasley-Murray, *John*, lxxxvii.

[69]E. Schwarz, "Aporien im vierten Evangelium," in *Nachrichten von der Koniglichen Gesellschaft der Wissenschaften zu Gottingen: Philologisch-historische Klasse* (Berlin, Ger.: n.p., 1907), pp. 342-72; (1908), pp. 115-88, 497-560 (who first suggested the theory); and Julius Wellhausen, *Das Evangelium Johannes* (Berlin, Ger.: Reimer, 1908), pp. 102-19. On the history of the identificaton of the sēmeia source, see Nicol, *Sēmeia in the Fourth Gospel*, pp. 9-14, and Schnelle, *Antidocetic Christology*, pp. 91-92 n. 105, who cite Schwarz.

[70]Cf. Walter Schmithals's introduction to Bultmann, *John*, pp. 6-7. Cf. Howard M. Teeple, *Literary Origins of the Gospel of John* (Evanston, Ill: Religion and Ethics Institute, 1974); J. Becker, "Wunder und Christologie: Zum literarkritischen und christologischen Problem der Wunder im Johannesevangelium," *NTS* 16 (1969-1970): 130-48. See the evaluation in D. Moody Smith, *Composition and Order of the Fourth Gospel: Bultmann's Literary Theory* (New Haven, Conn.: Yale University Press, 1965), and D. Moody Smith, "The Sources of the Gospel of John: An Assessment of the Present State of the Problem," *NTS* 10 (1963-1964): 336-51.

[71]A recent detailed discussion of the theory of the signs source is van Belle, *Signs Source in the Fourth Gospel*. Those proposing a signs source include, e.g., Schnackenburg, *St John*, 1:64-68; Becker, "Wunder und Christologie," pp. 130-48; Robert T. Fortna, *The Gospel of Signs: A Reconstruction of the Narrative Source Underlying the Fourth Gospel* (Cambridge, U.K.: Cambridge University Press, 1970); Robert T. Fortna, "Source and Redaction in the Fourth Gospel's Portrayal of Jesus' Signs," *JBL* 89 (1970): 151-66; Nicol, *Sēmeia in the Fourth Gospel*; Teeple, *Literary Origins*; D. Moody Smith, *Johannine Christianity* (Columbia, S.C.: University of South Carolina Press, 1984); Robert T. Fortna, *The Fourth Gospel and Its Predecessors: From Narrative to Present Gospel* (Edinburgh, U.K.: T & T Clark, 1988).

[72]Rudolf Bultmann, "Das Johannesevangelium in der neuesten Forschung," *Christliche Welt* 41 (1927): 503.

[73]Eduard Schweizer, *Ego eimi* (Göttingen, Ger.: Vandenhoeck & Ruprecht, 1939), pp. 82-112.

[74]Eugen Ruckstuhl, "Johannine Language and Style," in *L'évangile de Jean*, ed. Marinus de Jonge (Leuven, Bel.: Leuven University Press, 1977), p. 141.

[75]Nicol, *Sēmeia in the Fourth Gospel*, pp. 25-26.

[76]Fortna, *Gospel of Signs*, pp. 2-3.

[77]Anticipated by Wilhelm Wilkens, *Die Entstehungsgeschichte des vierten Evangeliums* (Zollokon: Evangelischer Verlag, 1958). See James M. Robinson, "Recent Research in the Fourth Gospel," *JBL* 78 (1959): 242-46, and "The Johannine Trajectory," in *Trajectories Through Early Christianity*, ed. James M. Robinson and Helmut Koester (Philadelphia: Fortress, 1971), pp. 247 and n. 25.

[78]For his proposal of the text of the signs source, see Fortna, *Gospel of Signs*, pp. 235-45.

[79]Beasley-Murray, *John*, p. xl.

[80]See Robinson, "The Johannine Trajectory," in *Trajectories Through Early Christianity*, pp. 247-52; Barnabas Lindars, *Behind the Fourth Gospel* (London: SPCK, 1976), pp. 28-42; and the review of Fortna by D. Moody Smith in *JBL* 89 (1970): 498-501.

[81]Cf. Alexander Faure, "Die alttestamentliche Zitate im 4. Evangelium und die Quellenscheidung

shypothese," *ZNW* 21 (1922): 107-9.

[82]In more detail, see Schnelle, *Antidocetic Christology,* pp. 150-64. See also Wolfgang J. Bittner, *Jesu Zeichen im Johannesevangelium: Die Messias-Erkenntnis im Johannesevangelium vor ihrem jüdischen Hintergrund* (Tübingen, Ger.: Mohr, 1987).

[83]Lindars, *Behind the Fourth Gospel,* p. 34.

[84]Mark W. G. Stibbe, *John as Storyteller: Narrative Criticism and the Fourth Gospel* (Cambridge, U.K.: Cambridge University Press, 1992), pp. 83-84.

[85]Cf. Donald A. Carson, "Current Source Criticism of the Fourth Gospel: Some Methodological Questions," *JBL* 97 (1978): 411-29, esp. p. 428.

[86]Nicol (Sēmeia *in the Fourth Gospel,* pp. 39-41), e.g., considers the stories of the first disciples (1:35-51) and Jesus and the Samaritan Woman (4:1-42) as possibly from the signs source. Van Belle (*Signs Source in the Fourth Gospel,* p. 376) concludes his detailed survey and study: "I am inclined to refuse the semeia hypothesis as a valid working hypothesis in the study of the Fourth Gospel." The theory of a discourse or revelation source has also rightly been received with some skepticism (e.g., Käsemann and Haenchen, cited by James M. Robinson, "Kerygma and History in the New Testament," in *Trajectories Through Early Christianity,* p. 52, and Lindars, *Behind the Fourth Gospel,* pp. 20-26), especially on the grounds that there is not the stylistic evidence to distinguish these possible sources from the hand of John (Eugen Ruckstuhl, *Die literarische Einheit des Johannesevangeliums* [Freiburg, Ger.: Paulus, 1951], pp. 203-19, following Schweizer, *Ego eimi*). Further, on reasons for the skepticism, see D. Moody Smith, "The Sources of the Gospel of John: An Assessment of the Present State of the Problem," *NTS* 10 (1963-1964): 336-51.

[87]Cf. van Belle, *Signs Source in the Fourth Gospel,* p. 388.

[88]Van Belle (ibid., p. 394) cites O. Cullmann, F. Roustang, W. Grundmann, R. Schnackenburg, R. E. Brown, M. Baron, W. Nicol and F. J. Moloney.

[89]See also Gerald F. Hawthorne, "The Concept of Faith in the Fourth Gospel," *BSac* 116 (1963): 117-26; Walter Grundmann, "Verständnis und Bewegung des Glaubens im Johannes-Evangelium," *KD* 6 (1960): 131-54; Schnelle, *Antidocetic Christology,* pp. 168-70. Cf. Culpepper, *Anatomy of the Fourth Gospel,* pp. 146-48.

[90]Cf. Brown, *John,* 1:530.

[91]So Jean-Pierrre Charlier, "La notion de signe dans le IVe Évangile," *RSPT* 43 (1959): 438, cited by Nicol, Sēmeia *in the Fourth Gospel,* p. 101.

[92]So Nicol, Sēmeia *in the Fourth Gospel,* p. 101.

[93]Cf. Schnelle, *Antidocetic Christology,* p. 170.

[94]Brown, *John,* 1:530.

[95]Cf. C. H. Dodd, *Historical Tradition in the Fourth Gospel* (Cambridge, U.K.: Cambridge University Press, 1963), pp. 234-35. See also Wellhausen, *Das Evangelium Johannes,* p. 16; Emanuel Hirsch, *Studien zum vierten Evangelium* (Tübingen, Ger.: Mohr, 1936), pp. 6, 48; Bultmann, *John,* p. 130. However, not all are convinced that Jn 2:23-25 is redactional (see the discussion in Schnackenburg, *St John,* 1:357-60). Indeed, there would still be the possibility that the core of the narrative is traditional (so Brown, *John,* 1:126-27).

[96]Cf. Dodd, *Historical Tradition,* p. 235.

[97]Cf. Ernst Haenchen, " 'Der Vater, der mich gesandt hat,' " *NTS* 9 (1962-1963): 208-16; Brown, *John,* 1:531.

[98]M. de Jonge, "Signs and Words in the Fourth Gospel," in *Miscellanea Neotestamentica,* ed. T. Baarda, A. F. J. Klijn and W. C. van Unnik (Leiden, Neth.: Brill, 1978), 2:121.

[99]Eduard Lohse, "Miracles in the Fourth Gospel," in *What About the New Testament?* ed. Morna Hooker and Colin Hickling (London: SCM Press, 1975), p. 65.

[100]Werner G. Kümmel, *Theology of the New Testament* (London: SCM Press, 1974), p. 300.

[101]Cf. Nicol, Sēmeia *in the Fourth Gospel,* p. 43.

[102]Brown, *John,* 1:531.

[103]So, e.g., Zane C. Hodges, "Untrustworthy Believers—John 2:23-25," *BSac* 135 (1978): 142.

[104]On "blessed," especially in relation to Johannine literature, see Brown, *John,* 2:553; David E.

Aune, *Revelation 1—5* (Waco, Tex.: Word, 1997), 1:10-11, 19-20. Note Bultmannn: "*Makarioi* does not refer to 'the blessing which true discipleship brings with it' (B. Weiss), but to the salvation which is given to the true disciples" (*John*, p. 476 n. 4).

[105]So Grundmann, "Verständnis und Bewegung des Glaubens," pp. 131-54. Cf. Culpepper, *Anatomy of the Fourth Gospel*, p. 147. See also, e.g., Ben Witherington, *John's Wisdom: A Commentary on the Fourth Gospel* (Louisville, Ky.: Westminster John Knox, 1995), p. 89.

[106]So Brown, *John*, 1:530.

[107]For a discussion of the meaning of *signs* here, arguing that they continue to refer to the miracle stories, see van Belle, *Signs Source in the Fourth Gospel*, pp. 398-404.

[108]Cf. Haenchen, " 'Der Vater, der mich gesandt hat,' " p. 208-16.

[109]See also Schnackenburg, *St John*, 1:357-58.

[110]So the discussion in Schnelle, *Antidocetic Christology*, p. 175.

[111]Contra Nicol, Sēmeia *in the Fourth Gospel*, pp. 99-106; Mark L. Appold, *The Oneness Motif in the Fourth Gospel: Motif Analysis and Exegetical Probe into the Theology of John* (Tübingen, Ger.: Mohr, 1976), pp. 94-102.

[112]Kümmel, *Theology of the New Testament*, p. 300. Cf. Jn 10:37-38; 14:11; cf. 4:48; 5:36; 6:26, 36.

[113]Jn 20:29; cf. 4:50; 12:48; 14:11a; 17:20. Kümmel, *Theology of the New Testament*, p. 301; cf. Sebald Hofbeck, *Semeion: Der Begriff des "Zweichen" in Johannesevangelium unter Berücksichtigung seiner Vorgeschichte* (Münsterschwarzbach: Vien-Türme, 1966), pp. 177-86.

[114]Cf. Nicol, Sēmeia *in the Fourth Gospel*, p. 106.

[115]Cf. William R. G. Loader, *The Christology of the Fourth Gospel* (Frankfurt: Peter Lang, 1989), p. 216.

[116]Cf. Marianne Meye Thompson, *The Humanity of Jesus in the Fourth Gospel* (Philadelphia: Fortress, 1988), p. 80. Cf. van Belle (*Signs Source in the Fourth Gospel*, p. 39), who notes that if this conclusion is correct, "we are not compelled to postulate a signs source whose theology of signs the evangelist transforms."

[117]Brown, *John*, 1:531.

[118]Following Schnackenburg (*St. John*, 2:71) and Beasley-Murray (*John*, p. 245), against Bultmann (*John*, pp. 610-11), Haenchen (*John*, p. 475) and Joachim Becker (*Das Evangelium des Johannes*, 2 vols. [Gütersloh: G. Mohn, 1979, 1981], 2:464), who identify these works with the words of Jesus on the basis of the association of words and works in verse 10. That Jesus should promise "greater" works is probably intended to include not the meaning that greater miracles will be performed (what could be greater than the resurrection of the dead!) but the meaning that the breadth and impact of the mission of the followers of Jesus would be greater. See Schnackenburg, *St. John*, 2:71-72.

[119]Brown, *John*, 1:531.

[120]Jn 11:2, 3, 12, 21, 27, 32, 34, 39.

[121]Jn 21:7, 12 (twice), 15, 16, 17, 20, 21.

[122]Cf. Otto Michel, "Der Anfang der Zeichen Jesu," in *Die Leibhaftigkeit des Wortes*, ed. Otto Michel and Ulrich Mann (Hamburg, Ger.: Furche, 1958), p. 19.

[123]Nicol, Sēmeia *in the Fourth Gospel*, p. 90.

[124]Ibid., p. 92.

[125]Cf. van Belle, *Signs Source in the Fourth Gospel*, p. 392, citing J. Konings, R. Schnackenburg, W. Wilkens, B. L. Blackburn, R. E. Brown, M. M. Thompson, F. J. Moloney, C. H. Giblin and J. Painter.

[126]Bultmann (*John*, pp. 101-2) argued from Jn 1:40-42, 47-48; 2:24-25; 4:17-19, as well as from the signs source, that Jesus is shown to be the *theios anthrōpos*. See also Jürgen Becker ("Wunder und Christologie: Zum literarkritischen und christologischen Problem der Wunder im Johannesevangelium," *NTS* 16 [1969-1970]: 141), who says that all the essential theological traits of the miracle stories in the signs source belong to the *theios anēr* concept of Hellenism. However, there is no clear typology of the *theios anēr* and little evidence of the use of the term in Hellenistic Jewish sources (see John Painter, *The Quest for the Messiah*, 2d ed. [Edinburgh,

U.K.: T & T Clark, 1993], p. 12, and §3.29). A more appropriate designation for Jesus in the signs source is "Son of God" (see Hans-Jürgen Kuhn, *Christologie und Wunder: Untersuchungen zu Joh 1,35-51* [Regensburg, Ger.: Verlag Friedrich Pustet, 1988], section 6).

[127]Thompson, *Humanity of Jesus in the Fourth Gospel,* pp. 56, 62-63; cf. Schnackenburg, *St John,* 1:525; Schnelle, *Antidocetic Christology,* pp. 166-67.

[128]So Schnackenburg, *St John,* 1:267.

[129]Ibid., 1:268.

[130]Whereas Matthew has nineteen stories and Mark and Luke each have twenty, John only has seven stories plus the one appended to the Gospel (21:4-14). Then in Mark, for example, the miracle stories account for about 200 of the 425 verses in the first ten chapters (so Alan Richardson, *The Miracle-Stories of the Gospels* [London: SCM Press, 1941], p. 36). In John, on the other hand, the seven stories account for only 120 verses out of the 520 verses of the Fourth Gospel up to the end of chapter 11.

[131]A point missed by, e.g., John Wilkinson ("A Study of Healing in the Gospel According to John," *SJT* 20 [1967]: 458-59), who on the basis only of the number of stories says that physical healing was not the primary work of Jesus in John.

[132]Culpepper, *Anatomy of the Fourth Gospel,* p. 60.

[133]This is highlighted in Leon Morris's analysis of the Gospel (*The Gospel According to John* [Grand Rapids, Mich.: Eerdmans, 1971], pp. 65-67), cited with approval by Witherington, *John's Wisdom,* p. 42.

[134]Cf. Brown, *New Testament Essays,* pp. 168-69.

[135]Cf. van Belle, *Signs Source in the Fourth Gospel,* pp. 391-92.

[136]Cf. ibid., p. 393.

[137]Cf. Nicol, Sēmeia *in the Fourth Gospel,* pp. 43-44.

[138]Cf. Burge, *Anointed Community,* p. 75 n.110.

[139]Cf. Eduard Schweizer, *"pneuma," TDNT* 6:438; Käsemann, *Testament of Jesus,* pp. 20-26.

[140]See Jn 2:4; 4:50 11:6. Cf. Nicol, Sēmeia *in the Fourth Gospel,* p. 43; Appold, *Oneness Motif in the Fourth Gospel,* p. 93 n. 2.

[141]Cf. Mk 3:7-12; 5:24-34; 6:53-56; contrast Mt 8:14-15; 9:1-8.

[142]Cf. Nicol, Sēmeia *in the Fourth Gospel,* p. 43.

Chapter 9: Miracles & the Historical Jesus

[1]John P. Meier, *A Marginal Jew: Rethinking the Historical Jesus,* 3 vols. (New York: Doubleday, 1991, 1994, forthcoming), 2:509-1038.

[2]The price for calling into question the historical value of the miracles has been high. Between 1727 and 1729 Thomas Woolston, a fellow of Sidney Sussex College, Cambridge, published six *Discourses on the Miracles of Our Saviour.* He maintained bluntly that, regarded as historical events, the miracles were so fantastic that no reasonable person could believe them. Thirty thousand copies were sold and evoked a response of sixty pamphlets and a trial for blasphemy before the Lord Chief Justice in the Guildhall, who sentenced him to pay a fine of one hundred pounds and a year's imprisonment. Unable to pay the fine he spent the remainder of his days, until 1733, in confinement. See William Neil, "The Criticism and Theological Use of the Bible, 1700-1950," in *The Cambridge History of the Bible: The West from the Reformation to the Present Day,* ed. S. L. Greenslade (Cambridge, U.K.: Cambridge University Press, 1963), pp. 245-46.

[3]In light of a 1989 opinion survey finding that about 82 percent of American respondents believed that today "miracles are performed by God," the number of readers holding this view is likely to be quite small. See George Gallup Jr. and Jim Castelli, *The People's Religion: American Faith in the 90's* (New York: Macmillan; London: Collier, 1989), p. 58. Cf. Laura Sessions Stepp in *The Washington Post,* March 22, 1992, p. A14, and Meier, *A Marginal Jew,* 2:520.

[4]Robert W. Funk and the Jesus Seminar, *The Acts of Jesus: The Search for the Authentic Deeds of Jesus* (New York: HarperCollins, 1998).

[5]See the brief, though helpful, discussion in N. T. Wright, *The New Testament and the People of God* (Minneapolis: Fortress, 1992), pp. 32-35.

[6]Roy Wood Sellars, *Critical Realism: A Study of the Nature and Conditions of Knowledge* (New York: Russell & Russell, 1916). See also Durant Drake et al., *Essays in Critical Realism: A Cooperative Study of the Problem of Knowledge* (London: Macmillan, 1920), which has been called the manifesto of the school, and Ben F. Meyer, *Reality and Illusion in New Testament Scholarship: A Primer in Critical Realist Hermeneutics* (Collegeville: Michael Glazier, 1994).

[7]Cf. Wright (*The New Testament and the People of God*, p. 35 [his emphasis]), in advocating the value of a form of critical realism, does not acknowledge the work of Sellars or the school that emerged in the final years of the nineteenth century and flourished up to to the beginning of the Second World War.

[8]F. H. Bradley, "The Presuppositions of Critical History" (1874), in *Collected Essays*, 2 vols. (Oxford, U.K.: Clarendon, 1935), 1:2. This issue will be approached again from a slightly different perspective. See the discussion of the tool of analogy at §9.6.

[9]Gerd Theissen, "Historical Scepticism and the Criteria of Jesus Research *or* My Attempt to Leap Across Lessing's Yawning Gulf," *SJT* 49 (1996): 147-76. Theissen deals with the issue of all our knowledge—including the greatest certainty—being hypothetical.

[10]Ben F. Meyer, *Critical Realism and the New Testament* (Allison Park, Penn: Pickwick, 1989), p. x.

[11]Cf. Wright, *The New Testament and the People of God*, pp. 44-46.

[12]See Keith Jenkins, *On "What Is History?"* (London: Routledge, 1995). See the review of Jenkins by Geoffrey Roberts, "Postmodernism Versus the Standpoint of Action," *History and Theory* 36 (1997): 249-60.

[13]Hans Kellner, "Introduction: Describing Redescriptions," in *A New Philosophy of History*, ed. Frank Ankersmit and Hans Kellner (London: Reaktion, 1995), p. 10.

[14]On our ability to recover an author's intentions, see, e.g., Mark Bevir, "The Errors of Linguistic Contextualism," *History and Theory* 31 (1992): 276-98.

[15]Hayden White, "Historical Text as Literary Artifact," in *The Writing of History*, ed. Robert H. Canary and Henry Kozicki (Madison: University of Wisconsin Press, 1978), p. 42.

[16]Hayden White, *The Content of the Form: Narrative Discourse and Historical Representation* (Baltimore, Md.: Johns Hopkins University Press, 1987), p. 170. See also F. R. Ankersmit, *Narrative Logic* (The Hague, Neth.: Nijhoff, 1983); L. O. Mink, "Narrative Form as a Cognitive instrument," in *The Writing of History*, ed. Robert H. Canary and Henry Kozicki (Madison: University of Wisconsin Press, 1978), pp. 129-49.

[17]Cf. Leon Pompa, "Philosophy of History," in *The Blackwell Companion to Philosophy*, ed. Nicholas Bunnin and E. P. Tsui-James (Oxford, U.K.: Blackwell, 1996), p. 434.

[18]Here I am dependent on David Carr, *Time, Narrative and History* (Bloomington, Ind.: Indiana University Press, 1986) and the summary of his postion in "Narrative and the Real World: An Argument for Continuity," *History and Theory* 25 (1986): 117-31. See the discussion of Carr in William H. Dray, "Narrative and Historical Realism," in *On History and Philosophers of History* (Leiden, Neth.: Brill, 1989), pp. 131-63.

[19]Carr, "Narrative and the Real World," p. 117.

[20]Cf., e.g., John M. Court, "The Philosophy of the Synoptic Miracles," *JTS* 23 (1972): 13.

[21]Cf., e.g., Mt 21:11, 46; Mk 6:4, 15; 14:65; Lk 7:16, 39; 13:33; 24:19; Jn 4:19, 44; 7:40, 52; 9:17.

[22]E.g., Mk 1:2-6; 9:11-13; Lk 16:16; Jn 1:6-8, 19-36.

[23]So A. E. Harvey (*Jesus and the Constraints of History* [London: Duckworth, 1982], p. 103), who notes that Otto Weinreich (*Antike Heiligungswunder*) adduces only a handful of miracle stories associated with pagan figures. The situation is similar with Jewish figures. See Paul Fiebig, *Jüdische Wundergeschichten des neutestamentlichen Zeitalters* (Tübingen, Ger.: Mohr, 1911).

[24]Werner Kahl, *New Testament Miracle Stories in Their Religious-Historical Setting* (Göttingen, Ger.: Vandenhoeck & Ruprecht, 1994), p. 236.

[25]Cf. Gerd Theissen and Annette Merz, *The Historical Jesus: A Comprehensive Guide* (London: SCM Press, 1998), p. 113.

[26]Meier, *A Marginal Jew* 1:167-95; Craig A. Evans, *Jesus and His Contemporaries* (Leiden, Neth.:

Brill, 1995), pp. 13-26, 213-27.

[27]The term may have been coined by J. B. Bauer of Graz. See Franz Mussner, *The Miracles of Jesus: An Introduction* (Notre Dame, Ind.: University of Notre Dame Press, 1968), p. 95 n. 30. On older work on investigating the historicity of the activities of Jesus, including Rudolf Pesch, *Jesu ureigene Taten? Ein Beitrag zur Wunderfrage* (Freiburg, Ger.: Herder, 1970), see Graham H. Twelftree, *Jesus the Exorcist: A Contribution to the Study of the Historical Jesus* (Tübingen, Ger.: Mohr; Peabody, Mass.: Hendrickson, 1993), pp. 130-35. See also Wright, *The New Testament and the People of God*, pp. 29-35, and Ben Witherington, *The Jesus Quest: The Third Search for the Jew of Nazareth* (Downers Grove, Ill.: InterVarsity Press, 1995), chap. 2.

[28]Robert J. Miller, "Historical Method and the Deeds of Jesus: The Test Case of the Temple Demonstration," *Forum* 8 (1992): 5-30.

[29]Adopting such an approach may accrue the description "postivistic," which, as Keith Windschuttle notes, is "the most pejorative insult to hurl in today's academic climate" (*The Killing of History: How a Discipline Is Being Murdered by Literary Critics and Social Theorists* [Sydney: Macleay, 1994], p. 186). However, in the context of our discussion, this positivism would need to be modified to what could be called a "critical" positivism in that I am attempting to be sensitive to such contributions to historiography made by, e.g., R. G. Collingwood, *The Idea of History* (Oxford, U.K.: Clarendon, 1946), and Wilhelm Dilthey, *Pattern and Meaning in History: Thought on History and Society*, ed. H. P. Rickman (New York: Harper & Row, 1962). On the debate between the positivists and the idealists in historiography, see the brief introduction in David Bebbington, *Patterns in History* (Leicester, U.K.: Inter-Varsity Press, 1979), chap. 7. See also Windschuttle, *Killing of History*, chap. 7. See also the discussion of the theses in the ensuing text, especially that of "Plausibility."

[30]Miller, "Historical Method," pp. 28-29.

[31]For a philosophical discussion of the issue, see James Cargile, "On the Burden of Proof," *Philosophy* 72 (1997): 59-83.

[32]Cf. Peter W. Ensor, *Jesus and His "Works": The Johannine Sayings in Historical Perspective* (Tübingen, Ger.: Mohr, 1996), pp. 264-65.

[33]For a discussion of how Middle Eastern people carefully preserve and pass on traditions, see Kenneth E. Bailey, "Middle Eastern Oral Tradition and the Synoptic Gospels," *ExpTim* 106 (1995): 363-67. For a case that the earliest Christians were concerned to remember Jesus and to pass on these memories, see James D. G. Dunn, "The Gospel as Oral Tradition," in *The Living Word* (London: SCM Press, 1987), pp. 25-43.

[34]As also understood by Meier, *A Marginal Jew*, 2:619-22.

[35]Miller, "Historical Method and the Deeds of Jesus," p. 26.

[36]Reginald H. Fuller, *The Foundations of New Testament Christology* (London: Lutterworth, 1965), p. 18; cf. Norman Perrin, *Rediscovering the Teaching of Jesus* (New York: Harper & Row, 1976), p. 39. See the discussion in Meier, *A Marginal Jew*, 1:171-74.

[37]Cf. David R. Catchpole, "Tradition History," in *New Testament Interpretation*, ed. I. Howard Marshall (Exeter, U.K.: Paternoster, 1977), p. 174. See also the discussion in Robert H. Stein, "The 'Criteria' for Authenticity," in *Gospel Perspectives 1: Studies of History and Tradition in the Four Gospels*, ed. R. T. France and David Wenham (Sheffield, U.K.: JSOT, 1980), pp. 240-45.

[38]See also Gerd Theissen and Dagmar Winter, *Die Kriterienfrage in der Jesusforschung: Vom Differenzkriterium zum Plausibilitätskriterium* (Göttingen, Ger.: Vandenhoeck & Ruprecht, 1997), pp. 241-47.

[39]Miller, "Historical Method and the Deeds of Jesus," p. 26.

[40]Ibid., p. 26.

[41]Pesch, *Jesu ureigene Taten?* pp. 25, 147, 151, 153-54.

[42]Mussner, *Miracles of Jesus*, pp. 27-28.

[43]Further, see Twelftree, *Jesus the Exorcist*, pp. 132-35.

[44]Arthur Marwick, *The Nature of History* (London: Macmillan, 1970), p. 136. In the third edition (1989), pp. 216-20, Marwick draws a distinction between witting and unwitting testimony. Further, see Twelftree, *Jesus the Exorcist*, pp. 134-35, and Craig Blomberg, "Concluding

Reflections on Miracles and *Gospel Perspectives*," in *Gospel Perspectives 6: The Miracles of Jesus,* ed. David Wenham and Craig Blomberg (Sheffield, U.K.: JSOT, 1986), p. 447.

[45]Ernst Troeltsch, "Über historische und dogmatische Methode in der Theologie," in *Gesammelte Schriften,* 4 vols. (Tübingen, Ger.: Mohr, 1913), 2:729-53, esp. p. 732; English translation: Ernst Troeltsch, *Religion in History* (Minneapolis: Fortress, 1991), pp.11-32, esp. p. 13. See also his "Historiography," in *Encyclopedia of Religion and Ethics,* ed. James Hastings (New York: Charles Scribner's Sons, 1914), 6:718.

[46]Marc Bloch, *The Historian's Craft* (Manchester, U.K.: Manchester University Press, 1954), p. 44.

[47]See Carl L. Becker, "Detachment," in *Detachment and the Writing of History: Essays and Letters of Carl L. Becker,* ed. Phil L. Snyder (Ithaca, N.Y.: Cornell University Press, 1958), pp. 3-29.

[48]See the discussion in Ted Peters, "The Use of Analogy in Historical Method," *CBQ* 35 (1973): 475-82; Ted Peters, "Jesus' Resurrection: An Historical Event Without Analogy," *Dialog* 12 (1973): 112-16; Marlin E. Miller, "Criticism and Analogy in Historical-Critical Interpretation," in *Essays on Biblical Interpretation,* ed. Willard M. Swartley (Elkhart, Ind.: Institute of Mennonite Studies, 1984), pp. 223-36, esp. pp. 229-36. Ben F. Meyer, *The Aims of Jesus* (London: SCM Press, 1979), pp. 17-19.

[49]Cf. Wolfhart Pannenberg, "Redemptive Event and History," in *Basic Questions in Theology,* 3 vols. (London: SCM Press, 1970), 1:45-46.

[50]Cf. Theissen and Winter, *Die Kriterienfrage in der Jesusforschung,* pp. 241-47.

[51]Graham H. Twelftree, "Jesus in Jewish Traditions," in *Gospel Perspectives 5: The Jesus Traditions Outside the Gospels,* ed. David Wenham (Sheffield, U.K.: JSOT, 1985), pp. 301-8; John P. Meier, "Jesus in Josephus: A Modest Proposal," *CBQ* 52 (1990): 76-103; Meier, *A Marginal Jew,* 1:56-88.

[52]E.g., *Ant.* 2:223, 285, 295, 345, 347; 3:1, 30, 38; 5:28; 9:58, 60; 10:214, 235.

[53]*Ant.* 3:38; cf. Ex 17:1-7.

[54]*Ant.* 9:58, 60; cf. 2 Kings 6:8-23.

[55]E.g., *Ant.* 2:91; 5:125; 6:171, 290; 9:14, 182; 10:21, 266; 15:379; *Ag. Ap.* 2:114.

[56]"It has been taught" is a cue-word designating a *baraita* tradition from the period A.D. 70 to 200. Morris Goldstein, *Jesus in the Jewish Traditions* (New York: Macmillan, 1950), p. 269 n. 2.

[57]Twelftree, "Jesus in Jewish Traditions," p. 324.

[58]Ibid.

[59]On the issue of Jesus' being charged with performing magic, which is only clear from the second century (cf. Quadratus in Eusebius *The History of the Church* 4:3:2; Justin Martyr *Dialogue* 69; Origen *CC* 1:68), see Twelftree, *Jesus the Exorcist,* §24, and esp. David E. Aune, "Magic in Early Christianity," *ANRW* II:23:2 (1980): 1507-57.

[60]Cf., e.g., Mk 9:38-39/Lk 9:49-50; [Mk 16:17]; Lk 10:17; Acts 16:18; 19:13-19; *PGM* 4:3019-20; cf. 1227; further, see Twelftree, *Jesus the Exorcist,* pp. 140-41.

[61]Cf. Pseudo-Philo *Liber Antiquitatum Biblicarum* 60; Josephus *Ant.* 8:46-49; Origen *CC* 1:6; cf. 1:67. See also Lucian *Philops* 13.

[62]Cf. *t. Ḥul.* 2:22-23; *y. Šabb.* 14:4:14d; *y. 'Abod. Zar.* 2:2; *b. 'Abod. Zar.* 27b.

[63]Cf. Justin, *Dial.* 30:3; 76:5; 85:2; *Apology* 2:6.

[64]For a discussion of the implications of Christian copyists being involved in the transmission of the works of Josephus, see Twelftree, "Jesus in Jewish Traditions," pp. 290-310.

[65]Nikolaus Walter, "Paul and the Early Christian Jesus-Tradition," in *Paul and Jesus: Collected Essays,* ed. A. J. M. Wedderburn (Sheffield, U.K.: JSOT, 1989), p. 60. For a history of the Jesus-Paul debate, see Victor P. Furnish, "The Jesus-Paul Debate: From Baur to Bultmann," in *Paul and Jesus,* pp. 17-50.

[66]Walter, "Paul and the Early Christian Jesus-Tradition," p. 61. There is the view that in 2 Corinthians 10—13 Paul is rejecting the Jewish peripatetic missionaries who have characterized Jesus as a miracle-working hero. In so doing Paul deliberately made no use of stories that portrayed Jesus as a miracle worker. So Hans-Wolfgang Kuhn, "Der irdische Jesus bei Paulus also traditionsgeschichtliches und theologisches Problem," *ZTK* 67 (1970): 295-320. However,

this would not explain why, throughout the letters in the New Testament, there is a paucity of information about Jesus' ministry and teaching. See the discussion in Leonard Goppelt, *Theology of the New Testament,* 2 vols. (Grand Rapids, Mich.: Eerdmans, 1982), 2:44-45.

[67]Rudolf Bultmann, *Theology of the New Testament,* 2 vols. (London: SCM Press, 1952, 1955), 1:188, cf. pp. 293-94.

[68]See the discussion in Walter, "Paul and the Early Christian Jesus-Tradition," p. 61.

[69]For what follows, see Seyoon Kim, "Jesus, Sayings of," *Dictionary of Paul and His Letters,* ed. Gerald F. Hawthorne, Ralph P. Martin and Daniel P. Reid (Downers Grove, Ill.: InterVarsity Press, 1993), pp. 486-87.

[70]See Rom 15:18-19; 1 Cor 2:4; 2 Cor 12:12; Gal 3:5; 1 Thess 1:5; and Stephan Schreiber, *Paulus als Wundertäter: Redaktinsgeschichtliche Untersuchungen zur Apostelgeschichte und den authentischen Paulusbriefen* (Berlin, Ger.: de Gruyter, 1996).

[71]David Wenham (*Paul: Follower of Jesus or Founder of Christianity?* [Grand Rapids, Mich.: Eerdmans, 1995], pp. 351-52) suggests that Phil 1:8 ("I long for you with all the deep yearning *[splagchnizomai]* of Christ," auth. trans.) may be another hint pointing in the same direction since the word *yearning* or *compassion* is also used of Jesus' attitude, sometimes in relation to those seeking healing (cf. Mt 9:36; 14:14/Mk 6:34; Mt 15:32/Mk 8:2; Mt 20:34). That is, it could be that Paul has been influenced by the miracle stories of Jesus.

[72]Wenham, *Paul: Follower or Founder?* pp. 81-83.

[73]So ibid., p. 351 n. 39.

[74]M and L may be only free compositions by Matthew and Luke, respectively, with no traditional material in them. See the discussions in Stephenson H. Brooks, *Matthew's Community: The Evidence of His Special Sayings Material* (Sheffield, U.K.: JSOT, 1987), esp. chap. 1, and Kim Paffenroth, *The Story of Jesus According to L* (Sheffield, U.K.: Sheffield Academic, 1997), chap. 1.

[75]Mt 11:4-5/Lk 7:22; 13:31-33.

[76]Mt 12:25-29/Mk 3:24-27/Lk 11:17-22; Mt 12:43-45/Lk 11:24-26.

[77]Mt 12:27/Lk 11:19.

[78]Mk 9:38-41/Lk 9:49-50.

[79]Mt 10:1/Mk 6:7/Lk 9:1; 10:1.

[80]So also, e.g., A. George, "Les miracles de Jésus dans les Evangiles synoptiques," *Lumière et vie* 33 (1957): 7-24; Marcus J. Borg, *Jesus: A New Vision* (San Francisco: HarperCollins, 1991), p. 59; John Dominic Crossan, *The Historical Jesus: The Life of a Mediterranean Jewish Peasant* (North Blackburn, Austl.: Collins Dove, 1993), pp. 310-11; Meier, *A Marginal Jew,* 2:630.

[81]So Rudolf Bultmann, "New Testament and Mythology," in *Kerygma and Myth: A Theological Debate,* ed. Hans Werner Bartsch, rev. and trans. Reginald H. Fuller (New York: Harper & Row, 1961), pp. 4-5.

[82]Rudolf Bultmann, *Jesus and the Word* (London: Collins/Fontana, 1958), p. 124 (his emphasis).

[83]Against this generally held view is that of Burton L. Mack (*A Myth of Innocence: Mark and Christian Origins* [Philadelphia: Fortress, 1988], pp. 75-77, 91-93, 215-24), who does not see any Gospel tradition having a basis in the life of the historical Jesus. See the discussion of Mack in Barry L. Blackburn, "The Miracles of Jesus," in *Studying the Historical Jesus: Evaluations of the State of Current Research,* ed. Bruce Chilton and Craig A. Evans (Leiden, Neth.: Brill, 1994), pp. 362-63 and n. 46.

Chapter 10: The Meaning of the Miracles for Jesus

[1]Cf. Ben F. Meyer, "Jesus' Ministry and Self-Understanding," in *Studying the Historical Jesus: Evaluations of the State of Current Research,* ed. Bruce Chilton and Craig Evans (Leiden, Neth.: Brill, 1994), pp. 337-52.

[2]Cf., e.g., Ben F. Meyer, *The Aims of Jesus* (London: SCM Press, 1979), pp. 154-58. On the false dichotomy between the words and deeds, see F. Gerald Downing, "Words as Deeds and Deeds as Words," *Biblical Interpretation* 3 (1995): 129-43.

[3]In dealing with what Jesus thought about the "kingdom," E. P. Sanders (*Jesus and Judaism* [London: SCM Press, 1985], p. 156) takes dealing with a range of Jesus' activities (which he

calls facts!) as the easier and more certain way forward. See also Marcus J. Borg, *Jesus in Contemporary Scholarship* (Valley Forge, Penn.: TPI, 1994), p. 12.

[4]Cf. the list in Sanders, *Jesus and Judaism,* p. 11.

[5]So Herbert Butterfield, *Man on His Past: The Study of the History of Historical Scholarship* (Cambridge, U.K.: Cambridge University Press, 1955), p. 97, relying on Lord Acton.

[6]See, e.g., Van Austin Harvey, *The Historian and the Believer* (London: SCM Press, 1967), p. 11.

[7]Rudolf Bultmann, *Jesus and the Word* (London: Collins/Fontana, 1958), p. 14. Cf. Karl Barth, *The Epistle to the Romans* (London: Oxford University Press, 1933), p. 30.

[8]See Borg, *Jesus in Contemporary Scholarship,* p. 187. Borg also briefly discussses Martin Kähler and Albert Schweitzer as holding similar views on the importance of the historical Jesus for faith and theology. See the brief discussion on Barth in John P. Galvin, " 'I Believe . . . in Jesus Christ, His Only Son, Our Lord': The Earthly Jesus and the Christ of Faith," *Int* 50 (1996): 376, where he draws attention to the Barth-Harnack correspondence: H. Martin Rumscheidt, *Revelation and Theology: An Analysis of the Barth-Harnack Correspondence of 1923* (Cambridge, U.K.: Cambridge University Press, 1972), esp. pp. 31, 35.

[9]Luke Timothy Johnson, *The Real Jesus: The Misguided Quest for the Historical Jesus and the Truth of the Traditional Gospels* (New York: HarperCollins, 1995), p. 141.

[10]Ibid., pp. 142-43. Cf. the interview by Carol Fellows with Bultmann cited in §1.2.

[11]Cf. Richard A. Burridge, "About People, by People, for People: Gospel Genre and Audiences," in *The Gospel for All Christians,* ed. Richard Bauckham (Grand Rapids, Mich.: Eerdmans, 1998), pp. 123-24. See also Richard A. Burridge, *What Are the Gospels? A Comparison with Graeco-Roman Biography* (Cambridge, U.K.: Cambridge University Press, 1992).

[12]See, e.g., John P. Meier, *A Marginal Jew: Rethinking the Historical Jesus,* 3 vols. (New York: Doubleday, 1991, 1994, forthcoming), 1:196-201.

[13]For what follows, see Borg, *Jesus in Contemporary Scholarship,* pp. 188-96.

[14]Ernst Käsemann, "The Problem of the Historical Jesus" (1953), in *Essays on New Testament Themes* (London: SCM Press, 1964), pp. 15-47.

[15]Norman Perrin, *Rediscovering the Teaching of Jesus* (New York: Harper & Row, 1976), p. 244.

[16]Ibid., p. 244.

[17]John Dominic Crossan, *Jesus: A Revolutionary Biography* (New York: HarperCollins, 1994), pp. 199, 200, and also in Jeffrey Carlson and Robert A. Ludwig, *Jesus and Faith: A Conversation on the Work of John Dominic Crossan* (Maryknoll, N.Y.: Orbis, 1993), pp. 3-4.

[18]From Borg, *Jesus in Contemporary Scholarship,* pp. 191-92.

[19]As set out by ibid., p. 191.

[20]Marcus J. Borg, "The Historian, the Christian, and Jesus," *TToday* 52 (1995-1996): 7.

[21]Borg, *Jesus in Contemporary Scholarship,* pp. 192-95.

[22]Martin Kähler, *The So-Called Historical Jesus and the Historic Biblical Christ* (1896; Philadelphia: Fortress, 1964), cited by Richard B. Hays, *The Moral Vision of the New Testament* (Edinburgh, U.K.: T & T Clark, 1997), p. 159.

[23]A. E. Harvey, *Jesus and the Constraints of History* (London: Duckworth, 1982), p. 105.

[24]See the collections of material by Paul Fiebig, *Jüdische Wundergeschichten des neutestamentlichen Zeitalters* (Tübingen, Ger.: Mohr, 1911); Otto Weinreich, *Antike Heilungswunder: Untersuchungen zum Wunderglauben der Griechen und Römer* (Geissen: Töpelmann, 1909); Rudolf Bultmann, *History of the Synoptic Tradition* (New York: Harper & Row, 1976), pp. 220-38; Werner Kahl, *New Testament Miracle Stories in Their Religious-Historical Setting: A Religionsgeschichtliche Comparison from a Structural Perspective* (Göttingen, Ger.: Vandenhoeck & Ruprecht, 1994).

[25]William Loader, "Challenged at the Boundaries: A Conservative Jesus in Mark's Tradition," *JSNT* 63 (1996): 45-61.

[26]Harvey (*Jesus and the Constraints of History,* p. 100) notes that "two stories sometimes cited from Lucian are told with the characteristic cynicism of that writer, and were clearly not intended to be taken too seriously; [*Philops.* 26; *Alex.* 24] and the one close parallel, which occurs in the

life of Apollonius of Tyana, [4:45] is accompanied by a comment of Philostratus to the effect that he is not sure himself whether it is to be believed."

[27] Harvey, *Jesus and the Constraints of History*, p. 100.

[28] See *b. Pesaḥ* 68a; cf. Str-B 1:557-60.

[29] So N. T. Wright, *Jesus and the Victory of God* (London: SPCK, 1996), p. 193.

[30] Reginald H. Fuller, *Interpreting the Miracles* (London: SCM Press, 1963), p. 37.

[31] Cf. Harvey, *Jesus and the Constraints of History*, p. 116, following Ernest Bloch (*Das Prinzip Hoffnung* [1959], p. 165): "the only kind of promise of a new future which can genuinely nourish human hope is that which bears a close relationship to the actual limitations of human existence, and which lies only just beyond the threshold of what we believe to be possible."

[32] Harvey, *Jesus and the Constraints of History*, p. 100, citing *b. Ber.* 34b; *b. Ḥag.* 3a.

[33] Cf. Morton Smith (*Tannaitic Parallels to the Gospels* [Philadelphia: SBL, 1951], pp. 81-84), who shows (against Paul Fiebig) the extreme paucity of Tannaitic parallels to any of Jesus' miracles.

[34] Harvey, *Jesus and the Constraints of History*, p. 101. Further, see the discussion in §10.13.

[35] Cf. Perrin, *Rediscovering the Teaching of Jesus*, pp. 130-31.

[36] Faith in relation to the miracles is mentioned only in Acts 3:16 and 14:9.

[37] Perrin (*Rediscovering the Teaching of Jesus*, p. 137) was prepared to go so far as to say that even though "we cannot, today, reconstruct a single authentic healing or exorcism narrative from the tradition we have, we are none the less entitled to claim that the emphasis upon the faith of the patient, or his friends, in that tradition is authentic." Cf. Jürgen Roloff, *Das Kerygma und der irdische Jesus* (Göttingen, Ger.: Vandenhoeck & Ruprecht, 1970), pp. 152-73.

[38] See Laurence J. McGinley, "The Synoptic Healing Narrative and Rabbinic Analogies," *TS* 4 (1943): 95; Gerd Theissen, *The Miracle Stories of the Early Christian Tradition* (Ediburgh: T & T Clark, 1983), pp. 130-32.

[39] Theissen, *Miracle Stories*, p. 140.

[40] Further, see Graham H. Twelftree, *Jesus the Exorcist: A Contribution to the Study of the Historical Jesus* (Tübingen, Ger.: Mohr; Peabody, Mass.: Hendrickson, 1993), pp. 145-46.

[41] See Twelftree, *Jesus the Exorcist*, p. 162 n. 21.

[42] See Joachim Jeremias, "*airō . . . ,*" *TDNT* 1:185 n. 1.

[43] See Josephus *Ant.* 14:22-24; *m. Ta'an.* 3:8; *b. Ber.* 33a, 34b; *y. Ber.* 9a; *t. Ber.* 2:20. Cf. Geza Vermes, *Jesus the Jew* (London: Collins/Fontana, 1976), pp. 69-72; Harvey, *Jesus and the Constraints of History*, pp. 106-7.

[44] So also Harvey, *Jesus and the Constraints of History*, p. 107.

[45] See also Twelftree, *Jesus the Exorcist*, p. 165. Werner Kahl (*New Testament Miracle Stories in Their Religious-Historical Setting* [Göttingen, Ger.: Vandenhoeck & Ruprecht, 1994], p. 79) refers to Jesus as a "bearer of numinous power" who did not need to come before his god as a suppliant or refer to a bearer of numinous power mightier than himself whenever he wanted to effect a healing.

[46] Harvey, *Jesus and the Constraints of History*, p. 109.

[47] From ibid., p. 112.

[48] Mt 9:32-34; 12:22-30/Mk 3:22-27/Lk 11:14-23.

[49] See Meier, *A Marginal Jew*, 2:407-11.

[50] Cf. Meyer, *The Aims of Jesus*, p. 155; also Joachim Jeremias, *New Testament Theology* (London: SCM Press, 1971), p. 14; James D. G. Dunn, *Jesus and the Spirit* (London: SCM Press, 1975), p. 44.

[51] Robert Shirock ("Whose Exorcists Are They? The Referents of *hoi huioi humōn* at Matthew 12.27/Luke 11.19," *JSNT* 46 [1992]: 41-51) has tried unsuccessfully, in my view, to overthrow the modern consensus and support an ancient view that the "sons" here are Jesus' disciples.

[52] E.g., Werner Kümmel, *Promise and Fulfilment* (London: SCM Press, 1957), pp. 105-6; Sanders, *Jesus and Judaism*, p. 134. On the various interpretations of these two verses, see W. D. Davies and Dale C. Allison, *The Gospel According to Saint Matthew*, 3 vols. (Edinburgh, U.K.: T & T Clark, 1988, 1991, 1997), 2:340-41.

[53]E.g., Meier, *A Marginal Jew*, 2:409-10. His case is not convincing, relying on the suggestion that there is a shift of audience from the "your" of verse 27 to the "you" of verse 28.

[54]As thought by Harvey, *Jesus and the Constraints of History*, p. 109.

[55]As suggested by C. C. Caragounis, "Kingdom of God, Son of Man and Jesus' Self-Understanding," *TynBul* 40 (1989): 230-31.

[56]As does Dunn, *Jesus and the Spirit*, p. 47, though see his point (b) there.

[57]See Marcus J. Borg, *Conflict, Holiness and Politics in the Teaching of Jesus* (Lampeter, U.K.: Edwin Mellen, 1984), p. 253.

[58]Cf. Helge K. Nielsen, *Heilung und Verkündigung: Das Verständnis der Heilung und ihres Verhältnisses zur Verkündigung bei Jesus und in der ältesten Kirche* (Leiden, Neth.: Brill, 1987), pp. 32-40.

[59]Jeremias, *New Testament Theology*, §11; James R. Butts, "Probing the Polling: Jesus Seminar Results on the Kingdom Sayings," *Forum* 3 (1987): 98-128.

[60]See further Twelftree, *Jesus the Exorcist*, p. 110.

[61]See Graham H. Twelftree, *Christ Triumphant: Exorcism Then and Now* (London: Hodder & Stoughton, 1985), chap. 4.

[62]Compare, e.g., George B. Caird, *New Testament Theology* (Oxford, U.K.: Clarendon, 1994), esp. chap. 4.

[63]Cf. Sanders, *Jesus and Judaism*, pp. 134, 136; James D. G Dunn, "Matthew 12:28/Luke 11:20—A Word of Jesus?" in *Eschatology and the New Testament*, ed. E. Hulitt Gloer (Peabody, Mass.: Hendrickson, 1988), pp. 29-49; Meier, *A Marginal Jew*, 2:413-17. Robert W. Funk, Roy W. Hoover and the Jesus Seminar (*The Five Gospels: The Search for the Authentic Words of Jesus* [New York: Macmillan, 1993], p. 330) gave this saying "a pink rating"; that is, the Jesus Seminar considered that "Jesus probably said something like this" (p. 36). We are still in the position expressed by Perrin, *Rediscovering the Teaching of Jesus*, p. 64: "The saying is, in fact, one of the very few sayings in the tradition, the authenticity of which has not been seriously questioned in more than half a century of intensive discussion of Jesus' eschatological teaching."

[64]See Gustaf Dalman, *The Words of Jesus* (Edinburgh, U.K.: T & T Clark, 1902), pp. 106-7; Meier, *A Marginal Jew*, 2:422-23.

[65]On the status of *egō* ("I") in the text, see the apparatus of the Greek New Testament.

[66]On the Jewish exorcists in the time of Jesus, see Twelftree, *Jesus the Exorcist*, §3.

[67]Contrast Martin Hengel, *The Charismatic Leader and His Followers* (Edinburgh, U.K.: T & T Clark, 1981), p. 64 n. 102.

[68]Cf. Deiter Trunk, *Der messianische Heiler* (Freiburg, Ger.,: Herder, 1994), p. 426, cited by Gerd Theissen and Annette Merz, *The Historical Jesus: A Comprehensive Guide* (London: SCM Press, 1998), p. 290.

[69]Cf. *Tg. Isa* 42:1-4. Further, see Erik Sjöberg, *"pneuma ... ," TDNT* 6:384.

[70]Cf. Davies and Allison, *Saint Matthew*, 2:339.

[71]Cf. Rudolf Pesch, *Das Markusevangelium*, 2 vols. (Freiburg, Ger.: Herder, 1980), 1:219.

[72]See Joachim Jeremias, *The Parables of Jesus* (London: SCM Press, 1972), p. 197.

[73]Cf. Funk et al., *The Five Gospels*, p. 51. The Gospel of Thomas §35 preserves a version of the saying. But this is of little help to us at present, for the question of the relationship between Q and Thomas remains an open question. See the discussion by Ron Cameron, "Thomas, Gospel of," *ABD* 6:536-38; G. J. Riley, "The *Gospel of Thomas* in Recent Research," *Biblical Studies* 2 (1994): 232-36; Bradley H. McLean, "On the *Gospel of Thomas* and Q," in *The Gospel Behind the Gospels: Current Studies on Q*, ed. Ronald A. Piper (Leiden, Neth.: Brill, 1995), pp. 321-45.

[74]See, e.g., *PGM* IV:3037-39; Twelftree, *Jesus the Exorcist*, p. 112.

[75]See James D. G. Dunn and Graham H. Twelftree, "Demon-Possession and Exorcism in the New Testament," *The Churchman* 94 (1980): 220 and n. 31, citing Is 24:21-22; *1 Enoch* 10:4-6; 1QS 4:18-19; cf. *1 Enoch* 54:4-6; Rev 19:20—20:15; *T. Sim.* 6:6; *T. Levi* 18:12.

[76]See Twelftree, *Jesus the Exorcist*, §23.

[77]See the commission in Mk 16:17, the parable of the wheat and the tares (Mt 13:36-43), the parable of the net and its explanation (Mt 13:47-50) and the parable of the sheep and goats

(Mt 25:1-46).

[78]See Twelftree, *Christ Triumphant*, pp. 80-81.

[79]See Is 24:21-22; *1 Enoch* 10:4-6, 12-13; 18:14—19:2; 21:6-7; 90:23-24; *Jub.* 5:5-10; 10:4-9. See also 2 Pet 2:4; Jude 6; Rev 20:1-3. Cf. George Foot Moore, *Judaism in the First Three Centuries of the Christian Era, the Age of Tannaim,* 3 vols. (Cambridge, Mass.: Harvard University Press, 1948-50), 2:338-45.

[80]The identity of the "host of heaven" (cf. Is 24:21) is not clear, but here it is probably the rebellious powers in heaven thought to be controlling or manipulating the heathen nations. Cf. Deut 32:8; Dan 10:13.

[81]A demonic figure. See David P. Wright, "Azazel," *ABD* 1:536-37; B. Janowski, "Azazel," in *Dictionary of Deities and Demons in the Bible,* ed. Karel van der Toorn et al. (Leiden, Neth.: Brill, 1995), pp. 240-48.

[82]On Duda'el, see Michael A. Knibb, ed. *The Ethiopic Book of Enoch,* 2 vols. (Oxford, U.K.: Clarendon, 1978), 2:87.

[83]Cf. *1 Enoch* 10:12-13; cf. 18:14—9:2; 21:6-10; 90:23-27; *Jub.* 5:6-10; 10:5-9.

[84]Further, on this passage, see Knibb, ed., *The Ethiopic Book of Enoch,* 2:87, and Matthew Black, *The Book of Enoch or 1 Enoch* (Leiden, Neth.: Brill, 1985), pp. 133-35.

[85]E.g., see René Latourelle, *The Miracles of Jesus and the Theology of Miracles* (New York: Paulist, 1988), p. 42.

[86]So, e.g., Dunn, *Jesus and the Spirit,* p. 59.

[87]That this beatitude belongs here, see Davies and Allison, *Saint Matthew,* 2:243.

[88]See also, e.g., Kümmel, *Promise and Fulfilment,* pp. 109-13; Karl Kertelge, "Die Überlieferung der Wunder Jesu und die Frage nach dem historischen Jesus," in *Rückfrage nach Jesus: Zur Methodik und Bedeutung der Frage nach dem historischen Jesus,* ed. Karl Kertelge (Freiburg, Ger.: Herder, 1974), pp. 183-89; Meyer, *The Aims of Jesus,* pp. 157-58.

[89]See Meier, *A Marginal Jew,* 2:132 n. 90.

[90]Ibid., 2:134-35.

[91]See Is 29:18-19; 35:5-6; 61:1.

[92]Contrast Pesch (*Jesu ureigene Taten?* pp. 41, 43, 44, 48), who thought that the Gospels did not contain any authentic sayings of Jesus about lepers being healed but were an expression of the early church's belief in Jesus as eschatological prophet.

[93]Cf. Dunn, *Jesus and the Spirit,* p. 59; James D. G. Dunn, "Messianic Ideas and Their Influence on the Jesus of History," in *The Messiah,* ed. James H. Charlesworth (Minneapolis: Fortress, 1992), pp. 373-76.

[94]See the summary discussion on the variety of meanings of the term in Davies and Allison, *Saint Matthew,* 1:312-14.

[95]See the discussion in John Nolland, *Luke 1—9:20* (Dallas: Word, 1989), pp. 328-29.

[96]N. T. Wright, *Jesus and the Victory of God* (London: SPCK, 1996), pp. 191-92.

[97]Following David R. Catchpole, *The Quest for Q* (Edinburgh, U.K.: T & T Clark, 1993), p. 172.

[98]Bultmann, *History of the Synoptic Tradition,* p. 112.

[99]For what follows, see Dunn, *Jesus and the Spirit,* pp. 70-71. Also on the authenticity of these woes, see Davies and Allison, *Saint Matthew,* 2:270-71.

[100]So Franz Mussner, *The Miracles of Jesus: An Introduction* (Notre Dame, Ind.: University of Notre Dame, 1968), p. 21.

[101]Ibid.

[102]Seán Freyne, *Galilee from Alexander the Great to Hadrian 323 B.C.E. to 135 C.E.* (Wilmington, Del.: Michael Glazier; Notre Dame, Ind.: University of Notre Dame Press, 1980), p. 361.

[103]This is not to deny that judgment and salvation were seen to hinge on the people's repentance. See Davies and Allison, *Saint Matthew,* 2:270-71.

[104]Mussner, *The Miracles of Jesus,* pp. 21-22.

[105]See Gustav Stählin, "*sakkos . . . ,*" *TDNT* 7:61-62.

[106]Mk 6:2, 5, 14; Mt 11:21, 23/Lk 10:13. See §8.5.1.

[107]See Dalman, *Words of Jesus,* p. 201.

[108]Cf. Dunn, *Jesus and the Spirit,* pp. 209-10.

[109]The verb *iaomai* ("I cure") occurs eleven times in Luke, four times in Matthew, once in Mark and three times in John. For those who affirm the historicity of this saying, see Bultmann, *History of the Synoptic Tradition,* p. 35, cf. p. 56; Vincent Taylor, *Jesus and His Sacrifice* (London: Macmillan, 1937), pp. 167-71; Harold W. Hoehner, *Herod Antipas* (Grand Rapids, Mich.: Zondervan, 1980), pp. 214-24. Others have attributed the saying to Lukan redaction: Adelbert Denaux, "L'hypocrisie des Pharisiens et le dessein de Dieu: Analyse de Lc., xiii, 31-33," in *L'évangile de Luc,* ed. Frans Neirynck (Gembloux, Fra.: Duculot, 1973), pp. 245-85; Martin Rese, "Einige Überlegungen zu Lukas xiii, 31-33," in *Jésus aux origenes de la christologie,* ed. Jacques Dupont et al. (Gembloux, Fra.: Duculot, 1975), pp. 201-25.

[110]Cf. Joseph B. Tyson, "Jesus and Herod Antipas," *JBL* 79 (1960): 245; Joseph A. Fitzmyer, *Luke X—XXIV,* (New York: Doubleday, 1981), p. 1030.

[111]Funk, et al., *The Five Gospels,* p. 348.

[112]See Davies and Allison, *Saint Matthew,* 2:577-78.

[113]See Robert A. Guelich, *Mark 1—8:26* (Dallas: Word, 1989), p. 411.

[114]Further, see Karl H. Rengstorf, *"sēmeion . . . ," TDNT* 7:208-38, and Morna D. Hooker, *The Signs of a Prophet: The Prophetic Actions of Jesus* (London: SCM Press, 1997), pp. 13-15.

[115]Cf. Hengel, *Charismatic Leader,* p. 58; Meyer, *The Aims of Jesus,* p. 158; Harvey, *Jesus and the Constraints of History,* pp. 111-12; Hooker, *Signs of a Prophet,* pp. 33-34.

[116]So Hooker, *Signs of a Prophet,* p. 34.

[117]See Marinus de Jonge, "The Use of the Word 'Anointed' in the Time of Jesus," *NovT* 8 (1966): 132-48; James H. Charlesworth, "From Messianology to Christology: Problems and Prospects," in *The Messiah,* ed. James H. Charlesworth (Minneapolis: Fortress, 1992), pp. 11, 13-29, also citing George E. Ladd, *A Theology of the New Testament* (Guildford and London: Lutterworth, 1974), p. 136.

[118]Cf. Markus Bockmuehl, *This Jesus: Martyr, Lord, Messiah* (Edinburgh, U.K.: T & T Clark, 1994), chap. 2; William Scott Green, "Introduction: Messiah in Judaism: Rethinking the Question," in *Judaisms and Their Messiahs at the Turn of the Era,* ed. Jacob Neusner, William S. Green and Ernest Frerichs (Cambridge, U.K.: Cambridge University Press, 1987), pp. 1-13. John C. O'Neill (*Who Did Jesus Think He Was?* [Leiden, Neth.: Brill, 1995]) argues to the contrary: that all Jews expected a single Davidic Messiah.

[119]For details, see Charlesworth, "From Messianology to Christology," pp. 7-8.

[120]See *Pss. Sol.* 17; 18; 4 Ezra 7:28-29; 12:31-34; 13:26; *2 Apoc. Bar.* 30:1-2; cf. *Odes Sol.* 41:15; Charlesworth, "From Messianology to Christology," p. 13.

[121]Cf. Meyer, "Jesus' Ministry and Self-Understanding," p. 345: "Jesus was the conscious bearer of a (indeed, of *the*) climactic and definitive mission to all Israel" (his emphasis).

[122]Meyer, "Jesus' Ministry and Self-Understanding," p. 351.

[123]E.g., Anton Fridrichsen and Herman N. Ridderbos, cited in Loos, *Miracles,* p. 282, and Rudolf Bultmann, *Jesus Christ and Mythology* (New York: Charles Scribner's Sons, 1958), pp. 12-13.

[124]See Jn 2:23; 4:54; 10:38; 12:18; 20:30. Cf. Richard H. Hiers, "Satan, Demons, and the Kingdom of God," *SJT* 27 (1974): 37-38; Anton Fridrichsen, *The Problem of Miracle in Primitive Christianity* (Minneapolis: Augsburg, 1972), pp. 63-72.

[125]Cf. Rudolf Bultmann, *Theology of the New Testament,* 2 vols. (London: SCM Press, 1952-1955), 1:7.

[126]Marcus J. Borg, "An Orthodoxy Reconsidered: The 'End-of-the-World Jesus,'" in *The Glory of Christ in the New Testament: Studies in Christology,* ed. L. D. Hurst and N. T. Wright (Oxford, U.K.: Clarendon, 1987), pp. 216-17.

[127]See those cited by Barry L. Blackburn, "The Miracles of Jesus," in *Studying the Historical Jesus,* pp. 373-74. See also the discussion in Twelftree, *Jesus the Exorcist,* pp. 166-71, and also Dermot Connolly, "Ad miracula sanationum apud Matthaeum," *VD* 45 (1967): 306-25, and Christian Dietzfelbinger, "Vom Sinn der Sabbatheilungen Jesu," *EvT* 38 (1978): 281-98.

[128]That the messiahs of early Judaism were not expected to be miracle workers, even though the

messiah does perform wonders in 4 Ezra 13, see Charlesworth, "From Messianology to Christology," p. 8.

[129]On the historical reliability of the report of Jesus' baptism reflecting an experience of the historical Jesus, see, e.g., Ben Witherington, *The Christology of Jesus* (Minneapolis: Fortress, 1990), pp. 150-52; Meier, *A Marginal Jew*, 1:168-70.

[130]Mk 11:27-33. See Joachim Jeremias, *New Testament Theology* (London: SCM Press, 1971), pp. 55-56.

[131]Cf. Is 35:5-6; Mt 11:2-6/Lk 7:18-23.

[132]Cf. Twelftree, *Jesus the Exorcist*, pp. 182-84; also Marinus de Jonge, "The Earliest Christian Use of *Christos:* Some Suggestions," *NTS* 32 (1986): 334-35.

Chapter 11: Jesus & Exorcism

[1]So also Reginald H. Fuller, *Interpreting the Miracles* (London: SCM Press, 1963), p. 37. Further, see chapter 16 and §17.12.

[2]For a more detailed treatment of this subject, see Graham H. Twelftree, "*EI DE . . . EGŌ EKBALLŌ DAIMONIA . . . ,*" in *Gospel Perspectives 6: The Miracles of Jesus,* ed. David Wenham and Craig Blomberg (Sheffield, U.K.: JSOT, 1986), pp. 363-68, and *Jesus the Exorcist: A Contribution to the Study of the Historical Jesus* (Tübingen, Ger.: Mohr; Peabody, Mass.: Hendrickson, 1993).

[3]E.g., Mk 1:32-34/Mt 8:16-17/Lk 4:40-41; Mk 3:10-11/Lk 6:17-18; Mt 10:1/Lk 9:1; cf. Mk 6:13; n. 5 below.

[4]See the discussion in the conclusions of chapter 17.

[5]Complete stories of healing are found at Mk 1:29-31, 40-45; 2:1-12; 3:1-6; 5:21-43; 7:31-37; 8:22-26; 10:46-52. The exorcism stories are Mk 1:21-28; 5:1-20; 7:24-30; 9:14-29. The distinctions of terminology and narrative set the exorcisms apart from the other healing stories. However, in that the stories deal with the restoration of health of individuals, we will treat them as a type of healing story.

[6]Origen *CC* 1:6, 67; *PGM* IV:3019-20, cf. 1227. Further, see Twelftree, *Jesus the Exorcist*, pp. 139-40.

[7]Mk 1:21-28; 5:1-20; 7:24-30; 9:14-29.

[8]Mt 9:32-33/12:22-24/Lk 11:14.

[9]Mt 12:24/Lk 11:15 and Mk 3:22.

[10]This saying is attested in a number of traditions. It is preserved in Mk 3:27 and followed by Matthew in 12:29. Q probably also has the saying, which is preserved in Lk 11:21-22. Cf. *Gospel of Thomas* 35 (on which see §10.12 n. 73).

[11]E.g., Rudolf Bultmann, *History of the Synoptic Tradition* (New York: Harper & Row, 1976), p. 25; Ernst Haenchen, *Der Weg Jesu* (Berlin, Ger.: Töpelmann, 1966), p. 327.

[12]E.g., 11QPsAp[a]4:4; Josephus *Ant.* 8:46-47; cf. *PGM* IV:3019 and see §9.7.1.

[13]See Adolf Deissmann, *Bible Studies* (Edinburgh: T & T Clark, 1901), pp. 197-98.

[14]See Gerhard Kittel, "*akoloutheō . . . ,*" *TDNT* 1:214. Further, see Twelftree, *Jesus the Exorcist*, p. 42.

[15]See Twelftree, *Jesus the Exorcist*, p. 42 n. 65.

[16]Mentioned in Acts at 5:16; 8:7; 16:16-18; and 19:11.

[17]Mt 28:18-20; Lk 24:46-49; Jn 20:21-23; Acts 1:8.

[18]Here we are not far removed from the conclusions of the Fellows of the Jesus Seminar, who "agreed that Jesus healed people and drove away what were thought to be demons." See Robert W. Funk and the Jesus Seminar, *The Acts of Jesus: The Search for the Authentic Deeds of Jesus* (New York: HarperCollins, 1998), p. 60.

[19]See G. A. Chadwick, "Some Cases of Possession," *Expositor* 6 (1892): 275. Cf. P. Pimental, "The 'Unclean Spirits' of St Mark's Gospel," *ExpTim* 99 (1988): 173-75.

[20]Further, see Graham H. Twelftree, *Christ Triumphant: Exorcism Then and Now* (London: Hodder & Stoughton, 1985), chap. 5.

[21]See 1 Macc 2:39-41; Str-B 1:618-19. See also *m. Yoma* 8:6. Cf. Str-B1:622-29; Eduard Lohse,

"*sabbaton...,*" *TDNT* 7:11-15.

[22]See Mk 1:23; 3:11; 5:6, 33; 9:20. Luke also pays no particular attention to this element in the exorcism stories: Lk 4:33, 41; 8:28; 9:42.

[23]See Harry M. Buck, "Redactions of the Fourth Gospel and the Mother of Jesus," in *Studies in the New Testament and Early Christian Literature,* ed. David E. Aune (Leiden, Neth.: Brill, 1972), p. 177.

[24]See Twelftree, *Jesus the Exorcist,* pp. 63-64, and Otto Bauernfeind, *Die Worte der Dämonen im Markusevangelium* (Stuttgart, Ger.: Kohlhammer, 1927), pp. 3-28.

[25]Bauernfeind, *Die Worte der Dämonen,* pp. 13-15.

[26]See Mt 2:23; 21:11; Acts 10:38; Jn 1:45.

[27]H. H. Schaeder, "*Nazarēnos...,*" *TDNT* 4:874.

[28]If Q is Palestinian in outlook (see David R. Catchpole, "The Mission Charge in Q," *Semeia* 55 [1991]: 147-74), we have further evidence that the term *Nazareth* was of little theological significance to Palestinian Christianity, for the word probably does not occur in Q. (See Richard A. Edwards, *A Concordance to Q* [Missoula, Mont.: Scholars, 1975]).

[29]Cf. Acts 19:13; *PGM* 4:3045-49.

[30]Nigel Turner, *A Grammar of New Testament Greek* (Edinburgh, U.K.: T & T Clark, 1976), p. 16.

[31]See *PGM* IV:1500, 2984-86; V:103-5; VIII:13; Twelftree, *Jesus the Exorcist,* p. 67 n. 57.

[32]William R. Domeris, "The Holy One of God as a Title for Jesus," *Neot* 19 (1985): 9.

[33]See, e.g., P. Oslo. 1:161-62; Twelftree, *Jesus the Exorcist,* pp. 69-70.

[34]See, e.g., *PGM* 4:3013-15; Philostratus *Life* 4:20; Twelftree, *Jesus the Exorcist,* p. 70.

[35]Mk 1:27; 10:24, 32.

[36]Cf. Rudolf Pesch, *Das Markusevangelium,* 2 vols. (Freiburg, Ger.: Herder, 1980), 2:143, 150-52.

[37]Cf. James D. G. Dunn, *Jesus and the Spirit* (London: SCM Press, 1975), pp. 76-77.

[38]Cf. Erik Peterson, *Eis Theos* (Göttingen, Ger.: Vandenhoeck & Ruprecht, 1926), pp. 183-222; Pesch, *Markusevangelium,* 1:124; Gerd Theissen, *Miracle Stories in the Early Christian Tradition* (Edinburgh, U.K.: T & T Clark, 1983), pp. 69-70.

[39]Funk and the Jesus Seminar, *The Acts of Jesus,* p. 61

[40]See Bruce M. Metzger, *A Textual Commentary on the Greek New Testament* (Stuttgart, Ger.: United Bible Societies, 1994), p. 72.

[41]John P. Meier, *A Marginal Jew: Rethinking the Historical Jesus,* 3 vols. (New York: Doubleday, 1991, 1994, forthcoming), 2:652.

[42]See the discussion in Robert A. Guelich, *Mark 1—8:26* (Waco, Tex.: Word, 1989), pp. 275-77.

[43]See the discussion in Twelftree, *Jesus the Exorcist,* §7.

[44]See the literature cited in Twelftree, *Jesus the Exorcist,* p. 75, and also M. P. Nilson, *A History of Greek Religion* (Oxford, U.K.: Clarendon, 1949), pp. 85-86.

[45]J. Duncan M. Derrett, "Contributions to the Study of the Gerasene Demoniac," *JSNT* 3 (1979): 5.

[46]See Twelftree, *Christ Triumphant,* chap. 5.

[47]See the discussion in Twelftree, *Jesus the Exorcist,* §7.

[48]See Morna D. Hooker, "On Using the Wrong Tool," *Theology* 75 (1972): 570-81.

[49]Although it is unlikely that this aspect of the story has its origin in Is 65:4-5, the overlap of vocabulary could support the view that these verses represent a midrashic rewriting of the story based on Is 65. See John F. Craghan, "The Gerasene Demoniac," *CBQ* 30 (1968): 529-31; Pesch, *Markusevangelium,* 1:286. It might be argued that the withering of the fig tree destroyed at least part of a person's livelihood.

[50]See Twelftree, *Jesus the Exorcist,* pp. 76-77.

[51]Cf. Diodorus Siculus 26:5 and, e.g., P. Oxy. 1666:5-6. See also H. Preisker, "*legiōn,*" *TDNT* 4:68.

[52]*PGM* 4:1067-68; 5:46.

[53]See, e.g., *PGM* IV:3019-20, 3046.

[54]Cf., e.g., *PGM* 4:3037-41; 13:242-44.

[55]See the discussion in Twelftree, *Jesus the Exorcist*, pp. 83-84.

[56]Cf., e.g., *PGM* 1:162; 4:3037-41; 13:242-44. See also Twelftree, *Jesus the Exorcist*, p. 84.

[57]The Jesus Seminar concluded only that "some vague historical event might lie behind the present narrative." See Funk and the Jesus Seminar, *The Acts of Jesus*, p. 78

[58]Dennis E. Nineham, *The Gospel of St Mark* (Harmondsworth, U.K.: Penguin, 1969), p. 201, citing Acts 13:46; 18:6; Rom 1:16.

[59]Cf. James D. G. Dunn, *Romans 1—8* (Dallas: Word, 1988), p. 40.

[60]See the discussion in Guelich, *Mark 1—8:26*, p. 385.

[61]Gerd Theissen, *The Gospels in Context: Social and Political History in the Synoptic Tradition* (Minneapolis: Fortress, 1991), p. 67.

[62]See Otto Michel, "*kuōn* . . . ," *TDNT* 3:1101-2. On the insult of being called a dog, see 1 Sam 17:43; 24:14; 2 Kings 8:13; Prov 26:11; Eccles 9:4; Is 56:10-11; also, though very late (eighth century), *Pirqe de Rabbi Eliezar* 29. Cf., e.g., S. G. F. Brandon, *The Fall of Jerusalem and the Christian Church* (London: SPCK, 1978), p. 33. Also see Petr Pokorný, "From a Puppy to the Child: Some Problems of Contemporary Biblical Exegesis Demonstrated from Mark 7.24-30/Matt 15.21-8," *NTS* 41 (1995): 323-24.

[63]W. D. Davies and Dale C. Allison, *The Gospel According to Saint Matthew*, 3 vols. (Edinburgh, U.K.: T & T Clark, 1988, 1991, 1997), 2:545.

[64]Cf. Philostratus, *Life*, 3:38; *b. Ber.* 34b.

[65]E.g., Meier, *A Marginal Jew*, 2:660-61. Funk and the Jesus Seminar (*The Acts of Jesus*, p. 97) reports that the Jesus Seminar voted by a slight majority (57 percent) that there was probably a historical core to this story.

[66]Cf. also Ferdinand Hahn, *Mission in the New Testament* (London: SCM Press, 1965), p. 32; Gerd Theissen, "Lokal-und Sozialkolorit in der Geschichte von der syrophönikischen Frau (Mk 7 24-30)," *ZNW* 75 (1984): 202-25; Davies and Allison, *Saint Matthew*, 2:544-45.

[67]E.g., Bultmann, *History of the Synoptic Tradition*, p. 211; Paul J. Achtemeier, "Miracles and the Historical Jesus: A Study of Mark 9:14-29," *CBQ* 37 (1975): 476-77; cf. also, Gerhard Petzke, "Die historische Frage nach den Wundertaten Jesu," *NTS* 22 (1976): 188.

[68]Meier, *A Marginal Jew*, 2:654.

[69]E.g., Petzke, "Die historische Frage nach den Wundertaten Jesu," pp. 202-4.

[70]Cf. Mk 1:23, 26; 3:11; 5:2-4; 7:25.

[71]See Mk 2:5; 5:34, 36; 10:52.

[72]See Twelftree, *Jesus the Exorcist*, pp. 95-96.

[73]Cf. Josephus *Ant.* 8:49; Philostratus *Life* 4:20; cf. C. Bonner, "The Violence of Departing Demons," *HTR* 37 (1944): 334-36.

[74]See Lloyd Gaston, *Horae Synopticae Electronicae* (Missoula, Mont.: Scholars, 1973), pp. 19, 72-74, 76, 78.

[75]On "inconsistencies" as indicators of redaction, see Robert H. Stein, "The 'Redaktionsgeschichtlich' Investigation of a Markan Seam (Mc 1.21f.)" *ZNW* 61 (1970): 78-79. If we take prayer to be an expression of faith (see §3.26), our certainty here is somewhat reduced.

[76]Cf. Achtemeier, "Miracles and the Historical Jesus," pp. 476-77; Pesch, *Das Markusevangelium*, 2:95; Meier, *A Marginal Jew*, 2:656. Funk and the Jesus Seminar, *The Acts of Jesus*, p. 109: "It is possible that the account . . . harbors some reference to an actual event."

[77]Cf. Gregory E. Sterling, "Jesus as Exorcist: An Analysis of Matthew 17:14-20; Mark 9:14-29; Luke 9:37-43a," *CBQ* 55 (1993), p. 492.

Chapter 12: The Crippled & Paralytics

[1]For the evidence, see A. E. Harvey, *Jesus and the Constraints of History* (London: Duckworth, 1982), p. 100.

[2]For the evidence, see ibid., p. 100.

[3]See, e.g., Jn 5:3-4; *m. Pe'a* 8:9; *b. Ketub.* 76b-68a; *b. Sanh.* 98a, b.

[4]So, e.g., Richard T. Mead, "The Healing of the Paralytic—a Unit?" *JBL* 80 (1961): 348-54;

Martin Dibelius, *From Tradition to Gospel* (Cambridge, U.K.: Clarke, 1971), pp. 66-67; Pesch, *Das Markusevangelium,* 1:151-52; Hans-Josef Klauck, "Die Frage der Sündenvergebung in der Perikope von der Heilung des Gelähmten (Mk 2,1-12 parr)," *BZ* 25 (1981): 223-48.

[5]Cf. Gerd Theissen, *Miracle Stories of the Early Christian Tradition* (Edinburgh, U.K.: T & T Clark, 1983), p. 164.

[6]So, e.g., H. van der Loos, *The Miracles of Jesus* (Leiden, Neth.: Brill, 1965), p. 443; Theissen, *Miracle Stories,* pp. 58-59.

[7]On blasphemy and God's prerogative to forgive, see Graham H. Twelftree, "Blasphemy," in *Dictionary of Jesus and the Gospels,* ed. Joel B. Green, Scot McKnight and I. Howard Marshall (Downers Grove, Ill.: InterVarsity Press, 1992), pp. 76-77.

[8]If the words are taken as a divine passive the situation is not changed. Mark has *aphientai,* an aorist present, indicating that Jesus was seen either to be forgiving the sin or speaking for God that, at that moment, the man's sins were forgiven. There is, therefore (contra Robert A. Guelich, *Mark 1—8:26* [Dallas: Word, 1989], p. 87), no conflict between this pronouncement (2:5) and the charge (2:7).

[9]Joachim Jeremias, *New Testament Theology* (London: SCM Press, 1971), p. 114, citing Mt 11:19; 18:27; Mk 2:15-17; Lk 7:18, 42; 15:2, 5, 9, 11-32; 18:14.

[10]See the discussion in §3.8 and n. 59 there.

[11]Cf. Morna D. Hooker, *The Son of Man in Mark* (London: SPCK, 1967), pp. 88-89. John the Baptist is said to appear "proclaiming a baptism of repentance for the forgiveness of sins" (Mk 1:4). In light of the Essene writings, it is likely that John was understood not to be forgiving sins but offering a process whereby people could be granted forgiveness by the Spirit. See the discussion in Guelich, *Mark 1—8:26,* pp. 19-20.

[12]Cf. Theissen, *Miracle Stories,* pp. 164-65. That it also fits into the framework of preaching about Jesus (see Klauck, "Die Frage der Sündenvergebung in der Perikope von der Heiling des Gelähmten [Mk 2,1-12 parr]," pp. 241-44) is not, in itself, an argument against historicity.

[13]Chester Charlton McCown, "Luke's Translation of Semitic into Hellenistic Custom," *JBL* 58 (1939): 213-16.

[14]Meier (*A Marginal Jew,* 2:729 n. 7) is right to reject the view that the man is lowered through the roof to hide the house's door from the demon that would be exorcised from the man, for the text does not support this understanding nor are the slight and distant parallels from India (adduced by Hedwig Jahnow, "Das Abdecken des Daches Mc 2,4 Lc 5,19," *ZNW* 24 [1925]: 155-58) at all helpful.

[15]Meier, *A Marginal Jew,* 2:680. See also, e.g., Pesch, *Das Markusevangelium,* 1:157-58; Joachim Gnilka, *Jesus von Nazaret: Botschaft und Geschichte* (Freiburg, Ger.: Herder, 1990), p. 133. Funk (Robert W. Funk and the Jesus Seminar, *The Acts of Jesus: The Search for the Authentic Words of Jesus* [New York: HarperCollins, 1998], p. 64) says that the voting of the Fellows of the Jesus Seminar leads to the conclusion that "the story reflects an incident in the public life of Jesus."

[16]Geza Vermes, *Jesus the Jew* (London: Fontana/Collins, 1976), p. 25.

[17]See *m. Yoma* 8:6. Cf. Str-B 1:622-29; Eduard Lohse, *"sabbaton . . . ," TDNT* 7:11-15. E. P. Sanders (*Jewish Law from Jesus to the Mishnah* [London: SCM Press, 1990], p. 13), who doubts the authenticity of this story, says that the implied definition of the Jewish regulations is "practising medicine is work."

[18]So Meier, *A Marginal Jew,* 2:682-83. Cf. Sanders, *Jewish Law,* p. 13. To the contrary Guelich, *Mark 1—8:26,* pp. 132-33.

[19]In Mark at 1:24; 2:22; 3:6; 4:38; 8:35; 9:22, 41; 11:18; 12:9. Cf. BAGD, *"apollumi,"* p. 95.

[20]See also Mk 6:19; 8:31; 9:31; 10:34; 12:5, 7, 8; 14:1.

[21]See Pesch, *Das Markusevangelium,* 1:195.

[22]Cf. Rudolf Bultmann, *History of the Synoptic Tradition* (New York: Harper & Row, 1976), p. 12. See also §10.10.

[23]Cf. Guelich, *Mark 1—8:26,* p. 135, against, e.g., Jürgen Sauer, "Traditionsgeschichtliche Überlegungen zu Mk. 3:1-6," *ZNW* 73 (1982): 199-200.

[24]So also Arland J. Hultgren, *Jesus and his Adversaries* (Minneapolis,: Augsburg, 1979), pp. 82-84;

Pesch, *Das Markusevangelium,* 1:195-96; W. D. Davies and Dale C. Allison, *The Gospel According to Saint Matthew* (Edinburgh, U.K.: T & T Clark, 1988, 1991, 1997), 2:316; contrast the results of the Jesus Seminar: "It is difficult to isolate any elements in the story that are not part of Mark's compositional scheme" (Funk and the Jesus Seminar, *The Acts of Jesus,* p. 69).

[25]See Mt 4:23-24/Mk 1:39; Mt 8:6/Lk 7:2; Mt 9:20/Mk 5:25; Mt 9:32/12:22/Lk 11:14; Mt 17:15/Mk 9:17.

[26]So, e.g., C. H. Dodd, *Historical Tradition in the Fourth Gospel* (Cambridge, U.K.: Cambridge University Press, 1963), pp. 194-95; Raymond E. Brown, *The Gospel According to John,* 2 vols. (London: Chapman, 1971), 1:193; Barnabas Lindars, *The Gospel of John* (London: Oliphants/Marshall, Morgan & Scott, 1972), p. 198; James D. G. Dunn, "John and the Oral Gospel Tradition," in *Jesus and the Oral Tradition,* ed. Henry Wansborough (Sheffield, U.K.: JSOT, 1991), p. 360; Udo Schnelle, *Antidocetic Christology in the Gospel of John* (Minneapolis: Fortress, 1992), pp. 87-91. On the relationship between John and the Synoptics, see chapter 12.7 n. 2.

[27]Bultmann, *History of the Synoptic Tradition,* pp. 38-39 (cf. §2.3).

[28]In any case there are increasing numbers of careful reports on the possibility of telepathic communication. See the popular report by Joseph Bullman, "While You Were Sleeping," *The Age* (Melbourne), July 11, 1998, pp. 29-32.

[29]See the discussion in Uwe Wegner, *Der Hauptmann von Kafarnaum* (Tübingen, Ger.: Mohr, 1985), pp. 409-18.

[30]Cf. John Nolland, *Luke 1—9:20* (Waco, Tex.: Word, 1989), pp. 313-14.

[31]Cf. Mt 15:28 and Lk 8:12-13.

[32]Cf. Jeremias, *New Testament Theology,* pp. 159-62.

[33]Cf. Reginald H. Fuller, *Interpreting the Miracles* (London: SCM Press, 1963), p. 32; Wegner, *Der Hauptmann von Kafarnaum,* pp. 403-28; Gnilka, *Jesus von Nazaret,* p. 133. Contrast the results of the Jesus Seminar in Funk and the Jesus Seminar, *The Acts of Jesus,* p. 46.

[34]Bultmann, *History of the Synoptic Tradition,* p.12, followed by E. P. Sanders, *Jewish Law from Jesus to the Mishnah* (London: SCM Press, 1990), p. 20. Cf. Dibelius, *From Tradition to Gospel,* p. 97.

[35]Cf. Jürgen Roloff, *Das Kerygma und der irdische Jesus* (Göttingen, Ger.: Vandenhoeck & Ruprecht, 1973), pp. 67-68.

[36]Cf. Ulrich Busse, *Die Wunder der Propheten Jesus* (Stuttgart, Ger.: Katholisches Bibelwerk, 1977), pp. 294-98; C. F. Evans, *Saint Luke* (London: SCM Press, 1990), p. 550.

[37]Funk and the Jesus Seminar, *The Acts of Jesus,* p. 319.

[38]See J. Duncan M. Derrett, "Positive Perspectives on Two Lucan Miracles," *Downside Review* 104 (1986): 274, 284 n. 14.

[39]Roloff, *Das Kerygma und der irdische Jesus,* p. 67 n. 59.

[40]See esp. *m. 'Erub.* 2:1-4; CD 11:5-6, and the evidence cited by Martin Hengel, *"phatnē,"* *TDNT* 9:53 n. 40.

[41]Ibid., 9:53.

[42]Cf. Ernst Haenchen, "Johanneische Probleme," *ZTK* 56 (1959): 46-50.

[43]See Joachim Jeremias, *The Rediscovery of Bethesda: John 5:2* (Louisville, Ky.: Southern Baptist Theological Seminary, 1966), and the discussion in Meier, *A Marginal Jew,* 2:729-30 n. 11.

[44]Brown, *Gospel According to John* 1:209

[45]See Maurice Baillet, Josef T. Milik and Roland de Vaux, *Discoveries in the Judaean Desert of Jordan III: Les petites grottes de Qumran* (Oxford, U.K.: Clarendon, 1962), pp. 211-302, pls. XLVIII-LXXI; Florentino García Martínez, *The Dead Sea Scrolls Translated: The Qumran Texts in English* (Leiden, Neth.: Brill, 1994), pp. 461-63.

[46]See C. H. Dodd, *Historical Tradition in the Fourth Gospel* (Cambridge, U.K.: Cambridge University Press, 1963), p. 174; Brown, *Gospel According to John* 1:209.

[47] Brown, *Gospel According to John* 1:209. Discussions in the Jesus Seminar led to a "gray" vote for this story—that is, it is possible but unreliable information for determining who Jesus was,

lacking supporting evidence (Funk and the Jesus Seminar, *The Acts of Jesus*, pp. 36-37, 383).

Chapter 13: The Blind

[1]See W. Schrage, "*tuphlos . . . ,*" *TDNT* 8:270-75.

[2]See, e.g., Is 35:5; 61:1; Lk 4:18; cf. 4Q521. See also Max Turner, *Power from on High* (Sheffield, U.K.: Sheffield Academic, 1996), chap. 9. On the term *messiah*, see the conclusions in §10.17.

[3]Acts 9:8-9, 17-18; cf. 13:11.

[4]Lk (4:18); 7:21-22.

[5]Reporting on the Jesus Seminar (Robert W. Funk and the Jesus Seminar, *The Acts of Jesus: The Search for the Authentic Deeds of Jesus* [New York: HarperCollins, 1998]), Funk says, "The Fellows by a narrow majority concluded that Jesus cured at least one blind person" (p. 103).

[6]See the lists in Vincent Taylor, *The Gospel According to St. Mark* (London: Macmillan, 1959), pp. 368-69.

[7]So E. Wendling, *Entstehung des Marcus Evangeliums* (Tübingen, Ger.: Mohr, 1908), p. 77; Rudolf Bultmann, *History of the Synoptic Tradtion* (New York: Harper & Row, 1976), p. 213.

[8]See the discussion in Robert A. Guelich, *Mark 1—8:26* (Dallas: Word, 1989), p. 429.

[9]So John P. Meier, *A Marginal Jew: Rethinking the Historical Jesus*, 3 vols. (New York: Doubleday, 1991, 1994, forthcoming), 2:692, citing Martin Dibelius, *From Tradition to Gospel*, 3 vols. (Cambridge, U.K.: Clarke, 1973-1987), pp. 86-87.

[10]Rudolf Bultmann, *History of the Synoptic Tradition* (New York: Harper & Row, 1976), p. 213.

[11]See Emil Schürer, *The History of the Jewish People in the Age of Jesus Christ* (Edinburgh, U.K.: T & T Clark, 1979), 2:172, for a discussion on the status of Bethsaida.

[12]Herman Strathmann, "*polis . . . ,*" *TDNT* 6:530.

[13]James F. Strange, "Beth-saida," *ABD* 1:692-93.

[14]Cf. Meier, *A Marginal Jew*, 2:693.

[15]Mk 7:31-37/Mt 15:29-31. In Luke this story is part of his great omission of material from Mark.

[16]See the discussion and material cited by C. K. Barrett, *The Gospel According to St John* (London: SPCK, 1978), p. 358; George R. Beasley-Murray, *John* (Waco, Tex.: Word, 1987), p. 155.

[17]See literature cited by BAGD, "*ptusma*," p. 727. On the widespread "magical" influence on popular tradition, see Clinton E. Arnold, *The Colossian Syncretism: The Interface Between Christianity and Folk Belief at Colossae* (Tübingen, Ger.: Mohr, 1995), chap. 1.

[18]Meier, *A Marginal Jew*, 2:693; cf. Funk and the Jesus Seminar, *The Acts of Jesus*, p. 103.

[19]See Taylor, *St. Mark*, p. 371.

[20]Cf. Ben Witherington, *Christology of Jesus* (Minneapolis: Fortress, 1990), p. 172.

[21]Cf., e.g., Rudolf Pesch, *Das Markusevangelium*, 2 vols. (Freiburg, Ger.: Herder, 1980), 1:420; Witherington, *Christology of Jesus*, pp. 171-72.

[22]Cf., e.g., Bultmann, *History of the Synoptic Tradition*, p. 213; Vernon K. Robbins, "The Healing of Blind Bartimaeus (10:46-52) in the Marcan Theology," *JBL* 92 (1973): 232.

[23]See the discussion in Pesch, *Das Markusevangelium*, 2:170.

[24]See Graham H. Twelftree, *Jesus the Exorcist: A Contribution to the Study of the Historical Jesus* (Tübingen, Ger.: Mohr; Peabody, Mass.: Hendrickson, 1993), pp. 183-85. Cf. Meier, *A Marginal Jew*, p. 689.

[25]Cf., e.g., Rom 1:3-4; 15:12; 2 Tim 2:18. See Dennis C. Duling, "The Promises to David and Their Entrance into Christianity—Nailing Down a Likely Hypothesis," *NTS* 20 (1974): 55-77.

[26]Meier, *A Marginal Jew*, 2:690. To the contrary, Funk and the Jesus Seminar, *The Acts of Jesus*, p. 119, express reservations about the historicity of the core of the story.

[27]See the list in Raymond E. Brown, *The Gospel According to John*, 2 vols. (London: Chapman, 1971), 1:378.

[28]See Mt 8:5-10; 9:28-29; 15:24-28; Mk 2:5-11; 3:1-6; 5:35-36; 7:27-29; 9:22-24; Lk 13:10-17; 14:1-6; Jn 4:46-54.

[29]Cf. Tertullian *De Bapt* 1 and the discussion in Brown, *John*, 1:380-82.

[30]See the discussion in Beasley-Murray, *John*, pp. 155-56.

[31]Further, see C. H. Dodd, *Historical Tradition in the Fourth Gospel* (Cambridge, U.K.: Cambridge University Press, 1963), p. 184.

Chapter 14: Raising the Dead

[1]See David F. Strauss, *The Life of Jesus Critically Examined* (Philadelphia: Fortress, 1972), p. 495. On the highly developed rationalism of H. E. G. Paulus, see Albert Schweitzer, *The Quest of the Historical Jesus* (London: Black, 1911), chap. 5. See also H. van der Loos, *The Miracles of Jesus* (Leiden, Neth.: Brill, 1965), pp. 564-65. Even in our own time the suspended animation view, or some variation of it, is common. Cf. Max Wilcox, "TALITHA KOUM(I) in Mk 5,41," in *Logia: Les paroles de Jésus. Mémorial Joseph Coppens*, ed. Joël Delobel (Leuven, Bel.: Leuven University Press, 1982), pp. 469-76, and those cited by Loos, *Miracles*, pp. 564-66.

[2]Strauss, *Life of Jesus*, p. 495.

[3]Gérard Rochais, *Les récits de résurrection des morts dans le Nouveau Testament* (Cambridge, U.K.: Cambridge University Press, 1981).

[4]See Philostratus *Life* 4:45; Lucian *Philopseudes* 26; the material cited by Str-B 1:560 and Loos, *Miracles*, pp. 560-63.

[5]Cf. Rudolf Bultmann, *History of the Synoptic Tradition* (New York: Harper & Row, 1976), p. 231.

[6]For what follows, see also John P. Meier, *A Marginal Jew: Rethinking the Historical Jesus*, 3 vols. (New York: Doubleday, 1991, 1994, forthcoming), 2:773-75.

[7]Ibid., 2:774.

[8]Ibid., 2:775.

[9]Cf. Murray J. Harris, " 'The Dead are Restored to Life': Miracles of Revivification in the Gospels," in *Gospel Perspectives 6: The Miracles of Jesus*, ed. David Wenham and Craig Blomberg (Sheffield, U.K.: JSOT, 1986), pp. 295-326.

[10]We will deal separately with the accompanying story of the woman with a hemorrhage at §16.5.

[11]As did, e.g., Rudolf Bultmann, *History of the Synoptic Tradition* (New York: Harper & Row, 1976), p. 215; Vincent Taylor, *The Gospel According to St. Mark* (London: Macmillan, 1952), p. 287.

[12]See Bruce M. Metzger, *A Textual Commentary on the Greek New Testament* (Stuttgart, Ger.: United Bible Societies, 1994), pp. 73-74. Cf. Rudolf Pesch, "Jaïrus (Mk 5, 22 / Lk 8, 41)," *BZ* 14 (1970): 252-56.

[13]The masculine form of "arise" *(kum)* rather than the feminine *(kumi)* is most likely original. At the time of Jesus, the masculine was used in popular speech, so it is more likely that a copyist would have changed the word to the correct feminine form than the opposite. Cf. Metzger, *A Textual Commentary*, pp. 74-75; Meier, *A Marginal Jew*, 2:785 and n. 55.

[14]See Elliott C. Maloney, *Semitic Interference in Marcan Syntax* (Chico, Calif.: Scholars, 1981), see index.

[15]Meier, *A Marginal Jew*, 2:786.

[16]See Karl H. Rengstorf, "*katagelaō* . . . ," *TDNT* 1:658-62.

[17]Harris, " 'The Dead are Restored to Life,' " p. 309, citing Alfred Edersheim, *Sketches of Jewish Social Life* (Grand Rapids, Mich.: Eerdmans, 1957), pp. 166-67. See also *m. Yebam.* 15:1, 4-6; 16:3-6.

[18]Robert W. Funk and the Jesus Seminar (*The Acts of Jesus: The Search for the Authentic Deeds of Jesus* [New York: HarperCollins, 1998], p. 83) report that the Jesus Seminar voted not to include this narrative information in the primary database in determining who Jesus was (cf. p. 36).

[19]See N. T. Wright, *Jesus and the Victory of God* (London: SPCK, 1996), pp. 531-32; Max Turner, *Power from on High: The Spirit in Israel's Restoration and Witness in Luke-Acts* (Sheffield, U.K.: Sheffield Academic, 1996), pp. 229-30, 244-64.

[20]Cf. Reginald H. Fuller, *Interpreting the Miracles* (London: SCM Press, 1963), p. 64. Cf. 2 Kings 4:8-37, where there is a similar story related to Elisha. However, the parallels are less close to Luke than to 1 Kings 17:7-24, so the 2 Kings story is even less help in determining the origin of the Lukan story.

[21]For more details, see Harris, " 'Dead Are Restored to Life,' " pp. 299-301.

[22]1 Kings 17:23/Lk 7:15. Cf. A. George, "Le miracle dans l'oeuvre de Luc," in *Les miracles de Jésus selon le Nouveau Testament*, ed. Xavier Léon-Dufour (Paris: Éditions du Seuil, 1977), pp. 52-53; Thomas L. Brodie, "Towards Unraveling Luke's Use of the Old Testament: Luke 7.11-17 an *Imitatio* of 1 Kings 17.17-24," *NTS* 32 (1986): 247-67.

[23]Cf. Turner, *Power from on High*, pp. 238-39.

[24]For more detail, see Harris, " 'Dead Are Restored to Life,' " pp. 300-301, and Meier, *A Marginal Jew*, 2:792-93.

[25]Bultmann, *History of the Synoptic Tradition*, p. 215.

[26]For more detail, see Harris, " 'The Dead Are Restored to Life,' " p. 302.

[27]See the discussion in Meier, *A Marginal Jew*, 2:791-93. For other, more remote, minor parallels, see Bultmann, *History of the Synoptic Tradition*, pp. 233-34.

[28]Contrast Funk and the Jesus Seminar, *The Acts of Jesus*, p. 288: "The Fellows of the Jesus Seminar were unanimous in their judgment that this story was the creation of Luke." For what follows, see Meier, *A Marginal Jew*, 2:794-95.

[29]See Joseph A. Fitzmyer, *The Gospel According to Luke I—IX* (New York: Doubleday, 1981), pp. 164-71. See also §15.3.

[30]The specific location of Nain is not known to be mentioned in any literature until about A.D. 200 by Origen (*selecta in Pss.* 88). The town has been excavated and found to have been walled, with a cemetery on the east side. See James F. Strange, "Nain," *ABD* 4:1001.

[31]See Rochais, *Les récits de résurrection*, pp. 21-30, discussed by Meier, *A Marginal Jew*, 2:795-96.

[32]So Alfred Edersheim, *Sketches of Jewish Social Life* (Grand Rapids, Mich.: Eerdmans, 1957), p. 170.

[33]Cf. Harris, " 'Dead Are Restored to Life,' " p. 299; Meier, *A Marginal Jew*, 2:798; contra Fuller, *Miracles*, p. 64; Rochais, *Les récits de résurrection*, p. 30.

[34]Funk, *The Acts of Jesus*, p. 409.

[35]B. F. Westcott, *The Gospel According to St John* (London: John Murray, 1896), p. 164.

[36]Loos, *Miracles*, p. 576; cf. Sandra M. Schneiders, "Death in the Community of Eternal Life," *Int* 41 (1987): 44-56; Jacob Kremer, *Lazarus: Die Geschichte einer Augerstehung* (Stuttgart, Ger.: Stuttgart, 1985); Jacob Kremer, "Die Lazarusgeschichte: Ein Beispiel urkirchliche Christusverkundigung," *Geist und Leben* 58 (1985): 244-58; Jacob Kremer, "The Awakening of Lazarus," *TD* 33 (1986): 135-38; Josef Wagner, *Auferstehung und Leben: Joh 11,1-12,19 als Spiegel johanneischer Redaktions—und Theologiegeschichte* (Regensburg: Pustet, 1988).

[37]See also the discussion in Rudolf Schnackenburg, *The Gospel According to St John*, 3 vols. (London: Burns & Oates, 1968-1982), 2:345-46.

[38]Mk 5:21-43/Mt 9:18-26/Lk 8:40-56.

[39]So Harris, " 'Dead Are Restored to Life,' " p. 312.

[40]So ibid., citing J. N. Sanders, *The Gospel According to St John* (London: Black, 1968), p. 276.

[41]Roderick Dunkerley, "Lazarus," *NTS* 5 (1958-1959): 321-27; Wilhelm Wilkens, "Die Erweckung des Lazarus," *TZ* 15 (1959): 22-39.

[42]Joseph A. Fitzmyer, *The Gospel According to Luke X—XXIV* (Garden City, N.Y.: Doubleday, 1985), p. 1131.

[43]Further, see Ernst Haenchen, *John*, 2 vols. (Philadelphia: Fortress, 1984), 2:69; Meier, *A Marginal Jew*, 2:822-31.

[44]Cf. Wilkens, 22-39, cited by Raymond E. Brown, *The Gospel According to John*, 2 vols. (London: Chapman, 1971), 1:429. See also C. H. Dodd, *Historical Tradition in the Fourth Gospel* (Cambridge, U.K.: Cambridge University Press, 1963), p. 230.

[45]Cf. Beasley-Murray, *John*, pp. 184-85. See also the various theories of the extent of the pre-Johannine source in Meier, *A Marginal Jew*, 2:862 n. 118, 867 n. 147.

[46]On the following paragraph cf., in particular, Mark W. G. Stibbe, *John's Gospel* (London: Routledge, 1994), pp. 101-3.

[47]Contrast Stibbe, *John's Gospel*, pp. 101-2.

[48]Ibid., pp. 101-3.

Chapter 15: Lepers Cleansed

[1]Stanley G. Browne, *Leprosy in the Bible*, 3d rev. ed. (London: Christian Medical Fellowship, 1979), p. 22. See also M. W. Dols, "Leprosy in Medieval Arabic Medicine," *Journal of the History of Medicine and Allied Sciences* 36 (1979): 314-33. Browne (*Leprosy*, p. 22) says that the confusion of what we call "leprosy" (their "elephantiasis") with *lepra*, the group of scaly skin conditions, seems to originate with the writings of Galen (A.D. 130-201).

[2]Rudolf Pesch, *Jesu ureigene Taten? Ein Beitrag zur Wunderfräge* (Freiburg, Ger.: Herder, 1970), pp. 52-87; Rudolf Pesch, *Das Markusevangelium*, 2 vols. (Freiburg, Ger.: Herder, 1980), 1:140-49.

[3]Ernst Käsemann, "The Problem of the Historical Jesus," in *Essays on New Testament Themes* (London: SCM Press, 1964), p. 37. Cf. §9.6.

[4]Brought to my attention in correspondence by Max Turner.

[5]Cf. René Latourelle, *The Miracles of Jesus and the Theology of Miracles* (New York: Paulist, 1988), p. 89; Robert A. Guelich, *Mark 1—8:26* (Dallas: Word, 1989), p. 72.

[6]Joseph A. Fitzmyer, *The Gospel According to Luke I—IX* (New York: Doubleday, 1981), pp. 572-73.

[7]See the Jewish material cited by Emil Schürer, *The History of the Jewish People in the Age of Jesus Christ*, 3 vols. (Edinburgh, U.K.: T & T Clark, 1973-1987), 2:448, 475-78.

[8]So also, e.g., John Dominic Crossan, *The Historical Jesus: The Life of a Mediterranean Jewish Peasant* (San Francisco: HarperCollins, 1991), pp. 321-23. Cf. Robert W. Funk and the Jesus Seminar, *The Acts of Jesus: The Search for the Authentic Deeds of Jesus* (New York: HarperCollins, 1998), p. 62: "The Fellows of the Jesus Seminar agreed by a narrow margin that Jesus cured the 'leper' of some form of dermatitis."

[9]See Christopher F. Evans, *Saint Luke* (London: SCM Press; Philadelphia: TPI, 1990), p. 623.

[10]Cf. Wilhelm Bruners, *Die Reinigung der zehn Aussätzigen und die Heilung des Samariters Lk 17 11-19: Ein Beitrag zur lukanischen Interpretation der Reinigung von Aussätzigen* (Stuttgart, Ger.: Katholisches Bibelwerk, 1977), pp. 297-306. For the opinion that the story is a pre-Lukan early church creation, see Hans Deiter Betz, "The Cleansing of the Ten Lepers (Luke 17:11-19)," *JBL* 90 (1971): 314-28.

[11]On the phrase, see Fitzmyer, *Luke X—XXIV*, pp. 1152-53.

[12]See the proposals in Bruners, *Die Reinigung*, pp. 149-63, and Pesch, *Jesu ureigene Taten?* pp. 117-19.

[13]Cf. Pesch, *Jesu ureigene Taten?* p. 118; John P. Meier, *A Marginal Jew*, 2 vols. (New York: Doubleday, 1991-1994), 2:704 (third volume forthcoming).

[14]See the list in Meier, *A Marginal Jew*, 2:705.

[15]Ibid., 2:705.

[16]So Rudolf Bultmann, *History of the Synoptic Tradition* (New York: Harper & Row, 1963), p. 33.

[17]Cf. Saul Nathaniel Brody, *The Disease of the Soul: Leprosy in Medieval Literature* (Ithaca, N.Y.: Cornell University Press, 1974), chap. 2; Peter Richards, *The Medieval Leper and His Northern Heirs* (Cambridge, U.K.: D. S. Brewer; Totowa, N.J.: Rowan & Littlefield, 1977), chap. 6.

[18]Funk and the Jesus Seminar (*The Acts of Jesus*, p. 330), say that the Fellows were virtually unanimous in designating this story as narrative material they would not include in the primary database for determining who Jesus was.

Chapter 16: Other Healings & Miracles of Nature

[1]Cf. William Neil, "Expository Problems: The Nature Miracles," *ExpTim* 67 (1955-1956): 369. Further, see §17.12.

[2]Cf. Detlef G. Müller, "Epistula Apostolorum," in *New Testament Apocrypha*, ed. Wilhelm Schneemelcher, rev. ed., 2 vols. (Cambridge, U.K.: Clarke; Louisville, Ky.: Westminster John Knox, 1991), 1:251, 253.

[3]See William Horbury, "The Temple Tax," in *Jesus and the Politics of His Day*, ed. Ernst Bammel and C. F. D. Moule (Cambridge, U.K.: Cambridge University Press, 1984), p. 265. Both Jewish

and pagan literature carry a number of stories of wealth discovered in fish. See the literature cited by Str-B 1:614 and Loos, *Miracles,* pp. 682-84.

[4]John P. Meier, *A Marginal Jew: Rethinking the Historical Jesus,* 3 vols. (New York: Doubleday, 1991, 1994, forthcoming), 2:884.

[5]Ex 30:13; Josephus *Ant.* 18:312; Horbury, "The Temple Tax," p. 265; Richard Bauckham, "The Coin in the Fish's Mouth," in *Gospel Perspectives 6: The Miracles of Jesus,* ed. David Wenham and Craig Blomberg (Sheffield, U.K.: JSOT, 1986), p. 219.

[6]See G. D. Kilpatrick, *The Origins of the Gospel According to St. Matthew* (Oxford, U.K.: Clarendon, 1946), p. 41; Robert H. Gundry, *Matthew* (Grand Rapids, Mich.: Eerdmans, 1982), pp. 355-57.

[7]Meier, *A Marginal Jew,* 2:883.

[8]Stephen Travis in private correspondence July 27, 1997.

[9]For what follows, see Bauckham, "The Coin in the Fish's Mouth," pp. 230-33.

[10]Cf. *t. Menaḥ* 13:21; *b. Pesaḥ* 57a.

[11]As does Meier, *A Marginal Jew,* 2:883-84.

[12]Cf. Mt 6:25-34/Lk 12:22-32; Mt 7:7-11/Lk 11:9-13.

[13]Bauckham, "The Coin in the Fish's Mouth," p. 234. In seeking to understand the miracle from a first-century perspective, I resist Bauckham's suggestion that we should consider these miracles as a third category alongside healings and exorcisms.

[14]See W. D. Davies and Dale C. Allison, *The Gospel According to Saint Matthew* (Edinburgh, U.K.: T & T Clark, 1988, 1991, 1997), 2:741-42.

[15]Robert W. Funk and the Jesus Seminar, *The Acts of Jesus: The Search for the Authentic Deeds of Jesus* (New York: HarperCollins, 1998), p. 222.

[16]Cf. C. H. Dodd, *Historical Tradition in the Fourth Gospel* (Cambridge, U.K.: Cambridge University Press, 1963), p. 225 and n. 7.

[17]Drawn to my attention by Stephen Travis in private correspondence July 27, 1997.

[18]R. T. France, *The Gospel According to Matthew* (Leicester, U.K.: Inter-Varsity Press; Grand Rapids, Mich.: Eerdmans, 1985), pp. 268-69.

[19]René Latourelle, *The Miracles of Jesus and the Theology of Miracles* (Mahwah: Paulist, 1988), p. 83.

[20]For some this is one of the leading candidates for an authentic eyewitness account finding its way into the Jesus tradition. See Barry L. Blackburn, "The Miracles of Jesus," in *Studying the Historical Jesus: Evaluations of the State of Current Research,* ed. Bruce Chilton and Craig A. Evans (Leiden, Neth.: Brill, 1994), pp. 356-57, and those he cites in n. 52.

[21]Funk and the Jesus Seminar, *The Acts of Jesus,* p. 59.

[22]Cf. David E. Aune, "Magic in Early Christianity," *ANRW* II.22.2 (1980): 1524: "The nature miracles . . . are generally regarded as legendary embellishments of the Jesus tradition." Cf. p. 1538; also, e.g., Rudolf Bultmann, *History of the Synoptic Tradition* (New York: Harper & Row, 1963), pp. 234-39; Marcus J. Borg, *Jesus: A New Vision* (San Francisco: HarperSanFrancisco, 1991), p. 67; Crossan, *The Historical Jesus,* pp. 320, 396-410.

[23]Adolf Harnack, *What Is Christianity?* (London: Williams & Norgate, 1901), p. 28.

[24]Funk and the Jesus Seminar, *The Acts of Jesus,* p. 77.

[25]Cf. Joseph Klausner, *Jesus of Nazareth: His Life, Times, and Teaching* (London: Allen & Unwin, 1929), p. 269, and other rationalist explanations mentioned by Loos, *Miracles,* pp. 639-40.

[26]Bultmann, *History of the Synoptic Tradition,* p. 235.

[27]See Bastiaan M. F. van Iersel and A. J. M. Linmans, "The Storm on the Lake: Mk iv 35-41 and Mt viii 18-27 in the Light of Form Criticism, 'Redaktionsgeschichte' and Structural Analysis," in *Miscellanea Neotestamentica,* ed. T. Baarda, A. F. J. Klijn and W. C. van Unnik (Leiden, Neth.: Brill, 1978), p. 21.

[28]Cf., e.g., Vincent Taylor, *The Gospel According to St. Mark* (London: Macmillan: 1952), p. 272.

[29]Cf. Jon 1:4, 5, 16. Citing Jerome, *Comm. in Matt.,* I.9 (PL 26, 55A), Robert M. Grant (*Miracle and Natural Law in Graeco-Roman and Early Christian Thought* [Amsterdam, Neth.: North-Holland, 1952], p. 169) says that the framework of the stilling of the storm is based on the

story of Jonah.

[30]See Job 12:15; Ps 33:7; 65:7; 77:16; 107:25-30; 147:18; Prov 30:4; Amos 4:13; Nahum 1:3-4.

[31]Cf. Leonhard Goppelt, *Typos: The Typological Interpretation of the Old Testament in the New* (Grand Rapids, Mich.: Eerdmans, 1982), pp. 72-73.

[32]E.g., Johannes Munck, *The Acts of the Apostles* (New York: Doubleday, 1967), p. 192. For a rationalizing discussion of the concept of power emanating from Jesus, see Eric E. May, " '. . . For Power Went Forth from Him . . .' (Luke 6,19)," *CBQ* 14 (1952): 93-103. Hence it is still possible to turn up rationalizations of this story, as in Davies and Allison (*Saint Matthew*, p. 124), who say, "The story of the woman with an issue could easily be understood in psycho-somatic terms. The capacity of the mind to heal many bodily infirmities is an established fact."

[33]See Graham H. Twelftree, *Christ Triumphant: Exorcism Then and Now* (London: Hodder & Stoughton, 1985), p. 114.

[34]See Gerd Theissen, *Miracle Stories of the Early Christian Tradition* (Edinburgh, U.K.: T & T Clark, 1983), p. 134.

[35]Theissen (*Miracle Stories*, p. 134) incorrectly says that the narrator stresses the woman's good intentions.

[36] Cf. Rudolf Pesch, *Das Markusevangelium*, 2 vols. (Freiburg, Ger.: Herder, 1980), 1:305-6. With reservations, the Fellows of the Jesus Seminar included this narrative in the database for determining who Jesus was (see Funk and the Jesus Seminar, *The Acts of Jesus*, p. 81).

[37]C. K. Barrett, *The Gospel According to St John* (London: SPCK, 1978), p. 271; cf. also Udo Schnelle, *Antidocetic Christology in the Gospel of John* (Minneapolis: Fortress, 1992), p. 115.

[38]See the chart in Raymond E. Brown, *The Gospel According to John*, 2 vols. (London: Chapman, 1971), 1:240-43.

[39]On the relationship between John and the Synoptics, see chaptaaer 7 n. 2.

[40]Mk 6:31, 32, 35; 8:5 and Jn 6:31. See Dodd, *Historical Tradition*, pp. 203-6.

[41]See the chart in Brown, *John*, 1:240-43.

[42]Contrary to most commentators, Robert Fowler (*Loaves and Fishes: The Function of the Feeding Stories in the Gospel of Mark* [Chico, Calif.: Scholars, 1978], pp. 68-90) has argued the opposite.

[43]See Meier, *A Marginal Jew*, 2:957-58 and n. 277.

[44]So ibid., 2:957-58.

[45]Cf. Ernst Haenchen, *John*, 2 vols. (Philadelphia: Fortress, 1984), 1:273-77.

[46]See also 1 Kings 17:8-16; 2 Kings 4:1-7. Cf. Pesch, *Das Markusevangelium*, 1:353-54.

[47]For what follows, see Meier, *A Marginal Jew*, 2:960-61.

[48]Ibid., 2:961.

[49]Indeed, as suggested by Brown (*John*, 1:248), there is no reason Jesus could not have intentionally conducted a feeding with Passover overtones.

[50]Bastiaan M. F. van Iersel, "Die wunderbare Speisung und das Abendmahl in der synoptischen Tradition," *NovT* 7 (1964): 182-83.

[51]E.g., Mk 2:15-17; Lk 19:5. Cf. Joachim Jeremias, *New Testament Theology* (London: SCM Press, 1971), pp. 115-16; E. P. Sanders, *Jesus and Judaism* (London: SCM Press, 1985), pp. 208-9.

[52]Ps 23:2. Cf. Ezek 34:23; Jer 23:4; *Pss. Sol.* 17:40. Cf. Gerhard Friedrich, "Die beiden Erzählungen von der Speisung in Mark. 6,31-44; 8,1-9," *TZ* 20 (1964): 10-22.

[53]Funk and the Jesus Seminar, *The Acts of Jesus*, p. 91.

[54]Ibid., p. 93.

[55]See Albert Schweitzer, *The Quest of the Historical Jesus* (London: Black, 1911), p. 41. Loos (*Miracles*, pp. 558-61) gives other bizarre examples.

[56]We will leave aside dealing with the Matthean story of Peter walking on the sea (Mt 14:28-32, on which see Reinhard Kratz, "Der Seewandel des Petrus [Mt 14,28-31]," *BibLeb* 15 [1974]: 86-101), for strictly it is not a miracle of Jesus.

[57]Taylor, *St. Mark*, p. 326.

[58]See the discussion of "the criterion of vividness of narration" in Meier, *A Marginal Jew*, 1:180-82.

[59]Taylor, *St. Mark*, p. 327.

[60]Cf., e.g., Job 9:8; 38:16; Ps 77:19-20; Is 43:16; Hab 3:15. Further, see Meier, *A Marginal Jew*, 2:914-19.

[61]Joseph A. Fitzmyer, "The Aramaic Background of Philippians 2:6-11," *CBQ* 50 (1988): 470-83.

[62]Cf. Jos. Keulers, *Het Evangelie volgens Mattheüs* (Roermond: Maaseik, 1950), cited by Loos, *Miracles*, pp. 658-59.

[63]For what follows, see Meier, *A Marginal Jew*, 2:920-24.

[64]E.g., C. H. Dodd, "The Appearances of the Risen Christ: An Essay in Form-Criticism of the Gospels," in *Studies in the Gospels: Essays in Memory of R. H. Lightfoot*, ed. Dennis E. Nineham (Oxford, U.K.: Blackwell, 1967), pp. 23-25; Brown, *John*, 1:254.

[65]Patrick J. Madden (*Jesus' Walking on the Sea: An Investigation of the Origin of the Narrative Account* [Berlin, Ger.: de Gruyter, 1997]) comes to the opposite conclusion.

[66]Meier, *A Marginal Jew*, 2:922-23.

[67]Ibid., 2:923, citing Jn 1:1-18; Phil 2:6-11; Col 1:15-20.

[68]Brown, *John*, 1:254.

[69]Cf. Jeremias, *New Testament Theology*, p. 87.

[70]In John 6:21 it is said only that "they wanted to take him into the boat." In Mark 6:51 the storm is said to cease immediately when Jesus got into the boat, a point not incompatible with the explanation offered here.

[71]Cf. a natural explanation by J. Duncan M. Derrett, "Why and How Jesus Walked on the Sea," *NovT* 23 (1981): 340-48.

[72]Paul N. Anderson (*The Christology of the Fourth Gospel: Its Unity and Disunity in the Light of John 6* [Tübingen, Ger.: Mohr, 1996], p. 183) goes so far as to say that a cluster of events from the life of Jesus such as this must have occurred.

[73]On the relationship between this story and the story of the blind man at Bethsaida (Mk 8:22-26), see §13.2.

[74]The use of this extremely rare word *(mogilalos)* may be due to the influence of its single use in the LXX at Is 35:5, which is reflected later in this story; cf. Mk 7:37. See J. H. Moulton and G. Milligan, *The Vocabulary of the Greek Testament* (London: Hodder & Stoughton, 1930), p. 415. Cf. §3.21.

[75]So Meier, *A Marginal Jew*, 2:758 n. 154.

[76]See the material cited by Joachim Jeremias, *"airō . . . ," TDNT* 1:185 n. 1.

[77]Cf. Joachim Jeremias, *The Prayers of Jesus* (London: SCM Press, 1967), pp. 72-78; James D. G. Dunn, *Jesus and the Spirit* (London: SCM Press, 1975), pp. 15-21.

[78]See those cited in Graham H. Twelftree, *Jesus the Exorcist: A Contribution to the Study of the Historical Jesus* (Tübingen, Ger.: Mohr; Peabody, Mass.: Hendrickson, 1993), p. 162 n. 21.

[79]On this and the view that these Aramaic words were considered magical, see Meier, *A Marginal Jew*, 2:759 n. 159, discussing Fred L. Horton Jr., "Nochmals *ephphatha* in Mk 7:34," *ZNW* 77 (1986): 101-8.

[80]Funk and the Jesus Seminar, *The Acts of Jesus*, p. 98.

[81]See William R. Telford, *The Barren Temple and the Withered Tree* (Sheffield, U.K.: JSOT, 1980), pp. 12-15 and, for what follows, pp. 234-38.

[82]Funk and the Jesus Seminar, *The Acts of Jesus*, pp. 122-23.

[83]See Acts 5:1-11; 9:1-9; 13:6-12. In later material, see the punitive miracles in *Infancy Gospel of Thomas* 3:1-3. See also the discussion in §5.27.

[84]Whereas this story may be an act of prophetic symbolism, it is still punitive in that Jesus appears to be punishing the tree for not having fruit (cf. Mk 11:13-14).

[85]Cf. C. E. B. Cranfield, *The Gospel According to Saint Mark* (Cambridge, U.K.: Cambridge University Press, 1966), p. 354.

[86]E.g., miracles performed at the hands of human figures: Ex 7:14—12:30; 14:23-31; 2 Kings 1:9-12; 2:23-24; 5:27; 2 Chron 26:16-21 (cf. 2 Kings 15:5); cf. 2 Macc 2:22-30. Other punitive miracles can be found at Lev 10:1-2; 2 Sam 6:6-7; Dan 4:1-37.

[87]See, e.g., Jer 8:13; Hos 9:10, 16-17; Mic 7:1; and Telford, *The Barren Temple and the Withered*

Tree, chap. 5.

[88] In private correspondence.

[89] Mt 21:12-17/Mk 11:15-19/Lk 19:45-48/Jn 2:13-25, a story generally taken to have its historical roots in the ministry of Jesus. Further, see E. P. Sanders, *Jesus and Judaism* (London: SCM Press, 1985), pp. 61-76.

[90] Cranfield (*Mark,* p. 356) quotes the earliest extant commentary on Mark by Victor of Antioch as saying that the withering of the fig tree was an acted parable in which Jesus "used the fig tree to set forth the judgement that was about to fall on Jerusalem."

[91] Cf. Brown, *John,* 2:1090.

[92] It is generally agreed that the reference to "the disciple whom Jesus loved" (Jn 21:7) is from the hand of the Fourth Evangelist. See those listed by Meier, *A Marginal Jew,* 2:989 n. 83.

[93] Günther Klein, "Die Berufung des Petrus," *ZNW* 58 (1967): 34-35.

[94] For a more detailed argument, see Meier, *A Marginal Jew,* 2:899-904.

[95] Cf. Funk and the Jesus Seminar, *The Acts of Jesus,* p. 280: "The evidence seems incontrovertible: the story as it stands in Luke is fiction not history."

[96] See, e.g., Mt 28:7, 16; Mk 14:28; 16:7; Jn 21.

[97] If this is the case, we may have in this story—as we may have in the story of the storm being suddenly calmed (the historicity of which I left open)—an example of what we defined in chapter one (§1.3) as a "coincidence" miracle.

[98] See the definition at §5.23.

[99] See BAGD, "*hudrōpikos,*" p. 832, and Loos, *Miracles,* pp. 504-8.

[100] Contrast Meier, *A Marginal Jew,* 2:711.

[101] See, e.g., Joseph A. Fitzmyer, *Luke X—XXIV* (Garden City, N.Y.: Doubleday, 1985) pp. 1038-39; Meier, *A Marginal Jew,* pp. 757 n. 147, 758 n. 148. Cf. Funk and the Jesus Seminar, *The Acts of Jesus,* p. 321.

[102] Bultmann, *History of the Synoptic Tradition,* p. 12. Funk and the Jesus Seminar (*The Acts of Jesus,* pp. 321-22) concluded that they would not include this story in the primary database in determining who Jesus was.

[103] Mt 26:51/Mk 14:47/Lk 22:50/Jn 18:10.

[104] Funk and the Jesus Seminar (*The Acts of Jesus,* p. 354) say that "the alterations and additions Luke has made to the story come from his own imagination."

[105] So, e.g., Fitzmyer, *Luke X—XXIV,* pp. 1447-48 and those listed there, and by Meier, *A Marginal Jew,* 2:761 n. 170.

[106] See Fitzmyer, *Luke X—XXIV,* p. 1448, and Fitzmyer, *Luke I—IX,* p. 114.

[107] Friedrich Rehkopf, *Die lukanische Sonderquelle: Ihr Umfang und Sprachgebrauch* (Tübingen, Ger.: Mohr, 1959), pp. 68-69, cited by I. Howard Marshall, *The Gospel of Luke* (Exeter, U.K.: Paternoster, 1978), p. 837.

[108] For a summary discussion of Luke's possible sources, see Marshall, *Luke,* p. 834, and Fitzmyer, *Luke X—XXIV,* p. 1448.

[109] Cf. Fitzmyer, *Luke X—XXIV,* p. 1448.

[110] See also Stephen T. Davis, "The Miracle at Cana: A Philosopher's Perspective," in *Gospel Perspectives 6: The Miracles of Jesus,* ed. David Wenham and Craig Blomberg (Sheffield, U.K.: JSOT, 1986), pp. 419-42.

[111] See Meier, *A Marginal Jew,* 2:934-35. See also the discussion by Davis, "Miracle at Cana," pp. 419-42.

[112] On the little information we have bearing directly on contemporary practice with regard to weddings, see J. Duncan M. Derrett, "Water into Wine," *BZ* 7 (1963): 80-97.

[113] See the discussion in Davis, "Miracle at Cana," pp. 422-24.

[114] Contra Meier, *A Marginal Jew,* 2:935.

[115] Here we are following Meier, *A Marginal Jew,* 2:936-47. Funk and the Jesus Seminar (*The Acts of Jesus,* pp. 327-28) say that "Johannine fingerprints are all over the narrative" and conclude "that the story is the creation of the author of the Fourth Gospel."

[116] Cf. Jn 2:1, 3, 5, 12; 6:42; 19:25-27.

[117]See Jn 2:9; 7:27; 8:14; 9:29, 30; 19:9.

[118]Cf., e.g., Jer 31:12; Hos 14:7; Joel 4:18; Amos 9:13-14.

[119]So Meier, *A Marginal Jew,* 2:942-44.

[120]Cf. Brown, *John,* 1:100.

[121]Meier, *A Marginal Jew,* 2:949 n. 252, citing W. Bauer.

[122]The objective of Davis, "Miracle at Cana," pp. 419-42.

[123]Cf. Derrett, "Water into Wine," p. 97.

[124]A. E. J. Rawlinson, *St. Mark* (London: Methuen, 1947), p. 60.

Chapter 17: Jesus the Miracle Worker

[1]So also John T. Carroll, "Sickness and Healing in the New Testament Gospels," *Int* 49 (1995): 132.

[2]See Gerhard Friedrich, *"kērussō . . . ," TDNT* 3:714, quoted in §1.6.

[3]Birger Gerhardsson, *The Mighty Acts of Jesus According to Matthew* (Lund, Swe.: CWK Gleerup, 1979), p. 15 (his emphasis).

[4]Jn 2:11; 11:4 (cf. 9:3), 40; 12:41, 43.

[5]Morna D. Hooker, *The Signs of a Prophet: The Prophetic Actions of Jesus* (London: SCM Press, 1997), p. 74: "All the Johannine signs focus . . . on the exaltation of Christ on the cross."

[6]Ernest Renan, *The Life of Jesus* (1863; London: Kegan Paul, Trench, Trübner & Co., 1903), p. 190.

[7]Norman Perrin, *Rediscovering the Teaching of Jesus* (New York: Harper & Row, 1976), p. 137.

[8]Renan, *Life of Jesus,* p. 196.

[9]Cf. Ben F. Meyer, "Jesus' Ministry and Self-Understanding," in *Studying the Historical Jesus: Evaluations of the State of Current Research,* ed. Bruce Chilton and Craig A. Evans (Leiden, Neth.: Brill, 1994), p. 345: "Jesus was the conscious bearer of a (indeed, of *the*) climactic and definitive mission to all Israel" (his emphasis).

[10]Cf. those cited by Barry L. Blackburn, "The Miracles of Jesus," in *Studying the Historical Jesus: Evaluations of the State of Current Research,* ed. Bruce Chilton and Craig A. Evans (Leiden, Neth.: Brill, 1994), pp. 373-74. See also the discussion in Graham H. Twelftree, *Jesus the Exorcist: A Contribution to the Study of the Historical Jesus* (Tübingen, Ger.: Mohr; Peabody, Mass.: Hendrickson, 1993), pp. 166-71.

[11]A. E. Taylor, *Philosophical Studies* (London: Macmillan, 1934), p. 349, also cited in §§1.3 and 2.2.

[12]Cf. C. Stephen Evans, *The Historical Christ and the Jesus of Faith: The Incarnational Narrative as History* (Oxford, U.K.: Oxford University Press, 1996), p. 145.

[13]Mk 10:46-52/Mt 20:29-34/Lk 18:35-43.

[14]Cf. Marcel Bastin, "Jesus Worked Miracles: Texts from Mt 8," *Lumen Vitae* 39 (1984): 132-36.

[15]John Macquarrie, *Principles of Christian Theology* (London: SCM Press, 1966), p. 225, cited also in §1.3.

[16]See also Mt 8:27; 9:1-8, 33; 12:23; 15:31.

[17]Cf. Joseph A. Fitzmyer, *The Gospel According to Luke I—IX* (Garden City, N.Y.: Doubleday, 1981), pp. 542-43.

[18]Cf. H. Baltensweiler, "Wunder und Glaube im Neuen Testament," *TZ* 23 (1967): 241-56.

[19]Mk 6:2, 5, 14; cf. 5:30; 9:39; 12:24.

[20]Cf. Michael Dummett, "A Remarkable Consensus," *New Blackfriars* 68, no. 809 (1987): 429-30; Joseph Houston, "Objectivity and the Gospels," in *Objective Knowledge: A Christian Perspective,* ed. Paul Helm (Leicester, U.K.: Inter-Varsity Press, 1987), pp. 147-65.

[21]Rudolf Bultmann, *History of the Synoptic Tradition* (New York: Harper & Row, 1963), pp. 218-44.

[22]Twelftree, *Jesus the Exorcist,* pp. 172-73.

[23]Cf. Reginald H. Fuller, *Interpreting the Miracles* (London: SCM Press, 1963), pp. 37-39; Blackburn, "Miracles of Jesus," pp. 370-72.

[24]See, e.g., Bultmann, *History of the Synoptic Tradition,* pp. 234-39; Günther Bornkamm, *Jesus*

of Nazareth (London: Hodder & Stoughton, 1960), p. 131; David E. Aune, "Magic in Early Christianity," *ANRW* II.23.2 (1980): 1524.

[25]See also Robert W. Funk and the Jesus Seminar, *The Acts of Jesus: What Did Jesus Really Do?* (New York: HarperCollins, 1998), p. 34.

[26]Mk 11:23/Mt 21:21; cf. 1 Cor 13:2; *Gos. Thom.* 48, 106. On the authenticity of the Gospel saying, see Perrin, *Rediscovering the Teaching of Jesus*, pp. 137-38.

[27]James D. G. Dunn, *Jesus and the Spirit* (London: SCM Press, 1975), p. 72.

[28]Blackburn, "Miracles of Jesus," p. 371.

[29]For what follows, see Gerd Theissen, *Miracle Stories of the Early Christian Tradition* (Edinburgh, U.K.: T & T Clark, 1983), chap. 3.

[30]Cf. G. Schille, *Die urchristliche Wundertradition: Ein Beitrag zur Frage nach dem irdische Jesus* (Stuttgart, Ger.: Calwer, 1967), pp. 24-27.

[31]Martin Dibelius, *From Tradition to Gospel* (Cambridge and London: Clarke, 1971), chaps. 3 and 4.

[32]See Laurence J. McGinley, "Form-Criticism of the Synoptic Healing Narratives," *TS* 3 (1942): 214, and Theissen, *Miracle Stories*, p. 82.

[33]Bultmann used this term *(apophthgemata)* for the pericopes in which authoritative sayings of Jesus formed the culmination of stories. See his *History of the Synoptic Tradition*, p. 11 and n. 1, and Stephen H. Travis, "Form Criticism," in *New Testament Interpretation: Essays on Principles and Methods*, ed. I. Howard Marshall (Exeter, U.K.: Paternoster, 1977), pp. 155-56.

[34]Bultmann, *History of the Synoptic Tradition*, pp. 11-39, 209-44. Cf. Theissen, *Miracle Stories*, pp. 82-83.

[35]So H. van der Loos, *The Miracles of Jesus* (Leiden, Neth.: Brill, 1965).

[36]See Otto Perels, *Die Wunderüberlieferung der Synoptiker in ihrem Verhältnis zur Wortüberlieferung* (Stuttgart: Kohlhammer, 1934), p. 70, cited by Theissen, *Miracle Stories*, p. 84.

[37]Gerhard Delling, "Zur Beurteilung des Wunders durch die Antike," in *Studien zur Neuen Testament und zum hellenistischen Judentum: Gesammelte Aufsätze 1950-1968*, ed. Ferdinand Hahn, Traugott Holz and Nicolaus Walter (Göttengen, Ger.: Vandenhoeck & Ruprecht, 1970), pp. 55-56, cited by Theissen, *Miracle Stories*, p. 84.

[38]Theissen, *Miracle Stories*, chap. 3.

[39]Of the many surveys, see, e.g., Albert Schweitzer, *The Quest of the Historical Jesus: A Critical Study of Its Progress from Reimarus to Wrede* (London: Black, 1911); James M. Robinson, *A New Quest of the Historical Jesus* (London: SCM Press, 1959); Ben F. Meyer, *The Aims of Jesus* (London: SCM Press, 1979), chap. 2; Colin Brown, "Historical Jesus, Quest of," in *Dictionary of Jesus and the Gospels*, ed. Joel B. Green, Scot McKnight and I. Howard Marshall (Downers Grove, Ill.: InterVarsity Press, 1992), pp. 326-41; N. T. Wright, "Quest for the Historical Jesus," *ABD* 3:796-802; Blackburn, "Miracles of Jesus," pp. 353-94; Marcus J. Borg, *Jesus in Contemporary Scholarship* (Valley Forge, Penn.: TPI, 1994); Ben Witherington, *The Jesus Quest: The Third Search for the Jew of Nazareth* (Downers Grove, Ill.: InterVarsity Press, 1995); N. T. Wright, *Jesus and the Victory of God* (London: SPCK, 1996), chap. 1; Gerd Theissen and Annette Merz, *The Historical Jesus: A Comprehensive Guide* (London: SCM Press, 1998), chap. 1.

[40]See Charles H. Talbert, *Reimarus: Fragments* (London: SCM Press, 1971), pp. 59-269.

[41]Schweitzer, *Quest of the Historical Jesus*, p. 186. Cf. the discussion at §9.5; §10.3.

[42]Johannes Weiss, *Jesus' Proclamation of the Kingdom of God* (1892, Philadelphia: Fortress, 1971), p. 76.

[43]Schweitzer, *Quest of the Historical Jesus*, p. 396.

[44]Ernst Käsemann, *Essays on New Testament Themes* (London: SCM Press, 1964), pp. 15-47.

[45]Ibid., p. 46.

[46]Ibid.

[47]See Robinson, *A New Quest of the Historical Jesus*.

[48]Brown, "Historical Jesus, Quest of," p. 337.

[49]For a review of the Third Quest, see John P. Meier, "Reflections on Jesus-of-History Research Today," in *Jesus' Jewishness: Exploring the Place of Jesus in Early Judaism*, ed. James H.

Charlesworth (New York: Crossroad, 1991), pp. 84-107; Borg, *Jesus in Contemporary Scholarship;* James H. Charlesworth, "Jesus Research Expands with Chaotic Creativity," in *Images of Jesus Today,* ed. James H. Charlesworth and Walter P. Weaver (Valley Forge, Penn.: TPI, 1994), pp. 1-41; and Witherington, *The Jesus Quest;* N. T. Wright, *Jesus and the Victory of God* (London: SPCK, 1996), chap. 3; Bernard Brandon Scott, "From Reimarus to Crossan: Stages in a Quest," *Currents in Research: Biblical Studies* 2 (1994): 258-80.

[50]So Stephen Neill and Tom Wright, *The Interpretation of the New Testament: 1861-1986* (Oxford, U.K.: Oxford University Press, 1988), p. 379. Cf. Witherington, *The Jesus Quest,* pp. 12-13.

[51]The term *Third Quest* was probably first used by N. T. Wright in Neill and Wright, *The Interpretation of the New Testament: 1861-1986,* pp. 363, 397-98. See also Meyer, *The Aims of Jesus,* pp. 16-20; James H. Charlesworth, *Jesus Within Judaism: New Light from Exciting Archeological Discoveries* (London: SPCK, 1988), pp. 26-28.

[52]Wright, *Jesus and the Victory of God,* p. 84. With an eye toward recent studies on the historical Jesus, Witherington *(Jesus Quest)* includes the following Third Questers: Markus Bockmuehl, Marcus J. Borg, Maurice Casey, John Dominic Crossan, F. Gerald Downing, James D. G. Dunn, Elisabeth Schüssler Fiorenza, Anthony E. Harvey, Richard Horsley, Marinus de Jonge, R. David Kaylor, Burton L. Mack, John P. Meier, E. P. Sanders, Peter Stuhlmacher, Gerd Theissen, Geza Vermes, Ben Witherington III and N. T. Wright.

[53]Sanders, *Jesus and Judaism,* p. 164, citing Morton Smith, *Jesus the Magician* (London: Gollancz, 1978), pp. 9, 11, 23-24. Cf. Martin Hengel (*The Charismatic Leader and His Followers* [Edinburgh, U.K.: T & T Clark, 1981], p. 66), who says that the miracles awakened "at least as much attention and enthusiasm as his preaching."

[54]See above on Mt 12:27/Lk 11:19 in §10.10. Also, on the perspective of the Gospel writers, see §§3.8, 9 and 5.9.

[55]So Witherington, *The Jesus Quest,* p. 116. Cf. Sanders, *Jesus and Judaism,* p. 318.

[56]Borg, *Jesus: A New Vision,* p. 60. See also Marcus J. Borg, "The Historian, the Christian, and Jesus," *TToday* 52 (1995-1996): 8-10.

[57]Borg, *Jesus: A New Vision,* pp. 67, 70.

[58]Ibid., p. 190.

[59]Cf. Borg, "The Historian, the Christian, and Jesus," pp. 8-10.

[60]Crossan, *The Historical Jesus,* p. 422. Cf. Witherington, *The Jesus Quest,* p. 64. Although Wright does not include Crossan in his list of twenty writers in the Third Quest (see chap. 17 n. 52), he mentions him in stressing that the compartmentalization of the writers in the various quests is far from watertight. See Wright, *Jesus and the Victory of God,* pp. 83-84.

[61]Cf. the summary of Crossan in Blackburn, "Miracles of Jesus," pp. 289-90.

[62]Crossan, *The Historical Jesus,* pp. 287-91.

[63]See Blackburn, "The Miracles of Jesus," pp. 391-92; cf. Howard Clark Kee, "A Century of Quests for the Culturally Compatible Jesus," *TToday* 52 (1995-1996): 21-23.

[64]Cf. Kee, "Century of Quests," p. 27.

[65]Echoing George Tyrrell (*Christianity at the Cross-Roads* [London: Longman, Green & Co., 1910], p. 44) in his comment on Adolf Harnack.

[66]Blackburn, "Miracles of Jesus," p. 392.

[67]James D. G. Dunn, "Jesus for Today," *TToday* 52 (1995-1996): 66-74.

[68]Cf. Bernd Kollmann (*Jesus und die Christen als Wundertäter: Studien zu Magie, Medizin und Schamanismus in Antike und Christentum* [Göttingen, Ger.: Vandenhoeck & Ruprecht, 1996]) also concludes that the exorcism and healing traditions in the New Testament are undervalued.

Bibliography

This bibliography is intended to draw attention to texts for further reading. The index will lead the reader to the works cited in this study.

General
Aune, David. "Magic in Early Christianity." *ANRW* II:23:2 (1980): 1507-57.

Bastin, Marcel. "Jesus Worked Miracles: Texts from Mt 8." *Lumen Vitae* 39 (1984): 131-39.

Betz, Hans Dieter. "The Early Christian Miracle Story: Some Observations on the Form Critical Problem." *Semeia* 11 (1978): 69-81.

Betz, Otto, and Werner Grimm. *Wesen und Wirklichkeit der Wunder Jesu: Heilungen—Rettungen—Zeichen—Aufleuchtungen.* Frankfurt am Main, Ger.: Peter Lang, 1977.

Blackburn, Barry L. "The Miracles of Jesus." In *Studying the Historical Jesus: Evaluations of the State of Current Research,* pp. 353-94. Edited by Bruce Chilton and Craig A. Evans. Leiden, Neth.: Brill, 1994.

———. "Miracles and Miracle Stories." In *Dictionary of Jesus and the Gospels,* pp. 549-60. Edited by Joel B. Green, Scot McKnight and I. Howard Marshall. Downers Grove, Ill.: InterVarsity Press, 1992.

Borgen, Peder. "Miracles of Healing in the New Testament: Some Observations." *ST* 35 (1981): 91-106.

Brown, Colin. *That You May Believe.* Grand Rapids, Mi.: Eerdmans; Exeter, U.K.: Paternoster, 1985.

Brown, Raymond E. "The Gospel Miracles." In *New Testament Essays,* pp. 169-91. Ramsey, N.J.: Paulist, 1965.

Brox, Norbert. "Magie und Aberglaube an den Anfängen des Christentums." *TTZ* 83 (1974): 157-80.

Court, John M. "The Philosophy of the Synoptic Miracles." *JTS* 23 (1972): 1-15.

Delling, Gerhard. "Botschaft und Wunder im Wirken Jesu." In *Der historische Jesus und der kerygmatische Christus,* pp. 389-402. Edited by Helmut Ristow and Karl Matthiae. 3d ed. Berlin, Ger.: Evangelische Verlagsangtalt, 1964.

———. "Das Verständnis des Wunders im Neuen Testament." *ZST* 24 (1955): 265-80. Reprinted in Gerhard Delling, *Studien zur Neuen Testament und zum hellenistischen Judentum: Gesammelte Aufsätze 1950-1968,* pp. 146-59. Edited by Ferdinand Hahn, Traugott Holz and Nicolaus Walter. Göttingen, Ger.: Vandenhoeck & Ruprecht, 1970.

Duprez, A. "Les récits évangéliques de miracles." *Lumière et Vie* 23 (1974): 49-69.

Fascher, Erich. *Kritik am Wunder: Eine geschichtliche Skizze.* Berlin, Ger.: Evangelische Verlagsanstalt, 1960.

Fridrichsen, Anton. *The Problem of Miracle in Primitive Christianity.* Minneapolis: Augsburg, 1972.

Fuller, Reginald H. *Interpreting the Miracles.* London: SCM Press, 1963.

Funk, Robert W. "The Form of the New Testament Healing Miracle Story." *Semeia* 12 (1978): 57-96.

Funk, Robert W., and The Jesus Seminar. *The Acts of Jesus: What Did Jesus Really Do? The Search for the Authentic Words of Jesus.* New York: HarperCollins, 1998.

Glöckner, Richard. *Neutestamentliche Wundergeschichten und das Lob der Wundertaten Gottes in den Psalmen: Studien zur sprachlichen und theologischen Verwandtschaft zwischen neutestament-*

lichen Wundergeschichten und Psalmen. Mainz, Ger.: Grünewald, 1983.

Grant, Robert M. *Miracle and Natural Law in Graeco-Roman and Early Christian Thought.* Amsterdam, Neth.: North-Holland, 1952.

Gutwenger, E. "Die Machterweise Jesu in formgeschichtlicher Sicht." *ZKT* 89 (1967): 176-90.

Harvey, Anthony E. *Jesus and the Constraints of History.* London: Duckworth, 1982.

Headlam, Arthur C. *The Miracles of the New Testament.* London: John Murray, 1914.

Hendrickx, Herman. *The Miracle Stories of the Synoptic Gospels.* London: Geoffrey Chapman; San Francisco: Harper & Row, 1987.

Hilgert, E. "Symbolismus und Heilsgeschichte in den Evangelien: Ein Beitrag zu den Seesturm-Gerasenererzählungen." In *Oikonomia: Heilsgeschichte als Thema der Theologie. Festschrift Oscar Cullmann,* pp. 51-56. Edited by Fely Christ. Hamburg-Bergstedt, Ger.: H. Reich, 1967.

Hislop, I. "Miracles and the Gospels." *Blackfriars* 39 (1958): 57-60.

Hobbs, E. C. "Gospel Miracle Story and Modern Miracle Stories." *ATR supplementary series 3 (1974): 117-26.*

Hodges, Z. C. "The Centurion's Faith in Matthew and Luke." *BSac* 121 (1964): 321-32.

Hooker, Morna D. *The Signs of a Prophet: The Prophetic Actions of Jesus.* London: SCM Press, 1997.

Hull, John M. *Hellenistic Magic and the Synoptic Tradition.* London: SCM Press, 1974.

Kahl, Werner. *New Testament Miracle Stories in Their Religious-Historical Setting: A Religions-geschichtliche Comparison from a Structural Perspective.* Göttingen, Ger.: Vandenhoeck & Ruprecht, 1994.

Kallas, James. *The Significance of the Synoptic Miracles.* London: SPCK, 1961.

Kee, Howard Clark. *Medicine, Miracle and Magic in New Testament Times.* Cambridge, U.K.: Cambridge University Press, 1986.

———. *Miracle in the Early Christian World: A Study in Sociohistorical Method.* New Haven, Conn.: Yale University Press, 1983.

Keller, Ernest, and Marie-Luise Keller. *Miracles in Dispute: A Continuing Debate.* London: SCM Press, 1969.

Kertelge, Karl. "Die Wunder Jesu in der Neueren Exegese." *Theologische Berichte* 5 (1976): 71-105.

Klein, Günther. "Wunderglaube und Neues Testament." In *Ärgernisse: Konfrontationen mit dem Neuen Testament,* pp. 13-57. Munich, Ger.: Kösel, 1970.

Kolenkow, Anitra Bingham. "Healing Controversy as a Tie Between Miracle and Passion Material for a Proto-Gospel." *JBL* 95 (1976): 623-38.

Kolping, Adolf. *Wunder und Auferstehung Jesu Christi.* Bergen-Enkheim: Kaffke, 1969.

Langevin, P.-E. "La signification du miracle dans le message du Nouveau Testament." *ScEs* 27 (1975): 161-86.

Latourelle, René. *The Miracles of Jesus and the Theology of Miracles.* Mahwah: Paulist, 1988.

Léon-Dufour, Xavier, ed. *Les miracles de Jésus selon le Nouveau Testament.* Paris: Éditions du Seuil, 1977.

———. "Parler de miracle aujourd'hui." *Études* 344 (1976): 437-54.

Linton, Olof. "The Demand for a Sign from Heaven (Mk 8, 11-12 and Parallels)." *ST* 19 (1965): 112-29.

Lohse, Eduard. "Glaube und Wunder: Ein Beitrag zur theologia crucis in den synoptischen Evangelien." In *Theologia Crucis-Signum Crucis,* pp. 335-50. Edited by Carl Andresen and Günter Klein. Tübingen, Ger.: Mohr, 1979.

Long, Burke O. "The Social Setting for Prophetic Miracle Stories." *Semeia* 3 (1975): 46-63.

Loos, H. van der. *The Miracles of Jesus.* Leiden, Neth.: Brill, 1965.

McKenzie, J. L. "Signs and Power: The New Testament Presentation of Miracles." *Chicago Studies* 3 (1964): 5-18.

Maertens, Jean-Thierry. "La structure des récits de miracles dans les synoptiques." *SR* 6 (1976-1977): 253-66.

Meier, John P. *A Marginal Jew: Rethinking the Historical Jesus.* 3 vols. Garden City, N.Y.:

Doubleday, 1991, 1994, forthcoming.

Menoud, Philippe-H. "La signification du miracle dans le Nouveau Testament." *RHPR* 28-29 (1948-1949): 173-92.

Merli, D. "Glauben und Vertrauen in den Wundererzählungen der Evangelien: Überlegungen zu einem biblischen Grundbegriff." *BibLeb* 14 (1973): 210-15.

Moule, C. F. D., ed. *Miracles: Cambridge Studies in Their Philosophy and History.* London: Mowbray, 1965.

Mussner, Franz. *The Miracles of Jesus: An Introduction.* Notre Dame, Ind.: University of Notre Dame Press, 1968.

O'Bréarúin, L. "The Theology of Miracles." *Ephemerides Carmeliticae* 20 (1969): 3-51.

O'Connell, Patrick. "Miracles: Sign and Fact." *The Month* 36 (1966): 53-60.

Perry, Michael C. "Believing and Commending the Miracles." *ExpTim* 73 (1961-1962): 340-43.

Pesch, Rudolf, and Reinhard Kratz. *So liest man synoptisch I-III.* Frankfurt am Main, Ger.: J. Knecht, 1975, 1976.

Petzke, Gerd. "Historizität und Bedeutsamkeit von Wunderberichten: Möglichkeiten und Grenzen des religionsgeschichtlichen Vergleiches." In *Neues Testament und christliche Existenz. Festschrift für Herbert Braun zum 70, Geburtstag am 4. Mai 1973,* pp. 367-85. Edited by Hans Dieter Betz and Luise Schottroff. Tübingen, Ger.: Mohr, 1973.

Pittenger, Norman. "On Miracle: I." *ExpTim* 80 (1968-1969): 104-7.

Polhill, John B. "Perspectives on the Miracle Stories." *RevExp* 74 (1977): 389-99.

Prenter, Regin M. "The Miracles of Jesus." In *The Gospel as History,* pp. 15-19. Edited by Vilmos Vatja. Philadelphia: Fortress, 1975.

Richardson, Alan. *The Miracle Stories of the Gospels.* London: SCM Press, 1941.

Robinson, Bernard. "The Challenge of the Gospel Miracle Stories." *New Blackfriars* 60 (1979): 321-35.

Rohrbach, Hans. *Mit dem Unsichtbaren leben: Unsichtbare Mächte und die Macht Jesu.* Wuppertal: R. Brockhaus, 1976.

Sabourin, Leopold. "The Miracles of Jesus (I): Preliminary Survey." *BTB* 1 (1971): 59-80.

Schille, G. *Die urchristliche Wundertradtion: Ein Beitrag zur Frage nach dem irdischen Jesus.* Stuttgart, Ger.: Calwer, 1967.

Schnackenburg, Rudolf. "Miracles in the New Testament and Modern Science." In *Present and Future: Modern Aspects of New Testament Theology,* pp. 44-63. Notre Dame, Ind.: University of Notre Dame Press, 1966.

Schrage, Wolfgang. "Heil und Heilung im Nuen Testament." *EvT* 46 (1986): 197-214.

Speigl, Jakob. "Die Rolle der Wunder im vorkonstantinischen Christentum." *ZKT* 92 (1970): 287-312.

Steiner, Anton, and Volker Weymann, eds. *Wunder Jesu.* Basel, Switz.: Reinhardt; Zürich, Switz.: Benziger, 1978.

Stolz, Fritz. "Zeichen und Wunder: Die prophetische Legitimation und ihre Geschichte." *ZTK* 69 (1972): 125-44.

Suhl, Alfred. *Die Wunder Jesu: Ereignis und Überlieferung.* Gütersloh, Ger.: Gerd Mohn, 1968.

———, ed. *Der Wunderbegriff im Neuen Testament.* Darmstadt: Wissenschaftliche Buchgesellschaft, 1980.

Suriano, Thomas M. "Christian Faith and the Miracles of Jesus." *Bible Today* 92 (1977): 1358-64.

Sweet, John P. M. "Miracles and Faith II: The Miracles of Jesus." *Epworth Review* 3 (1976): 81-91.

Taymans, F. "Faith, Miracles and Reason." In *Faith, Reason and the Gospel,* pp. 299-310. Edited by John J. Heaney. Westminster: Newman, 1961.

Theissen, Gerd. *Miracle Stories of the Early Christian Tradition.* Edinburgh, U.K.: T & T Clark, 1983.

Trautmann, Maria. *Zeichenhafte Handlungen Jesu: Ein Beitrag zur Frage nach dem geschichtlichen Jesu.* Würzburg, Ger.: Echter, 1980.

Weder, H. "Wunder Jesu und Wundergeschichten." *VF* 29 (1984): 25-49.

Wenham, David, and Craig Blomberg, eds. *Gospel Perspectives 6: The Miracles of Jesus.* Sheffield, U.K.: JSOT, 1986.

Wire, Antoinette Clark. "The Structure of the Gospel Miracle Stories and Their Tellers." *Semeia* 11 (1978): 83-113.

Zeilinger, F. "Zum Wunderverständnis der Bibel." *BLit* 42 (1969): 27-43.

Zeller, Dieter. "Wunder und Bekenntnis: Zum Sitz im Leben urchristlicher Wundergeschichten." *BZ* 25 (1981): 204-22.

Chapter 1: Objectives & Issues

Boobyer, George H. "The Gospel Miracles: Views Past and Present." In *The Miracles and the Resurrection: Some Recent Studies,* pp. 31-49. Edited by Ian T. Ramsey et al. London: SPCK, 1964.

Bron, Bernhard. *Das Wunder: Das theologische Wunderverständnis im Horizont des neuzeitlichen Natur-und Geschichtsbegriffs.* Göttingen, Ger.: Vandenhoeck & Ruprecht, 1975.

Brown, Colin. *Miracles and the Critical Mind.* Grand Rapids, Mich.: Eerdmans; and Exeter, U.K.: Paternoster, 1984.

Bultmann, Rudolf. *History of the Synoptic Tradition.* Rev. ed. New York: Harper & Row, 1976.

———. "The Question of Wonder." In *Faith and Understanding.* Philadelphia: Fortress, 1987.

Carlston, C. E. "The Question of Miracles." *ANQ* 12 (1971): 99-107.

Craig, William Lane. "The Problem of Miracles: A Historical and Philosophical Perspective." In *Gospel Perspectives 6: The Miracles of Jesus,* pp. 9-48. Edited by David Wenham and Craig Blomberg. Sheffield, U.K.: JSOT, 1986.

Culpepper, R. H. "The Problem of Miracles." *RevExp* 53 (1956): 211-24.

Dodd, C. H. "Miracles in the Gospels." *ExpTim* 44 (1932-1933): 504-9.

Hay, Eldon R. "Bultmann's View of Miracle." *LQ* 24 (1972): 286-300.

Holland, R. F. "The Miraculous." *American Philosophical Quarterly* 2 (1965): 43-51.

Kasper, Walter. "Zur naturwissenschaftlichen Problematik der Wunder Jesu." *Renovatio* 32 (1976): 172-73.

Maier, Gerhard. "Zur Neutestamentlichen Wunderexegese im 19. und 20. Jahrhundert." In *Gospel Perspectives 6: The Miracles of Jesus,* pp. 49-87. Edited by David Wenham and Craig Blomberg. Sheffield, U.K.: JSOT, 1986.

Mark, James. "Myth and Miracle, or the Ambiguity of Bultmann." *Theology* 66 (1963): 134-40.

Schilling, B. "Die Frage nach der Enstehung der synoptischen Wundergeschichten in der deutschen neutestamentlichen Forschung." *SEÅ* 35 (1970): 61-78.

Schwarz, H. *Das Verständnis des Wunders bei Heim und Bultmann.* Stuttgart, Ger.: Calwer, 1966.

Taymans, F. "Le miracle, signe du surnaturel." *NRT* 77 (1955): 225-45.

Chapter 2: The Possibility of Miracles

Ahern, Dennis M. "Hume on the Evidential Impossibility of Miracles." In *Studies in Epistemology.* American Philosophical Quarterly Monograph Series 9, pp. 1-31. Edited by Nicholas Rescher. Oxford, U.K.: Blackwell, 1975.

Alston, William P. "God's Action in the World." In *Divine Nature and Human Language: Essays in Philosophical Theology,* pp. 197-222. Ithaca, N.Y.: Cornell University Press, 1989.

Beckwith, Francis J. *David Hume's Argument Against Miracles: A Critical Analysis.* New York: University Press of America, 1989.

Broad, C. D. "Hume's Theory of the Credulity of Miracles." *Proceedings of the Aristotelian Society.* New Series 17 (1916-1917): 77-94. Reprinted in *Human Understanding: Studies in the Philosophy of David Hume,* pp. 86-98. Edited by Alexander Sesonske and Noel Fleming. Belmont, Calif.: Wadsworth, 1965.

Burhenn, Herbert. "Attributing Miracles to Agents—Reply to George D. Chryssides." *RelS* 13 (1977): 485-89.

Burns, R. M. *The Great Debate on Miracles.* East Brunswick, N.J.: Associated University Presses, 1981.

Byrne, Peter. "Miracles and the Philosophy of Science." *HeyJ* 19 (1978): 162-70.

Carter, James C. "The Recognition of Miracles." *TS* 20 (1959): 175-97.

Chryssides, George. "Miracles and Agents." *RelS* 11 (1975): 319-27.

Collier, John. "Against Miracles." *Dialogue* 25 (1986): 349-52.

Colwell, Gary G. "Miracles and History." *Sophia* 22, no. 2 (1983): 9-14.

Conway, David A. "Miracles, Evidence and Contrary Religions." *Sophia* 22, no. 3 (1983): 3-14.

Diamond, Malcolm. "Miracles." *RelS* 9 (1973): 307-24.

Dietl, Paul. "On Miracles." *American Philosophical Quarterly* 5 (1968): 130-34.

Erlandson, Douglas K. "A New Look at Miracles." 13 (1977): 417-28.

Evans, C. Stephen. *The Historical Christ & the Jesus of Faith: The Incarnational Narrative as History.* Oxford, U.K.: Clarendon, 1996.

Flew, Antony. *David Hume: Philosopher of Moral Science,* chapter 5. Oxford, U.K.: Blackwell, 1986.

———. *God and Philosophy,* chapter 7. London: Hutchison, 1966.

———. *Hume's Philosophy of Belief,* chapter 8. London: Routledge and Kegan Paul, 1961.

———. "Miracles." *Encyclopedia of Philosophy* 5 (1967): 346-53.

Gaskin, J. C. A. *Hume's Philosophy of Religion,* chapter 7. London: Macmillan, 1978.

Geivett, R. Douglas, and Gary R. Habermas, eds. *In Defense of Miracles: A Comprehensive Case for God's Action in History.* Downers Grove, Ill.: InterVarsity Press, 1997.

Gill, John B. "Miracles with Method." *Sophia* 16, no. 3 (1977): 19-26.

Hambourger, Robert. "Belief in Miracles and Hume's Essay." *Nous* 14 (1980): 587-604.

Hardon, J. A. "The Concept of Miracle from St. Augustine to Modern Apologetics." *TS* 15 (1954): 229-57.

Hesse, Mary. "Miracles and the Laws of Nature." In *Miracles: Cambridge Studies in Their Philosophy and History,* pp. 33-42. Edited by C. F. D. Moule. London: Mowbray, 1965.

Houston, Joseph. *Reported Miracles: A Critique of Hume.* Cambridge, U.K.: Cambridge University Press, 1994.

Hume, David. *On Human Nature and the Understanding.* New York: Collier; London: Collier Macmillan, 1962.

Johnstone, William. "The Concept of Miracle for To-day." *Theology* 63 (1960): 143-50.

Ladrum, George. "What a Miracle Really Is." *RelS* 12 (1976): 49-57.

Langtry, Bruce. "Hume on Miracles and Contrary Religions." *Sophia* 14, no. 1 (1975): 29-34.

———. "Miracles and Rival Religious Systems of Religion." *Sophia* 24, no. 1 (1985): 21-31.

Lapointe, Roger. "Qu'en est-il des miracles?" *Église et Theologie* 6 (1975): 77-96.

Larmer, Robert A. H. *Water into Wine? An Investigation of the Concept of Miracle.* Kingston and Montreal, Can.: McGill-Queen's University Press, 1988.

Lewis, C. S. *Miracles.* London: Collins/Fontana, 1960.

McKinnon, Alastair. " 'Miracle' and 'Paradox.' " *American Philosophical Quarterly* 4 (1967): 308-14.

MacNamara, Kevin. "The Nature and Recognition of Miracles." *ITQ* 27 (1960): 294-322.

Pannenburg, Wolfhart. *Basic Questions in Theology.* Vol. 1. London: SCM Press, 1970.

Nowell-Smith, Patrick. "Miracles—The Philosophical Approach." *Hibbert Journal* 48 (1950): 354-60. Reprinted in *New Essays in Philosophical Theology,* pp. 243-53. Edited by Antony Flew and Alasdair MacIntyre. London: SCM Press, 1955.

Odegard, Douglas. "Miracles and Good Evidence." *RelS* 18 (1982): 37-46.

Paley, William. "A View of the Evidences of Christianity." In *The Works of William Paley, D.D., Archdeacon of Carlisle,* pp. 198-286. 1794; London: Tregg, 1853.

Perry, M. C. "Believing the Miracles and Preaching the Resurrection." In *The Miracles and the Resurrection,* pp. 64-78. Edited by Ian T. Ramsey et al. London: SPCK, 1964.

Ramsey, Ian T. "Miracles: An Exercise in Logical Mapwork." In *The Miracles and the Resurrection,* pp. 1-30. Edited by Ian T. Ramsey et al. London: SPCK, 1964.

Rein, Andrew. "Repeatable Miracles?" *Analysis* 46 (1986): 109-12.

Robinson, Guy. "Miracles." *Ratio* 9 (1967): 155-66.

Sider, Ronald J. "The Historian, the Miraculous and Post-Newtonian Man." *SJT* 25 (1972): 309-19.

Smart, Ninian, *Philosophers and Religious Truth,* chapter 2. London: SCM Press, 1964.

Sobel, Jordan Howard. "On the Evidence of Testimony for Miracles: A Bayesian Interpretation of David Hume's Analysis." *The Philosophical Quarterly* 37 (1987): 166-86.

Sorenson, Roy A. "Hume's Scepticism Concerning Reports of Miracles." *Analysis* 43 (1983): 60.

Swinburne, Richard G. *The Concept of Miracle.* London: Macmillan, 1970.

————. "Miracles." *The Philosophical Quarterly* 18 (1968): 320-28.

————, ed. *Miracles.* New York: Macmillan; London: Collier Macmillan, 1989.

Taylor, A. E. *Philosophical Studies.* London: Macmillan, 1934.

Tennant, F. R. *Miracle and Its Philosophical Presuppositions.* Cambridge, U.K.: Cambridge University Press, 1925.

Wadia, P. S. "Miracles and Common Understanding." *The Philosophical Quarterly* 26 (1976): 69-81.

Walker, Ian. "Miracles and Coincidences." *Sophia* 22, no. 3 (1983): 29-36.

————. "Miracles and Violations." *International Journal for Philosophy of Religion* 13 (1982): 103-8.

Wallace, R. C. "Hume, Flew and the Miraculous." *The Philosophical Quarterly* 20 (1970): 230-43.

Ward, Keith. *Divine Action.* London: Collins, 1990.

————. "Miracles and Testimony." *RelS* 21 (1985): 131-45.

Wootton, David. "Hume's 'Of Miracles': Probability and Irreligion." In *Studies in the Philosophy of the Scottish Enlightenment,* pp. 191-229. Edited by M. A. Steward. Oxford, U.K.: Clarendon, 1990.

Yandell, Keith E. *Hume's "Inexplicable Mystery": His Views on Religion,* chapter 15. Philadelphia: Temple University Press, 1990.

Young, Robert. "Miracles and Credibility." *RelS* 16 (1980): 465-68.

————. "Miracles and Physical Impossibility." *Sophia* 11, no. 3 (1972): 29-35.

Chapter 3: The Miracles of Jesus in Mark

Achtemeier, Paul J. " 'And He Followed Him': Miracles and Discipleship in Mark 10:46-52." *Semeia* 11 (1978): 115-45.

————. "Gospel Miracle Tradition and the Divine Man." *Int* 26 (1972): 174-97.

————. "The Origin and Function of the Pre-Marcan Miracle Catenae." *JBL* 91 (1972): 198-221.

————. "Person and Deed: Jesus and the Storm-Tossed Sea." *Int* 16 (1962): 169-76.

————. "Toward the Isolation of Pre-Markan Miracle Catenae." *JBL* 89 (1970): 265-91.

Beauvery, R. "La guérison d'un aveugle à Bethsaïde (Mc 8, 22-26)." *NRT* 90 (1968): 1083-91.

Bauernfeind, O. *Die Worte der Dämonen im Markusevangelium.* Stuttgart, Ger.: Kohlhammer, 927.

Best, Ernest. "Discipleship in Mark: Mark 8:22-10:52." *SJT* 23 (1970): 223-37. Reprinted in *Disciples and Discipleship: Studies in the Gospel According to Mark,* pp. 1-16. Edinburgh: T & T Clark, 1986.

————. "The Miracles in Mark." *RevExp* 75 (1978): 539-54. Reprinted in Ernest Best. *Disciples and Discipleship: Studies in the Gospel According to Mark,* pp. 177-96. Edinburgh: T & T Clark, 1986.

Betz, Hans Deiter. "Jesus as Divine Man." In *Jesus and the Historian,* pp. 114-33. Edited by F. T. Trotter. Philadelphia: Westminster, 1968.

Betz, Otto. "The Concept of the So-called 'Divine Man' in Mark's Christology." In *Studies in New Testament and Early Christian Literature,* pp. 229-40. Edited by David E. Aune. Leiden, Neth.: Brill, 1972.

Blackburn, Barry L. "Miracle Working ΘEIOI ANΔPEΣ in Hellenism (and Hellenistic Judaism)." In *Gospel Perspectives 6: The Miracles of Jesus,* pp. 185-218. Edited by David Wenham and Craig Blomberg. Sheffield, U.K.: JSOT, 1986.

————. *Theios Anēr and the Markan Miracle Traditions.* Tübingen, Ger.: Mohr, 1991.

Boobyer, George H. "The Eucharistic Interpretation of the Miracles of the Loaves in St. Mark's Gospel." *JTS* 3 (1952): 161-71.

———. "Mark II, 10a and the Interpretation of the Healing of the Paralytic." *HTR* 47 (1954): 115-20.

Bornkamm, Günther. " 'Ο Πνεῦμα ἄλαλον.' Eine Studie zum Markusevangelium." In *Geschichte und Glauben*, 2:21-36. Munich, Ger.: Kaiser, 1971.

Burkhill, T.A. "Mark 3 7-12 and the Alleged Dualism in the Evangelist's Miracle Material." *JBL* 87 (1968): 409-17.

———. *Mysterious Revelation: An Examination of the Philosophy of St. Mark's Gospel.* Ithaca, N.Y.: Cornell University Press, 1963.

———. "The Notion of the Miracle with Special Reference to St. Mark's Gospel." *ZNW* 50 (1959): 33-48.

———. "The Syrophoenician Woman: Mark 7,24-31." *SE* 4 (=TU 102 [1968]): 166-70.

Cangh, Jean-Marie van. "Les sources de l'Évangile: Les collections pré-marciennes de miracles." *RTL* 3 (1972): 76-85.

Cave, C. H. "The Obedience of Unclean Spirits." *NTS* 11 (1964-1965): 93-97.

Chilton, Bruce. "Exorcism and History: Mark 1:21-28." In *Gospel Perspectives 6: The Miracles of Jesus*, pp. 253-71. Edited by David Wenham and Craig Blomberg. Sheffield, U.K.: JSOT, 1986.

Clavier, H. "La multiplication des pains dans le ministère de Jésus." *SE* 1 (=TU 73 [1959]): 441-57.

Corrington, Gail Paterson. *The "Divine Man": His Origin and Function in Hellenistic Popular Religion.* Frankfurt am Main, Ger.: Peter Lang, 1986.

Countryman, L. Wm. "How Many Baskets Full? Mark 8:14-21 and the Value of Miracles in Mark." *CBQ* 47 (1985): 643-55.

Danker, Frederick W. "Mark 1:45 and the Secrecy Motif." *Concordia Theological Monthly* 37 (1966): 492-99.

Derrett, J. Duncan M. "Mark's Technique: the Haemorrhaging Woman and Jairus' Daughter." *Bib* 63 (1982): 474-504.

———. "Trees Walking, Prophecy and Christology." *ST* 35 (1981): 33-54.

Dewey, Joanna. *Markan Public Debate: Literary Technique, Concentric Structure and Theology in Mark 2:1—3:6.* Chico, Calif.: Scholars Press, 1977.

Donfried, K. P. "The Feeding Narratives and the Marcan Community: Mark 6,30-45 and 8,1-10." In *Kirche: Festschrift für Günther Bornkamm zum 75 Geburtstag*, pp. 95-103. Edited by Dieter Lührmann and Georg Strecker. Tübingen, Ger.: Mohr, 1980.

Doughty, Darrell J. "The Authority of the Son of Man (Mk 2 1—3 6)." *ZNW* 74 (1983): 161-81.

Dowd, Sharyn Echols. *Prayer, Power and the Problem of Suffering: Mark 11:22-25 in the Context of Markan Theology.* Atlanta: Scholars Press, 1986.

Dwyer, Timothy. "The Motif of Wonder in the Gospel of Mark." *JSNT* 57 (1995): 49-59.

Ellenburg, B. Dale. "A Review of Selected Narrative-Critical Conventions in Mark's Use of Miracle Material." *JETS* 38 (1995): 171-80.

Elliot, J. H. "Man and the Son of Man in the Gospel of Mark." In *Humane Gesellschaft: Beiträge zu ihrer sozialen Gestaltung*, pp. 50-58. Edited by Trutz Rendtorff and Arthur Rich. Zürich, Switz.: Zwingli, 1970.

Farrer, Austin. "Loaves and Thousands." *JTS* 4 (1953): 1-14.

Fisher, Kathleen M., and Urban C. von Wahlde. "Miracles of Mark 4:35—5:43: Their Meaning and Function in the Gospel Framework." *BTB* 11 (1981): 13-16.

Fowler, Robert M. *Loaves and Fishes: The Function of the Feeding Stories in the Gospel of Mark.* Chico, Calif.: Scholars Press, 1978.

Friedrich, Gerhard. "Die beiden Erzählungen von der Speisung in Mark. 6,31-44; 8,1-9." *TZ* 20 (1964): 10-22.

Gallagher, Eugene V. *Divine Man or Magician? Celsus and Origen on Jesus.* Chico: Scholars Press, 1982.

Glasswell, M. E. "The Use of Miracle in the Markan Gospel." In *Miracles: Cambridge Studies in Their Philosophy and History*, pp. 151-62. Edited by C. F. D. Moule. London: Mowbray, 1965.

Hedrick, C. W. "The Role of 'Summary Statements' in the Composition of the Gospel of Mark: A Dialogue with Karl Schmidt and Norman Perrin." *NovT* 26 (1984): 289-311.

Heising, A. "Exegese und Theologie der alt- und neutestamentlichen Speisewunder." *ZKT* 86 (1964): 80-96.

Holladay, Carl R. *THEIOS ANER in Hellenistic—Judaism: A Critique of the Use of This Category in New Testament Christology*. Missoula, Mont.: Scholars Press, 1977.

Johnson, Earl S. "Mark VIII. 22-26: The Blind Man from Bethsaida." *NTS* 25 (1979): 370-83.

———. "Mark 10:46-52: Blind Bartimaeus." *CBQ* 40 (1978): 191-204.

Kazmierski, Carl R. *Jesus, the Son of God: A Study of the Markan Tradition and Its Redaction by the Evangelist*. Würzburg, Ger.: Echter, 1979.

Keck, Leander. E. "Mark 3 7-12 and Mark's Christology." *JBL* 84 (1965): 341-58.

Kee, Howard Clark. "The Terminology of Mark's Exorcism Stories." *NTS* 14 (1967-68): 232-46.

Kertelge, K. *Die Wunder Jesu im Markusevangelium: Eine redaktionsgeschichtliche Untersuchung*. Munich, Ger.: Kösel, 1970.

Kingsbury, Jack D. *The Christology of Mark's Gospel*. Philadelphia: Fortress, 1983.

———. "The 'Divine Man' as the Key to Mark's Christology—The End of an Era?" *Int* 35 (1981): 243-57.

Koch, D.-A. *Die Bedeutung der Wundererzählungen für die Christologie des Markusevangeliums*. Berlin: de Gruyter, 1975.

Kremer, Jacob. "Jesu Wandel auf dem See nach Mk 6,45-52: Auslegung und Meditation." *BibLeb* 10 (1969): 221-32.

Kuhn, H.-W. *Ältere Sammlungen im Markusevangelium*. Göttingen, Ger.: Vandenhoeck & Ruprecht, 1971.

Lamarche, Paul. "Les Miracles des Jésus selon Marc." In *Les Miracles de Jésus selon le Nouveau Testament*, pp. 213-26. Edited by Xavier Léon-Dufour. Paris: Éditions du Seuil, 1977.

Lane, William L. "*Theios Anēr* Christology and the Gospel of Mark." In *New Dimensions in New Testament Study*, pp. 144-61. Edited by Richard N. Longenecker and Merrill C. Tenney. Grand Rapids, Mich.: Zondervan, 1974.

Luz, Ulrich. "The Secrecy Motif and the Marcan Christology." In *The Messianic Secret*, pp. 75-96. Edited by Christopher Tuckett. 1965; London: SPCK; Philadelphia: Fortress, 1983.

Neugebauer, Fritz. "Die wunderbare Speisung (Mk 6, 30-44 parr.) und Jesu Identität." *KD* 32 (1986): 254-77.

Pimentel, Peter. "The 'Unclean Spirits' of St Mark's Gospel." *ExpTim* 99 (1987-88): 173-75.

Pokorný, P. "From a Puppy to the Child: Some Problems of Contemporary Biblical Exegesis Demonstrated from Mark 7.24-30/Matt 15.21-8." *NTS* 41 (1995): 321-37.

Ritt, Hubert. "Der 'Seewandel Jesu' (Mk 6, 45-52 par): Literarische und theologische Aspekte." *BZ* 23 (1979): 71-84.

Robbins, Vernon K. "*Dynameis* and *Sēmeia* in Mark." *BR* 18 (1973): 5-20.

———. "The Healing of Blind Bartimaeus (10:46-52) in the Marcan Theology." *JBL* 92 (1973): 224-43.

Sahlin, Harald. "Die Perikope vom gerasenischen Besessenen und der Plan des Markusevangeliums." *ST* 18 (1964): 159-72.

Schenke, Ludger. *Die Wundererzählungen des Markusevangeliums*. Stuttgart, Ger.: Katholisches Bibelwerk, 1974.

Schille, Gottfried. "Die Seesturmerzählung Markus 4 35-41 als Beispiel neutestamentlicher Actualisierung." *ZNW* 56 (1965): 30-40.

Schmithals, Walter. *Wunder und Glaube: Eine Auslegung von Markus 4,35-6,6a*. Neukirchen-Vluyn: Neukirchener, 1970.

Snoy, Thierry. "Les miracles dans l'évangile de Marc: Examen de quelques études récentes." *RTL* 3 (1972): 449-66; 4 (1973): 58-101.

———. "La rédaction marcienne de la marche sur les eaux (Mc.,6, 45-52)." *ETL* 44 (1968):

205-41, 433-81.

Starobinski, J. "The Gerasene Demoniac: A Literary Analysis of Mark 5:1-20." In *Structural Analysis and Biblical Exegesis: Interpretational Essays*, pp. 57-84. Edited by R. Barthes et al. Pittsburgh: Pickwick, 1974.

Steinhauser, Michael G. "The Form of the Bartimaeus Narrative (Mark 10.46-52)." *NTS* 32 (1986): 583-95.

Tagawa, K. *Miracles et Évangile: La pensée personnelle de l'évangéliste Marc.* Paris: Presses universitaires de France, 1966.

Thiering, Barbara E. " 'Breaking of Bread' and 'Harvest' in Marks' Gospel." *NovT* 12 (1970): 1-12.

Thissen, Werner. *Erzählung der Befreiung: Eine exegetische Untersuchung zu Mk 2, 1-3,6.* Würzburg, Ger.: Echter, 1976.

Thurston, Bonnie Bowman. "Faith and Fear in Mark's Gospel." *Bible Today* 23 (1985): 305-10.

Tiede, David L. *The Charismatic Figure as Miracle Worker.* Missoula, Mo.: Scholars Press, 1972.

Young, Robert. "Miracles and Epistemology." *RelS* 8 (1972): 115-26.

Zeller, Dieter. "Die Heilung des Aussätzigen (Mk 1, 40-45): Ein Beispiel bekennender und werbender Erzählung." *TTZ* 93 (1984): 138-46.

Ziener, P. Georg. "Die Brotwunder im Markusevangelium." *BZ* 4 (1960): 282-85.

Chapter 4: The Miracles of Jesus in Matthew

Birger, Gerhardsson. *The Mighty Acts of Jesus According to Matthew.* Lund, Swe.: CWK Gleerup, 1979.

Bornkamm, Günther. "The Stilling of the Storm in Matthew." In *Tradition and Interpretation in Matthew*, pp. 52-57. Edited by Günther Bornkamm, Gerhard Barth and Heinz Joachim Held. London: SCM Press, 1982.

Braumann, G. "Der sinkende Petrus: Matth. 14, 28-31." *TZ* 22 (1966): 403-14.

Burger, Christoph. "Jesu Taten nach Matthäus 8 und 9." *ZTK* 70 (1973): 272-87.

Connolly, Dermot. "Ad miracula sanationum apud Matthaeum." *VD* 45 (1967): 306-25.

Denis, A.-M. "La marche de Jésus sur les eaux: Contribution à l'histoire de la péricope dans la tradition évangélique." In *De Jésus aux évangiles: Tradition et rédaction dans les évangiles synoptiques*, pp. 233-47. Edited by Ignace de la Potterie. BETL 25. Gembloux: Duculot; Paris: Lethielleux, 1967.

Dermience, Alice. "La péricope de la Cananéenne (Mt 15, 21-28): Rédaction et théologie." *ETL* 58 (1982): 25-49.

Dupont, Jacques. "Le paralytique pardonné (Mt 9, 1-8)." *NRT* 82 (1960): 940-58.

Feiler, Paul Frederick. "The Stilling of the Storm in Matthew: A Response to Günther Bornkamm." *JETS* 26 (1983): 399-406.

Gatzweiler, K. "Les récits de miracles dans l'Évangile selon saint Matthieu." In *L'Évangile selon Matthieu: Rédaction et Théologie*, pp. 209-20. Edited by M. Didier et al. BETL 29. Gembloux: Duculot, 1972.

Greeven, Heinrich. "Die Heilung des Gelähmten nach Matthäus." *Wort und Dienst* 4 (1955): 65-78. Also in Joachim Lange, ed. *Das Matthäus-Evangelium*, pp. 205-22. Darmstadt: Wissenschaftliche Buchgesellschaft, 1980.

Heil, John Paul. "Significant Aspects of the Healing Miracles in Matthew." *CBQ* 41 (1979): 274-87.

Held, Heinz Joachim. "Matthew as Interpreter of the Miracle Stories." In *Tradition and Interpretation in Matthew*, pp. 165-200. Edited by Günther Bornkamm, Gerhard Barth and Heinz Joachim Held. London: SCM Press, 1982.

Hook, S. H. "Jesus and the Centurion: Matthew viii. 5-10." *ExpTim* 69 (1957-58): 79-80.

Kingsbury, Jack D. "Observations on the 'Miracle Chapters' of Matthew 8—9." *CBQ* 40 (1978): 559-73.

―――. "Retelling the 'Old, Old Story': The Miracle of the Cleansing of the Leper as an Approach to the Theology of Matthew." *CurTM* 4 (1977): 342-49.

Kratz, Reinhard. "Der Seewandel des Petrus (Mt 14,28-31)." *BibLeb* 15 (1974): 86-101.

Légasse, Simon. "L'épisode de la Cananéenne d'après Mt 15,21-28." *BLE* 73 (1972): 21-40.

———. "Les miracles de Jésus selon Matthieu." In *Les miracles de Jésus selon le Nouveau Testament*, pp. 227-47. Edited by Xavier Léon-Dufour. Paris: Éditions du Seuil, 1977.

Loader, William R. G. "Son of David, Blindness, Possession and Duality in Matthew." *CBQ* 44 (1982): 570-85.

Luz, Ulrich. "Die Wundergeschichten von Mt 8-9." In *Tradition and Interpretation in the New Testament: Essays in Honor of E. Earle Ellis for His 60th Birthday*, pp. 149-65. Edited by Gerald F. Hawthorne and Otto Betz. Grand Rapids, Mich.: Eerdmans; Tübingen, Ger.: Mohr, 1987.

Overman, J. Andrew. *Church and Community in Crisis: The Gospel According to Matthew*. Valley Forge, Penn.: TPI, 1996.

Thompson, William G. "Reflections on the Composition of Mt 8:1-9:34." *CBQ* 33 (1971): 365-88.

Vledder, Evert-Jan. *Conflict in the Miracle Stories: A Social-Exegetical Study of Matthew 8 and 9*. Sheffield, U.K.: Sheffield Academic, 1997.

Chapters 5—6: The Miracles of Jesus in Luke

Achtemeier, Paul J. "The Lukan Perspective on the Miracles of Jesus: A Preliminary Sketch." In *Perspectives on Luke-Acts*, pp. 153-67. Edited by Charles H. Talbert. Danville, Va.: Association of Baptist Professors of Religion; Edinburgh: T & T Clark, 1978.

Brodie, Thomas Louis. "Towards Unravelling Luke's Use of the Old Testament: Luke 7:11-17 as an *Imatatio* of 1 Kings 17.17-24." *NTS* 32 (1986): 247-67.

Bruners, W. *Die Reinigung der zehn Aussätzigen und die Heilung des Samariters Lk 17,11-19: Ein Beitrag zur lukanischen Interpretation der Reinigung von Aussätzigen*. Stuttgart, Ger.: Katholisches Bibelwerk, 1977.

Busse, Ulrich. *Die Wunder Propheten Jesus. Die Rezeption, Komposition und Interpretation der Wundertradition im Evangelium des Lukas*. Stuttgart, Ger.: KWB, 1977.

Delorme, Jean. "Luc v.1-11: Analyse structurale et histoire de la rédaction." *NTS* 18 (1971-1972): 331-50.

George, A. "Le miracle dans l'oeuvre de Luc." In *Les miracles de Jésus selon le Nouveau Testament*, pp. 249-69. Edited by Xavier Léon-Dufour. Paris: Éditions du Seuil, 1977.

Glombitza, Otto. "Der dankbare Samariter: Luk. xvii 11-19." *NovT* 11 (1969): 241-46.

Kirchschläger, W. *Jesu exorzistisches Wirken aus der Sicht des Lukas: Ein Beitrag zur lukanisches Redaktion*. Klosterneuburg: Österreichisches Katholisches Bibelwerk, 1981.

McCaughey, Terence. "Paradigms of Faith in the Gospel of St. Luke." *ITQ* 45 (1978): 177-84.

May, Eric. " '. . . For Power Went Forth From Him . . .' (Luke 6, 19)." *CBQ* 14 (1952): 93-103.

Menzies, Robert P. "Spirit and Power in Luke-Acts: A Response to Max Turner." *JSNT* 49 (1993): 11-20.

Meynet, R. "Au coeur du texte: Analyse rhétorique de l'aveugle de Jéricho selon saint Luc." *NRT* 103 (1981): 696-710.

Pilch, John J. "Sickness and Healing in Luke-Acts." In *The Social World of Luke-Acts: Models for Interpretation*, pp. 182-209. Edited by Jerome H. Neyrey. Peabody, Mass.: Hendrickson, 1991.

Talbert, Charles H. "Excursus B: Miracle in Luke-Acts and in the Lukan Milieu." In *Reading Luke: A Literary Theological Commentary on the Third Gospel*, pp. 241-46. New York: Crossroad, 1984.

———. "The Lukan Presentation of Jesus' Ministry in Galilee: Luke 4:31—9:50." *RevExp* 64 (1967): 485-97.

Turner, Max. "The Spirit and the Power of Jesus' Miracles in the Lucan Conception." *NovT* 33 (1991): 124-52.

Wilkinson, John. "The Case of the Bent Woman in Luke 13, 10-17." *EvQ* 49 (1977): 195-205.

Vogels, Walter. "A Semiotic Study of Luke 7,11-17." *Eglise et théologie* 14 (1983): 273-92.

Chapters 7—8: The Miracles of Jesus in the Fourth Gospel

Becker, Jürgen. "Wunder und Christologie: zum Literarkritischen und christologischen Problem der Wunder im Johannesevangelium." *NTS* 16 (1969-1970): 130-48.

Bernard, Jacques. "La guérison de Bethesda: Harmoniques judéohellénistiques d'un récit de miracle un jour de sabbat." *MScRel* 33 (1976): 3-34; 34 (1977): 13-44.

Berrouard, M.-F. "La multiplication des pains et le discours du pain de die (Jean 6)."*Lumière et Vie* 18 (1969): 63-75.

Bittner, Wolfgang J. *Jesu Zeichen im Johannesevangelium: Die Messias-Erkenntnis im Johannesevangelium vor ihrem jüdischen Hintergrund.* Tübingen, Ger.: Mohr, 1987.

Bligh, John. "Four Studies in St. John: I. The Man Born Blind." *HeyJ* 7 (1966): 129-44.

Boismard, Marie-Émile. "Le chapitre XXI de saint Jean: Essai de critique littéraire." *RB* 54 (1947): 473-501.

———. "Rapports entre foi et miracles dans l'évangile de Jean." *ETL* 58 (1982): 357-64.

———. "Saint Luc et la rédaction du quatrième évangile (Jn, iv, 46-54)." *RB* 69 (1962): 185-211.

Brodie, Thomas Louis. "Jesus as the New Elisha: Cracking the Code." *ExpTim* 93 (1981-1982): 39-42.

Busse, Ulrich, and Anton May. "Das Weinwunder von Kana (Joh 2,1-11): Erneute Analyse eines 'erratischen Blocks.'" *Biblische Notizen* 12 (1980): 35-61.

Cangh, Jean-Marie van. "Le thème des poissons dans les récits évangéliques de la multiplication des pains." *RB* 78 (1971): 71-83.

Cassian, Bishop. "John XXI." *NTS* 3 (1956-1957): 132-36.

Charlier, Jean-Pierre. *Le signe de Cana: Essai de théologie johannique.* Brussels: La Pensée Catholique, 1959.

Clark, Douglas K. "Signs in Wisdom and John." *CBQ* 45 (1983): 201-9.

Collins, Raymond F. "Cana (Jn. 2:1-12)—The First of His Signs or the Key to His Signs?" *ITQ* 47 (1980): 77-95.

Cortés, Juan B. "The Wedding Feast at Cana." *TD* 14 (1966):14-17.

Derrett, J. Duncan M. "Water into Wine." *BZ* 7 (1963): 80-97.

Dillon, Richard Joseph. "Wisdom Tradition and Sacramental Retrospect in the Cana Account (Jn 2,1-11)." *CBQ* 24 (1962): 268-96.

Dodd, C. H. *Historical Tradition in the Fourth Gospel.* Cambridge, U.K.: Cambridge University Press, 1963.

———. *The Interpretation of the Fourth Gospel.* Cambridge, U.K.: Cambridge University Press, 1968.

Ensor, P. W. *Jesus and His "Works": The Johannine Sayings in Historical Perspective.* Tübingen, Ger.: Mohr, 1996.

Feuillet, André. "The Theological Significance of the Second Cana Miracle." In *Johannine Studies,* pp. 39-51. Staten Island, N.Y.: Alba House, 1964.

Formesyn, R. "Le sèmeion johannique et le sèmeion hellénistique." *ETL* 38 (1962): 856-94.

Fortna, Robert T. *The Gospel of Signs.* Cambridge, U.K.: Cambridge University Press, 1970.

———. "Source and Redaction in the Fourth Gospel's Portrayal of Jesus' Signs." *JBL* 89 (1970): 151-66.

Gärtner, Bertil. *John 6 and the Jewish Passover.* Lund, Swe.: G. W. K. Gleerup; Copenhagen, Den.: Ejnar Munskgaard, 1959.

Geyser, A. "The Semeion at Cana of the Galilee." In *Studies in John Presented to Professor J. N. Sevenster on the Occasion of His Seventieth Birthday,* pp. 12-21. Leiden, Neth.: Brill, 1970.

Giblin, Charles Homer. "The Miraculous Crossing of the Sea (John 6. 16-21)." *NTS* 29 (1983): 96-103.

Gourgues, Michel. "L'aveugle-né: Du miracle au signe: Typologie des réactions à l'égard du Fils de l'homme." *NRT* 104 (1982): 381-95.

Grassi, Joseph A. "The Wedding at Cana (John II 1-11): A Pentecostal Meditation?" *NovT* 14 (1972): 131-36.

Haenchen, Ernst. "Faith and Miracle." In *SE* 1 (=TU 73 [1959]): 495-98.

Hahn, Ferdinand. "Sehen und Glauben im Johannesevangelium." In *Neues Testament und Geschichte: Historisches Geschehen und Deutung im Neuen Testament. Oscar Cullmann zum*

70sten Geburtstag, pp. 125-41. Edited by Heinrich Baltensweiler and Bo Reicke. Zürich, Switz.: Theologischer; Tübingen, Ger.: Mohr, 1972.

Hanson, A. T. "The Old Testament Background to the Raising of Lazarus." *SE* 6 (=TU 112 [1973]): 252-55.

Heekerens, Hans-Peter. *Die Zeichen-Quelle der johanneischen Redaktion: Ein Beitrag zur Entstehungsgeschichte des vierten Evangeliums.* Stuttgart, Ger.: Katholisches Bibelwerk, 1984.

Hennig, J. "Was ist eigentlich geschehen? Joh 2,11." *ZRGG* 15 (1963): 276-86.

Hofbeck, Sebald. *Semeion: Der Begriff des "Zeichens" im Johannesevengelium unter Berücksichtigung seiner Vorgeschichte.* Münsterschwarzach: Vier-Türme, 1966.

Jonge, Marinus de. "Signs and Works in the Fourth Gospel." In *Jesus: Stranger from Heaven and Son of God,* pp. 117-40. Missoula, Mo.: Scholars Press, 1977.

Kee, Howard Clark. "Myth and Miracle: Isis, Wisdom and the Logos of John." In *Myth, Symbol and Reality,* pp. 145-64. Edited by Alan M. Olson. Notre Dame, Ind.: Notre Dame University Press, 1980.

Kiley, Mark. "The Exegesis of God: Jesus' Signs in John 1-11." In *SBL Seminar Papers: 1988 Seminar Papers,* pp. 555-69. Edited by David J. Lull. Atlanta: Scholars Press, 1988.

Kuhn, Hans-Jürgen. *Christologie und Wunder: Untersuchungen Joh 1,35-51.* Regensburg, Ger.: Friedrich Pustet, 1988

Lamarche, Paul. "La guérison de la belle-mère de Pierre et le genre littéraire des évangiles." *NRT* 87 (1965): 515-26.

Lee, Dorothy A. *The Symbolic Narratives of the Fourth Gospel: The Interplay of Form and Meaning.* Sheffield, U.K.: Sheffield Academic, 1994.

Léon-Dufour, Xavier. "Autour de *sémion* johannique." In *Die Kirche des Angangs: Festschrift für Heinz Schürmann,* pp. 363-78. Edited by Rudolf Schnackenburg et al. Leipzig, Ger.: St. Benno-Verlag, 1977.

———. "Les miracles de Jésus selon Jean." In *Les miracles de Jésus selon le Nouveau Testament,* pp. 269-86. Edited by Xavier Léon-Dufour. Paris: Éditions du Seuil, 1977.

Léonard, Jeanne-Marie. "Notule sur l'Evangile de Jean: Le récit des noces de Cana et Esaie 25." *ETR* 57 (1982): 119-20.

Lieu, J. M. "Blindness in the Johannine Tradition." *NTS* 34 (1988): 83-95.

Linnemann, Eta. "Die Hochzeit zu Kana und Dionysios." *NTS* 20 (1974): 408-18.

Lohse, Eduard. "Miracles in the Fourth Gospel." In *What About the New Testament?* pp. 64-75. Edited by Morna Hooker and Colin Hickling. London: SCM Press, 1975.

Lütgehetmann, Walter. *Die Hochzeit von Kana (Joh 2,1-11): Zu Ursprung und Deutung einer Wundererzählung im Rahmen johanneischer Redaktionsgeschichte.* Regensburg, Ger.: Friedrich Pustet, 1990.

McCasland, S. Vernon. "Signs and Wonders." *JBL* 76 (1957): 149-52.

McNeil, B. "The Raising of Lazarus." *Downside Review* 92 (1974): 269-75.

Martyn, James Louis. *History and Theology in the Fourth Gospel.* Nashville: Abingdon, 1979.

Michel, Otto. "Der Anfang der Zeichen Jesu." In *Die Leibhaftigkeit der Wortes: Theologische und seelsorgerliche Studien und Beiträge als Festgabe für Adolf Köberle zum Sechzigsten Geburtstag,* pp. 15-22. Edited by Otto Michel and Ulrich Mann. Hamburg: Furche-Verlag, 1958.

Moloney, Francis J. "From Cana to Cana (Jn. 2:1-4:54) and the Fourth Evangelist's Concept of Correct (and Incorrect) Faith." *Salesianum* 40 (1978): 817-43.

Müller, Ludolf. "Die Hochzeit zu Kana." In *Glaube, Geist, Geschichte: Festschrift für Ernst Benz zum 60. Geburtstag,* pp. 99-106. Edited by Gerhard Müller and Winfried Zeller. Leiden, Neth.: Brill, 1967.

Neirynck, Frans. "John 21." *NTS* 36 (1990): 321-36.

Nicol, W. *The Sēmeia in the Fourth Gospel: Tradition and Redaction.* Leiden, Neth.: Brill, 1972.

Olson, Birger. *Structure and Meaning in the Fourth Gospel: A Text-Linguistic Analysis of John 2:1-11 and 4:1-42.* Lund, Swe.: C. W. K. Gleerup, 1974.

Painter, John. "John 9 and the Interpretation of the Fourth Gospel." *JSNT* 28 (1986): 31-61.

Parkin, V. " 'On the Third Day There Was a Marriage in Cana of Galilee' (John 2.1)." *IBS* 3 (1981): 134-44.

Pesch, Rudolf. "Das Weinwunder bei der Hochzeit zu Kana (Joh 2,1-12)." *TGl* 24 (1981): 219-25.

Quiévreux, François. "Le récit de la multiplication des pains dans le quatrième évangile." *RevScRel* 41 (1967): 97-108.

Reim, Günter. "Joh 9—Tradition und zeitgenössische messianische Diskussion." *BZ* 22 (1978): 245-53.

Riga, Peter. "Signs of Glory: The Use of '*Sēmeion*' in St. John's Gospel." *Int* 17 (1963): 402-24.

Rissi, Mathias. "Die Hochzeit zu Kana (Joh. 2, 1-11)." In *Oikonomia: Heilsgeschichte als Thema der Theologie. Festschrift Oscar Cullmann*, pp. 76-92. Edited by Fely Christ. Hamburg-Bergstedt: H. Reich, 1967.

Robinson, James M. "The Miracles Source of John." *JAAR* 39 (1971): 339-48.

Schmidt, Karl Ludwig. "Der johanneische Charakter der Erzählung vom Hochzeitswunder in Kana." In *Harnack-Ehrung: Beiträge zur Kirchengeschichte, ihrem Lehrer Adolf von Harnack zum seinem siebzigsten Geburtstage*, pp. 32-43. Leipzig, Ger.: Hinrichs, 1921.

Schnackenburg, Rudolf. *Das erste Wunder Jesu (Johannes 2, 1-11)*. Freiburg, Ger.: Herder, 1951.

———. "Zur Traditionsgeschichte von Joh 4, 46-54." *BZ* 8 (1964): 58-88.

Schnelle, Udo. *Antidocetic Christology in the Gospel of John*. Minneapolis: Fortress, 1992.

Schulz, A. "Das Wunder in Kana im Lichte des Alten Testaments." *BZ* 16 (1924): 93-96.

Schweizer, Eduard. "Die Heilung der Königlichen: Joh. 4, 46-54." *EvT* 11 (1951-1952): 64-71.

Smalley, Stephen S. "The Sign in John XXI." *NTS* 20 (1974): 275-88.

Smith, D. Moody. "The Milieu of the Johannine Miracle Source: A Proposal." In *Jews, Greeks and Christians: Religious Cultures in Late Antiquity. Essays in Honor of William David Davies*, pp. 164-80. Edited by Robert Hammerton-Kelly and Robin Scroggs. Leiden, Neth.: Brill, 1976.

Smith, Robert. "Exodus Typology in the Fourth Gospel." *JBL* 81 (1962): 329-42.

Smitmans, Adolf. *Das Weinwunder von Kana: Die Auslegung von Jo 2, 1-11 bei den Vätern und heute*. Tübingen, Ger.: Mohr, 1966.

Spicq, Ceslaus. "Il promo miracolo di Gesè dovuto a sua Madre (Giov. 2, 1-11)." *Sacra Doctrina* 18 (1973): 125-44.

Temple, Sydney. "The Two Signs in the Fourth Gospel." *JBL* 81 (1962): 169-74.

Tenney, Merrill C. "Topics from the Gospel of John: Part II. The Meaning of the Signs." *BSac* 132 (1975): 145-60.

Toussaint, Stanley D. "The Significance of the First Sign in John's Gospel." *BSac* 134 (1977): 45-51.

Walter, Nikolaus. "Die Auslegung überlieferter Wundererzählungen im Johannes-Evangelium." In *Theologische Versuche*, 2:93-107. Edited by J. Rogge et al. Berlin-Ost, Ger.: Evangelische Verlagsanstalt, 1970.

Whittaker, Molly. " 'Signs and Wonders': The Pagan Background." *SE* 5 (1968): 155-58.

Wilkens, Wilhelm. *Zeichen und Werke*. Zürich, Switz.: Zwingli, 1969.

Wilkinson, John. "A Study of Healing in the Gospel According to John." *SJT* 20 (1967): 442-61.

Windische, Hans. "Die johanneische Weinregel (Joh. 2, 10.)." *ZNW* 14 (1913): 248-57.

Chapter 9: Miracles & the Historical Jesus

Borg, Marcus. *Jesus in Contemporary Scholarship*. Valley Forge, Penn.: Trinity, 1994.

Calvert, D. G. A. "An Examination of the Criteria for Distinguishing the Authentic Words of Jesus." *NTS* 18 (1971-1972): 209-19.

Crossan, John D. "Why Christians Must Search for the Historical Jesus." *BibRev* 12 (1996): 34-39, 42-45.

Freyne, Seán. "Query: Did Jesus Really Work Miracles?" *The Furrow* 26 (1975): 283-86.

George, A. "Les miracles de Jésus dans les évangiles synoptiques." *Lumière et Vie* 33 (1957): 7-24.

———. "Paroles de Jésus sur ses miracles (Mt 11, 5 21; 12,27 28 et par.)." In *Jésus aux origines de la christologie*, pp. 283-301. Edited by Jacques Dupont. Leuven/Louvain, Ger.: Leuven

University Press, 1975.

Gutwenger, E. "Die Machterweise Jesu in formgeschichtlicher Sicht." *ZKT* 89 (1967): 176-90.

Harvey, Van Austin. *The Historian and the Believer: The Morality of Historical Knowledge and Christian Belief.* London: SCM Press, 1967.

Johnson, Luke T. "The Search for (the Wrong) Jesus." *BibRev* 11 (1995): 20-25, 44.

Kasper, Walter. "Zur historischen Problematik der Wunder Jesu." *Renovatio* 32 (1976): 78-79.

Kertelge, Karl. "Die Überlieferung der Wunder Jesu und die Frage nach dem historischen Jesus." In *Rückfrage nach Jesus: Zur Methodik und Bedeutung der Frage nach dem historischen Jesus,* pp. 174-93. Edited by Karl Kertelge. Freiburg, Ger.: Herder, 1974.

Latourelle, René. "Authenticité historique des miracles de Jésus: Essai de critériologie." *Gregorianum* 54 (1973): 225-62.

Lentzen-Deis, Fritzleo. "Die Wunder Jesu: Zur neueren Literatur und zur Frage nach der Historizität." *TP* 43 (1968): 392-402.

Lonergan, Bernard. *Method in Theology.* London: DLT, 1975.

McEleney, Neil J. "Authenticating Criteria and Mark 7:1-23." *CBQ* 34 (1972): 431-60.

Meyer, Ben F. *The Aims of Jesus.* London: SCM Press, 1979.

———. *Critical Realism and the New Testament.* Allison Park, U.K.: Pickwick, 1989.

———. *Reality and Illusion in New Testament Scholarship: A Primer in Critical Realist Hermeneutics.* Collegeville, Minn.: Michael Glazier, 1994.

Miller, Robert J. "Historical Method and the Deeds of Jesus." *Forum* 8 (1992): 5-30.

Mussner, Franz. "Ipsissima Facta Jesu?" *TRev* 68 (1972), cols. 177-85.

Nielsen, Helge Kjaer. "Ein Beitrag zur Beurteilung der Tradition über die Heilungstätigkeit Jesu." In *Probleme der Forschung,* pp. 58-90. Edited by Albert Fuchs. Vienna, Aus., and Munich, Ger.: Herold, 1978.

Pesch, Rudolf. *Jesu ureigene Taten? Ein Beitrag zur Wunderfrage.* Freiburg, Ger.: Herder, 1970.

Polkow, Dennis. "Method and Criteria for Historical Jesus Research." In *SBL 1987 Seminar Papers,* pp. 336-56. Edited by Kent H. Richards. Atlanta: Scholars Press, 1987.

Sabourin, Leopold. *The Divine Miracles Discussed and Defended.* Rome: Catholic Book Agency, 1977.

Schille, G., *Die urchristliche Wundertradition: Ein Beitrag zur Frage nach dem irdische Jesus.* Stuttgart, Ger.: Calwer, 1967.

Stein, Robert H. "The 'Criteria' for Authenticity." In *Gospel Perspectives 1: Studies of History and Tradition in the Four Gospels,* pp. 225-63. Sheffield, U.K.: JSOT, 1980.

Troeltsch, Ernst. "Historical and Dogmatic Method in Theology." In *Religion in History,* pp. 11-32. 1898; Minneapolis: Fortress, 1991.

———. "Historiography." In *Encyclopedia of Religion and Ethics,* 6:716-23. Edited by James Hastings. Edinburgh: T & T Clark, 1913.

Verweyen, Hansjürgen. "Die historische Rückfrage nach den Wundern Jesu." *TTZ* 90 (1981): 41-58.

Vögtle, Anton. "Jesu Wunder einst und heute." *BibLeb* 2 (1961): 234-54.

———. "The Miracles of Jesus Against Their Contemporary Background." In *Jesus in His Time,* pp. 96-105. Edited by Hans Jürgen Schultz. London: SPCK, 1971.

Wandsworth, Henry. "Event and Interpretation VII: Jesus the Wonderworker." *Clergy Review* 55 (1970): 859-67.

Wright, N. T. *The New Testament and the People of God.* Minneapolis: Fortress, 1992.

Chapter 10: The Meaning of the Miracles for Jesus

Blank, J. "Zur Christologie ausgewählter Wunderberichte." *Evangelische Erzeiher* 20 (1968): 104-28.

Dunn, James D. G. "Matthew 12:28/Luke 11:20—A Word of Jesus?" In *Eschatology and the New Testament: Essays in Honor of George Raymond Beasley-Murray,* pp. 29-49. Edited by W. Hulitt Gloer. Peabody, Mass.: Hendrickson, 1988.

Latourelle, René. "Originalité et Fonctions des miracles de Jésus." *Gregorianum* 66 (1985): 641-53.

Mearns, Chris. "Realized Eschatology in Q? A Consideration of the Sayings in Luke 7.22, 11.20 and 16.16." *SJT* 40 (1987): 189-210.

Meyer, Ben F. "Jesus' Ministry and Self-Understanding." In *Studying the Historical Jesus: Evaluations of the State of Current Research,* pp. 337-52. Edited by Bruce Chilton and Craig A. Evans. Leiden, Neth.: Brill, 1994.

Nielsen, Helge Kjaer. *Heilung und Verkündigung: Das Verständnis der Heilung und ihres Verhältnisses zur Verkündigung bei Jesus und in der ältesten Kirche.* Leiden, Neth.: Brill, 1987.

Pesch, Rudolf. "Zur theologischen Bedeutung der 'Machttaten' Jesu: Reflexionen eines Exegeten." *TQ* 152 (1972): 203-13.

Chapter 11: Jesus & Exorcism

Achtemeier, Paul J. "Miracles and the Historical Jesus: A Study of Mark 9:14-29." *CBQ* 37 (1975): 471-91.

Aichinger, H. "Zur Traditionsgeschichte der Epileptiker-Perikope Mk 9, 14-29 par, Mt 17, 14-21 par, Lk 9, 37-43a." In *Problem der Forschung,* pp. 114-23. Edited by A. Fuchs. Vienna: Herold, 1978.

Annen, Franz. "Die Dämonenaustreibungen Jesu in den synoptischen Evangelien." *Theologische Berichte* 5 (1976): 107-46.

———. *Heil für die Heiden: Zur Bedeutung und Geschichte der Tradition vom besessenen Gerasener (Mk 5,1-20 par.).* Frankfurt: J. Knecht, 1976.

Bächli, O. " 'Was habe ich mit Dir zu schaffen?' Eine formelhafte Frage im A.T. und N.T." *TZ* 33 (1977): 69-80.

Böcher, Otto. *Christus Exorcista: Dämonismus und Taufe im Neuen Testament.* Stuttgart, Ger.: Kohlhammer, 1972.

———. *Das Neue Testament und die dämonischen Mächte.* Stuttgart, Ger.: Katholisches Bibelwerk, 1972.

Burkill, T. A. "Historical Development of the Story of the Syro-phoenician Woman." *NovT* 9 (1967): 161-77.

———. "The Syrophoenician Woman: The Congruence of Mk 7 24-31." *ZNW* 57 (1966): 22-37.

Catherinet, F. M. "Demoniacs in the Gospel." In *Soundings in Satanism,* pp. 121-37. Edited by Francis J. Sheed. New York: Sheed & Ward, 1972.

Craghan, J. "The Gerasene Demoniac." *CBQ* 30 (1968): 522-36.

Cranfield, C. E. B. "St. Mark 9.14-29." *SJT* 3 (1950): 57-67.

Dermience, A. "Tradition et rédaction dans la péricope de la Syrophénicienne: Marc 7,24-30." *RTL* 8 (1977): 15-29.

Derrett, J. Duncan M. "Contributions to the Study of the Gerasene Demoniac." *JSNT* 3 (1979): 2-17.

———. "Law in the New Testament: The Syrophoenician Woman and the Centurion of Capernaum." *NovT* 15 (1973): 161-86.

———. "Legend and Event: The Gerasene Demoniac: An Inquest into History and Liturgical Projection (Mk 5, 1-20)." In *Studia Biblica II,* pp. 63-73. Edited by E. A. Livingstone. Sheffield, U.K.: JSOT, 1980.

Duling, D. C. "Solomon, Exorcism and the Son of David." *HTR* 68 (1975): 235-52.

Dunn, James D. G., and Graham H. Twelftree. "Demon-Possession and Exorcism in the New Testament." *Churchman* 94 (1980): 210-25.

Flammer, Barnabas. "Die Syropheonizerin: Mk 7,24-30." *TQ* 148 (1968): 463-78.

Guillemette, P. "Mc 1, 24 est-il une formule de défense magique?" *ScEs* 30 (1978): 81-96.

Haenchen, Ernst. "Die Komposition von Mk vii 27-ix 1 und Par." *NovT* 6 (1963): 81-109.

Hawthorn, T. "The Gerasene Demoniac: A Diognosis: Mark v. 1-20. Luke viii. 26-39. (Matthew viii. 28-34)." *ExpTim* 66 (1954-55): 79-80.

Hiers, Richard H. "Satan, Demons and the Kingdom of God." *SJT* 27 (1974): 35-47.

Hollenbach, Paul W. "Jesus, Demoniacs and Public Authorities: A Socio-Historical Study." *JAAR* 49 (1981): 567-88.

Howard, J. Keir. "New Testament Exorcism and Its Significance Today." *ExpTim* 96 (1984-1985): 105-9.

Käsemann, Ernst. "Die Heilung der Besessenen." *Reformatio* 28 (1979): 7-18.

Lamarche, Paul. "Le possédé de Gérasa (Mt 8, 28-34; Mk 5, 1-20; Lc 8, 26-39)." *NRT* 90 (1968): 581-97.

Léon-Dufour, Xavier. "L'épisode de l'enfant épileptique." In *Etudes d'Évangile*, pp. 183-227. Paris: Éditions du Seuil, 1965.

McCasland, S. Vernon. *By the Finger of God: Demon Possession and Exorcism in Early Christianity in the Light of Modern Views of Mental Illness.* New York: Macmillan, 1951.

Mussner, Franz. "Ein Wortspiel in Mk 1,2 4?" *BZ* 4 (1960): 285-86.

Pesch, Rudolf. "The Markan Version of the Healing of the Gerasene Demoniac." *Ecumenical Review* 23 (1971): 349-76.

———. " 'Eine neue Lehre aus Macht': Eine Studie zu Mk 1,21-28." In *Evangelienforschung: Aufsätze deutscher Exegeten*, pp. 241-76. Edited by J.-B. Bauer. Graz: Styria, 1968.

———. "Ein Tag vollmächtigen Wirkens Jesu in Kapharnaum (Mk 1,21-34, 35-49)." *BibLeb* 9 (1968): 61-77, 114-28, 177-95, 261-77.

Petzke, G. "Die historische Frage nach dem Wundertaten Jesu: Dargestellt am Beilspiel des Exorzismus Mark 9:14-29 Par." *NTS* 22 (1976): 180-204.

Russell, E. A. "The Canaanite Woman and the Gospels (Mt 15:21-28; cf. Mk 7:24-30)." In *Studia Biblica 1978: II. Papers on the Gospels*, pp. 263-300. Edited by E. A. Livingstone. Sheffield, U.K.: JSOT, 1980.

Sabourin, Leopold. "The Miracles of Jesus (II): Jesus and the Evil Powers." *BTB* 4 (1974): 115-75.

Schenk, Wolfgang. "Tradition und Redaktion in der Epileptiker—Perikope Mk 9 14-29." *ZNW* 63 (1972): 76-94.

Starobinski, Jean. "An Essay in Literary Analysis—Mark 5:1-20." *Ecumenical Review* 23 (1971): 377-97.

Stock, A. "Jesus and the Lady from Tyre: Encounter in the Border Distirct." *Emmanuel* 93 (1987): 336-39, 358.

Suhl, Alfred. "Überlegungen zur Hermeneutik an Hand von Mk 1,21-28." *Kairos* 26 (1984): 28-38.

Twelftree, Graham H. *Christ Triumphant: Exorcism Then and Now.* London: Hodder & Stoughton, 1985.

———. "ΕΙ ΔΕ . . . ΕΓΩ ΕΚΒΑΛΛΩ ΤΑ ΔΑΙΜΟΝΙΑ . . ." In *Gospel Perspectives 6: The Miracles of Jesus*, pp. 361-400. Edited by David Wenham and Craig Blomberg. Sheffield, U.K.: JSOT, 1986.

———. *Jesus the Exorcist: A Contribution to the Study of the Historical Jesus.* Tübingen, Ger.: Mohr, 1993.

Vencovský, Jan. "Der gadarenische Exorzismus: Mt 8, 28-34 und Parallelen." *Communio viatorum* 14 (1971): 13-29.

Wilkinson, John. "The Case of the Epileptic Boy." *ExpTim* 79 (1967-1968): 39-42.

Yamauchi, Edwin M. "Magic or Miracle? Disease, Demons and Exorcisms." In *Gospel Perspectives 6: The Miracles of Jesus*, pp. 89-183. Edited by David Wenham and Craig Blomberg. Sheffield, U.K.: JSOT, 1986.

Yates, Roy. "Jesus and the Demonic in the Synoptic Gospels." *ITQ* 44 (1977): 39-57.

Chapter 12: The Crippled & Paralytics

Diaz, José Alonso. "El paralítico de Betesda." *Biblia y Fe* 8 (1982): 151-67.

Ceroke, Christian P. "Is Mk 2,10 a Saying of Jesus?" *CBQ* 22 (1960): 369-90.

Dewey, Joanna. "The Literary Structure of the Controversy Stories in Mark 2:1-3:6." *JBL* 92 (1973): 394-401.

Dietzfelbinger, Christian. "Vom Sinn der Sabbatheilungen Jesu." *EvT* 38 (1978): 281-98.

Green, Joel B. "Jesus and a Daughter of Abraham (Luke 13:10-17): Test Case for a Lucan

Perspective on Jesus' Miracles." *CBQ* 51 (1989): 643-54.

Hamm, M. Dennis. "The Freeing of the Bent Woman and the Restoration of Israel: Luke 13.10-17 as Narrative Theology." *JSNT* 31 (1987): 23-44.

Haslam, J. A. G. "The Centurion at Capernaum: Luke 7:1-10." *ExpTim* 96 (1984-1985): 109-10.

Grigsby, Bruce. "Washing in the Pool of Siloam—A Thematic Anticipation of the Johannine Cross." *NovT* 27 (1985): 227-35.

Klauck, Hans-Josef. "Die Frage der Sündenvergebung in der Perikope von der Heiling des Gelähmten (Mk 2,1-12 parr)." *BZ* 25 (1981): 223-48.

Léon-Dufour, Xavier. "La Guérison de la Belle-Mère de Simon-Pierre." *EstBib* 24 (1965): 193-216.

Lohse, Eduard. "Jesu Worte über den Sabbat." In *Judentum-Urchristentum-Kirche: Festschrift für Joachim Jeremias,* pp. 79-89. Edited by Walther Eltester. Berlin, Ger.: Töpelmann, 1960.

Maisch, Ingrid. *Die Heilung des Gelähmten: Eine exegetisch-traditionsgeschichtliche Untersuchung zu Mk 2,1-12.* Stuttgart, Ger.: Katholisches Bibelwerk, 1971.

Mead, Richard T. "The Healing of the Paralytic—A Unit?" *JBL* 80 (1961): 348-54.

Noorda, Sijbolt J. "Illness and Sin, Forgiving and Healing: The Connection of Medical Treatment and Religious Beliefs in Ben Sira 38:1-15." In *Studies in Hellenistic Religions,* pp. 215-24. Edited by M. J. Vermaseren. Leiden, Neth.: Brill, 1979.

O'Toole, Robert F. "Some Exegetical Reflections on Luke 13,10-17." *Bib* 73 (1992): 84-107.

Reicke, Bo. "The Synoptic Reports on the Healing of the Paralytic: Matt. 9:1-8 with Parallels." In *Studies in New Testament Language and Text,* pp. 319-29. Edited by J. K. Elliott. Leiden, Neth.: Brill, 1976.

Sauer, Jürgen. "Traditionsgeschichtliche Überlegungen zu Mk 3 1-6." *ZNW* 73 (1982): 183-203.

Wendling, E. "Synoptische Studien: II. Der Hauptmann von Kapernaum." *ZNW* 9 (1908): 96-109.

Wrede, W. "Zur Heilung des Gelähmten (Mc 2,1ff.)." *ZNW* 5 (1904): 354-58.

Chapter 13: The Blind

Blank, J. "Die Heilung des Blindgeboren als Zeichen für Offenbarung und Krisis." In *Krisis: Untersuchungen zur johanneischen Christologie und Eschatologie,* pp. 252-63. Freiburg, Ger.: Lambertus, 1964.

Bornkamm, Günther. "Die Heilung des Blindgeborenen (Johannes 9)." In *Geschichte und Glaube,* part 2. *Gesammelte Augsätze,* 4:65-72. Munich, Ger.: Kaiser, 1971.

Howard, J. Keir. "Men as Trees, Walking: Mark 8.22-26." *SJT* 37 (1984): 163-70.

Mollat, Donatien. "La guérsion de l'aveugle-né." *BVC* 23 (1958): 22-31.

Riga, Peter J. "The Man Born Blind." *Bible Today* 22 (1984): 168-73.

Chapter 14: Raising the Dead

Baltz, Frederick W. *Lazarus and the Fourth Gospel Community.* Lewiston, N.Y.: Mellen, 1996.

Cadman, William H. "The Raising of Lazarus (John 10, 40-11, 53)." *SE* 1 (=TU 73 [1959]): 423-34.

Clark, W. Royce. "Jesus, Lazarus and Others: Rescuscitations or Resurrection." *Religion in Life* 49 (1980): 230-41.

Dunkerley, Roderic. "Lazarus." *NTS* 5 (1958-1959): 321-27.

Harris, Murray J. " 'The Dead Are Restored to Life': Miracles of Revivification in the Gospels." In *Gospel Perspectives 6: The Miracles of Jesus,* pp. 295-326. Edited by David Wenham and Craig Blomberg. Sheffield, U.K.: JSOT, 1986.

Kremer, Jacob. *Lazarus: Die Geschichte einer Aufstehun: Text, Wirkungsgeschichte und Botschaft von Joh 11,1-46.* Stuttgart, Ger.: Katholisches Bibelwerk, 1985.

Martin, James P. "History and Eschatology in the Lazarus Narrative, John 11.1-44." *SJT* 17 (1964): 332-43.

Paul, André. "La guérison de l'aveugle (des aveugles) de Jéricho." *Foi et Vie* 69 (1970): 44-69.

Pearce, Keith. "The Lucan Origins of the Raising of Lazarus." *ExpTim* 96 (1984-1985): 359-61.

Pesch, Rudolf. "Jaïrus (Mk 5, 22 / Lk 8, 41)." *BZ* 14 (1970): 252-56.
Pollard, T. E. "The Raising of Lazarus (John xi)." *SE* 6 (=TU 112 [1973]): 434-43.
Rochais, Gérard. *Les récits de résurrection des morts dans le Nouveau Testament.* Cambridge, U.K.: Cambridge University Press, 1981.
Sabourin, Leopold. "Resurrectio Lazari (Jo 11,1-44)." *VD* 46 (1968): 339-50.
Salas, Antonio. "La resurrección de Lázaro." *Biblia y Fe* 8 (1982): 181-94.
Schmitt, Armin. "Die Totenerweckung in 2 Kön 4, 8-37: Ein literaturwissenschaftliche Untersuchung." *BZ* 19 (1975): 1-25.
Stenger, Werner. "Die Auferweckung des Lazarus (Joh 11, 1-45): Vorlage und johanneische Redaktion." *TTZ* 83 (1974): 17-37.
Wilkens, Wilhelm. "Die Erweckung des Lazarus." *TZ* 15 (1969): 22-39.

Chapter 15: Lepers Cleansed

Betz, Hans Deiter. "The Cleansing of the Ten Lepers (Luke 17:11-19)." *JBL* 90 (1971): 314-32.
Boismard, M.-É. "La guérison du lépreux (Mc 1, 40 et par.)." *Salmanticensis* 28 (1981): 283-91.
Cave, C. H. "The Leper: Mark 1. 40-45." *NTS* 25 (1979): 245-50.
Elliott, J. K. "The Conclusion of the Pericope of the Healing of the Leper and Mark i.45." *JTS* 22 (1971): 153-57.
Neirynck, Frans. "Papyrus Egerton 2 and the Healing of the Leper." *ETL* 61 (1985): 153-60.
Paul, André. "La guérison d'un lépreux: Approche d'un récit de Marc (*1*, 40-45)." *NRT* 92 (1970): 592-604.

Chapter 16: Other Healings & Miracles of Nature

Bagatti, B. "Dove avvenne la moltiplicazione dei pani?" *Salmanticensis* 28 (1981): 293-98.
Barnett, Paul W. "The Feeding of the Multitude in Mark 6/John 6." In *Gospel Perspectives 6: The Miracles of Jesus*, pp. 273-93. Edited by David Wenham and Craig Blomberg. Sheffield, U.K.: JSOT, 1986.
Bartsch, Hans-Wener. "Die 'Verfluchung' des Feigenbaums." *ZNW* 53 (1962): 256-60.
Bauckham, Richard. "The Coin in the Fish's Mouth." In *Gospel Perspectives 6: The Miracles of Jesus*, pp. 219-52. Edited by David Wenham and Craig Blomberg. Sheffield, U.K.: JSOT, 1986.
Blomberg, Craig. "The Miracles as Parables." In *Gospel Perspectives 6: The Miracles of Jesus*, pp. 327-59. Edited by David Wenham and Craig Blomberg. Sheffield, U.K.: JSOT, 1986.
Braude, William G. "Jesus and His Miracles." *Bible Today* 58 (1972): 627-31.
Buse, Ivor. "The Gospel Accounts of the Feeding of the Multitudes." *ExpTim* 74 (1962-1963): 167-70.
Cantrell, Richard A. "The Cursed Fig Tree." *Bible Today* 29 (1991): 105-8.
Daube, David. *The New Testament and Rabbinic Judaism*, pp. 36-51. Salem: Ayer, 1984.
Davis, Stephen T. "The Miracle at Cana: A Philosopher's Perspective." In *Gospel Perspectives 6: The Miracles of Jesus*, pp. 419-42. Edited by David Wenham and Craig Blomberg. Sheffield, U.K.: JSOT, 1986.
Derrett, J. Duncan M. "Why and How Jesus Walked on the Sea." *NovT* 23 (1981): 330-48.
Hegermann, Harald. "Bethsaida und Gennesar: Eine traditions-und redaktionsgeschichtliche Studie zu Mk 4-81." In *Judentum-Urchristentum-Kirche: Festschrift für Joachim Jeremias*, pp. 130-40. Edited by Walter Eltester. Berlin, Ger.: Töpelmann, 1960.
Heil, John Paul. *Jesus Walking on the Sea: Meaning and Gospel Functions of Matt 14:22-33, Mark 6:45-52 and John 6:15b-21.* Rome: Biblical Institute, 1981.
Heising, Alkuin. *Die Botschaft der Brotvermehrung: Zur Geschichte und Bedeutung eines Christusbekenntnisses im Neuen Testament.* Stuttgart, Ger.: Katholisches Bibelwerk, 1966.
Herbert, A. G. "Historicity in the Feeding of the Five Thousand." *SE* 2 (=TU 87 [1964]): 65-72.
Iersel, B. M. F. van. "Der wunderbare Speisung und das Abendmahl in der synoptischen Tradition (Mk 6, 35-44 par.; 8, 1-20 par.)." *NovT* 7 (1964-1965): 167-94.
Iersel, B. M. F. van, and A. J. M. Linmans, "The Storm on the Lake: Mk iv 35-48 and Mt viii

18-27 in the Light of Form Criticism, 'Redaktionsgeschichte' and Structural Analysis." In *Miscellanea Neotestamentica*, pp. 17-48. Edited by T. Baarda, A. F. J. Klijn and W. C. van Unnik. Leiden, Neth.: Brill, 1978.

Kiilunen, Jarmo. *Die Vollmacht im Widerstreit: Untersuchungen zum Werdegang von Mk 2,1-3,6.* Helsinki, Fin.: Suomalainen Tiedeakatemia, 1985.

Knackstedt, J. "Die beiden Brotvermehrungen im Evangelium." *NTS* 10 (1963-1964): 309-35.

———. "De duplici miraculo multiplicationis panum." *VD* 41 (1963): 39-51, 140-53.

Kruse, Heinz. "Jesu Seefahrten und die Stellung von Joh. 6." *NTS* 30 (1984): 508-30.

Lamarche, Paul. "La tempête apaisée (Mc 4,35-41)." In *Révélation de Dieu chez Marc*, pp. 61-77. Paris: Beauchesne, 1976.

Lapide, Pinchas. "A Jewish Exegesis of the Walking on the Water." *Concilium* 138 (1980): 35-40.

Léon-Dufour, Xavier. "La guérison de la belle-mère de Simon-Pierre." In *Etudes d'Évangile*, pp. 123-48. Paris: Éditions du Seuil, 1965.

———. "La tempête apaisée." *NRT* 87 (1965): 897-922.

McEleney, Neil J. "153 Great Fishes (John 21,11)—Gematriacal Atbash." *Bib* 58 (1977): 411-17.

Masuda, Sanae. "The Good News of the Miracle of the Bread: The Tradition and Its Markan Redaction." *NTS* 28 (1982): 191-219.

Pesch, Rudolf. "Die Heilung der Schwiegemutter des Simon-Petrus: Ein Beispiel heutiger Synoptikerexegese." In *Neuere Exegese—Verlust oder Gewinn?* pp. 143-76. Freiburg, Ger.: Herder, 1968.

———. *Der reiche Fischfang: Lk 5,1-11/Jo 21,1-4. Wundergeschichte-Berufungerzählung-Erscheinungsbericht.* Düsseldorf, Ger.: Patmos, 1969.

Potterie, I. de la. "Le sens primitif de la multiplication des pains." In *Jésus aux origines de la christologie*, pp. 303-29. Edited by Jacques Dupont. Leuven, Bel.: Leuven University Press, 1975.

Richardson, Alan. "The Feeding of the Five Thousand, Mark 6:34-44." *Int* 4 (1955): 145-49.

Reicke, Bo. "The Synoptic Reports of the Healing of the Paralytic: Matt. 9:1-8 with Parallels." In *Studies in New Testament Language and Text: Essays in Honour of George D. Kilpatrick on the Occasion of His Sixty-fifth Birthday*, pp. 319-29. Leiden, Neth.: Brill, 1976.

Rigato, Maria Luisa. "Tradizione e redazione in Mc. 1,29-31 (e paralleli): La guarigione della suocera di Simon Pietro." *RivB* 17 (1969): 139-74.

Rissi, Mathias, "Voll grosser Fische, hundertdreiundfünfzig, Joh. 21,1-14." *TZ* 35 (1979): 73-89.

Robbins, Vernon K. "The Woman Who Touched Jesus' Garment: Socio-Rhetorical Analysis of the Synoptic Accounts." *NTS* 33 (1987): 502-15.

Romeo, Joseph A. "Gematria and John 21:11—The Children of God." *JBL* 97 (1978): 263-64.

Sabourin, Leopold. "The Miracles of Jesus (III): Healings, Resuscitations, Nature Miracles." *BTB* 5 (1975): 146-200.

Suriano, Thomas M. " 'Who Then Is This . . . ?' Jesus Master the Sea." *Bible Today* 79 (1975): 449-56.

Telford, William R. *The Barren Temple and the Withered Tree: A Redaction-critical Analysis of the Cursing of the Fig-Tree Pericope in Mark's Gospel and Its Relation to the Cleansing of the Temple Tradition.* Sheffield, U.K.: JSOT, 1980.

Chapter 17: Jesus the Miracle Worker

Allison, Dale C. "The Contemporary Quest for the Historical Jesus." *IBS* 18 (1996): 174-93.

Baltensweiler, H. "Wunder und Glaube im Neuen Testament." *TZ* 23 (1967): 241-56.

Best, Ernest. "Healing and the New Testament." *IBS* 5 (1983): 65-72.

Boring, M. Eugene. "The 'Third Quest' and the Apostolic Faith." *Int* 50 (1996): 341-54.

Brown, Raymond E. "Jesus and Elisha." *Perspective* 12 (1971): 85-104.

Carroll, John T. "Sickness and Healing in the New Testament Gospel." *Int* 49 (1995): 130-42.

Crossan, John Dominic. *The Historical Jesus: The Life of a Mediterranean Jewish Peasant.* North Blackburn, Austr.: CollinsDove, 1993.

——— "The Presence of God's Love in the Power of Jesus' Works." *Concilium* 10, no. 5 (1969):

34-40.

Davies, Stevan L. *Jesus the Healer: Possession, Trance and the Origins of Christianity*. London: SCM Press, 1995.

Graham, D. J. "Jesus as Miracle Worker." *Studia Biblica et Theologica* 4 (1986): 85-96.

Kasper, Walter. "Zur theologischen Bedeutung der Wunder Jesu." *Renovatio* 32 (1976): 172-73.

Kee, Howard Clark. "A Century of Quests for the Culturally Compatible Jesus." *TToday* 52 (1995-96): 17-28.

Kertelge, Karl. "Begründen die Wunder Jesu den Glauben?" *TTZ* 80 (1971): 129-40.

McArthur, Harvey K. ed. *In Search of the Historical Jesus*. London: SPCK, 1976.

Neil, William. "Expository Problems: The Nature Miracles." *ExpTim* 67 (1955-1956): 369-72.

Neill, Stephen, and Tom Wright. *The Interpretation of the New Testament: 1861-1986*. Oxford, U.K.: Oxford University Press, 1988.

Robinson, James M. *A New Quest for the Historical Jesus*. London: SCM Press, 1959.

Sanders, E. P. *Jesus and Judaism*. London: SCM Press, 1985.

Scott, Bernard Brandon. "From Reimarus to Crossan: Stages in a Quest." *Currents in Research: Biblical Studies* 2 (1994): 253-80.

Theissen Gerd and Annette Merz. *The Historical Jesus: A Comprehensive Guide*. London: SCM Press, 1998.

Tiede, David L. *The Charismatic Figure as Miracle Worker*. Missoula, Mo.: Scholars Press, 1972.

Witherington, Ben. *The Jesus Quest: The Third Search for the Jew of Nazareth*. Downers Grove, Ill.: InterVarsity Press, 1995.

Wright, N. T. *Jesus and the Victory of God*. London: SPCK, 1996.

Index

Authors

Subjects